Trial, Tribulation & Triumph

Trial, Tribulation & Triumph

Before, During, and After Antichrist

by

Desmond A. Birch

PUBLISHING COMPANY
P.O Box 220 • Goleta, CA 93116
(800) 647-9882 • (805) 692-0043 • FAX (805) 957-5133

©1996 Queenship Publishing

Library of Congress Number # 96-68461

Published by:
Queenship Publishing
P.O. Box 220
Goleta, CA 93116
(800) 647-9882 • (805) 692-0043 • Fax: (805) 967-5133
www.queenship.org

Printed in the United States of America
ISBN: 1-882972-73-2

Reviews of
Trial Triumph and Tribulation

Mike Schwartz: Catholic commentator and contributing author for such journals as *Triumph* and *Twin Circle:*

> *"The second half of Birch's book is a fast-paced summary ... Drawn entirely from the prophecies of canonized saints and others whose orthodoxy has been approved by the Church,* **these prophecies offer a gripping account of how the Antichirst will come to power, and how he will ultimately be defeated.** The author deals soberly and sanely with a topic which might easily be sensationalized.
>
> Each of the two introductory chapters ... is a brilliant contribution to some of the most crucial theological debates of our time. This book ... appears to be the first scholarly treatment of the subject of private prophecy."

Fr. Michael O'Carroll: Irish Theologian, at Blackrock College, County Dublin, Ireland, author of theological works such as *Mediatress of All Graces,* and Liturgical Press' five volume *Theological Encyclopedia:*

> "the Antichrist ... the Second Comming of Christ ... What will immediately precede this culmination? ... *there never have been so many alleged messages from on high, so many voices claiming to enlighten and reassure us on these very grave matters ... through all this ... we need a guide.* This is the task that Desmond Birch assumes and he discharges admirably.
>
> One is quite simply amazed at the completeness of his research. **This is *the* book that I shall certainly recommend to anyone who is interested in this important subject."**

Fr. William G. Most: Full Professor of Theology and Scripture at the Notre Dame (Pontifical) Institute's Graduate School. Author of such works as *The Consciousness of Christ* and *The Thought of St. Paul.*

> "(today) Many think the end of the world and the great Antichrist may be just around the corner, and that he will appear before the year 2000. Not a few deny there will be a personal Antichrist. A powerful aid [to remedy these errors] is now available in a solidly theological work, *Trial, Triumph and Tribulation,* by Desmond Birch.
>
> He [utilizes] chiefly four solid sources [the *Catechism,* Scripture, Tradition, and majority opinions of the Fathers]. Tradition ... as found in the documents of the Magisterium today, and in the virtually unanimous teaching of the early Fathers of the Church, *given when* they show by their words that they are passing on truths revealed from the beginning, from Christ Himself.
>
> **All of this Birch does, as we said, in a thoroughly scholarly, theological way.** ***Now there will be no excuse for false notions or denials on the Antichrist and the other last things.*** We are and should be extremely grateful to our author for this tremendous resource.

FROM THE PUBLISHER
October, 1996

The following review was produced for Queenship Publishing Company by Fr. Michael O'Carroll at Blackrock College in Ireland. American and Canadian readers will recognize Fr. O'Carroll as the author of the five volume theological encyclopedia published by Liturgical Press. Fr. O'Carroll's international reputation as a Catholic theologian well qualifies him to assess *Trial, Tribulation and Triumph* by Desmond A. Birch

This book of over 700 pages in semi-large format represents an immense volume of painstaking research. Not only because of the subject, but by its editing and layout, typography adapted and varied to match the sequence of topics, and well chosen sub-headings, it will be readable to anyone interested in its subject. The subject is one that must stir most people with Christian faith. How will our world end? How are we to understand or interpret all that is available to us in print or in oral testimony? The future stings our curiosity for the simple reason that it is certain to happen and it is, almost by definition, unknown. Then closer attention to the writings which command our respect and more than respect, the sacred books and the authoritative interpreters of them, discovers some certainties.

One of them concerns a person who, as the end approaches, will have maximum prominence: ***the Antichrist.*** It is a word often enough bandied about, prompting many different theories. Can we have anything firm to grasp? What about another event, ***the Second Coming of Jesus Christ,*** our Savior? what about those passages in the Gospel where he gives us the picture of the final, exhaustive verdict on the human story and all who have had a part in it? ***What will immediately precede this culmination?***

The human story in our generation is sorry and degenerate. Where the Christian religion had an allegiance socially coherent, rising to great heights in individual cases, we now have a void, a spreading attitude of rejection in the face of Christian teaching, precepts and promises. Call it apostasy, for that is what it is. Without entering on every aspect of our tragic times, we may note that the decline in religious belief and practice is felt in all the religions with a previously substantial following. People look for substitutes in sects which are numbered in thousands; they turn to drugs, the plague of our time;or worse still, they dabble in Satanism.

Is there nothing to give us hope and comfort? Whey, *there never have been so many alleged messages from on high, so many voices claiming to enlighten and reassure us on these very grave matters.* Through all that is open to our awareness or perception, *we need a guide.* This is the task that Desmond Birch assumes and he discharges admirably.

One is quite simply amazed at the completeness of his research. He takes the basic Biblical text, he has gone through the Fathers of the Church, and scrutinized private revelations through the centuries, that is in each century, sometimes in each decade. Themes which we have heard from time to time, such as the appearance of a great king, savior of Christian civilization, or three days of darkness over the earth, have a place in his carefully compiled anthology.

By the anthology is expanded, again and again, to give the author scope to expound correct methodology, to show the need for acceptance of the established norms of theological exposition, to state and vindicate the basic principles of sound theology, and of spirituality, which is a branch of the sacred science.

No opinion is forced here. what is stated is supported by what the author considers adequate evidence. So all that is relevant to the final phase of the human story is, as he sees things, set forth and documented. In accord with his orderly treatment of the subject, his essential theses are spelled out at the beginning of the book with lucidity. The reader is facilitated in mastering an important, most important, subject. This is ***the*** book that I shall certainly recommend to anyone who is interested in this important subject.

Michael O'Carroll, C.S.Sp.
Blackrock College, Dublin County,
Republic of Ireland

CONTENTS

FOREWORD

by

Fr. William Most

"There will come a time when people will not endure sound doctrine. With their ears itching, they will accumulate teachers according to their own liking. They will turn from the truth and be converted to fables." Hence St. Paul urged his great helper Timothy whom he left behind in the province of Asia, to preach the word in season and out of season. For earlier he had stopped in Miletus and called together the Presbyters and warned them that from their own midst would come ravening wolves (Acts 20: 29) that would come in, and not spare the flock. He had reason to warn about false teachers.

And with all this there are wars and rumors of wars. One can hardly contend that we are living in the period of peace promised by Our Lady of Fatima. So the flock is confused, and doctrine and the way of living are both in turmoil. In the U.S. today polls show only 30% of Catholics believe in the Real Presence, while at least 80% to 90% reject the teaching of the Church on contraception. And false teachers in Catholic universities and colleges hold sway, and often are able to oust the teachers who would follow the Pope.

Among other errors we find many holding false ideas about the Antichrist. Many think the end of the world and the great Antichrist may be just around the corner, and that he will appear before the year 2000. Not a few deny there be a personal Antichrist - this is just a name standing not for a person but for the forces of evil. Many priests and nuns who have read the latest book or have attended a workshop given by false teachers not only think this way, but teach others. And they are lauded for doing this, and ridicule those who would still dare to teach what the Church teaches. They say Vatican II has revolutionized all theology so that those trained before it no longer know much of anything. Formerly one could find the answer to almost any question about morality or doctrine just by asking any priest. Now if he/she wants to shop around a bit, there are teachers fit for itching ears that will assure them that anything goes.

The sovereign remedy for these evils is to follow St. Paul, and preach the truth in season and out of season. A powerful aid for this is now available in a solidly theological work, *The Trial, Tribulation, & Triumph Before, During, and After Antichrist* (TTT) by Desmond Birch. He tries to put before the reader chiefly four solid sources, utilizing the *Catechism of the Catholic Church* as a summary, which is based on Sacred Scripture itself and on Tradition.

The very notion of Tradition as a great source is unknown to many. We think of tradition with a small "t" and many think they can create their own traditions. To counter this our author explains with meticulous care what Tradition really is: it is the ongoing teaching of the Church as found in the documents of the Magisterium today, and in the virtually unanimous teaching of the early Fathers of the Church, *given when* they show by their words that they are passing on truths revealed from the beginning, from Christ Himself. For He did not leave the Church at sea. He did not tell the Apostles to write some books, give them out, and tell the people to figure them out for themselves. No. Our Lord left, as it were, a Supreme Court for teaching, and not a court that would ignore what He had taught, and would not invent instead new unconstitutionalities, even though they led to the murder of literally millions of the unborn.

To supplement these unanimous teachings, Birch presents majority opinions of the Fathers. And so as to fight fire with fire, he has sifted through a huge mass of alleged private prophecies, so as to come up with a small percent that do not impose themselves as a matter of divine faith but yet seem worthy of human assent.

All of this Birch does, as we said, in a thoroughly scholarly, theological way. Now there will be no excuse for false notions or denials on the Antichrist and the other last things.

So ,yes, Virginia, there will be an Antichrist, not the devil incarnate, but a most evil man having at his disposal all the powers of an evil fallen angel. Is this Antichrist just around the corner? There is impressive evidence to show Antichrist is not about to appear almost any day. So we must watch and pray, and utilize all resources, such as the TTT, to help us steer a course between the Scylla of false beliefs and the Charybdis of enticing errors. We are and should be extremely grateful to our author for this tremendous resource.

INTRODUCTION

Three Major Theses of This Book Are:

I. Belief that the Second Coming of Christ, the Antichrist, and/or some kind of a millennium are on the very near or immediate horizon is neither consonant with the Scriptures, nor Tradition (most particularly within the writings of the Fathers of the Church), nor, with a *broad overview* of Catholic private prophecy.

II. Belief that Antichrist could be a set of circumstances, or a movement, or a group of men is not consistent with Tradition, Scripture, nor especially the exegesis of the early Church writers including and extending to the great Fathers and later Doctors of the Church. Antichrist will and must come; he will be an individual man with a human soul. That doctrine is universally taught since the inception of the Church.

III. Mankind is approaching a rather unique period of its history *which is hope-filled.* According to Tradition, Scripture and the Fathers and Doctors of the Church, sometime between now and the advent of Antichrist mankind will most probably experience an age of peace. Private Catholic prophecy from Church-approved sources are consistent with this scenario (Fatima is only one of those sources).

Mankind will arrive at that Age of Peace in one of two ways;

(1) Through God's proffered easy way of the radical inner conversion of men and women, or,

(2) Through a Chastisement of rather dynamic proportions.

IV. This period of peace has absolutely nothing to do with any sort of "Millenium" theory. Any sort of Millenarianism or any "modified form" of it is absolutely rejected by the Church. Proofs of this will be developed from the earliest to the latest documents of the Church including all of the best modern studies of this subject.

1. The Antichrist

According to Tradition, Scripture, the commentaries of various Fathers and Doctors of the Church, and, a *broad understanding* of private Catholic prophecy, there will be many "antichrists" preceding ***the*** *Antichrist* who is an individual man. *The supreme or ultimate Antichrist foretold to come in the end times* cannot be a political, sociological, or religious movement, nor can he be a "group" of men. According to these same sources, he *is most probably* not coming by the year 2000 nor any time in the immediate future either.

That particular thesis (that *the Antichrist* must appear as an individual man) will be developed in this book through evidence from;

(1) Tradition, and
(2) Scripture, and
(3) In particular from the writings of the Fathers and Doctors of the Church.

These three will *only ancillarily* be expanded and amplified through,

(4) Private Catholic prophecy from approved sources -- canonized Saints, Blessed, and Venerable and other holy souls.[1]

Number 4 is described as "ancillary" because; private revelation can never be part of the deposit of faith, whereas, Scripture and Tradition are, and even exegesis of the Fathers can be when certain conditions are met.

---

1 "Venerable and Blessed" - two stages in the Church process leading up to being canonized a Saint.

2. Recent Causes for Concern

The author recently attended an international Catholic conference held in the U.S. The speakers included a star-studded list of U.S. and foreign Bishops including one foreign Cardinal. One of the few *lay* speakers said, "Just as St. John the Baptist ushered in the First Coming of Christ ... recent apparitions and messages of Our Lady are announcing that we are entering into a time of extreme difficulties ... and I am talking about Antichrist with a Capital 'A.'"[2] *This speakers alleged source for these statements were some private prophecies from sources which the Church has not approved.*

While that speaker (a published author on the subject of private prophecy) did not fully flesh out his thoughts, everyone definitely understood the speaker to be implying that the "Antichrist" and then the Parousia[3] (the Second Coming of Christ) are just around the corner. ***Let it also be clearly understood that none of the Bishops either said or implied any such thing!***[4] Those Bishop's were speaking in the same hope-filled vein as the Holy Father does about the world's future in the 3rd Millennium.

The Holy Father is very conversant with the subjects of both public and private prophecy. He has read the "Third Secret of Fatima." He is working fervently to prepare for the Third Millennium pastorally, liturgically, and theologically. *Would he be doing that if he thought the Antichrist or the end of the world were at hand?*

On the other hand, most Catholics who are promoting the theme that the Antichrist and possibly the Parousia are just around the corner have at least one thing in common; they have primarily received that idea from sources of (1) *private prophecy from some*

---

2 Quoted from hand-written notes taken by this author at that conference.

3 Most words which might not be immediately understood by some of the readers are explained in the Glossary at the back of this book. When such a word is encountered by the reader, he or she should immediately consult the Glossary.

4 However, the author personally knows some Ecclesiastics who have taken seriously the possibility that the Antichrist may be coming "in our time." And he respects them for their learning. They are neither ill-educated nor fools. As a matter of fact, they are generally well-read and very well-educated. The author simply believes that (similar to most Ecclesiastics of the late 20th century) they have not had the time nor opportunity to peruse the wealth of eschatological works and quotes from the Fathers and Doctors of the Church in this matter.

sources not approved by the Church[5] and on occasion, *(2) a serious misreading of Scripture.*

One of the central themes of this book is admirably generically summed up in the following words of St. Augustine.

> "He who indiscreetly announces the coming of Christ falls into a noxious error. Supposing that his prophecy is not justified by the event, men will not say that the event has been postponed, but they will say that it will never happen, which must prove very injurious to their faith."[6]

Augustine's approach also well applies to precipitous announcements of the arrival of the Antichrist. St. Augustine is also one of the most definitive voices in the early Church who condemns any form of Millenarianism as an untenable belief for a Christian. Belief in such a millennial theme (a one thousand year reign on earth of Christ with his Saints) is spreading primarily from the same sources attributed above to belief that the Antichrist is coming.

In the case of the spread of Millenial belief in Catholic circles, there are two additional factors;

(1) The recent dissemination of long-discredited claims that the first general or ecumenical Council of the Church, the Council of Nicea, taught this Millenial doctrine. This is being promoted primarily by some non-Catholic sources. But it is spreading from those non-Catholic sources into Catholic venues.

(2) A serious misreading of several statements in the documents of Vatican II. They are being misunderstood by some Catholics to support Millenial theory. From personal experience the author knows that this "misreading" is not limited to some of the laity, but also includes a small but growing number of priests.

A detailed portrayal of the history of this theological error of a "Millenium" is developed later in this book.

---

5 Of these, some have formally been declared not to be of a supernatural character, and others have simply had no judgment passed on them at this time.

6 Epist. 80 ad Heszch.

3. Tradition, Scripture, and the Fathers

How does a Catholic know how to interpret certain passages of Scripture - which by definition are of faith? How does a Catholic discern what things contained in private prophecies might be humanly credible. There are a number of tests which the Church applies in relation to judging private prophecies. One of the first key tests is whether the contents of such prophecies are compatible with doctrine contained in Revelation, as it is understood and taught by the Church.

As Vatican II teaches us, the two sources of Revelation are "sacred Tradition and sacred Scripture."[7] But those sources, Tradition and Scripture, must be understood and interpreted. This interpretation is very difficult in the case of prophetic texts from the Old and New Testaments.

4. A Key Role is Played by the Fathers of the Church

The writings left to us by the Fathers of the Church form a major part of Tradition. Also, the Church teaches us that under certain circumstances the "Fathers ..., are of supreme authority whenever they all interpret in one and the same manner any text of the Bible."[8] The Fathers play a major role in both sources of Revelation as they come to us through the Church. Most Catholics have only a vague idea of who the Fathers are. Many who are familiar with the Fathers of the Church, are at the same time not sure what their authority is.

Who the Fathers are and the extent of their authority will be fully described in Chapter 1. In Chapters 4 and 10 the reader will see how the Fathers interpreted, "in one and the same manner," certain prophetic texts about the end times. As the Church teaches, when that happens under certain circumstance, the Fathers are "of supreme authority" as to the meaning of Scriptural texts.

One such area relates to the Fathers' teachings about certain events which *must* precede *the* Antichrist. Consequently, those events

---

7 Dei Verbum #'s 9&10.

8 *Providentissimus Deus*

appear to be ones which must take place before Antichrist comes. Therefore, there would have to be something wrong with any private prophecy which claimed to foretell Antichrist's coming prior to those events. The Church ultimately decides that which is of faith in all areas of theology. Teachings about the end times is no exception. The Church searches the Fathers because of the following:

(1) The Church teaches that the two sources of Catholic belief are sacred Tradition and sacred Scripture.

(2) The Church also teaches that under certain conditions, the "*Fathers ..., are of supreme authority whenever they all interpret in one and the same manner any text of the Bible.*"[9]

(3) The Church has issued definitive eschatological[10] documents on only a few points of eschatological doctrine, (documents about the end times).

(4) In areas, and on specific eschatological issues, where the Church has not issued definitive statements, the Fathers are the first place to look for a Catholic answer.

Anyone not familiar with the various eschatological pronouncements of the Church, and certain eschatological writings of the Fathers -- such a person is ill-prepared to be discerning about any private prophecy concerning the end times. This is because such a person will not recognize when some claim in a private prophecy runs clearly counter to the definitive eschatological statements of the Church and the teaching of the Fathers. *In areas where the Church has not yet spoken definitively, the opinion of the Fathers is invaluable to determining the probability of an apparently eschatological private prophecy.*

5. Background to the Book

Over the past twenty-three years as time permitted, the author has gathered, studied, and correlated thousands of prophecies of

---

9 *Providentissimus Deus*

10 "eschatological" - things dealing with the last things, the end of time. See Glossary for a full definition.

the "latter times" and the "end times." The most important of those prophecies come from (1) Tradition and Scripture, and (2) *only very ancillarily*, private Catholic prophecy which is in concord with those from Tradition and Scripture.

As will be emphasized and reemphasized; a broad view of Catholic prophecy must begin in, and be rooted in, what the Vatican Council II Fathers reconfirmed and defined as the two sources of Revelation, sacred Tradition and sacred Scripture.[11] According to Catholic teaching, those are the only sources for what we believe in supernatural faith. Those two sources ended with the death of the last Apostle. Nothing else can be a matter of faith for a Catholic. Any private prophecies can hold interest for a Catholic only to the degree that they are in agreement with Public Prophecy from Scripture and Tradition.

6. A Compendium of Catholic Doctrine and Prophecy About the Latter and End Times!

This book is planned as a single volume edition so as not to discourage the non-academic reader. At the same time, it is planned to be sufficiently comprehensive to interest a serious scholar. For the reader who wishes greater detail in any of the areas discussed herein, excellent books are available in most good Catholic seminary or Catholic University libraries. (See Bibliography for some specific titles to look for.)

A. THIS IS A BOOK ON CATHOLIC PROPHECY AND DOCTRINE ABOUT THE LATTER AND END TIMES.

(1) This book is designed to be a compendium dealing with the totality of Catholic prophecy encompassing the entire scope of public revelation (Tradition and Scripture), and *only ancillarily*, private Catholic prophecy -- as it pertains to the "latter" and "end" times.

[11] *Dei Verbum*, #'s 9 & 10.

(2) Just to quote the entirety of Scriptural prophecies about the "latter" and "end" times would require a very large book in and of itself. Therefore the quotes herein from Revelation are themselves the result of a highly selective process.

(3) The Oral Tradition of the Church on this subject, much of which was subsequently committed to writing by the Church Fathers is voluminous. Many of the Fathers wrote entire books on the totality of apostolic Tradition (which includes the oral Tradition) which came down to them about the "latter and end times." *Some wrote entire works just on the specific subject of Antichrist alone.* Many of those books survive down to this day. So only a random sampling of those items can be presented in a one volume presentation.

(4) In the area of private prophecy: It takes entire volumes just to hold the prophecies of St. Hildegarde alone. The two volume Latin edition of her *Scivias Domini*[13] occupies 636 pages. Her *Divinum Operorum* is almost three hundred pages long. Her private letters (which contain many of her prophecies) cover roughly another 75 pages. That amounts to just under a thousand single spaced pages in order to quote the prophetic works of St. Hildegarde alone.

(5) **Therefore, in order to present an overview in a single volume edition, which also shows the mutual agreement between prophecies from Tradition and Scripture (and *only ancillarily* some private prophecy) it is patently obvious that a highly selective process is mandatory in all three areas.**

(6) Therefore the reader should not be surprised if (a) some particular "prophet" from the Old Testament has been excluded, or, (b) some private prophet approved by the Church is excluded. Well over 90% of the private prophets known to the author have been excluded from this volume.

---

[13] Corpus Christianorum, Continuatio Mediaevalis, XIII, *HILDEGARDIS SCIVIAS*, Turnholti, Typographi Brepols Editores Pontifici, MCMLXXVIII.

SUMMATION: Of the three areas containing "Catholic" prophecy, Tradition, Scripture, and private Catholic prophecy, it would probably take over three dozen very large volumes just to present the raw prophetic materials themselves. Few readers could or would take the time to read them, let alone to assimilate and analyze all those materials. Therefore, a highly selective pruning or selection process is necessary for a one volume presentation.

1. A Hypothetical Chronological Table of events prophesied to preceed the Parousia

Later in this book we will see various prophecies of events foretold to preceed the Second Coming of Christ - the end of the world. They come from several sources. Some are official teachings of the Church, things which one must absolutely believe as a Catholic. Others are those which are part of the traditional teaching of the Church - but which are not absolutely binding in faith. Next come those items which comprise the majority opinion of the Fathers, Doctors and theologians of the Church, but about which there are some Fathers and or some Doctors of the Church who disagree. Finally there are items which come strictly from private Catholic prophecy from Church-approved sources.

(1) ***Those which are binding in Faith are presented in bold italicized print.***

(2) **Those which are part of the traditional teachings of the Church - but which are not absolutely binding in faith are presented in bold print.**

(3) *Those about which there is a heavy preponderance of teaching among the Fathers and Doctors are presented in simple italicized print.*

(4) Those which represent private prophecy from Church-approved sources are presented in plain type.

The Table: A hypothetical or proposed chronology of these prophesied events, prophesied to preceed the end of time is presented at this time in order to help the reader assimilate and mentally organize the prophetic materials to follow.

The Minor Chastisement

(1) At some time in the future, the corrupt faithless age we live in now will come to an end either through repentance (immediately followed by an age of peace) -- or there will be a chastisement. This would be a Minor Chastisement preceding an Age of Peace. It is not the Tribulation of the Antichrist.

(2) If this chastisement is not averted through conversion, the "Latin (Western) Church" will be terribly afflicted by heresy and schism. This is prophesied to be primarily caused by a false intellectualism, which intellectualism presents itself in the form of "senseless questions and elaborate arguments" attacking the traditional teachings of the Church.

(3) The chastising elements will come in two forms, (a) Man- made and (b) Heaven-sent.

(4) Civil war breaks out in France and Italy at almost the same time.

(5) This will spread to general wars, and, famine and pestilence (the usual by-products of war).

(6) Earthquakes, tidal waves, floods and all other sorts of "natural" disasters will occur.

(7) Somewhere in all of this, an army composed of Russian troops invades Western Europe just when everyone thinks this impossible.

(8) England will suffer a terrible civil war which starts after the French and Italians have gone into theirs.

(9) The Pope will flee Rome in the company of several other cardinals and go into hiding, be found, and cruelly mur- dered.

(10) A man who will subsequently be known as a great saint will ultimately be elected pope near the end of the Chastisement. He will be heavily responsible for the French acceptance of a king to be their military and civil leader.

(11) The Great King will lead his forces (against terrible odds) and finally defeat these Russian and Prussian forces.

(12) Somewhere near the end of the Chastisement, God sends Three Days of Darkness.

(13) The three days of darkness probably occur sometime after final and total victory over the Russians and Moslems.

[If people repent, the chastisement is averted till a later time. In that case, the prophesied great king and the great pope come *near the end of an age of peace*.

In the latter scenario, the great king comes to usher in a final period of peace which lasts only as long as he lives. That is an alternate possibility. The prophecies simply do not give sufficient details for us to tell.]

2. The Age of Peace

(1) According to the prophecies, through a historically very unique series of events there will be a complete restoration of Christian Culture in the West.
(2) The Great King will be crowned Holy Roman Emperor by the reigning Pope.
(3) The Great King will establish Peace and justice in civil matters on almost a worldwide basis. The former disciplines of the Church are fully restored and order is re-established.
(4) *The Pope calls an Ecumenical Council* which will be viewed as the greatest in the history of the Church. The world is spiritually and materially prosperous as never before and many Jews, Mohammedans, heathens and heretics will enter the Church.
(5) Extended prosperity causes people to begin to grow lax in the practice of their faith.
(6) Wars and bad economic times break out again after some period of time during which the faithful fall into laxity.
(7) *Ten kings divide up the boundaries of a Roman Empire which had been established.*

3. The Major Chastisement - the Tribulation of Antichrist

(1) ***The gospel must be preached in the whole world (Matt. 24, 14; Mark 13, 10), even though many will not accept its message (Luke 18, 8).***
(2) ***Before Christ's Second Coming there will be a great apostasy or religious defection (Matt. 24, 10-12; Luke 18, 8; Thess. 2, 3j; 2 Tim. 3, 1-9), and the Antichrist will appear (2 Thess. 2, 3-12; 1 John 2, 18, 22; 2 John 7).***

(3) **The last (Roman) Empire, which has been divided up into "ten kingdoms" is dismantled by a great (but evil) military and political leader. Three of the ten kingdoms will not go along with this. They are crushed. See - Book of Rev. Ch. 13, Book of Dan. Ch. 7 & 8.** [See in St. Jerome's commentary on *Book of Daniel* that Antichrist will kill the three kings "who will not bow to him"]

(4) **The "False Prophet" arrives -- the Precursor of Antichrist. He will "ape" the role that St. John the Baptist performed in preparing the people for the arrival of the Messiah.**

(5) ***All of this prepares the way for the coming of the Antichrist.*** He begins his rise to power at about the age of 30. ***After he seizes total power he begins a three and one half year bestial persecution of the Church.***

(6) ***During this period, the Two Witnesses*** **(Enoch and Elias) who have never died but have been maintained in "Paradise"** ***return to the presence of men and preach to the people against Antichrist.*** **Elias preaches primarily to the Jews and Enoch primarily to the Gentiles. It is the arrival of these "Two Witnesses" which foreshadows the foretold conversion of the Jews to Christianity.**

(7) *Antichrist finally kills them by his own hand in Jerusalem and* ***their bodies lie in the street by his command for 3 & 1/2 days, at the end of which a voice from Heaven is heard by everyone present which commands the two witnesses*** **(Enoch and Elias)** ***to arise. to the surprise and stark terror of the onlookers, they do.***

(8) **The Jews as a nation will be converted after the full number of the Gentiles enter the Church (Rom. 11).**

(9) *Antichrist, stung again by this latest heavenly miracle, tries to restore his prestige with the Jews by simulating Christ's ascension from Mt. Olivet, and St. Michael casts him down screaming to his death.* (St. Thomas Aquinas & other Doctors teach this.)

B. THE FOUR LAST THINGS

(1) After the death of Antichrist, a short period of time of unknown duration is given to the remaining inhabitants of the earth to repent and accept Our Lord and the message of his Gospel.

(2) ***There will be a physical transformation of the universe (Matt. 24, 29; Mark 13, 24f; Luke 21, 25f), and the world will be purified by fire in the final general conflagration (2 Pet. 3, 5-7; cf. 1 Cor. 3, 13). Then only will the Son of Man appear in heaven (Matt. 24, 30; Mark 13, 26; Luke 21, 27).***[1]

(3) ***Then comes the end of the world and the Four Last Things; Death, the Last Judgement, Heaven, Hell,.***

C. AUTHOR'S FIRST MEETING WITH PRIVATE PROPHECY

In addition to prophecies from Tradition and Scripture, in this book there are some private prophecies which come from various sources approved by the Church. Some readers may be unfamiliar with this private prophecy. Prior to 1972, for the most part so was the author. His exposure to private prophecy was almost limited to that of the apparitions at Fatima.

In the fall of 1972 the author of this book returned home from an extended stint on a U.S. presidential campaign. Shortly thereafter, a dear friend offered him a small book on private Catholic prophecy. The friend asked him to read it and tell him what he thought of it. The book was read and reread rather quickly. Two weeks later they met again for lunch and the author told him that:

(1) The book had predicted that sometime in the foreseeable future (probably before the year 2000) that the Arabs would become a serious power with which the major Western Powers would have to contend.

---

[14] __*Catholic Biblical Encyclopedia, New Testament*, John E. Steinmueller, S.T.D., S.Scr.L., Consultor of the Pontifical Biblical Commission, Kathryn Sullivan, R.S.C. J., Ph.D. Research Professor of Sacred Scripture, Introduction by James-M. Voste, O.P., S.T.M., S.Scr.D., Secretary of the Pontifical Biblical Commission, Pub: Joseph F. Wagner, Inc. New York City, 1949, p. 142.

(2) The author felt that prediction highly improbable.
(3) Not content with just his own opinion, he had called several reliable "diplomatic contacts" and asked them what they thought. They had just laughed.

He subsequently told his friend that based upon the book's "Arab Power before the year 2000" thesis alone, that he had a hard time taking the book seriously.

That luncheon took place several months prior to the Arab Oil Embargo which began in very late 1972 and continued into 1973. That period saw Americans waiting in lines for gasoline for the first time since World War II. Within months, the Arabs had demonstrated they had real power. For this reason they had the serious attention of every U.S. citizen for the first time.

What the author had thought impossible by the year 2000 had happened in a matter of months. While it is difficult for people of the 1990's to remember, prior to the Arab Oil Embargo, only a handful of people in the West ever considered the role of the Arabs. Prior to that time the Arabs simply weren't considered to be "players" on the international stage. For the author that Embargo created an intellectual shock. That shock was the realization that prophecy *might have* indicated what political experts thought impossible.

At that point the author was also reminded of the fact that many highly specific prophecies made at Fatima in 1917 had subsequently come true. These two things in turn made the author reassess many of his previously held positions - which resulted in,

(1) He decided to reserve judgment on the subject of private Catholic prophecy until he had a chance to look further into the matter, and
(2) Further investigation eventually piqued his interest in the subject.

D. THE END OF THE SECOND MILLENNIUM - A TIME OF TREPIDATION

It is no secret that as we approach the end of the second millennium there is a general sense of foreboding amongst the populace of the Western world and particularly in the United States. Both that foreboding and the events which give rise to it are being written about in the secular press on a regular basis. For example, for those in the diplomatic corp., there is (1) the observed increasing conflict and threat of war in the Middle East (as there has continually been for the last fifty years) and in Central Europe, and (2) the political situation behind the former Iron Curtain which inspires anything but confidence for world stability.

1. Contemporary Lack of Optimism

A cursory look at recent history tells us that the West, in general, is not the land of optimism which it was a mere decade or two ago. Particularly in the USA, our newspapers are filled with stories of impending bank closures, terrorist attacks, gang attacks, the rise of internal hate groups, and particularly crimes of violence such as rape, robbery, and murder. There is also the continuous fear of a possible financial collapse. Should any serious observer of the current American scene be surprised if our citizenry is not hope-filled about America's immediate future?

Extensive polling data taken over the last decade clearly confirm that Americans (and Catholic Americans are no exception) are not as a group hope-filled about the entire world's immediate future either. And this lack of hope is *not* exclusively localized in the United States. As syndicated columnist George Weigel so aptly summed up the situation in late 1995:

> "And so at the end of a century of unparalleled cruelty the world slouches toward the third millennium, full of fear. The modern age, which began with the confident assertion of human "autonomy," is ending, paradoxically, with fear; human beings are afraid of themselves, afraid of their differences, afraid of their technology, afraid of the future."[15]

But there is justifiable hope. That is the ultimate message of this book! As the Holy Father keeps reiterating the words of Our Lord,

"BE NOT AFRAID!"

---

[15] Quoted from *Denver Catholic Register*, Vol. LXXI, No. 40, Denver, Co. U.S.A., Oct. 11, 1995, p. 6.

2. Many of Our Crises Were Predicted by a Few Ordinary People Twenty Years Ago

In the mid-1970's few Christians or Jews in North America were thinking about the themes of this book. But some pulpits resounded with warnings about the escalating divorce rate in Canada and especially in the U.S. There were also a significant number of social scientists who seemed equally concerned about the issue. Their collective warnings contained dire predictions of social disaster for our country if marriages did not begin to stabilize.

They were mutually predicting that massive divorce would produce a growing mass of socially unstable youth, that juvenile crime, violence, and other "anti-social behavior" would be one of the predictable fruits of such a development. But such people were viewed for the most part as extremist "peddlers of doom and gloom." *A civilization in which the majority was infatuated with the concept of "easy divorce" did not want to hear such a message.*

In the mid-1970's, despite the fact that America was the most powerful nation in the world, it had just lost the Vietnam War. But America was still the industrial giant of the world, the wealthiest nation on earth, and was "getting back to normalcy." However, a handful of people in the "Right to Life" movement seemed to be disturbed about the 1973 *Roe V. Wade* Supreme Court Decision. Some leading Protestant, Catholic, and Jewish clergy were predicting that a nation which legalizes the killing of babies could lose God's protection and suffer predictable dire consequences.

They predicted that a nation which would morally and philosophically stand still for legalized abortion would subsequently stand still for legalized euthanasia. They also predicted that a nation which legalized violence against unborn innocents would predictably find violence spreading and ultimately becoming pandemic in their land. These predictors of the 1970's were branded as radicals in the press. But even to "good" Catholics, Protestants and Jews, some of their rhetoric sounded somewhat shrill, somewhat similar to the storybook character "Chicken Little" alarmedly shouting that "the sky is falling."

A few voices were heard talking about the plight of the *inner city poor*. They were warning that a nation which had grown unconcerned about its poor would sooner or later have to face the issue one way or another. They warned that if something positive was not done, within a few years poverty would not be able to be kept comfortably hidden in minority ghettos, that we would find it penetrating into our non-ghetto streets. In the mid-1970's, this kind of talk was viewed as irresponsible, alarmist, and as an impossible prediction for "the industrial giant of the world."[16]

An even smaller number of American voices collectively associated all predicted problems from free-wheeling divorce, abortion, and a lack of concern for the poor with a creeping selfishness in the U.S.A. Some prominent individuals drew a relationship between this perceived selfishness and a nationwide drop in church attendance, a reduced belief in God and his precepts, and a failure to put those beliefs into action.

Those voices were again essentially treated by the secular press as religious fanatics. Even many good Christians and Jews thought they were going too far, were exaggerating the problems. But in retrospect, few of today's practicing Christians and Jews would think those predictions had been exaggerations. They may not be in total agreement as to all of the causes, but there is no disagreement as to the accuracy of those predictions of twenty years ago. Were they after all, just "lucky guesses"?

Unlike twenty years ago, national politicians, news analysts, and talk show hosts will now commonly speak of a national moral decline, unparalleled quantum increase in violence throughout the U.S.A., and the spread of poverty beyond the ghetto's into non-minority communities. Few of them, however, discuss or point out that this decline in morality, quantum increase in violence, and spreading poverty were being clearly and specifically predicted by many clergymen and a significant number of social scientists over twenty years ago. Even fewer will discuss a religious significance in these events.

None of those *predictors* twenty years ago claimed to be receiving prophecy from God. Knowing that all actions have consequences, they simply looked at the world around them with objec-

[16] If the reader does not remember this as an accurate portrayal of the mid-1970's, a short visit to his or her local library and the reading of daily newspapers from 1975 will refresh his or her memory.

tive vision and calculated what they felt to be a highly predictable outcome. But those predictors who were subjects of ridicule twenty years ago now *look* like prophets. The secular media either cannot or will not see that these consequences were clearly predicted over twenty years ago by "religious types of people."

Today, a few within the media will however discuss a few of the predictions which came from eminent social scientists of the late 1960's and 1970's. It would appear that the majority of today's media have confused separation of Church and State with a separation of God and State. This has separated most of the press from a dispassionate discussion of religious issues and themes as they relate to our national well-being.

With few exceptions, nothing has *truly* changed with politicians, news analysts, and talk show hosts. While they view it as their legitimate and respectable function to discuss the current moral decline, increased juvenile crime and violence, spreading poverty, etc., they still berate and ridicule people of strong religious conviction for publicly discussing and analyzing the selfsame events. In doing so they effectively removed *The Source* of morality and peace from the public forum. The opinion molders will not allow God into the terms of the debate. They are already reaping the first part of the whirlwind consequences of that decision. But they either cannot or will not see that.

The one piece of free speech that is not treated with respect by the large majority of the opinion molders is the observation that a turning away from God and His law is the basal cause of our problems. Absolutely nothing will raise their ire faster than such an observation. For the majority of public opinion molders of the West, discussion of secular or social science solutions to our problems are legitimate and respectable, while a religious discussion of solutions is not.

The majority of the predecessors of today's opinion molders contributed in large part to our predicted problems. They did so by ridiculing those who accurately predicted disastrous results for a national culture based primarily in secular humanism. The majority of their successors refuse a free discussion of the only realistic Solution. And Americans of several generations *freely* follow their lead. *The opinion molders did not put a gun to the people's heads.* People have freely chosen to limit the terms of the debate to those of secular humanism.

Some objective men and women from the ranks of both social scientists and religious leaders of the mid-1970's saw twenty years into the future by the light of limited human reason. Would it not stand to reason that people informed by the omniscient God, true prophets, could have seen much more, much earlier?

E. APOCALYPSE NOW? IS THIS THE TIME OF ANTICHRIST?

1. The Power of Suggestion

There is an old psychological adage to the effect that, when people are under great stress, they are highly subject to the power of suggestion. Over the last few years the author has spoken with several U.S. Bishops about an observable contemporary lack of an attitude of *hopefulness* in both the East and the West. It is generally more pronounced in the West. This is observable amongst both the ranks of the laity and clergy. That lack of hopefulness is generally a cause of stress.

Of particular concern to these Bishops is their observation that a rising number of their laity and some of their priests are beginning to consider the possibility that this, the end of the 20th century, could be the time of *the* Antichrist or the general time of the end of the world. This phenomenon is in large part due to the recent appearance of certain books which *strongly suggest* that the Antichrist is just around the corner, possibly arriving on the scene even by the year 2000 A.D., or if not then, within the following decade. Since Antichrist must precede the end of the world, if he is not coming soon, then neither is the Parousia - the Second Coming of Christ.

Someone might object that since Jesus said, "But of that day and hour no one knows,"[17] no one can state with any degree of surety that this either is, or is not, the time of Antichrist!

(1) in the quoted passage Jesus is *specifically* addressing the Parousia, His Second Coming, and the Final Judgment

[17] Matt. 24:36

of the World. He is saying that no one knows the day nor the hour of the Parousia. In that passage He is *not* addressing the subject of the coming of Antichrist.

(2) Another explanation is the difference between a positive and a negative.

Jesus told his disciples how they might positively identify, first, the circumstances surrounding the destruction of the Temple in Jerusalem, and second, the advent of Antichrist, and third, other events surrounding the end times. Our Lord finished this discussion with,

> "From the fig tree learn its lesson; as soon as its branch becomes tender and puts forth its leaves, you know that summer is near. So also, when you see these things taking place you know that he [Antichrist] is *near*, at the very gates."[18]

In other words, specific signs *are* given us through Our Lord's direct Revelation. The signs give us measuring tools by which we can *both positively and negatively* determine whether *the signs of the times* match those predicted to precede the coming of Antichrist.

The first prophesied event for which Our Lord gave us impending signs is the destruction of the Temple in Jerusalem (which happened in 70 A.D.). The second prophesied "signed" event includes the signs preceding the coming of the Antichrist. *We are told to watch for those signs.* When those signs are missing (that is what the author means by "negative" signs), then the conditions set down by Our Lord for Antichrist's appearance simply are not there. Therefore, when those signs are absent, it cannot possibly yet be the time of Antichrist.

2. Predecessors have Thought They Saw some or All of the Signs of the Antichrist

Conditions were so chaotic in the last decade of the 6th century that Pope St. Gregory *considered the possibility* that the end times might be approaching because *some* of the foretold "signs"

18 Matt. 24:32-33

of Antichrist were present, but not all. Pope St. Gregory said:

> "As the Scripture foretold, all the glory of the world has perished. Cities are overthrown, camps uprooted, churches destroyed; no tiller of the land inhabits our land. Among ourselves, the poor remnant who are left, the sword of man rages incessantly and the hand of God deals slaughter from above. The World destruction which we heard was coming, we now see before our eyes; the regions of the earth are become to us an open book."[19]

As we can see, St. Gregory stops just short of affirming the imminent coming of Antichrist.

Some Christians in the last decade prior to the year 1000 thought that terrible events were at hand. While the Church gave this opinion no credence, in certain portions of Western Europe significant numbers of individuals even sold their lands and entered monasteries and convents to await the "foretold" release of the Devil. In 1948 the great Christian scholar and philosopher, Etienne Gilson, observed in his academic paper, *The Terrors of the Year Two Thousand*,

> "These men of the tenth century knew at least what they feared. Not at all - as has been erroneously reiterated - the end of the world, but an event which, on the contrary, was to precede it by a sufficiently long interval of time which was announced prophetically in the Apocalypse, ch. 20, v. 7: 'Then, when the thousand years are over, Satan will be let loose from his prison, and will go out to seduce the nations that live at the four corners of the earth' - that is the meaning of Gog and Magog - 'and muster them for battle, countless as the sand of the sea.'"[20]

As Gilson points out, there were a significant number of people who were concerned about this possibility. But these fears were not limited to the uneducated. Even some scholars of the 10th century

---

19 *The Building of Christendom, A History of Christendom*, Warren H. Carroll, Christendom College Press, 1987, p. 189. [For the interested reader, Dr. Carroll's series of general Church History Texts is simply the very best available in the English language. It is also still in print.]

20 *The Terrors of the Year Two Thousand*, Etienne Gilson, St. Michael's College, Toronto, Canada, Garden City Press Cooperative, 1949, p. 11.

were concerned about some "current events" which might portend Satan's release.

Some in the early 19th century thought Napoleon was the Antichrist, while others (both Protestant and Catholic) in the middle of the 20th thought Hitler might be he. If they had consistently applied the "fig leaf" analogy, if they had been thoroughly familiar with the "signs" of Antichrist given us in Revelation, they would have known Antichrist could most probably not have come at their time. That is because some of the signs prophesied in Scripture and Tradition to precede Antichrist were missing. *All* the predicted fig-leaf *signs of the times* were not present. When some signs are missing, that is always a *negative* sign.

3. Signs from Tradition

One of the signs from Tradition should have most certainly excluded Adolph Hitler. The common teaching of Christian Tradition is that Antichrist will be of Jewish descent (eg., Sts. Irenaeus, Ambrose; Jerome, Augustine, Pope Gregory the Great, and Anselm), and will make his capital in Jerusalem. That same Tradition teaches that his two principal opponents, the "Two Witnesses"[21] spoken of in the Book of Revelation, will also be Jewish. Hitler was not Jewish,[22] Jerusalem was not his capital, and there were not "Two Witnesses" (Jewish or otherwise) who were prominently and publicly opposing him. Therefore, anyone remotely familiar with the totality of apostolic Tradition on Antichrist would have sensed that neither Adolph Hitler nor Napoleon could have been he.

No one positively knows the "day nor the hour" of the Second Coming, or even way ahead of time when the Antichrist will come. But we *are* given signs of serial events or *proximate* signs which are foretold to immediately precede Antichrist's coming. When some of those "signs" are absent, in the negative sense, we have reasonable assurance that his time cannot yet be.

---

21 Revelation 11:3-12.

22 However, a number of genealogists record that Hitler was 1/4 Jewish.

F. SPECIFIC EVENTS WHICH MUST PRECEDE THE PAROUSIA

1. Prophecies of "The End" and The Catholic Catechism

The power of suggestion: Prophecies from several recent "prophets" have even hinted that the Second Coming will happen by the year 1998 or 2000. *Is that either possible or probable*?

I. Scripture tells us of a number of events which must precede the Second Coming of Christ. The Church has studied and interpreted these Scripturally foretold events for almost two thousand years.

2. The Catechism of the Catholic Church

When a Catholic wishes to quickly determine the teaching of the Church on a subject, the best quick source is the 1994 *Catechism of the Catholic Church*. We will be quoting from this text throughout the book. The doctrinal value of the *Catechism* is addressed in its section entitled "The doctrinal Value of the Text." There, Pope John Paul II is quoted as saying about it,

> "The *Catechism of the Catholic Church,* which I approved June 25 ... I declare it to be a sure norm for teaching the faith and thus a valid and legitimate instrument for ecclesial communion." ... The catechism is given to them [Church's Pastors and the Christian faithful] that it may be a sure and authentic reference text for teaching Catholic doctrine and particularly for preparing local catechisms."[23]

It is obvious from the words of the Holy Father that what is contained in the *Catechism* constitutes the official teaching of the Church. In relation to the Second Coming, the *Catechism* states,

> **"The glorious Messiah's coming is suspended at every moment of history until his recognition by 'all Israel,'** for 'a hardening has come upon part of Israel' in their unbelief'

23 *Catechism of the Catholic Church*, Libreria Editrice Vaticana, St. Paul Books and Media, 1994, p. 5.

> toward Jesus.[568] ... The 'full inclusion' of the Jews in the Messiah's salvation, in the wake of 'the full number of the Gentiles'[571] will enable the People of God to achieve 'the measure of the stature of the fullness of Christ,' in which 'God may be all in all.[572]'" [24]

Here the *Catechism* clearly references the Scripturally foretold "full inclusion" or *mass conversion* of the Jews to Christ. The *Catechism* clearly teaches that the Second Coming of Christ cannot happen until the conversion of "all Israel." That is not a new teaching. It has been the traditional teaching of the Church since its infancy.

The sentence you are reading right now was written in 1996. The author sees no sign of an *en masse* conversion of the Jews. Until we see an *en masse* conversion of the Jews to Christ, you can rest assured that the Second Coming cannot happen. If that does not happen prior to the year 2000, then neither will the Second Coming. *If any alleged prophecy states otherwise, you can be absolutely certain that prophecy is not genuine, or, the prophecy has been grossly misunderstood by the "prophet."*[25]

II. The Reign of Antichrist must also precede the Second Coming of Christ. As the *Caetchism* teaches,

> "Before Christ's second coming the Church must pass through a final trial that will shake the faith of many believers.[573] The persecution that accompanies her pilgrimage on earth will unveil the 'mystery of iniquity' in the form of a religious deception ... The supreme religious deception is that of the Antichrist"[26]

As we can see, the Church teaches there will be an ultimate or "supreme" Antichrist, whose ultimate coming is clearly taught to precede the Second Coming of Christ.

---

[24] *Ibid.* #674, p. 176. The internal Footnote #568 cites Rom. 11:20-26 and Mat. 23:39. Footnote #571 cites Rom. 11:12, 25; cf. Lk. 21:24.

[25] As will be fully discussed later in the book, a genuine prophet can misunderstand or misinterpret something they hear in a genuine prophecy. In some ways and in some cases, a prophet can be the most poorly qualified person to interpret his or her received prophecy.

[26] *The Catholic Catechism,* #675, p.176.

The *Catechism* also confirms St. Paul's and St. John's teaching that there are many antichrists, but it also affirms the "supreme" Antichrist, whose coming must precede the Parousia. We are specifically told in the Book of Revelation that the reign of "the" Antichrist will last for three and one half years (1,260 days). *The constant teaching of the Fathers of the Church is that this figure is a "proper"*[27] *literal one, that it is not an allegorical number.* Additionally, Scripture speaks of a primary *False Prophet* who paves the way for Antichrist, and a great military leader who will help to prepare the way for him, who will be in the field performing certain publicly recognizable acts for some time preceding Antichrist.

III. As will be more amply demonstrated later, according to Scripture and Tradition, (especially the writings of the Fathers of the Church) prior to the Second Coming of Christ, we must see and experience,

1 The mass conversion of the Jews to Christ.
2 The Reign of Antichrist - which lasts three and one half years.
3 After the death of Antichrist, a time of unknown duration for a final repentance and conversion of the nations.
4 Prior to the coming of Antichrist, the appearance of the False prophet who will precede him, the appearance of the man destined to be his herald.
5 The appearance of a great military leader, who will militarily prepare the way for Antichrist. (This is not an exhaustive list of those things which must precede him. But it is enough for the moment to make our point.)
6 The "fullness" of the Gentiles. This has been universally interpreted to refer to St. Paul's reference to a general revolt or apostasy which is universal on the earth.

According to Scripture, Tradition (most especially the Fathers of the Church), *minimally*, the processes or events described above should take an absolute minimum of five years for completion. *As this is being written, it is already less than five years till the year 2000.*

---

[27] See definition in footnote in section on "Authority of the Fathers".

ADDITIONALLY: As to the Second Coming of Christ, according to the words of Our Lord, no one knows "the day or the hour, not even the angels in heaven."[28] Therefore if anyone claims to name the time of the Parousia well ahead of that event, any Christian may feel secure in the fact that that "prophet" is seriously mistaken in one way or another. This holds true no matter how prestigious the alleged "prophet" or "expert on prophecy" might be. Beware of either confused or false prophets - or their potentially confused interpreters!

3. The Predicted Signs of the Times of Antichrist

The predicted signs from the two sources of Revelation (Tradition and Scripture) on the coming of Antichrist and various commentaries thereon by Fathers and Doctors of the Church will be presented in this book. From that body of evidence, an exposition will be developed vis-a-vis why our present times are highly unlikely *immediately* to precede either the times of Antichrist, or the Parousia which follows sometime after him.

4. The First Sign

According to the Fathers of the Church, there are two most specific signs of the impending approach of Antichrist which are provided for us by Tradition and Scripture. The first sign is a universal or world-wide falling away from the faith. This concept is not only found in St. Paul, but also in the Apocalypse and many others books of both the Old and the New Testament. According to the Fathers and Doctors of the Church, this "apostasy" or "revolt" (as St. Paul calls it) is not something which will be merely regional. It will be worldwide.

5. The First "Sign" of Antichrist Appears to be Missing

Many recent prophecies claiming to announce the imminent arrival of Antichrist point out the heresy problems currently observ-

---

28 This does not theologically mean that Jesus Christ, the Second Person of the Blessed Trinity, did not also know this.

able in the Church. That thesis has a major flaw. It is geographically limited. The Christological apostasy or theological problems currently being experienced by those in the Western or Latin part of the Catholic Church are *not* being universally experienced in the East. The rather broad doctrinal error currently found in the West is **not** universally found in the East. Even in the West, in many parts of Africa, the Faith is thriving and the faith of the average believer is orthodox, faithful to the traditional teachings of the Church. This fact alone should make it obvious that this the universal revolt or apostasy spoken of by St. Paul does not yet exist.

That is why *prophesy* books currently being sold which appear to be predicting the rise of either the Antichrist or the Second Coming of Christ by the year 2000 are so unfortunate. Many people are becoming overly concerned or neutralized by an obsession created by these books. Very frankly, this type of theory can only be convincingly portrayed to those who are not current in their knowledge about the state of the Church around the globe. But there are people who *are* well-informed who still find this theory *psychologically* attractive. Why?

G. THE THEORY THAT ANTICHRIST IS COMING CAN BE EMOTIONALLY APPEALING

The idea that the Antichrist is "just around the corner" can have great emotional appeal, especially in very troubled times. We are all human and live in the human condition. If The Antichrist is just around the corner, then our troubles would end one way or another in a very short period of time. *They might end without our having to do anything. That is very attractive, because that idea relieves one of a great deal of personal responsibility.* That idea has a tremendous appeal for any human being no matter how brilliant, well-informed and well-educated. Education does not change our basic human nature.

The idea that "Antichrist is coming" can *subconsciously* (but erroneously) relieve us of our sense of personal responsibility to become or remain involved in an immoral world which does not want to hear a Christian moral message. If one thinks "it is all going to end tomorrow," then what is the point of announcing the Gospel, of shouting the good news from the rooftops? The "Antichrist is coming tomorrow" message can have great emotional appeal to people who are bone-tired from witnessing for Christ and working in the spread of His Gospel.

That message can give someone just the quasi-rational excuse he subconsciously needs to stop working so hard for the salvation of souls. While it can make people very attentive to the state of their own souls, and to shared *communio* with those who share their apocalyptic beliefs, it can also make them unmindful of their Christian missionary responsibility for the souls of others.

That is the dangerous appeal of this "Antichrist is just around the corner" message. Its subconscious effects are extremely subtle, and its appeal is clearly and presently dangerous to the health of the Body of Christ here on earth. *It has an alluring escapist appeal.* It is spreading, largely thanks to the aforementioned books. It cannot be ignored. It must be confronted and confounded by sound argumentation.

If we were living through a relatively peaceful era, rather than probably the bloodiest and most troubled in the history of mankind, today's people would not be nearly so susceptible to the power of suggestion. Our times, however, are extremely stressful. There has been no real peace in this century. It has been one constant struggle of wars, and political and financial disasters and tensions. The mass murders of our century are unchallenged as to their scale. People who have grown up in such an ambiance are almost by definition going to be highly susceptible to suggestion. It behooves us in times like these to present Christian truth clearly.

H. 1000 YEARS OF PEACE - A MILLENNIUM?

There is an additional problem attendant to those described immediately above. There is beginning to appear amongst the ranks of some contemporary Catholics a belief in the possibility of *a physical 1000-year reign of Christ, with his "saints"* here on earth. This type of belief is traditionally referred to as the "Millennium." Another variation of that theme is that when the present woes are over we have some kind of Scriptural guarantee of some kind of an era of peace of 1000 years duration. This theory also has an almost overwhelming "escapist" appeal in times of trouble. That last scenario is usually tied in to Millenium theories.

It is true that some of the early Eastern and Western Fathers of the Church adhered to some parts or all of that formulary.[29] But largely due to Origen[30] in the East, and Sts. Jerome and Augustine[31] in the West, it was ultimately totally discredited. It was rejected by the early Church in the 5th century under the alternate titles of "Chiliasm," "Millenarism," or "Millenarianism." That process is described in the following quotation,

> "...both Chiliasm [the teaching of a Millennium] and Montanism were declared heretical and were excluded from the universal church; for they both denied this vision [the "Christ is the end of the ages" vision] and awaited still another period of more definitive salvation to follow after the age of Christ."[32]

As the 1994 *Catechism of the Catholic Church* teaches,

> "The Church has rejected **even modified forms** of this falsification of the kingdom to come under the name of millenarianism, especially the 'intrinsically perverse' political form of a secular messianism"[33] [emphasis added]

---

29 Called "Millenarianism" or "Millenarism", or "Chiliasm,"

30 Millenarianism was abandoned by almost all the Eastern Fathers after the "anti-Millenarianist" writings of Origin (principal writings inter 220-251 A.D.). The heretic Apollinaris [beginning around 376 A.D.] was the last major Eastern advocate of Millenarism. In 381, he was condemned for his heresy *against* the "human truly rational soul in Christ" both by Pope St. Damasus at the Council of Rome, and by the Eastern Bishops at the Council of Constantinople. Another of his prominent teachings was Millenarianism. While not officially condemned at this council, this teaching had already been coming under increasingly consistent heavy attack from the Fathers of the Church, and was by this time generally looked upon disfavorably.

31 In the West, Millenarianism was over by the first quarter of the 5th century due in large part to the prestige and writings of Sts. Jerome & Augustine (Augustine at first accepted a modified form of Chiliasm but later rejected the entire Millenarianist doctrine [*De Civitate Dei*, XX,7]).

32 *The Theology of History in St. Bonaventure*, Joseph Ratzinger, English Edition-translated by Zachary Hayes, O.F.M., Franciscan Herald Press, Chicago, 1971, p. 96.

33 *Catechism of the Catholic Church*, Libreria Editrice Vaticana, St. Paul Books and Media, 1994., # 676, p. 177.

From the 5th century until the advent of the Anabaptists over a thousand years later, Millenarianism was for the most part a dead letter amongst Christians. With the advent of the 16th century Anabaptists, Millenarianism began to be resurrected.[34] Proof from history and documents of the Church (especially from the writings of Augustine and Jerome) will be presented later showing that; Millenarianism *even under modified forms* is "rejected" by teachings of the Church.

The same discussion will show that it is totally inconsistent with a comprehensive view of Scripture. In other words, Millenarianism only seems plausible when (a) certain Scriptural passages are either taken out of context, (b) misunderstood within context, or (c) both, and (d) the teachings from Tradition are totally unknown or ignored.

Unfortunately, conjecture about a literal 1000-year peaceful reign of Christ on earth is no longer limited to heirs of Anabaptist General Eschatology. Within the last fifty years, even a few legitimate Catholic Scholars have shown signs of reconsidering this teaching. *The cause of this reversal is unfortunately quite easy to identify*. It stems from a lack of understanding of the teachings from Tradition, particularly as found in the writings of the Fathers of the Church.

1. Tradition - In Part, the Writings of the Fathers

The Fathers of the Church obeyed St. Paul where he taught:

> "So then, Brethren, stand firm and hold fast to the *traditions* that you were taught by us, EITHER BY WORD OR BY OUR LETTER."[35]

---

[34] This led to many Doctors of the Church restating the traditional positions of the Church on this subject. See in particular the discussions of this subject in Bellarmine's *De Summo Pontifice* which are quoted later in this book.

[35] 2nd. Thessalonians, 2:15 RSV. Catholic Edition, 1965. In the current official Church Biblical text, the Latin *New Vulgate*, the text reads, "Itaque, fratres, state et tenete traditiones, quas didicistis sive per sermonem sive per epistulam nostram." That most accurately translates into, "Stand firm and hold fast to the traditions **which** you *have learned*, either by (our) word, or by our Epistle." "Didicistis" is the "perfect second person plural" form which comes from the root latin verb "to learn", not, "to teach.".

As we will read later, the Fathers sorted out many eschatological questions from what had been handed down to them both orally and in writing from the Apostles. The writings of the Fathers have not been sufficiently taught in most seminaries for years. That is a major part of the problem. Those who have thoroughly read the Fathers understand what was approved and what was condemned by those who were trained by the Apostles and their immediate successors who handed down those teachings. Nowhere is that more important than in the study of the end times.

Here, two old sayings are very apropos: "Those who refuse to learn from history are condemned to repeat its mistakes." "Those who fail to read have no advantage over those who cannot." Those who fail for one reason or another to read the Fathers, are unaware of (1) the ideas which they condemned as *not* being of apostolic Tradition, and (2) those which they approved as apostolic. Therefore, when one of the condemned ideas rises up again, the Patristic non-reader is not in a position to recognize it as a previously condemned theological error. That is one major reason so many heresies which the Fathers condemned as being inconsistent with the teachings of the Apostles are gaining new ground within the ranks of the Church.

I. DOES A CHASTISEMENT NECESSARILY SIGNIFY THE END OF TIME?

One of the major theses of this book is that it is, at the very least, highly improbable that this is the time of the Antichrist. The reason is that some of the signs of his imminent arrival which are given to us in Revelation simply are not here. There are *negative* signs of our times in relation to the advent of Antichrist.

Another major thesis is that many prophecies of Scripture, and of many highly credible prophecies of canonized Saints, Blessed, and Venerable, and other *Church-approved* sources conditionally predict a pre-Antichrist worldwide Chastisement of seemingly cataclysmic proportions. According to the prophecies, (1) whether that Chastisement happens at all, and (2) the degree of its possible severity, are (3) conditional upon people's cooperation with the grace of God in any given age. If such a Chastisement occurs because of lack of cooperation with grace, it is foretold to well precede and be less severe than the **Major Chastisement of Antichrist**.

1. A Minor Chastisement

This less severe Chastisement is often referred to as a **Minor Chastisement.** According to all the prophecies of a "minor" chastisement from approved sources, that Chastisement is avertable for any given point in history. When and if it occurs depends totally upon mankind. If it occurs (*it is conditional*) the Minor Chastisement will immediately precede a significant period of peace which is foretold to precede Antichrist;[36] i.e., such a **Minor Chastisement** would not be part of *the end of the world* or the specific *end times.* **It and the period of peace to follow it would precede the Antichrist and the ultimate end times.**

The prophesied impending signs of this *Minor* yet worldwide Chastisement do *appear* to be growing. Unlike the prophesied signs of the advent of the Major Chastisement of Antichrist, all the signs of the Minor Chastisement do *appear* to be at least *partially* in place. But appearances are often deceiving. Again, those signs of a Minor Chastisement are related to "conditional" prophecies. The conditions are that unless a significant number of people begin to seek out and cooperate with the will of God, at some time in the future there will be a chastisement. But even if it should happen, it will *not* be the tribulation of Antichrist.

2. Prophecy of the Antichrist is *Not* Conditional

There is nothing "conditional" about the Chastisement or Tribulation of an individual Antichrist. (*If the reader has previously been led to believe that the Antichrist is or can be something other than an individual man, please reserve judgment on this till later in the book.*) Antichrist's ultimate appearance is not in question - it is not conditional upon anything. According to public prophecies

---

36 Such a period of peace does not rest solely upon private prophecy but also has a strong basis in Tradition and Scripture. This basis from Tradition and Scripture will be developed later in the book.

contained in Revelation his inevitable appearance is only a matter of time. On the other hand, the Minor Chastisement could have been, and might still be totally averted, on condition of sufficient cooperation by mankind with the grace of God.

3. Prophecies About the 20th Century

Centuries ago, prophecies were written down which specifically named the time for their fulfillment as the twentieth century. *They come from sources which have been approved by the Church.* There are two themes which those prophecies have in common. They predict that ours will be an age in which "heresy" becomes rampant in the Church in the West. They predict that a major source of this heresy will be "senseless questions and elaborate arguments." They predict those questions and arguments which will be used to challenge even the most basic beliefs of Christianity - no matter how time-honored and venerable they might be.

4. Some Parts of this Book are Easier to Read than Others

The effects of *extreme* higher critics on the Church in the West are discussed in some detail in a latter portion of Chapter 1 (higher critical attacks on Tradition). Chapter 2 is entitled "Extremist "Higher Criticism" and its "Demythologizing" of REVELATION." Chapter 2 will also take some concentration on the part of the reader.

Reading the last portion of Chapter 1 and all of Chapter 2 with sufficient care will reap a heavy reward. Those who do so will have a much deeper understanding of contemporary problems being experienced by the Church. Most importantly, such a reader will have a much greater opportunity to decide for himself or herself whether centuries old prophecies about the 20th century are being fulfilled by today's extreme higher critics. But the reader who skips these materials in Chapter 2 should still understand much of the significance of such prophecies.

5. This Book Deals With Prophesied Events for Many Generations to Come

This book is both for *today and tomorrow*. It is *not* written merely to view possibilities of what will happen today and in the near future. It is *not* intended merely to extinguish some contemporary and unjustified fears of the improbable imminent appearance of Antichrist. Rather it covers:

(1) The sweep of those things conditionally prophesied to happen during our time,
(2) An apparently unconditional age of peace to follow sometime in the future. It is *apparently* an unconditional age, because such an age seems to be indicated both in Tradition and Scripture,
(3) The subsequent deterioration of that peaceful age,
(4) The evolution of that deterioration into the Reign of Antichrist, and then,
(5) Subsequent events up till the end of time.

But the ultimate thesis of the book is that our time is in particular a period for hope, it is not a period for fear. It is a book of hope for all who love God. It is a book of hope for us, our children, our grandchildren, and hopefully and possibly many generations to follow.

PROLOGUE

A. SIGNS OF OUR TIMES

This book might never have been completed *at this time* except for one event. That event is the recent circulation of books and alleged prophecies beginning in the late 1980's, which are leading many people to believe that (1) the coming of Antichrist, (2) the Second Coming of Christ, and (3) some form of Millennium are quite literally upon us. St. Paul admonishes us,

> **"Now concerning the coming of our Lord Jesus Christ and our assembling to meet him,** ***we beg you, brethren, not to be quickly shaken in mind or excited, either by spirit or by word*****, or by letter purporting to be from us, to the effect that the day of the Lord has come.** Let no one deceive you in any way; for that day will not come, unless the rebellion[1] comes first, and the man of lawlessness is revealed, the son of perdition, who opposes and exalts himself against every so-called god or object of worship, so that he takes his seat in the temple of God, proclaiming himself to be God. *Do you not remember that when I was still with you I told you this*?"[2]

St. Augustine comments on the indiscretion and dire consequences of those who precipitously announce the Second Coming of Christ,

> "He who indiscreetly announces the coming of Christ falls into a noxious error. Supposing that his prophecy is not justified by the event, men will not say that the event has

[1] Many early texts alternately translate "rebellion" as "revolt" or "apostasy."
[2] 2nd. Thessalonians, 2:1-6, RSV, Catholic Edition, 1965.

> been postponed, but they will say that it will never happen, which must prove very injurious to their faith."[3]

Those who are propagating the idea that the Antichrist, and/or the Second Coming, and/or some kind of a Millenium are events within the proximate future should seriously reread and prayerfully consider those words of St. Augustine. Following the publication of some of the above-mentioned books and alleged prophecies, the author received many letters and telephone calls from people throughout the United States asking him if he thought the Antichrist and the Second Coming of Christ could be events of the near future. One caller said to him, "If all of this is true, *what's the use*, since it's all going to be over in a few of years, anyway?"

That question set off alarm bells in the author's head. The man who asked it is a nationally- known figure who has a well-deserved reputation for remaining calm and collected under adverse circumstances. He is a very well-educated layman who additionally knows his Catholic doctrine quite well. But one of the books which intimate that Antichrist and the Second Coming were in the near future had **"shaken in mind or excited"** this normally cool-headed leader.

The author had previously discussed this problem with several U.S. Bishops. They had expressed concern about the deleterious effects of the faithful precipitously coming to anticipate the coming of Antichrist and/or the Second Coming of Christ. They also observed that this was a problem not just with the faithful, but also with some of their priests. The biggest problem is the "what's the use" reaction. Instead of evangelizing, many people who think that Antichrist is just around the corner tend to look for a place to hide and to ride out the storm. It is a quite natural, highly predictable human reaction.

1. Will Discussing the Subject Make Matters Worse?

There are some who advise not to write any more on the subject because that will only bring even more attention to it. To such people the author and some Bishops of his acquaintance would

[3] Epist. 80 ad Heszch.

respond with the proverb, "It does no good to attempt to close the barn door after the horse is out." In the U.S. alone, there are many hundreds of thousands of copies of very recent books in circulation which *are* leading people to believe that Antichrist and the Second Coming of Christ are in the immediate future. *The horse is already out.*

Ignoring a problem never solves it. The author personally knows a large number of people who have read one or more of these books. The large percentage of those readers have already become excited or disturbed in spirit by such reading. The circulation of the ideas in such books is now spreading rapidly, not diminishing. For any bishop who might be unaware of the scope of the problem, be assured that the spread is exponential, it is not just linear. And it is not limited to your laity, it is also spreading amongst some of your clergy.

2. Changes in Attitude in the Last Forty Years

Forty years ago, in the U.S. and Canada, horoscopes were laughed at by the vast majority of the population, probably 99% or higher. That is no longer the case. Forty years ago people who consulted psychics and mystics to "see" their future were laughed at by the same vast majority. The only contact normal people had with such a phenomenon was as a gag at a side-show tent at a carnival or a circus. That is also no longer the case in the U.S. and Canada.

Most of the citizens of both countries still do *not* consult horoscopes or psychics. But, due to the dramatic recent spread of such practices it is no longer looked upon as an *unusual* oddity to do so. As an example: The former U.S. First Lady, Nancy Reagan, has publicly admitted that she did so. U.S. President Reagan was regularly influenced in his decision making by his wife's consulting of a medium!

Over the last forty to fifty years ideas have been spread abroad *questioning* traditional belief about what is found in Scripture. Many Catholics, Protestants, and even Jews, who were affected by this "questioning" have lost their particular faith. As the modern expression goes, they became "unchurched." They lost their faith AND HOPE in whatever level they were at in the Judeo-Christian belief system.[4] The process began in France and Germany about ten years prior to its onslaught in the U.S. and Canada. Many of the Catholics and Protestants *who left their "church"* have sought to fill the natural hunger for eschatological knowledge of the future through mediums and horoscopes. This is happening throughout the West.

3. Catholics Who Stayed in Church

In a growing number of Catholics who remained in the Church, the questioning of traditional belief has lead to a totally subconscious reaction. As their psychological comfort found in certitude of Scriptural interpretation has been shaken, many have subconsciously sought more of that comfort and security in private prophecy. Certitude in faith can only come from Revelation. Intellectually, they know that private prophecy is not of faith. Despite that knowledge, because of contemporary confusion - it is nevertheless where many now seek some eschatological *certitudinal* comfort. Consequently, a growing number of Catholics are now becoming *engrossed* in private prophecy. Much of this prophecy is from unapproved sources.

4. The Solution Does Not Lie in Condemnation

As a rule, only those who teach a positive belief with authority can effectively teach a negation. The answer to the problem of overemphasis of private prophecy lies not in denigrating those Christians who have sought eschatological comfort in private prophecy. It lies in positive teaching of the eschatological teachings of the Church.

Perceived Confusion in the Church

God in His wisdom knows the strengths, weaknesses and needs of our human nature which he created. Every psychologist knows that fear of the unknown, particularly fear of the *future* unknown is

[4] For the Christians who are unaware of it, the Jewish religious communities have also suffered many losses through this process. The extreme higher critical theories attack traditional acceptance of both the Old and New Testaments.

an integral part of fallen man's psychological profile. In Scripture, God gave us *some* certain eschatological knowledge about the future. That eschatological knowledge is part of, and participates in, the Christian virtue of Hope. *Those Scriptural prophecies*, when properly understood, *sufficiently fill a deep-seated psychological need in man as God created him.*

That is why by itself, authoritative condemnation of *an over-emphasizing* of private prophecy will have no lasting affect. The answer to an *over-emphasis*[5] of private prophecy *lies in positive exposition of traditional Scriptural interpretation, especially in the preaching of the traditional eschatological teachings of the Church about latter and end times.*

5. Contemporary Lack of knowledge in General Eschatology

The *broad view* of prophesied future events which comes particularly through Revelation, only ancillarily expanded through approved Catholic sources, can be of great value in balancing a misguided view that Antichrist is "just around the corner." Only in an absence of this broad view has it been possible (1) for fears of an immediate coming of Antichrist to take hold, or (2) the equally erroneous idea that Antichrist will or can appear as something other than an individual man. (e.g., Many fears are abroad that the New Age Movement or some new world supergovernment could be the Antichrist.)

That absence of a broad view initially proceeds from a contemporary lack of consistent sound teachings from Tradition and Scripture on the end times. Such teaching is traditionally called General (vs. Individual) Eschatology. A balanced view of General Eschatology, generated from Tradition (particularly from the exegesis of the Fathers of the Church), and Scripture, indicates a significant series of events yet to precede Antichrist.

---

[5] This discourse is not meant to denigrate authentic private Catholic prophecy. As discussed earlier, the "Consecration" which Pope John Paul performed was a response to private revelation from Fatima. The Holy Father has even made a pilgrimage to Fatima. Here we are only discussing an emphasis on private prophecy which grows so strong that it begins to supplant the role of Revelation. Usually this happens without the person so affected even being aware of this shift of emphasis.

When the author was growing up in the 1940's and 1950's, he recalls that one usually got at least one sermon every couple of years with sound exegesis on the Antichrist and end times. The author unfortunately recalls hearing only a couple of such sermons in the last thirty years.[6] Those occurred within the last year at one parish. That, by definition, is almost a vacuum. Can the laity or even some priests be blamed for falling into an erroneous concept if they have not been effectively taught the sound one to counter it?

In addition to the public prophecy of Scripture and Tradition, private prophecies from canonized Saints, Blessed and Venerable and other approved sources, in ancillary consonance with Revelation, similarly indicate that a significant series of events await us before the appearance of Antichrist.

Private prophecies even of canonized Saints, or even those with the prestige of Fatima, are not of faith, and can only be mentioned with great prudence. But when properly labeled as *private prophecy* (which by definition is not of faith) they can be well-utilized in a book to counter unapproved private prophecies which are leading people into error. This is an example of effectively fighting fire with fire.

In the 1940's and 1950's many parish priests spoke of the prophecies of Fatima from the pulpit. This they did with the full permission of their Bishops. Those prophecies from an *approved* source predict "a certain period of peace for the world." That peace is prophesied to arrive prior to the apocalyptic events of Antichrist and the Parousia.

Several Bishops recommended to this author the completion of *this* book. These are several reasons:

(1) Most Bishops today are highly trepidatious (for very understandable reasons) about public discussion of non-approved private prophecy. When a Bishop does so *he most often winds up being quoted out of context.* Even if that were not a problem, most Bishops would not even want to dignify alleged prophecies that "Antichrist is just around the corner" by responding to them

---

[6] The author very recently heard those two sermons delivered by a parish priest from the pulpit at a Sunday Mass. There are some encouraging indications that in some quarters things may be beginning to turn around.

directly. This places a bishop in a "catch 22" situation. Many a bishop feels as if (to use a popular expression) he is "damned if he does, and damned if he doesn't." BUT IT MUST BE RESPONDED TO.

(2) People who have already been affected by precipitous apocalyptic fears generated by reading several recent "prophecy books" would probably discount the opinions of anyone who in principle scoffs at private prophecy.

(3) Therefore, combining #'s (1) & (2), who would be better suited to convincingly contend against *unapproved* sources which hint that Antichrist is just around the corner, than (a) a layman, (b) who is not a general "scoffer" at the charism of private prophecy?

Catholics who have fallen into the belief that the Antichrist and the Parousia are just around the corner have done so primarily from,

(1) Private prophecy from *unapproved* sources, and,
(2) In some cases, a consequent serious misreading of Scripture, heavily induced by #1.

TO THE READER WHO HAS BEEN SO SHAKEN: This author does *not* take private prophecies lightly. He most certainly does not laugh at prophecies emanating from Fatima and other approved sources which conditionally predict a future chastisement of mankind if man does not return to God. Such prophecies about a possible chastisement come from too many credible approved sources to be taken lightly. Fatima is only one of many such sources. *But that is an entirely different subject than the Antichrist and the Parousia.*

If such a Chastisement does takes place some day as conditionally prophesied, it will be monumental. According to statements of numerous canonized Saints, many people will erroneously come to the conclusion that it is the end of the world -- when it definitely is not. If such a Chastisement were to occur in our lifetime, a balanced view of both Revelation and only ancillarily -- approved private prophetic sources indicate it would not be part of the Parousia nor end of the world.

6. Can A Chastisement Happen Without Antichrist?

A balanced view of Eschatology requires a *primary* understanding of those things prophesied through the two sources of *Revelation, Sacred Tradition and Sacred Scripture.* The primary source for understanding those public prophecies correctly is through the writings of the Fathers and Doctors of the Church AND the constant eschatological teaching of the Magisterium.

Years ago it was normally sufficient in order to demonstrate the truth of something to a Catholic to prove it was from Tradition. Today, there is less understanding of the role of Tradition than there was even forty or fifty years ago. *Most contemporary Western Catholics are unaware of the teaching of the Church on the role of Tradition in determining what we are to believe.*

Most Catholics have not read nor correctly understood the teachings of Vatican Council II on Tradition. More specifically, compared with a few decades ago, a much smaller number of Catholics is aware of the authority and role of the Fathers of the Church in determining doctrine. That role is also clearly spelled out in the documents of Vatican Council II. Therefore, the role of Tradition and the Fathers is going to be generally developed in this book, and most specifically as it deals with the latter and end times.

Very secondarily, there are many prophecies which *appear* to relate to our time which come from the ranks of many canonized Saints, Blessed, and Venerable and other Church-approved sources. Their specific value lies in that they conditionally predict a future chastisement *which does not include Antichrist*, but rather, *a conditional chastisement which comes well before Antichrist.* It is a chastisement which can be averted by cooperation with grace.

7. A Limited View From Recent Prophecies

A view of prophecy whose *primary* understanding restrictedly comes from recent private prophecies (approved or not) could hardly produce a balanced picture. Such a view would be incredibly unbalanced. A balanced view of prophecy absolutely *requires* an anchoring in the sources of Revelation (Tradition and Scripture). Such a view depends on the exegesis of the Fathers and Doctors of the Church, and the constant eschatological teaching of the Magisterium. Only then, could private prophecy (which is not of faith) get a hearing in the light of that which is contained in Tradition and Scripture - as interpreted by the *teaching office* of the Church. **A balanced view of prophecy concerning the latter and end times is the intended object of this book. Such a view *must* be anchored in *Revelation - the source of our doctrinal and moral beliefs as Christians.***

The Church Does Not Denigrate Private Revelation

It will also be demonstrated that in the mind of the Church, a balanced view does *not* make light of nor denigrate the charism of private prophecy from canonized Saints, Blessed, Venerable, and other *approved* prophets known for the faithfulness of their lives. *Rather, a balanced view attempts to understand them within the guidelines set for us by the Church.*

B. OUR TIME IN PERSPECTIVE

At a retreat conducted by U.S. Archbishop Fulton J. Sheen in the late "1970's," he observed that from an historic perspective, in our age the Church and the world were suffering *in an almost unprecedented manner.* He said that of late we had been:

> "... surfeited with sociological, psychological, and theological surveys of what has happened to the Church, but they are not of much avail because cultural reasons do not explain what has happened, because the Church has undergone a great general crisis and particularly some degeneration in every country in the world. If there were cultural reasons, the effect would not be so universal. It can only be therefore, that there are some other causes besides the cultural and the natural at work. And one that is not to be neglected is the Demonic."[7]

[7] This quote is transcribed from the audio tape series, *Renewal and Reconciliation, Retreat Conferences by Archbishop Fulton J. Sheen*. Minister-O-Media, Inc. 1976. These are tapes of "conferences given by Archbishop Fulton J. Sheen for the priests of the Archdiocese of Washington, D.C., at *Loyola on Potomac Retreat House* during their annual priests' retreat" in 1976.

Sheen, quoting voluminous psychological studies conducted by Christian psychologists, gave three psychological signs of the Demonic; (1) Nudity, (2) Violence with contempt for life. (3) Schizophrenia, split mentalities. He gave the example of the possessed young man whom Jesus exorcised in the land of the Gadarenes who possessed all three symptoms. The young man was naked, was violent (he could not even be kept in chains). And thirdly, when Jesus asked him who he was, a voice answered, "We are legion."

Sheen then gave the Biblical or theological sign of the Demonic -- **CONTEMPT FOR THE CROSS.** He gave as one of many examples the fact that when Peter attempted to keep Jesus from the Cross, Jesus responded, "Get behind me, Satan."

Another of Bishop Sheen's observations was his famous quotation that, "Our dreams have been unholy." He was referring to the patent materialism of our age -- in that people in general are much more concerned about their homes, cars, material things, than they are about the state of their souls. As he pointed out, we in the West, particularly in the United States of America, have also been instrumental in exporting this mind set to the rest of the world. Our materialism and its companion rejection of the cross he observed were the cause of our general malaise.

In historical perspective, the West first embraced materialism -- which is incompatible with the Cross. As a culture the West subsequently rejected Christ and the Cross. This has left Satan free to work out his diabolical influence on our minds and hearts. When they rejected Christ and the Cross, they also rejected belief in Satan. As more than one theologian has pointed out, Satan has no greater advantage than that people fail to believe in his existence. Even military tacticians understand that the unseen enemy is always the most dangerous enemy.

C. THE ROLE OF FATIMA

To end Demonic influence and reduce Satanically inspired suffering in our age, in order to end the major problems of our age, God sent us a peace and prosperity plan for our century. On July 13, 1917 at Fatima, Portugal, Our Lady said that the key to Peace was inner conversion of the people, reparation, and Consecration to her Immaculate Heart and the daily Rosary. She even introduced herself as "The Lady of the Rosary."

1. Fatima Terms for Peace

Our Lady announced that she would "return" to ask for the Consecration of Russia to her Immaculate Heart, and for the "First Saturdays" of reparation. On June 13, 1929, Mary "returned" to Lucia and asked for the consecration of Russia to her Immaculate Heart, to be performed by the Pope in union with all the Bishops of the world. This was another of the things required for the "peaceful" conversion of Russia which would keep that country from spreading her errors throughout the world.

If this request was fulfilled in conjunction with the prior requests for conversion of hearts, the daily Rosary and Consecration to her Immaculate Heart, it would as promised usher in a peaceful conversion of Russia[8] and a general era of peace for the World. This request was passed on to the Papacy by Sr. Lucy, one of the seers at Fatima. Every Pope since Pius XI has publicly endorsed and recognized this two-part Fatima peace plan.

D. THE CONSECRATION

The Holy Father personally performed a Consecration of "the World" on March 25, 1984. Shortly before this date he sent a copy of the consecration to all the Bishops of the world and asked them to join him in this Consecration. It is common knowledge that the Consecration was generated by private prophecy emanating from the private revelations at Fatima. That fact alone should readily establish the accuracy of an earlier statement in this book:

> It will be demonstrated that in the mind of the Church, a balanced view also does *not* make light of or denigrate the

---

[8] This did not cast an aspersion on Russia. Rather, Russia is to serve a leadership role for other nations of the world on this road to inner conversion. This theme is developed more fully later in the book.

> charism of private prophecy from canonized Saints, Blessed, Venerable, and other 'approved' good Catholics known for the faithfulness of their lives. Rather, a balanced view attempts to understand them within the guidelines set for us by the Church.

We now give the salient portions of the text of the Consecration as they were reported in *L'Osservatore Romano* (the official Vatican Newspaper).

> "In a special way we entrust and *consecrate to You those individuals and nations* which particularly need to be thus entrusted and consecrated.
>
> The power of this consecration will last for all time and *embraces all individuals, peoples and nations.*
>
> In entrusting to You, O Mother, the world, all individuals and peoples, we also entrust to You this very *consecration of the world*, placing it in Your Motherly Heart." [all emphasis - the authors]

We have no idea how many of the Bishops complied with His Holiness' request. But the Holy Father did all that he felt he could at that time. The author has been personally told by an American Bishop that, "Very many (Bishops) did, perhaps a large majority; but not all."

The following point must be reiterated. The Consecration which the Holy Father performed in 1984 was a direct consequence of Our Lady of Fatima's requests for the Consecration of Russia. That fact was not publicly proclaimed as such at that moment. However, no knowledgeable Catholic either inside or outside the Vatican would challenge the validity of the point that it was done in response to Our Lady's request, as expressed to Sr. Lucia, and passed on to the Vatican.

1. Will the Consecration Generate Peace *Immediately*?

Early in 1990, as the Iron Curtain seemed to be lifting, many Catholics euphorically looked to this "lifting" as a sign of some kind of cessation of suffering in response to the 1984 consecration. The Berlin Wall came down, and peace talks in the Middle East appeared to be showing signs of fruition. In many Catholic circles these events were hailed as showing signs of the immediate ushering in of a new era of peace and prosperity.

But even though the U.S. was freed of the major economic burdens of the Cold War, economic problems have continued to escalate in the U.S. The world watched as instead of worldwide peace and prosperity, economic, social and political chaos enveloped the former Soviet territories. Peace remained fragile on the Palestinian scene, and the worldwide financial monetary systems started showing obvious cracks. For any keen observer of the geo-political and geo-economic scenes, the signs were and are of anything but immediately impending peace and prosperity.

Possibly these disappointments were caused by;

(1) The fact that the **other** Fatima requests for; conversion of hearts, Consecration to Mary's Immaculate Heart, and the faithful saying of the Rosary, and First Saturday Communions of Reparation, have ***not*** been fulfilled by a sufficient number of the faithful -- or,
(2) Also *a possibility -- that not a sufficient number of the bishops joined the Holy Father in the Consecration, or*
(3) It was performed too late to totally avoid the predicted results if it were not performed, or,
(4) All of the above.

In any case, there was never anything in the Fatima promises which indicated how long it would take for the Consecration to have its full effect.

2. The Western Response To The Soviet Collapse

The West through various government aid agencies continuously tells the former "Soviet" nations, and third-world nations, that their current financial crisis has been brought on by two major causes: (a) overpopulation, and (b) lack of an archetypal American free market system. Our preliminary suggested solutions for their problems are contraception and abortion. Our official advice to the emerging East and Third World Nations is to disregard God and his laws. As any practicing Catholic knows, the fruits of this are predictably hellish, and will bring nothing but more suffering to the East if they follow that advice.

We promise them that if they adopt our free market system every problem will ultimately solve itself. But how *can* we make this promise when our Western economies which *are* based on luxury oriented consumerism, are in increasing trouble? We promote to them McDonalds franchises and Hilton Hotels (which only their well-to-do can frequent). Of what avail is that to the majority of the Soviet populace which the news media show us standing in line to get a little bread? Of what use is that to the recently documented thousands of mothers in Moscow and other major Russian cities who have tragically turned to prostitution as a method through which they might merely feed their children?

The author has spoken to several Bishops from Russia and other former Soviet countries. While they are hopeful for the future, they are fully aware that "former" communists hold the reins of political power throughout much of the former Soviet Union. They are further aware that if the economic situation continues to deteriorate there, a nationalist expansionist direction could again come to the fore in those countries.

In other words, these Bishops know that the "peace" we are currently experiencing with the former Soviet Union needs to be fostered. They also realize that "peace" could still rather dramatically reverse itself. Catholics faithfully performing their daily duties within their state in life, saying Rosaries, making Saturdays of Reparation (as Our Lady has requested,) will do more to foster that peace than all the diplomatic and trade missions which Moscow and Washington can generate.

3. America's Growing Problems

The fact is, America's "free market system" is in growing economic trouble. We also have legalized abortion and promote it worldwide. Is there any practicing Christian who believes that God will reward anyone with peace and prosperity -- no matter what their economic system -- if legalized murder of innocents is also an integral part of that system?

We also practice contraception at home and promote it abroad. *As Mother Teresa and Pope John Paul II state, the birth control mentality inevitably leads to an abortion mentality.*[9] None are so blind as those who will not see. Should any Catholic need prophecy to tell them that God will not reward a nation which acts in such a manner? If a prophecy said that God was displeased by the current state of affairs in America, would this do more than confirm suspicions already in the mind of any believing Christian?

4. Pope John Paul II & Mother Teresa

Could anyone seriously deny that the U.S. as a national whole, and the West as a culture have collectively abandoned their Christian roots? Pope John Paul II has often stated that this abandonment is the basal cause of our increasing problems in the West. Just for an example of such abandonment, over 70% of the French described themselves as practicing Catholics in the late 1950's. As of November of 1990 that figure had dropped (it would be more accurate to say - plummeted) to 19%. In France, the eldest daughter of the Church, that constitutes a per capita decline of 50% of the total population in just four decades.

What is the cause of our massive problems in the Church and in the World? Bishop Sheen, Pope John Paul II, and Mother Teresa submit that it is due to the abandonment of the basic elements of our Christian faith. And what do Mother and the Pope indicate as the singularly greatest cause of this evil? ABORTION. Mother Teresa has said publicly what she has told the author privately,[10] that WE WILL NEVER HAVE PEACE AS LONG AS ABORTION IS THE PROBLEM IT IS TODAY.

And why do we have legalized abortion of an estimated 15 million babies in the world each year? Because we have abandoned God and His law. Euthanasia advocates are making steady headway in their push for legalized suicide in America. The name of the Euthanasiast, Dr. Kavorkian, is almost as well-known today as that of the Pope's. According to *Priests for Life* Magazine, -- in formerly

---

9 See the Holy Father's recent Encyclical, *Evangelium Vitae*.

10 In 1988, Mother Teresa stated this to the author during a private conversation on a plane trip from Denver, Co. to Edmonton, Alta. Ca.

Christian Holland "...doctors now routinely kill somewhere between five and ten thousand patients annually." We are now all too familiar with the growing influence of the Hemlock Society here in the U.S.

5. The Principal Cause of Lack of Peace

Of course we don't have peace -- or prosperity! ***We're in the murder business on a grand scale.*** Could anything ultimately explain this massive violence and carnage in formerly Christian nations besides the influence of the Demonic. And, should this surprise us? Something, anything, will rush in to fill a vacuum. When as Pope John Paul II observed, "the West abandoned its Christian roots," that very act created a vacuum! What happens when we abandon the culture of "The Gospel of Life" (Evangelium Vitae). Would it not seem logical that the "Culture of Death" would rush in to fill it?

This *should* answer a sometimes unstated question in the minds of many Western people who today ask, "Why do we have all these problems in our time?" As the Holy Father keeps saying, we have developed a "Culture of Death." *We are simply enjoying the fruits of that culture.*

E. FOREWARNED IS FOREARMED

God regularly forewarned His Chosen People in the Old Testament of impending events and dire circumstances. As we read in the New Testament, He commonly forewarned His people (examples: (1) the angel's message warning Joseph to flee with the Holy Family into Egypt, (2) the warning to the Magi in a dream not to return to Herod, or (3) Jesus' prophecy about the fall of Jerusalem, etc.). Would it not seem logical, even predictable, that our Good God in His love for us would give us some general prescience about the dangers of our age?

Indeed He has given us warning and directions for our time through four sources: Tradition, Sacred Scripture, the Magisterium (Papal warnings), and ancillarily, private Catholic prophecy. This is one of the theses of this book, that *He has so warned us* of the *dangers* and advised us of the *opportunities* of our age.

But now we must clearly make some basic distinctions. In this discussion of God's prophetic warnings, admonitions and directives for mankind, there will be an admixture of that which comes (1) from Tradition, and (2) from Scripture, (3) from the Magisterium, and ancillarily (4) from private Catholic revelation. That which comes from the Deposit of the Faith i.e., Oral Tradition, and Written Tradition (Scripture), we as Catholics are bound to believe as it is interpreted by the Magisterium, the Teaching Office of the Church.

That which comes from private revelation we do not have to believe; as a matter of fact, no Catholic can be required to believe in any private revelation. But, when private revelation comes from approved sources such as canonized Saints, Blessed and Venerable, and other reputable Catholics, **and**, it is consistent with living Tradition, Scripture, and the writings of the Fathers of the Church (all as interpreted and understood by the Magisterium) then shouldn't it be viewed by a practicing Catholic with an open mind?

Portier
St. Hilary
Rheims
St. Remigius
GERMANY
SWITZER LAND
FRANCE
Lyon
St. Ireneaus
Milan
St. Ambrose
St. Caesarius
Arles
AUSTRIA
SLOVAKIA
HUNGARY
SLOVENIA
CROATIA
ROMANIA
UKRAINE
Sea of Azov
RUSSIA
ITALY
Adriatic Sea
BOSNIA
SERBIA
Black Sea
GEORGIA
CORSICA
Rome
St. Justin Martyr
St. Hippolytus
BULGARIA
St. John Chrysostom
Constantinople
ALBANIA
MACE DONIA
SARDINIA
Tyrrhenian Sea
Phillipi
St. Methodius
Chalcedon
Council of - 451 A.D.
Nyssa
St Gregory of
Edessa
St. Ephraem
GREECE
Aegean Sea
Nicea
Council of - 325 A.D.
TURKEY
Ionian Sea
Smyrna
St. Polycarp
Nazianzus
St. Gregory of
Hippo
St. Augustine
Carthage
St. Cyprian
Tertullian
SICILY
Athens
Athenagoras
Ephesus
Council of - 431 A.D.
Antioch
Theophilus
SYRIA
TUNISIA
CRETE
Famagoste
St. Epiphanius
CYPRUS
Mediterranean Sea
LEBANON
St. Basil
Eusebius of
Caesarea
Damascus
St. John of
IRAQ
ISRAEL
Jerusalem
St. Cyril of Jer.
JORDAN
Bethlehem
St. Jerome
ALGERIA
Alexandria
St.Athanasius
St. Cyril of Al.
SAUDI ARABIA
LIBYA
EGYPT

CHAPTER 1

DEFINING OUR TERMS

Shortly after the author became interested in the subject of Catho-lic prophecy, he noticed that many late 20th century Catholics showed very little understanding of the theological status and importance of several things.

> FIRST: At that time, Catholics showed little interest in or knowledge about the prophetic books of both the Old and New Testament.
>
> SECOND: The same people showed little interest in or knowl-edge about that which comes to us through Tradition.
>
> THIRD: While not as critical, it was nevertheless signifi-cant that the same held true for the prophetic events, for example, at Fatima or Lourdes. American Catholics in particular had little knowledge about the respect shown by successive Popes for those events. Many of those who did know appeared to be confused about how to interpret this "Papal respect."

In an attempt to find the answer as to why practicing knowl-edgeable Catholics would not look at approved private prophecy with the same respect as numerous Popes, several issues became clear. In general, *most of the reticence* to look with an open mind

---

Map shows Names and locations of: three early Church Councils, Names & Locations of 27 Fathers and other ecclesial writers of the Church.

at private prophecy (e.g. from Fatima or Lourdes) or any number of apparitions which *are* approved by the Church *comes from a composite lack of full understanding in the following areas* -

(1) The interrelationship of the roles of the two sources of public Revelation (Tradition and Scripture), and their mutual teaching about private prophecy.

(2) *A lack of full understanding of the role and teaching of Tradition.*

(3) While the Church has *always* taught (a) that private prophecy is *not* a source of Revelation, and (b) that no Catholic has to believe in any specific private prophecy.

(4) The Church nevertheless teaches us that the charism of prophecy has a *Revealed* role in the ongoing life of the members of the Church -- which role specifically is for -- **"The direction of human acts,"** because, as Scripture says;

"When prophecy shall cease, the people shall be scattered abroad." Prov. 29:18[1]

A. THE SUBJECTS (DEFINITIONS) COVERED PRIOR TO THE PROPHECIES

1. Tradition & Scripture

One of the prime aims of this book is to demonstrate from both the sources of Revelation, Scripture and Tradition, that "the" Antichrist and the Parousia are most probably not just around the corner. Scripture holds much information on the subject of *the* Antichrist, and the Parousia (the Second Coming of Christ), and *Tradition contains even more*! But even when dealing with Scripture, how certain is the average Christian (whether Catholic or not) about that which is to be taken in the "*proper*" literal sense in Scripture, and that which is to be taken in a non-literal sense?

[1] Douay-Rheims edition of the bible.

How does today's Christian obtain the answers to many basic questions? e.g.,: Did Our Lord actually prophesy the destruction of the Temple in Jerusalem, then the destruction of the City itself, and then the rise of "*the* Antichrist" in the end times?[2] Did he confirm the actuality of the people of Nineveh having repented at the preaching of Jonas? Did he actually raise Lazarus from the dead?

Or are these just "literary devices" which have no significance for the modern Christian as he or she deals with the subject of the latter and end times? On what authority does a Christian in any sense believe in a *proper* literal (meaning word-for-word) "latter" or "end times"? Can Scripture in and of itself totally answer all questions such as these?

2. Our Questions Aren't New Questions

If *we* have honest questions about these issues, *can we believe that the early Christians were so bereft of intelligence that they did not have the same questions in their minds?* We know from certain passages of St. Paul and other sacred writers that the early Christians were vitally interested in these subjects.

Where did the first generations of Christians get their answers to these questions? Scripture tells us they got them from both apostolic oral teaching (part of Tradition) and Scripture, as understood and interpreted by their Bishops. Is there a large body of information about the "latter" and "end times" in the writings of the early Christian leaders? If so, how much of it are we to believe in faith?

Are contemporary Christians more certain, or are they less certain of their beliefs on these issues than the Christians of the early Church? If the average contemporary Catholic is less certain, what is the cause(s)? It does very little good to throw Scriptural quotations at

[2] We first know that Christ was a true prophet in that it is revealed of Him in Scripture -- e.g. "A prophet is without honor in his own land". In the sense that *merely* human prophets prophesy, Jesus' prophecy differed. As St. Thomas points out, the prophecy of merely human prophets comes through imperfect (incomplete) knowledge received through revelation by a man or woman. Human prophetic knowledge is imperfect in that it is limited to that portion which has been revealed to him or her by God. In the case of Jesus Christ, His prophecy of future events comes from perfect knowledge of the future held within the Hypostatic Union of his Divine and human natures. See Thomas Aquinas' *Disputed Questions on Truth.*

someone who might be confused as to what to believe in Scripture, or how to interpret or understand it. Similarly, if someone is even a little bit confused as to what Tradition is, it will accomplish little to throw quotations from Tradition at that person.

3. A Confusion Factor

If an extreme point of view, or school of thought, relating to basic understanding of Judeo-Christianity had been operative on many Catholic and Protestant university and seminary campuses for years, could and would that have a serious effect on the average practicing Christian? Could such extreme points of view have "filtered down to the pews" -- *without the average "pew Christian" understanding that process, how it works, how extreme it really is, and how seriously they may have been affected by it?* **These questions on the effects of "extreme higher criticism" will be partially answered toward the end of this Chapter, and more completely in Chapter 2.**

This book is designed for those who are seriously interested in what the Catholic Church traditionally teaches about the latter and end times! If the reader does not clearly understand,

(1) What the Catholic Church teaches Tradition and Scripture to be, and
(2) How the Apostles taught and the Magisterium continues to teach that the two sources of Revelation *are to be interpreted*, -- then,

it will accomplish little to cite prophecies from Tradition and Scripture other than to titillate the curiosity of the reader.

4. Vatican II - Tradition and Scripture -- They Are to be Equally Venerated!

There *is* some confusion amongst many members of the Church today on *the place and role of Tradition in Revelation.* If we wish to know what the Church teaches on this subject, the closest place to look is within the documents of Vatican II. In *Dei Verbum (the Word of God)*, #'s 9 and 10, we find;

"9. *Sacred Tradition and sacred Scripture, then,* ***are bound closely together****, and communicate one with the other. For both of them, flowing from the same divine wellspring, come together in some fashion to form one thing, and move towards the same goal.* Sacred Scripture is the speech of God as it is put down in writing under the breath of the Holy Spirit. *And* ***Tradition transmits in its entirety the word of God which has been entrusted to the Apostles by Christ the Lord and the Holy Spirit.*** It transmits it to the successors of the Apostles so that, enlightened by the Spirit of truth, they may faithfully preserve, expound and spread it abroad by their preaching. Thus it comes about that the Church does not draw her certainty about all revealed truths from the holy Scriptures alone. *Hence***,** *both Scripture and Tradition must be accepted and honored with equal feelings of devotion and reverence***.**"[3]

"10. Sacred Tradition and sacred Scripture make up a single sacred deposit of the Word of God, which is entrusted to the Church. By adhering to it the entire holy people, united to its pastors, remains always faithful to the teaching of the Apostles, to the brotherhood, to the breaking of bread and the prayers (cf. Acts 2:42 Greek). So, in maintaining, practicing and professing the faith that has been handed on there should be a remarkable harmony between the bishops and the faithful.

"But the task of giving an authentic interpretation of the Word of God, whether in its written form or in the form of Tradition,[4] ***has been entrusted to the living teaching office of the Church alone.***[5] Its authority in this matter is exercised in the name of Jesus Christ. Yet this Magisterium is not superior to the Word of God, but is its servant. **It teaches only what has been handed on to it.** At the divine command and with the help of the Holy Spirit, it listens to

---

3 Dogmatic Constitution on Divine Revelation, *Dei Verbum*, #9, *Vatican Council II, The Concilior and Post Concilior Documents, Vol 1.* Flannery, New Revised Edition, St. Paul Books & Media, Boston, 1992, p. 755.

4 Cf. First Vatican Council, *Dogm. Const. on the Catholic Faith,.*

5 Cf. Pius XII, Enclcl. *Humani Generis,* 12 Aug. 1950: *AAS 42* (1950) 569-569: *DENZ* 2314 (3886)

> this devoutly, guards it with dedication and expounds it faithfully. All that it proposes for belief as being divinely revealed is drawn from this single deposit of faith.
>
> "It is clear, therefore, that, in the supremely wise arrangement of God, *sacred Tradition, sacred Scripture and the Magisterium of the Church* are so connected and associated that *one of them cannot stand without the others.* Working together, each in its own way under the action of the one Holy Spirit, they all contribute effectively to the salvation of souls."[6] [Emphasis - author's]

Observe that the definition in #10 speaks of "a single deposit of the Word of God ... whether in its written form or in the form of Tradition." Here the Vatican II Fathers clearly reference St. Paul's "EITHER BY WORD OF MOUTH OR BY OUR LETTER."[7] ***In the Pauline sense, both sacred Tradition and sacred Scripture are part of the Church's Tradition.***

"Tradition" is not just the "Oral" Tradition and Scripture. "Tradition" also includes all the methods utilized by the infant Church to hand on intact those things which they had received from the Apostles. Fr. Hardon herein describes the extra-Scriptural sources of Tradition.

> "They are the (1) professions of faith, like the Apostle's and Nicene Creeds; (2) the Church's liturgy and unvarying practices since apostolic times; (3) *the writings of the ancient Fathers* and (4) archeological monuments *testifying to what Christians believed and how they worshipped over the centuries.* Yet all of these are only instrumental of the *organ* of Tradition in the Catholic Church's teaching authority, or *magisterium*, namely the bishops as successors of the apostles collegially united among themselves under the bishop of Rome."[8] [numbering & emphasis are the author's]

---

6 Ibid. 755-756.

7 2nd. Thessalonians, 2:15 RSV. Catholic Edition, 1965.

8 *The Catholic Catechism*, John A. Hardon, S.J., 1974, Doubleday & Co., P. 48.

5. Tradition and Scripture Are to be Interpreted in the Light of the Magisterium

Catholics are not free to attribute whatever they wish to interpretation of either Oral Tradition or Written Tradition[9] (Scripture), but rather that God gave us the Magisterium (Teaching Office) of the Church to show us the meaning of the deposit of the faith, to which Magisterium He entrusted His Word. That is the dogmatic teaching of the Church.

6. Without a "Magisterium" -- Confusion

Currently there are over 700 independent non-Catholic Christian denominations in the United States which claim to determine their faith from "Scripture alone." (Interestingly, nowhere in Scripture do we find such a "Scripture alone" teaching.) But, since they recognize no higher authority than themselves as individuals, these non-Catholic Christians also hold the rule of private judgment in interpretation of Scripture.[10]

This "private interpretation" doctrine is based originally upon *Luther's well-known position* that "*the Scriptures are clear even to the unlearned.*" ***Yet, the Scriptures themselves deny they are clear to the unlearned.*** As St. Peter tells us:

> "Just as our most dear brother Paul also, according to the wisdom given him, has written to you, as indeed he did in all his epistles, speaking in them of these things. **In these epistles there are certain things difficult to understand, which**

[9] Our English word, "Tradition", comes directly from the Latin word "Traditio", which is the nominative form of the verb "tradere" signifying to hand on or pass something on to someone else. Those things which were passed on (taught) by the Apostles, either orally or in written form, were called in Latin "traditiones" (traditions). That is what St. Paul means when he says, "Stand firm and hold fast to the *traditions* that you were taught by us, EITHER BY WORD OF MOUTH OR BY OUR LETTER." 2nd. Thessalonians, 2:15 RSV. Catholic Edition, 1965. When the author refers to "Oral or Written Tradition", it is in this Pauline sense referenced immediately above.

[10] There are some non-Catholic denominations which do not hold with the principle of private interpretation of Scripture.

> **the unlearned and the unstable distort,** ***just as they do the rest of the Scriptures***[11] ***also,*** **to their own destruction.** You therefore, Brethren, since you know this beforehand, be on your guard lest, carried away by the error of the foolish, you fall away from your own steadfastness."[12]

As we have just read in Scripture, *Sacred Scripture itself tells us that "the unlearned and the unstable" don't understand Scripture properly*, that "the unlearned and the unstable" "*distort*" its meaning "to their own destruction." Scripture says there is serious danger in private interpretation of the Scriptures.

So, it should not surprise us that the 700 previously mentioned American Christian denominations (which hold the "private interpretation" doctrine) cannot in many cases agree on the doctrinal or moral meaning of Scripture. That is why God gave us the Church to guide us in these matters. Because, the alternative is the doctrinal chaos on many basic issues observable amongst many of our beloved Separated Brethren. *That chaos is caused by private interpretation.*

7. The Same Thing Can Happen to a Catholic

When and if a "Catholic" begins to operate from the same private judgment premises as our Separated Brethren, he or she inevitably falls into that same chaos. That is why there is no room for private interpretation of Scripture (or Tradition) in the Catholic context.

---

11 The *New Vulgate* has "Scripturas", the Greek text reads "graphas". "Here St Peter classes St Paul's Epistles with the other inspired writings of the OT, showing how greatly he esteemed St. Paul's writings." [Quoted from: *A Catholic Commentary on Holy Scripture*, Editorial Committee: Dom Bernard Orchard - General Editor, Rev. Edmust F. Sutcliffe S.J. - Old Testament Editor, Rev. Reginald C. Fuller, - Secretary of the Catholic Biblical Association, Dom Ralph Russell - Hon. Secretary and Treasurer. Forward - Bernard Cardinal Griffin. Pub: Thomas Nelson and Sons, New York, 1953.]

12 II Peter, Chapter 3, verses 15-17.

B. WHAT IS TRADITION? APOSTOLIC SOURCES OF TRADITION

Today we experience a very interesting and provable contrast. If a pagan asked the average Catholic to explain what "Scripture" is, could the average Catholic intelligibly explain the basics of what the Bible is? We know the average Catholic could. But if he or she were asked to explain what Tradition is, could the average Catholic intelligibly explain it? Could they give you anything other than a vague description of something they really don't understand?

It is a fact that the average Catholic receives the majority of their understanding of the faith from Sunday sermons. Catholics regularly receive sermons on the Scriptures and on the subject of Scripture. But how long has it been since the Catholic reader has heard Tradition clearly described in a Sunday sermon? It is not particularly difficult to understand that what you never hear about, you don't understand, so you can't explain it to others.

If a Catholic does not know what Tradition is, how can he or she effectually understand that Revelation comes from two sources. When the Catholic does not understand what Tradition is, does that Catholic effectually (*by default*) become a person who thinks the faith comes from "Scripture alone"? Can a Catholic in this manner become non-Catholic in an extremely important part of his or her thinking -- without even knowing or suspecting it?

According to the *Catholic Encyclopedia*,

> "The Council of Trent ... held that *there are Divine traditions not contained in Holy Scripture, revelations made to the apostles either orally by Jesus Christ or by the inspiration of the Holy Ghost and transmitted by the Apostles to the Church.* Holy Scripture is therefore not the only theological source of the Revelation made by God to His Church."[13]

Why is this Apostolic "Tradition" so important to the subject of *this* Book? *Because there was a large body of eschatological*[14] *knowledge held by the Fathers of the Church about the "latter times" which had come to them orally from the Apostles.* Such

---

13 *Catholic Encyclopedia*, The Catholic Encyclopedia Press, Inc., 1913 Edition, Vol. 15, p.6.

14 Those things dealing with the very latter or end times.

knowledge is part of what the *Catholic Encyclopedia* is referring to in its statement quoted immediately above, that:

> "There are Divine traditions not contained in Holy Scripture, *revelations made to the Apostles either orally by Jesus Christ or by the inspiration of the Holy Ghost and transmitted by the Apostles to the Church.*"

That "Divine tradition," comes down to us through the organ of the Magisterium, many times having also been later committed to writing by the Church Fathers. This Oral Tradition adds a certain amount of knowledge to the Scriptural admonitions and warnings about latter times. Today, most Catholics are familiar only with the Scriptural side of this subject.

C. SCRIPTURE CONFIRMS ORAL TRADITION'S VALIDITY AND PROPHECIES OF END TIMES

As vitally valuable as its testimony is, it is not just the Magisterium of the Catholic Church which faithfully transmits to us the validity and relative importance of Tradition. *The Scriptures themselves clearly teach us of its existence*. St. Paul specifically discusses the existence of an Oral Tradition (teaching). In this particular case he is discussing that Oral Tradition specifically about the end times. By definition that Oral Tradition is extra-scriptural:

1. St. Paul

> "For the day of the Lord will not come unless the apostasy[15] comes first, and the man of sin is revealed, *the son of perdition* who opposes and is exalted above all that is called God, or that is worshipped; so that *he* sits in the temple and gives himself out as if *he* were God. ***Do you not remember that when I was still with you, I used to tell you these things?***"[16] [Emphasis - added]

---

[15] In some editions of the Bible, this word is translated as "revolt" or "rebellion."

[16] 2nd. Thessalonians, 2:3 *Greek Latin English New Testament Student's Workbook*, The Liturgical Press, Collegeville, MN., 1963, English text from Confraternity of Christian Doctrine, St. Anthony Guild Press, Paterson, N.J., 1958 Printing.

St. Paul further describes with what authority (in relation to Scripture) Christians are to hold these things he and the other Apostles orally handed on to them. St. Paul says,

> "So then, Brethren, stand firm and hold to the *traditions* that you were taught by us, *EITHER BY WORD OR BY OUR LETTER*."[17]

Anyone can *plainly see* that St. Paul Scripturally teaches Christians to view the oral (word) teaching with exactly the same authority and veneration as they do the written teachings. *He also makes vitally clear that they received prophecies of the end times in these oral instructions.*

It is not just St. Paul who speaks of the oral teachings or "Tradition" which the Apostles delivered to the early faithful. St. Jude-Thadeus[18] also exhorts the faithful to "remember" what they have already been orally taught about the latter and end times.

2. St. Jude Confirms Oral Tradition.

> "But as for you beloved, be mindful of [remember] *the words that have been spoken* beforehand *by the apostles* of our Lord Jesus Christ, who kept *saying* to you that at the end of time there will be scoffers, walking impiously according to their lusts."[19]

The author of *Jude* specifically uses the verb "said," versus *wrote*. Someone might object that could be just a manner of expression. That is also answered when the sacred author explains why he is writing his epistle.

> "Beloved, while I was making every endeavor to write to you about our common salvation, I found it necessary to write

---

[17] 2nd. Thessalonians, 2:15 RSV, Catholic Edition, 1965.

[18] The author is probably the Apostle, Jude-Thadeus, "brother" of Apostle James. This is the traditional view of the Church and is specifically attested to by Origen and Tertullian.

[19] *Jude*, 17. Latin/English/Greek interlinear Students workbook. p. 625. The specific Latin words in the New Latin Vulgate which are translated as "spoken beforehand" and "saying" are "Praedicta sunt" and "dicebant." There is *absolutely* no possible question about this referring to oral teachings vs. written communication.

> to you, exhorting you *to contend ernestly for the faith* ***once for all*** *delivered to all the saints.*"[20]

There is no single Biblical letter or Gospel which internally claims to deliver all of the mysteries of the faith. Neither does any Christian denomination of which the author is aware make such a claim for a single Biblical letter or Gospel. All true Christians (whether Protestant or Catholic) understand that the Bible must be accepted as a whole. Most importantly, no "Christian" claims that all the truths of the faith are contained in any single Epistle or Gospel.

It is highly improbable that all the other books of the Bible had even yet been written at the time of the composition of Jude (especially the Apocalypse).[21] It was definitely impossible at that time that all the "saints" could *all* have seen every book in the Bible. How then, can Jude speak of their contending for *a "faith once for all delivered to (all) the saints.*"?

The Apostles had to have first orally taught people by "word of mouth" prior to writing to them. Jude is writing to believing Christians *who have previously been orally catechized.* It is the totality of that catechization for which the author exhorts them "*to contend for the faith once for all delivered to all the saints.*" The Latin verb which is translated as "*delivered*" is "Tradita(e)," meaning those items of faith which already "have been *traditioned*," or "handed on." *It is a verb form used to describe an already completed action.*[22] He is writing to people whom he says have already received the faith "*once* [and] *for all.*"

Even if someone wishes to argue against all the best scholarship as to the date of the composition of Jude, and claim that it was the last New Testament book written, *so be it.* **That would not reduce the force of the arguments above in the slightest.** It is a highly demonstrable fact that even by the year 100 A.D., it was a very rare Christian community indeed which possessed copies all of the N.T. canonical "books."

---

[19] *Jude*, 3, p. 624

[20] St. Irenaeus tell us that, the Apocalypse (Book of Revelation) was written *towards* the end of the reign of the Roman Emperor Domitian, which occurred in 96 A.D. Victorinus (one of the "Fathers") tells us Domitian sent St. John into exile on the island of Patmos. Both St. Jerome and Eusebius also confirm this. All the above strongly confirms the traditional date of the composition of the Apocalypse for the year 95 A.D.

[21] A perfect passive participle.

But Jude previously tells the "saints," who have received "the faith ... delivered once for all," to contend for that faith. Again, how could a Christian have already received the complete faith for which to contend, when he or she did not possess all of the New Testament? The answer is quite simple. The totality of the faith had been "Traditum" (handed on to them) as St. Paul explains it, "EITHER BY WORD [OF MOUTH] OR BY OUR LETTER."

St. Paul clearly and unequivocally states that the apostolic "word of mouth" teaching is of equal importance and authority with teachings contained within the Written Word. There is no way around that conclusion unless someone wants to deny the authority of Scripture itself.

Not just St. Paul and St. Jude, but also St. John and St. Peter sent letters (now incorporated in Scripture) *reminding* the faithful of what they, the Apostles, had already **orally** taught them. This is especially apropos in relation to the subject of latter and end times. That fact clearly demonstrates to any reasonable person that more had to have been taught than what was later committed to the Scriptures. The point is that Oral Tradition, when it is consistently transmitted by the Fathers, is important to us just as the Scriptures are -- as St. Paul tells us.

D. WHAT CONSTITUTES "TRADITION."

This section identifies *the four elements of "Tradition."* Oral Tradition is one of those four elements. The Fathers of the Church transmitted much of that Oral Tradition of the Apostles by later committing it to writing. *For a full concise definition of the term "Fathers of the Church" as it is used in this book, see the Glossary in the back.*

TRADITION / SCRIPTURE

Our English word "TRADITION" comes directly from the Latin word "TRADITIO." That Latin noun derives from the Latin verb "TRADERE," which means to pass on, or hand something on. When this author sits at his supper table with his children and he wants one of them to pass him the salt, he sometimes says in Latin "trade mihi salem, si placeat tibi." In Latin that means "hand me the salt, please." The Latin verb "tradere" signifies to hand something on to someone else. That is what our English word "tradition" which is borrowed from the Latin "Traditio" means, something which has been handed down or on from one person (or generation) to another.

1. Early Understanding of the Word "Scripture" in the New Testament

When St. Paul says in the New Testament (N.T.),

> "So then, Brethren, stand firm and hold fast to the *traditions* that you were taught by us, *EITHER BY WORD [OF MOUTH] OR BY OUR LETTER"*[23]

by "traditions" St. Paul is *collectively* referring to the teachings which were "handed on" from the Apostles to these early Christian disciples. So, at the time of the Apostolic Church, when St. Paul made the statement quoted above, as Rev. Dix observed,

> "Originally *it* [*Tradition*] means any *Christian* teaching, as opposed to *graphi*, scripture, which means *only* the *Jewish scriptures of the O.T. The phrase 'Scripture and Tradition'* comes from the earliest age of the Church, and *means 'the whole of Revelation.'* It has no idea of 'oral' as against 'written.'"[24]

---

[23] 2nd. Thessalonians, 2:15 RSV, Catholic Edition, 1965. In the current official Church Biblical text, the Latin *New Vulgate*, the text reads, "Itaque, fratres, state et tenete traditiones, quas didicistis sive per sermonem sive per epistulam nostram." That most accurately translates into, "Stand firm and hold fast to the Traditions **which** you ***have learned***, either by (our) word, or by our Epistle." "Didicistis" is the *perfect second person plural indicative* form which comes from the root latin verb "to learn", not, "to teach.".

[24] *The Apostolic Tradition, of St. Hippolytus of Rome*, Rev. Gregory Dix, Monk of Nashborn Abbey, Society for Promoting Christian Knowledge, London, 1937, p. XLIII.

In other words, when Sts. Peter and Paul spoke in their letters of "Scripture" (Greek-graphi), their readers at that time immediately understood them to be speaking of the Old Testament. Those first century readers did not yet mentally associate the writings of the Apostles with the term "Scripture." To first century Christians,

(1) The word "Scriptures" specifically meant the Old Testament,

(2) The word "Tradition" meant all the teachings handed on to them by the apostles. The written teachings were bundled together with the oral teachings in their concept of the overall "Traditions" which St. Paul so clearly told them to "hold fast" to.

We know that the Epistles and Gospels were greatly venerated and read in the Christian assemblies from the beginning. The early Christians clearly understood the Old Testament to have been the fruit of directly inspired revelation from God. But what we do not know with any great degree of certitude is how the earliest Christians actually categorized "the Epistles" of the Apostles in relation to the Old Testament "Scriptures."

As late as 150 A.D., St. Justin (a Father of the Church) simply refers to the Epistles and Gospels as "*memoirs*" of the Apostles. This simply demonstrates that the word "Scripture" was probably not generally ascribed to them yet. It is not until shortly after 180 A.D. that the first clear description of them as "inspired "writings" comes to us from St. Theophilus, and, "he is the first [Father] to have clearly stated the inspiration of the N.T."[25] It would, however, be a serious mistake to make too much out of this.

Simply put, it simply took time for the Christians to mentally include the N.T. writings within the O.T. term "Scripture." Christianity's membership was initially formed out of Jewish converts. Therefore, the initial reference points of the Church were heavily Jewish. Within the Jewish tradition the term "Scripture" was exclusively associated with the Old Testament.

---

[25] *Patrology*, Berthold Altaner, Herder and Herder, New York, 1960, p. 133

2. Tradition and Scripture Basically Contain the Same "Doctrines"

What later Christians/Fathers would refer to as the "Unwritten Tradition" (apostolic teachings which were initially taught orally and not initially reduced to writing) teaches no doctrine which is not found at least in some seminal form in N.T. Scripture. And the New Testament teaches no doctrine which is not found in "Unwritten" Tradition. As St. Paul teaches us, both the Oral and Written "Traditions" are to be "held" with equal authority.[26] Why?

First of all, the Holy Spirit inspired him to so teach. But in the explanatory sense, sacred Tradition and sacred Scripture -- *which were "handed on" by the same Apostles* -- are necessarily complementary of each other. In certain cases the "Unwritten" Tradition clearly fleshes out a more detailed picture which Scripture describes in more elemental form. When this happens, it does not constitute a different or *new* doctrine. It is simply another teaching on the same doctrine.

In many cases in the N.T., one book (Written Tradition) fleshes out a doctrine only seminally taught in another N.T. Book(s). i.e., No one book of the N.T. contains the totality of the faith. Similarly, when "Unwritten Tradition" deals with a doctrinal matter, it can and often does provide further information on a Doctrine which is not explained in such detail in Scripture (Written Tradition). To know the doctrines which the apostles taught, it is necessary to know the totality of their teaching. What St. Paul is telling us is that **the totality of the faith** is to be found in **the totality of their teaching** which they taught as received from Jesus Christ and the Holy Spirit. So Paul writes:

> So then, Brethren, stand firm and hold fast to the *traditions* that you were taught by us, EITHER BY WORD [OF MOUTH] OR BY OUR LETTER[27]

---

[26] 2nd. Thessalonians, 2:15 RSV. Catholic Edition, 1965.

[27] Ibid.

3. Four Elements of What is Today Called "Tradition"

Most late 20th century Catholics are not sure they understand what the Church means by Tradition because its definition and content have not regularly been taught for the last thirty years. Consequently, the concept of what "Tradition" means (for the average contemporary Catholic) is vague in relation to their concept of what "Scripture" means - and they know it.

As Vatican II uses and defines the term in *Dei Verbum*, "sacred Tradition" is comprised of four basic elements. These elements are clearly described by Fr. Hardon in his 1974 *Catechism of the Catholic Church*, which we present again as follows:

> "They are the (1) professions of faith, like the Apostle's and Nicene Creeds; (2) the Church's liturgy and unvarying practices since apostolic times; (3) *the writings of the ancient Fathers* and (4) archeological monuments testifying to what Christians believed and how they worshipped over the centuries.
>
> "Yet all of these are only instrumental of the *organ* of Tradition in the Catholic Church's teaching authority, or magisterium, namely the bishops as successors of the apostles collegially united among themselves under the bishop of Rome."[28] [numbering is the author's]

As we can see, "Tradition" has even wider sources than the writings of the Fathers of the Church. The writings of the Fathers (*wherein they wrote down much of what they had received "from the Apostolic Tradition"*) do comprise a major portion of what the Council Fathers of Vatican II mean by "sacred Tradition."

One will find several common usages of the word "Tradition" in theological writings. For the most part, they are comprised of the following;

(1) Its broad four part sense as described by Fr. Hardon above, meaning the whole of Tradition.

---

[28] *The Catholic Catechism*, John A. Hardon, 1974, Doubleday & Co., P. 48.

(2) It's narrowest sense, when it is being used to describe "Oral Tradition" -- the Oral teachings of the Apostles such as St. Paul describes it.

(3) The "living Tradition" of the Church, the word's broadest sense, which is exemplified in the active teaching office of the Church, the Magisterium. This particular function or sense will be more fully explained by live examples later. It is also what Fr. Hardon is describing in his last paragraph of his definition.

E. THE AUTHORITY OF THE FATHERS.

The "Fathers of the Church" are quoted extensively in this book. The authority of the Fathers (when they universally teach the same doctrine) on a matter of faith or morals is very important to understanding the teachings of the Church on any subject. Nowhere is this more true than when the Fathers interpret specific Scripture passages. In his Papal Encyclical *Providentissimus Deus*, Pope Leo XIII states:

> **"The Holy Fathers**, 'to whom after the Apostles, the Church owes its growth -- who have planted, watered, built, governed, and cherished it' (Aug., C. Julian., II, x, 37) -- the Holy Fathers we say, **are of supreme authority whenever they all interpret in one and the same manner any text of the Bible,** ***as pertaining to the doctrine of faith and morals;*** **for their unanimity clearly evinces that such interpretation has come down from the Apostles as a matter of Catholic faith."** [emphasis added]

Other criteria are also laid down by Pope Leo in the balance of this lengthy encyclical. The *Catholic Encyclopedia* article on this encyclical comments on same and says:

> "Three conditions are, therefore, required in order that the patristic authority may be absolutely decisive: **first**, they must interpret texts referring to matters of faith or morals;

> **secondly**, they must speak as witnesses of Catholic tradition, not merely as private theologians; **thirdly**, there must be moral unanimity in their interpretation.
>
> **"This unanimity is *not* destroyed by the silence of some of the foremost Fathers,** and is sufficiently guaranteed by the consentient voice of the principal patristic writers living at any critical period, or by the agreement of commentators living at various times; *but the unanimity is destroyed if some of the Fathers openly deny the correctness of the interpretation given by others.*
>
> "But the encyclical warns us to treat the opinions of the Fathers with reverence, even if there is no unanimity: 'The opinion of the Fathers,' says the Holy Pontiff, 'is also of very great weight when they treat of these matters in their capacity of doctors (of the faith), unofficially.'"[29]

Pope Leo XIII faithfully expounds and echoes the Church's constant teachings about the authority of the Fathers as an authentic voice of Tradition. *In the West, it is probably only with the general rediscovery and understanding of this principle about the authority and teaching voice of the Fathers that a subsequent full appreciation of the traditional Doctrines of the Church can be effectively sought and understood.*

As the Bishops at Vatican II taught in speaking of Tradition and its relation to the Fathers of the Church,

> "The sayings of the Holy Fathers are a witness to the life-giving presence of this Tradition, showing how its riches are poured out in the practice and life of the Church, in her belief and in her prayer."[30]

In explaining the role played by the Fathers in interpretation and understanding Scripture the **Vatican II Fathers** said,

---

29 Catholic Encyclopedia, The Catholic Encyclopedia Press, Inc., 1913 Edition, Vol. 5, p.700

30 *Vatican Council II, The Concilior and Post Concilior Documents, Vol 1.* Flannery, New Revised Edition, 1992., Dei Verbum, p. 754

> "She [the Church] strives to reach day by day a more profound understanding of the sacred Scriptures, in order to provide her children with food from the divine words. **For this reason she [the Church] duly fosters the study of the Fathers, both Eastern and Western**"[31]

F. WHO ARE THE FATHERS OF THE CHURCH? - A VOICE OF HER TRADITION

Some of the Apostles' *Disciples*, men who were trained directly by one or more of the Apostles, are also "Fathers" of the Church. Such men are referred to as "*Apostolic* Fathers." (For the full definition of a "Father" -- See Glossary in the back of this book). **PARTICULAR EXAMPLE:** St. Polycarp was a disciple of St. John the Evangelist. Polycarp is also a Father of the Church. So St. Polycarp, who was trained by one of the Apostles, is referred to as an "Apostolic Father." The next generation of *Fathers*, who were directly trained by one or more of the disciples of the Apostles, are often called *SubApostolic* Fathers. Fathers who come after them are simply referred to as Fathers.

The chronological order of these titles is this: Apostles directly taught (1) *Apostolic Fathers* -- who taught (2) *SubApostolic Fathers* -- who taught the later (3) *Fathers*. However, it is most common to refer to all the Fathers collectively as "the Fathers of the Church."

An example: The apostolic Father, Polycarp wrote down some of what he received from apostolic Tradition. The SubApostolic Father, St. Irenaeus,[32] tells us about Polycarp:

> "[Polycarp] had been trained by the *apostles* and had conversed with many who had seen Christ."[33]

---

31 Ibid, p. 763.

32 Due to the rather late period within which Irenaeus wrote (roughly 180-200), most Patristic commentators do *not* list St. Irenaeus as a "SubApostolic" Father. This author does for one basic reason: Irenaeus learned directly from Polycarp. Irenaeus is only one teaching generation away from St. John the Apostle. Therefore he fits in that sense with the other SubApostolic Fathers.

33 *Adversus Haereses*, Irenaeus, 3.1.

St. Irenaeus personally wrote down much more of this oral teaching than Polycarp, much of which he specifically tells us came directly from St. John through St. Polycarp. **These oral teachings** (*when they meet certain other criteria*) **are part of Oral Tradition.**

1. The "Fathers" Committed Much of the Oral Apostolic Teaching to Writing

The following are examples of *some* writings of *some* Fathers. They do not comprise an exhaustive list of the *Fathers*. Nor are the included *examples* of particular Fathers writings' necessarily an exhaustive list of what those particular Fathers wrote. *These are simply examples* to demonstrate how the oral teachings of the Apostles were handed down from generation to generation.

Even some of the ***Apostolic*** **Fathers** committed part of this Oral Tradition directly to writing. Examples of such *Apostolic* Father's writings are, (1) Pope St. Clement of Rome (88-97 A.D. *Letter to the Corinthians*[34]), (2) St. Ignatius of Antioch (110 A.D. His *Letters to the 7 Churches*), and (3) St. Polycarp of Smyrna (135 A.D. *Second Letter to the Phillipians*).

Many ***SubApostolic*** **Fathers** committed even more of the Oral Tradition to writing - men such as, (1) St. Justin Martyr, (148-155 A.D. *First Apology*), (2) St. Irenaeus (180-199 *Against Heresies*), (3) Tertullian (200 A.D. *Demurrer Against the Heretics*),[35] (4) St. Hippolytus (215 A.D., *Apostolic Traditions*), (5) St. Clement of Alexandria (202 A.D. *Stromateis*), and (6) St. Cyprian of Carthage (251-256 A.D. *The Unity of the Catholic Church*).

---

[34] "To base Clement's title of Apostolic Father on his supposed association with St. Peter is at best somewhat tenuous. But whether or not he was Peter's convert, as the *Pseudo-Clementines* would have it; whether or not he was consecrated Peter's successor, and by Peter himself, as Tertullian would have it; still he is an Apostolic Father, and the title is firmly his, simply by reason of the fact that he is a man of the apostolic age." *The Faith of the Early Fathers*, W. A. Jurgens, The Liturgical Press, Collegeville, Mn. 1970, Vol. 1, p. 6.
However, Quasten lists Clement as of "Subapostolic times." *Patrology*, Johannes Quasten, Spectrum Publishers, 3 Vols., Utrech-Antwerp, Vol. 1, p. 45.

[35] Technically, Tertullian is not considered to be a "Father" because he did not remain orthodox, but died a Montanist heretic and schismatic. Whence the expression, "The Fathers *with* Tertullian and Origen".

Today, *almost no serious credentialed scholars (Catholic or otherwise) questions either the authenticity of, nor the basic dating of any of these documents.* According to the "Fathers," the "Traditions" in these writings emanate from two authoritative sources of that which had been "Traditum" ("handed on") from the Apostles; these two sources are *Oral* Apostolic Tradition, and the *Written* Apostolic Tradition. They testify that they passed both sources on exactly as they have received them (which is exactly what St. Paul admonished them to do).

Not everything which the Fathers wrote is something which came word-for-word to them directly from the Apostles. e.g., By the time of the SubApostolic Fathers many of them are beginning to develop commentaries (Scriptural exegesis) on the writings of the Old Testament (OT), and on many of the writings of the Apostles. Here especially we begin to find more and more original thought.[36] While they constantly quote the Apostles, they are less and less limiting themselves to parroting the word-for-word phrasing which has been passed down to them. More and more they become engaged in explaining and making understandable to the faithful those traditions which they the Fathers have received.

2. Potential Confusion in Usage of the Word, Tradition.

Contemporary Usage: Today, that which had been initially handed on *orally* by the Apostles is commonly referred to as part of "Tradition," while that which had initially been handed on *in written form* is referred to as "Scripture." **Actually, *in the Pauline sense, they are both "Traditions," things which have been "handed on."***

Usage of the Early Fathers: *That Pauline sense is certainly the usage of the early Fathers as they utilized the word "Tradition."* When the *early* Fathers used the word "Tradition" they used it in the collective Pauline sense, to collectively refer to Christian teachings

[36] It is original in that, in order to explain the Scriptures and to overcome heresies, much use begins to be made of analogous thought, and other teaching and exegetical methods. We find nevertheless, in their writings, that what the Fathers did pass on is constantly filled with and referenced to the Apostolic Tradition.

which had been handed on, "EITHER BY WORD OF MOUTH OR BY LETTER."[37] In other words, for the early earlier Fathers, "Tradition" was a collective noun. (See treatment of St. Irenaeus to follow shortly).

3. "Written Tradition" Begins to be Referred to as Scripture -- Along With the Old Testament

Some of the late *SubApostolic* Fathers and many of the later Fathers began also to distinguish between and refer to (a) the written sources of "Tradition" as Scripture, and (b) the oral sources of "Tradition" simply as "Tradition." Only gradually did the Christians begin to comprehend that their apostolic written works should be referred to as Scripture qua Scripture - right along with the Old Testament.

The following point is absolutely essential to an understanding of this process: Prior to the late second century, there were two major impediments to calling N.T. writings Scripture.

(1) What we now recognize as the N.T. writings only gradually came to be clearly identified as an integral whole such as the O.T. writings were. i.e., Originally, there was no recognized "list" of inspired N.T. writings. (There is no such list in the N.T. itself. This point will be developed more extensively later.)

(2) There were numerous pious writings which some members of the Church treated as the same type or genre as what we now accept to be inspired "Scriptural" writing.

Before the early Church and its Fathers could define all the N.T. writings as part of "Scripture," there had to be previous agreement as to what books were actually inspired writings --

---

37 2nd. Thessalonians, 2:15 RSV. Catholic Edition, 1965.

which ones were to be ultimately included in a N.T. Scriptural list or *canon*.

> "They [N.T. writings] were of course in circulation, but they really make good their position ... only with their canonization, *completed in essentials c.* A.D. 175-200."[38]

Again, the Apostolic and early SubApostolic Fathers, and even some of the *later* Fathers utilized the term "Tradition" in its collective Pauline sense. They used it to refer to the oral and the written teachings of the Apostles. Even some of the later Fathers occasionally did this. The different senses, distinctions, and usages of the word "Tradition" developed over a significant period of time.

4. A High Percentage of the Fathers Were Bishops

Of the selected Fathers whose works are cited a few paragraphs above, the majority were also Bishops of the Church. In chronological order they are -- Pope St. Clement of Rome, Ignatius of Antioch, Polycarp of Smyrna, Irenaeus of Lyons, Clement of Alexandria, and Cyprian of Carthage. When these Bishops of the infant Church state a teaching of the Church, or comment upon the liturgies they celebrated, or upon the Scriptures themselves, they commonly cite two sources, *Oral* and *Written Tradition*, as their authority. *And they state that they have received it as from the Apostles. This is universally true of the very earliest Christian writings available to us.*

Therefore, it is impossible for any reasonable man or woman (*who is also familiar with the contents of those writings*) to deny; (1) that the Apostles taught their disciples to receive their instruc-

[38] *The Apostolic Tradition, Of St. Hippolytus of Rome*, Rev. Gregory Dix, Monk of Nashborn Abbey, Society for Promoting Christian Knowledge, London, 1937, ff., p. XLIII. What does Rev. Dix mean by the statement," *completed in essentials*"? He is referring to the fact that there was still some disagreement about certain books which ultimately were accepted in the Church Canon as having been "inspired". This issue was not authoritatively decided until the late 4th century.

tion from both the Oral and Written Traditions of the Church, and (2) that the Apostles taught them to re-hand them on as being of equal authority.

5. The Concept of "Scripture Alone" is not Found in the Fathers, or Other Documents of the Infant Church -- Except Where They Condemn It as a Heresy

No intellectually honest individual - *who has also thoroughly familiarized himself or herself with the writings of the "Fathers"* - would claim that the infant Church ever accepted the doctrine or concept of "Scripture Alone." **That very concept of Scripture Alone is totally absent from and totally foreign to the Church of the Apostolic and SubApostolic Age.** When the subject of "Scripture Alone" did finally appear, it was universally rejected by the "Fathers."[39] The reader might wish to reflect upon this discussion when we later come to Karl Rahner's writings on the Catholic doctrine of Tradition.

6. Extant Writings of the Fathers

The examples given above are *only a random sampling* of some of the more prominent Patristic Writings of some Apostolic and SubApostolic Fathers on the subject of Tradition and Scripture. Many works from all three groups (Apostolic, SubApostolic, and "later" Fathers) have been lost in the course of time. In some cases, all we know is their title.

In all cases, when someone is referred to as a "Father," that signifies that at least some of his writing has survived. Sometimes all we have are fragments, or pieces of them. Sometimes, what we know of them is contained in the writings of another Father of Church. This usually happens when one Father quotes and comments on the writings of another Father.

---

[39] See the later discussions of this point in (1) the anti-Gnostic writings of St. Irenaeus, and (2) in the discussion of the "Council of Nicea" in the section on "higher critic" debunkers of Tradition.

Fortunately, many of the Patristic Writings have in one manner or another survived virtually intact (this is true of the "examples" given above). ***Those extant Patristic Writings are invaluable to a Christian who honestly wants to know the totality of what the Apostles taught their immediate disciples and successor Bishops.*** But not everything which is in them qualifies as tradition, qua "*T*radition."

It must also be noted that there are many supportive documents of the infant Church whose authorship is unknown. They are also treated as part of the traditional teachings of the Church. Included in such a list would for instance be the DIDACHE. Copies of this book are found from throughout the length and breadth of the Church by the year 170 A.D. Later we will be quoting from the DIDACHE and its teachings on the Antichrist.

7. "Tradition With a Capital /T/"

Here, another distinction must be made -- the distinction between what scholars refer to as *Tradition* with a /T/, or *tradition* with a /t/. The word *Tradition,* when used independently with a /T/ signifies something which is to be believed, compared with /t/ which refers simply to a custom or practice which is not necessarily a matter of Faith and/or Morals. In order for an item to qualify as *T*radition with a /T/, it must meet several criteria:

(1) The matter being described must fall within one of two categories, (a) articles of faith (things we are to *believe* as Christians), and/or, (b) Morals, (revealed Doctrine about what we may/should do, and may/should not do as Christians).

(2) The specific teaching must also for the most part be, (a) *held in common* by a number of "Fathers" who wrote on a specific subject, and, (b) it may *not* be specifically denied by even one of the "Fathers."

When there is "commonalty" amongst the Fathers in an area of Faith or Morals, then we usually have "*T*radition" with a capital letter "T."

8. St. Irenaeus: On Tradition

Today, there are both some confused Catholics and many non-Catholic Christians who say that "Tradition" (as the Church understands and explains it today) was an invention of the 4th and 5th century Church. *Nothing could be further from the truth.* A *thorough* reading of even the earliest Fathers will disabuse any intellectually honest individual of that notion.

In the second century the Gnostic heretics attempted to manipulate the understanding of many N.T. Scriptural texts to fit their doctrines. When that failed, they attacked the integrity of the Scriptures themselves. Consequently, St. Irenaeus (a Father of the Church) had to deal directly with the specific issues of Tradition and Scripture.

The SubApostolic Fathers of the Church (including St. Irenaeus) invoked against the Gnostics the total "Tradition" which had been received from the Apostles through the Apostolic succession of Bishops. Observe how St. Irenaeus speaks to these issues in *the late 2nd century*. It must be remembered that *Irenaeus is only one teaching generation removed from the Apostles*. He was a hearer of St. Polycarp, who in turn was a hearer of the Apostle John.

The following quotes come from Book Three of the five books of St. Irenaeus' *Adversus Haereses* (*Against Heresies*). He describes in one of his other works how he sat in the "house of Polycarp" (in Smyrna) listening to Polycarp's lectures and preaching. Irenaeus wrote these five books of *Against Heresies* between 180 and 199 A.D. in Lyon, France, (where he was Bishop).[40] St. Irenaeus writes,

> "When Scripture is used to demolish their [Gnostic] arguments, [the Gnostics] turn around and start accusing Scripture itself: they say that it is inaccurate and untrustworthy, that its language

[40] *The Faith of the Early Fathers*, W. A. Jurgens, The Liturgical Press, Collegeville, Mn. 1970, Vol. 1, p. 84.

is ambiguous, and that the truth cannot be extracted from it by people ignorant of their [secret] tradition."

[NOTE: Read this footnote carefully][41]

[Notice: That Irenaeus is (around 190 A.D.) already referring to N.T. writings as "Scripture." This is in accordance with the earlier quote from Rev. Dix about the canon being "*completed in essentials c.* A.D. 175-200."]

St. Irenaeus continues;

"But when we appeal to ***the tradition that comes from the apostles*, the tradition preserved in the Churches thanks to the succession of presbyters, *they oppose tradition*.** They claim to be wiser than not only the presbyters but the apostles themselves, and to have discovered the pure truth."[42] [emphasis - authors]

Notice Irenaeus' quote, "the tradition that comes from the apostles, the tradition preserved in the Churches thanks to the succession of the presbyters." One could not ask for a finer basal definition of "Tradition." Irenaeus *describes the Gnostic opposition to "tradition" as part of their Heresy!* Irenaeus continues,

"The tradition of the apostles, which had been manifested throughout the world, can be examined by all who want to see the truth. **We can enumerate the bishops instituted by**

41 Irenaeus' *Adversus Haereses* can be extremely difficult for someone to obtain a copy of. But it can be found in good seminary libraries in a number of sets of writings of the Fathers, such as the set, *Ancient Christian Writers*. For the reason of lack of ready access, the author has referenced these particular quotes as found in two sources, (1) from *Adversus Haereses* itself, and, (2) *from a paperback book which is currently in print*. That "paperback" is *The Scandal of the Incarnation, Irenaeus Against The Heresies*. [The references from that book are listed as SI...] This book can be ordered from Ignatius Press in San Francisco, California. The passages from *Adversus Haereses* which are quoted therein are "Selected and introduced by Hans Urs von Balthasar. THIS AUTHOR (of Trial, Tribulation & Triumph) HIGHLY RECOMMENDS TO THE READER THE PURCHASING AND CAREFUL READING OF THE *The Scandal of the Incarnation*.

42 *Adversus Haereses*, Book III, 1, 1., SI-p. 79.

the apostles in the Churches, and their successors down to our own day."[43]

Irenaeus demonstrates that he and his contemporaries are close enough to the Apostles that they can with precision validate the accuracy of (1) the *apostolic succession*, and (2) that the apostolic "tradition" of their teachings has been faithfully handed down.

9. Irenaeus Refutes the "Scripture Alone" Argument of Gnostics

Now, St. Irenaeus deals with the "Scripture Alone" argument! Despite what we might think today, it is not a new argument with Luther and Calvin. It was on occasion presented in late SubA-postolic times. But in each and every case "Scripture Alone" was denounced as a heresy in the infant Church. Irenaeus says:

> "What does this all come down to? Well, if controversy arises about some minor matter, should we not have recourse to the most ancient Churches, the one which had contact with the apostles, in order to obtain a sure and accurate resolution of the disputed issue? **And supposing the apostles had not left us their writings, *would we not then follow the order of tradition* which they handed down to the men to whom they entrusted the Churches?**
>
> "**Many of the barbarian** [illiterate] **nations who believe in Christ have given their assent to this order. *Salvation has been written in their hearts* (2 Cor. 3:3) *without paper and ink, by the spirit.*** Preserving the ancient tradition, they believe in one God, the Creator of heaven and earth and everything in them, and in Christ Jesus our Lord, who, in His superabundant love for His creation, condescended to be born of a virgin, uniting man to God through Himself, who suffered under Pontius Pilate, rose again and was taken up in splendor, who will come again in glory as Savior of those who are saved ... **Thanks to the ancient tradition of the apostles, they reject, even in thought, the lying inventions** [of heretics]."[44]

---

43 Ibid. Book III,1.. SI-P. 80.

44 Ibid, Book III, 4, 1-2, SI-p. 81.

As a living witness, Irenaeus is testifying to the following historic fact. In his time there were entire "barbarian" (without benefit of "paper and ink") nations, many of whose people were fully Christian. These "barbarian nations" were composed of people who were completely illiterate. Irenaeus tells us they had become Christian by "Preserving the ancient tradition."[45] In other words, they had been orally taught the basics of the Christian Faith and accepted it entirely through that oral instruction. *Salvation has been written in their hearts without paper and ink, by the spirit*. Irenaeus continues:

> "(147) **Since the tradition which comes down from the apostles exists in this way in the Church and abides among us**, let us return to the scriptural proof provided by those of the apostles who wrote the gospels."[46]

St. Irenaeus does not denigrate Scripture, he loves it. He beautifully describes the love and respect which the Church holds for both sacred Tradition and sacred Scripture.

NOTICE: He describes "the gospels" as part of the total tradition of the Church.

G. OUR LIVING TRADITION

Anyone familiar with the Scriptures knows that the exact meaning of certain Scriptural passages is not always immediately obvious. The early Christians, being no less intelligent than those of our day, realized the same thing. Therefore they sought the "exact meaning" of certain Scripture passages from the totality of Tradition.

---

[45] Irenaeus was a citizen of the Roman Empire. For citizens of the 2nd century Western Roman Empire, those other than the Greeks and Romans were often referred to as "Barbari." But this was not the only usage of the word. For instance, if a nation had no high culture in general, a "Roman" almost always specifically considered them to be barbarian. One of the first tests for culture was if they had a written language. That appears to be the sense within which Irenaeus is using the word here.

[46] *Adversus Haereses*. Book III, 5, 1., SP-p. 82

1. Tradition Explains Many Difficult Scripture Passages

As just one of hundreds of possible examples, what did Jesus mean when he said, "I and the Father are one." What did Jesus mean by that? Did Jesus mean that He is in actuality just another mode or appearance of the Father? That is how the third century heretic Sebellius interpreted, "I and the Father are one." Sebellius gathered many followers with that interpretation - which essentially eliminates the Trinity. He was ultimately excommunicated by Pope Callistus in 220 A.D. for that interpretation.

The modern Christian might respond against Sebellius, "The Father and the Son are of the same substance, but different in Person. Every Christian knows that." *Today,* "every Christian knows that." But *those formulas of faith commonly understood by modern Christians are not taken directly from Scripture.* Those formulaic distinctions did not exist until developed by the Fathers of the Church from the totality of apostolic Tradition. On several occasions heretics argued in error from Scripture alone. The Fathers (most of whom were also Bishops) counter-argued from the Pauline "traditions which have been taught to you, either by word or mouth, or by our Epistle."

2. Living Tradition

As the Fathers at Vatican II said,

> "The sayings of the Holy Fathers are a witness to the life-giving presence of Tradition, showing how its riches are poured out in the practice and life of the Church, in her belief and in her prayer. *By means of the same Tradition the full canon of the sacred books is known to the Church* and *the holy Scriptures themselves are more thoroughly understood and constantly actualized in the Church.*"[47] [Emphasis the author's]

The Church confirms the Apostolic and living Tradition of teachings coming down directly from the Apostles through the Fathers. That

---

[47] Dogmatic Constitution on Divine Revelation, *Dei Verbum*, #8, *Vatican Council II, The Concilior and Post Concilior Documents, Vol 1.* New Revised Edition 1992, p. 754.

living Tradition is thoroughly confirmed by a sound and thorough knowledge of Church history. Through the apostolic succession of Bishops transmitting the apostolic teaching down to our day, it is a *living* Tradition.

In the infant Church doctrinal and ethical decisions were based upon those apostolic teachings under the guidance of the Holy Spirit. It is on the same basis that those decisions continue to be made by the Magisterium to this day. This can be a difficult point to grasp without at least one concrete example.

3. The Canon of Scripture Itself Comes From Tradition

Some New Testament inspired writers refer to some of the other Biblical writings and/or writers. For instance, St. Peter's, "Just as our most dear brother Paul ... has written to you, as indeed he did in all his epistles"[48] is an example of one inspired writer referring by name to another. **Despite some of these cross-references, nowhere in the inspired Biblical texts themselves do we find anything even remotely approaching a list (canon) of the books to be included in what we now call the Bible.**

While it may appear to be obvious, it must be emphasized that the individual books of the Bible were not written as chapters of a book. They were separately written documents meant for a particular audience at a particular time. So how did the New Testament come into being. The Church simply collected the "inspired writings" into one book ("Biblia") at a much later date. That task was much more difficult than it might first appear.

There were some "apocryphal" books in circulation in the infant Church which were claimed to be the work of one of the Apostles. Some of them were out and out frauds and forgeries. There were also some spiritually and doctrinally sound but "non-inspired" books which some Christians thought should be included in a list of inspired books. Since the inspired texts in the Bible do not give us a list of the inspired writers, under the guidance of the Holy Spirit the Church worked through its received Tradition in determining which books should be included in a list (canon) of Scriptural "inspired" books.

---

[48] II Peter, Chapter 3, verses 15.

4. An Example of the Church's "Living Tradition" at Work

How did the Church decide which books were inspired and which ones were not? How did the actual process work? This is an excellent example of the "living Tradition" within the Church within a given period. By the fourth century, it had become necessary to provide a "canon" or list of the books from which Christians could draw certainty about which books contained the inspired Word of God.

Since the Scriptures themselves did not provide their own canon or list of books, the pro and con arguments in each case were based upon the totality of Tradition. Many discussions, meetings, synods, and councils of Bishops deliberated on this matter. Sometime between 380 and 382 A.D., Pope Damasus in Rome requested St. Jerome to assist him in the task of preparing a "canon" of approved books of both the Old and New Testaments. Pope Damasus after much prayer, and study of the apostolic Tradition, called a Council at Rome in 382. He presented a preliminary decree or "canon" of "inspired writings." The Council of Rome studied and agreed with this canon. Damasus published it in 382 as part two of *The Decree of Damasus*.[49]

Confirming the role of "apostolic Tradition" in this process, the 1994 *Catechism of the Catholic Church* says,

> "*It was by the apostolic Tradition that the Church discerned which writings are to be included in the list of the sacred books*. This complete list is called the canon of Scripture. It included 46 books from the Old Testament (45 if we count Jeremiah and Lamentations as one) and 27 of the New."[50]

---

49 This later came to be called the *Galasian Decree*. "It is now commonly held that the part of the *Gelasian Decree* dealing with the accepted canon of Scripture is an authentic work of the Council of Rome of 382 A.D., and that Gelasius edited it again at the end of the fifth century, adding to it the catalogue of the rejected books, the apocrypha." *The Faith of the Early Fathers*, Vol. 1, p. 404.

50 *Catechism of the Catholic Church*, Libreria Editrice Vaticana, St. Paul Books and Media, 1994, p. 34, #120.

The preliminary "canon" published by Pope Damasus was almost immediately accepted throughout the Church. Within a few short years:

> "The Council of Hippo (393 A.D.), the decisions of which were confirmed by the two Councils of Carthage (397 & 419 A.D.), determined the Canon exactly as it is today."[51]

The historic data from the Council records that the Canon of Carthage was sent to Rome for confirmation. The next recorded major "canon" event is the canon of February 20, 405, by Pope St. Innocent (the 1st). The canon, or list of sacred books to be included in Scripture, which he sent to Bishop Exsuperius of Toulouse, Gaul (France) is virtually identical to the one of Damasus.

In 1441 A.D., the Council of Florence stated the same canon as definitive. It is this same canon which the Council of Trent in the 16th Century solemnly defined as binding in Faith. That is the canon used in all Catholic Bibles today.

It is only on the authority of, and through the living Tradition of the Catholic Church that we even have a "Bible" today. This entire process, the Vatican II Council Fathers cryptically referred to in the following words,

> "*By means of the same Tradition* the full canon of the sacred books is known to the Church."[52]

In reference to the *New Testament*, the Traditional "canon" of Pope Damasus is the one used in all Christian Bibles today, whether Protestant or Catholic. *Its transmission to us is part of a reality which comprises more than a fixed set of formulae from the apostolic past passed on from the Apostles to their successors.*

---

[51] *A Companion to Scripture Studies*, Vol. 3, Rev. John E. Steinmeuller, S.T.D., S.Scr.Lld., Joseph F. Wagner, Inc., 6th. Printing, 1946, p. 76 [It should be noted however, that there are a number of other Church historians and Scripture scholars who attribute the first definitive Papal "list" to Pope Damasus circa 382/3 A.D. - having been issued by the Pope, even if there remains a historic question as to how soon this document was successfully circulated throughout the Church.]

[52] Dogmatic Constitution on Divine Revelation, *Dei Verbum*, #8, *Vatican Council II, The Concilior and Post Concilior Documents, Vol 1.* New Revised Edition 1992, p. 754.

POINT: It is through the continuum of the living Tradition of the Church that we can even point to any Scripture and state with confidence that it is the inspired Word of God. Without that living Tradition, *on whose authority would we accept those Scriptures today as the word of God?* Without the living Tradition of the Church transmitted to us through the authority of the Magisterium, how could we accept the Bible in all its parts as anything besides just another book? How can we, roughly nineteen centuries after the last of the books was written, know with certitude which books are supposed to be in the Bible and which ones are not? Without that *living* continuous testimony of the Church, we would just be taking those things on the authority of some contemporary man or woman.

5. St. Augustine Faced These Same Issues

St. Augustine is both a Father and a Doctor of the Church. His life and works come to us primarily from the early 5th century. Augustine (who had one of the brightest minds of his age) became Bishop of Hippo, in North Africa. There he wrote voluminously about the Christian faith, in turn becoming one of *its* most brilliant apologists and theologians. His writings in defense and explanation of the Christian faith are so lucid and beautifully written that many of them are read in literature courses in many secular universities to this day. His *Confessions* is the most famous example.

Augustine faced the basal issues of Tradition, Scripture, and the authority of the Magisterium. **He fully understood that Tradition and Scripture have to be transmitted to us, and that their instrument of transmission is the authority of the Church, the Magisterium.** In 397 A.D., Augustine wrote,

> "If you should find someone who does not yet believe in the Gospel, what would you answer him when he says, 'I do not believe'? **Indeed, I would not believe in the Gospel myself if the authority of the Catholic Church did not influence me to do so."**[53]

---

[53] *Against the Letter of Mani called "The Foundation"*, St. Augustine.

Amongst Catholics, only those who have lost their understanding of Tradition and its living process now wonder about the authority and accuracy of the Bible. *As Vatican II teaches us, if sacred Tradition falls, so must sacred Scripture.*

> "It is clear, therefore, that, in the supremely wise arrangement of God, *sacred Tradition, sacred Scripture and the Magisterium* of the Church are so connected and associated that *one of them cannot stand without the others.*"[54]

6. Scripture Canon of the Council of Trent

What was it caused the 16th century Council of Trent to Dogmatically define the canon of books to be included in Scripture as binding in Faith? Some 16th century "Reformers" were challenging the authenticity of several books in *both* the Old and New Testaments. For instance, one of them had deprecated a New Testament Book, the *Book of James*, calling it a "work of spiritual straw."[55] This was one of the first fruits of his theory of private interpretation,

---

[54] Dogmatic Constitution on Divine Revelation, *Dei Verbum*, #24, *Vatican Council II, The Conciliar and Post Conciliar Documents, Vol 1.* New Revised Edition 1992, p. 756.

[55] By the time Martin Luther made that statement, he was already teaching his "doctrine" of "salvation by faith alone." Luther denied the necessity of "works" for salvation. From its infancy, the Church has through the Fathers and the Magisterium always taught the necessity of *both* Faith and Works for salvation. The singularly most difficult (but not the only) Scriptural obstacle to Luther's "salvation by faith alone" doctrine is the Book of James, which says,
2:14 "What does it profit, my brethren, if a man says he has faith but has not works? Can his faith save him? 2:19 "You believe that God is one; you do well. ***Even the demons believe* - and shudder.**" 2:24 "You see that **a man is justified by works and not by faith alone.**"
Declarations such as these and many others in the "Book of James" which teach the necessity of works for salvation lead Luther to challenge and make disparaging statements about the Book of James such as saying "it is a work of spiritual straw". Luther and most of the other "Reformers" never understood the essential difference between the Doctrine of "Justification" and "Salvation". For a concise yet highly lucid exposition of this Doctrine, see Fr. Hardon's *Modern Catholic Dictionary*, John A. Hardon, S.J., Doubleday, New York, 1980. For a fuller discussion see the Dogmatic Canons and Decrees of the Council of Trent. The best edition available in good libraries is *Canons and Decrees of the Council of Trent*, original Latin text with English translation, Rev. H.J. Schroeder, O.P., B. Herder Book Co., 1941, pp. 29-50.

wherein one attempts to be one's own authority on such matters. This theory was going to terribly divide a portion of the Body of Christ.

The authenticity of the "Canon of Scripture" as received from the Fathers and the early Church was now for the first time being publicly consistently challenged, well over a millennium after the early Church had established that canon at least by 382 A.D.

Did the 16th century Council of Trent invent or decide upon their list of inspired books? No, under the guidance of the Holy Spirit it authoritatively witnessed to the decisions made by the early Church which had been passed on through the Church's living Tradition. The Council Fathers at Trent said:

> "If anyone does not accept as sacred and canonical the aforementioned books in their entirety and with all their parts, *as they have been accustomed to be read in the Catholic Church and as they are outlined in the old Latin Vulgate Edition, and knowingly and deliberately rejects the aforesaid traditions, let him be anathema.*"[56] [emphasis -authors]

The "Old Latin Vulgate" is essentially the work of St. Jerome which he began in 382 at the behest of Pope Damasus I. The Council of Trent then, on April 8, 1546, bound Catholics in Faith to accept what effectually is the late 4th century decision of the early Church. **This Decree of Trent clearly identifies the organ of transmission of the Canon of Scripture as "*aforesaid traditions.*"**

This is an excellent example of how a living traditional teaching of the Church can come to be formally defined as De Fide, binding in Faith. When this happens, Catholics are put on formal notice that, (1) something they *should* already believe, they now *must* believe in order to remain a Catholic in good standing.

Several other historical examples of the "living Tradition" of the Church in action are:

(1) The Council Fathers of the first General or Ecumenical Council of the Church theologically defined and pro-

[56] *Canons and Decrees of the Council of Trent*, Original Text with English Translations, Rev. H.J. Schroeder, O.P., Herder Book Co., 1941, (from the Decrees of the Fourth Session), p. 19.

tected the *true Divinity of Jesus Christ.* At the Council of Nicea in 325 A.D., they defined the "Son" as being "Homoousios" or "Consubstantial" with the Father. This doctrinal teaching was confirmed and approved by the 33rd. Pope, St. Sylvester - thus making it binding in Faith.

(2) The Council Fathers of the Third Ecumenical Council of Chalcedon theologically defined and protected the *true Humanity of Jesus Christ.* At the Council of Chalcedon in 451 A.D., they defined the "Son" Jesus Christ as consubstantial also with man "in one person and one hypostasis" (substance). This teaching was initially urged on the Council,[57] and subsequently confirmed and approved by the same 45th Pope, St. Leo the Great - thus making it binding in Faith.

Within "living Tradition," the Magisterium under the direction of the Holy Spirit, prayerfully considers all the Tradition that has come down from the Apostles. That "all" includes Scripture, the writings of the Fathers, the living Liturgies and unvarying practices of the Church since apostolic times, the various "Creeds," and the archeological monuments *testifying to what Christians believed and how they worshipped over the centuries.*

H. UNWRITTEN TRADITION

As stated earlier, the first teaching of the Apostles to any community or group of Christians was oral. After they had established a baptized community, as the New Testament tells us, they would move on to another area. Sometimes they also later returned to an established community for another visit. But as Scripture itself confirms, they often utilized a written method of follow-up communication with an established "ecclesia" (local assembly, community,

[57] *St. Leo's Tome*, was a document written and sent by Pope Leo to the Council Fathers at Chalcedon. When it was read to the assembled Fathers, they responded in chorus, "Peter speaks through Leo." In response, those fathers wrote their famous definition of the Hypostatic Union of Christ's true Divinity and true humanity "in one person and one hypostasis (substance)."

or church). Around the year 200 A.D., Tertullian (an authoritative Ecclesial writer of the Church) describes this process well

> "... the apostles, whom He [Jesus] sent forth to preach what he had revealed to them. But what they preached, that is, what Christ had revealed to them ... can be proved in no other way except through the same Churches which the apostles founded, preaching in them themselves *viva voce* [*with living voice*] as they say, *and afterwards by their Epistles*."[58]

Tertullian is here testifying from North Africa (in 200 A.D.) as to how they determine that which is *received doctrine* from the Apostles. *He clearly states that they determine this from both the Oral Tradition ("with living voice"), as well as from the Written Tradition ("by their Epistles").*

1. Tertullian Treats "Tradition" and Scripture Equally

A classic example from Tertullian of the meld between written and Unwritten Tradition is the following. In 208 A.D., in his work *The Soul*, Tertullian is describing the universal essential belief in his time of what we today call Purgatory.

> "In short, if we understand *that prison of which the Gospel speaks to be Hades*, and if we interpret the last farthing [penny] to be the light offense, which is to be expiated there before the resurrection [of the body], no one will doubt that the soul undergoes some punishment in Hades [Hades to be distinguished from - Gahenna, the eternal Hell], *without prejudice to the eternal resurrection.*"[59]

In another of his works written circa 211 A.D., *The Crown*, Tertullian tells us of the universal practice in his time of praying for those who had died in the faith, in order to assist them in release from "Hades" (Purgatory).

---

58 *The Demurrer Against The Heretics*, Tertullian, circa 200 A.D., [21, 2-3]

59 *The Faith of the Early Fathers*, William A. Jurgens, Liturgical Press, Collegeville, MN. 1970, Vol. 1p. 145, [Reverenced from Tertullians *The Soul*, written in Carthage North Africa circa 208 A.D.]

> "We offer sacrifices [Masses and fastings] for the dead on their birthday anniversaries."[60]

These examples from the writings of Tertullian are far from the only Patristic age testimonies to the above belief and practice of the young Church. From the above quotes of Tertullian we can learn at least three things:

(1) From the first quote we see that he draws no distinction between the authority of initial living voice teachings of the Apostles and the written Epistles. They are viewed as equally authoritative. His very words explicitly deny "Scripture Alone." His doctrine on this is virtually identical to that of St. Irenaeus in Gaul.

(2) In the second quote he recognizes that *many New Testament teachings are fleshed out in Unwritten Tradition* as testified to by the universal belief of the Church in a temporary place of purgation. He specifically references this teaching to the Scriptural quote - Matt. 5:26, "You shall not get out until you have paid the last farthing [penny]."

(3) The third quote cites the established practice of the Church validating that belief.

As we have previously read, Irenaeus contemporaneously (between 180-199 A.D.) tells us the exact same thing from Gaul (France) vis-a-vis the equal authority of what we call Tradition and Scripture. This *was* the universal belief and teaching of the infant Church.

As we know from Scripture, these apostolic letters were sometimes exhortations to continue strong in the faith, to stand up to persecution. Sometimes the intent was to strengthen them in a particular doctrine which had already been orally taught, sometimes a strong rebuke for unacceptable moral behavior. *But in none of these letters is there even a hint that all they had been taught about Faith and Morals was contained in any or all of those letters of Scripture.*

---

[60] Ibid. p. 151 [Referenced from Tertullian's *De Corona* (the Crown).]

2. The *"Disciplina Arcani"*

Was everything which had been orally taught by the apostles committed to writing shortly thereafter - even by the Fathers? The following may come as a surprise to some readers. But, *much of what had been taught by the Apostles was deliberately not committed to writing during the time of the infant Church.* ***This is a matter of public record!***

In the early Church there was a rule known as the "Disciplina Arcani," the "Discipline of the Secret." This had to do with keeping knowledge of the "*Sacred* (Revealed) *Mysteries*" of the faith from the non-Christian community:

(1) By late in the first century and early in the second, the authorities heard about Christians "Eating the Body and drinking the Blood" (of Christ) in Communion. In order to turn the mob against the Christians, the enemies of the Church subsequently began spreading rumors that the Christians were cannibals. That is actually a matter of historic record.

"Their [Christians'] supposed customs, principally accusations of cannibalism arising from a misunderstanding of eucharistic language, aroused scandal."[61]

(2) Additionally, the exhortations to love the "Sisters and the Brethren" (in the faith) were sometimes misunderstood, sometimes deliberately turned around and twisted as to their meaning. The enemies of the Church very early began to spread the calumny that the Christians were practicing incest. In order to counter these and other calumnies, some of the early Christian writers, called Apologists, wrote public lengthy defenses against these charges.

---

[61] *The Communion of Saints, An Examination of the Place of the Christian in the Belief, Worship, and Calendars of the Church*, Michael Pelham, Alcuin Club/SPCK, London, 1980, p. 4. For an example of a specific Christian defense against such spurious charges, see the *Supplication for the Christians* by Athenagoras of Athens (a Father of the Church) written circa 177 A.D.

Again, the Church attempted to keep knowledge of all of the "Sacred (Revealed) Mysteries" within the Church for several reasons,

(1) To avoid scandal, to avoid false interpretation (e.g., as in the false charges of cannibalism and incest), and also,

(2) In order to follow Our Lord's injunction, "Do not cast your pearls before swine."

However, what *was* taught, was openly known by every baptized Christian who had also received his or her first communion.[62] There was no "secret doctrine" *amongst the Christians themselves* about anything.

3. During the Roman Persecution

During that period between 64 A.D., to 313 A.D., the Romans during various periods of persecution raided Christian assemblies confiscating their Scriptures and Sacramentaries.[63] The Church therefore regularly refrained from putting the bulk of the Sacramental "Sacred Mysteries" in writing. And they did the best they could to physically protect their copies of the Scriptures.

If a Christian turned over a copy of some of the Scriptures or liturgical books to the Romans in order to avoid martyrdom, that Christian was automatically excommunicated from the Church. Such a "sinner" was called a "Traditor," a person who had "handed over" sacred writings.

However, *the Disciplina Arcani (Discipline of the Secret) did not come to an end with Constantine's Edict of Milan in 313 A.D.* Much of what was received of Apostolic Tradition was only gradually consigned to writing over a period of centuries after the end of

[62] Hippolytus, in his *Apostolic Tradition*, says, "But, if there is any other matter which ought to be told, let the bishop impart it **secretly** to those who have been communicated (been baptized, confirmed and received their first holy communion). He (the bishop) shall not tell this to any but the faithful and only after they have first been communicated." *The Apostolic Tradition, Of St. Hippolytus of Rome*, Rev. Gregory Dix, Monk of Nashborn Abbey, Society for Promoting Christian Knowledge, London, 1937., p. 43.

[63] In the East, they were usually called "Euchologions".

the Roman Persecution. Even after the persecution ended, elements of the "Apostles' Creed," and many items dealing with the Eucharistic Liturgy were only explained in part just prior to someone being baptized, and then more fully after receiving their first communion.

4. St. Cyril of Jerusalem

This is the case in 350 A.D. in St. Cyril of Jerusalem's *Mystagogic Catecheses.*[64] Witness Cyril's admonition (earliest possible date 348) to those already catechized, then Baptized, not to divulge any of the contents of the "Creed" and other Christian "mysteries" which will be explained to them -- *even to other catechumens who have not finished the catechetical process nor actually received the sacraments*.

> "Now when the Catechizing has taken place, should a Catechumen ask what the teachers have said, tell nothing to a stranger; *for we deliver to thee a mystery.*"[65]

This policy (*particularly* in relation to the "Creed") remained in effect for centuries. It is still so in the middle of the 5th Century as expressed in the writings of St. Augustine (circa 430 A.D.), St. Hilary (d. 449 A.D.), Pope St. Leo (circa 450 A.D), and in the *Gelasian Sacramentary,*[66] which all state that *by ancient tradition (as a matter of discipline - not as a matter of faith) the Creed in any form was to*

---

[64] Mystagogic Catechesis – "The instruction which is imparted to help candidates [for Baptism] to understand the meaning of what is said and what is done in the liturgy of his initiation into the Christian life is called "mystagogy", instruction in the meaning of the mysteries." Quoted from, *Christian Initiation, A Comparative Study of the Interpretation of the Baptismal Liturgy in the Mystagogical Writings of Cyril of Jerusalem, John Chrysostom, Theodore of Mopsuestia, and Ambrose of Milan*, Hugh M. Riley, Edited by Johannes Quasten, Vol. 17 of "The Catholic University of America Studies in Christian Antiquity, 1974, p. 2.

[65] *St. Cyril of Jerusalem's Lectures on the Christian Sacraments*, Edited by F.L. Cross, Pub: S-P-C-K, London 1951, Catechesis #22 (Mystagogical Catechesis #5), p. 47.

[66] The actual date of its original composition is unknown, but its earliest possible dating is the very late 5th century.

be learned by heart, and never consigned to writing. This matter of *discipline* only gradually changed over the next few centuries.

I. FURTHER EVIDENCE OF "UNWRITTEN TRADITION"

1. St. Basil, Unwritten Tradition

There is not room in a single volume book of this scope to do more than barely scratch the surface of the evidence for "*unwritten* Tradition" of teachings of the Apostles - which the earliest bishops passed on to their respective clergy and laity. Below are some quotes from St. Basil the Great (an Eastern Father of the Church), as commented upon by an Anglican scholar, Dr. Atchley. Atchley begins by directly quoting St. Basil from Basil's *On the Holy Spirit* (written in 374 A.D.). Atchley then adds further editorial comments of his own;

> [*St. Basil*] 'Which of the sacred writers of the New Testament has left us the words of the epiclesis at the consecration of the Bread of the Eucharist and the Cup of Blessing? For *we are not content merely with the words mentioned by the apostle or the gospel*, but utter before and after them *other words*, as having great power for the mystery, **receiving them from unwritten tradition.'**
>
> [*Atchley*] 'And this he concludes amongst the traditions handed down from the apostles, together with the use of the sign of the Cross, praying towards the East, and blessing the font, and several others.'[67]

Basil testifies to the fact that much of the Liturgical formulae of the Liturgy of the Eucharist primarily came from oral "Unwritten" Tradition "from the Apostles."

---

[67] *On The Epiclesis of the Eucharistic Liturgy and in the Consecration of the Font*, E.G. Cuthbert F. Atchley, Oxford University Press, London, 1935, p. 60. [The actual texts Atchley is quoting and commenting upon are from Basil's *De Spiritu Sancto*, as presented in Migne's *Patrologia Graeca.*]

These "*other words*" (extra-Scriptural words)[68] to which St. Basil refers are universally found throughout all the Rites of the early Church. **Where did that universality come from?** Certain *extra-Scriptural* words of the consecration appear in all the ancient Eucharistic liturgies of the Church. This "Eucharistic prayer, or *anaphora* is the core of the Divine Liturgy."[69] The very *universality* of the early use of these *extra-Scriptural* words throughout the young Church logically demonstrates that they could not have come through independent development.[70] The testimony of many of the Fathers (not just St. Basil) testifies to their teaching that it came through apostolic Tradition.

Could a theology which searches only the *exegesis* (commentaries on Scripture) of the Fathers (1) account for the *universality* of certain *extra-Scriptural* consecration formulas and major divisions or parts of the Eucharistic liturgy, (2) which are universally found throughout the earliest liturgical documents[71] of the Church of both the East and West, (3) which are not spelled out in Scripture? St. Basil and other Fathers say those formulas come from Unwritten Tradition.

Is it possible that in the West, the struggle during the last one hundred years to overcome the *exegetical extremes of Western rationalism and fundamentalism* has lead to an unanticipated side effect? Could it have inadvertently lead to (1) a Western academic neglect of sufficient contemporary study of the full role of Apostolic Tradition as described by the Fathers, (2) in particular of "Unwritten (Oral) Tradition" as described by the Fathers, (3) especially within the area of liturgical studies?

Searching of the Scriptural exegesis (explanation of Scripture) written by the Fathers is absolutely necessary and valuable. As won-

---

68 We are not just speaking of the Epiclesis, but of other extra-scriptural words of the consecration.

69 *The Byzantine-Slav Liturgy of St. John Chrysostom*, Rev. C. Kucharek, Alleluia Press, Allendale, N.J., 1971, p. 551.

70 There was a significant amount of "borrowing" of Eucharistic Prayers (in the East called "Anaphoras") at a later period. What we are talking about here is the consistency of certain non-Scriptural formulas for the consecration prior to the "borrowing", which *borrowing* did not significantly develop until after the Council of Nicea in 325 A.D.

71 The earliest full liturgy of the Mass which has survived intact is that of Hippolytus in his "Apostolic Tradition" from around A.D. 215.

derfully observed in September of 1993 by the Pontifical Biblical Commission,

> "Within the broader current of the great tradition, the particular contribution of patristic exegesis consists of this: to have drawn out from the totality of Scripture the basic orientation which shaped the doctrinal tradition of the church and to have provided a rich theological teaching for the instruction and spiritual sustenance of the faithful."[72]

This fresh emphasis on Patristic exegesis by the Commission has done the Church a great service, out of which much good will almost inevitably come. Due to the theme of the document, the Commission limits itself to observations of the role of patristic exegesis in contemporary understanding of Scripture. But that also *indirectly* raises anew another question which goes beyond the Scriptural Exegesis of the Fathers, it goes to other of their teachings which the Fathers say is also of Apostolic Tradition.

2. St. John Damascene

In the early Church, prayer (especially morning prayer) was universally said facing East in *both* the West and East. As St. Augustine says, "When we rise to pray, we turn East, where heaven begins."[73] This was *especially* true during the Liturgy of the Eucharist. It was a constant tradition for both the priest and the congregation facing the East during celebration of the Liturgy of the Eucharist.

In today's Eastern Church (both among Eastern Rite Catholics and the Orthodox) this tradition is still almost universal. Most homes of Eastern Rite Catholics have what is called an "Icon Corner." In some East-facing corner of their house they place an Icon (usually

---

[72] *The Interpretation of the Bible in the Church*, Pontifical Biblical Commission, Pub: Libreria Editrice Vaticana, Repub: Origins, CNS documentary Service, January 6, 1994, Vol. 23: No. 29, p. 516. [This commission, since shortly after Vatican II, is no longer a part of the magisterial office of the Church. Rather, it is now an association of scholars working closely with the Magisterium.]

[73] *Patrologia Latina*, 34:1277, *De sermone Domini in monte (The Sermon of the Lord on the Mount)* St. Augustine.

of Our Lord and/or His Mother). This "Icon Corner" is where the family gathers for household prayer. Most Eastern Rite Churches even today face the East.

Up until fairly modern time this was the *usual* custom for Churches in the Latin Rite as well. The people and the priest both faced East for most of the Liturgy.[74] Thus their prayer was directed to the East. But this was not absolutely universally practiced - there always were a few exceptions in both the East and West. **But *why* did they usually pray facing East?** Where did this /t/radition come from, what is its source? The last of the Fathers, St. John Damascene, tells us in his 8th century *De Fide Orthodoxa*,

> "And when he was taken up, He [Jesus] ascended to the East, and thus the Apostles worshipped Him and thus He shall come in the same way as they had seen Him going into heaven, as the Lord Himself said: "As the lightning cometh out of the east and appeareth even into the west: so shall also the coming of the Son of man be." And so while we are awaiting Him, we worship toward the East. **This is moreover, the unwritten tradition of the Apostles, *for they have handed many things down to us unwritten.***"[75] [emphasis and parens - authors]

[74] i.e., With rare exception, in the infant Church the priest *didn't* say Mass facing the people. The older readers will remember that prior to the 1960's, Latin Rite priests all said Mass facing the altar. i.e., The priest and the people were both facing the same way. Up until the Middle Ages most of the Latin Rite churches were built facing the East, just as they still for the most part do in the Eastern Rite. A rare "Eastern" exception was the Basilica which Constantine built in the 4th century at Tyre.
Most of the early "Western" exceptions (such as in Rome) are cases where the geography of donated land/building for a Church did not readily allow for a Western entrance. When that happened, the only way the priest could celebrate the Liturgy of the Eucharist facing East was to face the people. With those rare exceptions, the earliest Christian churches were set up with the altar, the priest, and the congregation facing East. So it wasn't a matter of the priest saying Mass with his back to the people. It was a simple matter of all liturgical prayer facing East. It was not considered either important or unimportant whether the priest faced the people. It was important that in offering the sacrifice of the Mass to God (not to the people) that he face East. This is still the almost universal practice in all the Eastern Rites.

[75] *De Fide Orthodoxa*, St. John Damascene, Pub.: The Fathers of The Church, Vol. 37, (Ed. Dr. Roy Deferrari, The Fathers of the Church, Inc., New York, 1958), pp. 353&354.

This particular "tradition" of praying facing the East was originally unwritten. Amongst others, Augustine and Basil wrote of it. *But its explanation* was not fully committed to writing till the 7th Century by St. John Damascene, the last Father of the Church. This tradition was one with a /t/. If it had been a religious precept taught as obligatory (with a /T/) there would not have been any early exceptions in either the East or West (which there were).

Again, the central point of this discussion is, "The volume of Patristic evidence for a sizable '*Unwritten Tradition*' as received from the Apostles is voluminous." Some of it is "tradition" with a with a lower case /t/ as is the case in St. Damascene immediately above. And some of it is tradition with a capital /T/ , as relates in part to the quotes from St. Basil a little earlier.

3. The Magisterium as Interpreter of Tradition

As with interpreting Scripture, *the decisions as to when the qualifications of "/T/radition" are met, and how they are to be specifically interpreted, are always ultimately reserved to the Magisterium of the Church.* This principle is taught in the documents of the earliest councils of the Church, and reiterated later by those of Trent, Vatican I, and Vatican II. It was also clearly recognized by Fathers of the Church. It is most beautifully expressed by St. Jerome in a letter to Pope Damasus wherein he is asking for the Pope's ruling on a difficult theological issue.[76]

4. St. Jerome

Jerome, a Father of the Church, specifically asks Pope Damasus for an *interpretation* of a specific Traditional teaching that has been passed on by the "Fathers" of the Church. Jerome says,

> "I must consult the Chair of Peter and the faith that was praised by the lips of the Apostle (St. Paul)."[77]

---

[76] He is asking about the Nicene "homoousios" definition, specifically, whether it is correct to refer to one or to three "hypostases" in conjunction with the one "ousia" (substance or essence) of God.

[77] *Ancient Christian Writers, The Letters of St. Jerome*, Vol. 1, Edited by Johannes Quasten & Walter Burghardt, S.J., The Newman Press, Westminster Maryland, 1963, p. 71.

Now Jerome explains the issue on which he is consulting thc Pope. In doing so, he *specifically* references the Papal authority to interpret even that which the Church has received from the "Fathers."

> **"by you (the chair of Peter) alone is the inheritance of the fathers preserved intact."**[78]

> "I speak with the successor of the fisherman and the disciple of the cross. Following none but Christ as my primate, I am united in communion with Your Beatitude -- that is, with the chair of Peter. Upon that rock I know the Church is built."[79]

This is quoted from a letter written by St. Jerome to Pope Damasus shortly before the death of Pope Damasus in late 384 A.D. As we can see, Jerome clearly understands that he is not free to put just any interpretation on what was received through apostolic Tradition. He understands and *clearly states* that is reserved to "Peter" as in Magisterium.

However, the status of something being of "Tradition" does not require that a formal *de fide* declaration has ever been made by the Church. Compared with the totality of that which we have received from the Apostles' Tradition, those items which the Church has gone to the trouble to formally define as being binding in faith constitutes a small percentage.

There is a contemporary current of thought amongst some, which says a Catholic has no obligation to believe in Faith anything outside of that which has been formally declared to be De Fide. That is *not* the traditional teaching of the Church. As discussed elsewhere in the book, the Church usually has gone to the trouble to define something as being "De Fide" only when (1) some heretical movement has loudly denied such a traditional teaching -- and (2) to such an extent that the Church senses that the situation is serious enough to warrant a formal definition of something being declared "Of Faith" ("De Fide").

It is normally sufficient when a specific interpretation has been part of the constant teaching tradition of the Fathers and Doctors of

---

[78] Ibid.

[79] Ibid. p. 71.

the Church and/or the universal ordinary Magisterium, that then a Catholic should accept such a teaching as being of "Tradition."

We have now concluded a brief synopsis of the teachings of the Catholic Church on Tradition and its relation to Scripture and to the Magisterium of the Church. We have seen that the Church substantially teaches the same things today about Tradition, Scripture and the Magisterium (in the documents of Vatican Council II and the contemporary Papal Encyclicals of Pope John Paul II) that she taught in the infant and SubApostolic Church. **This teaching is constant over two millennia.**

5. How Does All This Apply to the Reader of This Book?

An excellent example of how such a "teaching" could apply to the reader is the following: It is the constant teaching of the Fathers and Doctors of the Church that there will be *an* Antichrist who will appear as an individual man with a soul. Not one Father specifically denies this teaching. Once it is established in the mind of a Catholic that:

(1) This has been the constant teaching of the Church, and,

(2) Since this teaching is within the area of Faith and Morals, then,

(3) A Catholic can and should with confidence believe it to be part of Tradition.

Proof that the statement, "Antichrist is an individual," is a "constant teaching of the Fathers and Doctors" will be supplied later on. This specific "Antichrist appears as an individual" topic has been introduced here for purposes of example, example of how and why a Catholic should believe certain traditional teachings of the Church which have not been formally declared to be De Fide.

6. Attacks on Tradition in the Twentieth Century

As the reader is going to discover in later chapters, a number of prophecies which are already hundreds of years old speak of future attacks on the Catholic doctrine of Tradition. Some of them specifically predict such an attack for the 20th century. They further predict that this attack will come primarily from within the bosom of the Church. That is why the reader who wishes to fully appreciate the value and accuracy of those prophecies should read the next eleven pages with great care. Some of the material in those pages will require the reader to pay fairly close attention. But again, the reader who has read them with care will have an immensely greater appreciation for the upcoming prophecies about the 20th century.

J. VATICAN II VS. "HIGHER CRITICS" - TRADITION

Some of the Apostolic teachings were essentialized in various Creeds of the Faith. Much of it was certainly placed in the Church's various liturgies. Much of it was inscribed in early Christian inscriptions - e.g., such as on the walls of the Catacombs in Rome and at other grave sites of martyrs, in both the East and West. All of this transmits in part from the Apostolic Tradition.

In many cases what was passed on (traditum) orally from the Apostles was later committed to writing by the Fathers of the Church. When their teaching on a doctrinal or moral point of exegesis is not "specifically denied" by any of the Fathers, then we have a teaching "/T/radition," which, according to the teachings of the Catholic Church is of Faith. It is in these cases that the Council Fathers of Vatican II say,

> "Sacred Tradition and sacred Scripture, then, are bound closely together, and communicate one with the other. For both of them, flowing from the same divine wellspring, come together in some fashion to form one thing, and move towards the same goal. Sacred Scripture is the speech of God as it is put down in writing under the breath of the Holy Spirit. *And Tradition transmits in its entirely the word of God which has been entrusted to the Apostles by Christ the Lord and the Holy Spirit.* It transmits it to the successors of the Apostles so that, enlightened by the Spirit of truth, they may faithfully preserve, expound and spread it abroad by their preaching. Thus it comes about that the Church does

> not draw her certainty about all revealed truths from the holy Scriptures alone. *Hence, both Scripture and Tradition must be accepted and honored with equal feelings of devotion and reverence*."[80] (emphasis - added)

Both Scripture and reason confirm the essential existence and necessity of "Tradition" as part of the deposit of Revelation. And the Church of today solemnly defines that "essential existence and necessity" as a matter of Faith for a Catholic.

1. Higher Critics' Statements on Tradition

But in the West, there have been and are some other voices heard speaking from within the bosom of the Church about the role of Tradition. *And those voices are not consonant with the teachings of Vatican II on the role of Tradition.* Those voices have been causing confusion in the minds of many contemporary Catholics. Those voices are from amongst the ranks of extreme "higher critics."

Karl Rahner is a recognized leader of extreme "higher critics" and what is called by some, the "Contemporary Theological Movement." He is only one of many. But he is representative of much of their thought. His books have been centerpieces of the theology departments of many Catholic universities and seminaries. His reputation as a respected Catholic scholar is well-known in the academic community.

The following examples picked from Rahner's writings are not therefore meant to single him out as an individual. They are rather a way of demonstrating to the reader *the current reality of voices which are not consonant with the constant teachings of the Church on the role of Tradition.* Quoting Rahner is simply the most effective way to demonstrate the state of current thinking in a significant portion of the Western Catholic academic community. That thinking is not consonant with Vatican II. This type of "thinking" has caused a great deal of confusion in the mind of the average late 20th century Catholic.

---

80 Dogmatic Constitution on Divine Revelation, *Dei Verbum*, #9, *Vatican Council II, The Concilior and Post Concilior Documents, Vol 1.* New Revised Edition 1992, p. 755.

2. The "Trickle-down" Effect

A confusion amongst non-academic Catholics has occurred through a trickling down of Rahner's (and many of his theological look-alike's) thought as expressed in his writings. They have subsequently trickled down from university and seminary classrooms to the pulpits of many Catholic parishes. Rahner undoubtedly held his views in good faith, as do many of his students and admirers. But *good faith* or not, Rahner's thought, as expressed in his writings, has done significant damage to the average Catholic's acceptance and understanding of some of the constant teachings of the Church since the time of the Apostles. *This is particularly true about the Church's constant teaching on the definition and role of Tradition.*

Whether or not Rahner (or his theological look-alikes) intended the literal interpretation of many of his writings which have caused the subsequent "confusion" in many Rahnerian minds is not a subject proper to the themes or scope of this book. It is the bottom line effects of those writings we are discussing here.

In 1979, the author was taking a class at a Catholic seminary. At that time, he was writing a paper on "Tradition." During the research phase of the paper he was referred by the seminary's head librarian to Karl Rahner's *Sacramentum Mundi*. The librarian told the author, "This is the primary reference work the professors refer their theology students to." After reading the *Sacramentum Mundi*'s definition and description of "Tradition," the author remembers reporting back to his professor.

He told the professor that the definition of "tradition" in the *Sacramentum Mundi positively* defined "Tradition" with almost the exact words which Pope St. Pius X had condemned as heretical in the first decade of the 20th century.[81] He told the professor that *a* definition of Tradition which Pius X had condemned as part of the "Modernist Heresy" was almost exactly the definition used by Karl Rahner to describe orthodox Catholic belief.

When the author made this "discovery" he was already in his late 30's. He was old enough to know that from an orthodox Catholic perspective there was something radically non-traditional about Rahner's definition of Tradition. What happens to young

[81] This was part Pius X's condemnation of the Modernist Heresy.

inexperienced candidates for the priesthood when they are led to Rahner (or his theological look-a-likes) to find out "what the Church teaches"?

The major point is that many theology students imbued with the thought contained in Rahner's and his theological look-alikes writing *have* demonstrably understood those writings in a literal sense. Subsequently, they are confused and continue to spread that confusion. Again, the point is not to determine what Rahner actually believed, but to demonstrate that his writings are sufficiently obtuse to confuse many of his readers as to what the Catholic Church believes and teaches. And his writing is highly representative of the majority of extreme "higher critics."

3. Rahner on "Scripture Alone"

Rahner clearly states that 16th century Protestants (in their doctrine of "Scripture Alone") are part of "an equally authentic" Catholic "theological tradition";

> "It is our duty to take as seriously as possible *the Protestant principle of Scripture alone,* because that implies an authentic religious experience and *in my opinion, an equally authentic theological tradition which goes back to Catholicism of the past.*"[82] [emphasis - author's]

Karl Rahner wrote the passage quoted directly above in 1968, three years after the close of Vatican Council II. That was just one year after von Hildebrand wrote *Trojan Horse in the City of God* warning of the danger in many of the teachings of some extreme higher critics. Rahner's statement appears to run clearly contrary to what the Council Fathers defined in the Vatican II document, *Dei Verbum.* The following Conciliar definition was confirmed as official Church teaching when Pope Paul VI signed off on that Document.

82 *Sacra Scrittura e Teologia, in Nuovi Saggi I,* Karl Rahher, Ed. Paoline, Roma 1968.

> "Sacred Theology relies on the written Word of God, taken together with sacred Tradition, as on a permanent foundation."[83]

In none of the Vatican II documentation quoted above was the Council inventing Doctrine. Similar statements are to be found in the 19th century First Vatican Council, the 16th century Council of Trent, and at various councils and synods going back to the Sub-Apostolic Age.

4. The First Ecumenical Council of the Church Denied the "Scripture Alone" Argument

The Bishops at the **First** Ecumenical Council (the Council of Nicea in 325 A.D.) essentially had to do battle with the heretic Arius over the "Scripture alone" issue. At that Council Arius and several of his supporters were denying the full Divinity of Christ. They would have refused the Nicene Fathers the right to use the term "homoousios" (of the same substance) in defense of Christ's Co-Divinity with the Father. The Arians stated reason, because "it (the word "homoousios") is not found in Scripture."[84]

Of the 318 Bishops at Nicea, 315 ignored those Arian arguments and used the Greek "*Homoousios*" to describe Our Lord's Divinity as "of the same substance" *as the Father*. The Council Fathers denied the essentially "Scripture Alone" arguments of the Arians in order to save the Doctrinal Divinity of Christ by clearly defining it with the non-Scriptural word "Homoousios." i.e., Both the Father and Son are Divine. Jesus is not a "creature" of the Father, no matter what the Arians said. And the Faith is not based on "Scripture Alone" no matter what the Arians said.

---

[83] Dogmatic Constitution on Divine Revelation, *Dei Verbum*, #24, *Vatican Council II, The Conciliar and Post Conciliar Documents, Vol 1*. New Revised Edition 1992, p. 763.

[84] There were other arguments advanced against the word "homoousios". But it is an historic fact that the last ditch stand of Arius and his supporters *was* based upon the fact that that word does not appear in Scripture. Arius and his supporters were making the "Scripture Alone" argument as their last gasp attempt to stop the Fathers at Niceae from using it. It didn't work.

St. Athanasius (a Father of the Church, who was in attendance at the Council) wrote a surviving Epistle, *On the Decrees of Nicea.*[85] In this work he justifies the use of the expression "Homoousios," "although it is not found in the Scriptures."

Karl Rahner was very conversant with the histories of all the Ecumenical Church Councils. It is therefore difficult to see how (in light of the very First Ecumenical Council) Rahner could subsequently say,

> "It is our duty to take as seriously as possible the Protestant principle of Scripture alone, ... an equally authentic theological tradition which goes back to Catholicism of the past."[86]

As we have already read, in support of their heresy, not only the Arians in the 4th century but also the Gnostics in the 2nd denigrated the role of Christian Tradition and argued for Scripture Alone. **As an historian, Rahner (and his theological look-alikes) either knew - or should have known - that the "Catholic past" he referred to specifically rejected "Scripture Alone" from its very beginning.** He should have known this not just from the history of the Councils, but also from the writings of Fathers such as Sts. Irenaeus and Athanasius. The only place one will find "Scripture Alone" promulgated in relation to "Catholicism of the past" is in the words of its condemned heretics.

What exactly is Rahner saying "the Protestant principle of Scripture alone" is equal to? Most readers interpret that statement to mean that it is equal to the defined Catholic doctrine of "sacred Tradition and sacred Scripture." If that isn't what Rahner meant, what else could he have meant by it? Rahner's quoted statement on "tradition" is a classic example of the obtuse writings of "higher critics." After reading such statements, students at Catholic seminaries and colleges can easily become confused as to what the Church teaches.

---

85 P.G. 25, 415-476.

86 *Sacra Scrittura e Teologia, in Nuovi Saggi I,* Karl Rahher, Ed. Paoline, Roma 1968.

5. Rahner at Rome During Much of the Council

Rahner was in Rome during much of the Second Vatican Council. He was fully aware of the Doctrine on Tradition which the Council Fathers had reaffirmed and proclaimed. His above quoted statement (which, taken as it stands, was patently contradictory of the Council's Doctrinal statements on the role of Tradition) did not surprise those who had been astute observers at the Second Vatican Council. Rahner had been one of a number of "theologians" at the Council who had attempted to intervene in the matter of the Council Fathers confirming the constant teaching of the Church on the role of Tradition in Revelation.

Rahner was the general editor of the *Sacramentum Mundi, An Encyclopedia of Theology*. As its preface and introduction explain, the other contributing writers accept the responsibility for the contents. Yet, as general editor, Rahner's general responsibility for its contents cannot *credibly* be denied. However, if a reader prefers to attribute its contents to some of Rahner's theological look-alikes this author will not object. In the *Sacramentum Mundi*'s article on Tradition, it states under the subtitle *The Catholic Notion of Tradition:*

> "Further *it is very difficult* for the modern mind, with its *alert sense of the historical, to imagine that such truths of faith, not committed to Scripture, should have been preserved without error throughout the ages*, in spite of changes of culture and language. **Here a too hasty recourse to the assistance of the Holy Spirit would be out of place.**"[87] [emphasis added]

That statement was published over three full years after Vatican Council II. That statement implicitly runs directly contrary to (1) the teachings of the Fathers of Vatican II, particularly as expressed in the following statement:

> "And Tradition transmits in its entirely the word of God *which has been entrusted to the Apostles by Christ the Lord*

[87] *Sacramentum Mundi, An Encyclopedia of Theology*, General Editor - Karl Rahner, S.J., 6 Vols., English Edition, Herder & Herder, N.Y., Vol. 6, p. 271.

> *and the Holy Spirit.* It transmits it to the successors of the Apostles so that, **enlightened by the Spirit of truth**, they may faithfully preserve, expound and spread it abroad by their preaching."

The Council Fathers at Vatican II clearly have "recourse" to the Holy Spirit's enlightenment in the transmission of Tradition and its *preservation throughout the ages by the Holy Spirit.* This statement in *Dei Verbum* that the Holy Spirit faithfully *"transmits in its entirely the word of God"* is not a *new* doctrine!

And what is the relevance of this discussion to the major theme of this book? *Some of the most powerful quotes, which demonstrate that it is highly unlikely the Antichrist is coming in our time, come from part of Tradition.* They come from the writings of the Fathers. *Such writings are a major part of the Christian Tradition.* The understanding on the part of the average Western Catholic that, "Tradition" is one of the two sources of Revelation, has become badly confused by much of the writings of extreme "higher critics" such as Rahner. When this happens it deals a mighty blow to that Catholic's understanding of the authority of the Fathers of the Church.[88]

6. Cardinal Siri on Rahner and Tradition

In 1980, the Archbishop of Genoa, Joseph Cardinal Siri published his milestone work, *Gethsemane*. The following is quoted from the jacket of the English translation of *Gethsemane*,

> "The *L'Osservatore Romano* (the official Vatican Daily Newspaper) devoted an entire page to a review of this book by Raimondo Spiazzi. It is a supplementary guarantee of

---

[88] As stated earlier, the use of the word Tradition can be quite complex at times since it has several specific usages. There are at least two usages of the word Tradition involved in Vatican II's description of it as a source of Revelation. (1) The Oral Tradition in the Pauline sense (Hold fast to the traditions which have been handed on to you whether by [our] word of mouth", and (2) the sense within which St. Irenaeus uses it as a totality of all the teaching (whether from written or unwritten sources) which has come down from the Apostles; "Since the tradition which comes down from the apostles exists in this way in the Church and abides among us."

> the significance of a work which concerns not only a single diocese or a single country, but the universal Church."[89]

For a Catholic, that should establish the intellectual and faithful credentials of the book and its author.

In *Gethsemane*, Cardinal Siri makes the following statement,

> **"At the beginning of the Second Vatican Council a very sad event occurred: an attempt was made to deny one of the sources of Revelation** [Tradition] **saying there was only one source."**[90]

In order to make sure that there was no mistake as to his meaning, Siri went on almost immediately to say,

> **"He who denies Tradition its character as source** [of Revelation], **loses de facto the accurate reality of the Scripture. He who relativises the one also relativises the other."**[91] [parens - authors]

Rahner was in Rome during much of Vatican II. He knew the teaching of the Council on Tradition. It was common knowledge amongst those in attendance at the Council that Rahner was involved in what Cardinal Siri describes: "an attempt was made to deny one of the sources of Revelation [Tradition] saying there was only one source."

A major problem today is that most Catholics have never read the documents of Vatican II. But many of them have heard that if you understand Rahner and/or his theological look-alikes, that you understand Vatican II. Nothing could be further from the truth. We must rediscover and reread the documents of Vatican II in order to free our minds of the many current misunderstandings about what the Fathers at Vatican II said and did.

---

89 *Gethsemane: Reflections on the Contemporary Theological Movement*, Joseph Cardinal Siri, Archbishop of Genoa, Franciscan Herald Press, Chicago (in cooperation with, Editions De La Fraternite De La Tres Sainte Vierge Marie, Rome, Italy, 1981). The quote is from the jacket of the book.

90 Ibid. p. 31.

K. POPE JOHN PAUL II, ST. PAUL, ST. IRENAEUS, AND VATICAN II ON TRADITION

In his recent Encyclical, *Ut Unum Sint (That They Might be One)* The Holy Father has prayerfully given direction for Christian reunion. It deals heavily with union between Rome and her "Sister Churchs" (Orthodox) in the East. *While it is not the stated intent of the Encyclical, Ut Unum Sint* does give us most useful specific direction on how to work our way out of the morass of contemporary confusion caused by higher critics on the subject of tradition. *Not surprisingly, the Holy Father in seeking a most common ground for union of East and West has recourse to our common roots in "Apostolic Tradition."*

> "By engaging in frank dialogue, communities help one another *to look at themselves together in the light of the apostolic tradition*. This leads them to ask themselves whether they truly express in an adequate way all that the Holy Spirit has transmitted through the apostles."[92]

The Holy Father advises all to examine the "disagreements" between the "Sister Churches" and Rome from two key reference points:

> "The examination of such disagreements has two essential points of reference: sacred Scripture and *the great tradition of the church*."[93]

Both those statements naturally lead to a key synoptic statement from *Dei Verbum*,

> *"Tradition transmits in its entirely the word of God which has been entrusted to the Apostles by Christ the Lord and the Holy Spirit."*[94]

---

91 Ibid. p. 32.

92 *Origins*, CNS Documentary Service, June 8, 1995, p 54.

93 Ibid. p. 58.

94 Dogmatic Constitution on Divine Revelation, *Dei Verbum*, #9, *Vatican Council II, The Concilior and Post Concilior Documents, Vol 1.* Flannery, New Revised Edition 1992, p. 755.

The total apostolic Tradition, both written and unwritten, handed down and put into practice by the Church, continuously handed down to us today comprises our contemporary totality of Tradition.

The Holy Father then says something profoundly simple and beautiful in *Ut Unum Sint,*

> "The Church must breathe with her two lungs! ... Byzantium and Rome."[95]

This "two lungs" view can better help all of us to "express in an adequate way all that the Holy Spirit has transmitted through the apostles." All of this is somehow quite Pauline. In Paul's explanation from the apostolic era he initially tells us,

> "Stand firm and hold fast to the Traditions which you have learned, either by (our) word, or by our Epistle."

In a particular sense, if the Church is to "breathe with both lungs," it is imperative that we in the West rediscover the Church's constant teaching on the role of Tradition. Could anyone more profoundly express the two lunged sub-Apostolic view of the Faith than St. Irenaeus when he says,

> **"And supposing the apostles had not left us their writings, *would we not then follow the order of tradition* which they handed down to the men to whom they entrusted the Churches?**
>
> "Many of the barbarian [illiterate] nations who believe in Christ have given their assent to this order. ***Salvation has been written in their hearts* (2 Cor. 3:3) *without paper and ink, by the spirit.*** Preserving the ancient tradition, they believe in one God, the Creator of heaven and earth and everything in them, and in Christ Jesus our Lord, who, in His superabundant love for His creation, condescended to be born of a virgin, uniting man to God through Himself, who suffered under Pontius Pilate, rose again and was taken up in splendor, who

[95] *Origins*, p. 61.

> will come again in glory as Savior of those who are saved ... **Thanks to the ancient tradition of the apostles,"**[96]
>
> "Since the tradition which comes down from the apostles exists in this way in the Church and abides among us, ***let us return to the scriptural proof provided by those of the apostles who wrote the gospels."***[97]

Ireneaus was originally from the East, but living and presiding as a Bishop in the West, in Lyon, France. He had one foot and one lung in the East, and another foot and lung in the West. He understood the totality of Tradition and he venerated Scripture. He understood and breathed with both lungs before anyone knew there could be more than one.

Paul teaches, "Traditions which you have learned, either by (our) word, or by (our) Epistle." The Fathers at Vatican II express in *Dei Verbum* the sense of the totality of Tradition and love and respect for Scripture. And the Holy Father, Pope John Paul II clearly teaches "sacred Scripture *and the great tradition of the church,*" and, *"in the light of the apostolic tradition.*" In this sense, Paul, Irenaeus, the Fathers of Vatican II, and Pope John Paul II are one in this understanding of "breathing with both lungs" as it pertains to the understanding of Tradition.

In the Fathers and in *Dei Verbum*, a prayerful faithful search for our roots will assist all of us:

> *First*, in the West: in rediscovering and more fully appreciating the totality and means of transmission of "apostolic Tradition ... that the Holy Spirit has transmitted through the apostles." The West might find from the 2nd century a deeper appreciation of St. Irenaeus' "Since the tradition which comes down from the apostles exists in this way in the Church and abides among us."
>
> *Second*: in a similar manner, the East might well find in a renewed prayerful search of the Fathers and of *Dei Verbum*

[96] Ibid, Book III, 4, 1-2, SI-p. 81.
[97] *Adversus Haereses*. Book III, 5, 1., SP-p. 82

> a rediscovery and more full appreciation of the "keys of the Kingdom." They might also find in a two-lunged view a renewed internal energy for further development of a systematic "Orthodox Confession of Faith" from their rich theological traditions and mystical insights.

The key to success of breathing with both lungs, for both the East and West, most probably lies in a renewed, fresh, prayerful and completely open researching of what Irenaeus calls, **"the apostles ... *follow the order of tradition* which they handed down to the men to whom they entrusted the Churches."** The place for a Catholic to look for the Church's current understanding of tradition is within *Dei Verbum*, in the writings of the Fathers, and in many recent encyclicals of Pope John Paul II. In them the Catholic reader will find the constant teaching of the Church on the full role of Tradition.

How Does This Apply to the Reader of This Book?

I. In various Scripture passages dealing with the latter and end times (including the Antichrist and the Parousia) the interpretation of the Fathers of the Church specifically agree with one another in many matters of doctrine. In a number of instances the Fathers of the Church even *expressly declare* that *their statements originated with the Apostles and their disciples*. They often explicitly state that something is of constant tradition since the Apostles. Importantly, this is the case when dealing with the issue of whether *the* Antichrist is a specific individual. The reader will see further proof of this later in the book. A Catholic who does not understand the authority of the Fathers and Apostolic Tradition will not appreciate the importance of the Fathers' statements about the end times.

II. A reader of this book who does not truly understand the role of Tradition in the faith of the Church, that person will not understand the significance and importance of centuries old prophecies to be presented later in the book. Those prophecies appear to predict for our time a denigration of both the role of tradition, and the traditional teachings of the Church.

L. WHAT THE MAGISTERIUM, TRADITION, AND SCRIPTURE SAY ABOUT PROPHECY IN GENERAL - AND - ABOUT "PRIVATE" PROPHECY?

1. The Anti-Prophecy School

In order to establish a clear and common understanding with the reader, it is necessary that we be extremely frank in this particular case. There exists an anti-prophecy school of thought today which can even be found within the ranks of some in the Catholic Church. This "school" portrays as ridiculous the thought that someone by the power of God could know the future. This "school of thought" teaches that such prophetic power is something only to be believed in by the uneducated or the credulous. Therefore the question: is that either a reasonable position, or a faithful Catholic position?

Minimally, all true Christians and Jews, or Moslems for that matter, believe that God is omniscient, that He knows all things, that he is omnipotent - can do anything He wills. They further believe that we human beings are creatures, created by our God the Creator. Now since God knows all things, and can do anything He wills, what is ridiculous about His imparting a portion of that which He immediately knows about the future to one of His creatures, to some man or woman? Obviously, there is nothing erroneous in that logic -- nothing, that is, to someone who truly believes in the Omniscience and Omnipotence of God, and that He is the Creator of us all. Here we have been talking only about the reasonably possible, rather than the probable.

2. Definition(s) of Prophecy

Is it probable that God would have so wished or chosen to impart a portion of His immediate knowledge of all things to one of His creatures -- in this particular case, a portion of His knowledge of the future? If He did so choose, how would we know? *The only directly revealed infallible source of knowledge we have about the*

Will of God comes from the two sources of Revelation, Tradition and the Scriptures - (as interpreted by the Magisterium).

In the Bible, God Himself tells us through His sacred writers that He has on occasion chosen to so instruct some of His creatures about future events. In the Bible they are called prophets. Books written by them or about them and their prophecies we call the Prophetical Books of the Bible. In the Old Testament Prophetical Books, the prophets wrote or are written about in seventeen books which were composed over the course of about four hundred years roughly between 800 to 400 B.C.[98]

3. Arguments of Anti-Prophecy School

In order to circumvent the obvious significance of repeated references to the word "prophecy" in both the Old Testament and the New Testament, the anti-prophecy school engages in tortuous twistings and turnings in logic (or a lack of it). The "school's" most common argument is that "prophecy" merely signifies the explanation of current events, and that is all that St. Paul and the other sacred writers of the Bible meant to signify. *As just one counterexample*: There is no way a truly objective individual can reconcile that position with the Old Testament prophesies which "foretell" the coming of a future Messiah.

As we know, the Messianic prophesies were fulfilled to the letter in the details of the birth, life, passion, death and resurrection of Our Lord. Written physical copies of those Old Testament prophecies (particularly in the Greek Septuagint Version), have been unquestionably proven to exist from over two hundred years prior to the birth of Our Lord. Therefore, even if someone wishes to argue about the particular authorship of those books, how can he or she reasonably disclaim the existence of the prior prophecy per se of the fulfilled future? Again, total candor is called for in this case. When faced with this argument, most members of the anti-prophecy school usually attempt one or more of several tacks;

(1) They change the subject.

---

98 Details in, *The Book of Destiny*, Fr. Leonard Kramer, Buechler Pub. Co., Belleville, Il. 1955, p. 2

(2) They attempt to argue that the prophesies are ambiguous and could apply to any great leader (which argument a close look at the Messianic prophesies in Isaiah alone will demolish).

(3) They may attempt to argue that the Bible was actually written after the fact (a thesis which is demolished by the provably prior existence of the Greek Septuagint edition of the Old Testament from around 200 years prior to the birth of Our Lord).

(4) *Another **example** of this type of argumentation*, this time against *New Testament Prophecy*, is their claim that Jesus' prediction about the fall of Jerusalem never really occurred at all, that the "Book(s)" which make this prophetic claim were (or may have been) in fact written after Jerusalem fell in 70 A.D.[99] There is a major problem with that argument; historians of the period (including Eusebius Pamphilus, the Bishop of Palestinian Caesarea and the Father of Church History) records in 325 A.D. that the Christians of Jerusalem fled across the Jordan River to Pella in response to divine prophetic revelation.

THE CHRISTIANS WHO FLED JERUSALEM HAD TAKEN PROPHECY IN THE LITERAL "PRO-

---

[99] "According to a *Reply* of the Pontifical Biblical Commission of 26 June, 1912, this Gospel [of Luke] was written prior to the fall of Jerusalem which occurred in the year 70. The commission was even more specific than this about the date - arguing as follows: St. Luke, in the prologue to the Acts of the Apostles, expressly mentions his first book, that is, his Gospel. Therefore, the Gospel was obviously written before the Acts. Now the Acts end with a description of St. Paul's situation just before he is released from his first Roman imprisonment; which suggests that St. Luke finished writing the acts at that time. Since the date of St. Paul's release was the year 63, St Luke's Gospel must have been written at the latest in the year 62 or at the beginning of 63. Authors who tend to go for a date between 67 and 70 argue less convincingly." [Quoted from *The Navarre Bible, St. Luke's Gospel*, Four Courts Press, 1988, p. 18.]

> PER"[100] SENSE. THEY HAD NOT "*ASSUMED*" IT WAS SOME FIGURATIVE LITERAL FORM - AN ALLEGORY OR PARABLE. *HOW COULD THEY HAVE TAKEN SUCH A PROPHECY IN LITERAL "PROPER" SENSE UNLESS IT EXISTED PRIOR TO THE FALL OF THE CITY?* A full discussion of this event follows shortly. [NOTE: Carefully read footnote on the word "proper."]

This Christian response to the prophetic Scriptural admonition to flee the City of Jerusalem is attested to by many ancient Christian writers. St. Remigius[101] in commenting on Matt., V. 16, (*"Then they that are in Judea, let them flee to the mountains")* said in the late 5th cenury:

---

[100] The word "Proper", when applied to the "Literal" sense, does not necessarily signify "correct". The Fathers of the Church defined the word "literal" in a different sense than we do today in our common usage. As the Fathers of the Church defined the "literal" sense, it included the "*proper* (word for word) literal sense" and it included the "*figurative* literal sense". For the Fathers, a figurative meaning was considered to be one of the "literal" readings. So in this context the word "proper" does not refer either to "correct" or "incorrect". Rather, it refers to a "word for word" versus "figurative" reading.

An example of this would be where various Scripture passages refer to "the arm of God". For the Fathers, a "proper" reading would mean that the reader assumed from "the arm of God" that God has a physical arm (which would obviously be an incorrect reading). They rather, "figuratively" read such passages as a description of the "power" of God. The proper and the figurative meaning they further distinguished from various "accommodated" senses.

"The Fathers of the Church ... regarded the language of the Bible as truly human language, and therefore always endowed with a literal sense, whether *proper* or *figurative*. Where the patristic writers appear to reject the literal sense, they really exclude only the proper sense, leaving the figurative." Catholic Encyclopedia, 1913 edition, Vol. 5, p. 693.

This view has not changed. Faithful modern Scripture scholars approach the subject in much the same way. "**Every Part of Scripture has a Literal Sense",** i.e., "In interpreting Scripture we use the terms in a somewhat different way. We apply the term 'literal' to the sense of Scripture intended by the sacred writer, whether the words are to be taken in a proper or ordinary sense (without metaphor), or metaphorically. Thus 'literal' and 'metaphorical' of common parlance are both included under under the literal sense of Scripture. This difference of usage is made necessary by the fact that Scripture *is* different from other writings. ... In Scriptural terminology, however the former [ordinary sense] is called **literal proper** and the latter [metaphorical] the **literal improper** sense." *A Catholic Commentary on Holy Scripture,* pp. 54-55.

[101] Bishop of Rheims, France, baptized King Clovis with 3000 of his countrymen in 496 A.D.

> "All this we know now took place with the approaching desolation of Jerusalem. For as the Roman arms came on, all Christians who were in the Province, *warned,* as Ecclesiastical history relates, *by a divine sign, retreated a long way before them,* and crossing the Jordan came to the city of Pella, and remained there for some time under the protection of King Agrippa, of whom mention is made in the Acts of the Apostles."[102]

In addition to the warning of Scriptural prophecy, here is evidence of an additional "Divine Sign," a private immediate prophetical warning to the Christians to flee Jerusalem. Eusebius, St. Remigius, and St. Epiphanius have recorded this "Divine Sign" which was given to the Christians as an *additional* prophetical warning to flee Jerusalem. They do not record what the "Sign" was, only that it occurred in such a way that the Christians all clearly understood its meaning.

It could be that this "Divine Sign" is the same event which the Jewish historian, Josephus, records in his *Jewish Wars*, reports of "armed horsemen" appearing in the sky over Jerusalem making threatening gestures toward the city. Josephus, Eusebius, St. Remigius, and St. Epiphanius all record that the "Christians of Jerusalem" understood this "Divine Sign" in the light of Jesus' Scriptural warning of an impending sign of the destruction of the City. For the Christian inhabitants of Jerusalem, the "Divine Sign" or warning fleshed out the details of the "Scriptural sign" or warning.

God's warning to flee some particular city appointed for destruction did not originate with the early Christians in Jerusalem. Scripture informs us God sent angels to lead Lot out of Sodom, just as He warned the Jews to flee from ancient Babylon. In point of fact, **the only Christians that the "anti-prophecy" types can convince with their arguments are those Christians who have not had the opportunity to become thoroughly familiar with both Scripture and Tradition, and honest Church History.** This is not harsh or rash judgment. It is simply a necessarily candid factual analysis of the merits of the anti-prophecy arguments.

---

[102] *The Sunday Sermons of the Great Fathers*, Vol. 4, Translated and edited by M.F. Toal, Henry Regnery Co. 1964, p. 331.

St. Paul in his 1st letter to the Corinthians says:

> "Aim at charity, yet strive after the spiritual gifts, but especially that you may prophesy."[103]

> "He who prophesies speaks to men for edification and encouragement and consolation."[104]

> "Now I should like you all to speak in tongues but still more to prophesy. For he who prophecies is greater than he who speaks in tongues."[105]

And again, in his first letter to the Thessalonians;

> "Do not extinguish the Spirit. Do not despise prophecies. But test all things; hold fast that which is good."[106]

4. What Does St. Paul Signify by Prophecy?

The Magisterium, and the Church's greatest systematic theologian (St. Thomas Aquinas), tell us that St. Paul is including here the ability to foretell future events. We have additional Scriptural confirmations of the "Spirit-Given" charism to know the future through Divine Revelation. As two examples of N.T. prophecy of the future, the author of *Acts* tells us,

> "And now, behold, I am going to Jerusalem, bound in the Spirit, not knowing what shall befall me there, *except that the Holy Spirit testifies to me in every city that imprisonment and afflictions await me*." Acts 20:23

> "And coming to us he [Agabus] took Paul's girdle and bound his own feet and hands, and said, *Thus says the Holy Spirit*, 'So shall the Jews at Jerusalem bind the man who owns this girdle and deliver him into the hands of the Gentiles.'" Acts 21:11

It is really quite scholastically futile for anyone to claim that the "Gift of Prophesy" as described in the New Testament does *not*

[103] I Corinthians, 14:1.
[104] Ibid. 14:4.
[105] Ibid. 14:5.
[106] I Thessalonians, 5:19-21.

include the "ability to foresee future events" through the charism of Prophesy. Short of that, some will attempt to convince you that *if* there was a "Gift" in the sense of being able to foresee future events, that it was limited to the Apostles. But we have just read in Acts 21:11 wherein an individual (Agabus, who was not an Apostle) "revealed" the Apostle Paul's own future to that Apostle, told Paul things about the Paul's future which Paul himself did not know. Agabus prophesied about the future. And we learn in Scripture that what Agabus prophesied was fulfilled.

In *Lumen Gentium*, the Fathers of Vatican II confirm the charism of Prophesy for post-Apostolic times down to our day.[107] Those who argue against an extra-Apostolic or post-Apostolic charism of "Prophecy" can succeed only with an individual who really does not know his or her Scripture and/or the teachings of the Magisterium on this subject -- which teachings are constant since the time of the infant Church.

M. THREE DIVISIONS OR TYPES OF PROPHECY

In Paul's quote from Corinthians above, he is speaking **inclusively** *of all three divisions of prophecy.* According to the Magisterium, prophecy can be either an explanation of:

(1) The past, or,
(2) Present events or signs, or
(3) The legitimate foretelling of future events.

Note: *There have been such things as false apparitions and revelations and there will undoubtedly be more in the future. That is why St. Paul says, "test all things."*

1. St. Theresa of Avila

St. Theresa is one of the two female Doctors of the Church[108] and one of its greatest mystical theologians. She makes the same point as the one referred to by St. Paul immediately above when she says:

---

[107] (*Lumen Gentium*, Chapter 2, No. 12) There will be an enlarged discussion of this later.

[108] The other female "Doctor" is St. Catherine of Sienna.

> "Those who never receive extraordinary favors can *hardly* attach any belief in them. They should think of this -- that to believe everything in this respect is simplicity, *but, to believe nothing is audacity*."

There are many passages of Scripture besides those of St. Paul which ratify the authentic existence of private prophecy of future events. We read:

> "But Peter, standing up with the eleven, lifted up his voice and spoke to them: Men of Judea and all you who dwell in Jerusalem, let this be known to you, and give ear to my words. These men are not drunk as you suppose, for it is only the third hour of the day. But this (that you are witnessing) is what was spoken by the prophet Joel:
>
> "And it shall come to pass *in the last days, says the Lord, that I will pour out my Spirit upon all flesh;*
>
> *"And your sons and your daughters shall prophesy, and your young men shall see visions, and your old men shall dream dreams. And moreover upon my servants and my handmaids in those days will I pour forth of my Spirit, and they shall prophesy*."[110]

That the Scriptures recognize the *charism* of prophecy as a public and private entity is a point which will shortly be developed fully.

N. CHURCH'S OFFICIAL CONFIRMATION OF THE CHARISM OF PRIVATE PROPHECY

1. Vatican Council I Confirmed the Charism of Prophecy

> "Nevertheless, God has been pleased to supply, besides the interior aids of the Holy Spirit, external evidence of his revelation, namely divine acts, especially miracles and prophecies."[111]

---

[110] In Acts 2:14-18.

[111] (DSch 3009)

Notice: One thing should be well-noted. Today it is not uncommon to read either *some* Catholic or Protestant authors claiming that the charism of prophecy ended with the infant Church. *The Vatican II Fathers teach exactly the opposite in the passage below.*

2. Second Vatican Council

> "The Holy Spirit ... *distributes* special gifts among the faithful of every rank ... Such gifts of grace, whether they are of special enlightenment or whether they are spread more simply and generally, must be accepted with gratefulness and consolation, as they are specially suited to, and useful for, the needs of the Church ... **Those who have extraordinary gifts** ... Judgments as to their genuineness and their correct use lies with those who lead the Church and those whose special task is ***not indeed to 'extinguish the spirit'*** but to examine everything and keep that which is good."[112]

It is patently obvious the Vatican II Fathers are speaking in the present ongoing tense. They are describing a post-Apostolic gift which exists into the 20th century. *With their "extinguish not the spirit" passage from St. Paul's first letter to the Corinthians, the Vatican II Fathers are specifically confirming the charism of prophecy in this reference.*

Many Catholics have also never read the pronouncements of many Popes, or great Saints, or Fathers and Doctors of the Church on the subject of the charism of prophecy. Consequently they are unaware that the majority of such types who have spoken on private prophecy of future events hold the charism of authentic private prophecy in great respect.

The Catholic Encyclopedia

The encyclopedia defines prophecy (and references its position from DSch 3009) in the following manner:

> "As the term is used in Mystical theology, *it applies both to the prophecies of canonical Scripture and to private*

112 (*Lumen Gentium*, Chapter 2, No. 12)

prophecies. ***Understood in its strict sense, it means the foreknowledge and foretelling of future events,*** though it may sometimes apply to past events of which there is no memory, and to present hidden things which cannot be known by the light of natural reason. *St. Paul speaking of prophecy in I Cor., XIV, does not confine its meaning to predictions of future events, but includes under it Divine inspirations concerning what is secret, whether future or not.*"[113]

We can see from this that despite what some would have us believe, that when St. Paul speaks of the gift of prophecy, in the Catholic teaching, he is definitely including the ability to foresee future events. That is what the Church has constantly taught since its inception.

3. Pope John Paul II on St. Thomas

St. Thomas Aquinas, the Angelic Doctor, is publicly acclaimed by dozens of Popes as the greatest systematic theologian of the Catholic Church. As reported in *L'Osservatore Romano*, *Pope John Paul II* said in a major address on Sept. 29, 1990, about Aquinas:

> "We should hope for and foster in every way possible, the constant and deeper study of the philosophical, theological, ethical, and political doctrine which St. Thomas left as a heritage to the Catholic schools **and which the Church has not hesitated to make her own."**

4. St. Thomas Aquinas

According to St. Thomas Aquinas, future prophecy is divided into two subdivisions, namely that of foreknowledge and that of predestination. (See Summa II-II, Q clxxiv, A.1).[114] In the quote below St. Thomas gives us the sum and substance of the purpose of private prophecy.

---

[113] 1913 Edition, Vol. XII

[114] The interested reader may find Thomas' full discussion of this in Vol. 2 (II) of, *Summa Theologica, St. Thomas Aquinas, First Complete American Edition*, Translated by Fathers of the English Dominican Province, Benzinger Bros. Inc. New York, 1947. pp. 1906-1912 contain all of Q. 174.

"For prophecy like other gratuitous graces is given for the good of the Church." [115]

"Accordingly, if we speak of prophecy as directed to the Godhead as its end, it progressed according to three divisions of time, namely before the law, under the law, and under grace. ***As regards the guidance of human acts***, the prophetic revelation varied not according to the course of time, but according as circumstances required, because as it is written *(Prov. XXIX. 18), 'When prophecy shall fail, the people shall be scattered abroad.'* **Wherefore at all times men were divinely instructed about what they were to do, according as it was expedient for the spiritual welfare of the elect."**[116]

"The prophets who foretold the coming of Christ could not continue further than John, who with his finger, pointed to Christ actually present. Nevertheless, as [St.] Jerome says on this passage, 'This does not mean that there were no more prophets after John. For we read in the *Acts of the Apostles* that Agabus and the four maidens, daughters of Philip, prophesied.' John, too, wrote a prophetic book about the end of the Church; and *at all times there have not been lacking persons having the spirit of prophecy, not indeed for the declaration of any new doctrine of faith,* ***but for the direction of human acts."***[117]

5. Pope Benedict XIV

One previously made point should be reemphasized. The Church has always counseled caution when dealing with a specific private revelation but she also counsels against total incredulity. Simply as examples let us quote from Pope Benedict XIV:[118]

"The approval given by the Church to a private revelation is nothing else than the permission accorded after careful

115 Summa Pt. II-II, Q. 172 Art. 4.
116 Ibid Q. 174 Art. 6.
117 Ibid Obj. 3.
118 It should be noted that Benedict XIV wrote this treatise prior to being elected Pope. It was written under his previous title of Cardinal Lambertini.

examination, to publish this revelation *for the instruction and the good of the faithful*. Even if they are approved by the Church one must not and one cannot grant the assent of Catholic Faith to such revelations."

"In keeping with laws of prudence, one must give them the assent of human belief [assensus fidei humanae], in that such revelations are probable and piously credible. Consequently it is possible to refuse to accept such revelations and to turn from them, as long as one does so with proper modesty, for good reasons, and without the intention of setting himself up as superior."

"Though an assent of Catholic faith be not due to such revelations, they, however, deserve a human assent, according to the rules of prudence, by which they are probable, and piously credible, as the revelations of Blessed Hildegarde, St. Bridget, and St. Catherine of Sienna."[119]

Notice: Benedict is not limiting authentic prophecy to *these particular* Saints and "Blessed," (*at the time that Benedict wrote this, Hildegard had not yet been accorded the accolade Saint*) rather Benedict uses the word "as" in the sense of "such as," the revelations of Bl. Hildegarde, St. Bridget, and St. Catherine.

6. Contemporary Church Acknowledgment of the Charism of Private Prophecy

In addition to the pronouncements of Vatican I and Vatican II on the subject, does the Church today practically acknowledge as possible the existence of genuine, contemporary, private prophecy? On February 25, 1978, Cardinal Seper published a four page document entitled *Norms of the Holy Congregation for the teaching of the Faith concerning the procedure for judging of presumed apparitions and revelations*.

This document instructs local bishops who have such a presumed apparition or revelation occurring within their diocese on

[119] *De Servorum Dei Canonizatione et Beatificatione*, Lib. II. Cap. 32, No.11.)

how to rapidly issue either a Certification of Supernaturality to the event or one of non supernaturality. The Church would not issue such instructions to its Bishops if the Church did not believe in the existence of a post-Apostolic charism of private prophecy - which is operative to this day.

7. St. Theresa of Avila

Doctors of the Church besides St. Thomas describe the charism of private prophecy. *St. Theresa of Avila even personally claimed the gift of prophecy*. The following are some of her quotes on the subject:

> *"What I said about the prophecies concerning this house, and other prophecies I shall mention, as well as other things were all fulfilled.* Some the Lord told me three years before they came about -- others more than three years, others less. I always told them to my confessor and to this widow friend of mine whom I had permission to tell ... these persons know I am not lying; nor may God ever permit me to lie, for in no instance would I speak anything but the complete truth -- and how much more in matters so serious."[120]
>
> Notice: *Here St. Theresa is claiming for herself the gift of prophecy in the sense of foretelling the future.*
>
> **"Some individuals, seem to be frightened at the very mention of visions or revelations. I do not know why they think a soul being lead in this way by God is on a dangerous path, nor what is the source of this alarm."**[121]

St. Theresa describes her gift of prophecy in many places in her writings. There is no misunderstanding that she is claiming to be a recipient of the charism of private prophecy.

---

[120] *St. Theresa of Avila, Collected works*, ICS Publication, Institute of Carmelite Studies, Washington, D.C., 1976. P. 301.

[121] *Fire Within*, Ignatius Press, San Francisco, 1989, P. 247.

"At other times the Lord warns me of some dangers I'm in, or of other persons, and about things of the future - three or four years in advance very often - all of which have been fulfilled."[122]

O. PURPOSE OF *PRIVATE* PROPHECY

Above in St. Thomas we found encapsulated the whole reason for the charism of prophecy, it is ***"for the direction of human acts."* And St. Thomas confirms that this charism of the foretelling of the future occurs "at all times."** Our Lord's place of birth, the miracles He would perform, what race and tribe He would be born of, where His ministry would take place and the manner of His death, ALL THE SIGNS BY WHICH THE MESSIAH COULD BE RECOGNIZED, were all foretold in public prophecy in the Old Testament. Peter's brother Andrew, after he had met Our Lord, proceeded to tell Peter that, "We have found the Messiah."[123]

How did Andrew know what the Messiah was? How did Andrew know or suspect that Jesus was the Messiah? Obviously grace was at work, but he also knew what the Old Testament prophecies foretold of the Messiah, and the manner of His life. Andrew knew that Jesus met the elements about the Messiah contained in the Scriptures. Did the Pharisees who rejected "the cornerstone" also know these prophecies?

Everyone in Palestine and its surrounding territories knew about the "Jewish" prophecy of the coming of a Jewish Messiah. King Herod was an Edomite. He was a Jew by religion but was not of a Jewish bloodline. The Romans had imposed a non-Jew, Herod, upon the Jewish Nation as its king.[124] Even Herod, a non-Jew, knew

[122] *St. Theresa of Avila, Collected works*, Washington, D.C., 1976. P. 225.

[123] John 1:41

[124] How did Herod come to be a Jew by religion? "John Hyrcanus (Hasmonean Judean High Priest and leader king? d. 104 B.C.) having entered Idumea [the land of the Edomites], did not expel the foreigners as the Machabees ordinarily had, but obliged them to embrace Yahwism by accepting circumcision." *The History of Israel*, Giuseppi Ricciotti, Vol. 2, The Bruce Publishing Co., Milwaukee, 1955. pp. 283-284. See also Josephus' *Antiquities.*

the prophesies of a Messiah. And he believed them. When the Magi appeared announcing their search for the promised Messiah, Herod panicked. His fear of being displaced as King by the foretold Jewish Messiah is specifically what lead him to murder all the Jewish baby boys under two years of age in the hopes of killing the prophesied Messiah.

Within the context of prophecy of future events is also how the Apostles later understood the providence of the Angel appearing to Joseph in a dream. The Angel prophesied that baby Jesus was in danger, and told Joseph to flee into Egypt. Historical records demonstrate that this Jewish *Messiah Prophecy* was such common knowledge that, not only the Roman provincial governors, but even the common Roman soldiers knew about it. The pharisees and scribes were, had to be, just as conversant as Andrew was with these prophecies. But unlike Andrew and Peter they rejected the "Cornerstone."

The Christian community of Jerusalem fled the city sometime in the winter of 68 A.D.[125] As they saw the "Zealots" in Jerusalem preparing for a war with Rome, they remembered Jesus' announcement to His apostles about the future destruction of Jerusalem. We read at the beginning of Luke 13,

> "And as he came out of the temple (in Jerusalem), one of his disciples said to him, 'look, Teacher, what wonderful stones and what wonderful buildings!' And Jesus said to him, 'Do you see these great buildings? There will not be left here one stone upon another, that will not be thrown away.'"[126]

While that statement clearly foretells the destruction of the Temple, it does not necessarily refer to the rest of Jerusalem. But Jesus filled in those details in another prophecy.

[125] *The Founding of Christendom, Vol. 1, A History of Christendom*, Warren Carroll, Christendom College Press, Front Royal, VA. Vol. 1., P. 446 fn.#148. In this footnote, see Carroll's argument for this flight having taken place in the Winter of 68 A.D.

[126] Luke 13:1-2 RSV.

> *"But when you see Jerusalem surrounded by armies* [by an earthenwork wall];[127] *then know that its desolation has come near. Then let those who are in Judea flee to the mountains; and those who are inside the city depart; and let not those who are out in the country, enter into it."*[128]

Ricciotti records that during Titus' siege of Jerusalem, that he finally surrounded Jerusalem with an earthenwork wall. Josephus, a non-Christian Jewish secular historian (who was an eye-witness to the events he describes), tells us in his *Jewish Wars* that the Temple was completely destroyed during the destruction of Jerusalem by Titus' army in 70 A.D. In his account we discover that the majority of the city's population either starved to death during the siege, or was later slain when the Roman General Titus' troops finally broke into the city.

---

[127] The *New Vulgate* Latin more accurately reads, "circumdabunt te inimici tui vallo" "your enemies encircle you with an earthenwork wall". That is specifically what the Roman Commander Titus did. In 67 A.D., Titus built a series of Garrisons in the Palestinian countryside around the city of Jerusalem. In the summer of 69 A.D., he tightened the circle by building a series of "earthworks" for "siege engines" around the city. By the summer of 70 A.D., Jews were exiting the city at night through open spaces in the Roman fortifications to scavenge food. Then they would return into the city before dawn. This scavenging was extending the Jews' ability to withstand the Roman siege. Therefore, Titus built a fortified earthenwork wall (called a "vallo") completely encircling Jerusalem in just three days. That "wall" was used to keep supplies from entering Jerusalem. It was with this tactic that Titus finally weakened the defenders of Jerusalem such that the Romans could successfully storm the walls of Jerusalem. As we can see, Our Lord's prophecy was extremely specific - describing enemies encircling Jerusalem with an "earthenwork wall'.

It was on the top of that earthenwork wall (vallo) within the sight of the city that the Romans crucified Jews who subsequently attempted either to escape Jerusalem or to scavenge for food. At one point, the Romans were crucifying an average of 500 captured "escapees" a day. That only stopped when the Romans "ran out of wood" with which to build crosses. (For full details and description of the siege and fall of Jerusalem see Josephus' "*Jewish Wars*" and Riciotti's *History of Israel.*).

For those who did not attempt to escape, only starvation awaited them, and, "From a single gate of the city (Jerusalem), no less than 115,880 bodies were thrown out in less than three months." *History of Israel*, Ricciotti, Vol. 2, p. 431-435.

[128] St. Luke 21: 20-21.

Eusebius Pamphilius, the first Church historian (who also was Bishop of the Church at Palestinian Caesarea) recorded in 325 A.D., how the Christians of Jerusalem escaped its fate.

> "The whole body, however, of the Church at Jerusalem, ... removed from the city, and dwelt at a certain point beyond the Jordan, called Pella."[129]

Two centuries later St. Epiphanius twice recorded that the Christians of Jerusalem (who had taken future prophecy into account, i.e., who did not despise that prophecy) left the holy city before its downfall. We have earlier quoted St. Remigius recording this flight of the Christian inhabitants of Jerusalem in response to prophetic warnings.

Those who have known, believed, and have not despised prophecy, have seldom been taken completely off guard by cataclysmic events, either in Old or New Testament times. In the case above, it saved the Church at Jerusalem from sharing in the horrible fate of those who remained in the City.

Private prophecy holds an honored place in the history of the Church. Of the devotions which the Catholic readers have been taught since they were children: such as the practice of saying the Rosary (as we pray it today), the wearing of the Brown and Green Scapulars, the Miraculous Medal, as well as the devotions to the Sacred Heart of Jesus and the Immaculate Heart of Mary, these and many others COME FROM PRIVATE REVELATION. Priests *have and utilize* written prayers for the purpose of installing people with the Brown Scapular for the first time. These prayers are authorized by the Church and are rooted in the Church's acceptance of a devotion which emanates from approved private revelation.

Some orders of priests and nuns wear the Rosary as an official part of their religious habit. If the Church looked with disfavor on the fruits of approved private prophecy -- would it sanction all of these religious practices which have flowered out of private prophecy? Would Pope after Pope speak positively about, and some even

---

[129] *History of the Church*, Eusebius of Caesarea, completed in 325 A.D. Eusebius the first "Church Historian" clearly records the fact that the Christians fled Jerusalem prior to its fall to the Romans on Aug. 10, 70 A.D.. This flight most likely occurred in the Winter of 68 A.D.

make pilgrimages to the Shrines at Fatima or Lourdes? Those who try to convince a reasonable Catholic that all private prophecy is to be despised or rejected simply do not have a leg to stand on.

P. CHRISTIANITY IS ESSENTIALLY AN HISTORIC AND PROPHETIC FAITH

Catholics and Protestants, or Jews, who actually believe in the historic reality of various Biblical events, figures, miracles, and prophecies have been under attack by some academics for years. That is no secret. The same thing holds true for those who believe in any substantive way in God's direct Divine intervention in human affairs. In this century this is primarily the fruit of an extreme "Higher Criticism," or, the "Contemporary Theological Movement."

"Higher Criticism" schools of thought employed in the study of Scripture have been active since before the turn of the century. The movement initially grew up amongst some Rationalist Protestant intellectuals in the 19th century. The *more moderate branches* of this school (whether Protestant or Catholic) *have* clearly done Scripture studies valuable service in some areas. However, in both the Catholic and Protestant venues of this "Higher Criticism" movement, there are branches which tend toward extremes. Those extremes are related to what is described later as the "Contemporary Theological Movement."

1. Judeo-Christianity Begins in History and Prophecy

As the Apostles and Fathers of the Church clearly understood, Christianity and its root predecessor, Judaism, are radically different from all other religions. First, prior to the time of Yahweh revealing Himself to the Jewish people and forming His Covenant with them, religions of the world were religions without an historic perspective.

At the very beginning of the Jewish faith, God makes a prophecy to Abraham in which He promises this old man that he and his elderly wife (who is beyond childbearing years) will have descendants more numerous than the sands of the sea. **The Judeo-Christian faith functionally begins in prophecy and history.**

> "When Abram was ninety-nine years old Yahweh appeared to him and said, I am El Shaddai (the almighty God), live in my presence, and be perfect, and I shall grant a covenant between myself and you, and make you very numerous. And Abram bowed to the ground.
>
> "God spoke to him as follows; 'For my part, this is my covenant with you: you will become the father of many nations. ... I shall make you exceedingly fertile. I shall make you into many nations, and your issue will be kings. And I shall maintain my covenant between myself and you, and your descendants after you, generation after generation, as a covenant in perpetuity, to descendants after you."[130]

Abram, renamed by God Abraham, does not understand how this can come about since he and his elderly wife have no children, so God explains and prophesies to Abraham,

> "As regards your wife Sarai, ... I shall bless her and moreover give you a son by her."[131]

This Jewish faith, anchored in the Old Covenant, began in an identifiable historic event with God revealing Himself to man, ***with God prophesying man's future to him.*** **The quintessential beginning of Judeo-Christianity is absolutely rooted in prophecy of future events.** Therefore, how can anyone who claims to be Christian or of the Jewish Faith deny the possibility of God partially sharing His foreknowledge of future events with man? How can they deny it and call themselves either Christian or Jew?

2. Comparative Religion vs. the Facts

"Comparative Religion" classes in Western universities most often imply that the Jewish faith was simply an adapted form of preceding religions of the Middle and Far East, and that the story

---

130 *New Jerusalem Bible*, Doubleday, 1985 Edition, Gen. 17:1-7.

131 Ibid. Gen 17:15.

of Abraham is therefore at least partially based in myth. Any close look at that statement shows that it is academically and historically bankrupt for the following reasons. **In none of the preceding religions:**

(1) *Is there a history of "God" revealing Himself to man, nor*
(2) *Is there a companion series of prophecies for the future development of that religion delivered by that God.* (The other religions of the time taught about alien *gods* - god*s* remote and removed from man.)
(3) Nor is there a sense of linear history (the O.T. prophecies reveal a linear line of historicity), nor,
(4) In any other religion is their "god(s)" **a "God" of hope and love**, nor,
(5) Does other religions' god(s) reveal Himself as the Creator of the universe. (Judeo-Christianity uniquely teaches that God's Creation is real [not illusory], and that it is Good [not evil]). The Old Testament tells us that God looked at His Creation, and saw "that it was good."

At least these five elements are totally unique and *absolutely central* to the Jewish religion. Not one of them appears in any surrounding or previous religion. They are *not* borrowed from any other religion as many extreme "higher critics" would have us believe.

The classic "Epic of Gilgamesh" and the religious culture from which it springs are commonly taught to be one of the progenitors of Jewish "myths/beliefs." But the "Epic of Gilgamesh" teaches an utter despair in death, an ultimate black void *within which there is no hope.* In the Old Covenant, God expresses His love and affection for the people of His Covenant. The very first thing He gives is hope. This hope is not copied from surrounding religions; *it was historically unique with God's promise to Abraham and his descendants.* Again, this religion of hope and God's love for His people begins in an historic fact - *with prophecy of future facts.*

With the Coming of the Messiah, hope springs Eternal in the loving Redemption of Man by God who assumes the human flesh of His creatures. This is another major difference. The Judeo-

Christian faith teaches an historic fact that **THE ONE GOD** is the sole Creator of the Universe, and that the CREATOR loves those beings He has created.

He loves His CREATURES so much that He comes down from Heaven to save them. He is not a remote alien God as in other religions of the period. His Coming He has prophesied through His prophets of old. He has fulfilled this historic prophecy through the Coming of His Son. *Christianity is absolutely, ineffably, an Historic religion. History is at the very heart of the Christian Faith.* These are far from original thoughts but they must be stated and restated anew in this time when they are rarely heard.

Q. THE LINEAR HISTORICITY OF JUDEO-CHRISTIANITY

The tremendous culture of the Greeks with their worthwhile blossoming of philosophy, their love of and search for wisdom, that culture had little to no sense of history - as the religious Jew or Christian understands the term. With the exception of their epic poems, the Greeks had no truly historic literature. They had no historic line tracing man's existence. There were only mythic epic snapshots taken from disparate moments. The linear historicity of Judeo-Christianity *is* unique. It is demonstrably not an imitation of or borrowing from surrounding culture, rather, it is their antithesis. Where pagan cultures and religions have isolated snapshots of tragedy and despair, Judeo-Christianity has historic linearity of hope. Pagan cultures and religions and Judeo-Christianity are basally exact opposites.

One of the major problems for historians of the East is the virtual total lack of ancient historic records as such in the areas of the Eastern religions. That absence is a logical consequence of their religious beliefs. Those religions for the most part view man as endlessly treading on an endlessly spinning wheel in a highly illusory world. Their view is totally cyclic. *What point is there in recording a repeating cycle*? As we of the West understand the term, the East had no sense of historicity. That is the reason why (compared with the West) there is not any significant amount of historical data in the early phases of Eastern religions and cultures.

The only sense of "prophecy" in Eastern religions is that everything is taught to repeat itself over and over again.[132] True prophecy relates to historic events which are successively sufficiently unique to be later identified as a fulfilled prophecy. That uniqueness is totally non-cyclic. This type of revealed prophecy uniquely exists in the Judeo-Christian religion.

1. Judeo-Christianity Begins in Prophecy of Future Historic Events

Christianity views man's existence as a linear historical reality in a world created by a loving Creator. That world has a procession of prophesied unique events from its beginning to its prophesied end. As Christopher Dawson stated it so well,

> "The Christian interpretation of history is derived from a different source. It is Jewish rather than Greek, and finds its fullest expression in the primary documents of the Christian faith -- the writings of the Hebrew prophets and in the New Testament itself.
>
> "Thus *the Christian view of history* is not a secondary element derived by philosophical reflection from the study of history. *It lies at the very heart of Christianity and forms an integral part of the Christian faith.*"[133]

Dawson goes on to explain and emphasize the dynamic difference in this Christian "historic view" and theology, from those of other "religions."

> "For Christianity, together with the religion of Israel out of which it was born, is an historical religion in a sense to which none of the other world religions can lay claim -- not even Islam, though this comes nearest to it in this respect.

---

[132] Someone might object that the "state of Nirvana" is an exception. It is not. Nirvana describes oblivion of self. Linear historical Judeo-Christianity describes hope and the possibility of eternal happiness for an individual -- not his oblivion.

[133] *Dynamics of World History*, Christopher Dawson, Edition of Sherwood Sugden & Company, 1978, p. 234

> "Hence it is very difficult, perhaps even impossible, to explain the Christian view of history to a non-Christian, since it is necessary to accept the Christian faith in order to understand the Christian view of history, **and** *those who reject the idea of a divine revelation are necessarily obliged to reject the Christian view of history as well.*"[134]

Without further evidence one could reasonably ask whether this "historic" Christian view is a 20th century invention, or a modern view and perspective which may or may not have been held by the young Church. That "question" about whether this historic view is a *totally* modern view, discovery, or "invention" is one of the unproven theses of many "higher critics" who attempt to "demythologize" the Christian faith.

There can be no question that someone living in the second millennium of the Church has a more systematized "historic" view than in previous times. This is particularly so in the last two centuries. *However, we are not speaking of the advance in the historical sense or understanding of modern man. We are also not speaking of our greater availability of historical data with which to develop a more thorough eschatological understanding. We are speaking only of that tendency amongst some to imply through overstatement that the early Church had little to no historical sense at all - particularly within the course of Revelation.*

Against this overstatement lies the view that the Fathers of the early Church had a *basally* historic view of God's Revelation. How much they individually felt they could learn from a theological study of such history - that is another subject. Augustine took the position that such a *learning* process was impossible.[135] But, there remains

---

[134] Ibid.

[135] Again, we are not discussing a learning process which is ongoing from this view. Augustine, for instance, held that little or nothing could be learned from the study of history, qua history, because we learn from "universals", but historic events are not universals. But, the very fact that Augustine took the position he did is proof positive that the historic view *was* understood. Vide, *The Theology of History in St. Bonaventure*, Joseph Ratzinger, English Edition-translated by Zachary Hayes, O.F.M., Franciscan Herald Press, Chicago, 1971, p. 76.

a serious question as to whether Augustine therein represents the thought of *all* the Fathers on this subject - particularly some of the Eastern Fathers.

R. PATRISTIC SENSE OF HISTORY AND PROPHECY

1. Athenagoras of Athens

Athenagoras was a Father of the Church. He was one of the great lay Apologists. Around *177 A.D.* he composed his *Embassy,* which he addressed to the Roman Emperors Marcus Aurelius Antoninus and Lucius Aurelius Commodus. The stated purpose of Athenagoras' *Embassy* was to defend the Christians against three false charges of "atheism, cannibalism, and incest."[136] In his defense against the charge of atheism, he points out the ridiculousness of Athenian and other pagan gods, *in that they were created by man.*

In the course of this line of defense he points out (1) that Christians are being called atheists because they will not sacrifice to pagan gods, but (2) that the pagan gods cannot be god(s) since they were created by men. In the section on the "gods" of Athens, he argues that he knows who created these Athenian gods -- and most importantly -- ***when they did it***.

> "*... Homer and Hesiod preceded me by four hundred years, not more.* They established the Greek theogony and gave the gods names, appointing their rank and functions and describing their appearance."[137]

These "gods" which Athenagoras describes were nothing more than statues which the Athenians actually worshipped -- *as statues*. Athenagoras argues that they cannot be gods since he even knows the identity of the sculptors who made these pagan statues.

---

[136] "godlessness, Thyestean banquets, and intercourse such as Oedipus practiced." *Ancient Christian Writers*, Vol. 23, Edited by Johannes Quasten, Newman Press, Maryland. p. 32.

[137] *Ancient Christian Writers*, Vol. 23, Edited by Johannes Quasten, Newman Press, Maryland. p. 47.

> **"The time interval**, then, since statues and statue-making began is so short that I am able to mention the name of *the craftsman of each god*."[138]

As we can see, *in 177 A.D. Athenagoras has a clear and highly refined sense of the linearity of history*. He even utilizes the phrase "time interval" between earthly historic events. *He* is not describing isolated historic events.[139] He goes on to argue to the Emperor that the one Christian God (unlike their pagan man-made "gods"), (1) is timeless - because, (2) He exists from eternity, and (3) exists in Himself totally outside of this world and its chronological history, and (4) has revealed Himself to man through the "Spirit of prophecy."

2. St. John Chrysostom

There are many statements from other Fathers of the Church which testify to the early Christian understanding of the linearity of earthly history. A thorough reading of Irenaeus' writings (primarily from 181-199 A.D.) leads one to the inescapable conclusion that his view of Revelation was also at its core "historic." One of the clearest Patristic expressions of an "historic" view comes from St. John Chrysostom in 390 A.D. In his commentary on the Gospel of St. Mathew, St. John therein describes the sweep of God's Revelation of Himself and His plan for man's salvation in *purely historic terms*,

> "What then could be equal to these Good Tidings [this Good News]? ..."
>
> **"Therefore he hath called the *history* of Good Tidings ..."**
>
> **"But what are these [historic] points? Such as follow; That God became man, that He wrought miracles, that He was crucified, that He was buried, that He rose**

[138] Ibid., p. 48.

[139] This point is extremely important since many modern commentators are extremely fond of pointing out that the Fathers had *no sense* of the continuum of history. Some did not. But this cannot be said of Athenagoras.

> **again, that He ascended, *that He will judge*, that He hath given commandments tending to salvation, that He hath brought in a law not contrary to the Old Testament, that He is a Son, that He is only-begotten, that He is a true Son, that He is of the same substance as the Father,"**[140] [emphasis - author's]

St. John Chrysostom, a Father and Doctor of the Church, *in 390 A.D.* fully understood that the essential reality of the Glad Tidings (Good News or the Gospel) *processes in a linearity of events.*

In Chrysostom's commentary, the incarnation, miracles, passion, death, resurrection, ascension, the Eternal Divinity and present glory of Christ are presented as historic fact *in specifically chronological historical order*. In the same breath with which he proclaims the history of the Good News of Christ's Messianic mission on earth, Chrysostom then *immediately proclaims the Revealed prophesy of the future Judgment to come*. Who could deny that St. John understands the historic linearity of revealed Christian prophecy?

Nor is this author unique in seeing that the Fathers of the Church had a sense of the historical in their belief, exegesis, and catechesis. In his landmark work, *Christian Initiation,* Hugh Riley sums up the Mystagogic Cathechesis of the four Fathers (1) St. Cyril (Bishop of Jerusalem), (2) St. John Chrysostom (Bishop of Constantinople), (3) Theodore of Mopsuestia, (Bishop of Mopsuestia), and (4) St. Ambrose (Bishop of Milan).

> "Not merely on the occasion of, but in and through the ceremonies is the candidate [Baptismal] brought face to face with the drama of ***the whole Christ, active in himself and in history***, the Christ of the *OT*, the Messiah, Jesus of Nazareth in His life, death, and resurrection, the glorified Lord, Christ united here and now with the candidate in his own conversion, his *metanoia*, his transformation from not seeing to seeing, from belief to unbelief.
>
> "This recapitulation of the life of Christ, His passion, death, and resurrection, as well as its foreshadowing in the

140 *The Homilies of St. John Chrysostom, Archbishop of Constantinople, on the Gospel of St. Mathew*, Oxford, John Henry Parker, The Frederick Field Edition, 1843, pp. 4-5.

> *OT* and its consummation in the eschaton of glory, is interpreted and explained [in the baptismal instructions of these early bishops]"[141]

It is quite common today to hear extreme "higher critics" overstating their case by claiming/implying that the Fathers had little to no sense of history. That is an insupportable tenet for anyone who is truly familiar with the Fathers.

3. St. Jerome

The reader will encounter many eschatological comments from St. Jerome in this book. Jerome's knowledge of history was broad and detailed. Jerome constantly refers to historical innacuracies found in the writings of the enemies of the Church. As Fr. Murphy states in his classic *A Monument to St Jerome,*

> "Jerome was actually haunted by an historical sense. It permeates his Scriptural commentaries. It is continually betraying itself in his letters and controversies.[142]
>
> *"Jerome grasped its* [history's] *indispensability in permitting the Western Christian to orientate himself in the course of world history, and thus facilitate his study of the Scriptures and of the milieu of profane knowledge.*"[143] [emphasis added]

4. Cardinal Newman

This same process, *the reality of prophecy and its fulfilled history* was freshly observed by the great Cardinal Newman in 1878. As he stated in the introduction to his famous *Development of Doctrine in the Christian Church,*

---

[141] *Christian Initiation, A Comparative Study of the Interpretation of the Baptismal Liturgy in the Mystagogical Writings of Cyril of Jerusalem, John Chrysostom, Theodore of Mopsuestia, and Ambrose of Milan*, Hugh M. Riley, Edited by Johannes Quasten, Vol. 17 of "The Catholic University of America Studies in Christian Antiquity," 1974, pp 41&42.

[142] *A Monument to St. Jerome*, Edited by Francis X. Murphy, C.SS.R. - Forward by Cardinal Tisserant, Sheed and Ward, New York, 1952, p. 116.

[143] Ibid. p. 118

> "... considering that *prophecy* had already determined that it [Christianity] was to be a power visible in the world and sovereign over it, *characters which are accurately fulfilled in that historical Christianity* to which we commonly give the name."[144]

When *strictly limiting ourselves* to *a discussion of the Patristic view of prophecy and the linearity of its historic fulfillment,* it is virtually identical to Newman's in the late 19th century. As we have seen in Chrysostom (and as could be shown in many other Fathers) this historic Christian view of the interrelationship of prophecy and its fulfillment in history is hardly a modern invention!

True, the Patristic view lacked a theology of history as such. It also did not have a "historic consciousness" in any sense as fully developed as our own.[145] But to state that the early Church, and particularly the Fathers, had little to no sense of history in prophecy, in relation to Revelation, is to betray a woeful ignorance of the writings of the Fathers.

> "Despite the different attitudes toward the world and despite the different ways in which Christianity consequently is translated into concrete reality, nevertheless, a common historical consciousness remains alive [in the period of the Fathers]."[146]

Whether we are (1) reading the First Covenant as revealed, initiated, and presented to Abraham in the Jewish Tradition, or (2) the New Testament "Good News" of the Gospel as proclaimed to us today, *their uniquely Judeo-Christian historic and unchanging character, and the prophetic nature of its future events are inseparable.*

God in His Gospel reveals to us facts about the past, present and future. The average Christian's historic view of man *is linear*, it is not despairingly cyclic, and that is initially unique

---

144 *Development of Christian Doctrine*, John Henry Cardinal Newman, Longmans, Green and Co. New York, 1927, p. 5.

145 *The Theology of History in St. Bonaventure*, Joseph Ratzinger, p. 107.

146 Ibid. p. 96. [However, it must not be assumed from this that it was fleshed out or even fully understood such as our modern "historical consciousness" or "sense". And it was not universally written about by all the Fathers.

to Judeo-Christianity.[147] In the Christian view, even much of the future is historic *fact* revealed to man in prophecy, only yet to be lived out in the lives of future generations of men and women. ***The future Antichrist and Parousia are part and parcel of the Christian view of history*. The Antichrist and the Parousia are as historically certain to a Christian as Christ's passion, death and resurrection.** Prophecy of future historic events is inseparable from Christianity.

There is no doubt that the average believing Christian views history as it travels in a straight chronological line. That line traverses God's creation of the angels, of the World, its first human inhabitants - Adam and Eve in the Garden, then His creation of each one of us. From there the Christian view travels on to the eschaton, Final Judgment and then to either our eternal happiness with Him in Heaven, or its alternative.

God does not reveal to us our individual eternity which He (being Omniscient) immediately knows. He has revealed to us what is necessary; that through His gift to us of free will — by His grace — our eternal destiny is (by His grace and mercy) in our own hands. God simply pre-knows the choices we will individually make through the power of free will which He has created within us.

If the Gospel's basic message in His Revelation were not essentially historic, then it would be a myth. As St. Paul says, "And if Christ has not risen, vain then is our preaching, and vain is your faith."[148] From the above reflections it becomes predictable that *those who would most effectively attack the Christian faith in its 20th & 21st century context, they will attack both its real historicity and its uniquely prophetic nature. Credible Christianity as revealed to us is inconceivable outside of its uniquely historic and prophetic context.* And that context includes prophecy of future historic events.

God's Covenantal Revelation with man, from its very beginning with Abraham, *specifically exists within a prophetic context*. There

---

[147] There are some scholastic exceptions to this. e.g., St. Bonaventure (and a few others) also in a real sense attempted to learn from the history of God's salvation by viewing it from the point of view of one giant completed circle. But this "cyclic" view was not *endlessly* cyclic such as in many Oriental religions. There was only one cycle which began in the Alpha and ended in the Omega-eschaton.

[148] 1 Cor. 15:14.

are those who today publicly wear the label "Christian" and/or "Catholic" who essentially deny and attack both the historic and prophetic elements of God's Revelation to man. If Judeo-Christianity is not based in true history and prophecy, then it is as its rationalist enemies claim, based in myth. Whether the "attacker" knows it or not, he or she who attacks the authenticity of the historic *and/or prophetic elements of Christianity attacks the Christian Faith at its very roots.*

CHAPTER 2

EXTREMIST "HIGHER CRITICISM" AND ITS "DEMYTHOLOGIZING" OF REVELATION

A. THE "MODERN THEOLOGICAL MOVEMENT"

Many of the prophecies which appear later in this book appear to deal very specifically with the effects of extreme higher criticism *in the 20th century*. These prophecies will not be nearly as understandable or poignant for the reader who has not read this chapter. However, ***SOME OF THE CONTENTS OF THIS CHAPTER REQUIRE CAREFUL READING.*** **FOR THE READER WHO SO WISHES, THE GENERAL CONTENTS CONTINUE AT THE BEGINNING OF CHAPTER 3.**

1. Every Man or Woman of the West Has a Right *and a Need* to Know the Effects of Extreme Higher Criticism

Whether one is an ally or an enemy of "higher criticism," *everyone has a need and a right to know what follows*. We intend to show how the ideas of the extreme "higher critics" have affected all of us. If one is a "Western" adult (from North or South America, or Western Europe) he or she has been affected by extreme higher criticism. Whether Catholic, Protestant, Jewish, an agnostic, or professed atheist, all "Westerners" have been greatly affected by "higher criticism" either directly or indirectly in much of their spiritual decision-making over at least the last twenty to thirty years.

"Extreme Higher Criticism"

The effects of "extreme higher criticism" and the "Contemporary Theological Movement" are the major cause of several contemporary problems for the *average* Western Catholic. As the reader will later discover, *these effects* have been *specifically* foretold for the 20th century by many prophecies of canonized Saints, Blessed and Venerable, prophecies which are now hundreds of years old. These prophecies predict that in the 20th century, heresy (engendered by a false intellectualism) will affect many of those in the Latin Rite. In order to fully understand those effects, one has to be aware of their various causes. According to the prophecies, the major cause of our faith problems in the 20th century will be **"senseless questions and elaborate arguments"** created by a false intellectualism.

2. Effects of A False Intellectualism

One major effect of "higher criticism" and/or the "Contemporary Theological Movement" is: today's Catholics *on average* do not hold the same degree of *certainty* about a number of traditional Church teachings which their Catholic parents and grandparents held. Those teachings include (but are not limited to):

(1) The historicity of Biblical accounts of Our Lord's miracles and prophecies,
(2) Miracles performed by the Apostles, and,
(3) In general, the historicity of the New Testament,
(4) The charism of prophecy, and,
(5) Traditional Christian doctrine in general.

Does the reader doubt the claim in item (5)? Cardinal Bernardin of Chicago has recently reported a very in-depth poll showing that 70% of the U.S. "Catholics" no longer believe in the "Real Presence" of Our Lord in the Sacrament of Communion, in the sense of "Transubstantiation." This is the belief that after a validly ordained priest consecrates the bread and wine, that the bread and wine actually change into the Body and Blood of Christ. That is a daily miracle.

The Western technical theological expression of this is that they truly *substantially* become the Body and Blood of Our Lord, and only the "accidental" appearances of bread and wine remain.

> **NOTE to readers from the Eastern Church:** The author is aware of some Eastern Rite Catholics and Eastern Orthodox objections to *what they perceive as the Thomistic/Aristotilean terms* "Transubstantiation" and "matter and form."[149] The major point the author is making is not about the technical theological terminology employed. The point is the drop in the number of Western Catholics who believe in the reality of the *change* of the bread and wine into the Body of and Blood of Christ. This reality *was* until quite recently accepted by the vast majority of Western Catholics. The testimony of the Fathers of the Church is replete with specific confirmations that belief in the basic tenets of that "*change*" goes right back to the teachings of the Apostles. This is well-documented in many sources. This belief and fact are succinctly encapsulated by the Eastern priest/scholar, Fr. Popivchak (an Eastern Rite priest).[150]

What could account for such a Western dramatic loss in belief and understanding of such a central doctrine of the Faith in just three decades? And why is that so important to the subject of this book?

---

149 "The Eastern Church is marked even today by the rather lively debate on whether the 'western philosophical tradition (source and mother of the Russian 'religious philosophy' of the 19th and 20th centuries), rather than the Hellenic, must supply theology with its conceptual framework' or whether a 'return to the Fathers' and the 'permanent and the eternal value of Hellenic categories' must be rediscovered." Quoted from *Peter Mohila, Metropolitan of Kiev (1633-47) Translation and Evaluation of His "Orthodox Confession of Faith (1640),* (Doctoral Dissertation of) Rev. Ronald Peter Popivchak, Catholic University of America, Department of Theology, Washington, D.C., 1995, p. 129.

150 Ibid. p. 128. "Traditional theologians, either Eastern or Western ... can hardly deny the basic reality or meaning of the word [Transubstantiation]. The Church Fathers used a wide variety of terms to express this same reality." Popivchak now quotes numerous equivalent expressions from St. Irenaeus, Athanasius, Cyril of Jerusalem, Gregory of Nyssa, John Chrysostom and Ambrose in support of his statement about the apostolic origins of this "reality."

That "loss" is important because *it is a waste of time to throw eschatological Mysteries from Tradition and Scripture at people who no longer know what to believe about the most central Mystery of the Faith.* If a Catholic begins to lose faith in the greatest miracle of all, the daily transformation of mere bread and wine into the Body and Blood, Soul and Divinity of Our Lord - everything else begins to fall. Once a central domino begins to totter it is only a matter of time before a *line* of dominoes goes down.

3. The Confusion Factor

In the West, there *is* general confusion amongst the faithful concerning what the Church teaches concerning the interpretation of Scripture. *That is a fact. At least in private*, that fact is not denied by a number of priests and theologians of the authors acquaintance. That confusion extends at least in part to many orthodox members of the laity *as well as many of the clergy.* There is an observable confusion as to what to take literally, or merely allegorically in Scripture, *confusion at a level which absolutely did not exist even thirty or forty years ago.*

Many of the more orthodox members of the Latin Rite will publicly dramatically state that they are not confused in this. But within their own hearts, they know that on average, they are no longer as certain of what the Church teaches about many Scriptural interpretations as their parents and grandparents were.

4. Is Contemporary Loss of Faith a Result of Confusion or Informed Denial?

Many Western Catholics are confused as to what the Church teaches on many central issues of Faith. Such people have not heard the fullness of the doctrinal beliefs of the Church consistently preached to them in Faith for the last thirty years. ***How can one reject something one has never clearly heard preached!*** In many cases the preaching they *have* heard from pulpits has been doctrinally confused. In a doctrinal vacuum of confused preaching, isn't subsequent confusion in the minds of the faithful a predictable gradual byproduct?

For all the reasons stated so far in Chapter 2, it is imperative to understand the teaching and affect of the Modern Theological Movement.

B. EXTREME HIGHER CRITICISM - ITS UNBELIEF

The "unbelief" of the extreme "higher critics" was described very succinctly and accurately by Dr. Deitrich von Hildebrand in 1967. In the introduction to his now famous *Trojan Horse in the City of God*, Dr. Hildebrand wrote,

> "if we then turn to a number of articles by Catholic priests and laymen published in recent years, we cannot escape the impression that these writers not only have lost their Catholic faith, but also no longer understand the very nature of religion *based on divine revelation*."[151]

The extreme "higher critics" (whom von Hildebrand and others have written of) are fond of "debunking" the following:

(1) Prophecies,
(2) Divine intervention in human history,
(3) Miracles (*Scriptural or otherwise*), and,
(4) The role of Tradition.
(5) In general, debunking the historicity of many Biblical figures, events and prophecies.

We have already discussed their debunking of Tradition in the previous chapter. The effects of that "debunking" in items 1-3 and 5 are developed in the following discussion.

1. A Catholic Must Believe in the Existence of the Charism of Prophecy of Future Events

Public prophecies in Revelation of future events, as they are understood and taught by the Magisterium, are part of what a Catho-

[151] *Trojan Horse in the City of God*, Dr. Deitrich von Hildebrand, Franciscan Herald Press, Chicago, 1967, p. XI.

lic must believe. Some examples of such prophesied "predestined" events are:

(1) The Old Testament prophecies of the coming Messiah.
(2) The New Testament prophecies concerning the Parousia and the Final Judgment.

Both the Parousia and the Final Judgment are articles of Faith included in the Creed which is said at the Liturgy of the Eucharist. **The source of these two *Predestined*[152] "articles of Faith" is the Scriptural public prophecy of their future actualization.**

2. Our Lord Scripturally Confirms the Existence of Inspired Prophecy of Future Historical Events

The *actual existence of the Charism or Gift of Prophecy*, a special gift of the Holy Spirit as it is revealed and described in Scripture is something in which a Catholic must believe. This is one of the special gifts of the Holy Spirit which Scripture reveals to us is given to certain individuals of God's choosing. That gift in many cases includes the ability to foresee some future events.

The Church's traditional doctrine on this point is best found in the constant teachings of the Fathers, Doctors, and the Magisterium. The documents of both the First and Second Vatican Councils authenticate the Church's belief in this gift, and describe the gift itself.

Our Lord directly appealed to, and Divinely confirmed this Charism of the Prophecy of Future Events when He directly claims the Old Testament prophecies of His own "coming" into the world.

> Then He said to them, "These are my words which I spoke to you, while I was still with you, that ***everything written about me in the law of Moses and the prophets and the psalms must be fulfilled."*** Then He opened their minds to understand the Scriptures, and said to them, "Thus it is writ-

---

152 "*Predestined*" in the Thomistic sense. As discussed earlier, St. Thomas describes those prophesied events as "predestined" which, "takes place when God reveals what he alone will do, and what He sees present in eternity and in His absolute decree."

> ten, that the Christ should suffer and on the third day rise from the dead, and that repentance and forgiveness of sins should be preached in His name to all nations, beginning in Jerusalem. You are witnesses of these things. And behold, I send the promise of my Father upon you, but stay in the city, until you are clothed with power from on high."[153]

Herein Our Lord directly confirms the Old Testament prophets, and their prophecies of His coming, His suffering, His death, and His rising on the third day. He points out that they all came true - AS PREDICTED. He thus demonstrates to man the historical accuracy of Scriptural prophecy of future events.

Our Lord even closes this passage with a prophecy of His own about the imminent coming of the Holy Spirit on Pentecost. JESUS CHRIST UNEQUIVOCALLY CONFIRMS THE GOD-GIVEN GIFT OF PROPHECY OF FUTURE EVENTS. THEN IN THE SAME BREATH HE HIMSELF PROPHESIES. **If someone wishes to question or deny the God-given gift of prophecy he must question or deny both the direct testimony of Jesus Christ and His recorded acts.**

3. The Historicity of Revelation

Later, we will discuss what is contained in the private prophecy of many canonized Saints, Blessed and Venerable. But *here in this section, we are discussing*; (1) *only things contained within public Revelation*, (which includes its public prophecy) and, (2) how we respond to that Revelation. The purpose of this discussion is to demonstrate the following,

(A) In relation to what is contained in Revelation, the belief system of the average Western Christian in the last few decades has been seriously affected/impaired by extreme elements of "higher criticism." And Catholics are no exception to these effects/impairments.

(B) These effects of extreme "higher criticism" are the cause of the *average* Catholic's today not holding the same

---

[153] Luke 24:44-49.

degree of certainty (as did that Catholic's parents and grandparents) about the Biblical historical accounts of Our Lord's miracles and prophecies, miracles performed by the Apostles, and in general, the historicity of the New Testament.

(C) The "impairment" of their certainty about even public prophecy contained in Revelation, naturally results in extreme incredulousness concerning the prophecies of canonized Saints or Fatima (even though Popes of this century have publicly expressed confidence in Fatima and John Paul II has even gone on pilgrimage there).

(D) That contemporary incredulousness renders its victims deaf to any authentic charismatic prophecy, (1) the existence of which contemporary charism the Magisterium confirms, (2) which the foremost systematic Theologian of the Catholic Church, St. Thomas Aquinas, tells us that God grants to men "at all times" for "the direction of human acts."

While the Catholic "higher critics" will not usually publicly admit it, **most *extreme* "Higher Critics" do *not* personally believe that:**

(1) Anyone by the power of God ever legitimately predicts the future -- not even Jesus Christ through and within His Hypostatic Union,
(2) Jesus ever personally performed any miracles in His earthly life,
(3) The Bible is (in any serious form) a reliable accurate historic documentary,
(4) The Bible is a Divinely Inspired document (at least in any meaningful sense of the word),
(5) Sacred Tradition is to be equally "venerated" with sacred Scripture.

At the same time, these extreme "Catholic" critics publicly portray themselves as fully Catholic. When they also enjoy Catholic positions of teaching authority, that causes great confusion amongst the faithful about what Catholicism is and what it teaches.

THE "CATHOLIC" PROBLEM: Many of these "extreme critics" who are fairly described in items 1-5 above, publicly and consistently present themselves as fully Catholic. *They may even wish to believe that they can be fully Catholic* at the same time that they dissent from the teaching of the Magisterium on serious matters of Faith and Morals. But by the norms of Magisterial Teachings of the Catholic Church which go back to the infant Church - they are not, objectively speaking, fully Catholic.

Again, few *extreme* higher critics, who are academics, publicly and forthrightly present the fact that their personal beliefs are at variance to the teachings of the Magisterium. *The extreme critics' fellow Catholic academics often know that he or she dissents from the teachings of the Church. But a "critics" lack of full disclosure about their dissent is disastrous for their students. It leaves their average Catholic student with substantially less than sufficient information by which to judge if what they are being taught is "Catholic."*

When such a "critic" teaches doctrine contrary to the Magisterium, that predictably results in *confusion* amongst his or her Catholic students as to what the teachings of the Church really are. *That phenomenon is ultimately the major cause of confusion in the Church today.* That confusion is fairly described and predicted for our century by many prophecies which will be presented later in the book.

C. HOW DOES "CRITICAL" "UNBELIEF" SHOW ITSELF?

One example: many "extreme higher critics" *openly* "postulate" as to whether Jesus actually predicted the fall of Jerusalem. They "wonder" whether Scriptural portrayals of Jesus' prophecy are merely "literary devices" which were created after the fall of Jerusalem.

There are times when absolute candor is necessary, and this is one of them. When all of the academic verbiage is peeled off, in this case, such a "higher critic" is essentially saying some of the writers of sacred Scripture knowingly *created out of thin air* those descriptions of Jesus' prophecy of future historic events. We are not judging as to the various *critics* intent when they do this. We are speaking only of the bottom line conclusions reached by their students.

Sometimes those conclusions are caused by an ambiguous statement, e.g., "Some Scripture scholars have engaged in research as to whether Jesus actually predicted the fall of Jerusalem or whether it was later employed as a literary device to impart a religious message." (Bottom line: Jesus never made the prophecy, it never happened.) At other times it appears within some form of a question, "Is there any way that anyone can truly ascertain whether Jesus actually made this prophecy or whether this was a later literary devise employed by the sacred writer." (Bottom line: an implication through a subtle question that the sacred writer invented this story - i.e.., it never *really* happened.) In this specific case, isn't "literary device" a polite euphemism? To use an old expression, "A rose by any other name is still a rose."

It would be unfair and inaccurate to sweep all "higher critics" into the same "unfaithful" net. The above refers only to consistent higher critic "debunkers" of the Church's traditional teaching on; (1) Divine Prophecy, (2) the possibility of the miraculous (3) any serious historicity of any substantive kind in the Bible (4) Divine Inspiration of the contents of Tradition and Scripture in any meaningful sense of the word.

1. One Western Heretical Example

The author first became personally aware of the extent of heresy amongst some Latin Rite higher critic scholars in 1966. He was a university student when one evening he went to a coffee house in Seattle, Washington, with several friends who were attending local colleges and universities. All were either Protestant or Catholic. They had heard that the guest speaker that night was one of the Department Heads from Seattle's Diocesan Major Catholic Seminary. Since this coffee house did not have a reputation for catering to Christians, they wished to attend and hear what this Catholic scholar had to say.

Toward the end of his talk the priest announced that "Jesus probably did not know he was God until He died on the cross." The author (and his Christian friends) were stunned. He was particularly embarrassed since the girl he had fallen in love with was with him. She was a very good Lutheran. He had been hoping against hope that somehow she would become a Catholic. But he saw the look in her eyes when the first Catholic priest she had ever listened to uttered those words. He feared that any chance of her becoming Catholic was lost.

Then his friends and he had their first "meaningful" ecumenical experience. All of them, Lutherans, Baptists, and the Catholic, went after that priest in the question and answer session which followed. The author remembers going to particular pains to demonstrate to this girl that Catholics believed in Christ's eternal Divinity *and in His eternal knowledge of His Divinity* every bit as much as she did. Despite what she had heard that night, by the grace of God she became a Catholic several years later and is now the author's bride of 26 years and mother of six.

The point is that what was then a shock has now become more commonplace. It is no longer a shock or unusual to hear even some parish priests express confusion or doubt about just when Christ "discovered" or "knew" that He was God, or to conjecture how much He knew about his Divinity at any given point in His earthly life.

A very good friend of the authors hosted a Christmas party several years ago, to which he invited many members of his parish as well as the parish priest. In the midst of the party, the priest stated that Jesus did not know he was God until he died on the cross. At this point, the atmosphere "grew very heated." It got so bad that "it looked like the priest and one of the parishioners were going to come to blows." The party came to a rather abrupt ending.

In making such statements about Christ's lacking knowledge of His Divinity, such men betray an ignorance of the Church's constant teachings on the reality of the Hypostatic Union.[154] Some Catholic "scholars" are now heard to imply that only uneducated Catholics (the implication is that such *uneducated* Catholics are pious simpletons) believe that the "Person" Jesus Christ knew He was God throughout His entire earthly ministry. In actual fact, a supposedly *educated* Catholic should know better, should know that even in His perfect manhood Jesus Christ had full knowledge of his

[154] See Glossary for "Hypostatic Union."

Divine Union with the Word from the moment of the Incarnation onward. If they knew any Church history they would also know that to deny this is closely related to two of the earliest condemned heresies, Nestorianism and that of the Agnotae.

2. There are No New Heresies

Should a truly educated Christian be capable of making such a basic theological mistake as that described above? In order to fully demonstrate the falsehood of denial of Christ's knowledge of his Divinity we will now quote from only five of a host of available sources.

(1) St. Thomas Aquinas' *The Disputed Questions on Truth.*
(2) The *Faith of the Early Fathers*, by Fr. William A. Jurgens.
(3) Third, St. Cyril of Alexandria's *On the Holiness and Consubstantiality of the Trinity.*
(4) Pope Vigilius' *Constitutum* from 553 A.D.
(5) Pope Pius XII's Encyclical *Sempiternus Rex* from 1956.

3. Christ's "Consciousness" and St. Thomas Aquinas

St. Thomas Aquinas authoritatively answered this question about whether Christ knew He was God. In his *Disputed Questions on Truth*, in the section on *The Knowledge of Christ*, Aquinas addresses the question of what St. Luke means in his Gospel when he says, "And Jesus advanced in wisdom." Thomas distinguished between the "uncreated knowledge" in the Divinity of Christ, and the created knowledge in the Perfect Man Christ.

> "Just as we say that there are two natures in Christ [one human and one Divine], so, also, we say there are two kinds of knowledge: created and uncreated."[155]

> "Although in Christ there is only one substantial subject [One Person due to the Hypostatic Union], in Him there are two natures, so, two activities."[156]

---

[155] *The Disputed Questions on Truth*, St. Thomas Aquinas, Henry Regnery Company, Chicago, 1953, Vol. 2., p. 398.
[156] Ibid. pp. 399 & 400.

Discussing the level of knowledge held by Christ in His human nature, Aquinas says:

> "Therefore, Christ [in His human intellect] had this perfection of knowing things in their own nature *through the infused knowledge given him by God*"[157]

In discussing the communication of knowledge between Jesus Christ's Human and Divine natures, Thomas says:

> "*The [human] soul of Christ* enjoyed a greater privilege than any [other] created intellect. For in the Word [Christ's Divine Nature] it [His human nature] *sees all things, present, past, and future*."[158] [emphasis added]

St. Thomas summed up his technical theological defense of this *position,* (*which is also the traditional teaching of the Church on this subject*) in the following manner. At the very end of the discussion concerning in what sense Christ could grow in knowledge within His assumed human nature, St. Thomas says:

> "For that matter, even in this knowledge [created knowledge] Christ could not advance in so far as the habit is concerned, since such knowledge by the nature of its genus cannot extend to more things than Christ knew through it. **But in the Gospel it is said that He "advanced in wisdom"** ***with reference to experience of those things which he [already] knew in the habit.***"[159] [emphasis the author's]

This is the traditional theological teaching of the Church on this subject. Anyone who says that Christ did not know He was God until He died on the Cross, clearly denies the traditional teaching of the Church, and the dictates of reason applied to Revelation on this subject.

---

[157] Ibid. p. 407.

[158] Ibid. p. 412.

[159] Ibid. p. 424.

4. Fr. Jurgens on Modern Nestorianism

Fr. Jergens' *Faith of the Early Fathers*, is a three volume series on the writings of the Fathers of the Church. This three volume set is the best read scholarly *summary* of Patristic writings in today's English speaking Church. It was originally published in 1979. Because of popular demand it is still in print, and is available from The Liturgical Press, Collegeville, MN.

In his commentary on the Nestorian Heresy (which began early in the 5th century A.D., Jurgens says:

> "Nestorianism taught that the Man Jesus, by the virtuous conduct of His life, came Himself to *deserve* union with the Divine Majesty.
>
> "If the latter notion seems very similar to the rather *common ideas of our own time to the effect that Christ only came gradually to realize that he was God and perhaps was not fully aware of it until He was hanging on the cross* -- is this the same as saying that His Divinity was only gradually actualized and that perhaps it was not fully actualized until he was hanging on the cross? -- *possibly it is because Nestorianism is not nearly as dead an issue as some suppose*, and *there is an effective revival of it among some "Catholic theologians even today,* ***Heresies never die; they just change their names.*** I cannot recall any modern heresy that is really new; nor do I know of any ancient heresy that has been slain outright."[160]

Here we have a very broadly respected Catholic scholar and theologian telling us that ideas similar to the 5th century Nestorian Heresy are "common" as of 1979 -- common especially amongst "some Catholic theologians." But they were relatively uncommon even fifteen years prior to Jurgens' books. The "gradual realization" theological theory which Jurgens describes as *"an effective revival"* of the Nestorian heresy, is today a common thread in the writings of many extreme "higher critics."

---

[160] *The Faith of the Early Fathers Vol.* 3, *A source-book of theological and historical passages from the writings of St. Augustine to the end of the Patristic Age*, W.A. Jurgens, Liturgical Press, Collegeville, MN, 1979, p. 198.

The heretical "idea" which Jurgens tells us was "common" among "some theologians" in 1979, is now in the mid 1990's even heard at the level of a significant number of parish priests. Consequently, In the last fifteen years that heresy has filtered down another level. In order to further examine Jurgens' case, it will be advantageous to the reader to review *other aspects* of that Nestorian Heresy -- which according to Jurgens is alive and well again in the late 20th century.

On Christmas Day, 428 A.D., Bishop Nestorius of Constantinople publicly denied that Mary could be "Theotokos" (God-bearer), later saying that she could only have been "Christokos" (Christ-bearer). Nestorius was stating that Mary could only be the bearer of the Lord's human nature. *Nestorius explained (as part of his logical rationale) that no sinful mortal could bear God.*

Nestorius' statement was correct as it stands, but he completely missed the point! He was denying/overlooking the possibility of Mary's Immaculate Conception -- which the Church much later declared to be De Fide.

At the Ecumenical Council of Ephesus in 431 A.D., the Church responded to Nestorius' denial of the title "Theotokos" by:

(1) Formally declaring Mary to be "Theotokos" (God-bearer)
(2) Declaring that the two natures of Christ are truly joined "in one person and one hypostasis," and
(3) Condemning both Nestorius' heresies about Our Lady and Our Lord, and excommunicating Nestorius.[161]

5. St. Cyril of Alexandria, Father and Doctor

The authority of St. Cyril is described by Quasten, ***"In his Trinitarian works he intends to sum up in a systematic presentation the teaching of the Church Fathers."***[162] As many of Fathers of the Church did, St. Cyril went to great effort to defend the Divinity of Christ against heretics.

One of the tactics of those heretics was to attempt to misuse Scripture in order to disprove Christ's Divinity. In his *On the Holy and Consubstantial Trinity*, Cyril confronts such a misinterpretation of Matt. 24:36 "But of that day and hour no one knows, not even the angels of heaven, nor the Son, but the Father only." [It should also be observed that, "Other ancient authorities omit (the phrase) *nor the Son.*"[163]]

The text which St. Cyril possessed obviously contained the phrase "nor the Son." St. Cyril tells us that "heretics" use this phrase in order to deny Jesus' Divinity. In his *On the Holy and Consubstantial Trinity,* probably written shortly before the outbreak of the Nestorian Heresy in 428, he says they do this by the device of asking this question,

---

161 See *The Building of Christendom, A History of Christendom,* Warren Carroll, Vol. 2, P. 92-94, & *History of the Councils,* Hefele, Vol. III, P. 44,45. "Council of Ephesus." *Catholic Encyclopedia*, 1913 Edition, "Nestorius."

162 *Patrology*, Johannes Quasten, (Prof. of Ancient Church History and Christian Archeology, Catholic University of America), Vol. 3. , Spectrum Publishers Utrecht-Antwerp, 2nd Printing, 1963, p. 135

163 Quoted from commentary in *The Navarre Bible, The Gospel of St. Matthew,* Four Courts Press, 1988, p. 198.

> "So in what manner, they inquire, is the Son similar to the Father in essence, since He declares Himself to be ignorant of the date of the end of the world?"[164]

Cyril definitively responds to that question for many pages. The following are a few highlights of several questions and statements of Cyril in answer to this question "Haereticorum" (of heretics):

> "If He [Jesus] is the creator of the world and of time, which He assuredly is : How is it estimated among you [heretics] that He is ignorant of the day and the hour? In what manner is it possible that that which He made, He does not know? Therefor the things said by Him to His disciples must be investigated. ***From these things it shall be easily shown that He knew the day and the hour, as God;***"[165] [emphasis added]

We are quoting St. Cyril extensively to demonstrate several things. *The first*, this questioning of Christ's consciousness of His Divinity and His specific knowledge about the future is not a new one thought up by 20th century extreme higher critics. Contemporary higher critics who attempt to question the knowledge of Christ are wasting their time whipping a theological dead horse. All the *major* ramifications of this argument were understood by the 4th and 5th century Fathers of the Church. *The second* is that in quoting Cyril on this issue, we also quote a compendium of the Fathers who went before him, as Johannes Quasten has informed us.

Now St. Cyril makes a classic explanation of Jesus' statement that "the Son" doesn't know "the day nor the hour, no one except the Father." He shows that in the light of Scripture, *the Holy Spirit has to know*. Therefore, if the Holy Spirit knows, then Jesus could

---

[164] *Patrologiæ Cursus Completus, Series Graeca*, Vol. 75., Migne, Paris au Petit-Montrouge, 1857-1866, p. 369. Author's translation of Migne's Latin text which reads, "At quomodo, inquiunt, erit similis Filius Patri secundum essentiam, cum dicat se nescire diem consummationis saeculi. Investiganda igitur sunt quae ab ipso discipulis dicta sunt. E quibus facile constabit ipsum et diem et horam novisse, ut Deum."

[165] Ibid. pp. 369 & 370. "Si ipse est conditor saeculorum, et temporum, atque hoc vere ita est : quomodo unum diem atque horam ignorare vobis censetur? Quomodo item ea quae fecit, nescire potest? Investiganda igitur sunt quae ab ipso discipulis dicta sunt. E quibus facile constabit ipsum et diem et horam novisse, ut Deum."

not have *literally* meant that no one but the Father knows! So, there must be another explanation of Jesus' statement.

> *"The enemies of Christ* [heretics] *must be strongly asked why, when the Savior spoke about the angels and the Son, nowhere did he make an mention of the (Holy) Spirit?* Because He did not say : the Spirit doesn't know, but "the angels don't know, and neither does the Son"; this is the point - simply: [*In that statement*] *he did not apply* [*extend*] *that statement to the Godhead.* It is clear that, he spoke of the angels because they are creatures. *In truth, He did not wish to tell the disciples a certain ineffable aspect of the Divine Economy* (*Gk. oikonomia*) [adaptation, disposition, arrangement, or management] *and plan* : "Who has known the mind of the Lord and who has been His counselor?" and lest He seem to wish to conceal something from them, and by this means to grieve them, ***He said*** *that this* [the day and the hour] ***the Son didn't know - speaking about Himself in a more human way,*** *as a man :* ***and in the meantime, keeping knowledge of ALL things to Himself, as God.*** *For the same reason, He didn't say the Spirit* [who is also God] *doesn't know."*[166]

St. Cyril now gives a further explanation of why Jesus said what He did,

> If therefore, the Word of God is found to have said something humble about Himself *in respect to the incarnation,* heretics would use it to object to His Divinity and would interpret what He said to gainsay His Divinity. But if when He became flesh, ***He spoke in a human way, in order that He might show himself to be truly man; how would it not be fitting to relate the things which he spoke - in a human way?*** For this

[166] ibid. p. 370 "Interrogandi sunt hostes Christi, quamobrem Servator cum angelos et Filium nominarit, Spiritus mentionem nusquam fecerit? Non enim dixit : Non novit Spiritus, sed, "Non norunt angeli, ne- que novit Filius"; atque hoc quidem, ***simpliceter : non adjecit, Dei.*** Manifestum igitur est quod angelos ignorasse dixerit, ut creaturas. *Cum vero discipulis id dicere nollet, ob eneffabilis quamdam divine administrationis et consilii rationem* : "Quis enim novit mentem Domini, aut quis consiliarus ejus fuit?" ne videretur illos hoc celare velle eoque nomine illos moerore afficere, dixit, ne Filium quidem hoc nosse; humano more de se loquens, ut Deus. Idcirco enim non dixit, Spiritus ignorare."

is to accommodate Himself to THE ECONOMY WHICH HE RECEIVED, (namely the incarnation).[167]

After pages of argument after argument demonstrating how and why Jesus (in His Hypostatic Union) ***did*** know the "day and the hour," St. Cyril concludes with this statement,

> **"He who says the Son, as Word, is ignorant of the day and the hour, cannot avoid blasphemy.** ***Because if He (Jesus) knows the Father, as He himself testifies : what can keep Him from knowing everything about the end of creation?"***[168]

Cyril, as the rest of the Fathers, refuses to have Christ divided up. For Cyril and the Fathers Christ must be seen in his Incarnation and its Hypostatic Union of the two natures of the one Person of Christ, the union of His truly Divine and truly human natures. Again, "the one Jesus Christ, true Son of God, and true Son of man,"[169] cannot be divided up.

Cyril does not utilize the theological terminology of later systematic theologians to discuss how Christ in His rational human soul knows. However, St. Thomas Aquinas does,

> "Therefore, Christ [in His human intellect] had this perfection of knowing things in their own nature *through the infused knowledge given him by God*"[170]

6. Pope Vigilius

In the wake of the Nestorian Heresy, which erroneously taught there were two persons in Christ, there arose a new threat, the

---

[167] Ibid, "Si ergo ante incarnationem Verbum Dei humile aliquid de se dixisse reperitur, divinitatem ejus objurgent, et contra eam dictum interpretentur. Sin vero cum factus est caro, humano more locutus est, ut vere se hominem esse ostendat, quo pacto non sit consen- taneum ad humanitatem referre quae humano more dixit. Hoc enim est sese administrationi quam suscepti, sive incarnationi, accomodare.

[168] Ibid. "Qui dicit Filium, quatenus est Verbum, ignorare diem illum et horam, blasphemiam evitare non potest. Si enim novit Patrem, sicut ipsemet testatur: quid obstat quominus etiam finem creationis norit?"

[169] Pope Vigilius from "DS 419."

[170] *The Disputed Questions on Truth*, p. 407

Monophysite Heresy. This heresy denied two natures to Christ, declared that He had only one nature which was divine, They denied that Christ had a truly human nature. Out of that Monophysite Heresy another heretical splinter group formed called the Agnotae. In the words of Dr. Warren Carroll, this was a group,

> "who (like many modern heretics) denied Christ's divine knowledge when He was a man on earth"[171] [parens - Dr. Carroll's]

As Fr. William Most, a contemporary theologian and Scripture scholar observes, "Against such erroneous thinking Pope Vigilius hurled an anathema in his *Constitutum* of May 14, 553 A.D.,

> 'If anyone says that the one Jesus Christ, true Son of God, and true Son of man, was ignorant of future things, or of the day of the last judgement, and says He would know only as much as the divinity dwelling in Him *as in another* made known to Him: let him be anathema.'"[172] [italics added]

Pope Vigilius' phrase, "divinity dwelling in Him *as in another*" is referring to the Agnotae heretical teaching that the Divinity of Christ only "dwelled" in, but was not joined to, the human nature of Christ. They denied that there was a Hypostatic Union of Christ's truly Divine and truly human natures which was a full and unbreakable union.

Many higher critical scholars state that therefore Pope Vigilius' anathema cannot apply in their case. They say their questioning of Christ's knowledge within his human nature is not the same as the position of the Agnotae. We now turn to our 20th century Pope Pius XII to answer that objection of the extreme higher critics.

7. Pope Pius XII

By the early 1950's, the question of the knowledge of Christ in his "early ministry" was being hotly debated. The extreme higher

---

171 *The Building of Christendom, A History of Christendom*, Warren H. Carroll, Christendom College Press, 1987, p. 200.

172 *The Consciousness of Christ*, William G. Most, Christendom College Press, 1980, p. 137. Fr. Most quotes Pope Vigilius from "DS 419."

critics were again calling into question the knowledge of Christ. In 1951, Pope Pius XII issued his Encyclical, *Sempiternus Rex*. In that document he refers to those who "misuse" the definition of the Council of Chalcedon in the following manner,

> "They so insist on the state and condition of the humanity of Christ that it seems to be considered as a subject, as it were, in itself, *as if it did not subsist in the person of the Word.*"[173]

Pius XII clearly readdresses, within our 20th century context, the problem of those who question the knowledge of Christ, who say that "He did not know." They can only do so by attempting to divide "the person of the Word." As the Church constantly teaches, that way leads to error.

8. The Importance of "Neo-Nestorianism" and "Neo-Monophysitism"

Why did we single out in this discussion the contemporary heresy of challenging Our Lord's knowledge during His "earthy ministry"? Many extreme higher critics claim *Christ was ignorant* (till He died on the cross) of the fact that He was Divine. If a Christian begins to believe that Jesus Christ didn't even know He was God until He died on the Cross -- how much credence would he or she place in Christ's Knowledge which He expressed in eschatological prophecies made prior to His death? In other words, if Jesus Christ didn't even know He was God, why would anyone believe He knew enough to prophecy *about signs preceding the rise of Antichrist - which He told us to watch for?*

9. One Heresy Cannot Exist in Academic Isolation

One heresy always breeds others. Neo-Nestorianism, Neo-Agnotaeism and the other heresies they have generated have spread (1) initially among extreme higher critic academics, (2) then down to the level of some parish priests, and (3) are now trickling down to the level of the lay Catholic in the pew.

---

[173] AAS 43 (1951) 638.

Those heresies are definitely beginning to impact many peoples ability to faithfully accept public prophecies contained in Revelation. That is why it is so important from the perspective of this book to understand first, the thinking of the extreme higher critics - and second, *to understand the impact their thought has now begun to have on the faithful.* One of its major effects is at least partial impairment of the average Catholic's ability to faithfully fully accept even public prophecy from Revelation.

D. RAHNER'S AND OTHER HIGHER CRITICS' "DE-MYTHOLOGIZING THEOLOGY"

How have the extreme higher critics come to challenge so many doctrines taught by the Church since its infancy? The extreme higher critics have gone through a mental process of attempting to make rational all the mysteries of faith. In the case of Karl Rahner, we earlier discussed how this led him to state views which ran clearly contrary to some of the teachings of Vatican Council II on Tradition. Here a point must be made. Most of the really questionable theology in Rahner came from the post-Vatican II part of his career. There is no denying the existence of some valuable contributions made by him earlier in his career.

But there is also no denying that when Karl Rahner reached that point where his rationalization process could not be reconciled with the Traditional Christian view, he wrote,

> "The theology of the future must be a demythologizing theology"[174]

If the reader is somewhat confused as to just exactly what Rahner means by that, now Rahner removes all doubt,

> "A 'demythologizing theology' well understood must realize that propositions such as: '*there are three persons in one God*' -- '*God sent his son into the world*' -- '*We are saved by the Blood of Christ*;' are purely and simply incomprehensible to modern man, if they remain in the ancient style

[174] *Gethsemane*, p. 349.

of theology and of the proclamation, the point of departure and the arrival point of the Christian statement. *They make the same impression as the pure mythology in a religion of times past.*"[175]

1. Rahner is Only One of Many

Rahner is not the first to propagate this theme. He had both predecessors and contemporaries in this. In 1967, Deitrich von Hildebrand commented on Teilhard de Chardin's almost identical statements about making religion "relevant" to modern man,

> "The 'new theologians,' the 'new moralists,' welcome Tielhard's views because they share his *historical relativism* -- his conviction that *faith must be adapted to 'modern man.'*
>
> "But it is astonishing, on the other hand, that many faithful Christians are carried away by Tielhard -- that they fail to grasp *the complete incompatibility of his teaching with the doctrine of the Church.*"[176] [emphasis added]

Vis-a-vis Rahner's previous quote concerning relevancy to modern man: Sts. Peter and Paul and Mary Magdalene, Martin Luther and John Calvin and Queen Isabella of Spain, Blaise Pascal, Nobel Prize winner Mother Teresa, Pope John Paul II and Billy Graham all have at least one thing in common. They *have comprehended* and continue to comprehend every single thing which Karl Rahner stated "modern man" finds "incomprehensible." These men and women from the Apostolic era, the Renaissance, the age of "the enlightenment" and the 20th century (including many members of its scientific community) equally find God's Revelation highly comprehensible *through the eyes of Faith. They have believed His revealed Mysteries in Faith.*

God's Revealed word about (1) the Mystery of His Incarnation with its Sacrifice of His Only-begotten Son, and (2) that "we are saved by the Sacrificed Blood of Christ," are ***Mysteries*** **which can *only* be comprehended, accepted, and believed through the eyes**

---

[175] Ibid. p. 350.

[176] *Trojan Horse in the City of God*, Dr. Deitrich von Hildebrand, Franciscan Herald Press, Chicago, 1967, p. 244.

of Faith. They cannot be rationalized. They can only be believed through the eyes of Faith.

But for Karl Rahner and other extreme higher critics who attempt to plumb the depths of revealed Mysteries with logic, (when those Mysteries are *fully* comprehensible only to their Revealor) -- *for such rationalist "logicians" - those Mysteries predictably become "incomprehensible*." That failure *to comprehend* is based in the attempt to *fully* understand Omniscience when we are not omniscient, the desire to *fully* understand Omnipotence when we are not omnipotent.

Their very first flaw is failing to accept Divine Mysteries for what they are, Mysteries. You cannot "make *fully* rational" a Divinely revealed Mystery. Their basic premise upon which all their thinking rests is that you can somehow *fully* rationalize these Mysteries. When we understand this basic "flaw" of the "higher critics," then we have the key to the extreme "higher criticism" vault. They do not initially approach God's revealed Word from a point of faith. No matter how good their intentions, they initially approach it from an over-intellectualized rationalism.

Consider again that Rahner's theology texts and those of his theological look-alikes have been the theological flagships for the large majority of Western European and North American Catholic Universities and Seminaries for at least the last thirty years. Those texts in those institutions have played a large role in the formation of the majority of our contemporary "academics."

There are flaws in the premises and logic of the "Contemporary Theological Movement" every step of the way. A large number of those calling themselves "Catholic theologians" (whom you will encounter today on North American or Western European campuses) were to a significant degree intellectually formed in the flawed premises and conclusions of the extreme higher critics.

Those who fully accepted Rahner and other "higher critics" are now themselves "higher critics," and members of what Cardinal Siri calls the "Contemporary Theological Movement." The "critics" have framed the thought of many of our priests, leading to their acceptance of Rahner's "Demythologizing Theology." From there it has since trickled down from pulpits to the laity. That has resulted in great confusion about what the Church officially teaches as part of her doctrine. That confusion has had a particularly deep impact on the ability of the faithful to fully accept public prophecy from Revelation in Faith. Now let us return for an even closer look at the thought of Karl Rahner.

E. RAHNER'S ASCENDANCE CHRISTOLOGY VS. THE INCARNATION

THE INCARNATION IS THE CENTRAL DOCTRINE OF CHRISTIANITY! If someone in a teaching position of respect and authority is confused on this doctrine, or writes in a confusing manner on this doctrine - that person confuses people about the central doctrine of the Christian Faith. All Christian issues/doctrines spin off and around the Doctrine of the Incarnation! Therefore, discussing nuances about any other doctrinal issue with a person who has become confused about the Incarnation becomes an exercise in futility.

The theology of the Incarnation is cryptically described in the following:

> "[The Incarnation is] The union of the divine nature of the son of God with human nature in the person of Jesus Christ. The son of God assumed our flesh, body and soul, and dwelled among us like one of us in order to redeem us. His divine nature was substantially united to our human nature."[177]

If the Son of God did not do this, then we are not redeemed in the Blood of Christ. If that did not happen, then we are without hope. If the Incarnation did not happen as described above, as St. Paul says, "our faith is in vain." That is why the Incarnation is *THE* central doctrine of the Christian Faith.

Rahner taught an "ascendance" Christology in which Christ, as He gradually became aware of His own existential reality, drew closer and closer to God. Concomitantly, Rahner taught that the Scriptural teachings of Sts. Paul and John had altered what Rahner *claims* was an original "Ascendance" Christology of the initial Christian understanding of Christ. Rahner says,

[177] *Modern Catholic Dictionary*, John A. Hardon, S.J., Doubleday, 1980, p. 272.

> "The Christology of today, in the announcement and theological reflection, must in some way *take up again* - and preach - that story of the 'Ascendance Christology,' which already in the frame of the New Testament, *passing with an enormous rapidity from the experience of the historic Jesus to the formulae of the descent of the Christology of Paul and John, has been* ***transformed*** *into a doctrine of the Incarnation of the pre-existent Son-Logos.*"[178] [emphasis added]

A "plain English" translation of Rahner above: In effect, Rahner is saying that Sts. Paul and John *changed* (that is what the verb "*transformed*" means) what Rahner claims was,

(A) An *original* doctrine of "**Ascendance Christology**" - into
(B) The doctrine of the **"Descent Incarnation."**

Rahner says Sts. Paul and John changed (A) into (B). Again, it is common knowledge amongst students of Scripture that, within the writings of Sts. Paul and John are to be found those passages which most fully and graphically state the Doctrine of the Incarnation.

1. Sts. Paul and John vs. Rahner

Paul and John (and the Church) **teach that God descended to become Man. Rahner teaches that a man who gradually became more godlike ascended to become God.** These two positions, exclusively taken as such, are ultimately opposed to each other, a fact which Rahner clearly states and understands. That is why Rahner wants to "take up *again*" (sic) a doctrine different than that of the Gospels of Paul and John and the constant teaching of the Church since the time of the Apostles.

Rahner's almost parenthetical remark "*passing with an enormous rapidity*" is an obvious literary device of his own to get around a basic fact; *there is no historic evidence that what Paul and John taught constituted any change.* Has Rahner herein merely been quoted out of context? Is he being misunderstood on this point - that Paul and John changed an original Gospel message? There are

178 *Sacramentum Mundi*, Karl Rahner, Vol. 4, col. 492.

numerous passages in the writings of Rahner which say the same thing and are just as explicit. The following is another example;

> "A current, systematic Christology cannot however take its natural point of departure in that theological understanding of Jesus Christ. That at base is also valid for the *more ancient* Christological assertions of the **pre-Pauline** Scriptures."[179]

What in the world does Rahner mean by "more ancient"? In one paragraph he asserts that the transition from "Ascendance Christology" to "Incarnation Christology" happened with "*an enormous rapidity*." In another, he refers to a "more ancient" Christological assertion. *One cannot have it both ways.* In any case, there is no denial of or contraposition of the Incarnational Christology in "pre-Pauline" Scripture. That entire line of thought is an artificial construct of the "higher critical" mentality. As will presently become evident, Rahner is here beginning his own rather unique "Scripture alone" approach.

The Scriptures themselves tell us that the Christology which the Apostles taught came to the Christian converts not just in written form. Prior to sending letters to Christians, the Apostles had to have Christians to send letters to. First, they had to personally meet and orally teach the first Christians the Faith. Scripture and common sense attest to that fact. Then, and only then, did they send them letters and Gospels.

Rahner pretends that;

(1) Since some of the later Gospels have some explicit Christological details not contained in some earlier Gospels,

(2) That is proof that there was a change in doctrine. *That logic can only be based*

- (a) In a Scripture alone premise, which
- (b) Further pretends that the Scriptures as inspired by God were not intended by Him *to be used as an integral whole.*

---

179 *Sacramentum Mundi*, vol. 4, col. 194.

2. Pope John Paul II on Responsibility of Exegetes

In 1993, the Pontifical Biblical commission issued a document called *The Interpretation of the Bible in the Church.*[180] On April 23, 1993, the Holy Father related the contents of this document to the two major predecessor documents on Scriptural interpretation (exegesis) of the last one hundred years. They were, (1) Pope Leo XIII's *Providentissimus Deus* from 1893, and (2) Pius XII's *Divino Afflante Spiritu* from 1943.

In his address, Pope John Paul II observed that both documents wanted to protect the Church from two extremes ,

> "*Providentissimus Deus* wanted especially to protect Catholic interpretation of the Bible from the attacks of rationalistic science, on the other hand, *Divino Afflante Spiritu* was primarily concerned with defending Catholic interpretation from attacks that opposed the use of science by exegetes and that wanted to impose a non-scientific, so-called 'spiritual' interpretation of Sacred Scripture."[181]
>
> The Pope next observed one central feature of both documents, "4. In both cases ... the Magisterium went to the heart of the problem and thus showed (let us note this at once) **the Church's faith in the mystery of the Incarnation.**"[182]

The Holy Father returns to this theme later, and reemphasizes the harmony of the two key encyclicals of the past one hundred years on this interpretation of Scripture in regards to the Incarnation.

> "Consequently, the two Encyclicals require that Catholic exegetes remain in full harmony with the mystery of the incarnation, a mystery of the union of the divine and human in a determinate historical life... The Church of Christ takes the realism of the incarnation seriously"[183]

---

180 "The Pontifical Biblical Commission, in its new form after the Second Vatican Council, is *not* an organ of the teaching office, but rather a commission of scholars.

181 *Address of His Holiness Pope John Paul II and Document of the Pontifical Biblical Commission*, Libreria Editrice Vaticana, 1993, p. 9.

182 Ibid. p. 10.

183 Ibid. p. 13 & 14.

3. The Wisdom of God vs. the Wisdom of the World

The Rahnerian approach to the Incarnation described above is patently rationalistic. It is not only *not* consistent with traditional Catholic teaching - it has also crossed beyond the boundaries of foundational Protestant belief. *Faith in the constancy of the basics of what Christians have been taught since the Apostolic kerygma nowhere enters into Rahner's analysis!* He does not start his analysis from Faith. He starts it from a cold rationalism which attempts to understand Mysteries of Faith through limited human intellect.

True Catholics and Protestants start a search for understanding of Scripture from a position of Faith. Please observe that the author is not stating that Rahner had no Faith, he is simply stating that Rahner did not start his analysis of Scripture from the point of Faith in *Jesus Christ Crucified*. St. Paul tells us what will happen in that case,

> "Has not God made foolish the wisdom of this world? For since, in the wisdom of God, the world did not know God through wisdom, it pleased God through the folly of what we *preach* to save those who believe. For Jews demand signs and Greeks seek wisdom, but we preach Christ crucified, a stumbling block to the Jews and folly to the Gentiles, but to those who are called, both Jews and Greeks, Christ the power of God and the wisdom of God."[184]

Even a believing Christian who attempts to make rational and analyze God's Revelation from the perspective of the "wisdom of the world," rather than beginning their analysis in Faith ("in the wisdom of God) -- will be "made foolish." We are not speaking here of valid Christian exegesis (which by definition is scholarship which begins in Faith in *Christ Crucified*). We are speaking of those who attempt to analyze "the wisdom of God" in His Revelation through the perspective of "the wisdom of this world." *That process is just as doomed to failure for a professed Christian as it is for a pagan. That is what happens when one attempts to make the Mysteries of Faith totally rational to the human mind. Mysteries are Mysteries. They can only truly be seen through the eyes of Faith.*

It is one thing to study philosophy in order to gain a most valuable tool for a thorough understanding of theology. That process is

[184] I Cor. 1: 20-24.

both necessary and valid for a real theologian. But that tool must be at the service of theology - not its master. Our age is plagued with "Christian" scholars who for one reason or another have failed to make this distinction.

4. Attempting to Know God Outside Himself

Attempting to know God outside Himself, outside His Revelation, is not a new problem. The Gnostics did it in the first few centuries of the Church. Some Medieval theologians attempted it from a purely philosophical point of view.[185] "Attempting to know God outside Himself" was of particular concern to St. Bonaventure.[186] In his writings he centralizes his thought and method in a humble searching of Scripture in Faith in Christ crucified.

Bonaventure fully understood the concept of the "Theology of History." He had a highly developed "historical sense." He could easily have held conversation with today's extreme higher critics on these vital issues. Yet he would not have agreed with them for one basic reason. He would have understood they were (as Cardinal Siri put it in 1980) attempting to know God outside Himself.

Bonaventure would easily have told today's extreme higher critics what was wrong with their method - especially when they are attempting to understand Scripture. It is same thing which is generally wrong in every one of their speculations. Their approach to it is fundamentally flawed. Bonaventure tells us that any attempt to truly understand either,

(1) God and/or His creation (through observation of that creation), or
(2) Scripture

which fails to begin, continue, and finish in prayerful faith in Christ crucified is useless. In other words, the philosopher or Scripture scholar who clinically steriley inspects Scripture will come away with little true understanding of its content or its ultimate Author.

In his *Itinerarium,* Bonaventure describes the six steps of how one gets to know God. Whether one is merely at the level of attempt-

[185] We are *not* speaking here of Thomas Aquinas. Here we are speaking of the extreme Aristotelians of the Averoistic type who were the people St. Bonaventure truly directed some of his polemics against.

[186] Declared a Doctor of the Church by Pope Sixtus V in 1487.

ing to know God though "His traces in the Universe" or studying His Scripture, the same approach is required for true understanding. He now describes the fourth step,

> "4. First, therefore, I invite the reader to cry out in prayer through Christ crucified, by whose blood we are cleansed from the filth of sin. **Let us not believe that it is enough** to read without unction, to speculate without devotion, to investigate without wonder, to observe without joy, to act without godly zeal, to know without love, to understand without humility, to strive without divine grace, or to reflect as a mirror without divinely inspired wisdom. ... I am supposing that *the mirror offered by the outside world is of little or no value*."[187]

Is this an old-fashioned idea, somehow out of fashion in that it emanates from the late 13th century? Is it relevant today? Pope John Paul has recently reiterated this timeless truth,

> "Indeed, to arrive at a completely valid interpretation of words inspired by the Holy Spirit, one must first be guided by the Holy Spirit and it is necessary to pray for that, to pray much, to ask in prayer for the interior light of the Spirit and docilely accept that light, to ask for the love that alone enables one to understand the language of God"[188]

Bonaventure was fully trained and skilled in the philosophy of the Greeks. And he had respect for the Greek philosophers. But he clearly understood how unbridled philosophy could impede theology. Bonaventure is writing to and for Christians of all ages and predicts disaster for those who do not understand that God cannot be successfully approached and understood through sterile purely academic inquiry. *Bonaventure has herein also described the major dilemma of the extreme higher critics of our age*. Bonaventure is repreaching what Paul states:

---

[187] *The Works of Bonaventure, Mystical Opuscula*, Translated from the Latin by Jose de Vinck-Doctor Louvain University, St. Anthony Guild Press, Patterson, N.J., 1960. Quoted from the Prologue to *The Journey of the Mind to God*, pp. 7&8.

[188] *Address of His Holiness Pope John Paul II and Document of the Pontifical Biblican Commission*, p. 15.

> "Has not God made foolish the wisdom of this world? **For since, in the wisdom of God, the world did not know God through wisdom,** it pleased God through the folly of what we *preach* to save those who believe. For Jews demand signs and Greeks seek wisdom, but we preach Christ crucified, a stumbling block to the Jews and folly to the Gentiles, but to those who are called, both Jews and Greeks, Christ the power of God and the wisdom of God."[189]

Those who seek to know God strictly from an approach which begins outside prayer and God's sources of Revelation, who attempt to make totally rational His sources from outside those sources, they are doomed at the least to failure, and at the worst to personal disaster. As Pope John Paul II recently stated,

> "Catholic exegesis must be careful not to limit itself to the human aspects of biblical texts."[190]

5. Common sense arguments against Rahner et al.

Common sense tells us the following: neither Paul nor John orally taught nor wrote in a vacuum. Even by the time Paul was writing, there were quite literally thousands of Christians who had been personally previously taught by other Apostles. If Paul had attempted to introduce a new, different, or "changed" Christological doctrine - there would be a record of the resultant challenges to his teachings everywhere.

There was no challenge - because there was no change. If the written teaching of Paul on the Incarnation had been a "change" - at the very least - Peter would have challenged Paul on it. Some of the other disciples would surely have protested in the case of John's Christological writings if those writings had constituted a new or changed doctrine.

The earliest written records of what the early Christians actually did believe is exactly what the Apostles taught as a continuum, a totality, a whole. There was and is no single oral instruction, or letter or book of Scripture, which pretends to contain all Christian

[189] I Cor. 1: 20-24

[190] *Address of His Holiness Pope John Paul II*, p. 14.

doctrine. All that which was taught both orally and in written form constituted a whole. *Rahner is apparently attempting to analyze what was taught based upon his own rather unique interpretation of Scripture alone, while ignoring the existence and catechetical reality and effect of the initial apostolic oral instruction.*

Rahner presents absolutely no evidence (outside of his own conjecture and that of other extreme higher critics) for his thesis that what Paul and John wrote down is a "transformation" (change) of doctrine. Sts. Paul and John do give more details on the fullness of the Doctrine of the Incarnation than some of the earlier inspired writings. Paul's Incarnational *writings* come from almost three full decades after the death of Our Lord. By that time the early Docetist/ Gnostic heretics were denying the reality of Jesus' earthy life and His Divine Incarnation.[191]

---

[191] From Apostolic times the Church struggled with "Docetists" (who had Gnostic tendencies), and Judaizers. All three groups tended to overlap in many of their beliefs. The Judaizers held that Christians must still be bound by the elements of the Mosaic Law of the Old Testament. Some of the "Judaizers" were sincere Christians who were confused about the necessity for observance of the Law of Moses. Others however, also *were* Gnostic heretics. Most of those Jews had also been heavily "Helenized" -- they had been imbued with Greek Philosophy which was for the most part of a Platonic stripe. They tended to interpret Christian Revelation through pagan Greek philosophy rather than validly utilizing philosophy to verbally systematize the Christian Mysteries contained in Revelation.

These 1st century "Gnostics" (not to be confused with the highly systematic 2nd century Gnostics with whom St. Irenaeus contended), who claimed to have an elevated "Gnosis" (knowledge), claimed to be able to supplant or modify the commonly received Gospel message with their higher Gnosis, or knowledge, and became highly "boastful" about this. [Just exactly who and what these "1st century "Gnostics" were is subject to lively debate.] The "Docetists" claimed that Christ only appeared to suffer and die, that such suffering was therefore illusory. (See "Docetism" in Glossary). By the time that St. Paul wrote his "Incarnational" "Gospel" (which "Gospel" he tells us was directly revealed to him by Jesus Christ), the Church was struggling mightily against Docetist philosophy which was specifically denying the reality of the Incarnation, denying that Christ (God) truly became man. Most Docetists were not Christians as such, but were attempting to infiltrate the Christian communities with their philosophy. The highly Incarnational aspects of the writings of Paul and John (under the inspiration of the Holy Spirit) even more deeply immersed Christians of the Apostolic age in the Mystery of the Incarnation, and immunized them from the philosophy/heresies of the Docetist/Gnostics (which heresies most specifically denied the possibility/ reality of the Incarnation).

Later when St. John wrote his Gospel, that Gnostic problem had gotten even worse. *If* one wishes to get into the *conjecture game* as to why Paul and John give more detail on the Doctrine of the Incarnation -- it is much more probable that they did so under the inspiration of the Holy Spirit - in order to defend the *already constant* Church teaching on Christ's Divinity against the emerging Gnostic heretics. Von Balthasaar comments on this specific point;

> "In their epistles, St. Paul and St. John had already begun the struggle against Gnosticism, which in their time was in its early stages. Even so, it [gnosticism] was already showing its pernicious tendencies: promoting its seductive secret knowledge in the Christian communities, confusing simple believers, and *spreading the first dangerous 'pluralism' within the unity of the Faith.*"[192]

All of the early Christian writers taught that Scripture had to be read and understood as a whole, *and in the total light of that which had been received from the total Apostolic Tradition.* Rahner fails to see written Revelation as an *integral* whole. Worse, he fails to consider and integrate the Oral Teachings (part of Tradition) with the written (Scripture) as an integrated whole. These are two fruits of the "higher critical" mechanical approach to Revelation.

6. Modern Day Gnostics

Many late 20th century theological writers have commented on the similarities between the Gnostic heretics of the early Church and the extreme "higher critics" of the 20th century. Many have even coined them "modern day Gnostics." The greatest theologian of the Church at the end of the second century was St. Irenaeus. He began his *Adversus Haereses* (Against Heresies), around 180 A.D. It is one of the Patristic classics. It was primarily written to combat the Gnostic heretics of *his* day. It should be rementioned that Irenaeus was trained by St. Polycarp, who was trained by the Apostle John. A Bishop, St. Irenaeus is only one teaching generation away from the Apostles.

---

[192] *The Scandal of the Incarnation, Irenaeus Against the Heresies*, Selected and Introduced by Hans Urs von Balthasaar, Ignatius Press, San Francisco, 1990, p. 7.

In a study and modern presentation of the highlights of Irenaeus' *Against Heresies*, Hans Urs von Balthasaar commented:

> "So-called gnosis (knowledge) was an enormous temptation in the early Christian Church. By contrast, persecution, even the bloodiest, posed far less of a threat to the Church's continuing purity and further development. Gnosticism had its roots in late antiquity, drew on oriental and Jewish sources, and multiplied into innumerable esoteric doctrines and sects. Then, like a vampire, the parasite took hold of the youthful bloom and vigor of Christianity. **What made it so insidious was the fact that the Gnostics very often did not want to leave the Church. Instead, they claimed to be offering a superior and more authentic exposition of Holy Scripture**."[193] [Emphasis - authors]

7. Development of the Doctrine of the Incarnation

If there was one singular central doctrinal highlight of the Gnostic heresy, it was its denial of the Doctrine of the Incarnation. St. Irenaeus understood this very clearly, and he locked-in on this aspect of Revelation and defended the Doctrine of the Incarnation ***as expressed in Revelation***. Von Balthasaar further comments on this:

> "Gnosticism is radically anti-Christian, Irenaeus, with great perspicacity understood this, and showed it up for what it was. For him, Christianity is about the divine and spiritual Word becoming flesh and body. ***The redemption depends on the real Incarnation*, the real suffering on the Cross, and the real resurrection of the flesh.** All three of these are a scandal for Gnosticism. ... the main object of Irenaeus' anti-Gnostic polemic is the salvific character of the Incarnation of God's son and word."[194]

Irenaeus was one of the first real theologians to begin an attempt to systematize a theology of the Incarnation. The *seeds* of this theology are replete throughout sacred Scripture and sacred Tradition. But the specific theological definition and description

[193] *Ibid*, p. 1.
[194] Ibid. p. 3.

had to be developed by the first great Christological theologians. This *process of development* is basically true of all theology.

(1) **Many doctrines** (not just the Incarnation) **are germinal in Revelation.** A true understanding of them must (in prayer) be thought out with the brains which God gave us. For example: earlier we discussed the "*I and the Father are one*" quote of Our Lord.

(2) What does "*I and the Father are one*" mean? **Early Christians** had minds just as questioning as our own. **They sought to understand this revealed doctrine.** Solid Christians in prayer, lead by the Holy Spirit, began to develop a sound theology of the Trinity from this and other related speculations.

(3) Did it mean that there was no real difference between the Father and the Son? That is what the heretic Sebellius and those who followed him thought. **Heretical claims** that Christ was merely another "mode" of the Father **further lead faithful bishops/theologians to clearly and accurately begin to develop the Church's understanding of the essence of the true "Personhood" of Christ - The Doctrine of the Incarnation**.

Someone might ask, why didn't God spell out the total answer for us in the Bible? First of all, that question would betray a misunderstanding of Revelation. Revelation includes Tradition - as Scripture tells us. Someone might then respond, OK, why didn't God spell out the detailed answer for us in *Tradition and Scripture*?

8. Development of Doctrine in General

One of the answers to that question is as follows: individual men *wrote entire books to answer just this one question:* what does "The Father and I are one" mean? There are thousands of basic questions which occur to the intellect of man as he contemplates God's Revealed Word. You could not get the "total" answers to all these questions in the space of ten sets of the *Encyclopedia Brittanica*. Even if you could, how many Christian people could and would read all of it? How may Christians who read it all could and would understand *all of it*?

God gives us varying degrees of intellect. But none of us are omniscient. He gives us faith in his Revealed Word - in sacred Tradition and sacred Scripture. As we study His Revelation we are all humbled by our lack of understanding. That gift of humility leads us to understand the need for an authoritative interpreter and teacher of Revelation - the Magisterium. If we will but ask for increased humility, we can be obedient to that Magisterium, whose function, a humble intellect tells us is necessary. God gave us intellects to faithfully work within that framework.

Because of intellect, we can also understand the genius of Cardinal Newman as he cryptically describes the seed of doctrinal development:

> **"(1) No one doctrine can be named which starts complete at first** [vis-a-vis its theological development and full understanding], **and (2) gains nothing from the investigations of faith and (3) the attacks of heresy."**[195]

Even the attacks of heresy ultimately work toward the greater glory of God. Even heretical attacks ultimately lead the Church to greater understanding of God's Revealed Word.

9. St. Paul's "Gospel" - On the Incarnation

Rahner, when accepting the Christological message of Scripture *only up to Sts. Paul and John,* is very similar to a calculus student saying he was only going to accept calculus up to the point that they teach "differential equations," or a Christian or Jew saying he is only going to accept the first five of the Ten Commandments. St. Paul says;

> **"For I would have you know, brethren, that the gospel which was preached by me is not man's gospel. For I did not receive it from man, nor was I taught it, but it came through a Revelation of Jesus Christ."**[196]

[195] *Development of Christian Doctrine*, John Henry Cardinal Newman, Longmans, Green and Co. New York, 1927, p. 68.

[196] Galatians 1:11-12, RSV. Catholic Edition, 1965.

We cannot have it both ways. St. Paul clearly states that Jesus Christ directly revealed His "gospel" to Paul. What St. Paul writes does not reasonably allow for his Gospel being part of "divinely revealed allegories." Paul's words *directly contradict the following theory* wherein Scripture in general is seen as a case where,

> "God causes some strong and unusual spiritual commotion [in the soul of the sacred writer] which they of their own ingenuity, consciously or unconsciously, seek to utter and embody in allegories"[197]

In order for Rahner to be right, St. Paul has to be either deluded or a liar, and the Church wrong in her traditional teaching on this point. That is the logical choice which Karl Rahner's own words leave us with. *Rahner asks us to believe what Rahner says, based on Rahner's authority, in the place of what Scripture and the constant teaching Tradition of the Church tell us is based on God's authority.* Rahner says that instead of preaching an "Incarnational" (God-made-man-in- the-flesh) Theology, he wants an "Ascendental (Man-gradually-became-God) Christology" preached.

Rahner's writing leaves one with a choice between believing either the Apostle to the Gentiles and the Church's constant teaching over two millennia, or Rahner. What is said here is in no way meant to judge Rahner's intent or motives. There can be no way of knowing if Rahner perceived that his words forced that type of a choice. But St. Paul gives us direction on what to do if someone should appear to give us such a choice,

> *"But even if we, or an angel from heaven, should preach to you a gospel contrary to that which we preached to you, let him be accursed.* As we have said before, so now I say again, If any one is preaching to you a gospel contrary to that which you received, let him be accursed."[198]

---

[197] *From Newman to Congar*, Aidan Nichols, O.P., T&T Clark, Edinburgh, Scotland, p. 125. Nichols is quoting from *The Vitality of Christian Dogmas and Their Power of Evolution: A Study in Religious Philosophy*, A. Sabatier, 1898 English Edition.

[198] Galatians 1:8-9. RSV Catholic Edition, 1965.

Paul does not allow that his kerygmatic message is efficacious only for a time. Paul teaches his "gospel" for all time with no delimitation. Paul allowed no time in the future when his "gospel" which "*came through a Revelation of Jesus Christ*" might be changed. We are not allowed to do so even if someone such as Rahner thinks Paul's "gospel" is "*simply incomprehensible to modern man.*" That statement is typical of "higher critical" thinking which has been instrumental in forming many of our priests and laity for years.

10. St. John's Gospel - On the Incarnation

We have seen some of what Rahner objects to in Paul. Now let us look at St. John's Christology in his Gospel in order to see what Rahner is objecting to in John.

At the very beginning of St. John's Gospel, we read,

> "In the beginning was the Word, and the Word was with God, *and the Word was God*. **He was in the beginning with God, all things were made through him, and without him was not made anything which was made.**
>
> "In him was life, and the life was the light of men. The light shines in the darkness, and the darkness has not overcome it.
>
> "There was a man sent from God, whose name was John. He came for testimony, to bear witness to the light, that all might believe through him. He was not the light, but came to bear witness to the light. The true light that enlightens every man was coming into the world.
>
> "He was in the world, and the world was made through him, yet the world knew him not. He came to his own home, and his own people received him not.
>
> "**But to all who received him, who believed in his name, he gave the power to become children of God;** who were born, not of blood nor of the will of the flesh nor of the will of man, but of God.

***"And the Word became flesh and dwelt among us*, full of grace and truth; we have beheld his glory, glory as of the only Only-begotten[199] of the Father."**

(John bore witness to him, and cried, "This was he of whom I said, 'He who comes after me ranks before me, for he was before me.")

"And from his fullness have we all received, grace upon grace.

"For the law was given through Moses; grace and truth came through Jesus Christ.

"No one has ever seen God; the *Only-begotten*[200] who is in the bosom of the Father, he has made him known." [emphasis - authors]

---

[199] Author's change in the text from, *The Navarre Bible, St. John's Gospel, in the Revised Standard Version and New Vulgate with a commentary by the Faculty of Theology, University of Navarre*. So far this quote is word for word that of the RSV English edition as printed in the *Navarre Bible*. The RSV translates the Greek "monogenous" as "Son." Today, this is becoming quite commonplace -- but it is not accurate.
"Monogenous" has only one possible translation into English, and that translation is "Only-begotten" or possibly "Only generated." That is why all the English translations (either Protestant or Catholic) up until the last few years translated "Monogenous" as "only begotten" -- or less accurately as "One-begotten" -- because there is no other possible accurate translation. It is highly inaccurate to translate that word as "Son."
Even those not particularly familiar with Greek will recognize the prefix "Mono" as meaning "Only" or "One." The Greek "genous" signifies "begotten" or "generated" Many of our English words which have "Mono" for a prefix are direct imports from the Greek, e.g. "Monotheistic" signifying "Believing in One God." The author's reference of "Monogenous" is from the Greek text in *Greek Latin English New Testament Student's Workbook*, The Liturgical Press, Collegeville, MN., 1963, p. 244.
Additionally, the official Biblical Text of the Catholic Church since 1979, the *New Vulgate*, translates "Monogenous" as "Unigenitus" which also directly translates into English as "Only-begotten." Various "Creeds" of the Church since the 2nd General Council of the Church, (the Council of Constantinople in 381 A.D.), have the word "Son" after "Only-begotten" thus rendering, "Only-begotten Son." That was St. John's clear meaning. But no one had previously dared to drop "Only-begotten."

[200] Identical explanation to footnote immediately above, the author has again translated "unigenitum" as Only-begotten.

St. John tells us that, "In the beginning was the Word" and that "the Word was God." He further tells us that this Word is "Jesus Christ" and that " all things were made through him, and without him was not made anything which was made." John tells us that "the Word" Jesus Christ is God, the Creator of the Universe. Again St. John tells us that this "Word became flesh and dwelt among us," thus removing any doubt as to what and to Whom he is referring. According to John, God descended and became perfect man in the flesh. This Jesus Christ is the Incarnational God-in-the-flesh. This John unequivocally teaches in his Gospel.

St. Paul in like manner tells us,

> "For God has done what the law, weakened by the flesh, could not do; sending his own Son in the likeness of sinful flesh and of sin"[201]

> **"Make sure no one captivates you with the empty lure of 'philosophy' of the kind that human beings hand on, based on the principles of this world and not on Christ.** ***In him, in bodily form lives divinity in its fullness.***"[202] [emphasis -authors]

> "He is the image of the unseen God, the first-born of all creation, for in him were created all things in heaven and on earth: everything visible and invisible, thrones, ruling forces, sovereignties, powers - *all things were created through him and for him.*"[203]

> "He exists before all things and in him all things hold together, *and he is the Head of the body, that is, the Church.*"[204]

Sts. Paul and John are in total agreement that Jesus Christ is God Incarnate, God in the flesh. They teach an Incarnational Christology which says, God the Creator became Man. St. Paul tells us he received this doctrine in a direct revelation from "Jesus Christ."

---

[201] Romans 8:3 RSV Catholic Edition, 1965.
[202] Colossians 2:8-9. New Jerusalem Bible, June 18. 1985 Edition.
[203] Ibid. 1:15-16.
[204] Ibid. 1:17-18.

That is specifically what Rahner confronts in saying he wants its opposite "Ascendance Christology" preached.

Rahner also wants us to stop using phrases such as "We are saved by the Blood of Christ." But that is exactly what Tradition and Scripture tell us to preach. How could anything be more central to the Gospel message. In taking these stands, whether he intended it or not, *Rahner ranges himself with the 2nd century Gnostics with whom St. Irenaeus had to do theological battle.*

It is THE central message of Christianity which Rahner wants us to stop preaching! Rahner likewise wants us to stop preaching "Three persons in one God," and "God sent his Son into the world." These catechetical formulae are at the heart and soul of the Faith for any Christian. But Rahner wants them replaced. Many seminarians and theology students have taken Rahner's advice quite literally.

If in fact we followed Rahner's advice, what would be left of the central core of God's New Testament Revelation? How could it any longer honestly be called "Preaching the Gospel"? And why is this so important? As stated repeatedly before, Rahner's theology texts (and those of his theological look-alikes) are the centerpieces of many of the Catholic colleges and seminaries in the West. That teaching has affected all of us through the "trickle-down" affect. Given all of the above, it is difficult to conceive that Rahner understood the concept of the Divine Inspiration of Scripture in any sense of the word that would not strip it of all substantive meaning within the traditional Christian concept. That is particularly true in the cases of the writings of Sts. Paul and St. John.

Cardinal Siri gives his analysis of this situation in the following manner;

> "It is not therefore a question here [*with Rahner*] of the delicate nuances and images often ineffable through which at times one intimately lives the Mystery of the Incarnation, the mystery of a man conceived in the womb of a woman by direct intervention of God.
>
> "Rahner's discourses as a whole concern the intellectual and spiritual course of a man [*Jesus*] conceived naturally, and that cannot be called «incarnation.» *That theory*, [*of Rahner's*] *whether one wants it or not, is the negation of the*

Incarnation and the alteration of the reality of Christ."[205] [Parens. & emphasis - authors]

In contraposition to Rahner's convoluted expressions of his Christology, we present the following quote from Cardinal Archbishop Siri who therein presents the traditional teaching of the Church on the reality of the Doctrine of Christ's Incarnation:

> "This fundamental truth of the reality of the Incarnation constitutes a general criterion through which all subjects, questions, themes regarding the whole economy of Redemption must be seen and understood. *Thus the mystery of the Church, its origin and its constitutional reality are founded on the Incarnation.*"[206]

11. Vatican II Fathers Contradict Rahner's Ideas

There are many other theological areas within which Rahner wrote in a confusing manner, particularly in his Post-Vatican II period. They include (but not limited to); (1) the Immaculate Conception, (2) the definition and function of grace, (3) the definition of Inspiration, (4) the Church's definitions of Articles of Faith (and Rahner's concomitant problematic definition/understanding of pluralism), (5) distinctions between God and man, (6) the very concept of a constant Apostolic Kerygma, and in particular, (7) Rahner constantly brought into question the Church's doctrine on Tradition, and (8) both Paul and John's Doctrine of the Incarnation.

Contrary to the expressed thought of Rahner, the Council Fathers at Vatican II begin the very first sentence of their *Dogmatic Constitution on Divine Revelation* with words from the introduction in St. John's Gospel,

> "The sacred synod assents to the words of St. John, who says, 'We proclaim to you *the eternal life* which was with the Father and was made manifest to us -- that which we

---

[205] *Gethsemane: Reflections on the Contemporary Theological Movement*, Joseph Cardinal Siri, Archbishop of Genoa, Franciscan Herald Press, Chicago (in cooperation with, Editions De La Fraternite De La Tres Sainte Vierge Marie, Rome, Italy, 1981). p. 283 & 284.

[206] Ibid. p. 290.

> have seen and heard we proclaim also to you, so that you may have fellowship with us; and our fellowship is *with the Father and with his Son Jesus Christ*.'" (John 1:2-3)[207] [emphasis - authors]

The Council Fathers also chose to begin *Dei Verbum*'s New Testament section with three quotes from the Gospel of John and two from Paul. The first paragraph of "The New Testament" section includes one each from Paul and John,

> "For when the time had fully come (cf. Gal. 4:4) the Word became flesh and dwelt among us full of grace and truth." (cf John 1:14).[208]

SUMMATION: The Council Fathers at Vatican II under the inspiration of the Holy Spirit chose to open their document on Revelation with an Incarnational Christological quote from the beginning of the Gospel of St. John. They followed that up with two more "Incarnational" quotes, one each from Paul and John in the first paragraph of *Dei Verbum*'s section on the New Testament. Could there have been any greater tribute to the Incarnational Christology of Sts. Paul and John which is the constant teaching of the Church? Could there be a clearer contradiction to the Christological theories of Karl Rahner and his extreme higher critic look-alikes?

Some of the Christological theories of Rahner were known in their germinal stages prior to Vatican II. But the Council Fathers under the inspiration of the Holy Spirit (in contraposition to Rahner et al's theories) reaffirmed the timeless Apostolic Kerygma of Sts. Paul and John. Where then do extreme "higher critics" find a basis for one of their favorite charges, that those who seriously disagree with Rahner's Christology are "Pre-Vatican II"? In fact, if anyone is "Pre-Vatican II," it would have to have been Karl Rahner (died in 1984) whose Christological views (as expressed in his writings) the Conciliar documents contradicted.

---

[207] Dogmatic Constitution on Divine Revelation, *Dei Verbum*, Prologue, *Vatican Council II, The Conciliar and Post Conciliar Documents, Vol 1.* Flannery, New Revised Edition 1992, p. 750.

[208] Ibid. 760.

From St. Irenaeus in the 2nd century, to the Council Fathers at Vatican II, to von Balthasaar's expressed Christology above, we have faithful Catholic theology repudiating the Christology and exegetical positions of Rahner. We can either follow the thinking of Rahner and his theological look-a-likes, or we can follow the constant teaching of the Church as reaffirmed by the Fathers at Vatican II.

12. Rahner as Only One of Many "Higher Critics"

Why is this discussion of Rahner's writing so important?

Rahner is quite representative of the thought of the Extreme higher critics. One has to work very hard indeed to put an orthodox traditional interpretation on much in the later writings of Rahner. That fact explains the serious potential for doctrinal confusion in the mind of the readers of *both* Rahner and his theological look-alikes.

The potential for theological confusion in the "higher critical" approach to Scripture and Tradition has now filtered down to millions of Catholics in both their approach to, and understanding of both sacred Scripture and sacred Tradition. In the last thirty years, where is the Western Catholic (particularly in the U.S. and Canada) who has not heard sermons and homilies which speak of the Reality of Christ's Incarnation in a confused manner.

That confusion is one of the fruits of extreme higher criticism. *Rahner has been quoted so extensively here because (1) he is the most "respectable" of the extreme "higher critics" in the academic world, and (2)* his written theological works have been used more extensively in Catholic Universities and Seminaries than any other higher critic.[209] Expose the potential dangers in the views of the most representative, the most quoted, and the most respectable member of a group -- and you usually expose the dangers inherent in the entire group.

Was Rahner just honestly confused, in some manner not able to see the Traditional Christological forest for the trees? Did he not see the *real* points of departure? Only God knows. As for his

[209] Of late Rahner is gradually being replaced by other extreme higher critics. Beware of his replacements!

look-alikes (just as examples) we could have easily shown virtually the same Christological expressed thought in the writings of Hans Küng, Schillebeeckx, or Tielhard de Chardin (and many others). In their basic approaches to the Doctrine of the Incarnation, the innerancy and historicity of Scripture in any meaningful sense of the word, Tradition, miracles, or prophecy, they were all coming from the same *basic* rationalistic positions.

13. Extreme Higher Critics Meant Well, But Their Theology is Confusing the Faithful

The point is; *all of these men can be at least implicitly quoted on many sides of the same issue from various points of their careers and from various points of their works*. That is one of the *confusion factors* in their writings. However, the constant teaching of the Church is not confused at all. Just as examples, the Church constantly and *clearly* teaches that;

(1) God actually "descended" and fully became man in Christ,
(2) Tradition is to be equally accepted and honored as source of Revelation with Scripture,
(3) the *four* Gospels must be understood as a whole,
(4) they in turn must be understood within the totality of Scripture taken as a whole,
(5) God's Revelation in the Apostolic Kerygma remains not only relevant but essential for all time,
(6) the Magisterium under the guidance and protection of the Holy Spirit is the authoritative interpreter of God's Revelation.

14. Their Later Works are More Problematical

Again, on Christology and many other issues, it is not unusual to be able to quote these men from various stages of their academic careers on both or many sides of the same issue. In many cases, it is the later works of these men which betray the most problematic areas of their views of God's Revelation, and the development of doctrine out of that Revelation. When one exposes their dangerous expressions or questions in theology in their later work, one is frequently questioned for not having pointed out their at least one time expressed "belief" in certain Dogmas of the Church.

15. Specially Addressed to Academics and Theologians

[If the general reader wishes to do so, he or she can easily jump ahead to the next section entitled, "Rahner's Method."]

This is no longer merely an academic theological issue which affects only academics. It has now become a pastoral issue. In the interests of clarity, this author understands that at least at one point in their careers, each one of the above mentioned men has clearly stated his adherence to the traditional teachings of the Church on each one of the subjects discussed. Let it also be clearly understood that this author truly believes those various statements of orthodoxy to have been made sincerely and genuinely. It is also understood that these men were not mutual theological/philosophical clones, that there were significant differences in the approach and conclusions made by these men on a significant number of theological issues.

16. Historic Imminentism

But they also mutually wrote things which have lead to disastrous consequences for the belief systems of many Christians through the trickle-down effect. Küng, Schillebeeckx, and de Chardin, also were close to Rahner in his "Historic Imminentism." This concept alone has been understood by many seminarians such that:

(1) Because man is historically evolving in his existential reality, then

(2) What was theologically true for man in the past [while it may have been true for him then] does not necessarily theologically apply for men of later generations,

(3) Therefore our theological reality develops within the historical context and experience of man within his own individual historic and cultural setting. *There is* an

implicit subjectivism in all of this (whether intended or not) which can easily tend toward questioning of objective perception of the Articles of Faith,

(4) All of this has confused very many seminarians as to whether the doctrines the Church once taught She still holds.

(5) Once such seminarians become parish priests, this leads to hesitation to preach many doctrines of the Church clearly. In worse scenarios, it leads to what the laity often refer to as "flaky sermons."

***At this level it is no longer just an academic issue*! It is also a pastoral issue!** Whether these authors have been rightly or wrongly understood by the parish priests who previously studied them in seminary is not at issue here. The issue is that this understanding as expressed in sermon, homily, and catechetical expression has now begun to have a disastrous effect on many of the faithful. For many laity, it has subsequently become a pitched battle to teach, preserve, and protect the basic Faith of their children from various sermons, homilies, and catechetical teaching of some parish priests. AGAIN, AT THAT LEVEL THIS IS NO LONGER JUST AN ACADEMIC OR THEOLOGICAL ISSUE. IT HAS BECOME A PASTORAL ISSUE THAT INVOLVES THE CHURCH AT THE LEVEL OF THE INDIVIDUAL MEMBERS' BASIC FAITH SYSTEM.

There are measures of truth in the higher critics' historic imminentist position, in the sense that systematic theology developed gradually, and understanding of the totality of that "system," under the guidance of the Holy Spirit, increased over a period of time within that system. There *is* a theology of history recognized even by as early a theologian as St. Bonaventure. But what is also true is that, *the full concept of the expressed truths of the basics of the Apostolic Kerygma which will last till the end of time* seems to have *practically* escaped many leading higher critics.

They all at one point or another express their belief in the continuum of that Kerygma, but their particular view of "historic consciousness" and the concept of a theological staged evolution appears in a certain sense to be almost Joachimistic.[210] Such individuals write, talk, and give lectures and homilies which can readily lead to the conclusion that there is nothing timeless about specific doctrinal reality in the Apostolic Kerygma!

---

210 Joachim of Fiori - 12th century Cistercian Abbot and mystic. There is no question he intended to be entirely orthodox. In the year of his death (1202 A.D.) he submitted all of his writings to "the examination of (Pope) Innocent the III, but died before any judgement was passed."

However, later, some of his teaching was formally condemned "by Pope Alexander VI in 1256." The teaching which caused the most stir was that on the "Eternal Gospel."

Joachim's Scriptural exegesis held that there were three distinct periods of the Church corresponding to the Three Persons of the Blessed Trinity. The first period or state was that of the Old Testament which was the stage of the Father. The second was that of the New Testament (corresponding with the Son) which would end some time "soon."

"Joachim held that the second period was drawing to a close, ... and the third epoch would actually begin with some great cataclysm which he tentatively calculated would befall later in 1260."

Joachim held that the third period to come would be "the Kingdom of the Holy Spirit, *a new dispensation* of universal love, which will proceed from the Gospel of Christ, but transcend the letter of it, and in which there will be no need of disciplinary institutions." He interpreted this time of the "eternal Gospel" from a strained reading of the Book of Revelation 14:6. It is this which many extreme "higher critics" have in common with Joachim: a new age of the Church wherein Joachim anticipated that "disciplinary institutions" would disappear and the "Eternal Gospel" would "transcend the letter of the Gospel of Christ." It is in that sense that the author described their position as "almost Joachimistic."

It was this particular "eternal Gospel" teaching (concerning a new, in some ways theologically unique, and final age in the Church) which ultimately lead to a formal condemnation of some of Joachim's teaching. It also lead many 13th century Franciscans into some extreme theological positions which St. Thomas Aquinas specifically contended with in his *Summa Theologica*. (In Pt. 1-II, Q. 106 Art. 4, **St. Thomas says, "Nevertheless, we are *not* to look forward to a state wherein man is to possess the grace of the Holy Spirit more perfectly than he has possessed it hitherto, especially the apostles who *received the first fruits of the Spirit, i.e., sooner and more abundantly than others*"**) [This is quoted from *Summa Theologica*, St. Thomas Aquinas, First Complete American Edition, Vol. 1, Translated by Fathers of the English Dominican Province, Benzinger Bros. Inc. New York, 1947, p. 104])

Also, St. Bonaventure himself (while subscribing to some other positions of Joachim) had to suppress some Franciscan schools of thought which had proceeded from the "Eternal Gospel" teachings of Joachim. All of the quotes in this footnote not assigned to the *Summa Theologica* are taken from the 1913 edition of the *Catholic Encyclopedia*, Vol. 8, p. 407.

There *is* a legitimate study of Doctrinal Development as opened by Cardinal Newman that is *not* at root "rationalist." But these men have, perhaps without intending it, ultimately approached Doctrinal Development through avenues heavily tainted with rationalism. This is not just the opinion of this author. As stated earlier, Cardinal Seri performed an almost definitive study of that general process in his book *Gethsemane*. Cardinal Seri intends to be charitable, but he also calls a spade a spade.

Most faithful academics approach these men with the time-honored academic method of seeing first and foremost their achievement, and what they accomplished. For very good reason, academics are chary about harshly judging another academic. They are justifiably especially nervous about appearing to over-simplify the positions of a theologian or academic. Also, with charitable intention they tend to understate criticism of another theologian or academic. That approach is advisable and admirable within the confines of the academic community.

However, in the case of many of the extreme higher critics, their theories have now effectively penetrated out of the academic community down to the level of the pews. It has now become a pastoral issue. Therefore, charity towards one's fellow academic must now be especially balanced with that charity which in justice must be applied to the pastoral reality and needs of the non-academics. It may now be time to look more closely at and reassess the actual effect and pastoral fruit of the writings of the extreme higher critics.

Who would attack Aidan Nichols, O.P.'s sympathy for the academic? In his *From Newman to Congar* he justifiably expresses his admiration for the great and genuine theological insights of Rahner (especially in his early years), Schillebeeckx, and many other higher critics. But he is led to make the following observation about Schillebeeckx:

> "Schillebeeckx's new theological method carries with it, in addition to the promise of rich insight into the gospels and their spiritual application to the present, *seeds of destruction not found in the more classical theological terrain which he has abandoned.* Most notably: *here revelation and salvation tremble on the brink of absorption into the sea of*

> *human consciousness at large*. Refusing the luxury of an metaphysic, how can one state the difference between the Church's liturgical remembering of Jesus and say, Herbert Marcuse's critical remembering of Orpheus?
>
> "Where our own topic, that of doctrinal development, is concerned, *it is difficult to think that the later Schillebeeckx has left sufficient room for the rôle of the Church's public doctrine in his account of Christian believing*. While not denying - indeed, affirming - the christological and Trinitarian dogmas, he has ceased to seek their re-formulation, leaving them in the main, to one side as conceptual icons that tempt one to pure contemplation rather than the engaged mysticism of political commitment. Such an emancipatory and critical praxis will find greater encouragement in **a new christology *founded rather on the Synoptic Gospels than on the Gospel of John*.** Although Schillebeeckx regards the conciliar christology as a faithful reflection, within the Greek patristic framework, of the original New Testament kerygma, proclaiming as it does a Jesus who is at once wholly on God's side and wholly on ours as well, he considers it, nevertheless, a unilateral development, which set restrictive limits to the image of Jesus in the later Church. *For the later Christology is too frequently merely occasioned by the concrete Jesus of history*:
> [Italics - authors]"[211]

Nichols book deals specifically with the subject of *Doctrinal Development*. Most of his observations in *From Newman to Congar* about Rahner *are based upon Rahners earlier work*. Most of the quotes from Rahner which the reader has previously seen in *Trial, Tribulation & Triumph* come from Rahner's later work.

Does not Rahner in his later work also want, "a new christology *founded rather on the Synoptic Gospels than on the Gospel of John*." Doesn't a careful scrutiny of the later works of Rahner display many similarities with those elements which Nichols observes in the later Schillebeeckx as "seeds of destruction"? From the vantage point of pastoral theology, what has been the cumulative

[211] *From Newman to Congar, The Idea of Doctrinal Development from the Victorians to the Second Vatican Council*, Aidan Nichols, O.P., T&T Clark, Edinburgh, Scotland, 1990, p. 272.

affect of the writings of a whole host of those of the *Contemporary Theological Movement?*

17. Rahner's Method

In the mid-20th century Rahner and many other "higher critics" came to hope that if one man could amass sufficient knowledge of a sufficient number of subjects -- and hold them together long enough for analysis, then they could make knowledge of Creation and Creator more fully rational. They ultimately hoped to comprehend and make rational the Christian Mysteries and their respective formulas of Faith. They thought that then man could arrive at true "objective" knowledge of these subjects. They had obviously long since lost sight of the Christian fact that those Christian formulae are based on God's Revelation to man of God's *Mysteries*. Despite their protestations to the contrary, they appear to have lost full sight of that fact that the Omniscient God's revealed Mysteries are, by definition, beyond the full comprehension of non-omniscient man.

The intelligence of man *either before or after the "Fall in the Garden"* can be likened to a Royal Gnat riding on the elephantine back of God's Revelation. As long as the gnat understands his limitations and stays put, he can with the elephant's aid see from a great height. He may not even fully comprehend the full significance of the blades of grass so far below him. But he will comprehend much more than a gnat who has lost his full appreciation of the vantage point he enjoys from that "back." A gnat who lacks that appreciation and actually hops down quickly becomes lost in those blades of grass. His vision becomes obscured by their now relatively immense size.

In the end, the higher critics who had inadvertently hopped down amongst the blades of data grass, one by one became frustrated with this "information gathering" method and subsequent analysis attempt. Ergo, Rahner's lament that ultimately he had to give up on the possibility of one man acquiring sufficient knowledge and subsequently being capable of synthesizing it sufficiently to put all the pieces together. Rahner finally concluded that no man was smart enough to do that, which lack of intellect he called man's "gnosologic concupiscence."

Rahner describes his perception of this phenomena in the following manner;

> "What else can man do in his situation characterized by a 'gnosologic concupiscence' (which does not allow the enormous mass of learning to be elaborated or synthesized) but withdraw towards this original center; **a center of this kind must exist**."[212] [parens are Rahner's, emboldened emphasis added]

The "center" he is looking for can be quickly found in a *faithful climb* back up onto the "elephantine back of God's Revelation." Once there, the impossibility of omniscient understanding on the part of man[213] is no longer frustratingly implicitly required nor expected. But the view is once again simply mystically spectacular.

---

212 *Motivatione della fede oggi in Teologia dall'esperienza dello spirito*, Nuovi Saggi VI, ed. Pauline, Roma 1978, PP. 26-27.

213 Note: Rahner's "gnosologic *concupiscence*" phrase acknowledges mans limited intelligence and understanding here on earth. Perhaps unintentionally, he describes the fact that, since the fall of Adam, man at best has limited intelligence. Rahner's usage of the word "concupiscence" *almost* sounds Thomistically Catholic. The phrase "gnosologic concupiscence" is a classic example of Rahner's mastery at utilizing words in such a way that they have an almost Thomistic "sound," even when within Rahner's context they have no fully traditional *Catholic* significance. (See Glossary - "Concupiscence")

Both the Fourth Lateran and the First Vatican Councils teach that even after man is raised to the Beatific Vision, God is "Incomprehensible" to man (DNG. 428, 1732). "Although the blessed see God, they do not comprehend Him, because God is absolutely incomprehensible to every created intellect, and He cannot grant to any creature the power of comprehending Him as He Comprehends Himself." (*Catholic Encyclopedia*, 1917 Ed. Vol. 7, p. 172.)

After the "fall" of man in the Garden (which Rahner also did not describe with fully Catholic clarity) even that intelligence which Man originally received from God is flawed through the concupiscence consequent from Original Sin. All of the above Rahner vaguely appears to allude to with the term "gnosologic concupiscence."

Even if Rahner was truly referring in some manner to Original Sin with his term "gnosologic concupiscence," Rahner does not thereby address the root problem in his dilemma. That root problem is that even before the "fall of man," before his concupiscence, man did not have omniscience, did not possess sufficient intellect to "comprehend" God, or all God's Divinely revealed Mysteries *in a moment*. Genesis tells us of God having to explain many things to the still innocent Adam in the Garden. From this we learn that man could not fully comprehend *in a moment* the Divinely revealed Mysteries of our Creator even prior to the concupiscence entailed in the subsequent "fall."

Rahner's last phrase "*a center of this kind must exist*" sounds possibly like a painfully heart-rending prayer of a man who has somehow become lost, at least suspects it, and is hoping against hope to find his way home. If that be the case, such a man is not to be deprecated, but prayed for, because "*But for the grace of God, there go I.*" If someone has *not* hopped down from the elephantine back of God's Revelation as traditionally taught by the Church, he or she can only thank God.

It is important that we reemphasize a major point. No judgment is being passed upon what was in Rahner's or any higher critics' heart, or upon their intellectual honesty. *Similarly*, Origen was one of the most prominent 3rd century Fathers of the Church. His Scriptural studies and exegesis as well as his commentaries on the sacraments are avidly studied by scholars to this day. He provided the Church with a great record of the theological thought and understanding of his time. No true modern scholar believes that Origen ever *intended* to be anything but totally orthodox, nor do they deny his genuine genius.

Yet the fact remains that centuries after his death a fair number of his teachings were ultimately condemned by three General

---

[213 cont.] As Fr. William Most explains, "The human soul, and so the human consciousness of Jesus, did enjoy the beatific vision from the first moment of [His] human conception. That vision made known to Him the day and hour of the parousia. *In itself, the beatific vision contains all knowledge* [with the exception of *comprehending God as he comprehends Himself* - as taught by 4th Lateran and 1st Vatican Councils*]. Yet any created soul, human or angelic, even the human soul of Jesus, is finite. Hence, at any given moment, it will not contain infinite knowledge* . So, in itself, that vision could omit a given point such as the parousaic day and hour. Mk 13:32 tells us that such is the case with the angels. However, the Magisterium insists that Jesus, even as man, did know the day and the hour." *The Consciousness of Christ*, 1980, p. 144.

A fully Catholic explanation of the phenomenon which Rahner is attempting to describe is this; (1) Only God is Omniscient. (2) What Rahner et al. were attempting ultimately required omniscience. (3) Therefore, they were pre-doomed to failure.

As with many "higher critics," in the later Rahner there appears to be a lack of understanding of just how limited the intelligence of even the smartest man is. This, coupled with a seeming lack of a truly full appreciation for what a Divinely Revealed Mystery is, leads to many predictably questionable theological conclusions.

Councils of the Church.[214] That does not mean that Origen did not do his best in his own mind to obey God and understand His Revelation. The same must in charity be assumed for the extreme higher critics.

Similarly, Rahner's writings have not been formally condemned by a council, nor publicly repudiated by a Pope. Yet many Catholic scholars wonder whether it is only a matter of time until one of the above happens. But even if that were to happen, that would not objectively demonstrate that Rahner was not, (1) brilliant (which he definitely was), and (2) essentially a man of good will toward Christ and his Church. Only God can read hearts.

Prior to the ensuing quote, we should mention that Rahner made continued use of Hegelian Dialectic throughout his works. Books have already been written and new ones are currently being composed on the ramifications of his "Hegelian" aspect. The quote below is from C.S. Lewis, an Anglican Christian who deeply appreciated and understood both the strengths and weaknesses of our 20th century, of its struggles with the concept of truly objective knowledge and/or certitude in theology and philosophy. In the 3rd book of his Trilogy, Lewis wrote the following piece of dialogue about a man who had walked much the same intellectual/philosophical road as many extreme "higher critics."

---

[214] It is still a bone of contention amongst scholars as to whether Origin meant to teach certain doctrines as teachings of the Church, or whether he was simply recording some of his personal "speculations" wherein he discussed ideas such as "the pre-existence of souls" or a "final apocatastasis." In either case, his extremely allegorical interpretation of Scripture coupled with his dualistic Platonic philosophy lead him to conclusions which are incompatible with the message of the Gospel. Many of his ideas (and certainly the fruits of his extremely allegorical approach) led some of his later admirers such as Eusebius of Caesarea into trouble; e.g., it is quite possible that such "ideas" contributed to the Semi-Arianist position of Eusebius of Caesarea. Once some of Origin's ideas had been clearly critically brought to the fore by a man of the stature of St. Jerome, it was probably only a matter of time until a formal condemnation was forthcoming.

It is in this same vein that many contemporary Catholic scholars believe that once Cardinal Siri had published *Gethsemane*, that it became only a matter of time before some Council or Pope begins a process which will end in the condemnation of many of Rahner's ideas, at least as some of them are expressed in his writings.

> "Therefore he knew that everything was lost. It is incredible how little this knowledge moved him. It could not, because he had long since ceased to believe in [objective] knowledge itself. He had passed from *Hegel* into Hume, thence through pragmatism, and thence through logical positivism, and out at last into the complete void. The indicative mood now corresponded to no thought that his mind could entertain."[215]

F. THE EFFECT OF RAHNER ET. AL. ON OUR GENERATION - ON OUR BELIEF SYSTEM AND CAPACITY FOR BELIEF

The working majority of those in Western Europe and North America who today are called "theologians," were to one degree or another formed in or affected by the thought of Rahner and his theological look-alikes. Many of them accept Rahner et al.'s thought one hundred percent. Working back from that extreme end of "higher criticism" one can and does find a veritable rainbow of theological positions, with varying degrees of their faith accepted as in its traditional expression. The "rainbow" varies all the way from 100% "Rahnerian" down to "critical" Catholics who unquestionably express their faith in terms which are fully resonant with the teachings of the Magisterium.

1. Higher Critic's Portrayal of Magisterial Catholics

A significant number of even the faithful "higher critics" can tend to portray those we shall call "historicitists" as being ill-informed, poorly educated, credulous, or even ridiculous. *For the purposes of this discussion*, "historicitists" are defined as people who accept a significantly higher percentage of Biblical events, personages, and prophecies as literally factual versus allegorical than most "higher critics" so accept. As a result of higher critics inaccurate portrayal of "historicitists," many historicitists involuntarily become almost

---

[215] *That Hideous Strength*, Third Book of the Trilogy, C.S. Lewis, McMillan Publishing Co., Third Publishing, 1973, p. 353.

publicly defensive/apologetic about belief in the revealed events and figures contained in Tradition or Scripture.

As discussed above, a significant portion of the most extreme representatives of the "higher criticism" school currently enjoy positions of standing in Catholic colleges, seminaries, most diocesan catechetical schools, and other Catholic academic circles. In such posts, *higher critics have enjoyed the power of position now for twenty to thirty years or more*. This in many ways has resulted in conveyance of the general impression that those who disagree with them are ignorant of modern Scriptural research. Consequently, many Catholics who today tend *generally* to believe in the historicity of the Bible, have in the last twenty years been marginalized; portrayed as remnants of unscholarly positions. Yet nothing could be further from the truth.

2. The Church and Historicity of Scripture

We examine the case of Jonas here not because anyone's faith will rise or fall on the issue, but because it is the classic example wherein "higher critics" overstate their case. Again, as of this writing, any Catholic is legitimately allowed to take either an "historic Jonas" or an "allegoric Jonas" position (or any modified combination thereof). And no Catholic may challenge the "good standing" within the Church of any individual Catholic who takes either position. *The problem is not with Catholic "good standing" on this issue, but with intellectual and academic respectability and credibility.*

This section deals primarily with *that* academic respectability and credibility issue, as it relates to "generally" believing in the historicity of the Bible. Again, as used in this book, the term "historicitists" refers to Catholics who would, *as examples*, generally believe,

(1) in the reality of the direct miracles of Our Lord,
(2) the existence of a "first couple" (which Scripture describes as Adam and Eve -- and therefore such a "believer" would automatically reject "Polygenism"[216]),

---

[216] If the reader is unfamiliar with this term, see Glossary.

(3) that Jesus actually rose from the dead just as Scripture describes it,
(4) that Peter actually cured the cripple as described in Acts,
(5) that Paul was blinded on the road to Damascus and subsequently received back his sight,
(6) that Jesus actually prophesied the fall of Jerusalem (and therefore concomitantly that this "prophecy" was not invented by a Scriptural author after the fact),
(7) that Peter actually by the power of God struck Ananias and Saphira dead.
(8) They would also in many cases consider it possible, some even probable, that the Biblical story of Jonas is essentially an historical account.

The above are only a few examples.

A historicitist is generally a believer in the traditional teachings of the Church. As a rule the historicitist will determine his understanding of a Scripture passage in the following manner:

(1) When the traditional interpretation of the Church on a given passage is quite literal "proper", and,
(2) When evidence to the contrary of that "proper"[217] (meaning word for word) traditional interpretation is no stronger than some "scholarly opinions," then,
(3) Such a historicitist is going to *generally* hold with the Church's traditional "proper" interpretation of specific Scripture passages as the most prudent course.

3. A "Historicitist" is not a Blind Literalist

When we speak of the "generally believing" Catholic "historicitist," we are definitely *not* talking about rigid word-for-word literalism such as the earth cannot possibly be more than six or seven or eight thousand years old, or that God absolutely created the world in six physical days, no more, no less. When we speak of the historicitist position, we are *not* talking about a person who

[217] Again, see the footnote discussion of "proper" as "word-for-word" in the section on "The Authority of the Fathers."

universally applies a "proper" (word-for-word) literalist historicity in cases which no serious Catholic scholar, no matter what his or her position, would take seriously.

Again, we are talking about the type of person who merely holds with the traditional Scriptural exegesis of the Church. The Council of Trent bound all Catholics to this view with one of its Dogmatic Canons!

> "Furthermore, to check unbridled spirits, it [the Council of Trent] decrees that no one relying on his own judgment shall, in matters of faith and morals pertaining to the edification of Christian doctrine, distorting the Holy Scriptures in accordance with his own conceptions, presume to interpret them contrary to that sense which holy Mother Church, to whom it belongs to judge of their true sense and interpretation, has held and holds, ***or even contrary to the unanimous teachings of the Fathers.***"[218] [emphasis - authors]

Therefore, where that traditional exegesis attributes the "proper" (word-for-word) literal meaning to a Scripture passage, that is the interpretation which the faithful "historicitist" accepts.

We are also talking about a person who approaches Scripture following the instruction of St. Cyril of Jerusalem,

> "Prepare your own heart to *receive* doctrine, to have fellowship in holy mysteries."[219]

---

[218] *Canons and Decrees of the Council of Trent*, Original Text with English Translations, Rev. H.J. Schroeder, O.P., Herder Book Co., 1941, (from the Decrees of the Fourth Session), pp. 18 & 19. Here the Council is talking specifically of matters of "faith and morals." Many "higher critics" have used that as a door through which to drive theological trucks. They attempt to put the Magisterium in the position of having the burden of proof to demonstrate line-by-line that an interpretation of a particular Scripture passage is specifically dealing with Faith and Morals. With this method, they have chipped away at Christian belief in the general historicity of the Bible. Every Biblical event becomes for them an opportunity to question that event's and the Bible's historic authenticity.

[219] *St. Cyril of Jerusalem's Lectures on the Christian Sacraments*, Edited by Lady Margaret Professor of Divinity, University of Oxford, S.P.C.K., London, 1951, Cat. 16, p.51.

A "historicitist," while he or she believes that modern Scriptural research has been valuable, does not then however perfunctorily believe that all the Fathers of the Church were naive rustics - they follow the instructions of Trent and Leo XIII in this matter.

The historicitist also does not believe that doctrines the Fathers of the Church said they received from Apostolic Tradition, have now in the 20th century, somehow *automatically* become fair game for 180 degree turnarounds - as some higher critics would have it. Some would specifically single out the Scripture scholar, Raymond Brown, as an example of such an extreme higher critic. His effect on Catholic academics in North America has simply been immense over the last two decades.

G. MODERN "HISTORICITIST" SCRIPTURE SCHOLARS

Simply as an example, we are now going to quote Fr. Steinmueller on the Book of Jonas. We will do so simply because the extreme higher critics portray "historicists" as credulous people. Their favorite example of this is that such people would consider the possibility that the story of Jonas has an historical basis, and that it is not totally allegorical.

The "historicitist" knows the Magisterium has never dogmatically stated whether Catholics must believe Jonas to be either an historic or allegorical figure. This leaves contemporary Catholics "free" to believe one way or the other. And no "historicitist" Catholic would go to his death to defend the "historicity" of Jonas -- because he or she knows that his or her faith does not stand or fall on the issue.

But until or if the Church should ever bindingly declare the story of Jonas to be allegorical, most historicists would simply stand by the traditional teaching of the Church on this issue.

1. Fr. Steinmueller

One of the greatest Scripture scholars of the 20th century is Rev. Father John E. Steinmueller, S.T.D., S.Scr.L.[220] Fr. Steinmueller served as Professor of Religion at Queen of the Holy Rosary Novitiate, and was then for many years professor of Sacred Scripture and Hebrew at the Seminary of the Immaculate Conception, at Huntington, N.Y. He is the author of the three volume set, *A Companion to Scripture Study*, which *in its 6th printing* was described in part in the following manner in 1948:

> **"Volume I of this work**, on 'General Introduction,' **is rapidly attaining the position of *the standard* book on its subject in English**. Volume II (Special Introduction to the Old Testament) is, possibly of even greater practical value."[221]

In his discussion of the "literary character" of the Book of Jonas Fr. Steinmueller said,

> "Scholars are not in agreement with regard to the literary character of the book. Many non-Catholics regard the book as a legendary story based upon ancient myths and folk-tales, or as an allegorical composition. Other modern critics together with some Catholics (e.g., Gigot, 1906, Van Hoonacker, 1908, Lesàtre, 1909, Tobac, 1921) consider the book as a parable with or without an historical background to impart with some religious teaching.
>
> "*The historical character of the book has always been maintained by Jewish* (cf. Josephus, *Antiq.*, IX, 10, 2) *as well as Christian tradition.*

---

[220] After graduating from St. John's Seminary, he received four years of advanced Theological studies at Innsbruck University, Austria. He went on to the Lateran Seminary in Rome for an additional year, and then the Pontifical Biblical Institute for the next three years, at the end of which he received his S.Scr.L. Upon graduation he proceeded to the Middle East and Egypt where he conducted extensive Biblical research including much original work in Geography of the Holy Land.

[221] Quoted from the jacket of Vol. 1.

> "*Our Lord alludes to the narrative of the fish, not as a popular tradition or as a parable, but as an historical fact,* to serve as a type of His own death and resurrection."[222]

Several things are instantly observable in these remarks of Steinmueller. *First*, he has clearly defined what this author calls the "historicitist" position; *The historical character* of the book *has always been maintained by Christian tradition*. **What the Church has traditionally taught to be historical, the "historicitist" is usually going to accept unless the Church should solemnly change that position.** *Second*, when Fr. Steinmueller published these words in 1948, today's positions of "higher critics" about Jonas being merely an allegorical figure or a type, or a parable (or some combination thereof) were nothing new. Steinmueller even quotes works of some "Catholic" men who held such positions going back to 1906.

2. The Central Issue is Basic Belief in the Historicity of the Gospel

As examples: The miraculous accounts of (1) the Resurrection of Our Lord and (2) the raising of Lazarus from the dead are based on the authority/credibility factor of -- the Revelation of God. **Both miracles are recounted in the Gospel of St. John.** Most extreme "higher critics" *at least subtly question* the historicity of these accounts. The Fathers of Vatican II definitively stated:

> "The Church has always and everywhere maintained, and continues to maintain, the *apostolic origin of the four Gospels* ... the fourfold Gospel, according to Mathew, Mark, Luke and John."[224]

> "Holy Mother Church has firmly and with absolute constancy maintained and continues to maintain, *the four Gospels just*

---

[222] *A Companion to Scripture Studies*, Steinmueller, Vol. II, *Special Introduction to the Old Testament*, Joseph F. Watner, Inc., 6th. Printing, 1948, p. 289.

[224] Dogmatic Constitution on Divine Revelation, *Dei Verbum*, #18, *Vatican Council II, The Conciliar and Post Conciliar Documents, Vol 1.* p. 761-762.

> *named, whose history she unhesitatingly affirms*, faithfully hand on what Jesus, the Son of God, while he lived among men, really did and taught for their eternal salvation, until the day when he was taken up."[225]

The extreme "higher critics" almost to a person challenge (even if subtly) that basic concept of the historicity of the Gospels as reaffirmed and defined by the Council Fathers of Vatican II.

3. Higher Critic Scripture Scholars Have Performed Valuable Service to the Church

Many Catholic higher critical Scripture scholars of the 20th century have done invaluable service for the Church. Many *totally* rationalist students of Scripture abandoned a vision of Scripture which could in any way be compatible with traditional Christian (Catholic or Protestant) beliefs. Someone had to counter their completely rationalist arguments on many key issues. That task fell to many Catholic scholars one might fairly describe as higher critics.

A few examples from amongst many: (1) their analysis of the Dead Sea Scrolls, and (2) the Egyptian Nag Hammadi Gnostic texts has been invaluable.[226] These two sets of manuscripts were both discovered in the 1940's. Their work on the Dead Sea Scrolls has destroyed the earlier rationalist claims that the Gospel of John came out of influences from Eastern pagan religions. Their work on the Nag Hammadi texts has destroyed the rationalist claim that the Gospel of John is borrowed from Gnostic texts and thought. As observed by Fr. Raymond Brown about academic discoveries from such research,

> "The theory that [the Gospel of] John borrowed from such Gnosticm is implausible; more likely the second-century

---

[225] Ibid. #19, p. 761

[226] It must also be understood that many of the other Catholic Scripture scholars who worked on these projects could not be fairly described as "higher critics." But Catholic higher critics played an invaluable role.

Gnostics drew from John, and not vice versa."[227] [parens added]

But there is another side to the higher critical coin. Certain speculations of many of the Catholic extreme higher critics have also done much harm, *especially once those speculations filtered down to the pew*. Such speculations have caused many to wonder how much of the Bible was inspired by God. How much of it is from the imagination of men? The Church unerringly teaches that all Scripture is inspired by God. But much of the higher critical speculation has confused the laity and (let us be frank) even many priests about what to believe in this area.

4. Raymond Brown

The following statement and questions by Fr. Raymond Brown (himself a higher critic Scripture scholar) are cases in point. Fr. Brown says and asks,

> "Tridentine statements[228] that Christ instituted seven sacraments (DBS 1601) and that by the words 'Do this in remembrance of me' Christ ordained the apostles priests (DBS 1752) *represent an interpretation of the general thrust of the whole NT* for the life of the Church. They do not and will not answer historical-critical questions such as:
>
> Did the historical Jesus have a clear idea of a sacrament?
>
> *In his earthly life how many of what we call sacraments did he consciously envision? Before his death did Jesus actually utter the words 'Do this in commemoration of me'* (missing in Matthew's and Mark's account of the Last Supper),[229] *or*

227 *The Gospel and Epistles of John, A Concise Commentary*, Raymond E. Brown, S.S., The Liturgical Press, Collegeville, MN., 1988, p. 15.

228 Statements issuing from the 16th century Council of Trent.

229 The reader has earlier read one of the Church Fathers, St. Basil, answer that question. St. Basil (amongst other Fathers) clearly states that these and other Scriptural words associated with the consecration and eucharistic prayer came down from the apostles in "unwritten tradition." Fr. Brown's questions are also phrased in the same implied "Scriptura sola" context as Rahner.

> *is that a post-resurectional interpretation of the implication of his Last Supper based upon the eucharistic practice of the primitive churches known to Luke* (22:19) *and Paul* (ICor 11:25)? *Did the Jesus of the earthly ministry think of any of his followers as cultic priests and did he think of the eucharist as a sacrifice?*
>
> "These questions are best answered, not by citing church doctrine phrased by people who were neither asking nor answering them, but by studying the Gospels historically and seeking to pierce behind the professions of the early faith to the circumstances of Jesus' ministry and his world view."[230] [Emphasis added]

If Christ did not even "envision" (foresee?) sacraments, if he did not "think" that His Apostles would be priests who would teach "Eucharist as a sacrifice," how could He have been the Hypostatic Union? For someone who answers Brown's questions in the negative, what are the chances that person perceives Christ to have been aware of His Divinity from the moment of conception onwards? Consider the belief of a person who wonders with Fr. Brown, "*Did the Jesus of the earthly ministry think of any of his followers as cultic priests*"?

5. Where is Brown Going? Is He Merely Asking Questions – or is He Arguing for Ignorance in Christ During his Earthly Ministry?

Where is Fr. Brown going with all of this? Perhaps he tells us in another of his books, *Jesus God and Man.* We will quote the full paragraph of Fr. Brown in order to show his complete context.

> "But when all is said and done, the great objection that will be hurled again and again against any exegete (or theologian) who finds evidence that Jesus' knowledge was limited is the objection that in Jesus Christ there is only one person, a divine person. And so, even though the divine person acted

[230] *The Critical Meaning of the Bible*, Raymond E. Brown, S.S., Paulist Press, New York/Ramsey, 1981, pp. 40 & 41.

> through a completely human nature, any **theory that Jesus had limited knowledge** seems to imply a limitation of the divine person. Perhaps the best answer to this objection is to call Cyril of Alexandria, that Doctor of the Church to whom, more than any other, we are indebted for the great truth of the oneness of person in Christ. It was that ultra-orthodox archfoe of Nestorianism (two persons or powers in Christ) who said of Christ, **"We have admired his goodness in that for love of us he has not refused to descend to such a low position as to bear all that belongs to our nature, INCLUDED IN WHICH IS IGNORANCE."**[231] [emboldenment has been added, the all-caps and parens are Brown's]

Fr. Brown is obviously defending the "theory that Jesus had limited knowledge." He even appeals to the Church Father (Cyril) of whom he says, "more than any other, we are indebted for the great truth of the oneness of person in Christ." This is supposed to validate Brown's theory of ignorance in Christ. Brown says in the footnote for this quote from Cyril,

> "[92] *PG 75, 369.* We do not mean to suggest that Cyril grappled with the problem of Jesus' limited knowledge in the way in which that problem is treated today, but only that *the admission which Cyril makes* is significant." [emphasis added]

6. An Appeal to Cyril of Alexandria?

Brown's footnote is at best an understatement of the actual situation. The reader cannot tell from that footnote that Brown's quote from Cyril is the last half of the final sentence of a long and complex paragraph. *In that paragraph Cyril totally defends the knowledge of Christ.* The italicized words below are the first half of the sentence which Fr. Brown has omitted.

---

[231] *Jesus God and Man*, Raymond E. BRown, S.S., The Bruce Publishing Co., Milwaukeee, Wi. 1967, pp 101-102. Taken from the section entitled "HOW Much Did Jesus Know?"

> *"But it is not appropriate from this expression of the Word of God to rashly reproach Him with ignorance*;" [See reference after next quote]

There are some differences between the way Fr. Brown and this author translate the same passage of Cyril, but that is a minor matter. Cyril's entire paragraph reads,

> "In a place in Scripture, the Savior said to His Father: 'Father, the hour has come, glorify your Son.' If therefore He knew exactly the hour, which He said had come, *what stands in the way of Him knowing that hour, which, as a man, He said Himself to be ignorant of*? - it is that which befits the humanity [of Christ], which however He totally knew as God! *But it is not appropriate from this expression of the Word of God to rashly reproach Him with ignorance*; **but rather, to wonder at His burning love for the human race, *impelled by which love,* He did not refuse to reduce Himself to such a lowly state, that He might take upon himself all that is human, one of the things of which is ignorance."**[232]

Fr. Brown takes his quote (the emboldened text above) from Cyril's *Assertion 12* in his *Consubstantiality of the Holy Trinity*. In the almost 400 word context of *Assertion 12 which precedes the quote given by Fr. Brown, Cyril is totally defending the knowledge of Christ*. It is entirely devoted to defending the knowledge of the Christ against those who misunderstand and misuse Matt. 24:36, where Jesus says concerning His Second Coming,

> *"Concerning the day and the hour no one knows, not the angels of heaven, nor the son, none but the Father alone."*

---

[232] Patrologiæ Cursus Completus, Series Graeca, Vol. 75., Migne, Paris au Petit-Montrouge, 1863, p. 370. Migne's Latin Text reads, "Servator alicubi ad Patrem suum ita ait : 'Pater, venit hora, glorifica Fulium tuum' si ergo exacte novit horam, quam venisse dicit, quid obstat quominus et illam norit, quam, ut homo, ignorare se inquit, quod id humanitati conveniat, norit autem omnino ut Deus? At non oportet ob hanc vocem Verbum Dei incusare, et ignorantium temere illi objicere; sed potius mirari amorem quo erga humanum genus flagravit, quo impulsus non recusavit ad tantum humilitatem sese demittere, ut omnia nostra susciperet, quorum etiam unum est ignorantia."

At the very beginning of *Assertion 12*, Cyril explains that its purpose is to answer "An objection of heretics" who misinterpret Matt. 24:36, and therefore ask,

> "So in what manner, they inquire, is the Son similar to the Father in essence, since He declares Himself to be ignorant of the date of the end of the world?"[233]

Cyril now immediately establishes the entire context of *Assertion 12, which is the solution or answer to this objection of heretics to Christs's divinity*. Cyril writes,

Solution to the objection.

> "If He [Jesus] is the creator of the world and of time, which He assuredly is : How is it estimated among you [heretics] that He is ignorant of the day and the hour? In what manner is it possible that that which He made, He does not know? Therefor the things said by Him to His disciples must be investigated. **From these things it shall be easily shown that He knew the day and the hour, as God; even though, manifesting His humanity, He says that He is ignorant.**"[234]

This last emboldened quote is the entire point Cyril intends to make in *Assertion 12.*

Cyril says the statement in Matthew 24:36 was merely an expression of "the Word" from the Word's assumed humanity. With the limited theological terminology available to Cyril at that time, he understands and argues that Jesus Christ cannot be divided. At one point he explains,

> "If therefore, the Word of God is found to have said something humble about Himself *in respect to the Incarnation,*

233 Ibid. p. 69 "At quomodo, inquiunt, erit similis Filius Patri secundum essentiam, cum dicat se nescire diem consummationis saeculi"

234 Ibid. p. 370. "*Solutio objectionis.* Si ipse est conditor saeculorum, et temporum, atque hoc vere ita est : quomodo unum diem atque horam ignorare vobis censetur? Quomodo item ea quae fecit, nescire potest? Investiganda igitur sunt quae ab ipso discipulis dicta sunt. E quibus facile constabit ipsum et diem et horam novisse, ut Deum ; tametsi, humanitatem suam ostendens, ignorare se dicat."

> heretics would use it to object to His Divinity and would interpret what He said to argue against His Divinity. But if *when He became flesh, He spoke in a human way, in order that He might show himself to be truly man; how would it not be fitting to relate the things which he spoke - in a human way?*"[235]

Cyril repeatedly speaks of Christ as one, as both God and man in the Incarnation. For Cyril, Christ cannot be divided.

That is the sum and substance of St. Cyril's argument. And that is the argument which immediately precedes the half sentence quote given by Fr. Brown. By perhaps inadvertently quoting Cyril this badly out of context, Brown makes Cyril appear to do exactly what Cyril says no one can or should do -- *"rashly reproach Him [Christ] with ignorance."*

As a matter of fact, Cyril goes on for another five lengthy pages to defend the full knowledge of the indivisible Christ. At one point Cyril makes the following statement,

> **"He who says the Son, as Word, is ignorant of the day and the hour, cannot avoid committing blasphemy.** ***Because if He knows the Father, as He himself testifies : what can keep Him from knowing everything about the end of creation?"***[236]

Higher critics might attempt to object that Cyril is only talking about Christ as Word, and that therefore they are free to impute ignorance to Christ in His human nature. They can say it, but they cannot thereby legitimately bring Cyril to their defense. Because as the reader has seen, Cyril ceaselessly argues for the indivisibility of Christ. Here, Cyril is directly quoting the expression of Christ in his earthly mission, wherein Christ states that He "knows" the

---

[235] Ibid. "Si ergo ante incarnationem Verbum Dei humile aliquid de se dixisse reperitur, divinitatem ejus objurgent, et contra eam dictum interpretentur. Sin vero cum factus est caro, humano more locutus est, ut vere se hominem esse ostendat, quo pacto non sit consen- taneum ad humanitatem referre quae humano more dixit."

[236] Ibid. p. 371 "Qui dicit Filium, quatenus est Verbum, ignorare diem illum et horam, blasphemiam evitare non po- test. Si enim novit Patrem, sicut ipsemet testatur: quid obstat quominus etiam finem creationis norit?

Father. One cannot successfully appeal to Cyril in any manner that divides up Christ.

St. Cyril had to work without benefit of the theological terminology and tools developed over thirty years later in 451 A.D. by Pope St. Leo the Great[237] and the Council of Chalcedon, later refined even more by systematic theologians such as St. Thomas Aquinas. The most amazing part of Cyril's arguments is that he was able to make them as theologically lucid as he did with the limited tools of theological vocabulary available to him.

If St. Cyril had possessed the theological vocabulary and tools of a later age, he would most probably have written with Thomas Aquinas in the 13th century,

> "Therefore, Christ [in His human intellect] had this perfection of knowing things in their own nature *through the infused knowledge given him by God.*"[238]

And Cyril would most probably, after seeing the statements of many 20th century higher critics, have written with Pope Pius XII in 1951,

> **"They so insist on the state and condition of the humanity of Christ that it seems to be considered as a subject, as it were, in itself,** ***as if it did not subsist in the person of the Word.*****"**[239]

Neither Fr. Brown nor any other higher critic can legitimately appeal to Cyril of Alexandria in support of their questioning of the

[237] In his "Tome," Leo the Great in effect discovered or created the concept of personhood, or personality, as we understand it today. Previous to that, the Latin word "persona" and its Greek counterpart only signified "mask" or "appearance." As Leo redefined the word, "persona," it meant "person," as we have basically understood the word ever since. Cyril is writing this *Assertion 12* roughly 33 years prior to the development by Leo of our modern understanding of the word "person." That term and the concept it represents were not yet available to St. Cyril. Therefore, we cannot expect him to describe the Hypostatic Union in the language of the "one person of Christ." But given that limitation of available vocabulary, Cyril did an amazing job of describing the reality of Christ's knowledge in and through the reality of the Incarnation.

[238] *The Disputed Questions on Truth*, p. 407

[239] *Sempiternus Rex*, AAS 43 (1951) 638.

knowledge and/or consciousness of Christ. Because Cyril made no "admission" (as Fr. Brown erroneously claims), because, like Leo the Great, Thomas Aquinas, and Pope Pius XII, St. Cyril refused any attempt to divide up Christ.

7. Has This Academic Challenging of the Consciousness of Christ Developed into a Pastoral Issue?

Once one begins to be confused about the knowledge and/or consciousness of Christ, then it is usually only a matter of time before one becomes troubled and confused by all the other issues and questions posed by Fr. Brown and his theological look-alikes. Fr. Brown couches his previously quoted list of questions in *The Critical Meaning of The Bible*, in the following context,

> "What a passage *means* is the issue for the Church - not the semi-historical issue of what it *meant* to the person who wrote it."[240] [emphasis - Brown's]

But many would respond to Fr. Brown that such speculation about what the person who wrote it *meant*, such speculation inevitably filters down to the faithful. The Holy Father, John Paul II, has recently commented upon the *pastoral consequences* and aspects of exegesis.

> "Exegetes will be keen to remain close to the *preaching* of God's word, both by devoting part of their time to this ministry and by maintaining relations with those who exercise it and helping them with publications of pastoral exegesis *(cf Divino afflante Spiritu: EB, n. 551)*. ***Thus they will avoid becoming lost in the complexities of abstract scientific research which distances them from the true meaning of the Scriptures.*** **Indeed, this meaning is inseparable from their goal, which is to put believers in a personal relationship with God.**"[241]

---

[240] *The Critical Meaning of the Bible*, Raymond E. Brown, p. 40.

[241] *Address of His Holiness Pope John Paul II and Document of the Pontifical Biblican Commission*, 1994, p. 17.

The average "go to Mass on Sunday" Catholic will never read any of Fr. Brown's books. They will never read his questions as *collectively* posed in his book, *The Critical Meaning of the Bible.* But if they did see them collectively stated, what would be the reaction of the average "go to Mass on Sunday" Catholic? Would the majority of them choose someone who asks such questions (particularly about the knowledge of Jesus Christ) to instruct their children in the Faith? Do those questions offend their Sensus Fidei, their sense of the Faith? If so, are they automatically wrong and the Fr. Browns of this world right?

But there is a broader question. As he poses *the Questions,* what collective effect have those questions of Raymond Brown and his theological look-alikes had on the lay faithful over the last several decades? When such questions singularly filter down to the pew, do they as John Paul II admonishes, help "*to put believers in a personal relationship with God*"?

The sheer numbers of Catholics in the U.S. during the 1970's and 1980's who gradually stopped practicing their faith is staggering. That phenomenon and its cause has been the subject of continued debate and discussion in the U.S. for the last quarter of a century. The majority of *lay Catholics* who did stay in active participation in the Church have little doubt as to its primary cause. They saw that cause over and over again in their friends who left.

The major cause was (and still is) a subtle calling into question of traditional teachings of the Church from pulpits across our land. That questioning has radically shaken (in a tragic number of cases destroyed) the faith of many lay Catholics. They didn't *read* the questions collectively phrased in a higher critic's book. They *heard* them singularly implicitly presented over and over again from pulpits. The pulpit questions used in that process were previously framed by extreme higher critics. They were later expressed from pulpits (and in articles in many diocesan newspapers) by priests who had learned them from higher critics in seminaries and Catholic universities.

Later in this book we will see centuries-old Catholic prophecies about future "senseless questions and elaborate arguments."[242] A

[242] From the point of view of the faithful, are not quasi-Nestorian questions about Christ's knowledge senseless?

number of those prophecies even predict a time when as a result of such "senseless questions and elaborate arguments,"

> "no principle at all, however holy, authentic, ancient, and certain it may be, will remain free of censure, criticism, false interpretations, modification, and delimitation by man."

As the reader will later see, these prophecies also predict that as a result, the ranks of the faithful will be devastated. Interestingly enough, some of them specifically predict such a phenomenon for the 20th century.

H. THE CHURCH'S TRADITIONAL INSTRUCTIONS ON INTERPRETATION OF SCRIPTURE

Prophecy, public and private, is the major subject of this book. If an individual has any difficulty believing in (a) the accuracy and historicity of Scripture in general, and (b) prophecy of future events foretold in both the Old and New Testaments, what possibility is there that he or she will intellectually accept the traditional teachings of the Church on many points of doctrine -- especially about the latter and end times. Is there even less possibility they will seriously consider private prophecies from an approved source such as Fatima?

Fatima involved a public miracle witnessed by 70,000 people. In order to consider the possibility of a specific authentic approved source such as Fatima -- almost by definition a Catholic must be previously secure in his or her belief in public prophecy of Tradition and Scripture which *is* required by faith.

I. EXTREME HIGHER CRITICISM - NOT MODERN OR NEW

Extreme higher critics often present their various theses as the result of late 20th century discovery and research. But the arguments of the extreme "higher critics" were very old and well-known long before Fr. Steinmueller (who was quoted earlier). His exposition on their theories demonstrates that the arguments of the higher critics were old by mid-20th century.

We have quoted eminent contemporary theologians such as Cardinal Seri, and Dr. Deitrich von Hildebrand on extreme higher criticism. These contemporary late 20th century theologians fully recognized the danger in the extreme allegorical positions of the higher critics.

Those observations were understood by even earlier 20th century scholars. The following is quoted from the papers and minutes which were presented at the first General Meeting of "The Catholic Biblical Association of America" at St. Louis, MO, on October 9th & 10th, of *1937*.

> "It has been aptly said of *critics of the rationalistic type* "qui corticem rodunt, medullam vero non attingunt." ["Those who only gnaw at the bark of the tree will never get at its heart."][243] They miss the vital issue, forgetting that the Bible is a "book written within and without." There can be no vivisection, for one and the same letter by human hand carries the divine message. *It is one thing to examine, analyze, and explore with all scientific means available the true and original text and meaning. This is true exegesis.*
>
> "... It is another thing to analyze, dissect, and reduce to its ultimate elements every letter, line, and document with the avowed purpose of baring "the earthly" of "the heavenly." This is going beyond sound exegesis. *It is performing an autopsy on a corpse rather than a diagnosis on a healthy living body.*"[244]

Thus the major theses and approach of the rationalist "critics" was well-described and condemned by these American Scripture scholars in 1937. There is absolutely nothing new about the approach/arguments of the extreme higher critics even in the first half of this century.

---

243 Author's translation from the Latin.

244 *Proceedings of The Catholic Biblical Association of America, First General Meeting,* The Abbey Press, Meinrad, Ind. 1938, from the first article, *Nova et Vetera*, by Very Rev. Thomas Plassmann, O.F.M., p. 11.

1. Many Arguments of the Higher Critics are So Old the Church Fathers Specifically Combated Them

We have already demonstrated that by the middle of this century the vast majority of the central arguments of the extreme higher critics were recognized as shopworn by 20th century usage. We have also seen that many of them are to be found in the writings of 2nd, 3rd, 4th and 5th century condemned heretics, such as the Gnostics, Arians, Nestorians and Agnotae.

2. 3rd Century Arguments of the Pagan, Porphyry

Many of these heretical arguments are originally found in the writings of Pagan opponents of Christianity from the patristic period. Porphyry's arguments serve as an excellent example. Porphyry was a Pagan. He was also a vicious opponent of the Christian faith.

His attacks on Christianity are contained in his fifteen books entitled *Against the Christians* (written around 270 A.D.). Porphyry's arguments were so well-known to the Fathers of the Church that: his very name had become a term of opprobrium by the Council of Nicea in 325.[245] In the early 5th century, St. Jerome discusses St. Methodius' *Books Against Porphyry,*[246] in which Methodius apparently[247] gave systematic answers to Porphyry's attacks.[248] Methodius wrote them well prior to his death in 311 A.D.

We will be discussing Patristic exegesis on the *Book of Daniel* at some length later in this book. Therefore, the extreme higher critical attacks on the historicity and veracity of the *Book of Daniel* hold additional significance for the reader. Fr. Steinmueller cryptically

[245] At the end of the Council, the Emperor Constantine "wished to annihilate the name of the Arians [heretics] and ordered them in the future to be called Porphyrians, because Arius had imitated Porphyry in his enmity to Christianity." *History of the Councils*, von Hefele, Karl Joseph, 5 Vols., T&T Clark, Edinburgh, 1883-1896. AMS English Edition reprint, Ams Press, Inc. New York, 1972, Vol. 1, p. 297 [Hefele's footnote reads, "Cf. the Letter of Constantine to the Bishops, etc., Socrates, i.9, p. 32, ed. Mogunt]

[246] *De Viribus Illustribus* and also Jeromes *Commentary on the Book of Daniel*

[247] *Against Porphyry* is unfortunately one of those of Methodius' works which is lost. All we know about it is from the few surviving fragments and commentaries of other Fathers such as St. Jerome.

[248] *Patrology*, Johannes Quasten, Vol. 2, p. 137.

presents these critical arguments, and the answers to them, in the following,

> "*The critical thesis.* **-- Modern critics, following the opinion of the pagan Neo-Platonic philosopher, Porphyry** (d. 303 A.D.), **maintain that the Book of Daniel is a pseudepigraphic work composed during the Machabean period by a religious Jew, who wished to encourage his pious coreligionists during the persecution of Antiochus IV Epiphanes** (175-164 B.C.) The arguments, which they adduce, are insufficient to prove their thesis.
>
> "They assert, that the miracles and prophecies recorded in the book are outside the realm of historical and authenticated facts, and belong to subjective rather than objective knowledge. *But such a preclusion is a denial of the possibility of divine revelation, miracles, prophecies, and thus begs the question.*"[249]

Fr. Steinmueller goes on from here to thoroughly discredit the balance of the arguments of what Steinmueller refers to as "Modern critics" on the *Book of Daniel.* The pretense of "Modern critics" that the Fathers were unaware of these basic arguments, and therefore could not take them into account is absolutely historically ludicrous. The Fathers knew them in their basic form, academically discredited them, then totally rejected them.

Most important for our discussion is *Steinmueller's final conclusion* about this ancient pagan argument *which has been resurrected by our extreme higher critics*. He says what their argument ultimately boils down to "*is a denial of the possibility of divine revelation, miracles, prophecies, and thus begs the question.*" Steinmueller is absolutely correct.

But this implicit "denial" is not limited to extreme higher critics' arguments about the *Book of Daniel.* This implicit "denial" is at the base of much of their exegesis. This denial is not new, and it is not particularly scientific. Pagan sworn enemies of Christianity such a Porphyry[250] regularly used such arguments to attack the Christian claim for "*divine revelation, miracles, prophecies.*" It is

---

249 *A Companion to Scripture Studies*, Vol 2, p. 273-274.

250 Porphyry was far from the only Pagan writer to use these arguments against Christianity.

in many ways much easier to deal with the stipulated opposition of a Porphyry.

But, it is not Steinmueller alone who sees similarities between extreme higher critics and Porphyry, the 3rd century pagan antagonist of Christianity. The 1913 *Catholic Encyclopedia* comments on Porphyry's *Against the Christians*,

> "Only a few fragments, preserved in the works of the Christian Apologists, have come down to us. From these it appears that *he directed his attack along the lines of what we should now call historical criticism* of the Old Testament and comparative study of religions."[251]

It was arguments from Porphyry's "historical criticism" attack on the book of Daniel which Fr. Steinmueller says the *modern* critics adhere to.

Beyond these observations of Fr. Steinmueller and the *Catholic Encyclopedia*, the most prestigious 20th century patrologist, Johannes Quasten, observed,

> "Porphyry made much of the supposed contradictions in the Gospels about the genealogies of Jesus and about the accounts of the Resurrection."

As we can see, the bulk of the "modern" arguments are as old as the hills. All these sources quoted above are from the ranks of some of the most respected Catholic scholars and sources of our 20th century. They indicate three critical areas of similarity between the arguments of 3rd century pagans such as Porphyry, and the basic arguments of some the more extreme "Modern" critics. These are three key facets to their basic arguments (1) a type of historical criticism which works not from faith but out of scepticism, (2) an infatuation with a study of "comparative religion" which implies that Judeo-Christianity instead of being historically unique, borrowed heavily from other religions, and (3) "supposed" contradictions in the Gospels.

Is the reader getting a sense of *deja vu*? There is quite a set of similarities between the basic arguments of 3rd century pagans and those of modern extreme higher critics. And the Fathers of the

---

[251] *Catholic Encyclopedia*, 1913 Editioon, Vol. 10, Article on "Neo-Platonism," p. 743.

Church were aware of and combated all of them. THERE IS ABSOLUTELY NOTHING NEW ABOUT THE BASIC ARGUMENTS OF THE EXTREME HIGHER CRITICS. THEY GO BACK AT LEAST TO THE ANTICHRISTIAN ARGUMENTS OF THE 3RD CENTURY PAGANS.

Later we will be quoting extensively from the commentary of St. Jerome on the Book of Daniel. It is a common ploy of contemporary higher critics to claim that Fathers of the Church, such as St. Jerome, were unaware of the basic arguments of today's higher criticism. They thereby imply that it is a waste of time to read the Scriptural exegesis of men such as St. Jerome.

Interesting enough, Jerome begins his prologue to his commentary on Daniel with reference to Porphyry's historical criticism of the Old Testament. He references Porphyry's claim that the Book of Daniel was not written by Daniel or anyone of his time, but rather was written by a Jew at the time of the Seleucid King, Antiochus Epiphanes IV. Jerome points out that Bishop Eusebius of Casearea and Apollinaris have already written books which dispensed with Porphyry's arguments. He adds that Bishop Methodius had done the same prior to them.[252]

3. Higher Critical Arguments Against the Consciousness of Christ is Central to Their Position

The most dangerous specific point of the extreme higher critics is their challenging of the "consciousness" or knowledge of Christ. It is the most dangerous because most people who begin to doubt His knowledge predictably begin to have other consequent doubts. Such people regularly tend to become very shaky in their belief system vis-a-vis the teaching of the Magisterium.

As we have already seen, most of the questions of extreme higher critics about the knowledge of Christ are anything but new, *they are ancient*. Those questions were also framed in very similar language by both pagans and heretics of the fourth and fifth cen-

[252] *Corpus Christianorum, Series Latina*, Vol. LXXV A, S. Hieronymi Presbyteri Opera, Pars I, Opera Exegetica 5, Commentariorum in Danielem, Libri III <IV>, Pub: Turnholti, Typographi Brepols, Editores Pontifici, pp 771-772. [The Prologue actually begins, "Porphyry wrote twelve books against the Prophet Daniel."]

turies, particularly by late Nestorian, Monophysite, and Agnotae heretics. This is not meant to be a harsh judgment. It is simply a matter of historic record. For a deeper understanding of this point, the author highly recommends to the reader Fr. William Most's 1980 book, *The Consciousness of Christ*.

4. The Value of Knowing Church History

If more Catholics knew more honest Church history, including the history of the heresies and errors with which the Church, and her Fathers and Doctors, have had to contend over almost two millennia, it would then be much more difficult for an old heresy to obtain a new foothold in the minds of modern Catholics.

5. The Historically Demonstrable Importance of Marian Doctrine

An additional item of note for the reader: today as in the past, *those who fall into any number of current Christological heresies about Our Lord, have (as Nestorius did) usually already denied or questioned one or more of the Church's traditional teachings about His mother, Mary*. That is a historically demonstrable fact. On the other side, those (such as St. Cyril of Alexandria) who remain faithful to the Church's traditional teachings about His mother seldom fall into Christological or Trinitarian heresies. Mary *is* the "Mother of Good Counsel." Show me a heretic on a Christological doctrine, and nine times out of ten, you will have shown me a person who has *previously* denied a Marian doctrine.

One of the major points of this entire section is this; heresy is *common* today only in the Latin Rite in the West. The contemporary Eastern Rite faithfulness to Christological doctrine well may be due to the great devotion of Eastern Rite Catholics to the "Theotokos," the "God-bearer," Mary our Mother. As the reader will later see, private Catholic prophecy *has* accurately foretold a heretical problem in the Latin Rite of the Catholic Church for the 20th century. Hundreds of years in advance, Sor Marianne de Jesus Tores, Ven. Holshauser, and others made highly *specific* prophecies about future heresy in the Latin Rite. If that which we see occurring today in the

Latin Rite does not fit that bill, one can only imagine with horror what might.

That is why Our Lady, and devotion to her, hold such a central promise for the Church in the West today. Not surprisingly, the private revelations at Lourdes and Fatima strongly suggest Marian devotion as a central key to a solution of our problems in the West.

J. VATICAN II'S DEI VERBUM, AND ITS DEFINITIVE CURRENT NORMS ON "LITERARY FORMS" AND THEIR ROLE IN SCRIPTURE

The phenomena we are currently experiencing with problems emanating from the theories of extreme higher critics were well-known prior to Vatican II. Amongst other problems, the Fathers at Vatican II had two major extremes to overcome. Ironically, they both centered around different aspects or extreme views of the Doctrine of the Mystical Body.

The first extreme: In one sense, the Council Fathers had to quicken and enliven the almost quietistic individualism which had crept into much of the Church. Where it occurred, this individualistic view of the Church stifled a full sense of Christian community. The "kiss of peace" *was* universally practiced in the early Church. Due to some historically demonstrable abuses it had gradually ceased to exist. But the vitriolic opposition which arose in some quarters at its reintroduction in the West in the form of the "handshake of peace" -- *that vitriolic type* of opposition could not have arisen if this quietistic individualism were not a problem.[253]

The second extreme: The Council Fathers had to enlighten the modernist arm of higher criticism which stifled a desire for a deep

[253] The author is not discussing valid arguments about the best placement of the Kiss of Peace in the Liturgy. The early Church prominently featured the Kiss of Peace. But they had it shortly after the Gospel, where it would not break up nor break into the specific Eucharistic celebration. Here, the author is talking only about the extreme individualist reaction which resisted intercommunion with one's fellow Christians at Mass. That was only symptomatic of a deeper lack of understanding of the full doctrine of the Mystical Body. Initially, the author was one of that class.

personal relationship with the GodMan Christ. This was primarily evidenced at that time among many academics and Catholic intellectuals. It was evidenced in their ultra-rationalistic view of God's Revelation, and of the Church which He instituted, and the pronouncements of its Magisterium. Their view of the world was extremely humanistic. That view ultimately looks to Man almost to the exclusion of God. It could fairly be described as rampant secular humanism parading around in Christian clothes.

VATICAN II CITED ST. AUGUSTINE'S EXPERTISE ON LITERARY FORMS

Over against extreme rationalistic views of God's Revelation, the Council Fathers gave us *Dei Verbum*. It reminds all of us that the basics of the Apostolic Kerygma are in full force and effect for all time. Dei Verbum stressed the importance of a deep and prayerful respect for and understanding of sacred Scripture. Observe the following manner with which the Council Fathers singled out St. Augustine as a Scripture scholar who understood the various modes of expression of the sacred writers of Scripture.

> "In determining the intention of the sacred writers, attention must be paid, *inter alia,* to 'literary forms for the fact is that truth is differently presented and expressed in the various types of historical writing, in prophetical and poetical texts,' and in other forms of literary expression. Hence the exegete must look for that meaning which the sacred writer, in a determined situation and given the circumstances of his time and culture, intended to express and did in fact express, through the medium of a contemporary literary form. (7)"[254]

The "(7)" at the end of the quote above refers the reader of *Dei Verbum* to a footnote which reads, "St. Augustine, *De Doctr. Christ.*, III, 18, 26; *PL* 34, 75-76." What that footnote tells us is that the

[254] Dogmatic Constitution on Divine Revelation, *Dei Verbum*, #9, *Vatican Council II, The Conciliar and Post Conciliar Documents, Vol 1.* Flannery, New Revised Edition 1992, p. 757.

distinctions of literary form just described were understood and explained by St. Augustine. They reference his work *On Christian Doctrine* in demonstration of this.

Many Fathers of the Church (most specifically St. Augustine) were thoroughly familiar with the subject of various literary forms. Yet many "higher critics" pass off the Fathers of the Church as if they had no sophistication in these matters.

1. St. Augustine - His Role

Augustine began his *City of God* in 413 A.D., completing it in 426, four years before his death.[255] We will be liberally quoting from that work to demonstrate that Augustine was no blind "literalist." He and other "Fathers" of the Church are regularly portrayed by some "higher critics" as men who meant well, were sincere, but were ignorant of the basic "literary form" distinctions made by modern Scripture scholars. *But that does not resonate with the historic record.*

Augustine did intellectual and theological battle with both extreme literalists *and* extreme allegorists most of his episcopal life. He and many other "Fathers" had a keen appreciation for the different senses of Scripture. For example: In dealing with "literalists" who wished to have a Scriptural "day" always to signify a single physical day, Augustine responded,

> "but no one who reads the Scriptures, however negligently, need be told that in them 'day' is customarily used for [a] 'time.'"[256] [parens - authors]

In arguing against the "Millenarian" literalists who held with a thousand year physical reign of Christ with the Saints here on earth, he first said,

---

[255] *The Faith of the Early Fathers, Vol.* 3, *A source-book of theological and historical passages from the writings of St. Augustine to the end of the Patristic Age*, p. 97.

[256] *Basic Writings of Saint Augustine*, Edited by Whitney J. Oates, Chrm. Dept. of Classics, Princeton University, Random House, New York. Vol. II, p. 508. [Section on *The City of God*, Bk. 20, Chpt 29.]

> "Those who on the strength of this passage, have suspected that the first resurrection is future and bodily,[257] have been moved, among other things, specially by the number of a thousand years, as if it were a fit thing that the saints should thus enjoy a kind of Sabbath-rest during that period."[258]

Later on he comments,

> "They who do believe them are called by the spiritual Chiliasts, which we may literally reproduce by the name Millenarians.
>
> *"It is a tedious process to refute these opinions point by point*: we prefer proceeding to show how that passage of Scripture should be understood.[259]
>
> "Now the thousand years can be understood in two ways... or he [the Sacred Writer] used the thousand years as an equivalent for the whole duration of this world, employing the number of perfection to mark the fullness of time."[260] [parens - authors]

Does Augustine sound like a literalist? *Many scholars throughout the ages have accused Augustine of pushing allegorism about as far as it can authentically be pushed.* Augustine explains that he used to hold with some literalist views of the Millenarians, "for myself, too, once held this opinion."[261] He demonstrates he is capable of admitting a prior mistake. As he matured his exegesis became that of one who could more clearly distinguish between the "proper" literal, allegorical and accommodated senses of Scripture. At this point (in the quotes above and below) only a few years prior to his death, we are dealing with the matured Augustine.

---

257 Augustine believes in the resurrection of the body, which is an article of faith. He is referring to those who thought there would be in a sense two full resurrections. In a confused way they believed there would be a first resurrection wherein the bodies of the saints were not perfected bodies. These Millenarianist heretics believed in some kind of a sensual "banquet heaven" on earth prior to the glory of heaven (This is very similar to some aspects betrayed in Muslim eschatology and also to beliefs of certain Fundamentalist Christian sects today).

258 Ibid. p. 518.

259 Ibid.

260 Ibid.

261 Ibid.

In other passages Augustine patiently attempts to explain that yes, certain Scriptural passages do have an allegorical meaning as their first meaning, or serve as a parable, or an "accommodated" meaning. As an example of this, in explaining one particular use of the number "10" in the Book of Daniel, Augustine gives the following explanation;

> "...as totality is frequently symbolized by a thousand, or a hundred, or seven, or other numbers, which it is not necessary to recount."

Augustine understands the various senses of Scripture very well. [*NOTE*: When one reads the books of many contemporary "higher critics," wherein they patronizingly explain that the Hermeneutics[262] of the Fathers were well-intentioned but naive, one can gradually come to wonder to what degree those critics have themselves ever actually read the original texts of those Fathers -- Fathers such as Gregory Nazianz, Chrysostom, Basil, Cyril, Augustine, and Jerome, each of whom explained many different senses of Scripture in their exegesis.]

2. St. Jerome

Some higher critic Scripture scholars who are better read in the Fathers will admit the obvious, that Jerome had (for his time) a surprising appreciation for textual criticism. But it is also quite common to hear extreme higher critics making broad sweeping claims that the Fathers universally lacked a "historical sense" with which to critically read and interpret Scripture. Jerome is just one of several counterexamples. In his *Commentary on Isaiah* (after appealing to the historian, Josephus, to support one of Jerome's Scriptural interpretations) Jerome says,

> "And we say this, not condemning the tropological [figurative] sense, but because ***the spiritual interpretation must follow the order of history,*** which, many forgetting, they wander off into the most obvious errors against the Scriptures."[263]

[Note: There are those who say St. Jerome *only* uses the word "history" *historia* to designate the *literal* vs. the *spiritual (or figurative)*

[262] If the reader is unfamiliar with this term, see Glossary.

sense – that he is not referring to actual history. This is *absolutly* not the case. Jerome uses the word "history" to designate both literal historic facts *and* the literal proper sense. e.g., see also his commentary on Ez. 42:13.]

3. St. Augustine and Jerome Not Alone

The Church has constantly singled out St. Augustine as a fine exegete in that he understood there were various senses, meanings, and manners of speaking in Scripture. But the Church has never implied that he was the only Father who possessed an acute sense for this. Here we will give but one brief example from many of the other Fathers who possessed this sense for the varied meanings in Scripture.

St. John Chrysostom, one of the most famous and prestigious of the Fathers, was a brilliant preacher, theologian, and Scripture scholar. In his commentary on St. Paul's letter to the Roman's (11:11 "But through their [the Jews] trespass salvation has come to the Gentiles, so as to make Israel jealous"). Here Chrysostom writes,

> "But we must not take what is said here literally, but get acquainted with the spirit and the object of the speaker [St. Paul] and what he aimed to compass [express]. Which thing I ever entreat of your love [which is what I always encourage of you to do]."[264]

Does St. John Chrysostom herein sound like some country bumpkin who is unaware of various modes and expressions to be found in Scripture? We could give similar examples from many of the other Fathers.

In Scripture studies today, it is extremely rare to find individuals who are very broadly read in the Fathers. And should this surprise us? If as a theology student one has been pre-convinced by his professors that the Fathers had no real knowledge of or appreciation for various senses of Scripture -- why bother -- except out of idle curiosity?

---

263 *Commentarium in Isaiah*, St. Jeronimus, Patrologia Latina, 24.

264 *The Homilies of St. John Chrysostom, on The Epistle of S. Paul The Apostle To The Romans*, Pub: A Library of The Fathers, James Parker & Co., Oxford., England, Third Edition, 1877, p. 342.

As demonstrated above, Augustine had a full appreciation for the various "senses" of Scripture.[265] Anyone who has read his Scriptural commentaries quickly becomes aware that Augustine frequently argues for a non-"proper" (a non-word-for-word) interpretation of many many passages. It is in this knowledge that we can be absolutely assured that where Augustine intentionally takes the "proper" word-for-word literal meaning of a Scripture passage as its first meaning, that he views that literal meaning as its best and primary meaning, and often states that interpretation's actual advent to be from apostolic teaching.

Augustine Cited the "Historicity" of the Final Judgment, and Cites Jonas in this "Historicity" Context

In giving exegesis on the Final Judgment, Augustine portrays Christ as confirming the literal existence of Jonas, including the prophecy which Jonas preached to the Ninevehns. Interspersed throughout Augustine's following commentary are his Scriptural references.

> "The Savior himself, while reproving the cities in which He had done great works, but which had not been believed, and while setting them in unfavorable comparison with foreign cities, says,
>
> *'But I say to you, It shall be more tolerable for Tyre and Sidon at that day of judgment than for thee.'* (Mat. 11:22)
>
> And a little later He says,
>
> *'Verily, I say unto you, It shall be more tolerable for the land of Sodom in the day of judgment than for thee.'* (Mat. 11:24)
>
> Here he [Jesus] most plainly predicts that a day of judgment is to come. And in another place he says,

---

[265] There is no question that a more full "sense" of scripture have been more fully differentiated by modern Scriptural research. But that is an entirely different position than one which virtually writes the exegesis of the Fathers off as outdated and useless. And that is effectively what most of the extreme higher critics have done.

'The men of Nineveh shall rise in judgment with this generation, and shall condemn it: because they repented at the preaching of Jonas; and behold, a greater than Jonas is here. The queen of the south (Sheba) shall rise up in the judgment with this generation, and shall condemn it: for she came from the uttermost parts of the earth to hear the words of Solomon; and behold a greater than Solomon is here."[266]

Could it possibly be clearer that Augustine believes Our Lord to have literally confirmed the historic reality of Jonas preaching to the Ninevehns within this passage? And we have seen that the Fathers of Vatican II held Augustine up as a model of exegesis in that he understood the various modes and senses of Scriptural expression.

Augustine does not limit himself to defending Jonas' preaching to the Ninevites. He also specifically defends the account of Jonas surviving three days in the belly of a large fish. In a letter to a friend, Augustine answers the question of a mutual acquaintance about this Christian belief,

> "The answer to this is that either belief must be withheld from all divine miracles, or there is no reason why this should not be believed. ... as our friend has not asked the question whether it should be believed that Lazarus was raised on the fourth day or whether Christ himself rose on the third day, *unless perchance he thinks it easier for a dead man to be raised from the tomb* [Lasarus or Jesus] *than for a living man* [Jonas] *to be preserved in the great belly of a beast."*[267]

Many of the other Fathers and Doctors spoke just as strongly concerning the historicity of the Jonas Biblical account, including, but not limited to, St. Jerome (PL 25, 1132), and St. Gregory of Nazianzen (PG 35, 505-8, 953). When drawing a comparison between Jonas (and the fish) and Christ's resurrection, St. Cyril of Jerusalem say, "If the former is credible, so is the latter; if the latter is incredible, so is the former." i.e., Cyril says that Christians

[266] Ibid. Chapter 19, p. 512.
[267] Patrologia Latina, 33, 382

who believe in the resurrection after three days we should have no trouble believing in the historicity of the Jonas account.

4. A Catholic Commentary on Holy Scripture

In 1953, the 1300 page *A Catholic Commentary on Holy Scripture* was published. It was the end product of over fifty of the most prestigious Scriptural exegetes of the second half of our century. They come from England, Ireland, Germany, Australia, Malta, Canada, many others in teaching residence at Rome's Pontifical Biblical Institute, and from the U.S.A. In its Foreward, Bernard Cardinal Griffin enthusiastically supports this great work. These men were totally in harmony with Pope Pius XII's spirited defense of scientific Scriptural research in his *Divino Afflante Spiritu.* These men were *not* hostile to scientific studies in Scriptural research. *They themselves were Textual Critics, Historico-Critics, Form Critics, etc.* However, they also understood the indispensability of the *Analogy of Faith* and *Tradition* in sound exegesis.

The *Commentaries* section on the *Book of Jonas* was written by E. F. Sutcliffe, S.J., M.A., L.S.S., Professor of Old Testament Exegesis and Hebrew, Heythrop College. Sutcliffe observes with Steinmueller,

> "Until recent times, however, the historical character of this book was never seriously doubted within the Church."[268]

As Steinmueller, Sutcliffe refers to Van Hoonecker and others who had been attacking the historicity of *Jonas.*

Sutcliffe launches a scholarly defense of the historicity of the *Book of Jonas.* He cites every major argument of the extreme higher critics against its historicity (alleged "bizarre" miracles, time of a narrow nationalistic outlook - i.e. the claim that it is post-exilic in origin, lack of some historic detail expected in a historic narrative

---

[268] *A Catholic Commentary on Holy Scripture,* Foreward by; Bernard Cardinal Griffin, Archbishop of Westminster, Editorial Committee - Dom Bernard Orchard M.A. (Cantab), Rev. Edmund F. Sutcliffe S.J., M.A. (Oxom.), L.S.S., Rev. Reginald C. Fuller D.D., L.S.S. Secretary of the Catholic Biblical Association, Dom Ralph Russell D.D., M.A., Pub: Thomas Nelson and Sons, New York, 1953. p. 669.

- e.g., place where Jonas landed, didactic fiction - due to lack of Assyrian monuments to record a conversion of Ninevites, etc.). Then Sutcliffe systematically scholastically answers those objections. It is no exaggeration to state that Sutcliffe strongly argues in favor of the historicity of *Jonas*.

From Fathers and Doctors such as Augustine, Jerome, Gregory Naz. and Cyril of Jerusalem, to the modern scripture scholars such as Sutcliffe and Steinmueller, from the early 5th century to the 20th, we have presented experts stating that it is "respectable" to believe in the historicity of Jonas. *We have not done so to make a specific issue out of the Jonas controversy -- which is not an article of faith.* We have done so simply to make the following point: It is neither a sign of being naive nor credulous to *generally* accept the historicity of the Bible. It is the Traditional Catholic stance.

K. OVERALL CONCLUSIONS OF THIS CHAPTER

This whole discussion began with a defense of the possibility and reasonableness of a true Catholic Scripture scholar (or an average believer for that matter) *(1) generally believing in the historicity of the Bible, and (2) in the equal authority of Tradition, and particularly (3) in the authority of the opinions of the Fathers of the Church (4) in accepting the traditional teachings of the Church on all points of doctrine.*

In summation, the singularly best place a contemporary Catholic can look for guidance in these areas is from the actual documents of the Second Vatican Council, and *The Catechism of the Catholic Church*. From within these documents the following conclusions can be drawn:

(I) The Christological positions and the incredulosity of extreme higher critics about (1) Biblical miraculous events in general, and (2) the historicity of the Gospels in particular; such incredulosity is repudiated by the documents of Vatican II and *The Catechism of the Catholic Church.*

(II) The extreme higher critics' deprecation of the existence of a charism of prophecy of future events in Scripture (Agabus, etc.) was contradicted by the same Council Fathers.

(III) The extreme critics' raw skepticism relating to the possibility of a *contemporary* charism of prophesy is likewise repudiated by the Council Fathers.

OVERALL CONCLUSIONS FOR THE PUPOSES OF THIS BOOK: a 20th century *false intellectualism* has generated some highly questionable theoogy in our time. At this point in history, that *false intel lectualism* is challenging many of the basic teachings of the Church. Some of it is sufficiently questionable to have been branded by many sound Catholic theolo gians[269] as neo-Gnostic, neo-Arian,neo-Nestorian,and neo-Pelagian. Much of this *false intellectualism* has generated a *raw skepticism* among extreme higher critics. That scepticism (and or confusion generated by it) has now traveled to many of the laity. This has happened through the "trickle-down effect" - from college and seminary, to the pulpit, to the pew.

When the reader gets to the specific prophecies about the twentieth century, it might be fruitful to think back to this chapter. See if there is not an increible simlarity between that which was foretold about us centuries ago, and what has actually come to pass. See if the rhetoric of today's extreme higher critics does not fit what the prophecies predict of; "senseless questions and elaborate arguments" which will devatate the faith of an entire generation. As the reader shall see, several approved Catholic prophets have specifically predicted all of this for the 20th century!

---

[269] Amongst such sound theologians is Joseph Cardinal Ratzinger.

CHAPTER 3

SIGNS OF OUR TIMES

We possess the predictions of many Saints that in later times apparitions and revelations from Our Lady would rapidly increase. And as a matter of fact, Joseph Cardinal Ratzinger, PREFECT FOR THE SACRED CONGREGATION FOR THE DOCTRINE OF THE FAITH recently stated in the *Ratzinger Report*:

> "One of the signs of our times is that the announcements of 'Marian apparitions' are multiplying all over the world."

Such an increase of Marian apparitions has been foretold of "latter times" by innumerable canonized Saints eminently including St. Louis Grignon de Montfort. A caution: *in every period wherein authentic private prophecy from approved sources abounds, alleged apparitions which are subsequently declared by the Church to be false also usually appear in equal or even much greater abundance.*

1. Fatima

The first major Marian apparition formally approved by the Church in this century was that of Fatima. In 1917, 70,000 people at the Cova da Iria near Fatima, Portugal, saw the sun turn like a pinwheel in the sky. They were there because the three seers had announced that Our Lady had promised a miracle for that day. Our Lady subsequently prophesied to the three peasant children, Francisco, Jacinta, and Lucia that World War I would soon end.

She also told them that if people did not stop sinning that a second and worse world war would soon begin DURING THE REIGN OF POPE PIUS XI and that Russia would spread its errors throughout the world. As predicted, the next Pope was named Pius XI, the Second World War did initialize during his reign - just as predicted, and Russia did spread her errors. These and other prophecies made that day have subsequently come true. As Pope Pius XII said, "The time for disbelieving in Fatima has long since ceased."

Many Popes have publicly expressed their private belief in Fatima and Pope John Paul II has even gone on pilgrimage there. Yet we as Catholics are *not required* to believe in Fatima either as an apparition or in its prophecies. The same holds true for any other private apparition, revelation, locution or message. Vis-a-vis Revelation, we as Catholics are only required to believe in the deposit of Faith -- what is contained in Tradition and Scripture. *It is the question of the prudence of adhering to only the bare necessities of our Faith which is the issue here.*

While it cannot be and must not be a source of Faith, nor a primary source of our Christian Virtue of Hope, private Catholic prophecy does hold much hope and consolation for the practicing Christian. Over and over again the private prophets have stated that threatening prophecies are sent as warnings to the bad -- *but as consolations and encouragements to the good.* As St. Luke said when discussing prophecy of apocalyptic events, "When you see these things begin to take place, lift up your heads, for your redemption is at hand."[270] *The logical conclusion is that the Christian who in principle rejects all private prophecy misses out on a great deal of consolation.*

---

[270] Lk. 21:28

A. DISCERNMENT OF SPIRITS

1. Not All Prophecy is Authentic

The author personally has doubts about a number of alleged private prophets. Just as an example: Nostradamus, a 16th century physician, eventually made his living as an astrologer. He claimed to be able to predict the future of his wealthy clients by reading the stars. The "quatrains" of Nostradamus have been studied assiduously by his devotees for years.

Astrology has been condemned by the Church from its infancy. The reason is that astrology essentially denies the doctrine of free will.

> "...as at the Council of Trent, which expressly forbade the faithful to read books on astrology dealing with 'future contingent achievements, with fortuitous events and such actions as depend on human freedom, but daring to claim certitude about their occurence.'"[271]

Nostradamus claimed to be able to predict the future from the movement of the stars. He practiced for a living that which stands condemned by the Church. However, according to St. Thomas Aquinas, even a great sinner could be used as a prophetic instrument by God.[272] However, St. Thomas and the Magisterium also teach us that in the area of private prophecy it is much more prudent to only consider prophecies from those known for the sanctity of their lives.

The author has never read or heard of a Pope or Bishop speaking enthusiastically or respectfully about Nostradamus. But the "prophecies" of Nostradamus are very widely read today by the general public. The reader may confirm this by checking any major book store in North America. It could be just a coincidence that the same

---

271 *The Catholic Catechism*, John A. Hardon, S.J., Doubleday & Co., 1974, p. 46.

272 *The Disputed Questions on Truth*, St. Thomas Aquinas, Henry Regnery Company, Chicago, 1953, Vol. 2, Question XII,, Article V "Is Moral Goodness Required for Prophecy?", pp. 128-132.

"world" which rejects Scriptural prophecy and the Magisterium, promotes Nostradamus.

2. Authentic Catholic Prophecy Tells Man of His Responsibilities

Despite the prophetic track record of Fatima, most of this "world's" general public would not even think of reading the prophecies of its three little seers. Those Fatima prophecies tell us that the cause of our centuries massive problems are our sin and general faithlessness to God's Revelation. Every prophetic event of our century which the Church has confirmed as emanating from "supernaturality" has revealed that our wars and disasters are caused by mankind's contemporary increasing sinfulness. They confirm that man is personally responsible for the suffering of mankind in such wars and disasters. There is not one exception to that statement.

The world will promote the sensationalism of Nostradamus, but it draws back in horror from and rejects Fatima's moral message of personal responsibility. The majority of people who will excitedly run after fire trucks to a conflagration, will usually not go and listen to a fire marshal giving a presentation on fire safety. The majority of those who will raptly watch a television report on the AIDS epidemic, usually have little time for a program which proves that its *primary* (not exclusive) causes are two sinful acts, immoral sex and drug abuse. They don't want to hear that ninety-nine percent of AIDS infections would never occur if people simply obeyed God's law.

Interestingly, *many* approved private prophecies predict epidemics of horrible new diseases for our time. They also identify the cause as serious sin and rejection of God. Even many good "Catholics" think it is judgmentalism to make such statements. But *approved* prophecies predict these epidemics and state their cause to be the sin of man. How can it be *judgmental* to repeat an approved prophecy which states such things?

The author helped to found, and for years has done volunteer work at a house for men dying of AIDS. This house is run by Mother Teresa's Missionaries of Charity. All the nuns and the lay volunteers who work in this house love in Christ those who are dying there.

They also see first hand what is causing 99% of the AIDS epidemic. The cause is various violations of God's laws.

The nuns and volunteers also see the price in suffering which is regularly paid for such violations. Yet those nuns and volunteers never judge those dying of AIDS. They love them and care for them in Christ. The prophecies first and foremost contain pleas for man to return to God's law. For those who do so return, there is in many ways a predictable reduction in suffering. That return is the only place wherein mankind can find any measure of true happiness on this earth. God loves us. That is why He sends His Mother with pleas and the warnings that if man does not obey God, then man will bring the consequences upon mankind.

3. Prophecy Selection Process in This Book!

The Scriptures almost self-select themselves in that the Fathers, Doctors, and Theologians of the Church long ago established which were the most important prophetical items in Scripture.
The writings of the Fathers on prophecy are *primarily* contained in their expositions;

(1) on the Book of Daniel,

(2) on some other Old Testament prophetic books,

(3) on the Apocalypse,

(4) and in their general catecheses and expositions of that which they had received from Apostolic Tradition.

Many of the Fathers also wrote of their personal "opinions" (which they almost always separately label as such) based upon that Tradition. It is primarily from within the writings of the Fathers that the prophecies from Tradition are found. The Fathers present such in their exegesis on the Scriptures and within their works which are specific to the end times and the Antichrist. The author has culled from those Patristic writings the ones which most clearly demonstrate that the Antichrist most probably is not coming in our time. Those writings indicate a rather lengthy series of events yet to occur prior to the coming of Antichrist.

Those *Prophecies from Tradition and Scripture* are presented to the reader in Faith. The private "opinions" of the Fathers *which are not matters of faith*, but which according to the teaching of the Church "is also of very great weight" are herein presented as such. The actual prophecies themselves contained in Tradition and Scripture are of course totally consistent with one another. **Prophecies from Tradition and Scripture form the base from which private prophecy can and must be measured for consistency with the traditional teachings of the Church.** If one is not conversant with both the teachings from Tradition and Scripture on this subject, how can one begin to weigh a private prophecy for consistency with the traditional teachings of the Church on general eschatology?

Vis-a-vis selection, the private prophecies present an even more difficult problem in that their composite size is larger than the Scriptural and Traditional prophecies and their Patristic expositions combined. So they could not all be presented in any case. For that reason, *choice of the private prophecies presented had to be the most drastically selective.* **The easiest and most logical selective method was first, to almost exclusively limit the selections from private prophecy to those which have had some form of ecclesial approbation or another.** But this is not as great a loss as some might imagine.

Recent non-approved private prophecies add nothing *substantially* new to that which is contained in prophecies which already do have Church approbation. *The singular exception is that some of the recent prophecies from unnapproved sources appear to claim that the Antichrist and the Second Coming of Christ are close at hand.* In the light of Tradition and Scripture and a broad view of private prophecy from *Church-approved* sources, that is most probably not the case. That which is new and of principal interest in several recent approved prophecies (e.g. Akita) is a renewed and dramatically heightened sense of urgency in prophetic warnings about *a chastisement*.

Limiting the private prophecies to those from sources which have Church approbation also relieves this author of the dangers inherent in attempting to anticipate the judgment of the Church.

Private prophecies from approved sources are presented for the reader to weigh and consider their compatibility or non-compatibility with that which *is* of faith - that which comes from Tradition and Scripture. Their "approval" merely signifies that they are not "natural" in origin and that there is nothing contrary to Faith and Morals in them.[273]

Many of the older approved prophecies set an order or understandable system to the prophesied events. The most recent prophecies tend to present pieces of information in a manner similar to a very large and very complex jigsaw puzzle - from which the puzzle *picture* to help one put it together is missing. Without the overall picture from Tradition and Scripture, supplemented in part by private prophecies from canonized Saints, Blessed and Venerable, even the newer approved prophecies tend to present a bewildering jumble of pieces.

Once an individual has seen the overall picture which comes from Revelation (Tradition, Scripture) and also from private prophecies from approved sources, he or she has a good measure against which to judge those which are unapproved. The vast majority of the people who have studied private prophecy are totally *unaware* of the content of the vast body of prophecy from Tradition and the writings of the Fathers. There are several reasons for this.

(1) They have never had the opportunity to physically see those prophecies from Tradition and the writings of the Fathers.

(2) Many of those prophecies appear only in relatively rare books which normally are found only in the finest of very large Catholic libraries.

---

[273] Given the almost constant Papal approval of Fatima and its events, and the prophecies which emanated from there, given Pope John Paul's pilgrimage there, Fatima would appear to have a very special place of honor within the ranks of private prophecy. But even Fatima is not part of the Deposit of Revelation. Each and every Catholic must understand that even a Papal approbation or pilgrimage does not place an "of Faith" stamp of authority or authenticity on any private revelation. If this is the case, then why study *approved* prophecies? Because the Magisterium and Popes have done so. They study them not for the discovery of new doctrine, but for discernment in "the direction of human acts." Theirs is a good example to follow.

(3) Many of them are in print only in Latin or Greek, of particular importance being the following three works, *Patrologica Graeca*, *Patrologia Latina*, and the *Corpus Christianorum Continuatio Mediaevalis*. A significant percentage of the materials in those works have never been translated into English. Where they have, the English translations are in many cases difficult and/or expensive to get access to.

(4) Even for one fluent in Latin and Greek, their composite size comes to hundreds of very large volumes. BUT, even if they were all in English, few readers could or would take the time to search out the prophetic elements contained in those hundreds of volumes.

Therefore the author has culled the best from them *for the purposes of a single volume overview*, and (in many cases) presents them here for the first time in the English language. Again, how does one measure or discern a private prophecy (*particularly if it is unapproved*) if one does not have the comparative scale of all the prophecy from Tradition and Scripture? That problem is expanded when one also lacks the exegesis by the Fathers of the Church -- *men who were in direct possession of the body of Oral Tradition which had come down from the Apostles*.

4. Private Prophecy Selection Criteria for This Book

They are:

(1) The included private prophecies are limited (for the most part)[274] to those which have received some form of ecclesial approbation or another.

(2) Private prophecies have been especially selected with an eye to those *which amplify or expand on specific*

[274] Some of the older prophesies are difficult in this area. The Church has not always had the norms for approbation which She now utilizes. Therefore the older prophecies have not necessarily undergone the current legal screening processes. In those cases, where traditional attribution is all that is available, it is quoted as it is traditionally presented.

prophecies and themes which come from "sacred Tradition and sacred Scripture."[275]

(3) This is particularly so in relation to prophecies about the "latter times" and the "end times."

(4) Particular emphasis has been accorded to such prophecies which come from the Saints, Venerable and Blessed of the Church, along with those of some of Her non-canonized Popes. That process should increase the credibility of such prophecies in the eyes of the Catholic reader. This is especially applicable for any reader who may for the first time be discovering the concept of the actual existence of "genuine" private prophecy.
Today's heavily formalized and legalized process for dealing with private prophecies goes back only a few centuries. Also, the legal process as we know it today to declare someone either a canonized Saint, or Blessed, or Venerable does not go back to the earlier prophecies, so then, when dealing with,

(a) prophecies or exegesis of individuals who are not officially canonized or declared by the Church (under today's processes) to be either Saints, Blessed or Venerable, [e.g., Sts. Cyril of Jerusalem, John Chrysostom, John Damascene, Hildegard], and/or

(b) prophecies which are much over 100 years old, whether they come from Saints, Blessed or Venerable or not;

In cases (a) and (b) immediately above, special attention has been laid on those prophecies which subsequently received written "approbation" as to being "credible" or free from religious error -- either (1) through being declared by the Church to be a Father, Doctor, or canonized Saint, (2) through imprimaturs from Bishops on printed texts of their prophecies, or (3) were simply publicly fostered as such by the Bishop of the alleged "prophet," or were advanced/promoted by the superior of their religious order, and/or abbots and abbesses of monasteries of the respective prophets.

[275] *Verbum Dei.*

5. Discernment Tests

As repeatedly stated, there are such things as false apparitions. Sometimes the visionary or locutionist is simply deluded, sometimes he or she is actually lying, sometimes he or she has been tricked by spirits far from holy. As an example of the opposite, we have already read from St. Theresa of Avila, including her specific claim to being a recipient of the charism of private prophecy. Her spiritual companion, St. John of the Cross, was also an expert on this subject.

The 1989 book, *Fire Within*, summarizes the teachings of both of St. Theresa and St. John on locutions and visions. The author of *Fire Within* first describes the two "extreme views" on this subject (extreme credulity and extreme unbelief), and then summarizes the views and rules of St. Theresa and St. John on this subject.

> "Granted that our two saints [St. Theresa of Avila and St. John of the Cross] avoided both extremes, we need still to ask what exactly their outlook was on alleged cases of divine enlightenment. We may summarize their views in four statements.
>
> **"The first is that divine interventions are normal gifts given whenever God sees fit to give them. They are not rare.**
>
> "Their second principle may surprise many of those who are happy with the first, ... namely, **illusion and deception are not rare, either.**
>
> **"Their third principle is the logical consequence of the first two: the need for objective ecclesial discernment."**[276]

How can we, as St. Paul says when referring to private prophecy, "test all things; hold fast that which is good."[277] As Sts. Teresa and John of the Cross point out, the most prudent rule is to wait for the "ecclesial discernment" of the Church. However, it can take centuries for the Church to declare someone a Saint, and/or his or her prophecy "credible."

---

[276] *Fire Within*, Thomas Dubay, F.M., Ignatius Press, 1989, pp. 246&247.
[277] 1 Thess. 5:21.

What does a prudent individual do in the meantime. The Church has prudential rules by which She judges whether it is likely that a prophecy comes from God. We can prudently, privately as individuals, apply *some* of the same rules while prudently waiting for definitive statements from the Church. The following are a short excerpt of some of those rules:

(1) Will the prophet obey when silenced by competent Church authority such as his local Bishop? There has never been a case in the entire history of the Church when an *alleged* "prophet" who turned out to be an *authentic prophet*, was ever disobedient to his or her appropriate Bishop or religious superior's order of silence. [That rule consistently holds true only where such bishop or superior was in full union with Rome]. On occasion, an individual Bishop's decision has been overruled by a successor. *But even this has never happened in a case of initial disobedience* to a Bishop or superior who was in full union with Rome.

Obedience to ecclesial authority is the oldest, first, and most reliable *negative* "test" of a "prophet." i.e., proven disobedience *always* strongly signals the high probability of non-authenticity. As Scripture says, "Obedience is superior to sacrifice." Even the three little children of Fatima were at one point temporarily ordered to silence. They were immediately obedient, and only spoke respectfully of their superiors who had given the order of silence. When God wills a prophecy or locution to be made public, *He* arranges hearts, minds, and events such that it happens.

(2) Has the "prophet" ever wished for or willed to have the gift of prophecy? This is a tool to determine whether there is a *possibility* that his imagination is fulfilling the wish.

(3) Does the "prophet" appear to remain calm in the face of the revelation? Genuine revelations usually produce a sense of calm and peace in the recipient rather than agitation or panic. When calm and peace are missing, it is not a good sign.

(4) Does the recipient of the message remain open to the idea that it might be a delusion? If so, this is a *good* sign. As St. John of the Cross says, a prudent recipient takes even a skeptical view of such revelations, *because legitimate prophets are usually aware that they can be deluded.*[278] This understanding comes from their honest sense of humility.

(5) Has the "prophet" ever accepted money or personal favors in exchange for prophecy? If so, that is almost a sure sign something is amiss.

(6) Do the "prophet's" predictions tend to come true? This can be difficult to determine in the case of "conditional" prophecies. There have been cases wherein even canonized saints have misunderstood a timeline which was given for a prophecy. *"For centuries it has been a clear papal teaching that even a canonized saint who has reported a private revelation which has been approved by the Church for acceptance by the Faithful may have introduced some personal element that is subject to error or distortion."*[279]

(7) Is there anything relating to doctrinal or moral theology in the prophecy which is inconsistent with the traditional teachings of the Church? (If there is, the chances are the prophecy is not from God.) *However*, sometimes the prophet does not clearly understand what he or she was told.[280] Only the Church through her official representatives, Her Bishops, can sort this type of thing out.

(8) Is the alleged prophet sound of mind and emotionally stable? This question is best totally left to ecclesial

---

[278] See the section in *Fire Within* on St. John's commentary of "Locutions" for a full discussion.

[279] *A Still, Small Voice*, Fr. Benedict J. Groeschel, C.F.R., Ignatius Press, San Francisco, 1992, p. 27. Fr. Groeschel states that this "injection" is involuntary in a legitimate prophet.

[280] Ibid. p. 131 "Although prophecy is gift of the Holy Spirit, the Holy Spirit is not given in the gift of prophecy, but only with the gift of charity."

professionals. But in some cases, the instability is so obvious that the average non-professional can clearly observe it in the *alleged* prophet.

(9) Does the person lead a morally upright life? Has the alleged apparition appeared to increase the prophet's sense of humility and docility to direction from ecclesial superiors. One can find books that lay this condition down as a rule. But that is in error. Many sound theologians (including St. Thomas Aquinas) have observed that sanctity is not necessary in an authentic prophet.

Sanctity or goodness is not an absolute requirement, since as St. Thomas aptly points out "In the Gospel of St. Mathew (7:22), this statement is put in the mouth of the damned: 'Lord, have we not prophesied in thy name...?' Therefore, prophecy can exist in evil men."[281] But the Church chooses in her wisdom, in the main, only to deal with those of decent moral character when involved in the areas of private prophecy.

(10) LASTLY: For private individuals in their private judgments, if the local Bishop (or especially any higher authority) has merely expressed some reservations about a prophet, and this reservation has not been overruled by higher Church authority, prudence should tell one to be very cautious.

6. How (as St. Thomas Says) Could a Bad Person be a Legitimate Prophet

St. Thomas sends us directly to Scripture for the answer of that question, to a passage in the Gospel of St. Matthew. As with all of Scripture, this passage must be understood within the totality of the book within which it is written and the totality of Scripture itself. The passage Thomas refers us to is contained in our Our Lord's discussion of the Final Judgement. Jesus paints some striking contrasts in Matt 7:22-23 as to whether goodness of life is required for a genuine prophet.

[281] *Disputed Questions on Truth*, Vol. 2, p 129.

> "**Not everyone who says to me, Lord, Lord, shall enter the Kingdom of heaven, but he who does the will of my Father in heaven.** On that day many will say to me, Lord, Lord, **did we not prophesy in your name,** and cast out demons in your name, and do many mighty works in your name?
>
> "And then I well declare to them, 'I never knew you; depart from me you evildoers.'"

How could this be; that men and women who prophecy or cast out demons in the name of Christ, that God does not "know" them? They are obviously Christian believers because Jesus even says that they will appeal to having performed these deeds in His very name. Obviously, they have faith, and they have *apparently* put that faith into practice with deeds, or, works. So what could possibly be left? The answer lies within our Lord's statement,

> "Not everyone who says to me, Lord, Lord, shall enter the Kingdom of heaven, but **he who does the will of my Father in heaven.**"

Central to an understanding of this Gospel message is Our Lord's description of the separation of the sheep from the goats on the day of judgement. It reads,

> "When the Son of man comes in his glory ... Before Him gathered all the nations, and he will separate them one from another as a shepherd separates the sheep from the goats, ... [to the sheep] on his right hand, 'Come, O blessed of my Father, inherit the kingdom prepared for you from the foundation of the world; for I was hungry and you gave me food, I was thirsty and you gave me to drink, I was a stranger and you welcomed me, ... Truly I say to you, as you did it to one of the least of my brethren, you did it to me.'"

> " ... to those [the goats] at his left hand, 'Depart from me, ***you cursed***, into the eternal fire prepared for the devil and his angels; for I was hungry and you gave me no food; I was thirsty and you gave me no drink, I was a stranger and you did not welcome me, naked and you did not clothe me,

> sick and in prison and you did not visit me... Truly, I say to you, as you did it not to one of the least of these, you did it not to me.'"[282]

Jesus tells us several things about those who are *guaranteed* to get to heaven (including prophets).

(1) Mat. 7:22 They have faith. They are people who know the Lord. They say, "Lord, Lord."
(2) Matt 25:31-46. They have lived that faith in good deeds for their fellow man (of which Our Lord gives examples), good deeds without which Jesus clearly says they are "cursed."
(3) Yet He tells us that not all who have both faith and works have done "the will of my Father in heaven." So what is necessary besides faith and works?
(4) He tells us earlier in Mathew in the beatitudes. There He guarantees us, **"Blessed are *the pure in heart*, for *they shall see God*.**[283] There is the guarantee.

In the Gospel of Matthew we learn that when the "pure in heart" hear the message of the Gospel, they accept the gift of faith in belief. Those with a pure heart live that faith in good deeds, without which deeds even those with faith are "cursed." ("you cursed ... I was hungry and you gave me no food.") They perform these deeds out of love for God *and their fellow man*[284] for God's greater glory.

CONCLUSIONS: It is not necessary to be righteous in the sight of the Lord to be an authentic prophet. Our Lord tells us some authentic prophets will even go to hell.

---

[282] Matt. 25:31-46 - *Revised Standard Version, Catholic Edition.*

[283] Matt. 5:8. Thank you, Fr. Cliff.

[284] "If anyone says 'I love God,' and hates his brother, he is a liar; for he who does not love his brother whom he has seen, cannot love God whom he has not seen. And this command we have from Him, that he who loves God should love his brother also. 1 John 4:20-21. Quoted from Navarre Bible - English text from Revised Standard Version, 1987.

In other words, we cannot presume to privately judge the genuineness of the prophetic charism of an individual from the apparent goodness or lack thereof of someones life. Our Lord even tells us that some genuine prophets will not make it to heaven.

7. Some Recent Books Appear to Support Disobedience

There are several recently published books which seem to encourage a kind of disrespect for the juridical decisions of Bishops in these matters. While the authors probably mean well, these books specifically publicly challenge the Bishops for not having approved more of the recent alleged visions. Unfortunately, the above mentioned books are beginning to have a predictable effect on some of the faithful.

> **NOTE:** The author has on recent occasions heard individuals (who are enamored of a specific alleged "prophet") question some Bishop for a declaration of non-supernaturality in relation to that specific prophet or visionary. In virtually every case, these individuals have read one or more of the books mentioned above.
>
> Every Christian can prayerfully receive a gift of discernment from the Holy Spirit. But a Bishop is granted special gifts of discernment by the Holy Spirit for the exercise of his episcopal office, part of which office is official discernment of alleged apparitions.
>
> For obvious reasons those special episcopal gifts are not granted to those outside the episcopate -- non-bishops have no direct need to exercise those "special" episcopal gifts. Common sense should tell any Catholic (lay or sacerdotal) that they should tread lightly when challenging the decisions of a bishop who has such special gifts.

On the other hand, *there is absolutely nothing wrong with a respectful appeal to higher authority, or a respectful request of the local ordinary for a reexamination of a cause.* But openly questioning a Bishop's juridical decisions in such a matter is never a fruit of the Holy Spirit. Positive criticism of an *apparently* mishandled aspect of an investigation can still be handled with due respect. The proper forum for such respectful criticism is in the ecclesial process -- not in the streets.

8. Disobedience is a Slippery Slope

God gave us the Church to guide us in spiritual matters. When we reject that guidance we can place ourselves in a very dangerous spiritual position. *Experience shows that a spirit of disobedience in one area can readily transfer rather quickly to others.* Church history shows us hundreds of examples of those who almost imperceptibly traveled from disobedience in an area of discipline -- to disobedience in an area of Doctrine. That is a faithful Catholic's worst nightmare. **Disobedience, once begun, is a deceptively slippery slope.**

If the vision or locution is legitimate, and God wants it to be approved, God will arrange hearts and circumstances for approbation without any *undue* assistance from the faithful. One of the many things a discerning Bishop looks for in an alleged apparition is a faithful, respectful, following developing around the prophet. When the followers or admirers of an alleged prophet show less than full respect for the Bishop's decisions (or lack of same) or even for the caution or reticence of the Bishop, this leaves one of the required signs of authenticity missing. Bishops apply the rule, "By their fruits you shall know them."

The local faithful should show the same spirit of obedience an *authentic* prophet always shows to the decisions of their Bishop. **A supporter of an alleged prophet can flunk the same obedience test which is given to visionaries.** And when supporters of an alleged prophet are disobedient or disrespectful, to use a popular expression "they are shooting themselves in their own foot." They are hurting the cause of their *alleged* prophet when they produce a sign of disobedience. Supporters are one of the fruits of the alleged prophet. "By their fruits you shall know them."

B. CONDITIONAL PROPHECIES

"Conditional" prophecies usually contain some proviso(s) that unless certain things occur that something else will occur in consequence. For example: amongst other things, it was prophesied at Fatima that unless many people say their Daily Rosary and sinners cease offending Our Lord, that Russia would spread its errors

throughout the world. In addition there was the request for the "First Saturdays of Reparation," that if people did not comply with these requests a second and even more terrible world war would break out following the end of World War I.

People did not in general comply with those requests, and Russia as a consequence did spread her errors, and WW II did break out and was "even more terrible" than WW I. According to the prophecies of Fatima, *if enough people had met the Fatima "conditions" for peace, the major world crises which we now face would not have come to pass*. Further, according to several approved prophecies, if people will now put into effect those prayers, Rosaries, acts of reparation, Holy hours, etc., the events about to be described will also not come to pass. Short of that they will be greatly ameliorated, or they will be put off for another age in the future. This is a prime example of what is meant by a "conditional" prophecy.

Usually the "condition" amounts to this; whether the prophesied event takes place or not depends upon how the people respond to God's requests and grace. **There have been times in history when people did cooperate with grace and a "conditionally" threatened event did not materialize or was forestalled till a later time.** Another similar example of a conditional prophecy comes from the Old Testament. Jonas was told to go to the city of Nineveh and preach a chastisement, which would be withheld if the Ninevehns met a certain class of "conditions." Scripture tells us the Ninevehns met those conditions. According to Scripture, being lead by their King the Ninevehns performed public penance. For this reason Scripture tells us God spared them and their city.

A somewhat similar series of experiences happened to St. Vincent Ferrer, which experiences we will read of later.

C. PROPHECY OF FOREKNOWLEDGE, AND PROPHECY OF PREDESTINATION

Conditional prophecies can be a confusing concept. The "condition" has to do with future cooperation or lack of cooperation on the part of men. Many of the prophecies the reader will see in the chapters to come are purely conditional prophecies. The following passage from the *Catholic Encyclopedia* succinctly describes this concept. In this quote the encyclopedia is discussing St. Thomas Aquinas' theology on this subject. What we call conditional prophecies, St. Thomas refers to as "prophecies of foreknowledge."

According to St. Thomas Aquinas, *future* prophecy is divided into two subdivisions, namely that of (1) foreknowledge, and that of (2) predestination. (See Summa II-II, Q clxxiv, A.1).[285] As the Catholic Encyclopedia comments:

> "According to Thomas ... *that* [prophecy] *of foreknowledge*, takes place when God reveals future events *which depend upon created free will* and which He (God) sees present from eternity. They have reference to life and death, to wars and dynasties, to the affairs of the Church and State, as well as the affairs of individual life. That prophecy of predestination takes place when God reveals what he alone will do, and what He sees present in eternity and in His absolute decree."[286]

The encyclopedia article just quoted then immediately goes on to describe private prophecies of Pope St. Pius V, St. Edward the Confessor, St. Paul of the Cross, and then says:

> "There are many other private prophecies concerning the REMOTE and PROXIMATE signs which will precede the General judgment and concerning Antichrist, such as those attributed to St. Hildegarde, St. Bridget of Sweden, Venerable Anna Maria Taigi, the Cure of Ars, and many others." [1913 Edition, Vol. XII]

One previously made point should be reemphasized. The Church has always counseled caution when dealing with a specific private revelation. But as the reader can see from the article above, she also counsels against total incredulity.

---

[285] The interested reader may find Thomas' full discussion of this in Vol. 2 (II) of, *Summa Theologica*, St. Thomas Aquinas, *First Complete American Edition*, Translated by Fathers of the English Dominican Province, Benzinger Bros. Inc. New York, 1947. pp. 1906-1912 contain all of Q. 174.

[286] 1913 Edition, Vol. XII.

1. St. Thomas' Classification of Prophecy.

According to St. Thomas there are several ways to classify prophecies. The first of them has to do with time. Thomas speaks of three timelines of prophecy.

(1) Those which make known "hidden things of the past"
(2) Those which explain contemporary events
(3) The last category is prophecy of future events.

It is this third category of "future events" into which all conditional prophecies fit. Thomas further breaks that third category into two further classes.

(1) *Prophecy of predestination - takes place when God reveals what He alone will do*, and what He sees present in eternity and in His absolute decree.

(2) *Prophecy of foreknowledge - takes place when God reveals future events which depend upon created free will* and which He (God) sees present from eternity. ALL CONDITIONAL PROPHECY FITS INTO THIS CLASS.

So when we speak of "conditional" prophecies, we are speaking of one class of what St. Thomas calls "prophecy of foreknowledge." These are prophecies which depend as to their outcome on how people will exercise their free will in the future. If they cooperate with God's grace, a certain event or development will or will not take place. Conditional prophecies state conditions. They do not tell you whether people will meet those conditions.

2. Not All Private Prophecy of "Foreknowledge" is Conditional

Many prophecies contain a mixture of both conditional, and non-conditional prophecies. For instance; in 1917, at Fatima Our Lady is reported to have unconditionally foretold that the War (World War I) would end within a short period of time. There were *no* conditions attached to this prophecy. She foretold that the War would end shortly and it did.

But she went on to prophecy a number of other events (for example World War II), whose outcome would totally depend upon how people responded to a call for inner conversion, prayer, and repentance. In other words, not all private prophecy of the future is prophecy of "foreknowledge" (conditional) prophecy. Some of it is conditional and some of it is unconditional - proceeding both from God's justice *and* His Divine Mercy. But, as the reader will soon discover, the majority of prophecy over the last hundred or two hundred years from sources approved by the Church has been conditional.

Another apparently *unconditional* prophecy made at Fatima contains a total message of hope. Our Lady is reported to have said, "In the end my Immaculate Heart will triumph, and a certain period of peace will be granted to the world."

D. DO "EDUCATED" CATHOLICS BELIEVE IN THE CONTEMPORARY CHARISM OF PRIVATE PROPHECY?

You have already read numerous statements from Scripture, Tradition, and the Magisterium stating that authentic "private prophecy" of future events exists. Most particularly, the Fathers at Vatican II were for the most part very well-educated men. The documents they wrote confirmed the Church's constant belief in this charism. Scripture actually predicts that the charism will exist until the end of time. You will read the claims to the gift of "prophecy" by many canonized Saints, Blessed and Venerable, and Fathers and Doctors of the Church. We have even read the words of one of the most prestigious Doctors of the Church, St. Teresa of Avila, personally claiming for herself the charism of private prophecy.

There are *many* academics of the author's personal acquaintance who privately have no problem with the subject of private prophecy. But due to the volatility of the subject, many of them do keep this belief quiet in academe. Given the known list of Church Fathers, Doctors, Popes and canonized Saints who have spoken positively on the subject of the charism of private prophecy, it is a mystery to the author why so many otherwise solid Catholics visibly show signs of nervousness merely when the subject even comes up.

One academic who is public about his views is Rev. Benjamín Martín Sánchez, *Doctor of Sacred Scripture* at the University of Salamanca, Spain. In speaking of "private prophecies," he says in the Prologue to his book, *The Last Times*;

> "I must confess that these prophecies have greatly attracted my attention because, even though many of them are widely separated in time, **they maintain unity and agree with those of Divine Scripture.** In general, they warn us of a judgment of nations, a great chastisement, which will overcome all humanity, *to be followed by a long period of peace and universal well-being*."[287]

This book is a message of hope, there is nothing in it for a good Christian to fear! **"BE NOT AFRAID!"** According to the prophecies, the world awaits "a long period of peace and universal well-being."

If Popes did not also believe in the charism of private prophecy, would many Popes since 1917 have promoted devotion to Our Lady of Fatima? Would (as mentioned earlier) Pope John Paul II have made a pilgrimage there?

E. A FINAL CAVEAT

1. Some Recent *Alleged* Prophecies are at Variance With the Broad Catholic Spectrum of Prophecy

Several recent prophecies appear to predict the approach of Antichrist, the approach of the Second Coming of Jesus Christ, and of the end of the world. To the best of the author's knowledge, not one of those prophets nor their prophecies is currently approved by

[287] *Public And Private Prophecies About The Last Times*, Published by Opus Reginae Sacratissimi Rosarii, 1972, Rev. Benjamin Martin Sanchez, p.8.

the Church. As will be demonstrated in the materials to follow, *the apparent content of such prophecies stands in direct contradiction to the broad spectrum of prophecy from Tradition and Scripture, as well as private prophecy from canonized Saints about our period in history.*[288]

That is why, if one is going to read private prophecy it is imperative that the reading be broad and not limited to recent unapproved private prophecies. **Without a *broad* perspective from Tradition and Scripture, one has no reliable scale from which to measure an unapproved prophecy for possible authenticity.**

---

[288] There is always the possibility that these recent seers are simply misunderstanding what they have been told.

CHAPTER 4

AN OVERVIEW OF PROPHECIES OF A CHASTISEMENT, A GREAT KING, AND A RESTORED HOLY ROMAN EMPIRE

A. OVERVIEW - BEGINS WITH A CAVEAT:

The following remarks must be born in mind when dealing with any or all of the private prophecies contained in this book. The author's primary purpose in presenting them is *not* to induce readers to become engrossed in private prophecy. As stated in the Introduction, the primary purpose is the following:

(1) Some recent *alleged* private prophecies claim to show that Antichrist and/or the Second Coming of Christ (the Parousia) are just around the corner.

(2) Those ideas are spreading and must be combated.

(3) Those ideas are not consonant with revealed Doctrine that comes to us from Tradition and Scripture.

(4) That entire premise is also not consonant with the Scriptural exegesis of the Fathers.

(5) THAT IDEA IS *NOT* EVEN CONSONANT WITH A BROAD OVERVIEW OF APPROVED PRIVATE CATHOLIC PROPHECY.

The primary purpose of reproducing private Catholic prophecies from Church-approved sources contained in this book *is to fight fire with fire*. They show that Catholic prophecy from sources approved by the Church predict *many* events yet to come in this world prior to the coming of Antichrist and then the Parousia! Many of those privately foretold events are in total agreement with events foretold in Scripture and Tradition. This fact alone should disabuse any reader of the notion that Antichrist is "just around the corner" - especially if the reader has been lead to that notion by private prophecy from *unapproved* sources.

A large number of these "private prophecies" from approved sources are highly conditional in nature. Consequently, even they may, or may not, happen at all. Some of them appear to be unconditional (such as the Fatima prophecy of a period of peace). But no private prophecy under any set of conditions can be of supernatural faith.

1. Even Authentic Prophets Can and Do Sometimes Misunderstand That Which They Have Received in Prophecy

Any number of private prophets have been absolutely wrong in *some* of their prophecies, at the same time that they were right in others. *In some cases*, this error was due to the fact that the prophet did not perceive that the prophecy was conditional. However, that does not explain all of the errors in individual private prophecies.

There are recorded cases wherein the "prophet" has simply, clearly, misunderstood what was told to him or her. St. Catherine Laboure is one famous case in point. She accurately predicted the specific dates of some major events years in advance. She was also wrong on one or two others. The reader of private prophecies needs therefore to exercise a particular reserve in regarding *any single prophecy*. It is also advantageous when examining any singular prophecy, even of a canonized Saint, to be generally familiar with private prophecies of all the Saints, Blessed and Venerable. *Therefore, the author has repeated several times the absolute necessity for a "broad view" of Catholic prophecy which includes Tradition and Scripture.*

2. Necessity of a Broad View of Prophecy

Why do prudent people usually not consider a radical medical procedure without a second or third corroborating medical opinion? The reason is that individual doctors can and do make mistakes. Similarly, individual prophets, even canonized Saints can and do make mistakes in understanding what has been revealed to them. Therefore, the most prudent course is simply to:

(1) FIRST AND FOREMOST: Get a *broad* overview of prophecy contained in **both** Tradition and Scripture. We have already discussed the relationship of Tradition and Scripture. Most "Catholic" 20th century books on the subject of prophecy are almost devoid of the prophetic elements from Tradition and the exegesis of the Fathers.[289]

(2) Compare an *alleged* prophecy with those of Tradition and Scripture to see if as Fr. Sanchez observes, it maintains "unity and agreement" with them. If it does not, there is possibly a problem with the alleged "prophet," or a problem with the prophets understanding of what was revealed to them. In either case, that poses a serious problem with the prophecy as it is expressed. *An alleged prophecy which is not in full doctrinal unity and agreement with Tradition and Scripture as understood by the Church virtually never gets approved by a Bishop.*

[289] There appears to be a strong possibility that many of the Catholic writers on this subject have been unaware of (rather than ignored) the vast body of material contained in Tradition on the subject of prophecy for latter and the end times. Almost the only way one becomes aware of these materials is in reading a substantial number of the writings of the Fathers.

(3) Obtain a *broad* overview of private prophecies of canonized Saints, Blessed, and Venerable dealing with "latter times." *There is often an internal "unity and agreement" within prophecies of the Saints, Blessed and Venerable dealing with latter or end times.*[290] If a particular private prophecy is not in "unity and agreement" with those of canonized Saints, Blessed, and Venerable (in cases where enough detail is prophesied to see a unity which exists among them) experience shows that there is probably some kind of "problem" with that prophecy.

(4) Therefore, an alleged prophecy which does not appear to be in doctrinal unity and agreement with previous prophecies of canonized Saints, Blessed and Venerable is similarly almost never subsequently approved by a Bishop. *But this is not because the Bishop compares alleged prophecies with approved ones.*

Rather, the reason is that prophecies of Saints, Blessed and Venerable are firstly, almost by definition authentic, and secondly, such Saints, Blessed and Venerable have a consistently much better track record of properly interpreting and understanding that which is revealed to them. They tend to be in harmony with the traditional teachings of the Church.

Therefore, if an alleged prophecy does not appear to be in unity and agreement with those traditional teachings, the odds are much higher that the alleged prophecy is (a) either not authentic, or (b) has been seriously misunderstood by the alleged recipient of that prophecy.

[**An example** would be; if an alleged prophet said it had been revealed to him or her that the Devil would be the actual physical father of the Antichrist. That is a metaphysical impossibility, as well as being outside the

---

[290] Their unity and agreement is not usually as broad as that of the totality of Tradition and Scripture. This is primarily because much of the prophecy of the Saints, Blessed and Venerable is narrower in scope than that which is found in the totality of Scripture and/or Tradition. Nevertheless, such unity and agreement does exist in a number of cases.

traditional teaching of the Church.[291] Yet, a few *alleged* private prophets have stated such as being revealed to them. This specific subject (of the Devil actually fathering the Antichrist) is discussed by the Fathers, the majority of whom doctrinally condemned the idea, pointing out that it is of Tradition that the Antichrist will be a spiritual son of the Devil, but cannot, and will not be his physical son. Therefore, if some alleged prophet claimed that Antichrist would physically be sired by the Devil, this would be an example of an *alleged* prophecy which is either (a) not authentic, or (b) the prophet has seriously misunderstood what was revealed to them.[292]]

There are a number of details about Antichrist and the end times contained in the prophecy of canonized Saints, Blessed, Venerable, and other "approved" sources about the end times and the Antichrist. These details are normally consistent with what we receive from Tradition and Scripture and the Scriptural exegesis of the Fathers. But even when these "details" from private prophecy (1) add more

---

291 As observed by St. Augustine, human generation, outside the laws of nature, is a work of *creative power* and belongs to God alone. The direct power of Creation is unique to God and exists only within His Pure Act. Satan is a spiritual being - having been *created* by God as an angelic spirit without a body. He is creature of the Creator - as we are. It is therefore outside Satan's *created* nature to possess the power to create anything. When human parents come together and a child is born of that union - the parents are the instruments of a Divinely created and specifically appointed *instrumental* power created in them by God. The *instrumental* power to initiate human life, as created in man and woman by God - which man and woman exercise by the power of God - *God did not create/place that instrumental power in Satan*. Therefore, it is metaphysically impossible for Satan to sire a human child.

When the Holy Spirit "overshadowed" the Blessed Virgin Mary in creating the God/Man Jesus Christ (the Incarnation) - God exercised His Divine *exclusive* Creative power through the Holy Spirit. In order for Satan even to instrumentally create a human life, that would require that God through a singular exception would create in an evil spirit (Satan) the instrumental power to sire the human Antichrist. That would require that God participate in an evil act. *That is an impossibility.* **That is why the Fathers are unanimous** (with the possible exception of Origin [who thinks Antichrist might be an incarnate Demon], and Hippolytus [who thought he might be the Devil himself]) **that Antichrist is a man born of a natural human union.**

292 Numerous statements of various Fathers on this specific subject will be quoted later on in the Chapter on the Antichrist.

information on certain events foretold in Revelation, and (2) are consistent with what we receive from Revelation and the Scriptural exegesis of the Fathers, (3) they are still not of faith.

More Safety in Numbers

But as to determining what is "piously credible," when a multiplicity of prophecies from "approved" sources concur on a detail, then there is much less chance of error. This is because the odds are against a number of prophecies (from Church-approved sources) making exactly the same error in interpreting and/or understanding what was revealed to them. That is why a "broad view" of private prophecy from approved sources is so valuable to a proper understanding of such prophecy.

Therefore, when an *alleged* prophecy is (1) in unity and doctrinal agreement with Tradition, Scripture, and the exegesis of the Fathers, and (2) is consistent with the private prophecies of Canonized Saints, Blessed and Venerable and other "approved" prophets, and (3) the local Bishop has not expressed reservation or doubt about an alleged apparition, (4) then there is the beginning of a reasonable ground for what Pope Benedict XIV called "human (not religious) faith" in the revelation. When we do so it is because it is as Benedict XIV says, "piously credible."

Some might think that all of the above is an arbitrarily strict set of conditions. ***Do prudent individuals settle for less assurance vis-a-vis corroborating diagnosis when their physical life is at jeopardy?***

3. Reserving Judgement

The prophecies at Fatima, Portugal, were viewed by most people as simply incredible when they were first discussed in 1917. If it had not been for the accompanying Miracle of the Sun being seen by 70,000 witnesses, one wonders even how many Catholics would have taken them seriously at the time. Yet with one exception, every conditionally predicted event in the first two secrets has already come to pass. Since the Third Secret has not been made public, we cannot know about its contents with any certitude.

There are several central themes to the historic sweep of the private Catholic prophecies. Some of them will seem simply incredible to the 20th century reader. A serious student or scholar (Catholic or non-Catholic) always reserves judgment until the entire case for a thesis has been presented. This can be mentally difficult to do when a thesis appears quite radical. With the exception of the eschatological prophesies about the events surrounding the Antichrist and the Parousia, the following prophecies of a "Chastisement" are "conditional prophesies." By Catholic definition, they can be averted or at least ameliorated by sufficient cooperation with grace.

4. Planned Order of Presentation

Many prophets do not cover prophesied events either in chronological order, or in great depth. Others are limited to the future of a particular country or city. It is in putting all their prophecies together that an apparently recognizable pattern emerges. *Here we will take one private prophet out of historical order only because her prophecy covers quite a sweep of history -- including a definite chronology of events.* Later, you will see the same chain of events predicted for country after country causing a worldwide pattern to emerge.

5. Nursing Nun of Belay

The following prophecies of this nun are presented at this particular point because they do present an overall picture of a series of conditionally prophesied events for some future time. They show at least a proposed pattern for the pieces of a jigsaw puzzle.

Sr. Bertina Bouquillon is otherwise known as the Nursing Nun of Belay. This holy woman was born in 1800 in Saint Omer, France, and died in 1850. She made her vows in St. Louis Hospital as a nursing sister in 1822. *She received the stigmata of Christ* and had the charism of prophecy. The stigmata is the spiritual gift and penance of bearing one or more of the wounds of Christ on one's person. Stigmatics quite often also receive the gift of prophecy.

The following prophecy of Sister Bouquillon was written sometime between 1828 and 1830 and was entrusted to Fr. Fulgence, the Chaplain of the Trappist Monastery of Notre Dame des Gardes, near Angers, France. Among other things she declared:

> "Once again the madmen seem to gain the upper hand! They laugh God to scorn. Now, the churches are closed; the pastors run away; the Holy Sacrifice ceases.
>
> "The wicked try to destroy everything; their books and their doctrines are swamping the world. But the day of the justice is come. *Here is your King*; he comes forward amidst the confusion of those stormy days. Horrible times! *The just and the wicked fall!*
>
> "There was also a great battle, the like of which has never been seen before. Blood was flowing like water after a heavy rain. The wicked were trying to slaughter all the servants of the Religion of Jesus Christ. After they had killed a large number, they raised a cry of victory, but *suddenly the just received help from above.*
>
> "A saint raises his arms to Heaven; he allays the wrath of God. *He ascends the throne of Peter*. At the same time, the Great Monarch ascends the throne of his ancestors. All is quiet now. Altars are set up again; religion comes to life again. What I see now is so wonderful that I am unable to express it."

This series of events described by Sr. Bertina describes most of the major events associated with what some people call "The Minor Chastisement." It ends with a reference to a lasting period of worldwide peace which will come after a tribulation or chastisement. And that period of peace precedes the *Major Chastisement* associated with Antichrist. There has been no lasting age of peace between the early 1800's and today. Sr. Bouquillon continues:

> "All these things shall come to pass once the wicked have succeeded in circulating large numbers of bad books.
>
> "The end of time is approaching and the Antichrist will not delay his coming. *We will not see him, nor those who follow us, but those who come after the latter, will be under his dominion*."

Sister Bertina finishes the above text with the statement:

> "The *beginning* of the last period of the world will not occur in the nineteenth, but the twentieth century."[293]

6. Prophecy: Beginning of Last Period of Church Begins in 20th Century

Sr. Bertina says the "*beginning*" of the last period begins in the 20th Century. The "last period" could be a short century or two or thousands of years. Neither Revelation, the exegesis of the Fathers, *nor* "approved" private prophecy clearly states anything in this matter. In every period of trial for the Church and the World, many people ponder over whether Antichrist is on the immediate horizon. In the year 1000, there was a general panic throughout Christendom. Many of them believed that Satan was about to be unchained after having been bound for a thousand years. Had they thoroughly looked at their Tradition, Scripture, ancillarily confirmed by private prophecy, they would have known better.

The author does not believe that Antichrist is about to make his appearance. Oral Tradition, Scripture, and private prophecies say he comes after many more future events. In other words, these "approved" prophecies are definitely *not* predicting the end of the world for our time. They describe a "*beginning*" of a final stage of the world of unspecified length, but according to "approved" prophecies, of significant duration.

7. There is at Least One "Period of Peace" Before Antichrist

This prophecy of Sister Bertina's was given at this point to indicate a possible chronology of foretold events *after which* comes Antichrist. After all, *the last period of the world which she describes could last a 1000 years -- or more*. We have no way of knowing. According to this and many other prophecies, **at some point in the future BEFORE THE COMING OF ANTICHRIST we will**

[293] *Voix Prophetiques*, Curicquo, 1872, Vol. 1, p. 472.

have a period of almost universal peace and general prosperity -- both for the world and for the Church. This is a message of hope similar to Our Lady of Fatima's promise of a "certain period of peace." ***Our Lady said this peace will come after the conversion of Russia.*** **"BE NOT AFRAID!"**

8. Russia is Not the Only Country Which *Needs* Conversion

While there are many faithful Christians in both the East and the West, the Christians are now a minority in both areas. Most of Western Europe and much of North America is now considered by the Vatican to be "missionary territory." That is not an exaggeration. That is a fact. That is how low the practice of Christianity has fallen in these previously Christian lands of the West.

This is one of those cases where extreme candor is required. There is an internal ecclesial diplomatic problem currently developing within the Body of Christ. Many Russians feel that their country is being somehow denigrated by Western prayers for its conversion. They think that this somehow implies that we think they are less Christian than the West. Nothing could be further from the truth. The sacrifices made by Christians behind the former Iron Curtain, respectively shame many Christians of the West for their Western lack of similar sacrifice for the faith.

9. An Open Appeal to the Russian Bishops

Please do not consider our Western prayers for the conversion of Russia as an insult. They are actually a compliment. The author thinks it possible (in the light of private prophecy) that Russia may be the first country to experience a predicted mass reconversion to Christianity.

The "missionaries" who come back from Russia tell us that on average your people are much more open to the message of the Gospel than we Westerners. They tell us your people are simply not as absorbed with the lure of materialism to the degree that our people are. Therefore, if a "mass conversion" is to begin, it will most easily begin in the East. **In the light of the prophecies of**

Fatima, Russia's mass conversion may have to happen for you -- before a mass conversion happens for us in the West.

If the above analysis is correct: God in His omniscience foreseeing for our time Russia's openness to the Gospel -- as well as its recently won freedom for the Church in Russia to proclaim the Gospel; He providentially instructed Our Lady of Fatima to especially request prayers for Russia's conversion. Since your people are so open to the Gospel message at this time, that only makes sense.

Seen from within this context, in praying for the mass conversion of Russia we of the West are praying for Russia to *lead the way to conversion.* Within this context, it is our ultimate compliment to the Russian people.

B. DOES ANTICHRIST COME AT END OF A ROMAN EMPIRE?

As stated earlier, recent books have appeared to hint that Antichrist may be on the immediate horizon. The following prophecies briefly address the high improbability of that scenario. This "B." section is a brief introduction to statements of Fathers and Doctors of the Church vis-a-vis demonstration that Antichrist is most probably not coming soon.

This brief introduction of this subject - events to proceed Antichrist - is opened at this time for the following reason:

Many of the prophecies the reader is about to encounter concerning a "Chastisement" sound so earthshaking, that one could conclude that they refer to the time of Antichrist. They do not. Other events must happen prior to his coming. That is the reason for this brief introductory section. It includes some key statements from five Fathers and Doctors of the Church, Sts. Augustine, Ephraem, Cyril of Jerusalem, John Chrysostom, and Jerome. The purpose is to authoritatively introduce some events foretold by the Fathers of the Church to precede the coming of Antichrist. Shortly after this introduction on Antichrist, we shall begin with a survey of writings of various Catholic prophets (many of them canonized Saints) dealing with the development of a great Catholic Kingdom and King in latter times.

This Christian King is prophesied to precede Antichrist. We have just heard Sr. Bouquillon predict the arrival of a Great Monarch. That Great Monarch is the "Great King." The other prophecies say he will be the last, or one of the last of the Holy Roman Emperors. Here some remarks are in order.

As we will subsequently see, it was consistently taught by the Church Fathers and Doctors through Oral Tradition (and it is in part described in the Apocalypse) that before Antichrist came ten kings would control the Roman Empire. This the Fathers and early Doctors said was one of the signs to watch for. *Many of them say that this* (besides being based in Scripture) *is generally of Apostolic Tradition.*

The author is well aware that those "Traditional" and Scriptural quotations could be strictly mystical in nature. But the Fathers (when discussing this matter) specifically deny the mystical interpretation and many say the *proper* literal one is of Apostolic Tradition. The listener will have to judge for himself or herself after hearing the totality of these prophecies. We are going to partially develop this theme at this point in our presentation *in order to initially assure the reader that the following prophecies of a Chastisement are not referring to the imminent arrival of Antichrist.*

1. Proximate and Remote Signs

Our Lord, St. Paul, St. John, and many others give us two classes of "signs" to watch for as some prophesied event approaches. These signs are normally divided by scholars into the two classes of "remote" and "proximate" signs. Remote signs are those which occur some period of time prior to another prophesied event. An example of such a "remote" sign is the foretold break-up of an Empire prior to the coming of Antichrist. However, the rise of the Scripturally infamous individual "False Prophet" who (according to Scripture) immediately prepares the world for Antichrist; that would be classed as a proximate[294] (meaning near in time) sign.

[294] Our English word "Proximate" comes from the Latin word "Proxima" which signifies "near," "close by," or "neighbor." (e.g. Our English word "approximate.")

2. Scriptural Proximate Signs of Antichrist

St. Paul in 2 Thessalonians, Ch. 2, Verse 3 gives *two signs as to the impending approach of Antichrist. The first sign* is Scripturally described as the "revolt," or "apostasy," depending upon which English translation one reads. However it is translated, it describes a general falling away from the Christian Faith by Christians. This is the interpretation of Sts. Augustine-Father & Doctor, Venerable Bede-Dr.,[295] St. Anselm-Dr., St. Thomas Aquinas-Dr., Liranus Estius-F., and others.

The second sign is interpreted by a multitude of the Fathers and Doctors vis-a-vis a final destruction of the Roman Empire. This is the opinion of Tertullian, Lactantius-F, St. Cyril of Jerusalem-F&D and St. Jerome-F&D, who says, "It is the common opinion among Christian Writers." That is also the interpretation of St. Ambrose-F&D, St. John Chrysostom-F&D, St. Augustine, St. Prosper-F, St. Primatius-F, Theophilatus-F, Eucomenius-F, Aimon-F, St. Rupert-F and many other ancient Church writers. St. Ephrem of Syria-F&D, also, says, "When the Roman Empire has been abolished, the world shall be destroyed." This *was* (as St. Jerome assures us) what all the "ecclesiastical writers hand down (tradiderunt)."

C. SECOND SIGN - AUGUSTINE AND OTHER FATHERS ON THE FINAL DESTRUCTION OF THE ROMAN EMPIRE

1. St. Augustine (5th Century)

The author is aware that for many a reader, what is about to be presented is going to sound so bizarre that many readers will be tempted to reject the concepts presented as impossible. The author

[295] From this point on, "F&D" signifies that a personage mentioned is both a Father and a Doctor of the Church. Likewise, "F" signifies that a person is a "Father of the Church," "Dr." or "D" signifies he or she is a Doctor of the church.

asks the reader to reserve judgment on what he or she is about to read until he or she has seen all the evidence.

We will start out with the only negative Patristic evidence of which the author is aware. The only slightly possible Patristic exception to the "opinion" that Antichrist comes with a final destruction of a Roman Empire is St. Augustine. St. Augustine at one point authoritatively said, "There is no doubt that St. Paul in these words spoke of the abolition of the Roman Empire at the coming of Antichrist." Here St. Augustine indicates that this is from Apostolic Tradition. However, Augustine later somewhat modified that view.

When Augustine later wrote his *City of God* around 428 A.D., he was one of the few to understand that the old Roman Empire truly was dying. In general, people just could not believe that the Roman Empire could fall. The sack of the city of Rome by Alaric the Goth in 410 A.D. sent intellectual and psychological shock-waves throughout the "civilized" world. Shortly thereafter, Jerome wrote from Bethlehem that "If Rome can fall, what is safe?"

The Eastern Empire was experiencing severe trials, the Western Empire was still precariously in place, but Augustine was a realist. He understood that the "Roman Empire" as it had basically existed for at least six hundred years was passing away.[296] Possibly he made subsequent modified statements on the subject of Antichrist coming at the collapse "of the Roman Empire" with all of this in mind. Consequently, some will tell you that Augustine completely reversed himself in the book *City of God* on his position of Antichrist coming with the final destruction of the Roman Empire. As we shall see, he really did not.

Opinions that Augustine so reversed himself are based on the following passage from his *City of God*, wherein he is discussing those things leading up to the Reign of Antichrist -- and here he is commenting on how certain prophecies from the *Book of Daniel* related to that issue:

[296] The Western Empire would "die" a half century later with the ascendance of King Odovocar of Rome in 476 A.D. The Eastern Empire was already showing signs of change which would culminate in its evolution into the Byzantine Empire.

> "Some have interpreted these four kingdom's as signifying those of the Assurians, Persians, Macedonians, and Romans. *They who desire to understand the fitness of this interpretation may read Jerome's book on Daniel*, which is written with a sufficiency of care and erudition."[297]

Some commentators interpret the above passage to mean that Augustine, since he says "Some have interpreted" to mean that Augustine is now implying that he clearly disagrees with them. And we can see how someone (without further information) could reasonably come to that conclusion.

But, we have earlier seen that Augustine is perfectly capable of admitting when he has made a mistake in the past - such as he did when he admitted that he had previously held some Millenarist views,

> "... for myself, too, once held this opinion."

If Augustine was intending to patently repudiate his previously stated views that Antichrist comes at the end of the Roman Empire, why would he not just say so, as he did in the same book about his previous Millenarist views? Publicly correcting a view which he has previously held is consistent with his style, method, and humility throughout all of his works. This he does at various places in both his *Confessions* and his *Commentaries on The Psalms*.

The answer as to Augustine's meaning may lie in the fact that there is an alternate interpretation for this passage. When Augustine says, "They who desire to understand the *fitness* of this interpretation," could he not just as reasonably be stating that it is a "fit" or reasonable interpretation? Additionally, Augustine said in the preceding Chapter of Book 20,

> "Some think that the Apostle Paul referred to the Roman Empire, and that he was unwilling to use language more

---

[297] *Basic Writings of Saint Augustine*, Edited by Whitney J. Oates, Chrm. Dept. of Classics, Princeton University, Random House, New York. Vol. II, p. 548. [Section on *The City of God*, Bk. 20, Chpt 23.]

> explicit, lest he should incur the calumnious charge of wishing ill to the empire ... so that in saying 'For the mystery of iniquity doth already work,' he alluded to Nero, whose deeds already seemed to be as the deeds of Antichrist."

So far Augustine sounds like he might be reversing himself. But a little later on in the same work in further discussing this specific issue he says,

> "I frankly confess that I do not know what he [Paul] means."

In other words, Augustine has gone from being personally positive on this point to being open on it. But in no way can anyone claim that he now "specifically denies"[298] his former position about which he previously had no doubt. *On the contrary*, he says,

> "... **However, it is *not* absurd to believe that these words of the apostle, 'Only he who now holdeth, let him hold until he be taken out of the way,' refers to the Roman Empire.**"[299]

Does that sound as if Augustine has definitively changed his previously held view that Antichrist comes at the end of the Roman Empire, or at least that it is a reasonable possibility? There can be no question of his specifically "denying" this position. He did not! Therefore the "specifically denies" criteria contained in *Providentissimus Deus* is not met by this statement of Augustine. Therefore this position of Augustine cannot invalidate the "commonalty" or "universality" rule of Leo XIII concerning the Fathers.

The above should solve any apparent riddle concerning Augustine's statements about Antichrist's coming after the final destruction of the Roman Empire. In any case, Augustine does not in his

---

298 According to Pope Leo XIII in his Encyclical *Providentissimus Deus*, unanimity in the Fathers on a given point of faith or morals is not destroyed unless at least one Father "specifically denies" that teaching.

299 *Basic Writings of Saint Augustine*, Edited by Whitney J. Oates, Chrm. Dept. of Classics, Princeton University, Random House, New York. Vol. II, p. 538. [Section on *The City of God*, Bk. 20, Chpt 19.]

City of God repudiate his earlier quoted statement that Antichrist's coming at the final destruction of the Roman Empire is a common opinion or tradition. *He has ample opportunity to do so, and he never readdresses that issue.*

Of the Fathers who directly commented on the meaning in this passage, Augustine is the only one who does not positively state that St. Paul was referring to a Roman Empire. But Augustine does not deny it either. Even he goes so far as to say that "it is *not* absurd to believe that these words of the apostle, 'Only he who now holdeth, let him hold until he be taken out of the way,' refers to the Roman Empire." Now we shall see some specific examples of what other Fathers said.

2. St. Ephraem, Father and Doctor, (4th/5th Centuries) Specifically Refers to a *Latter* Roman Empire

St. Ephraem, an early 5th century Syrian Deacon, is both a Father and a Doctor of the Church. His theological writings and preachings on the Holy Spirit gained him the title, "Harp of the Holy Spirit." In commenting on *the latter times* preceding Antichrist, Ephraem said (1) God shall establish a period of peace, (2) during which a "kingdom of the Romans" shall be established, (3) after which the people become decadent, (4) which ushers in the period of the Antichrist.

> "*Then the Lord from his glorious heaven shall set up his peace*. And *the kingdom of the Romans* shall rise in place of this latter people, and establish its dominion upon the earth, even to its ends, and there shall be no one who will resist it. After iniquity shall have [subsequently] multiplied, and all creatures have become defiled, then Divine Justice shall appear, and shall wholly destroy the people, and coming forth from perdition, *the man of iniquity* shall be revealed upon the earth, the Seducer of men, and the disturber of the whole earth."[300] [emphasis - author's]

[300] *The Sunday Sermons of the Great Fathers*, Vol. 4, Translated and edited by M.F. Toal, Henry Regnery Co. 1964, p. 355.

If this statement is authentic Ephraem,[301] it may well be the key to eventual understanding of a multitude of statements of other Fathers on this subject. It is probably the most perspicacious quote from any of the Fathers on this subject. St. Ephraem is stating this position about sixty years prior to St. Augustine's writing his *City of God.* It is imperative to recognize that St. Ephraem is not talking about the Roman Empire existing at his time. He is talking about some future "Kingdom of the Romans" of a "latter people." This kingdom shall be established during some great God-given period of peace which God Himself will directly establish.

3. St. Cyril of Jerusalem (4th Century)

There are many detailed, absolutely specific statements from Fathers of both the Eastern and Western Church to the effect that it is of Tradition that Antichrist comes at the end of a Roman Empire. *St Cyril,* Bishop of Jerusalem, both a Father and Doctor of the Church, states such clearly, *and assures us this is not his private prophecy* with these words, " We prophesy not, for we are not worthy;"[302]

---

301 Sebastian P. Brock and Edmund Beck, two eminent contemporary Syriac Scholars are in doubt as to whether this is an "Ephraem composition". Both scholars have independently studied the various works attributed to St. Ephraem. They basically categorize those works in three groups, (1) works definitely attributable to Ephraem, (2) those where his authorship is in doubt, and (3) Those which are definitely not authentic works of Ephraem's. They both class this sermon in the "in doubt" category.

But this should not make us reject this sermon out of hand. For many years, many competent scholars seriously questioned St. Cyril of Jerusalem's authorship of the last five "catechesis". Many first-rate scholars openly denied Cyril's authorship. But once again the *catecheses* are now generally accepted as Cyril's work by most scholars. Therefore, given the absence of a definitive "non-authentic" classification, this sermon is presented at it appears in Fr. Toals text.]

302 *The Catechetical Lectures of S. Cyril, Archbishop of Jerusalem,* A Library of the Fathers, Oxford. p. 186. (Jurgens selection referenced immediately below begins shortly after this quote. So this is taken from the complete Oxford series.

> "[15,11] ... since the true Christ is to come a second time, the adversary makes use of the expectations of the simple, and especially of those of the circumcision [the Jews]; and he brings in a certain man who is a magician, and who is quite expert in sorceries and enchantments of beguiling craftiness. **This *one* shall seize the power of the Roman Empire, and shall falsely style himself Christ.** By the name of Christ he shall deceive the Jews, who are expecting the Anointed (71); and he shall seduce the gentiles by his magical illusions."
>
> "[12] This afore-mentioned Antichrist is to come when the times of the Roman Empire have been fulfilled and the end of the world is drawing near. There shall rise up together ten kings of the Romans, reigning in different parts, perhaps, but all reigning at the same time. After these there shall be an eleventh, the Antichrist, who by the evil power of magic [false miracles] shall seize upon the Roman Power. Of the kings who reigned before him, three shall be humble (72), and the remaining seven he shall have as subjects under him... He shall display against all men, and especially against us Christians, a spirit that is murderous and most cruel, merciless and wily. For three years and six months only shall he be the perpetrator of such things."[303]

St. Cyril now immediately tells us the source of the quote above,

> "Now these things we teach not of our own ingenuity ... **that this kingdom is that of the Romans, has been the *tradition* of the Church's *interpreters*."**[304]

Amongst other things, St. Cyril is specific and clear that it is "the tradition" that, (1) Antichrist is an individual ("one"), (2) who comes at the end of the "Roman Empire." Cyril could not be clearer on these two points. *St. Cyril, within his office as Bishop of Jerusalem, in 350 A.D. is formally teaching these two points as*

[303] *The Faith of the Early Fathers, Vol. 1*, Jurgens, The Liturgical Press, Collegeville, MN. 1970, pp. 357-358.

[304] *The Catechetical Lectures of S. Cyril, Archbishop of Jerusalem*, A Library of the Fathers, Oxford. p. 190.

being received doctrine. And he is formally teaching them to his catechumens whom he is shortly to baptize.[305] Cyril informs us that these points are based in Scripture (especially in the *Book of Daniel*), interpreted in the light of received Tradition.

St. Cyril's statement to that effect does not absolutely prove the case.[306] Cyril after all could individually have been mistaken on this point. *But, he is not the only Father of the Church to make the same point.* The teaching *T*radition of this point (that it is of Apostolic Tradition) has a very broad base amongst the Fathers.

4. St. John Chrysostom – The Golden Mouth (4th Century)

Both a Father and a Doctor of the Church, St. John (nicknamed Chrysostom) is acclaimed by all as one of its greatest Saints, preachers, and is unquestionably one of the most prestigious of the Fathers,[307] and is certainly one of the Church's most quoted theologians. St. John's nickname "Chrysostom" signifies "Golden Mouth" in Greek, which gives us a clear idea of his capabilities as a preacher. St. John says,

> "In the same way as those kingdoms which existed before the Roman Empire were destroyed (the Babylonian by the Persian, the Persian by the Greek, the Greek by the Roman), **so will the Roman Empire be destroyed by Antichrist. This will happen when the Roman Empire shall have been divided into ten kingdoms**."[308]

Here we have another Father and Doctor of the Church, teaching the exact same points as St. Cyril did roughly four decades earlier -- that Antichrist comes at the end of a Roman Empire. He also confirms

305 Catechesis 15 was one of the last Catecheses delivered to the Catechumens just prior to Baptism. [Again, some scholars debate whether this was delivered by St. Cyril or his successor, Bishop John. But most recent scholars now admit Cyril's authorship.] This catechetical instruction was delivered by St. Cyril during Holy Week of either 348, 349, or 350 A.D. Jergens says it is most probable that it was in 350.

306 This is because it requires a multiplicity of Fathers stating something before the Church accepts it as Tradition with a capitol /T/.

307 St. John Chrysostom is one of the "Four Great Eastern Fathers," the others being Sts. Gregory Nazianzus, Basil, and Athanasius.

308 Vide St. Chrysostom's commentary *On II Thess.*

there being ten kingdoms or inheritors of that Empire in place at the time of the arrival of Antichrist. That is consistent with identical statements about "ten kingdoms" found in the Apocalypse and the Book of Daniel. There is consistency and form in all of this.

5. St. Jerome (4th Century)

Another Father and Doctor of the Church, he is one of the Church's earliest great Scripture scholars. At the request of Pope Damasus in 382, he began the translation from the Greek of the first authorized vernacular edition of the Bible in Latin. Jerome began by translating the four Gospels. His completed Latin translation of the entire Bible was called the Vulgate. Jerome was the greatest Scripture scholar of his age.

St. Jerome SPECIFICALLY says that prior to the advent of Antichrist ten kings (rulers) *will divide the Roman Empire between themselves*. As previously quoted, he also says that, "It is the common teaching among Christian Writers" that the 2nd great sign of the impending approach of Antichrist comes with the final destruction of the Roman Empire. **St. Augustine specifically refers his readers to the statements of St. Jerome we are about to see on this point.**

St. Jerome on the Final Empire

As stated earlier, St. Jerome is often said to say, "It is the common opinion among Christian Writers." What *exactly* is this "common teaching" of which St. Jerome speaks. In his commentary on the *Book of Daniel,* St. Jerome explains this in depth, saying it is the **teaching** of "all ecclesiastical writers."

> "Therefore, let us state what all the ecclesiastical writers [omnes scriptores ecclesiastici] have passed down [tradiderunt]: At the consummation of the world [consummatione mundi], when the Kingdom of the Romans has been destroyed, when ten kings shall have divided the territory of the Romans between themselves, an eleventh [man] shall rise to [the kingship of] a small kingdom, who when he shall have overcome three of the ten kings, i.e., the king[s] of the Egyptians, of the Africans, and of the Ethiopians and

> consequently as we learn more manifestly - whom he shall have killed, the other seven kings shall submit their necks to the victor [the eleventh king]."[309]

St. Jerome then tells us just who this eleventh king is:

> "Nor do we think him to be the Devil or a demon (as some others do), but one of mankind in whom Satan shall dwell totally ... his mouth uttering great boasts, for he is *the man of sin the son of perdition, such that he will seat himself in the Temple as if he were God."* [Here Jerome is directly quoting from St. Paul's description of the Antichrist in 2nd. Thessalonians, 2:15][310]

Jerome could not possibly be any clearer that this individual member of mankind, the "eleventh king," is the Antichrist. He even points out the error of some who think he will be the devil incarnate or a demon.

---

309 *Corpus Christianorum, Series Latina*, Vol. LXXV A, *S. Heironymi Presbyteri Opera, Pars I, Commentariorum in Danielem*, Pub: Turnholti, Typographi Brepols, Editores Pontifici, 1964, p. 844.

Author's translation from, "Ergo dicamus quod omnes scriptores ecclesiastici tradiderunt: in consummatione mundi, quando regnum destruendum est Romanorum, decem futuros reges qui orbem *romanum [some manuscript texts read romanorum] inter se diuidant, et undecim surrecturum esse paruulum regem qui tres reges de decem regibus superaturus sit, id est Aegyptiorum regem et Africae et Aethiopiae sicut in consequentibus manifestius discimus, quibus interfectis etiam septem alii reges victori colla submittent."

310 Ibid. "ne eum putemus, iuxta quorundam opinionem, uel diabolum esse uel daemonem, sed unum de hominibus in quo totus satanas habitaturus est corporaliter. *Et os loquens ingentia: Est* enim *homo peccati, filius perditionis, ita ut in templo Dei sedere audeat faciens se quasi Deum."*

The Strength of This Teaching

A critic could say that all the men just quoted, Sts. Cyril, Jerome, Chrysostom, (all Fathers and Doctors of the Church) and Hippolytus and St. Ephraem (another Father and Doctor) are mistaken in this. But as Jerome states, it is "handed down by all the ecclesiastical writers." We have already read Augustine's final statement that this position "is not absurd." Short of a definitive statement from the Magisterium in this matter it remains a traditional teaching of the Church.

The author is not saying a Catholic in good standing cannot debate this point. *However, the burden of proof therefore in any controversy (as to whether this is the major teaching tradition of the Church on this point) is upon the critic*, not upon the Christian who believes the massive testimony of these quoted Fathers, especially Jerome when he testifies it is the teaching "of all ecclesiastical writers." This opinion as to where the burden of proof lies is not just the opinion of this author. As the reader will discover, many later Doctors of the Church such as St. Robert Bellarmine state this conclusion in even stronger words than this author.

This concludes our short introduction on this subject. Its purpose is to encourage the reader to reserve judgment on the private prophecies about to be introduced. Other Fathers will be quoted later in support of a *final Roman Empire* in the section on the proximate signs of Antichrist. If the Fathers of the Church held that Antichrist would come with the "final destruction" of the Roman Empire, and a number of them taught it as received doctrine, how incredible could it be for there to be at least one last "Holy Roman Emperor" at some time in the future? Does not an Empire, by definition, require an Emperor?

6. Continuum of Empire?

St. Jerome is able to say it is the common teaching that the Antichrist will come with the final destruction of the Roman Empire simply because so many Fathers said it. St. Augustine (Jerome's contemporary) was the only Father who was not sure on this point. But he also specifically states that "it is not absurd." No Father clearly held (let alone clearly stated) a contradictory opinion to that of Jerome and the other Fathers.

The Church has never formally "defined" the Fathers to have been right on this point. The same observation can be made on many traditional teachings of the Church. But every Pope and every Ecumenical Council teaches us that we are to steep ourselves in the teachings of the Fathers. It is primarily with the "apparent" end of the Holy Roman Empire that modern Catholic scholars have generally begun to *patronizingly ignore* the teachings of the Fathers of the Church on this subject.

The latter Fathers such as St. John Damascene explained in reference to the prophecies about Antichrist coming at the end of the "Roman Empire," that in their personal opinion, the Byzantine Empire was an extension (in the eschatological sense) of the Roman Empire. The *Holy* Roman Empire began when, on Christmas day 800 (A.D.), Pope Leo III crowned Charlemagne Emperor in St. Peters. Some later Doctors of the Church expressed the opinion that the Holy Roman Empire was a chronological Christian extension of the "Roman Empire" as Scripturally described.

However, it must be added that St. Thomas[311] and some other Medieval theologians stated their "opinion" that the prophetic "Roman Empire" was best interpreted in a strictly spiritual sense. But even later Doctors of the Church such as St. Robert Bellarmine specifically held with the literal interpretation. St. Cajetan, Suarez, Cornelius Lapide, and St. Peter Canisius held the same view. **The literal interpretation on this point did *not* die with the Fathers of the Church as some would have us believe.**

The reader who knows his or her history may be thinking, "But even the Holy Roman Empire was destroyed with the deposition of Emperor Francis by Napoleon in 1806. Why then has Antichrist not yet come?" Many of the *approved* prophecies contained herein state clearly that a Holy Roman Empire will flourish again some time in the future. This is one possible explanation.

---

[311] Vide Aquinas' Commentary of 2 Thess. Chpt. 2.

[NOTE: As previously stated, there is a Scriptural basis for the Antichrist's coming at the end of a final Empire or kingdom. If the reader is not familiar with the Father's Scriptural references to the "Fourth Empire," the interested reader should at least carefully read the *Book of Daniel* and the *Book of Revelation* to become familiar with the multiple references therein to such an Empire. As only a few examples: see Daniel 2:39-43]

There is nothing in the Scriptures which says there will be no break in the "Fourth Empire," which "Empire" or "Kingdom" the Fathers interpreted to be in some manner a Roman Empire. *St. Ephraem specifically tells us it will be a separate latter kingdom.* As a matter of fact, when the Western Roman Empire ended in 476 A.D., there was definitely a period of transition during which one could claim that "Roman" Empire ended. One cannot build a case for an unbroken line of Roman Empires. In the light of good history that is a fantasy.

7. Later Doctors and Theologians - Robert Bellarmine

Later Doctors and theologians (including St. Robert Bellarmine,[312] Suarez, and Sts. Cajetan and Peter Canisius) were fully aware of the allegorical arguments and interpretations on this subject. But that did not discourage them from holding to the traditional teachings of the Fathers of the Church on this subject. The Scriptures (the Books of Daniel and the Apocalypse) simply say that Antichrist comes with the final end of what Scripture describes as a final Empire, which the Fathers further described as a "Roman Empire" or "Roman Kingdom." They do not specify under what conditions and/or circumstances.

How do we evaluate this data?

According to Tradition (as explained by the Fathers and many Doctors), immediately preceding Antichrist there will be a Roman Empire in place. This leaves us with two options.

[312] The specific quote from Bellarmine is given later in the Chapter on Antichrist.

(1) The Fathers were misguided or misunderstood that point of exegesis, and this is not part of Apostolic Tradition -- though, Sts. Jerome, Cyril of Jerusalem, Chrysostom, Hippolytus, and others clearly claim that it is, or

(2) despite our best contemporary prognostications, a "Roman" Empire of some kind or other will surface some time in the future.

There are also dozens of private prophecies from *modern* times by canonized Saints, Blessed, and Venerable, which specifically state that this will be the case. They provide many details which simply sound incredible unless one is familiar with the teachings of the Fathers of the Church on this subject.

Much of what follows might strike the listener as simply and literally incredible. *But the prophecies of Fatima made in 1917 sounded equally incredible to many people of that era.* Yet today, most of the prophecies of the first two "secrets" of 1917 have *already* come to pass in less than seventy-five years.

D. THE GREAT KING AND THE HOLY ROMAN EMPEROR TO COME

The coming of a great king who will lead the forces of Christianity to an age of peace in those latter times prior to Antichrist is one of the extremely common threads which run throughout the prophecies. This man is variously predicted to defeat Russian, Prussian, and Arab and/or Middle Eastern forces in wars yet to come. According to the prophecies, he will eventually be anointed Holy Roman Emperor by a saintly Pope.

1. Credible Private Prophecies or Pious Legends?

There are books which describe *all* prophesies about a future Great King or military leader as simply pious "legends" which were created in the Middle Ages. A few of those books go on to take the position that these "legends" were simply the products of nationalistic "prophecy wars." It is postulated that all such prophecy emanated from claimants cynically vying for the residence of a Great King eventually occurring in their own native land.

However, the best historic record demonstrates the original "great monarch" prophecies emanate from true saints (such as Sts. Caesarius and Remigius). Those original prophecies described a future "king of the Franks." The prophecies about a "great monarch" *which do not appear to be authentic* seem at the very least to be a subsequent reaction to original genuine prophecy. There are other prophecies (which *are* most probably genuine) which speak of great monarchs or leaders for other countries such as Poland, Germany and Spain.

The "great monarch" could hardly lead in a vacuum. He would have to have associates leading the Christian forces of other countries. The majority (not all) of the prophecies which are branded as prophecy wars are most probably prophecies describing military leaders who evolve into "lieutenants" of the "Great King."

2. Reliable Sources

This author has labored to check *reliable* Catholic scholarly sources in order to exclude questionable prophecies. Just two examples of such exclusions are Joachim of Fiori,[313] and his latter emulator, Telesphorus of Cozensa. One can find Joachim's and Telesphorus' alleged prophecies in many older books on private

---

[313] He is alternately known as "Joachim of Flora" and "Merlin Joachim." **"He himself always disclaimed the title of prophet."** His alleged prophecies are actually taken from his "interpretation of Scriptural prophecy, with reference to the history and the future of the Church."

His basic approach claimed that there were "three ages" of the Church, the second of which was about to come to an end. A third period would come, "the Kingdom of the Holy Spirit; a new dispensation of universal love, which will proceed from the Gospel of Christ, but will transcend the letter of it, **and in which there will be no need of disciplinary institutions.**"

He calculated that the third period would begin with some cataclysm, "which he tentatively calculated would befall in 1260." His teaching was sufficiently flawed that "certain doctrines of Joachim were condemned by the Lateran Council in 1215. In 1256, Pope Alexander IV solemnly condemned a work of Joachim's extreme followers, which condemnation also "condemned the teaching of Joachim himself." Joachim was a highly trained and competent theologian. He made one major mistake, his theology of the "Eternal Gospel" - which will be discussed later in this book. [All quotes are from the 1913 Edition of the *Catholic Encyclopedia*, Vol. 8, p. 407.]

prophecy. As discussed earlier, Nostradamus is also excluded. Similarly, the alleged prophecies of St. Malachy as to "a list" or index of all the Popes from his day down to the end of time have been excluded.[314]

These are but four examples of exclusion of certain types of alleged prophecies from this book. Where there is serious *reliable* scholarly Catholic evidence that an alleged prophet or prophecy is not to be accepted - that prophet and or that prophecy has not been included. Also, in cases of a possibly genuine original prophecy for which there is substantive evidence that it has been subsequently altered or tampered with - they have been excluded.

But this author has *not* accepted (as *reliable*) the opinions of those "scholars" who subtly but very consistently denigrate the subject and possibility of genuine Catholic "prophecy" in general. *Such "scholars" are in fact themselves totally unreliable in this area.* Their flagrant scepticism blinds them to the possibility of genuine Catholic prophecy when it actually occurs - cases such as St. Teresa of Avila or the Curé of Ars. As a result, such "scholars" cast a blanket indictment on ALL prophecy - both public and private. Therefore, their stated negative opinion in any given case cannot have any objective weight or merit.

The problem: this type of "scholar" is almost never intellectually honest enough to forthrightly state his or her *general* anti-prophecy position. Instead, they merely appear to find fault with all prophecy. Most extreme "higher critics" fall into this category.

There are two major problems with opinions of such "scholars" vis-a-vis a "Great King."

(1) The authors of books who take a blanket "pious Legends" approach to such prophecy may be totally sincere. But many canonized Saints have made similar or identical prophecies. So when such authors make such blanket indictments, no mature Catholic will take such "scholars" seriously.

---

[314] In the opinion of this author, there is sufficient evidence of major "interpolation" of these prophecies.

(2) Another major problem with such a "scholar's" analysis is their thesis that *all* "Great King" prophecy is a product of "nationalistic prophecy wars." However, a significant number of prophets who predict a French Monarch are from countries other than France, such as Italy, Germany, and England. An Italian, German, or English man or woman predicting a "Great King" or a "Last Holy Roman Emperor" for France, does not sound like much of a nationalist.

(3) Most such anti-"Great Monarch" books also betray a general condescension toward and animus against the possibility of anyone's prophetically foreseeing any future events! Such books almost never *openly* deny the existence of the charism of prophecy. However, that unstated premise soon becomes intuitively obvious to the astute reader.

Item (3) is the most serious from a Catholic point of view. These authors also tend to show the same condescension toward evidence from the Tradition of the Fathers of the Church or Scriptural prophecy. Such authors deride the Patristic exegesis concerning a "Roman Empire" (Holy or otherwise) which is in existence just prior to the coming of Antichrist. In order to declare the prophecies of these saintly prophets as ridiculous, they logically must also declare the teachings of the Fathers as ridiculous.

E. 20TH CENTURY SELF-ASSURANCE AND SKEPTICISM

As the reader shall discover later on, dozens of canonized Saints, Blessed and Venerable, have predicted such a "Great Catholic King" for some time in the future. We, of the late 20th century, predictably have a hard time believing such a radical change in governmental forms could yet take place in the West. But before we intellectually assume such a position, we should review some history.

The United States of America currently has a republican form of government patterned after the "Roman Republic" which preceded the rise of the Roman Emperors. *The founding fathers of the U.S., clearly and publicly stated that they patterned our form of government after the Roman Republic which existed prior to the time of Christ.* To that republican form they added a written constitution. Many of their statements on this subject are found in the *Federalist Papers*.

Consider the following scenario: If anyone had told Europeans at the height of the Middle Ages that the majority of the western world would one day return to republican forms of government (such as that of the Roman Pre-Christian Era) most[315] Medieval Christians would have thought this highly unlikely. In a similar manner, most 20th century Americans or Europeans would view a Western return to monarchical forms of government in the future as improbable. The reason for this is that most civilizations view their own customs, governmental forms, and economic systems as normative and progressive. The Western people of our era are no exception to that rule.

1. World History of Governmental Forms

The prophecies state that sometime in the future, the world and particularly Western Europe will again return to monarchical forms of government during a period of extreme turmoil. *Tumultuous times have historically lead to strong forms of centralized government.* Monarchy is simply one of those forms. In the last 2,500 years the strongest Western Governments have unpredictably interchanged between monarchies, oligarchies, dictatorships, republics, and other varied forms of representative government.

As just one example; Rome began as a city ruled by (1) a monarchy (753 B.C), (2) changed to a city-state (Italian Peninsula) ruled by a republic (509 B.C.), (3) became an empirial dictatorship (44 BC-Julius Caesar), (4) switched back to monarchy (476 AD-King Odovocar), existed in one form of monarchy or another (papal states, kings, dukes, etc.) until (5) the Renaissance (at which point many of the Italian "city-states" were governed by oligarchies and

[315] There were a number of Italian city-states which were nominally republics. But many of them were in actual fact oligarchies. Never-the-less, citizens of those city-states might not have been shocked to hear that Republics would some day again be popular.

or small republics), and (6) back again to a national republic in the 19th century. When contemporary Italians are asked what form of government they have, the answers can be as varied as the number of Italians you ask. They can and do alternately say democratic, socialist, centrist, leftist, republican, etc.

The "modern" move back to republics began with the United States and France in the late 18th century. **Most civilizations view their contemporary body politic as progressive and normative**. But the history of governmental forms has developed primarily as unpredictable occurrences. Despite the outdated theories of Oswald Spengler and Toynbee, there is no historically demonstrable and therefore predictable pattern to it except that times of chaos usually lead to *some* form of strong centralized government. Rather than thinking that monarchy is a futuristic impossibility, *it might be better for a good student of history to remember that history demonstrates the unpredictability of governmental forms.* We now move to a historical prophetical development of the Great Monarch.

Some people are misinterpreting some recent alleged prophecies as signs of the impending arrival of the Antichrist and/or the Parousia. But, private prophecies from church-approved sources almost universally indicate *a substantial series of events which are yet to happen before the rise of the Antichrist, they especially predict an age of peace to come before the Antichrist.*

This map has many (but not all) of the names and locations of private prophets which appear in this book. Names of many Saints, Blessed and Venerable, and other approved sources, and names of many Catholic chroniclers of prophecies from the early and Medieval Church. *As the reader shall see, these older prophecies from approved sources are in complete concord with the later ones indicating an extensive series of events* (particularly an age of peace) *yet to occur prior to the coming of the Antichirst.*

CHAPTER 5

CHRONOLOGICAL PROPHECIES OF A GREAT KING, HIS RELATIONSHIP TO A CHASTISEMENT

The reader is almost immediately going to see prophecies predicting a great "Chastisement" or "Chastisements" of the human race which come at some age prior to Antichrist. The very term "Chastisement" causes many to shudder. Many react with a question as to why God would treat mankind like that, couldn't He find an easier way? Why would he have to "Chastise"?

The answer is in some ways complex, but in others quite simple! Parents who love their children use both the "carrot and the stick" to encourage their children to do the right thing, to pick up their room, do their homework, stop arguing with their siblings, be home on time, etc. We are God's children. The gulf between God and all humans (His children) is immense beyond comparison with the relationship between us earthly parents and our little ones. If earthly parents wisely use both the "carrot" and then as a last resort the "stick" with their physical children, what would make us believe it would or could be any different in God's relationship with all His children?

When the "carrot" isn't working for a parent, *what* makes him or her turn to other methods with his or her own children? If they didn't love them, would they bother to try something else when the carrot doesn't work? Parents take the time and effort to try things other than carrots because of their love for their children. Parents who do not go to that much time and effort predictably wind up with wayward children. God deals with mankind out of the *ultimate* parental love.

The above argument is logical, rational, reasonable, and is "common sense" to any seasoned parent. But it is not the only reason for us to believe that God will chastise us in order to correct us *for our own good.* Both Scripture and the Tradition passed on by the Fathers tell us the same thing. As the New Testament's Hebrews 12:6 tells us,

> "He whom the Lord loves, he chastises, and he scourges every son he receives."[316]
>
> [Reader: Please be *sure* to read the footnote on this quote - as it has application throughout this book.]

The author of the Epistle to the *Hebrews* herein tells us by the inspiration of the Holy Spirit that the cause of such chastisement is God's love for us. Should this surprise us? Even in sports there are endless popular sayings which express the same or

---

[316] (Author's translation) The *Douay-Rheims* text is, "For whom the Lord loveth, he chastiseth; and he scourgeth every son whom he receiveth." The New Jerusalem Bible reads, "for the Lord trains those he loves. and chastises every son he accepts." While the *RSV* says, "For the Lord disciplines whom he loves, and chastises every son whom he receives." As the reader can see, *there are significant differences between these translations*!

The *Douay-Rheims* is accurate but archaic, and *The New Jerusalem* shrinks from using the accurate verbs ("scourges" or "whips"), the *RSV* is better, but still reverses the respective verb order. Therefore the author has translated the text directly from the current official Biblical *New Vulgate* Latin text.

It is no secret that virtually all of the currently authorized English language texts have defects which bother many serious Catholic Scripture scholars. Many of the defects are minor. But this is one of those cases wherein none of the current authorized versions (e.g. *RSV* & *New Jerusalem*) accurately carry the original sense of the text. Whenever (in the author's opinion) this is the case, he has rendered a modern English translation directly from the *New Vulgate.* Wherever the author has done so, he will clearly identify it as such.

The *New Vulgate* is a direct revision of the venerable Latin *Vulgate* of St. Jerome: On April 22, 1979, by the Apostolic Constitution, *Scripturum Thesaurus*, Pope John Paul II promulgated the *New Vulgate* text as the Church's new official Biblical text. The *New Vulgate* text reads, "quem enim diligit, Dominus castigat; flagellat autem omnem filium, quem recepit."

similar themes: "No pain, no gain." "No guts, no glory." In business, the trades, and in academia the expression "we learn more from our failures than we do from our successes" is a commonly heard theme. Failure in trials is painful. But isn't that how we in our human nature learn and grow in our earthly lives? Why would the spiritual life be any different? The limitations of human nature's learning process do not change.

St. Augustine gives us the same message in his exegesis on the Psalms. In his Psalmic commentary he leads up to his final conclusion which makes the same point: trials produce good fruits. He says in his *On the Second Part of Psalm 9,*

> "And because Antichrist will attain such a pitch of empty glory and be allowed to take such action against all men, *and especially against God's saints, that at length some of the weak will indeed suppose God does not trouble about human affairs, the Psalmist ... goes on to express the groaning, so to speak, of those who ask why the judgement is delayed...*
>
> "Hence the Psalmist hints at the cause of the delay in the words, *'while the wicked man is proud, the poor is set on fire.'*
>
> *"It is truly wonderful to see with what earnestness and what firm hope God's little ones are enkindled to upright living when in contest with sinners."*[317]

The reader will notice that the "Chastisement" Augustine is describing is something which God allows to happen. It is nothing God directly sends to man. Most of what is contained in the prophecies relating to a Chastisement deals with what man does to man - not with what God does to man. The reader will repeatedly observe that in relation to the conditional Chastisement(s) which are threatened, if and when it happens God will allow a Chastisement as a Divine Mercy. And it will be a correction more than a punishment, because He loves us!

---

[317] *Ancient Christian Writers, St. Augustine on the Psalms, Vol. I, Psalms 1-29,* Translated and annotated by Dames Scholastica Hebgin and Felicitas Corrigan, *Benedictines of Stanbrook, England,* The Newman Press, Westminster, Maryland, 1960. pp. 125-126.

1. St. Methodius (4th Century)

St. Methodius was a Bishop and ecclesiastical author whose date of birth is unknown. He died a martyr, probably in the year 311 A.D. The earliest accounts of him are found in St. Jerome's *De Viribus Illustribus*. A prolific writer,[318] according to St. Jerome, Methodius was Bishop of Olympus in Lycia and died a martyr during the last Roman persecution. Methodius is the earliest of the Fathers to allegedly specifically mention the rise of a Great King in the latter times. He prophecies:

> "A day will come when the enemies of Christ will boast of having conquered the whole world. They will say: 'Christians cannot escape now!' **But a Great king will arise to fight the enemies of God. He will defeat them, and peace will be given to the world, and the Church will be freed from her anxieties."**[319] [read critical footnote]

---

[318] Only 3 of his works are extant.

[319] *The Revelations of St. Methodius*. BUT, Vide-*Ancient Christian Writers*, Vol. 27, p. 10. "*The Revelations of St. Methodius*, an apocalypse which *may* have originated in Syria in the seventh century. It was extremely popular in a Latin version in the Middle Ages. but its authenticity was suspect even to Robert Bellarmine, *De scriptoribus ecclesiasticis* (1613)."

[Despite some scholarly "doubts" concerning its authenticity, the author does not find their argumentation to be definitive. The criticisms used to attack its authenticity are primarily fourfold: (1) the fact that it is not directly referenced by commentators of Methodius' period such as Eusebius, Jerome or Rufinus, and, (2) that the language utilized appears in places to be later than the early 4th century. (3) that the earliest "copy" appears in a 7th century Syriac manuscript (thereby creating the suspicion that it was "invented" three centuries after the death of Methodius) (4) that there is no evidence of any other contemporary writing of such an apocalyptic vein -- vis-a-vis a future Catholic King (another supposed argument for a post-Methodius invention) -- and the *Revelations* appear to be written in a different style than Methodius' other works.

Responses: (1) The commentaries contemporaneous with St. John Chrysostom directly specifically referenced only a couple of *Baptismal Instructions* attributable to St. John Chrysostom. Yet, today, the eight "Baptismal Catecheses" discovered as a set by Wenger in Russia in 1955 are widely accepted even though only a couple are mentioned by any of his (Chrysostom's) contemporaries. (This is one of many such examples in Patristic studies).

(2) We do have *a parallel Patristic situation* in the Deir Belizeh Manuscript (8th century manuscript discovered in 1907 - which many scholars currently "attribute" to a 3rd century "original"). If that assessment is accurate, this also supplies us with evidence of a "Creed" appearing in writing in a Eucharistic Liturgy **two centuries prior to anything previously known**.

Even in some Patristic writings where authenticity is certain, it can sometimes be difficult to determine what is from Oral Tradition or from their own private prophecy. When that is the case, all we "know" is that it is one or the other. There is also the problematic of interpolations with some of the older prophecies.

The above prophecy of St. Methodius is challenged by many scholars.[320] Such men state that this prophecy dates from 7th or the end of the 6th century rather than the beginning of the 4th. If that be so, that does not mean that the prophecy is invalid, but merely that it would most probably belong to an anonymous 6th century prophet.

Although Christendom has suffered many dark moments since the beginning of the fourth century, (physical invasions by Attila the Hun, the Moslems, Napoleon, Communist invasions/expansions of the 20th century, etc.) never has there been a time when its enemies

---

319 cont. (3) The "late usage" Syriac could readily be explained (in the author's opinion) merely by the translation process per se from the original (Greek?) to Syriac (not all copyists of non-Scriptural manuscripts were literalists). Also, other Patristic commentators date the manuscripts from the 6th century rather than the 7th.

(4) While it was not uncommon for theologians in Methodius' time to write apocalyptic works, Methodius' *basal* theological approach in all his writing (e.g. in his *Symposium*) was apocalyptic/eschatological in nature. i.e, (with full understanding that the following begs the question) if the prophecy is genuine, then which came first, the eschatological apocalyptic view, or the private revelation? Style Argument: Many "higher critics" have also used such arguments to discredit the Apostles Paul and John's authorship of certain books in Scripture which nevertheless, according to the best testimony of Tradition, were in fact written by Paul and John.

In any case, whether Methodius actually wrote it or not, the prophecy is presented here as one of the earliest alleged predictions of a "Great Christian King" of which the author is aware.

320 "Interpolation" means to interpret. Sometimes copyists "thought" they saw a previous copying error and attempted to correct it. When there actually was no previous error that constitutes one type of interpolation. But this word is also sometimes used as a polite phrase in scholarly journals to discuss the possibility that someone actually tampered with, (usually added something to, sometimes removed something from) a writing of some kind (theological works, exegesis, personal correspondence, or prophecies, etc..) In other words, the word "interpolation" does not *necessarily* imply malice on the part of the "interpolator," because many of them are also accidental errors. Many others are poor interpretations made in translation. Another specific example is when a "copyist" accidentally includes "marginal notes" made by a previous copyist in the actual body copy of a manuscript).

could boast of having conquered the whole world. If this prophecy is accurate, this is something still to come.

2. St. Remigius (5th Century)

He was the Bishop of Rheims, France, and baptized King Clovis with 3000 of his countrymen in 496 A.D. According to Hincmar, the famous Archbishop of Rheims who lived in the ninth century, St. Remegius made the following prophecy to King Clovis on Christmas Eve of 494 A.D. The following quote is a translation from the original Latin of Ven. Cardinal Boronius. Cardinal Baronius, a protégé of St. Phillip Neri was the father of *modern* Church History. He spent almost forty years researching and compiling his *Annales.* That is a twelve volume history of the Church covering the period up to 1198 A.D. (beginning of the papacy of Pope Innocent III).

The last volume of the *Annales* was published in 1607 shortly before Baronius' death. In the course of his research, "The libraries of Rome yielded to his diligent quest a host of unpublished documents."[321] One of those documents which Baronius found contained the following prophecy of St. Remegius which had been previously recorded by Hincmar, Bishop of Rheims.

> "Take notice that the Kingdom of *France* is predestined by God for the defense of the Roman Church which is the only true Church of Christ. *This kingdom shall someday* be great among the kingdoms of the earth, and shall *embrace all the limits of the Roman Empire*, and shall submit all other kingdoms to its own scepter."

Comment: So far in history, France, while at times quite powerful, has never held this vast a breadth of geographic territory under its hegemony. It has never "embraced all the limits of the Roman Empire." If this prophecy is accurate, this event is still to come.

3. St. Caesar of Arles (6th Century) Father

A Father of the Church, according to Jurgen's *Faith of the Early Fathers*, "Caesar was probably the greatest moral teacher of

321 *Catholic Encyclopedia*, 1913 Ed., p. 305

the Western Church between Augustine of Hippo and Bethold of Regensburg," In his battle against the heresy of Semi-Pelagianism, "he presided over the Second Council of Orange in 529 A.D., which Council condemned Semi-Pelagianism."[322] Shortly thereafter, Rome ratified all of the definitions of the Faith and condemnations of heresy conducted by the Council of Orange. St. Caesar became the Bishop of Arles, France in 502 A.D. and was perhaps the strongest single factor in keeping Gaul (France) out of the hands of those hostile to the Church.

The prophecy to follow is taken from a copy of the *Liber Mirabilis*, printed in 1524. The older copies are entitled *The Prophecies of St. Caesarius*.[323]

> "When *the entire world*, and in a special way France, and in France especially the provinces of the north, of the east, and above all that of Lorraine and Champagne, shall have been laid waste by the greatest miseries and trials, then the provinces shall be comforted by a prince who had been

---

322 *Faith of the Early Fathers*, Vol 3. p. 282.

323 Jurgens does not list the *Liber Mirabilis* either as a work of St. Caesar or one containing his words, but presents only selections from some of St. Caesar's sermons. For three reasons, this is not unusual. First, Jergens is primarily concerned with presenting the personal writings of the Fathers. The *Liber Mirabilis* was not written by St. Caesar, but rather claims to be a compilation of his and other prophecies. In many cases, the "prophecies" of early saints were carried for centuries through oral tradition alone.

In the case of St. Methodius, Jurgens, Quasten, and others call into question some works which they think were actually written at a later date with no historical basis. It is in this vein that Jurgens as a regular course meticulously lists "spurious works" or those of "questionable authenticity" of the Fathers (those not attributable to the claimed source, or where such claim is in question). He lists no "spurious works" either for St. Caesar himself, or attributable to his words. The *Liber Mirabilis* (and its predecessors) were such well-known works, that it seems (1) it is highly unlikely that it would have escaped the attention of such a thorough-going scholar as Jergens, (2) it is unlikely that if he thought it to be "spurious" or of "questionable authenticity" that he would not have made a reference to that fact.

Volume four of Quasten's *Patrology* is no help either since it deals with Latin Patristic literature only up until the Council of Chalcedon in 451 A.D. (St. Caesar was born in 470). Since the author could find no authoritative figure stating a work this famous to be "spurious," or the calling of its authenticity into question, the following prophecies are simply presented as they appear in the *Liber Mirabilis*.

> exiled in his youth, and who shall recover the crown of the lilies. This prince shall extend his dominion over the total universe.[324]
>
> "At the same time, by the will of God, a most holy man shall receive the Papacy, who will be most perfect in every spiritual perfection. This Pope will have with him the great Monarch, a most virtuous man, who shall be an eminent leader of the holy line of French Kings. This great Monarch shall assist the Pope in the reformation of the whole earth. Many nations and their princes that are living in error and impiety [at that time] shall be converted, and an admirable peace shall reign among men during many years, because the wrath of God shall be appeased through their repentance, penance, and good works. There will be one common law, only one faith, one baptism, one religion.
>
> All nations shall recognize the Holy See of Rome, and shall pay homage to the Pope. *But after an extended period of time* fervor will cool, iniquity will abound, and moral corruption shall become worse than ever before, which shall bring upon mankind the last and worse persecution of Antichrist, and the end of the world."

As discussed more fully in the footnote about this text, there are problems in absolutely definitively establishing its attribution to St. Caesar, but there is *no* question as to its antiquity. In the absence of any strong evidence that it is spurious, it is presented as contained in the *Liber Mirabilis*. It is totally consonant with dozens of other prophecies of unquestionable authenticity from canonized Saints which say exactly the same thing.

This prophecy has the earliest claimed date of origin for *all the basic elements* of those prophecies. They all contain prophecy of;

(1) toward the end of time *but well prior to Antichrist*, the world will be very troubled,
(2) which troubles are ended for a time by a great temporal ruler, a great Monarch or King,
(3) who works closely with a very great and saintly Pope,

[324] The Latin reads "Dominabitur per universum orbem."

(4) together they reestablish peace in the world which *lasts for a significant period of time*,
(5) at the end of which time the people go bad because they cannot withstand the temptations that come with continued peace and prosperity,
(6) as a result of their becoming worse than "ever before," Antichrist comes.

That is the pattern which is consistent throughout many prophecies from many different centuries, from many different countries, from people in many different walks of life.

4. St. Catald(us) (7th Century)

An Irish Monk, circa 680, resigning his post as a teacher at the great school of Lismore in Ireland, undertook a pilgrimage to Jerusalem. On his way home, while traveling through Italy, "he was chosen to become Bishop of Taranto." To this day he is the "Titular Saint" of the Taranto Cathedral. St. Cataldus says,

> "The Great King will wage war till he is 40 years of age ... He will assemble great armies, and hurl back the tyrants out of his empire."[325]

A. THE GREAT MEDIEVAL TEACHING TRADITION OF A GREAT KING TO COME

1. Rabanus Maurus (9th Century)

Rabanus Maurus was not a prophet. But he was a most thorough chronicler of both prophecy and Oral Traditions in Western Europe coming from the Patristic Era. He studied in Tours under the famed scholar Alcuin. After completing his studies, he returned home to Fulda (in present day Germany) where, in 822, he was elected Abbot of its famous Benedictine Monastery. According to the *Catholic Encyclopedia*, upon his return,

[325] *The Prophets and Our Times*, Rev. Richard G. Culleton, 1941, p. 125.

> "[He] became teacher, and later headmaster of the monastic school of Fulda. His fame as teacher spread all over Europe, and Fulda became the most celebrated seat of learning in the Frankish Empire. . .Rabanus was probably the most learned man of his age. In Scripture and Patristic knowledge he had no equal, and was thoroughly conversant with canon law and liturgy."[326]

Later he was appointed Archbishop of Mayence. The following statement is recorded in Colvenerius' 1647 Latin Edition of Maurus' writings.

> "Our principal Doctors [teachers of the Faith] agree in telling us, that towards the end of time one of the descendants of the kings of France [Gaul] shall reign over all the Roman Empire; and that he shall be the greatest of the French Monarchs, and the last of his race. After having governed well his kingdom, he shall go to Jerusalem, and lay down his sceptre and crown on Mt. Olivet. This shall be the conclusion of the *Roman and Christian* Empire."

There is a veritable chain of some of the most learned men of Europe who continuously repeat this as a teaching tradition throughout Europe about a last great French King (or King of the Franks). *These statements do not come just from Frenchmen. They come from all over Europe*, just as later prophecies of a latter day Great French Catholic King come from many nations besides France, nations such as Germany and Italy to name two.

2. St. Anselm (11th Century)

St. Anselm is one of the most celebrated historical figures of the Church. As a scholar, theologian, and Christian philosopher, he played a major role in bridging the gap between the early Middle Ages and the great Scholastic Age of the Church. His fame as a theologian was universal throughout Christendom. When Pope Urban II called the "Council of Bari" in October of 1098 to deal with one of the most thorny theological issues of the day (the procession

[326] *Catholic Encyclopedia*, 1913 Edition, Vol. 12, p. 617.

of the Holy Spirit), "Anselm was called by the Pope to a place of honor and bidden to take the chief part in the discussion."[327]

Anselm's father was a Lombard (Northern Italian), and his mother a Bergundian (was from France). Anselm, born circa 1034, began his serious religious studies in 1057 under Lanfranc, who was one of the most celebrated scholars of the period. Anselm became a monk in the Benedictine Abbey of Bec in 1060 and was elected its Prior in 1063, then was elected Abbot in 1078.

In 1066, the Normans under William the Conqueror had taken England at the Battle of Hastings. Subsequent to that, the Normans controlled England -- even to a very large degree ecclesiastically. Lanfranc then became Archbishop of Canterbury. After the death of Lanfranc, Anselm succeeded him as Archbishop of Canterbury, after which he fought for the Canons of the Lateran Council against "lay investiture" and in general, the right of the Church in England to be freed of the interference of the English (Norman) King. His most famous book *Cur Deus Homo* (Why God Became Man), is a classic, is still in print and is well-known and read by a wide range of people to this day.

Anselm, as several of his scholastic contemporaries did, wrote an alleged eschatological work on Antichrist and the end of time. What is of particular importance to us is his deserved fame as the leading scholar of his age and one of its greatest theologians. Additionally, he is a Doctor of the Church. Shortly we will be quoting from a text copy printed in the 1976 edition of the *Corpus Christianorum, Continuatio Mediaevalis*, (Body of [writings of] Christian authors, the Medieval Continuation). The editors of this work strongly find against an authorship by Anselm. We shall state several of their objections, and then comment.

In the *Corpus Christianorum*'s introduction, the editors begin by objecting that they cannot find any proof that the manuscript(s) attributed to Anselm actually originated in England ("*Some copies of almost every manuscript of almost every version are found there currently, but relatively little seems to originally proceed from an English Scriptorium.*") Of the twenty-two different manuscripts which were obvious copies of an original source document, nine of them attribute their authorship to St. Anselm, and thirteen are

[327] *Catholic Encyclopedia*, 1934 Edition, Vol. 1, p. 548.

anonymous. Evidently (since during the *presumed general period of its composition* Anselm would have been residing in England as Archbishop of Canterbury) the editors further presumed that it would have to have been written in England. If this is their presumption, it is not a safe one.

Anselm's most famous work *Cur Deus Homo* was begun in England, but the lion's share of it was completed in the summer of 1098 at the Italian Monastery of Telese. *Cur Deus Homo* was a full-length book specifically written for publication and consumption by the general public. Anselm therefore carried the completed manuscript back with him to England where it was published. On the other hand, the *De Antichristo* is written in the form of a short epistle or letter (less than ten pages in length) *which appears to have been addressed to a private party*. If that is the case, and if it was written during either of Anselm's two extensive trips through Europe after having become Archbishop of Canterbury, there is absolutely no reason to assume that he would have bothered to make a copy of a letter and then have carried it back to England. The editors also admit that the great scholar, Trimethius, in his *Catalogue of Church Writers* which was written in 1531, attributes the work to St. Anselm. But, the editors of the Corpus Christianormum also object that the "editors" of Anselm's work (most of whom were English Benedictine monks) did not mention the *De Antichristo* as one of Anselm's works. *Again*, this could also be easily explained if Anselm had in fact written it *as a private letter* in France, but never brought a copy to England.

A final observation: As stated earlier, no extant commentaries contemporaneous with St. John Chrysostom directly specifically referenced any but a couple of his *Baptismal Instructions*. Several of his scriptural commentaries likewise go unmentioned by his contemporaries. Yet, today, the *eight* "Baptismal Catecheses" discovered by Wenger in 1955 are widely accepted though eight are not mentioned by any of his (Chrysostom's) contemporaries.

This is one of many such examples of contemporaneous listings of the works by some ancient writer (which list omits one or more of them which are accepted today as authentic). If the same "tests" which the editors of the *Corpus Christianorum* apply to "Anselm's" *De Antichristo* were applied to Chrysostom's *Baptismal Instructions*, Chrysostom's authorship of most of his currently accepted

"Catecheses" might well be questioned by many scholars instead of being almost universally accepted as his work.

In any case, the quotations below are presented from the *Corpus Christianorum, Continuatio Mediaevalis*, as translated by this author from its Latin text of the *LIBER ANSELMI DE ANTI-CHRISTO*.

> "Certain Doctors[328] truly say, that one of the kings of the Frankish [Roman] Empire shall possess it in its entirety ["ex integro"], which King shall live in the last time and shall be the greatest and last of kings. Who after he shall have happily governed his Kingdom, shall come to Jerusalem and lay down his scepter and crown on Mount Olivet. He shall be the last and consummate [Emperor] of the Roman and Christian Empire.
>
> "And immediately thereupon [after he lays down scepter and crown], according to the sentence of Paul, they [the Doctors] say Antichrist shall come."[329]

Notice that the author (whether Anselm or not) is not presenting this as his *private prophecy. Its greatest value lies in its testimony concerning a teaching tradition at the time of Anselm.* That teaching tradition relates to prophecy of a last Roman "Frankish" Christian Empire and Emperor -- and that teaching tradition is centrally tied to "the sentence of Paul." Some characteristics of this particular "teaching tradition" are almost unique in the history of the Church

[328] "Doctor," "teacher of the Christian Faith, whose authority is greatly venerated." quoted from *A Latin-English Dictionary of St. Thomas Aquinas*, Roy J. Deferrari, Ph.D., LL.D., L.H.D., Dr. Ed., St. Paul Editions, 1960. In order to translate this Latin "Doctores," which Anselm utilized in the very late 10th century, the author has referred to St. Thomas Aquinas' usage in the late 13th and early 14th centuries. In the period of both Anselm and Aquinas, the ecclesial term "Doctor" (as it is used here) meant an eminent teacher of the Christian Faith.

[329] *Corpus Christianorum, Continuo Mediaevalis*, Vol. 45, p. 164 *Liber Anselmi De Antichristo*, "Quidam vero doctores nostri dicunt, quod unus ex regibus Francorum imperium ex integro tenebit, qui in nouissimo tempore erit et ipse erit maximus et omnium regum ultimus. Qui postquam regnum suum feliciter gubernauerit im monte Oliveti sceptrum et coronam deponet. Hic erit finis et consummatio Romani simulque christiani imperii. Statimque secundum Pauli sententiam, Antichristum dicunt esse adfuturum."

- which makes it rather difficult to definitively characterize it. Later, we shall hear canonized *German, Italian, and French Saints privately* prophesying the identical elements central to this "teaching Tradition."

Anselm's alleged prophecy is not a personal prophecy per se

A major point to be gleaned from all of this is that the concept of this "Frankish" Roman Empire is no "Frankish" or French academic conspiracy (as some "scholars" have maintained). At the time of Anselm, a future "Frankish Roman Empire" had for some time been predicated throughout Western Europe. It was so common (from England to France to Italy) that no well-educated person of the period would have intellectually balked at the idea that St. Anselm might have recorded its historic existence. **A careful reading demonstrates it is *not* presented by its author as his own personal prophecy.** If the scholars who fight attribution of this document to Anselm once grasped that fact, much of their resistance to Anselm's authorship would probably melt away.

This author is not taking a position adamantly asserting Anselm's authorship of the document quoted above. Again, that is not the major purpose of presenting its text. The purpose is to further demonstrate that this prophecy of "a last Roman 'Frankish' Christian Empire" *is part of a constant teaching tradition at the time of Anselm*, not only in France but also throughout much of Western Europe -- which tradition goes back to *at least* the 5th century.

3. Monk Adso(n) (10th Century)

The Abbot Adso was a famous chronicler of many lives of the Saints and most specifically of their traditions and prophecies. He was born into a noble Gallican family around 930. He was one of the great French scholars of his period, some of whose works are also quoted in the *Corpus Christianorum, Continuo Mediaevalis*. A contemporary of St. Anselm, he simply states what was almost universally accepted as a teaching tradition in his time. (There are some writers who fairly strongly imply that the authorship of the Anselm's *De Antichristo* is actually none other than Adson's).

> Some of our Teachers [*Latin - "Doctores"*] say that a king of the Franks will possess the entire Roman Empire. He will be the greatest and the last of all Monarchs. After having wisely governed his kingdom, he.will go in the end to Jerusalem and will lay down his scepter and his crown upon the Mount of Olives. Immediately afterwards, Antichrist will come.[330]

B. A RETURN TO PRIVATE PROPHECIES OF A GREAT KING

1. St. Thomas a'Becket (12th Century)

A close friend of King Henry II of England, Thomas a'Becket was appointed Archbishop of Canterbury by King Henry. Henry believed that because of their friendship he could subsequently manipulate the Church in England. After Thomas' appointment, he continued in the tradition of St. Anselm's resistance to secular interference in the Church, and began the way of perfection of his soul. For his resistance to Henry's attempts to usurp the rights of the Church he was martyred. St. Thomas says:

> "A knight shall come from the West. He shall capture Milan, Lombardy, and the three Crowns. He shall then sail to Cyprus and Famagoste and land at Jaffa, and reach Christ's grave where he will fight. **Wars and wonders shall befall till the people believe in Christ toward the end of the world."**[331]

Notice that St. Thomas says wars and wonders will precede a resurgence in belief in Christ during the latter times. If we remember that the fortunes of Christianity have generally been on a gradual downhill slide vis-a-vis popular acceptance for at least the last 250 years, it may be reasonable to assume that this prophecy is for the future.

2. St. Hildegard (12th Century)

Here we will extensively detail the credentials of Hildegard since, in the author's opinion, they are the strongest from amongst

---

[330] *Corpus Christianorum, Continuo Mediaevalis*, Vol. 45.
[331] *Catholic Encyclopedia*, 1910 Edition.

the ranks of private prophets. Born in the year 1099 A.D., she had miraculous visions from the age of three. At the age of five, she joined a Benedictine convent located at Bingen, Germany, on the Rhine River. She was responsible for numerous miraculous cures. While she learned to speak Latin fluently, she had never previously been taught to read or write either her native German or Latin.[332]

She became Mother Superior of her convent in 1137 A.D. In 1141, when she was 42 years of age, as she herself tells us;

> **"And it was given to me to understand and see, not with my corporal eyes, the Holy Scriptures, all the deep and dark secrets of the Prophecies of all the Prophets before Christ and above all, the Gospels of the New Testament, and all the works of the Son of God, I understood."**[333]

She reports she was ordered by a heavenly messenger to write all of the things that she had seen and heard. As she could neither read nor write, she was (according to her own sworn account) miraculously gifted with ability to write in Latin. The result was two of her more famous books, *Scivias Domini* and *Divinorum Operorum*. Faithful copies of the Large Codices containing these and all her writings exist at Oxford, another in France, and another in Italy.

St. Bernard was a correspondent of St. Hildegard's. On the occasion of a visit of Pope Eugenius III to Germany, Bernard appealed to the Pope to investigate the writing of St. Hildegard. The Pope agreed to begin such investigation. Pope Eugenius called the Cardinals from the principal Christian nations of Europe to hold a regional council at Rome with the Pope presiding. At that time, he then sent a certain number of theologians (actually a commission of Bishops) under the direction of Archbishop St. Henry of Verdun to investigate the matter thoroughly.[334]

---

[332]The reader can find scholars who challenge this. However, Hildegard by her own testimony certifies the truth of the statement. The "Scholars" who challenge her statements about her previous illiteracy are euphemistically calling Hildegard a liar. That leaves the reader with two choices. Believe some contemporary scholars, or St. Hildegard.

[333] *The Life and Prophecies of St. Hildegarde of Bingen*, Frank J. Bendish, Carlton Press, Inc., New York, 1971, p. 19. Alternate spellings of St. Hildegard's name are common. Sometimes is it spelled "Hildegard" and others "Hildegarde."

[334] *Ibid.*, pp 20 & 21.

The appointed delegation arrived at the convent, conducted the investigation, returned to Rome, and recommended to Pope Eugenius that Hildegard's prophetic gifts were genuine. St. Bernard who was present reminded the Pope that Hildegard was a chosen vessel and that the light of her wisdom should not be hidden beneath a bushel basket. Pope Eugenius shortly afterward sent a letter to Saint Hildegard. The author has edited the pertinent passages as quoted below:

> "Eugene, Servant of servants, sends greetings and his blessing to his daughter, the virgin Hildegard. 'We are amazed, daughter, at your message and the more I ponder over your words, the more I wonder... **But I also rejoice that God even in our times works such marvels and reveals Himself to you, making known dark secrets of the future ... It is my will that you do what God has commanded you to do. Write and speak as He wills** ... But in all things be humble and prudent. **I shall approve of your works by a Papal Bull.**'"[335]

Pope Eugenius died before he promulgated that Bull. But to the best of the author's knowledge, such an accolade has been granted to no other private prophet by a Pope since the beginning of the Church.

A cautionary remark: This was not a blanket endorsement by Pope Eugenius of all the "works" of St. Hildegard. She wrote on many subjects. Some of her works, for instance those on medicine and science, were clearly limited to the scientific understanding of her time. She also wrote a number of musical and poetic compositions which were not included in Eugenius' endorsement. *Pope Eugenius is quite specific about what works he is talking about. They are those which "make known dark secrets of the future."* And as stated elsewhere in this book, Eugenius is not considering her prophetic works to be accepted in any sense other than that of strictly "human faith," human understanding. Eugenius fully knows and understands that they could not be matters of faith since they are private revelation.

[335] Ibid. pp. 21 & 22.

The list of Hildegard's correspondents and various individuals who sought her advice include but is not limited to: Popes Eugenius III, Anastasius IV, Adrian IV, and Alexander III, King Conrad III, Emperor Frederick, St. Bernard, 10 archbishops, nine bishops, forty nine abbots and provosts of monasteries, twenty three abbesses, and many priests, teachers, monks, nuns and religious communities.

Returning to the prophecies of St. Hildegard

St. Hildegard, who is a German, prophesies of France:

> **"Peace will return to the world when the White Flower again takes possession of the throne *of France*.** During this period of peace, people will be forbidden to carry weapons, and iron will be used only for making agricultural implements and tools. Also during this period, the land will be very productive, and many Jews, heathens, and heretics will join the Church"[336]

As promised, here is a prophecy by someone who is not French, about a great future leader in France. The white flower which Hildegard speaks of is the well-known symbol of the French Monarchy and also of the Bourbon Royal family. If this seems unclear to the reader it will later become evident when it is placed side by side with other similar prophecies. As stated elsewhere in the prophecies, the Great King is prophesied to be a legitimate heir to the French throne. At no time since Hildegard has iron only been used for agricultural implements and tools. And there has been no time when "many Jews, heathens, and heretics" have joined the Church. If this prophecy is accurate, this is an event yet to come. Hildegard continues:

> "For the latter times will be more evil and corrupt in the eyes of God. The children of God will be persecuted by means most hateful in the eyes of God. *The Throne of THE LAST ROMAN CATHOLIC EMPIRE Will crumble,* and the scepter will fall out of the trembling hand of him who sits on the throne. [By this time the Great King will be a very

[336] *Catholic Prophecy*, Yves Dupont, Tan Books and Publishers, 1971, p. 17.

> old man]. Hence all justice will cease, or will be trodden under foot." [The above is quoted from *a letter to the Holy Roman Emperor, Conrad,* in the year 1159.][337]

Hildegard goes on to say that almost immediately after the death of this king comes Antichrist. It is also interesting to note that *Hildegard uses the specific term* ***"the last Roman Catholic Empire."*** Hildegard herein confirms through the charism of prophecy what was earlier stated circa 1103 (allegedly) by St. Anselm as being what the "Doctors truly say." This prophecy of Hildegard is also foretold in many other prophecies, that the crowning of a last Great Monarch as Holy Roman Emperor by some future Pope will usher in a great age of peace and prosperity. Almost immediately upon his death comes the reign of Antichrist. This is also consonant with Scriptural prophecy relating to the latter times. There will be more on this Scriptural connection later.

Someone may reasonably object that no matter what Hildegard's credentials are, she could have misunderstood these revelations. That is not at all uncommon with those who receive private revelation. As a matter of fact, the private prophet almost always views the revelations through the conditions of his or her personal background. The education, life experiences, personality type, many factors can and do contribute to how a mystic receives/understands a message.

But even if we are predisposed to understand that Hildegard might have interpreted a purely spiritual meaning in a literal manner, *would that explain the fact that dozens of other Church-approved mystics have received basically the same message - and understood it in basically the same way?* One finds Catholic scholars and authors who attempt to explain away the individual prophecies of certain great Saints with the argument that they misunderstood the private revelation they received. What these authors never come to grips with is the fact that dozens of Church-approved mystics have received messages which they understood in exactly the same way.

All the mystics who predict a future Great Monarch have different "conditioning" in their particular backgrounds. What are

---

[337] *The Life and Prophecies of St. Hildegarde of Bingen*, Frank J. Bendish, Carlton Press, Inc., New York, 1971, p. 97.

the odds that they could all misunderstand the same message in exactly the same way? On a purely empirical basis, the statistical odds against that set of circumstances would be immense. Yet, one must logically admit the outside possibility even if it is extremely small. These prophecies are presented to the reader such that the reader can reach his or her own conclusions as to the *probability* of a common *mis*understanding. In the author's experience, this argument gives pause even to professed agnostics and atheists.

There is the same actual "possibility" that the Fathers of the Church also commonly misunderstood that their teachings about a final collapse of the Roman Empire prior to Antichrist was of Apostolic Tradition. And that is much more important than any consideration of private prophecy, because what a private mystic says can never (in and of itself) become a matter of Faith. Until the Church should finally say something definitive on the writings of the Fathers about a final collapse of a Roman Empire (and it is quite possible it may never do so) one cannot *absolutely* rule out either the possibility that the Fathers were correct, or that they were mistaken in this. Only the Magisterium, the teaching office of the Church could ever make an absolute positive or negative ruling in this area.

3. Werdin D'Otrante (13th Century)

He was an abbot of a monastery in Otranto, a city in the Province of Lecce in Southern Italy. Abbot Werdin died in 1279.

> "The Great Monarch and the great Pope will precede Antichrist. **The nations will be at war for four years and a great part of the world will be destroyed.** The Pope will go over the sea carrying the sign of Redemption on his forehead. The Great Monarch will come to restore peace and the Pope will share in the victory. Peace will reign on earth."[338]

This is one of the few prophecies which gives us a determinate period for the Chastisement -- about 4 years.

[338] *Catholic Prophecy*, p. 74

4. John of Vatiguerro, (13th century)

> "Spoilation, pillaging, and devastation of that most famous city which is the capital and mistress of France will take place when the Church and the world are grievously troubled. The Pope will change his residence and the Church will not be defended for twenty five months or more because, during all that time, there will be no Pope in Rome, no emperor and no ruler in France. But, after this, a young captive Prince shall recover the Crown of the Lilies and shall extend his dominions all over the world."[339]

5. St. Vincent Ferrer (14th Century)

St. Vincent, who died in 1419, was a contemporary of St. Catherine of Sienna. He was publicly honored as the greatest Canon lawyer of his time as well as one of its greatest theologians. For over 30 years he had and used an equivalent of the gift of tongues almost daily.

> "It was at Genoa, that people first realized the existence of a daily miracle which had been worked continuously for four or five years... Everywhere he [St. Vincent] went he was understood by all ... Once it was realized what was happening it was not long before this remarkable phenomenon was being discussed with enormous interest right through the town ... What language was the preacher using, for all were ready to swear that he was using their native tongue?
>
> "At last a deputation of the learned men of Genoa put the question to Vincent himself.
>
> 'You are all wrong and all right, my friends,' said the friar with a smile, 'I am speaking Valencian (a Spanish dialect), my mother tongue; for, except for Latin and a little Hebrew, I know no other Spanish [sic - language]. It is the good God who has rendered this intelligible to you.'
>
> "This fact was juridically attested at the process of the saint's canonization by more than a hundred witnesses;

[339] Ibid. p. 28.

> they say that it was not merely the general sense that they understood, but they could appreciate every turn of expression ... Furthermore, distance made no difference to them, for those on the outskirts of the huge crowds could hear as distinctly as those who were close to the pulpit."[340]

He healed the blind, deaf, lame, those who were possessed, etc. His public miracles were in the thousands. He also specifically preached a call to repentance in order to put off the end times. His travels, prayers, miracles and works to a great measure brought a loose-living age back to a more serious practice of the Faith.

A few documented stories of his life will help to emphasize the power of the Saint and also to explain why his gift of true prophecy is difficult to deny.

In 1374, he was living in the Convent of Saint Catherine at Barcelona. He was finishing his studies as a Dominican master of Logic. It was there that his apostolic work saw its beginning; 1374 was also the commencement of the era of his public miracles, cures, and gift of tongues (on almost a daily basis), prophecies, raisings from the dead, etc., which only ended with his death.

During 1374, as the result of drought and several bad harvests, the Kingdom of Aragon suffered severely from famine and the pestilence. Vincent, who was already beginning to be known in Barcelona as a preacher, predicted the arrival of some ships from Flanders to break the famine.

> *"Have confidence,"* he cried, *"rejoice in God. Before night two ships laden with corn will make port, the harbingers of abundant supplies."*[341]

The people were very angry. They thought he was either deranged or making it up. His brother Dominicans at the priory were even more annoyed, and told him so. The prior said to him:

> "For the future, Brother Vincent, you may dispense yourself from making any sort of prophecy, anything in fact which

---

340 *Angel of the Judgement, A Life of St. Vincent Ferrer*, S.M.C., Ave Maria Press, Notre Dame, Indiana, 1953,, pp. 137-138.

341 Ibid. p. 29.

> singles you out from the rest of the community. Singularity is a curse which leads to spiritual pride and the death of the soul."[342]

Vincent instantly obeyed. But that evening the grain-filled ships arrived. This, St. Vincent's first recorded prophecy, had come true. A short time later St. Vincent was near a prison in process of being constructed. A mason on the scaffolding missed his footing and fell off the edge.

> "'*Brother Vincent, save me,*' yelled the falling mason. Vincent, remembering the order against miracles said, '*Stay where you are until I come back,*' The mason stopped falling and hung in midair, Vincent hurried back to find his prior and told him, '*A mason who is falling off a roof has asked me to help him. He is waiting until I have your permission.*' A few minutes later, a messenger the prior had sent to the scene hurriedly returned confirming Vincent's account, and announced that a huge crowd of people were standing beneath the stone mason watching him suspended in mid-air over their heads. The Prior said to Vincent, '*Go back and finish it off, since the miracle is already worked, and the street full of people.*' Vincent returned and said before the large crowd which had gathered, '*The prior says you may come down.*'"[343]

The man at once floated gently earthward. This miracle was witnessed by thousands of people. Not surprisingly, this incident also ended the ban on St. Vincent's performing acts "which singled him out from other people."

On Oct. 3, 1408, he was preaching one day in Salamanca on a hill called the Mount of Olives. He was assuring his hearers that the Day of Judgment was near and he proclaimed himself the Messenger or "Angel" of the Judgment spoken of in the Apocalypse. Several of the listeners began to scoff at him. During the sermon a funeral procession passed by and Vincent called upon the dead woman to testify to the truth of this statement: He said:

---

[342] Ibid. p. 30.
[343] Ibid. p. 31

> *"Dead woman, arise and tell these people whether or no I am the Messenger of the Apocalypse sent to preach the advent of the Last Day."*[344]

The woman rose in her coffin, sat up and answered:

> *"Yes, Father, you are the Messenger."*

And immediately the body fell back again rigid and lifeless. The veracity of this event is testified to by numerous witnesses, again, who testified at his canonization proceedings. The official Church account of his canonization refers to him as "The Angel of the Judgment."[345]

St. Vincent became God's messenger at a time when Western Europe had sadly fallen from its Christian glory at the height of the Middle Ages. Frankly, large tracts of mainland Europe were in a desperate spiritual situation -- e.g., in major portions of Germany, in Savoy, in France and the Alpine countries, "in Lombardy [Northern Italy], [there were] nine valleys full of heretics." According to his biographer,

> "There were, therefore, two classes of unbelievers with whom Vincent had to deal: the Vaudois or Cathari, who taught that neither priesthood, sacraments nor sacramentals were of the slightest use toward salvation, claiming that their own unauthorized preaching and the witness of their pseudomortified lives should take their place; the others were pagans pure and simple (Sun-worshippers)."[345]

This religiously squalid state of affairs could not last. So God sent his messenger to preach Chastisement if people would not come back to the true faith, amend their lives, and do penance. It might be interesting for the reader to compare the disclosures of late

---

[344] Ibid. p. 100. Most of the prophecies of St. vincent quoted in this book, also appear in, *Histoire de Saint Vincent Ferrier.*

[345] The best scholarship indicates that St. Vincent was not claiming to be the specifc Angel of the last judgement spoken of in Rev. Ch. 19:9. As Fr. Kramer explains in *The Book of Destiny* (pp. 208_211) (see also Fr. Stanislaus Hogans' *Life of St. Vincent Ferrer*); St. Vincent most probably declared himself to be the "Eagle" flying in midheaven in Rev. 8:13. "Then I looked, and I heard an eagle crying with a loud voice, as it flew in midheaven, 'Woe, woe, woe to those who dwell on the earth, at the blasts of the other trumpets which the three angels are about to blow."

[346] *Angel of the Judgment,* p. 87.

14th century Europe with those of the United States and Western Europe today. Then it might not surprise one if, once again, God should threaten a Chastisement in our time. God is never mocked or ignored for long.

St. Vincent openly, publicly, stated that Jesus Himself had ordered him to preach the end of the world.[347] Like Jonas, Vincent preached of coming disaster. He also called for repentance to avoid it. **St. Catherine of Sienna** and quite literally dozens of other Saints were preaching close to the same message of repentance at exactly the same time. *When the people answer a call to repentance, God always responds.* While they didn't become Saints, the large number of the people of Western Europe of that period went through a substantial spiritual turnaround and met the terms of the conditional prophecy foretold by St. Vincent. God relented.

We of the late 20th century should also remember this event in reviewing the prophecies which follow. Threatened chastisement for our time can also be stopped, forestalled to a later period, or ameliorated, if we will but sufficiently correspond with grace.

Vincent's prophecies for "latter times" follow immediately, but we will hear much more from him later about the Antichrist and the "end times" immediately preceding him.

> "Armies from the West, East, and North will fight together in Italy, and the Eagle shall capture the false king, and all things shall be made obedient unto him, and there shall be a new reformation in the world."[348]

Comment: *One of the common pseudonyms for The Great King or Monarch in private prophecy is the "Eagle."*[349] Numerous prophesies speak of a Russian invasion of Italy and subsequent sack of the City of Rome. They also speak of a "Christian" army which will then drive a Russian army out of Italy. It must be remembered

---

[347] Ibid. pp 96-101.

[348] *Catholic Prophecy*, p. 31.

[349] This term "Eagle" was also used in a few prophecies in clear reference to Napoleon Bonaparte. But it is relatively easy to separate the "eagle" references which referred to Napoleon from those which refer to a future great king. The ones which referred to Napoleon predicted events which were clearly attributable to subsequent events in the career of Napoleon. They are also uncomplimentary to that "eagle." The ones which refer to a future Catholic monarch are clearly complimentary.

that in none of this is any one nation the proverbial "good guy" or the "bad guy." As we have already heard, and will hear more of in other prophecies: there will be "pro" and "anti" Christian Frenchmen, Germans, Italians, Poles, Spaniards, Ukrainians, Russians, Englishmen, etc.

A broad overview of all the prophecies related to this event does **not** indicate that all Russians will support this army. It simply confirms that an anti-Christian army composed primarily of Russian (and Prussian) troops will invade Western Europe and eventually sack Rome. *This invading army will also have the assistance of many anti-Christian Frenchmen and Italians.* There is nothing in these prophecies which single out one country in toto and declare it to be bad or good. The prophecies make it clear there will be a discernible admixture of anti- and pro-Christian forces in all countries engaged in this future prophesied conflict.

6. St. Bridget of Sweden (14th Century)

St. Bridget is one of the greatest mystics in the history of the Church. From the age of seven she showed signs of receiving special graces which gave her understanding beyond her years. At the age of thirteen she was married and then bore eight children. One of her daughters is St. Catherine of Sweden. After the death of her husband, St. Bridget founded an order of nuns, the Briggitines. In 1349 A.D. she traveled to Rome and (with the exception of a pilgrimage to the Holy Land) remained there until her death in 1373. In 1370 Pope Urban V confirmed the rule of her congregation. She was canonized a Saint on October 7, 1391 by Pope Bonafice IX.

Her *Revelations* have been extremely well-known throughout the Church to this day. The reader will remember that they are specifically referenced in the *Catholic Encyclopedia* as those which are piously credible. Pope Urban VI encouraged the multiplication of copies of St. Bridget's *Revelations.* Pope Benedict XIV listed her as piously credible in his *De Servorum Dei Canonizatione et Beatificatione*. Finally, Pope Pius IX publicly blessed them in 1862.

St. Bridget prophesied:

> "This most unhappy war will end, when an emperor of Spanish origin will be elected who will in a wonderful manner be victorious through the sign of the Cross ... He will restore the Church in Santa Sophia [in Constantinople], and all the

earth shall enjoy peace and prosperity; and new cities will be erected in many places."[350]

This is one of many references to a future Spanish Emperor. There are several possible explanations. The prophecies of a French Monarch which the reader will see later all state that the Monarch comes from outside of France to become first a great military leader of French Christians. They say he then becomes an Emperor and resides in France, that he is a descendent of the French royal line. He could be all of this and a Spaniard by birth. The royal families of Europe have been so intermarried for centuries that virtually anyone who is a member of any European royal family could probably claim at least a distant relationship to the French throne.

7. St. Francis of Paula (15th Century)

Francis was the founder of the religious Order of Minims. He was born at Paula in Cambria, Italy, in 1416 A.D. He was known throughout his life for abundant miracles. On one famous occasion, St. Francis was in need of transport from the coast of Italy across the six mile Strait of Messina to Sicily. Since Francis had no money with him, he asked a ferryman to carry him across "in the name of holy charity." The ferryman gruffly refused whereupon Francis spread his cloak on the water and sat down on it.

To the amazement of the ferryman and other bystanders, according to the *Catholic Encyclopedia*, "St. Francis of Paula did so on his cloak crossing over the straits from Italy to Sicily." (Also related in *Signs and Wonders*-p.3). This particular event was honored by Pope Pius XII in 1943 when he made St. Francis "Patron of all Italian Sea Workers."[351] Again, **"He had an extraordinary gift of prophecy: thus he foretold the capture of Otranto by the Turks in 1480, and its subsequent recovery by the King of Naples."** (As a matter of fact, witnesses at his canonization process testified that he had prophesied the specific day - over three months in advance for July 28, 1480.[352]) Also, he was gifted with the "discernment

[350] *Life and Revelations of St. Bridget*, Klarus, Regensburg, Mainx, 1833, vIII, p. 168.

[351] *St. Francis of Paula, The Wonder Worker* P.206.

[352] Ibid. p. 80.

of consciences."[353] He immediately knew the state of the soul of everyone he met.

His *recorded witnessed* miracles of the raising of the dead are more numerous than those of any other Saint. That is one of the things which lead to his canonization a mere 14 years after his death, in 1519 A.D. *At his canonization hearings there were multiple witnesses to 7 raisings of the dead.*[354] He repeatedly cured the blind, exorcised demons, and also many times repeated the miracle of the multiplication of loaves of bread for people in need. "The Saint's gift of prophecy was second only to his power of performing miracles, and he was fully aware that both were gifts from God,"[355]

As a matter of fact, St. Francis is one of many saints (including St. Teresa of Avila) who specifically claim the gift of prophecy. In one letter he says:

> "...the spirit of prophecy is granted to me **often** to foretell most wonderful events in relation to the reformation of the Church of the most High."[356]

St. Francis prophesies that Antichrist will destroy the Roman Empire. Francis also speaks in a series of letters to Simeon de Limena, Count of Montalto in great detail of a future Great Monarch who will be a Roman Emperor. Limena was a great patron of St. Francis' order and also a great military protector of the Church.

St. Francis predicts to Limena that one of his descendants will be the "Great Monarch." Through the course of these multiple letters we discover that this future monarch will not be a precocious saint. As a matter of fact, in his youth he will lead a dissolute life and then go through an inner conversion. St. Francis tells us:

> "One of your posterity shall achieve greater deeds and work greater wonders than your lordship. That man will be a great sinner in his youth, but like St. Paul he shall be drawn and converted to God."

Several potentially confusing things are now told about this future Monarch. He is described as founding a new religious order.

---

353 Catholic Encyclopedia, 1913 Edition.

354 *St. Francis of Paula, The Wonder Worker*, See all of Chapter 25, pp. 195-200.

355 Ibid. p. 74.

356 From a hand-written letter of St. Francis to Simeon Limena signed "Friar Francis di Paulo" and dated "5th February, 1482."

To the reader this may sound like he also becomes a priest. That is not the case. What happens is that he founds a religious order, part of which contains military men who take religious vows. He will be the head of the military arm of this order. In this sense it will be like the Knights Templar of the Middle Ages.

> **"He shall be the founder of *a new religious order different from all others***. He will divide it into three strata, namely military knights, solitary[357] priests, and most pious hospitalliers.[368] This shall be the last religious order in the Church, and it will do more good for our holy religion than all other religious institutions."[359]

In another letter to Limena, St. Francis expounds upon the role of this future "Great Monarch," in which he says:

> "From your lordship will be born [here he is speaking of a future descendant] the great leader of the Holy Militia of the Holy Spirit which shall overcome the world, and shall possess the earth so completely that no king or lord shall be able to exist, except he belongs to the Sacred Host of the Holy Ghost. These devout men shall wear on their breasts, and much more within their hearts, the sign of the living God, namely the cross."[360] [It becomes clear from other prophecies that it is from this that they will receive their popular name "the cross-bearers."]

In this same letter just quoted, St. Francis refers to this future military leader as the "Great Monarch." This specific title is seen over and over again in hundreds of prophecies of a future military and political leader of the Christians at some time in the future. Other titles which are applied to the same man are "Emperor," and "Great King."

> "He shall ... destroy all tyrants and heresies. **There will be one fold and one shepherd**. He shall reign until the end of

---

357 [priests who live solitary religious lives]

358 [individuals who do everything from care for the sick and dying to caring and providing for weary travelers]

359 Quoted from his Aug. 18, 1496 letter to Simeon Limena.

360 Quoted from a letter from St. Francis to Milena dated February, 5, 1492.

> time. On the whole earth there will be twelve Kings, one Emperor and one Pope."[361]

This is one of the few prophecies which gives a clue as to when the time of "one fold and one shepherd" might be. As we can see from the context, this "Great Monarch" is also foretold to be an Emperor. Since the time of St. Francis, no Catholic King has emerged who has annihilated all heretics, or one whose influence has spread over the whole world. Nor has there been a time of "twelve kings, one emperor, one Pope and a few princes." So this prophecy must be for the future.

8. Venerable Bartholomew Holzhauser (17th Century)

Holzhauser was born in Longanau, near Augsburg, Germany, in 1613. According to the 1910 *Catholic Encyclopedia*, he was "a parish priest, ecclesiastical writer, and founder of a religious community... On 9 July, 1636, he received the degree of Doctor of Philosophy, then studied in theology, in which he merited the baccalaureate on 11 May, 1639." After being ordained he served as a parish priest at Ingolstadt. During that period "he attended lectures at the university [of Ingolstadt] and was declared licentiate of Theology on 14 June, 1640."

He rapidly rose in the service of several Bishops, serving first as a simple parish priest, then as a district "Dean" in the Diocese of Salzburg, then under Archbishop John Phillip at Mainz, then Bingen on the Rhine, and finally as Dean of the District of Algesheim.

In 1640 he founded a religious "Institute" for parish priests.[362] The purpose of this institute was for the reform of the regular clergy. While its members took no special vows, it had a "rule" and its members (even parish priests) were to live in community in diocesan seminaries. After being approved by the local Bishop, "... in 1643, Holzhauser took control of the seminary at Salzburg. Pope Innocent XI approved of his [Holzhauser's] communities on 7 June, 1680. Af-

---

[361] *Apocalypsin*, Cornelius a Lapide, his commentary on Apoc. 17, 17. Here, Lapide quotes from a letter of St. Francis de Paul written Aug. 13, 1496 to Simon of Limena, Lord of Montalti.

[362] In Rome it is known as the "Institutum clericorum saecularium in communi viventium."

ter this the community spread to Poland, Sicily and Spain. In Rome a house had [previously] been assigned to him by the Pope."[363]

Holzhauser was prolific writer. Two of his works are now referred to which are quoted in several places in this book, they are his *Apocalypsin* which is a commentary on the Book of the Apocalypse, and his *Visions*. The *visions* were presented to Emperor Ferdinand III and to Maximilian of Bavaria in 1646. There are ten visions described in this book. One of those visions is about England. In this vision, Holzhauser accurately foresaw the execution of Charles I. He also prophesied that in the near future, Catholic priests would be prohibited for a period of 120 years from saying Mass in England - under pain of death. In fact, such a law was soon enacted in England and was not repealed until exactly 120 years later.[364] "This seems to have been fulfilled, for prohibition of Mass under the penalty of death was enacted in 1658, and partially recalled in 1778."[365]

As the reader can see, Ven. Holzhauser was no rustic or credulous fool. He was judged by his several Bishops as sufficiently well trained in both philosophy and theology to teach those subjects in several seminaries. Also, his insights as to the practical difficulties of the life of a parish priest were highly esteemed by several Popes. Similarly to the Cure of Ars (St. John Vianney - the Patron Saint of parish priests), Holzhauser regularly dealt with the practical details of parish life. As the Cure, he appears also to have been graced with special gifts of prophecy. His biographies (and the documents for his cause of canonization in Rome) attribute miraculous cures to him. His ten visions were evidently also part of his special gifts. Holzhauser says:

> "The fifth period of the Church, which began circa 1520,[366] will end with the arrival of the Holy Pope and of the powerful Monarch who is called "Help From God" because he will restore everything [in Christ]."[367]

---

[363] Ibid.

[364] *The Christian Trumpet*, also see article in the 1910 *Catholic Encyclopedia.*

[365] 1910 *Catholic Encyclopedia*, Vol. 7, p. 440.

[366] This date for the most part coincides with the beginning of Protestantism.

[367] *Apocalypsin*, Bartholomew Holzhauser, 1850, page 69.

9. Rudolph Gekner (17th Century)

Taken from his works printed in Augsburg in the year 1623, the following is from the chapter entitled "*The Waves of the Mystical Bark*."

> "A Great Prince of the North with a most powerful army will traverse all Europe, uproot all the republics, and defeat all the rebels. His sword moved by divine power will most valiantly defend the Church of Jesus Christ."[368]

When Gekner made this prophecy, the massive surge to return to republican forms of government in Europe had not yet begun, it was still over a century away.

10. Capuchin Friar (18th Century)

This prophecy is preserved in the library of the Capuchin Fathers in Genzano between Albano and Vetri near Rome. It was transcribed from a copy dated 1776.

> *"A scion of the Carolingian race*, by all considered extinct, will come to Rome and behold and admire the piety and clemency of this Pontiff, who will crown him, and declare him to be the legitimate Emperor of the Romans. He shall destroy the Ottoman (Arab) Empire and all heresies. With the assistance of God and of the Pope, he will cooperate in the reformation of abuses; he will assume the direction of temporal governments; he will assign a decent pension to the Pope and also the bishops and clergy. And they all will live in peace which shall last till the End of Time."[369]

Here again we see a common occurrence, a non-Frenchman prophesying a future King/Emperor who will most probably be of French blood. "Carolingian" refers to descendants of Charlamagne.

---

358 *The waves of the Mystical Bark*, p. 310.

369 *Catholic Prophecy*, p. 34

11. Fr. Nectou (18th Century)

Fr. Nectou was the Jesuit Provincial in the Southwest of France for many years. The priests who knew him all regarded him as a Saint and a prophet. He prophesied the suppression of the Jesuit order well before its occurrence in 1773.[370] After the suppression occurred as he predicted, he lived as a secular priest in Poitiers. His public reputation for holiness during this period induced a young grieving mother whose baby had just died to bring it in hope to Fr. Nectou. It was attested by several witnesses that he raised the baby from the dead and returned it to its mother.

Fr. Nectou also foretold the upcoming French Revolution, as his associate, the Abbe Raux testified, "in the most minute and circumstantial manner ... all the horrible events of the first French Revolution."[371] Fr. Nectou died in 1777. *He described the chastisement as "like a little general judgment*." He made this prophecy around 1760,

> "A man disliked by France will be placed on the throne; a man of the House of Orleans will be made king. It is only after this event that *the counter-revolution* will begin."[372]

In the 1800's, following the French Revolution the term "counter-revolutionary" was principally applied to those who wished freedom for the Catholic Church and an end to its persecution by the French Socialists, Free Masons, and Communists. When Fr. Nectou made this prophecy, the *French Revolution* and the *Reign of Terror* had not yet occurred. Fr. Nectou predicted them. *The political term, "counterrevolutionary" had not yet even been invented.* But Fr. Nectou through his gift of prophecy anticipated these future political developments.

The "Revolution" he predicted contains the same revolutionary spirit which has ever since persecuted the Church physically, psychologically, financially, and in its material security and freedom. This persecution has occurred under the guises of Classical Liberalism,

---

370 *The Christian Trumpet*, Fr. Pellegrino, ("With Superior's Permission), Thos. B. Noonan & Co. Boston, 1873, p. 55&56.

371 Ibid. p. 46

372 Ibid.

Rationalism, Socialism, Free Masonry, Communism, Nazism, and Fascism, to name a few. What all these ideologies have in common is an anti-Christian, specifically Anti-Catholic spirit. What Father Nectou is predicting is that the reign of the Great King will usher in the final victory of the Church over the specific "Revolutionary Spirit" of the last two and one half centuries.

12. Brother Louis Rocco (19th Century)

> "A Great King will arise after a period of terrible wars and persecutions."[373]

13. Nursing Nun of Belay (19th Century)

> "A saint raises his arms to Heaven; he allays the wrath of God. He ascends the throne of Peter. At the same time, *the Great Monarch ascends the throne* of his ancestors. All is quiet now. Altars are set up again; religion comes to life again. What I see now is so wonderful that I am unable to express it."[374]

14. St. John Vianney, The Curé of Ars (19th Century)

St. John died in 1859. The Curé is the official patron Saint of all parish priests in the Catholic Church. He was so slow in his studies that he could not master even the rudiments of Latin (which mastery was then required before ordination to the priesthood). An ordination exception was made for him by his Bishop and he was assigned to a remote French parish in Ars, France. There, his miracles (such as a grain bin that kept miraculously refilling itself) became famous throughout the country.

The Devil even physically assaulted him because of the good the Curé was doing. A short time before his death in 1859, the Curé made the following prophecies to a young man who was questioning the Cure about his (the young man's) possible vocation. It must be remembered that the prophecies of St. John Vianney are viewed

[373] *Catholic Prophecy*, p. 12.
[374] Ibid. p. 51.

(even by official Church publications) with relatively high regard. As quoted earlier from the *Catholic Encyclopedia*, "prophecies ... such as those attributed to St. Hildegarde, St. Bridget of Sweden, Venerable Anna Maria Taigi, the Curé of Ars, and many others.[375] The following prophecy of the Curé provides a rare historical view of the Great King in relation to other events. It was given sometime in August, 1859.

> **"The enemy** (the Prussians) **will allow the burning of Paris**, and they will rejoice at it, but they shall be beaten; they shall be driven entirely from France. Our enemies shall return, and will destroy everything in their march. They shall arrive near Poitiers without meeting any serious resistance, but there they shall be crushed by the defenders of the West, who shall pursue them. From other directions their provisions shall be cut off, and they shall suffer very serious losses. They will attempt to retire towards their country, but very few of them shall ever reach it.
>
> *"The Communists of Paris, after their defeat, shall spread themselves through all France,* and will be greatly multiplied. They shall seize arms; they shall oppress the people of order. **Lastly, a civil war shall break out everywhere.** These wicked people shall become masters in the North, East and Southwest of France. They will imprison very many persons, and will be guilty of more massacres. They will attempt to kill all the priests and all the religious. But this shall not last long. People will imagine that all is lost; but the good God shall save all. It will be like a sign of the last judgment ... God **shall come to help;** *the good shall triumph when the return of the king shall be announced***.** This shall reestablish a peace and prosperity without example. ***Religion shall flourish again better than ever before.***"[376]

At no period since this prophecy has there been a massacre of French priests as predicted by the Curé, and Paris has not been burned. Also, religion has not flourished as never before in France. There has also been no time since St. John Vianney made this prophecy

---

[375] *Catholic Encyclopedia*, 1913 Edition, Vol. XII.
[376] *Christian Trumpet*, pp. 87&88.

that the Communists have been driven out of Paris. Again, this would have to be of the future. Interestingly enough, Blessed Anna Maria Taigi, an Italian, makes an almost identical prophecy about a French civil war.

15. Abbe Souffrand (19th Century d. 1828)

> "During the reign of the Great King, the noblest virtues will be practiced throughout the world, and the land will yield abundant crops."[377]

Numerous prophecies talk of an almost unprecedented fertility of the land after a chastisement during the reign of a "Great King."

16. Sister Marianne (19th Century)

This holy nun lived in the convent of the Ursulines in Blois. She gave many prophecies throughout her life of short term future events. Shortly before her death in 1804, she predicted (1) the fall of Napoleon I, and his brief return from the Island of Elba, (2) the restoration of the Bourbon Dynasty in France, and the French Revolutions of 1830 and 1848.

> "It is then that the Prince shall reign, whom people did not esteem before, but whom they shall then seek. The triumph of religion will be so great that no one has ever seen the equal. All injustices will be made good; civil laws will be made in harmony with the laws of God and of the Church. Education in the schools will be most Christian, and **THE WORKERS' GUILDS WILL FLOURISH AGAIN.**"[378]

Many of the prophecies speak of the fact that the Great King at first will not be well-liked, especially by many of the French clergy.

17. The Ecstatic of Tours (19th Century)

She was a nun living in Tours, in France. In the year 1882, using a nom-de-plume, her spiritual director published her revelations in a book called *La Vielle de la Victoire du Christ* (On the Eve of the

---

377 *Catholic Prophecy*, Page 14.
378 *Catholic Prophecy*, p. 50.

Victory of Christ). The following excerpts come from the prophecies made in 1872 and 1873.

> *"The French people will ask for the good King*, he who was chosen by God. He will come, this saviour whom God has spared for France, this king who is not wanted now because he is dear to God's Heart. He will ascend to the throne; he will free the Church and reassert the Pope's rights."[379]

Obviously, between 1872 and now, the French people have not asked for a king. Also, by the 1870's, popular desire for a Monarchy was dead in France. This prophecy was no appeal to a popular sentiment.

18. Blessed Anna-Maria Taigi (19th Century)

A confidant of several Popes, she was an adviser to Pius IX. She saw the entire world, its past, present, and future in a mystical golden globe. That particular gift lasted for 47 years. People (including Popes, cardinals and priests) began to take her seriously after she accurately predicted the deaths of several Roman prelates. Her purpose in doing so was to help them get their spiritual affairs in order. *She predicted numerous major historical events which subsequently have come to pass.*

About her prophetic gifts, in resume, she predicted the abdication of Charles IV, King of Spain, the fall of Napoleon, the exact date of the liberation of Pope Pius VII, the death of the Father General of the Trinitarian Order who was assassinated in Spain by Napoleon's troops, the news of which didn't reach Rome until a month later, which proved all the details she had prophesied about his last moments. She also predicted years in advance the future election of Cardinal Mastai as Pope Pius IX. These are but a small sampling of specific prophecies of Anna Maria, all of which are attested to in the files of her case prior to her beatification in 1920.

Furthermore, *she prophesied through divine revelation the exact day of Napoleon's death on the Isle of St. Helena*. The news of Napoleon's death did not reach his own mother, Maria Letizia

---

[379] Ibid. p. 37.

(who lived in Rome a short distance away from the house of Anna Maria Taigi) until two months after his death.

Blessed Anna Maria also announced that a great chastisement would fall upon Rome, a punishment that would consist of a terrible plague which would break forth the day after her death, and from which her children would escape. Such is exactly what happened.

When Pope Leo XII was on his death bed Anna Maria Taigi was asked to pray for him and she answered: "The Pope will not die, but Monsignor Strambi should prepare himself since he has offered his life for the Pope and Our Lord has accepted his generous offering." People in Rome were perplexed. They knew the gifts of Anna Maria, but the facts were that the Pontiff was right then in his death agony and Msgr. Strambi was in perfect health. A few days later, Leo XII was out of danger and suddenly Msgr. Strambi became ill and died.

Blessed Anna Maria further prophesied:

> "France shall fall into a frightful anarchy. The French shall have a desperate civil war in the course of which old men themselves will take up arms. The political parties, having exhausted their blood and their rage without being able to arrive at any satisfactory understanding, shall at the last extremity agree by common consent to have recourse to the Holy See. Then the Pope shall send to France a special legate ... In consequence of the information received, his Holiness himself shall nominate a most Christian king for the government of France."[380]

Several things are striking about this prophecy. First, monarchy was already long gone in France when Anna Maria made this prophecy. Therefore, Anna Maria is predicting something which comes sometime after our time, sometime after 1996. Second, it is most interesting that here we have an Italian woman prophesying concerning the future of France. St. Hildegard, a German, made the same prophecy about a future French King.

As we will discover, the fortunes of France are integrally tied in these prophecies to the rest of the world. What are the chances

[380] *The Prophets and Our Times*, Rev. Jerald Culleton, Taft, Ca., Imp. Bishop Phillip G. Sher, 1941, p. 194.

that St. Hildegard and Blessed Anna Maria and many other Catholic mystics made exactly the same "*mistake*" in understanding the prophecies which they received? It is possible. But how probable is it?

Anna Maria's prophecy explains that the French will again seek a monarchy. How could this happen? It is explained by her words, "The political parties, having exhausted their blood and their rage without being able to arrive at any satisfactory settlement, shall agree at the last extremity to have recourse to the Holy See." In other words, the rebellious and irreligious French will have come totally to the end of their rope. It could only be in absolute desperation that a majority of the French people (at least as they have been since the time of Anna Maria) would turn to the Papacy for anything.

As a final comment on this phase of the prophecies, there is a remarkable similarity, contiguity, and form which develop over the course of many centuries and throughout many countries. In many cases these prophecies came from those who had never ventured outside their cloister from the time that they were in their early youth. It is difficult to explain away this contiguity by arguments of chance or a Catholic academic conspiracy. *All of this may sound improbable or bizarre to the listener, as it once did to the author.* But, it was his discovery of Catholic prophecy which disclosed to him the possible answer to a burning question from his college days:

> "How, since the Fathers and Doctors predicted that soon after the end of the (Holy?) Roman Empire, the Antichrist would come, WHY HADN'T HE ALREADY COME?"

C. COMMON OBJECTIONS TO: (A) "THE FATHERS," AND (B) PRIVATE PROPHECIES

(A) THE FATHERS: We find reference to a final Roman Empire in writings of the Fathers which fall into two classes.

(1) Scriptural Exegesis - their commentary on specific passages of Scripture.

(2) In their Catechetical instructions, general instructions, homilies, apologetical writing such as defenses against heresy, etc. Here they commonly speak of that which comes to them in "the order of tradition" (to use St. Irenaeus' phrase).

(3) The teaching about a final Roman Empire was very broadly taught. That is why and how St. Jerome could say *without fear of contradiction from his contemporaries* -- it is "handed down" by "all the ecclesiastical writers."

This should reasonably answer the objection that the Fathers were confused or just wrote whatever came into their heads (when they talked about a final Roman Empire)

There is a second objection raised by a few that these documents are later inventions. They have no validity to anyone familiar with the thoroughness of Patristic studies over the last one hundred and fifty years. To those who have heard such a charge we would answer.

> *First:* To serious scholars from many different faiths (some are even agnostics), the authenticity of the vast majority of the key texts attributed to the Fathers are simply not in question.
>
> *Second:* numerous Fathers who were greatly separated by distance and time, who lived in both the East and the West, made exactly the same statements about the Antichrist's coming after a final collapse of the Roman Empire. *The consistency and form of their statements are readily observable to anyone who has read them with any care.*

Similarly, theories that these and other statements of the Fathers were later inventions of the Catholic Church (you can actually find such statements in some publications, which for charitable reasons, we will not name here) are ludicrous to any serious student or scholar of the 3rd or 4th centuries. Just how one interprets the specific writings of these Fathers -- true scholars may and do disagree on here and there amongst themselves, but no serious "student or scholar" of the period challenges the authenticity of the vast majority of these documents.

(B) PRIVATE PROPHECIES: Attempts to explain away the statements of the Fathers also do not explain the fact that literally dozens of canonized Saints (many of whom were illiterate and/or lived in secluded cloisters all of their adult lives) have reiterated *corroborating chains* of their privately prophesied events through century after century. The statements of the Fathers about received doctrine and prophecies about a final collapse of a final Roman Empire, and their exegetical expositions on prophetical Scripture imply the possibility of a latter restoration of some kind of "Roman" Empire.

Several private prophecies of canonized Saints specifically state that there will be a latter *restoration* of the Holy Roman Empire and that there will be at least one last Holy Roman Emperor. The authenticity of the authorship of such prophecies of canonized Saints (e.g., St. Hildegard, St. Vincent Ferrer, St. Francis of Paula, and St. John Vianney) at least over the last eight hundred years is scholastically unquestionable.

We are left with the options that:

(1) the prophecies are genuine,
(2) all of the Fathers and Saints throughout the centuries who attested to some form of this tradition were deluded or mistaken *in exactly the same way*, or
(3) that they were all liars and part of a massive Catholic conspiracy which has spanned seventeen centuries, within which they all managed to tell exactly the same lies.

A conspiracy theory is always tendentious at best. But a seventeen century conspiracy scenario which managed to escape proof of its existence *would* be pushing credulity to the limit.

It must be admitted that it is not beyond the realm of possibility that in some manner, statements about a literal reinstitution of the Holy Roman Empire and a last Emperor are mystical expressions of some future truth. But one also has to perform extreme mental gymnastics to consistently conclude a "mystical expressions" interpretation.

For an intellectually honest and reasonably well-educated person, it finally gets down to a calculus of probabilities. Can all of the above merely be explained away in the mind of the reader? It *is* possible to explain away any singular prophecy listed above. That is a fact. But how does one explain away the massiveness and consistency of the witness (1) of so many individuals (2) from so many centuries (3) and so many countries (4) from such varying backgrounds? *What is the probability that there is that much smoke and not some kind of a real fire?*

In the light of the consistent statements of the Fathers, and the repeated consistent prophecies of great Saints of the Church, a literal understanding of the more modern prophecies of a "reinstitution" of a latter Roman Empire at least provides a most interesting hypothesis, in lieu of any other explanation the author has read or heard.

CHAPTER 6

THE THREE DAYS OF DARKNESS

Another major event consistently foretold in prophecy is a period of three days of darkness which will cover the entire earth. Several Scriptural quotes from prophetic books in the Bible speak of a darkness, but none speak of a three day period. This "three days" of darkness does not appear to occur in either Tradition or Scripture. Its basis appears to be limited to that of private prophecy.

1. Padre Pio Did *Not* Predict Three Days of Darkness

As the reader is about to see, numerous approved Catholic prophets, including canonized Saints have predicted such a specific event. But a subsequent problem may have developed. There are printed materials containing prophecy of three days of darkness which attribute such a prophecy to Padre Pio. But the author has in his possession sworn documents from the Capuchin Order stating that no such prophecy ever emanated from Padre Pio. All the author's attempts to track down an authentic source from Padre Pio have led to the conclusion that; some person(s) either accidentally or willfully created these attributions of such a prophecy to Padre Pio.

Many other prophecies from unapproved sources have appeared in recent years alleging to prophesy "three days of darkness." Some of those alleged sources appear to be *extremely* doubtful as to authenticity.

This may be a question of "copy-cat" prophecies. Since a possible copy-catism may have developed, any prophecy from recent *unapproved* sources alleging to predict the three days should be carefully examined (a) in light of the discernment tests, and particularly (b) for consistency with the body of history related to that event in other prophecies from approved sources. There are numerous historic cases of delusion of alleged prophets by forces less than holy. That phenomenon will undoubtedly be repeated.

2. Many Approved Prophets Have Predicted the Three Days of Darkness

Does this mean that all prophecy related to three days of darkness are questionable or inauthentic? The answer to that question is a resounding NO! The *Catholic Encyclopedia* itself refers respectfully to those who have attained to the rank of Venerable and Blessed, who have specifically foretold such an event. One obvious example of this is the writings of Blessed Anna Maria Taigi. Another prophecy of this event was made by a Carmelite nun whom Pope John Paul II beatified in 1983 as Blessed Mary of Jesus Crucified. Therefore the author begs the informed reader to reserve judgment on this issue until he or she sees the stature of the people approved by the Church who have made such prophecy about the "three days of darkness."

If the three days of darkness has no basis in Tradition or Scripture, then why present it here? There are several reasons:

(1) It is one of numerous privately prophesied events foretold to precede the coming of Antichrist - along with numerous other prophesied events which do have a basis in Tradition and/or Scripture.

(2) Many private prophecies of even canonized Saints which had no specific factual basis in Tradition and/or Scripture have come to pass. They were fulfilled as prophesied. They were obviously sent by God "for the direction of human acts." This is the role which St. Thomas Aquinas teaches us is proper to private prophecy.

If this event should come to pass, it could happen very soon, or many years later. There is absolutely nothing in the various prophecies of this event from approved sources which specify a time within which it happens. When this prophecy is understood within the context of other events foretold to surround it, it is also obvious that this is a conditional prophecy. Therefore it may or may not come to pass - in that it depends upon human correspondence with grace. *But,* (1) *If* this event is part of a foretold worldwide Chastisement, (2) if that conditional chastisement should occur, (3) it must occur near the end of that chastisement. The reasons for that statement will become more apparent after reading these prophecies.

The following is a small sampling of Saints and other devout Catholics who claimed the gift of prophecy and foretold this specific event. This event and other prophecies may sound in the dictionary sense of the word, "fantastic," but the practicing Catholic is faced with the opposite phantasm - that of alternately believing that canonized Saints and other good Catholics who are in exact agreement on specific points of prophecy and who claim that God revealed such to them, are all either deluded, crazy, or liars. How does one reconcile the two horns of the dilemma?

The solution seems to lie in simply keeping an open mind and not denigrating with what St. Peter Canisius calls "a rash and disdainful spirit,"[381] what has been foretold. In the same spirit, St. Francis de Sales comments on the words of St. Paul, *'Charity believeth all things,'* and St. Francis further comments, "Charity does not readily believe others lie, and more so, when one is treating of holy souls."[382]

3. St. Caspar (Jasper) Del Bufalo (19th Century)

Canonized in 1954, St. Caspar was the founder of the Order of the Missionaries of the Precious Blood, which order was approved in 1815. This Order of Priests' special mission was to have a "house" for its priests in the "most neglected and wicked town or district in a diocese." In 1821, Pope Pius VII personally requested Caspar to found six houses in the City of Naples which had become "a nest of crime" by that time. "Various miracles had been worked by Don

[381] *Public And Private Prophecies About The Last Times*, Published by Opus Reginae Sacratissimi Rosarii, 1972, Rev. Benjamin Martin Sanchez, Theology Dept., University of Salamanca. p.8

[382] Ibid.

Caspar during his lifetime, ... in fact a long list of cures and other miraculous occurrences."[383] St. Caspar prophesies the following:

> "The death of the impenitent persecutors of the Church will take place during the three days of darkness. He who outlives the darkness and the fear of these three days will think that he is alone on earth because the whole world will be covered with cadavers."[384]

4. Blessed Mary of Jesus Crucified, (19th Century)

The foundress of a Carmelite convent at Bethlehem, her nickname is the "Little Arab." She died in 1878, and was beatified by Pope John Paul II in 1983.

> "During a darkness lasting three days the people given to evil will perish so that only one fourth of mankind will survive."[385]

5. The Ecstatic of Tours

> "There will be earthquakes and signs in the sun. *Towards the end darkness will cover the earth.*"[386]

6. Palma Maria (19th Century)

Palma Maria was an Italian woman born in 1825. Widowed at the age of twenty eight, she later received the stigmata in her hands, feet, and side on May 3, 1865. Similar to a number of other graced souls,[387] she lived on the Blessed Sacrament alone for the last ten years of her life. She made a long series of prophecies concerning local affairs in Italy. She predicted the rise of particularly "anti-Catholic" "Republican" governments for France, Spain, and Italy well in advance of the events. She had the following to say about the three days of darkness.

---

[383] *Butler's Lives of the Saints*, Vol. 1, p. 25.
[384] *Catholic Prophecy*, p. 79.
[385] Ibid.
[386] Ibid. p. 37.
[387] Such as St. Nicholas of Fluh.

> "There shall be three days of darkness. Not one demon shall be left in hell. They shall all come out, either to excite the wicked murderers, or to dishearten the just. This shall be frightful! frightful! but a grand cross shall appear, and the triumphs of the Church will make people quickly forget all evils."[388]

This is another of the prophecies which clearly indicate that the "three days" will come at the end of a period of great tribulation. They are followed by some kind of triumph for the Church. This is also only one of many prophecies which state that in some mystical manner, a cross "shall appear." Some of the prophecies state it shall appear in the sky. Some indicate that it shall remain where it appears till the end of time as a reminder to man of God's love and mercy.[389]

7. Venerable Isabel (Elizabeth) Canori-Mora (1774-1825)

As a seer of the Tribulations of the "latter times" of the Church Venerable Isabel was favored with the gifts of vision and of proph-

---

[388] *The Christian Trumpet*, p. 114.

[389] If a new permanent sign were to be left, it would not be without precedent. We learn in the Old Testament that prior to the time of Noah there had never been a rainbow observed by man. The O.T. informs us that God left this sign as a confirmation of his covenant with man never to destroy the earth again with a flood. (Many modern critic Scripture scholars say this is just poetic language to deliver a spiritual message). Up until the last thirty years even many Christian members of the scientific community thought the flood account must be either a "literary device" or a pious legend. However, there is now mounting evidence of a general flood having occurred, which in many aspects is in basic accord with the Biblical account.

Even non-Christian scientists are now seriously considering the "green house effect" as a rationally possible explanation for numerous archeological anomalies. The "green house" theory conjectures that until some point in time, the earth was completely covered by some kind of cloud, or mist or fog layer. A rainbow requires direct sunlight hitting droplets of water thus creating a prismatic separation of all the colors of light into the colors of the rainbow. If at some point much of this airborne moisture began to massively precipitate out as rain, that could then provide for direct sunlight hitting the earth for the first time. Much more interesting to the Christian or Jew is that such a massive precipitation would also provide a physical science explanation for part of the Biblical account of the flood (the Bible also says that waters erupted from the earth itself). It is an interesting theory.

ecy. She died in Rome on Feb. 5th, 1825 where she was also born. She joined the Third Order of Franciscan Trinitarians in 1820. She was well-known in the city for her predictions about current events and also had the gift of miraculous cures.

We learn from the documents prepared for her beatification process that she freed the young Count John Maria de Mastai Ferreti (the future Pope Pius IX) from epilepsy, a disease which up until that time had kept him from entering the priesthood. Isabel prophesies,

> "As soon as St. Peter, the prince of the Apostles, had gathered the flock of Jesus Christ in a place of safety, he reascended into heaven, accompanied by legions of angels. Scarcely had they disappeared, *when the sky was covered with clouds so dense and dismal that it was impossible to look at them without dismay. On a sudden there burst out such a terrible and violent wind, that its noise sounded like the roars of furious lions. The sound of the furious hurricane was heard over the whole earth.* Fear and terror struck not only men, but the very beasts."[390]

Elisabeth Canori-Mora does not mention the duration of, but predicted a period of darkness caused by an immensely thick cloud cover with resultant hurricanes. As the reader will later see, she also predicted massive conflict which appears to occur in the same time frame. This is one of the prophecies which leads to the conclusion that the three days of darkness are an integral part of a "chastisement" which is even larger in scope. If this is the case, then the three days must come at the end of such a chastisement.

8. Blessed Anna-Maria Taigi

Anna-Maria specifically prophesies a three day duration for the period of darkness. She also gives many other details surrounding its occurrence.

> "God will ordain two punishments: one, in the form of wars, revolutions and other evils, will originate on earth; *the other will be sent from Heaven.* There will come over all the earth

[390] *Christian Trumpet*, p. 180.

> an intense darkness lasting three days and three nights. Nothing will be visible and the air will be laden with pestilence, which will claim principally but not exclusively, the enemies of religion... Only blessed candles can be lighted and will afford illumination...
>
> "*All the enemies of the Church, secret as well as known, will perish over the whole earth during that universal darkness,* with the exception of a few, whom God will soon after convert. The air shall be infected by demons who will appear under all sorts of hideous forms."[391]
>
> "After the three days of darkness, St. Peter and St. Paul, having come down from heaven, will preach in the whole world and designate a new Pope. A great light will flash from their bodies and will settle upon the cardinal, the future Pontiff [Pope]. Then Christianity will spread throughout the world. He is the Holy Pontiff, chosen by God to withstand the storm. At the end, he will have the gift of miracles, and his name shall be praised over the whole earth."[392] [The above is quoted from the Beatification documentation on Bl. Anna Maria.]

Not just Elizabeth Canori-Mora tells us that St. Peter and St. Paul are somehow directly involved with events surrounding the three days of darkness. We now have another holy soul, Anna Maria telling us the same thing. As one studies more and more of these prophesies, it becomes increasingly difficult to dismiss them as the work of overactive imaginations. There is a clearly recognizable pattern to them. And this pattern is to be found amongst practicing Christians who were known for their forbearance and common sense. None of them had reputations for anything but stability - while many of those around them were losing their heads. These two women were living through times which led many others to panic and despair.

---

391 *Public And Private Prophecies About The Last Times*, Rev. Benjamin Martin Sanchez, Pub: Opus Reginae Sacratissimi Rosarii, University of Salamanca, 1972, p. 47.

392 Ibid.

A. GOD'S PROVIDENCE, GRACE, AND FREE WILL

Perhaps it is time to emphasize what Bl. Anna Maria Taigi said above, that the bulk of the suffering during the chastisement is "manmade." That "bulk" will originate on earth. According to this and many other prophecies, it is only some events during the "three days of darkness" that are directly sent from Heaven. It is an established point of theology that all "events" which occur on earth fall into two categories, (1) those things which God wishes to happen, and, (2) those things which He allows to happen. In all of God's providence, He does not interfere with man's free will. He can and does inspire every man and woman by grace to do good, to cooperate with the will of his Maker; but God will never enforce His will on anyone to do anything.

To observe this principle in operative force, let us look at two rather famous Scriptural examples which are fairly comprehensive in their scope; that of the Egyptian Pharaoh in the story of the Book of Exodus, and that of Saul of Tarsus. This comparison encompasses a broad sweep of history in that Pharaoh is one of the central figures from the Old Testament, with Saul of Tarsus (St. Paul) filling the same description in the New Testament.

These two men have the following characteristics in common:

(1) both were very well-educated by their own civilization's educational standards,

(2) both were extremely strong-willed men with natural leadership ability who were in positions of varying authority and power, and,

(3) both were keenly observant of events and circumstances around them (as can be reasonably gleaned from the Scriptural descriptions of their response to events),

(4) both were obviously gifted with high intelligence.

In both cases, God graphically, miraculously, demonstrates to them His Being and His power. God's will for both men is that they obey His orders, -- and in both cases He dramatically demonstrates by means of a miraculous event (in Pharaoh's case many miracles) the proof of what His Divine will is in their lives.

Saul, later to be known as the Apostle Paul, responds to God's very first call to him on the road to Damascus. Over and over again, Pharaoh rejects God's will in his life and despises God's grace which is presented to him in the form of repeated public miracles. God wills that both be saved. One cooperates with God's grace and the other does not.

Amazingly enough, the one who does not cooperate is given chance after chance after chance. Finally, Scripture tells us that the Holy Spirit "hardened Pharaoh's heart" (withdrew further grace from him) and that subsequently Pharaoh turned his face to the wall and died. Why did Pharaoh reject so much grace, reject so many miraculous events from God intended for his conversion? We cannot understand it. Its cause is what St. Paul generically describes as the "mystery of iniquity." Man can be his own worst enemy.

Is Pharaoh alone in this rejection of God's grace? When the miracles shown to Pharaoh are re-presented to man today through God's Word in the Bible, some men and woman rationalize their way around it. When God publicly demonstrated His power and His will before seventy thousand people at Fatima in 1917, how many people responded to His call in faith?

In the prophecies to follow, we shall hear of repeated grace-filled warnings (including manifestations every bit as dramatic as those given to Pharaoh) from God through signs and events He has already given and will continue to give to mankind. Some men and women will respond. Others will not. The difference between the two is, as St. Paul tells us, a mystery.

B. A RETURN TO PROPHECIES ABOUT THE THREE DAYS OF DARKNESS

1. The Ecstatic of Tours (19th Century)

Now we will give the complete quote (partially quoted above) to put the three days into its proper chronological perspective. It appears from all these prophecies that the three days of darkness is not all of a sudden sprung on the human race in a period of relative calm. It seems to occur toward the end of a period of tribulation.

> "Before the war breaks out again, food will be scarce and expensive. There will be little work for the workers, and fathers will hear their children crying for food. There will be earthquakes and signs in the sun. *Towards the end darkness will cover the earth.*"[393]

Many of the prophecies say that the three days of darkness come "towards the end" of the chastisement. It is sent by God as a mercy to stop the man-made carnage and suffering.

2. Marie de La Fraudais (19th/20th Century)

Marie was a French laywoman who had received the stigmata of Our Lord. The holiness of her life was attested to by all who knew her.[394]

> "There will come three days of complete darkness. Only blessed candles made of wax will give some light during this horrible darkness. One candle will last for three days, but they will not give light in the houses of the Godless. Lightning will penetrate your houses, but it will not put out the blessed candles. Neither wind, nor storm, nor earthquake will put out the blessed candles."[395]

Marie is the only seer who describes this event who states that the candles must be of wax. In this sense it is not consistent with the others.

---

393 *Catholic Prophecy*, p. 37.

394 There is one exception to this observation. At one point the author read a commentary on stigmatics. The author of that article stated something to the effect that there had never been a "stigmatic" who did not remain constant and persevere to the end. But then that author added, "with the unusual exception of Marie Julie." This author has been unable to relocate that article - he has not been able to check out what the comment "with the unusual exception of Marie Julie" might have been referring to.

395 *Catholic Prophecy*, p. 76.

3. Sister Elena Aiello (20th Century)

Sister Aiello was *foundress of the Calabrian nuns.* She was also *a stigmatic* and endured much suffering to save the souls of others. She personally foretold to Benito Mussolini at least twice that if he did not change his course he would end in disaster. Sister Aiello died in 1961. She stated she received the following message from Our Lady on or near Good Friday, April 16th, 1954.

> "Clouds with *lightning rays of fire and a tempest of fire* will pass over the whole world and the punishment will be the most terrible ever known in the history of mankind. It will last 70 hours [three days]. The wicked will be crushed and eliminated. Many will be lost because they will have stubbornly remained in their sins. Then they will feel the force of light over darkness. The hours of darkness are near."[396]

This prophecy sounds almost identical to that of Elizabeth Canori-Mora. It speaks of "clouds" and a terrible storm. Elizabeth refers to it as a worldwide hurricane. This prophecy does not specifically refer to "three days" of darkness. However, 70 hours is within two hours of a full three days. This does not sound like nuclear war, it sounds like a natural event precipitated by God. If this prophecy is compared with the other prophecies of three days of darkness, it seems very highly reasonable that this is the context of this prophecy. **This prophecy and that of Isabel Canori-Mora specifically use the word "clouds."**

There are a myriad of other prophecies on the same subject. Suffice it to say that a number of canonized Saints and stigmatics have prophesied this event in addition to literally dozens of other Catholic non-canonized prophets who have identically described the same event.

[396] *Public And Private Prophecies About The Last Times*, p. 42.

4. Sr. Agnes, the Stigmatic Nun of Akita, (20th Century - 1980's)

The specific events surrounding Sr. Agnes and her prophesies were attested to by her bishop, Bishop Ito of Niigata, Japan. Sr. Agnes was similarly told,

> "Fire will fall from the sky and will wipe out a great part of humanity."[397]

This prophecy sounds strikingly similar to that of Sr. Elena Aiello quoted above. It is anything but certain, but the "fire" may well be the massive lightning referred to in the other prophecies (only a few of which are presented in this book).

A FINAL CAVEAT: AS WITH ALL PRIVATE PROPHECY CONTAINED IN THIS BOOK THERE ARE THREE MAJOR POINTS TO CONSIDER:

(1) Since they are from private prophecy - none of them are "of faith."

(2) These prophecies on the three days of darkness are *conditional*, whether or not they come to pass depends upon mankind's cooperation with the grace of God.

(3) They are *not* presented to engross the reader in private prophecy. *Rather*, they are presented *to demonstrate that "approved" prophecies predict many events yet to come in the history of mankind prior to the coming of Antichrist*. They are presented to inoculate the reader against the spreading rumor/suspicion that the Antichrist is just around the corner.

[397] *Akita, The Tears and Messages of Mary*, Rev. Teiji Yasuda, Pub: 101 Foundation, Asbury, N.J., 1989, p. 77.

CHAPTER 7

A MINOR CHASTISEMENT WHY US? WHY HERE?

In prophecy after prophecy, (both Scriptural and private) *the term chastisement keeps repeating itself.* These references are highly complex and can be confusing. In the last book of the New Testament, the "Apocalypse," or "Book of Revelation," the Chastisement or great tribulation of Antichrist is determined to be of three and one half years duration. Yet, there are seven years of Chastisement mentioned in those passages -- which appear to be two periods of three and one half years duration.

Some scholars believe that the first three and one half years merely refers to a period of the foretold specific "False Prophet" who will precede Antichrist and prepare the way for him. In this period, the "False Prophet" will ape the role of St. John the Baptist. (John first prepared Our Lord's way. He immediately foretold the presence of the Christ with the words "Behold the Lamb of God.") But, it is also highly possible that the first three and one half years refers to a period prior to the "False Prophet," that it is a period of chastisement which will well *precede* the time of Antichrist.

As is common knowledge amongst Scripture scholars, *especially* in the prophetic works of Scripture, one sentence often holds a complexity of meanings, i.e. both literal and allegorical, material and spiritual, and on occasion the same phrase refers to a multiplicity of events which have something in common.

It is entirely possible that the descriptions of the composite of two periods of three and one half years of chastisement foretold in the Apocalypse refers both to,

(1) a three and one half year preparation period for the Antichrist by the "False Prophet," as well as the three and one half year persecution of Antichrist,

(2) it refers also to another earlier chastisement to well precede the age of Antichrist.

It is the opinion of the author that what is specifically referred to are at least two different chastisements, i.e., the Apocalypse is referring to chastisements in two different periods which probably are;

(3) **A Minor Chastisement** which precedes the first Age of Peace, the Age of Mary, and,

(4) **The Major Chastisement of Antichrist** which follows the Age of Mary, but which Major Chastisement also ushers in a final period of peace (after the death of Antichrist). That period of peace is given to the world for conversion to Christ and His Church and for repentance.

This opinion of two separate periods of chastisement has been held over the years by a wide number of students of prophecy as well as by many Scripture scholars. The reason is the following; there are a large number of ancillary Scriptural "Prophecies" which make little or no sense (or appear to be mutually contradictory) when interpreted from the point of view of one contiguous seven year period which is made up of two successive three and one half year chastisements. But these self-same Scriptural "Prophecies" make a great deal more sense once the thesis of two separate chastisements (separated by a significant period of time) is predicated.

The Minor Chastisement is sometimes described in private prophecy as of "about" four years duration to come in the latter times. It is a time of purification. Some of those who are good Catholics will suffer and die also. But they will die with peace in their hearts such as the early Christian martyrs did. It is important again to remember that it is not possible to mention here even a large minority of the prophecies concerning this Chastisement. There are literally many hundreds of them from dozens of countries. Their contents are highly repetitive in nature. We set the stage for this discussion with an initial quote from one of the seers of Fatima.

The child Jacinta, one of the three children at Fatima, said something she repeated on her death bed:

> "If men will repent, God will pardon them, but if they do not amend their lives, there will come upon the earth the most terrible chastisement ever known."

How did Jacinta know this? Do we believe she would or could make it up? How would a child of Jacinta's age and background create such a story? When they first received the prophecy about praying for the conversion of Russia, these three peasant children of Fatima prayed for what they thought was a "woman" named "Russia." They did not even know that Russia was the name of a country. These children were not sophisticated enough to make up a story about a chastisement.

A. WHY US, WHY HERE?

Many people who find out about these prophecies for the first time ask why this could happen to us in the United States. If we cannot see why God would chastise the United States, possibly the answer lies in the Scottish Poet Robert Burns' poem, *The Louse*.

> "Oh would some power, the gift he give us, to see ourselves as others see us."

In a 1989 address given by Archbishop (now a Cardinal) Bevilacqua of Philadelphia to a conference of Consortium Perfecta Caritate, he was commenting upon the spiritual condition of the U.S. He described a conversation he had with a young girl in Czechoslovakia in the summer of 1989. At that time, while still under the repression of the Czechoslovakian Communist Government, thousands of young Cheks were crowding the Czeckoslovak churches. She said to the Archbishop,

> "When you see the Pope and report to him, tell him that we young people love him very much. We are grateful for our persecutions because it has brought us closer to God and the Church. But if this cross is ever removed from us -- we are afraid what will happen to us."

The Archbishop further described his talk with her,

> "She was obviously speaking strangely of the culture of *some of the Western Countries and particularly this nation [the U.S.].* She was afraid that in such a vacuum [of newfound freedom] that all of the materialism and hedonism of the U.S. would sweep into Czeckoslovakia."

Archbishop (now a Cardinal) Bevilacqua related that one year later he spoke with a young Hungarian living in the U.S., and that he remarked to him that it must have been very difficult to keep the Faith during the Communist repression. The young man responded,

> "Yes, it was very difficult. But the great difficulties we faced under the previous Communist regime is nothing compared to the difficulties the young people have with their faith here in the United States. I watch television and I read the magazines. When I see a young person in your country that has the faith and practices it, I say to myself, that is a miracle. I don't see how anyone can have the faith here."

COMMENT. If these two young people from behind the Iron Curtain are right (as the author suspects that they are) should any of us be surprised if God takes strong action to cure the situation? We have all heard the term "quiet desperation." That term aptly applies to most SERIOUS Catholic parents with young children today. The author is one of them. Trying to protect our children from moral evil today is a veritable nightmare for the majority of us.

1. There are Precedents to Our Situation - Seeing Ourselves as Other See Us

People seldom see themselves as others see them. Even people looking back on their own lives usually see past events much more clearly than when they were actually living them. There are usually a few people within a given generation who possess an accurate objective vision of events around them. Men and women with such "vision" can usually see that men in any generation are their own worst enemy. One of these people with "vision" was St. Cyprian of Carthage.

2. St. Cyprian on Chastisement

The Roman Emperor Decian's persecution of the Christians was drawing to a close in 251 A.D. The Church in North Africa had enjoyed a significant period of relative peace prior to the "Persecution of Decius." Shortly after he has returned from exile, St. Cyprian, Bishop of Carthage and a Father of the Church writes to his flock explaining the cause of "The persecution,"

> "*If we want to know what made us fall* [fall subject to the persecution], *we can learn how to heal our wounds.* The Master [Jesus] wanted to make trial of his household; and *because the long years of peace had undermined our practice of the way of life which God had given us*, our languid faith -- I almost said our *sleeping* faith ... Each one was intent on adding to his inheritance. *Forgetting what the faithful used to do under the Apostles and what they should always be doing,* each one with insatiable greed was engrossed in increasing his own property. Gone was the devotion of bishops to the service of God, gone was the clergy's faithful integrity, gone the generous compassion for the needy, gone all the discipline in our behavior.
>
> "If that is what we have become, what do we not deserve for such sins, when the judgement of God warned us long since, saying, **'If they forsake my law and walk not in my judgements: if they profane my statutes and observe not my commands: I will visit crimes with a rod, and their transgressions with scourges.'**
>
> "We had already been told this and [been] warned beforehand. But heedless of established law and customary discipline, *we brought it upon us by our sins that we should*

have to face correction for our contempt of God's commands, and should have our faith put to sterner tests."[398]

This is St. Cyprian's analysis of what led to their persecution. Every essential element dealing with the cause and effect of chastisement is present in his analysis.

(1) He says that they could not spiritually withstand extended prosperity and peace.

(2) In every level of the Church, they fell into materialism and the cares of the world, and

(3) through materialism they lost their zeal for the faith.

It matters not whether we call what they went through a persecution, trial, tribulation, or a chastisement. All these nouns well describe the "Persecution of Decian." Cyprian tells us that it was caused by "Forgetting what the faithful used to do under the Apostles." They stopped living their faith properly. *Stated simply, their faith stopped being the most important thing in their lives.*

3. Individual Exceptions Do Not Break a General Rule

There were many individual exceptions as Cyprian states in other places. But Cyprian's description certainly generally described the Christians in North Africa of that period. He even says they had been forewarned. Cyprian goes on to say that God allowed the Persecution of Decian as a "correction" to bring Christians back to their senses. Could they not see their condition till after their "correction"? Evidently not. In other words, the persecution was a Divine Mercy to bring people to their senses and thus *to save souls.*

4. Similarities to Our Civilization?

We have heard St. Cyprian discussing his own civilization. Can we see the truth in the observations of the American Archbishop

398 *Ancient Christian Writers*, St. Cyprian, *The Lapsed*, The Newman Press, Westminster, MD. 1957, p. 16.

and now Cardinal Bevilacqua, the Hungarian young man, and the Chek girl about our civilization? *Can we see ourselves as others see us?* But our condition is nothing unique or novel. Human nature is constant, it does not change! As St. Cyprian describes them, do we sound essentially different from the people of North Africa in the middle of the 3rd century? They received a "chastisement" -- AS A DIVINE MERCY to bring them back to the practice of their faith!

There are many other trials or chastisements which have occurred across the seventeen centuries intervening between St. Cyprian and ourselves. There have been great Saints in each case forewarning the Christians of what would happen if they did not return to a faithful practice of their faith. In a few cases, the people have listened and the threatened chastisement was averted. In the majority of cases where the Christians did not, after a chastisement there have been great Saints like Cyprian telling the people why it happened. These respective Saints have explained that God allowed a chastisement to happen in order to bring Christians to their senses. Thus these "chastisements" were Divine Mercies, sent in order to save souls.

If we see ourselves as others see us, then this should be viewed as the first step to recovery. It should not be viewed as a source for depression. St. John Chrysostom once counseled the people of Antioch at a time when they had begun to see their faults. They were facing the potential wrath of an emperor for acts performed in their city. Chrysostom described the psychological reality of the resultant sadness of the pending disastrous situation thusly:

> "So indeed does the cloud of sadness, when it stands before our souls, refuse to admit an easy passage for the word, but chokes it, and restrains it forcibly within. And this not only with those who speak, but with those who hear; for as it does not suffer the word to burst forth freely from the soul of the speaker, so neither does it suffer it to sink into the mind of those who listen, with its native power.
>
> "Therefore also the Jews of old time, while slaving at the mud and bricks, could not listen to Moses, while he repeatedly told them great things respecting their future deliverance; sadness making their minds inaccessible to the address, and shutting up their sense of hearing.

"But afford me your attention! Lend me your ears awhile! Shake off this sadness! .... For should the Lord see that His words are heard with sincerity; and that our love of divine wisdom stands the trial of the difficulty of these times, He will quickly take us up again, and will make out of the present tempest a calm and happy change. **For this too is a thing in which it behooves the Christian to differ from the unbelievers, the bearing of all things nobly;** ***and through hope of the future, soaring above the attack of human evils.***"[399]

[399] *The Homilies of S. John Chrysostom, Archbishop of Constantinople, "On the Statues," to the People of Antioch*, The Library of the Fathers, Oxford, John Henry Parker, London, 1856, p. 36. [Sermons delivered in March/April of 387 A.D.]

CHAPTER 8

CHRONOLOGY OF PROPHECIES CONCERNING A MINOR CHASTISEMENT

As already stated in the book, Tradition and Scripture predict a substantial series of events - prior to the rise of Antichrist - many of which do not appear to have yet occurred. The specific interpretations of those prophecies as to their being merely figurative, or allegorical, vs. literal, those interpretations can only be made by the Magisterium. Ancillary to those predictions of latter times to be found in the two sources of Revelation, we ancillarily have approved private prophecy - which cannot be confused with or *faithfully* put on the same level with Tradition and/or Scripture.

Those approved "private prophecies" however, have a contiguity, system, and form, which appears to be very consonant with Revelation. Those who have been led by *unapproved* private prophecy to believe that the advent of Antichrist is almost upon us will find that *approved* prophecies usually lead to the exact opposite conclusion. A reasonable faithful Catholic is most probably going to put much more stock in the approved prophecies of canonized Saints, Blessed, and Venerable, than he or she will in that which is unapproved. That is the major, but not the only, purpose in the presentation of prophecies from *approved sources*.

Additionally, these approved prophecies give a running analysis of causes of the major problems of our age. Much of that analysis is shockingly foreign to our 20th century ways of thinking. When it appears "shocking," a reader might ask himself the following: If our 20th century ways of thinking are truly enlightened and progressive, then why has the world situation gradually deteriorated over the course of this century? Could correct thinking produce the butchery of 20th century Nazism, Communism, and Fascism? Could it lead to the ever-increasing tragedy of our civil wars, or to the growing instabilities in our currencies and economies? These are a few examples of questions which gradually lead an objective observer to the conclusion that much of our 20th century thinking has been flawed.

Prior to launching into the prophecies of a "chastisement," the following caveats should be voiced. A long series of such prophecies are about to be presented which are worded with a sense of great urgency. They agree with each other on detail after detail. Interestingly, many of these urgent prophecies are already hundreds of years old.

What can be discerned from dozens of these prophecies covering centuries which warn of a terrible future chastisement? The basic points which may be gleaned from them are these.

(1) *These prophesies are conditional.* They depend upon man's cooperation with God's grace as to their outcome. Therefore, no one except God knows when and if such a chastisement might come about. *They are not about the time of Antichrist! They are about a period of time which well precedes him.*

(2) Every previous writer on these prophecies with which the author is familiar has gotten into a "guessing game" as to when a "chastisement" might come to pass. **Every single one of them has been wrong. There is not one single exception.**

(3) Some specific prophecies *have* come to pass; e.g., specific prophecies from Fatima about individual events prophesied to lead up to a potential "chastisement" (if people did not repent). Events such as (a) World War II (WW II), (b) the "sign" which warned of its impending beginning, (c) Russia spreading her errors, *have* come to pass specifically as predicted. But not one commentator on these prophesies accurately interpreted ahead of time just *when* these events would actually occur.

(4) Included as an extension of those Fatima predictions was one of an impending great "chastisement," conditioned upon whether people repented. As a young child one of the three "seers" at Fatima made the following prediction, which she also repeated on her deathbed, ***"If men will repent*, God will pardon them, but *if they do not* amend their lives, there will come upon the earth the most terrible chastisement ever known."**

Given the proven track record for the accuracy of prophecies given at Fatima, the odds are extremely high that this is an accurate prophecy.

But **this Fatima prophecy** raises several issues. As we can see, it **is one hundred percent** ***conditional***. Will men repent in time? We do not know. If mankind does not repent, is this prophecy for the near future? We do not know. The prophecy is already over six decades old and WW II has been over for fifty years. *This prophecy is a classic example of what is called a conditional prophecy!* Its outcome is conditional based upon whether or not men cooperate with the grace of God, and to what degree. Have men led morally better lives since the end of WW II? Ask anyone fifty or sixty years of age that question and they will laughingly tell you "NO." Yet a "chastisement" still has not yet come.

In the light of these prophecies the best course of action is to take the forthcoming prophecies to heart, amend our lives, and determine that we will participate as fully as possible in the Holy Father's call for a "New Evangelization." It is actually possible that some reader of this book might be inspired to such a positive degree that that person's cooperation with God's grace would turn them into a great Saint. Might such a person actually turn out to be the straw that turned the tide against the actuality of a "chastisement"?

A more realistic more hopeful scenario is that a substantial number of readers might be sufficiently inspired to experience a dramatic "inner conversion" whether they actually ever became a canonized Saint or not. And *that general inner conversion of many people is what Our Lady has asked for at apparition after apparition***.** She has not asked just for a handful of heroic Saints. In the name of her Son she has asked for a large number of ordinary people like us to go through inner conversion, to become more holy in the way we live our lives. According to Our Lady, the aversion of a "chastisement" does not depend upon the ubiquitous "George" becoming St. George. This time we cannot "let George do it." As Vatican II tells us, we "are all called to sanctity."

As a matter of fact, as one reads these prophecies one idea keeps coming to the fore. It is the concept that even if dozens of people on each continent are headed for canonization -- *THIS TIME* IN HISTORY THAT WILL NOT ASSUAGE OUR LORD. THIS TIME HE WANTS *US*. EITHER WE GIVE OURSELVES TO HIM FREELY, OR WE GET A CHASTISEMENT.

1. The Prophecy of Premol (5th Century)

This prophecy has been mentioned by every serious chronicler of the prophecies over the last 1500 years. Read this prophecy carefully!

> "Everywhere there is war! Peoples and nations are pitted against each other. War, war, war! Civil and foreign wars! Mourning and death everywhere! Famine over the whole world. Will Lutetius [Paris] be destroyed? Why, O Lord, dost Thou not stop all this with Thy arm? **Must also the elements be the instrument of Thy wrath?** Enough, O Lord, enough! The cities are destroyed, the natural elements are set loose, the earth quakes everywhere. But mercy, mercy for Rome! But Thou hearest not my entreaties, and Rome also collapses in tumult. **And I see the king of Rome with his Cross and his tiara, shaking the dust off his shoes, and hastening in his flight to other shores. *Thy Church, O Lord, is torn apart by her own children.* One camp is faithful to the fleeing Pontiff, the other is subject to the new government of Rome which has broken the Tiara.** But Almighty God will, in His mercy, put an end to this confusion and *a new age will begin. Then, said the Spirit,* ***this is the beginning of the End of Time."***[400]

Notice the quote, "Thy Church, O Lord, is torn apart by her own children." As will become clear from other prophecies, this proph-

[400] This prophecy is anonymous. No one today knows who it is attributable to. But there are many manuscript copies dating back to the late 5th and early 6th centuries.

esied internecine Church warfare is integrally tied to the Papacy. Any keen observer of the modern scene knows that the distinct camps in our present struggle are polarized for or against the Pope and the Papacy.[401]

Copies of this prophecy were extant throughout the early Church. By itself it might mean nothing. But its content is repeated over and over again by later Catholic prophecies to follow. These prophecies talk of the Pope having to take flight from Rome shortly before an Age of Peace, the Reign of Mary. The descriptions of earthquakes and major disturbance of the elements is also oft-repeated in these prophecies.

2. St. Malachy, (12th Century)

> "Ireland will suffer English oppression for a week of centuries, but will preserve her fidelity to God and His Church. At the end of that time she will be delivered, and the English in turn must suffer severe chastisement. *Ireland, however, will be instrumental in bringing back the English to the unity of Faith.*"[402]

Here again we see a prophet seeing centuries into the future, anticipating the British persecution of the Irish. *How could St. Malachy in the 1100's have foreseen that England would separate from the unity of the Faith four centuries later?*

This was not an event which could have been anticipated through astute secular observation of events. For centuries prior to King Henry VIII forcibly removing England from allegiance to Rome and beginning the Church of England, that country was the singularly most Papally obedient member of Christendom, and its most prosperous member. Without Divine inspiration how could anyone have foreseen a separation from Rome for such a country?

[401] There are several periods of Church history since this prophecy was first recorded which might possibly meet some of its descriptions. However, the expression, *"this is the beginning of the End of Time"* sounds much more like some event yet to occur sometime in the future.

[402] Unlike the "list" of future Popes attributed to St. Malachy, which also may have been heavily interpolated over the course of time, there is little doubt that this prophecy actually comes from the Saint himself. There is also no credible evidence that it has been tampered with.

Later we will see another prophecy which predicts that in addition to the Irish, the French will assist the English in restoring order and returning to the Faith after a chastisement.

3. St. Edward the Confessor (11th Century)

St. Malachy was not the only prophet to foresee England's separation from the Church of Rome. Just a few years prior to him, in 1066, St. Edward received the following revelation on his death bed:

> "St. Ælred, Abbot of Recraux, in Yorkshire, relates that a short time before his happy death, this holy king was wrapt in ecstacy, when two pious monks of Normandy, whom he had known in his youth, during his exile in that country, appeared to him, and revealed to him what was to happen in England in future centuries, and the cause of the terrible punishment. They said:
>
>> "The extreme corruption and wickedness of the English nation has provoked the just anger of God. When malice has reached the fullness of its measure, God will, in His wrath, send to the English people wicked spirits who will punish and afflict them with severity, by separating the green tree from its parent stem the length of three furlongs. But at last this same tree, through the compassionate mercy of God, and without any national (governmental) assistance, shall return to its original root, reflourish, and bear abundant fruit."[403]

As is observed in the footnote, the genuineness of this prophecy is sufficiently established that the *Catholic Encyclopedia* quotes it as an example of such. This prophecy has traditionally been treated with respect by Vatican scholars. Every commentator on this prophecy has concluded that in his reference to "separating the green tree from its parent stem," St. Edward is foreseeing Henry VIII separating England from the Roman Catholic Church in the 16th century. It is interesting to note that the National (Government) of England is foretold to have no role in the return of England to Roman allegiance. As a matter of fact, a number of

---

[403] *Catholic Encyclopedia*, 1913 Edition, Vol. 12, p. 475.

prophecies specifically state that England will be reevangelized by the French and Irish after England has suffered a terrible and very specific chastisement.

4. Bishop Christianos Ageda (12th Century)

> ***"In the 20th century* ... there will be wars and fury which will last long;** provinces divested of their people and kingdoms in confusion ... In diverse places the ground shall be untilled, and there shall be great slaughters of the nobility [& upper class] ... There shall be great mutilations of kings and rulers, The right hand of the world shall fear the left and the north shall prevail over the south."[404]

Here we read of a Bishop seeing centuries into the future. He gives an accurate compendium of many of the horrors of this the 20th century. He clearly sees eight centuries in advance that:

> (1) the world will still be here, that the end of time will not have come about,
>
> (2) that the world will be strife torn, with great overthrows of nobility and previously ruling classes, and
>
> (3) that the right will fear the left.

This is an interesting prophecy. As an item of interest, the political terms right and left did not even exist in the 12th century. If this is what the saintly bishop is alluding to, it is an amazing article of his prophecy.

THESE PROPHECIES ARE HIGHLY SPECIFIC AND THEY CAME TRUE AS FORETOLD

There is nothing vague in the time-line of this last prediction of Bishop Christianos -- it specifically names the 20th century. Remember that Sr. Bouquillon also specifically stated that the

[404] *The Prophets and Our Times*, p. 148.

beginning of the last period of the world will revolve around the 20th century. Later we will see another chain of highly detailed prophecies about the 20th century from Sister Marian de Jesus Torres which she delivered in the 17th century in Equador. They also came true in extraordinary detail.

Eight centuries in advance Bishop Christianos specifically predicted the slaughter of the upper class for the 20th century. Anyone minimally conversant with the history of our century knows about its slaughter of the upper class by various "Communist" revolutionaries. The upper class victims alone during seventy years of Marxist class warfare, first in Russia, and afterwards in China, Cambodia, Laos, Vietnam, Cuba, Nicaragua, Hungary, Poland, Czechoslovakia, Yugoslavia, East Germany, Latvia, Estonia, Lithuania, Byelorus, Ukraine, Georgia, Romania, Kazakhstan, Siberia, and many other countries has run close to a hundred million. That by definition is a "slaughter of the upper class" which is unique in the entire history of the world. Again, Bishop Christianos predicted it eight centuries in advance.

It is common to hear the statement "prophecies are so vague that anyone could have predicted them." In the case of common or commercial "prophets" who *sell* their "prophecy" to pulp magazines for the consumption of the gullible, this is consistently so. Such prophecies *on average* are correct about half the time or less. Most of the readers could guess correctly fifty percent of the time on such prognostications.

One can make similar comments on pathetically thin devices such as horoscopes which are written so vaguely that they can fit anyone. Again, any one of the readers could probably do as well. This "fifty percent accuracy" type of prophecy causes an understandably humorous reaction on the part of educated people when the general subject of "prophecy" comes up. But such hilarity can only occur in relation to approved Catholic prophecy when such "educated people" are unfamiliar with how specifically detailed authentic Catholic prophecy often is.

Most of the prophecies quoted herein contain elements which are highly specific in nature. They tend to be fulfilled to such a degree that when one of them does not come true we are surprised (and when that happens it is usually due to it having been a conditional prophecy). But there is a ready explanation for the highly specific nature and the high rate of accuracy of the predictions made by Catholic prophets contained in this book. To the best of the author's knowledge, all the prophecies contained in this book contain one form of ecclesial approbation or another. Also, these prophets claim they received their prophecy either directly from God, or from one of his messengers, such as Our Lady.

5. St. Hildegard (12th Century)

> "At this time, as a punishment for their sins Christians especially will attempt armed resistance [to those who at that time are persecuting Christians], sensing no concern about the death of their bodies. A powerful wind will rise in the north carrying heavy fog and the densest cloud of dust by divine command, and it will rage against them (the persecutors of the Christians) and it will fill their throats and eyes so that they will cease their savagery and be stricken with a great amazement.
>
> "Then within the Christian people the holy Godhead will accomplish signs and wonders as it accomplished them at the time of Moses with the pillar of cloud and as Michael the Archangel did when he fought the heathen for the sake of Christians.
>
> "Because of Michael's help, God's faithful children will march under his protection. They will decimate their foes and achieve victory through God's power. ... As a result of this, a large number of heathens will join Christians in true faith and they will say, 'The God of the Christians is true God, because such wondrous works have been accomplished among the Christians.'"[405]

Some explanation may be needed to explain the full content of the above prophecy received in a vision by Hildegard. Many prophecies explain that during a future chastisement, the forces of the Christians shall be terribly outnumbered. These prophecies indicate that in the beginning they lose almost all their battles.

[405] *Divinum Operorum*, Visio 10, Heading 24.

But, when they finally win against monumental odds, it will happen in such a way and manner that both the Christian victors and their defeated enemies are left in no doubt that the victory is due to Divine intervention.

The appearance of this "storm" or "strong wind" which carries a think fog and dust evidently arrives in such a vivid wondrous manner, and at such a beneficial time for the Christians, that all observers attribute it to the hand of God. There are other prophetic references to a fog which will be so thick that it will stop a horrible battle. There is also indication in these prophecies that other wondrous events will accompany this "storm" of fog and dust which Hildegard describes.

> "Before the comet comes, many nations, the good excepted, will be scourged by want and famine. The great nation in the ocean that is inhabited by people of different tribes and descent will be devastated by earthquake, storm, and tidal wave. It will be divided and, in great part, submerged. That nation will also have many misfortunes at sea and lose its colonies."[406]

Most serious students of the prophecies consider the reference to a "great nation" to be a reference to England -- if this prophecy is generally about our times. Hildegard continues:

> "By its tremendous pressure the comet will force much out of the ocean and flood many countries, causing much want and many plagues. All coastal cities will live in fear, and many of them will be destroyed by tidal waves, and most living creatures will be killed, and even those who escape will die from horrible diseases."[407]

> "For in none of those cities does a person live according to the laws of God. ***Peace will return to the world when the white flower again takes possession of the throne of France***. During this period of peace, people will be forbidden to carry weapons, and iron will be used only for making agricultural

[406] *Catholic Prophecy*, Yves Dupont, Tan Books and Publishers, p. 16 & 17.
[407] Ibid. p. 17.

implements and tools. Also during this period, the land will be very productive, and many Jews, heathens, and heretics will join the Church"[408]

The reader has heard this last paragraph quoted earlier. It is repeated so that the reader can determine the chronological context. There has been no historic period since this prophecy was made that tidal waves were a problem worldwide for coastal cities. This prophecy devolves around the same framework within which she discusses the arrival of the great king to come. There has also been no intervening period during which "many Jews, heathens, and heretics" have joined the Church. Within the full context of the work this is quoted from, it is a conditional prophecy.

6. Brother John of the Cleft Rock (14th Century)

> **"At that time, the Pope, with the cardinals will have to flee Rome** in trying circumstances to a place where he will be unknown. He will die a cruel death in this exile. *The sufferings of the Church will be much greater than at any previous time in her history* ... God will raise a holy Pope over whom the Angels will rejoice. Enlightened by God, this man will reconstruct almost the entire world through his holiness."[409]

Here we find the oft-repeated description of a Pope fleeing Rome during which there will be a great chastisement causing much suffering to the Church -- a situation which is saved by a succeeding great Pope ruling from Rome whose influence will be worldwide.

7. St. Nicholas of Fluh (15th Century)

St. Nicholas was canonized by Pope Pius XII in 1947. A layman with a wife and ten children, after 20 years of married life he was called by God to live the life of a hermit and prophet. He was viewed as a Saint by his contemporaries. A native of Switzerland, through

---

[408] Ibid.

[409] *The Prophets and Our Times*, p. 29.

his prayerful and diplomatic interventions, he quite literally saved the Swiss from annihilating themselves in bloody civil wars of the 15th century. No pacifist, but a courageous man of God, he said,

> "Meet with force those who make war on right, answer this violence with violence; fight valiantly, defend your country and its freedom like men of valour, but restrict yourselves to the defensive."[410]

As a soldier he fought in two major wars in defense of his country.

He lived on nothing but the Blessed Sacrament for the last twenty and one half years of his life, as was attested to by his bishop.[411] Fearlessly, he personally put up with continual physical assaults by the devil. Beyond that, on many an occasion he also had to deal with a creature which appeared terrorizing his wife and youngest children in the guise of a black dog with one eye in the center of its forehead.

He had the gift to read consciences. He had the gift of public miracles. As only one example: On August 15, 1468, an out of control fire was consuming the village of Sarnen. The townspeople could not stop the fire. They sent a messenger to St. Nicholas and he went, "to a high spot and made the sign of the cross in the direction of the fire, which died down immediately." **St. Charles Borromeo** built a chapel to commemorate this event on this exact spot 100 years later in 1570.[412]

A true prophet, *he predicted the exact date of his own death for his 70th birthday* (St. Benedict's Day, 1487) *over 20 years in*

---

410 *Brother Nicholas*, G. R. Lamb, Sheed & Ward, P. 154.

411 If the reader has never heard of this phenomenon before, it is not unique to St. Nicholas of Fluh. There is an extensive list of canonized saints who have experienced this. It usually occurs after they have reached a high degree of mystical prayer and contemplative union with God. It usually begins simply with an increasing loss of appetite for normal food and consequent reduced consumption of food. But unlike extended fasting, there is usually no concomitant loss of weight. At the same time they experience an increased desire to receive, and love for, the Blessed Sacrament. For most of the saints who receive this intervention, they gradually get to the point where food itself is not consumed at all. At most, they truly consume one communion host per day. No human being could live on that without Divine intervention. Again, it is far from unique with St. Nicholas.

412 *Brother Nicholas*, p. 151 & 152.

advance. As predicted, he died on his 70th birthday. He predicted the rise of the Protestant revolt in Switzerland for a time shortly after his death. He had predicted:

> "But there will come a time when another faith begins, and blessed will be those who bravely reject it. . . There will be a change of religion so near to Obwald that you will be able to take water to it in a jug held with one finger."[413]

Fifty years later, the Canton of Berne, Switzerland which ran alongside Obwald, had abandoned the Catholic Faith and become Protestant. Objectively speaking, Protestantism was an attack on the teachings of the Church from the outside. In speaking of prophecy for the *further* future which he said would be marked by attacks on the Church from within its bosom, he said;

> "An unhappy time is coming, of *revolt and dissension in the Church*. Oh my children, do not let yourselves be led astray by innovations. Rally and hold fast. Stay on the same road, the same footpaths as your pious fathers trod. *Preserve and maintain what they have taught you*. It will be enough if your resist the attacks, the tempests, the hurricanes that will arise with such violence."[414]

Again on another occasion, St. Nicholas prophesied,

> "The Church will be punished because the majority of her members, high and low, will become so perverted. The Church will sink deeper and deeper until she will at last seem to be extinguished, and the succession of Peter and the other Apostles to have expired. But, after this, she will be victoriously exalted in the sight of all doubters."[415]

Notice the phrase referring to the Church having sunk so low that "the succession of Peter and the other Apostles" will appear "to have expired." At no time (with the possible exception of the mid4-

---

[413] Ibid, P. 71.
[414] Ibid. P. 72.
[415] *Catholic Prophecy*, p. 30.

th century during the Arian Heresy[416]) have things sunk anywhere near so low. This is obviously something for the future.

This prophecy also warns us not to be led astray by innovations, to hold fast to the Faith of our fathers. If our age had held fast,

(1) would 80% of Catholics in the United States of child bearing years be practicing contraception?

(2) would 70% of American Catholics be telling pollsters that they disagree with the Church's teachings on Transubstantion which produces the Real Presence of Christ in the Eucharist?

This last question points out an ultimate irony in the contrast between our age and those where the majority have held fast. The Eucharistic Liturgy is *the* central theme which runs through the writings of the Fathers of the Church. From the beginning of the Church the Patristic writers emphasize the doctrine that receiving Communion at the Eucharistic Liturgy involves the reception of the true Body and Blood of Christ. In America today, 70% of the "Catholics" deny the Reality of that which St. Nicholas completely believed in and solely lived on for the last "twenty and one half years of his life."

As a contemporary reference for the readers, these prophecies were given over a period roughly thirty to fifty years after those of St. Vincent Ferrer. **Most importantly, St. Nicholas of Fluh also gives us hope. He predicts a virtually universal triumph for the Church after having suffered worldwide humiliation.**

---

[416] St. Jerome commented at one point that "one morning the world awoke and groaned finding itself Arian." But the Arian problem was most severe in the Episcopacy. As another historian has commented upon the period, when in 358 A.D. Bishop Ossius was put on the rack by Arians and semi-Arians at the age of 103, the number of orthodox (faithful) bishops who were still in possession of their own dioceses could be counted "possibly on the fingers of one hand." But the majority of the laity were faithful, no matter how many of their faithful bishops had been jailed, exiled, or murdered.

8. Ven. Sor Marianne de Jesus Torres[417] (17th Century)

In 1984, the author traveled to Quito, Equador, for the specific purpose of finding a lost book of the life and prophecies of Sor (Sister) Marianne de Jesus Torres. It had been lost since before the turn of the 20th century. After requesting Our Lady to help him in the search, the author "found" the prophecies that some residents of Quito had been searching for over a twelve year period. He personally witnessed the "finding" of the missing book, and took photos of many of its pages. Through an equally "fortuitous" event, the author subsequently came upon an English translation of a copy of the *Caudernon* (a biography of Sor Marianne containing many of her prophecies) which is quoted from in this book. The author has personally visited and researched the convent, statue, archives, etc., which are described in the following section.

Sor Marianne was born in the Spanish Province of Viscaya in 1563 and died in the Franciscan convent of the Immaculate Conception in Quito, Ecuador, in 1635. She was one of the foundresses of that convent which was the first for nuns in the New World. She traveled to the Equador in 1576 with her aunt, Mother Maria, who would be the first superior of this new foundation. *Sor Marianne exercised an almost continual gift of prophecy*, amongst which included predicting two and a half years in advance the exact date of the death of the Bishop of Quito for March 24, 1612.

Like St. Nicholas of Fluh, she predicted the exact date of her own death, which took place over 25 years later. She also predicted that in a little over two centuries, Ecuador would cease being a Spanish colony and would become a free Republic, which subsequently happened two centuries later on August 10, 1809. Virtually the whole world had monarchical forms of government in the early 1600's, so her prediction was viewed as improbable at the time.

---

[417] The title "Venerable" is to be found in printed materials about her in Equador. The author has been unable to determine whether this is of local custom or whether this is an official title ceded to her by Rome.

She also predicted that the;

> "Dogma of the faith of the Immaculate Conception will be proclaimed during a time when the Church will be strongly attacked."[418]

This came to pass 250 years later on December 8, 1854. At that time the Pope was quite literally a prisoner in the Vatican, and the Church was under constant attack from revolutionaries throughout Europe. Sor Marianne also predicted the declaration of the doctrine of the Assumption, which subsequently occurred 350 years later on November 1, 1950.

Her charity was simply incredible. Our Lord informed Marianne that one of her nuns was in the clutches of Satan. He told Marianne that the only thing that could save this poor nun from eventually going to Hell was if someone was willing to suffer the pains of HELL for five years for her. Marianne volunteered. Our Lord said to her:

> "I desire hearts like yours, my beloved spouse, for the salvation of souls. And such hearts will I always find in this my beloved convent. Have no fear. I will be your secret strength. You will suffer the five years in hell, and in exchange, the soul of your sister is already saved. She will first suffer a severe illness, in which you will take care of her in order to win and convert her, suffering the harshness of her abusiveness treatment. But after standing before the judgment seat and realizing her bad life, she will recover, and your hell will begin."

Her biographer goes on to state, "Marianne also saw the judgment through which this religious would pass, *where she would be condemned to remain in Purgatory until the day of the final judgment, though she was saved from the pains of Hell*." Our Lord revealed to several of her fellow nuns what Marianne's experi-

[418] From the English translation of an unpublished manuscript of the *Compendium* the *Caudernon*. The author has this uncopyrighted English translation in his possession. All of the quotes on Sr. Marianne come from this manuscript.

encing of the pains of Hell was like. The description of this takes two pages in her biography, but the following sentence will give a slight description. "The keenness of her senses were sharpened and quickened, so that she would suffer both physically and morally the pains of this loss (of hope) and experience the feeling of a condemned soul."

The author has yet to narrate this account to a devout Catholic who did not shudder just thinking about personally going through such an ordeal -- even to save a soul.

Sister Marianne's prophecies are highly directed at the 20th century.

The following is quoted from a compendium of the *Caudernon*, a book written about the life of Sister Marianne de Jesus Torres by the Friars Francisco Anquita, and Angel Francisco Perez, who were her confessors for many years. Fr. Anquita knew Sor Marian well for a long period of time and even heard her last confession just a few hours before her death. The *Compendium* of the *Caudernon* also utilizes some sources taken from the lives of seven other nuns who founded the Convent of the Immaculate Conception in Quito, Ecuador. The *Compendium* was written by Padre Frei Bartolome Ochoa de Alacano y Gamboa.

On one occasion Sister Marianne saw Our Lord emerge from the tabernacle, suffering as he did at Golgotha. The Blessed Virgin was shedding tears at his feet. St. John and Mary Magdalene were also there. Sister Marianne believing that she was the cause of Our Lord's suffering said;

> "*Lord am I the guilty one?*" Then her Guardian Angel said, "*No, You are not to blame. Arise and approach, for God desires to reveal a great secret.*"

Again, she asked Our Lady if she (Marianne) was the cause of Our Lady's sadness. Our Lady responded;

> "*No, it is not you, but the criminal world.*"

9. Punishments Foretold for the 20th Century by Sr. Marianne

Then while watching Our Lord's agony on the Cross, God the Father said;

> *"THIS PUNISHMENT WILL BE FOR THE 20TH CENTURY."*

Then she saw three swords over the head of Christ. On each was written

> **I shall punish heresy, blasphemy, and impurity.**

Sister Marianne was further lead to understand that all of this specifically applied to the 20th century. Then Our Lady asked her:

> "*My daughter, will you sacrifice yourself for the people of this time?*" Marianne said, "*I am willing.*" And immediately the swords moved away from the agonizing Christ and buried themselves in the heart of Sister Marianne, who fell as if dead through the violence of the pain."

One does not need to be an expert to know that "heresy, blasphemy, and impurity" are three scourges of the 20th century. Particularly in this its last decade, those three items have reached proportions which no one could have foreseen even forty years ago through unaided reason alone. This is simply not the same Western world it was a mere forty years ago.

For instance, the flaunting of impure behavior has become epidemic. Could any reader over the age of fifty have predicted in the 1950's that by the 1990's a large percentage of our youth would be openly living together outside of wedlock, and publicly talking about it without shame? Could anyone have predicted the level of social problems generated by the shear volume of "single parent" families which have resulted from this century's sexual revolution? Could someone have then foretold that leading social scientists would now be openly agonizing in our news media over how to deal with the problems of youth in these families?

Problems of this scope would not even exist except for our contemporary sexual revolution against God's laws on *impure* behavior. Pope John Paul II has repeatedly warned and expressed his concern to the world that the fruits of this sexual revolution are destroying not just the morals, but the entire social fabric of the West. He repeatedly states what the majority of Western social scientists only now are coming to see, that the stability of the two-parent family is the social glue which holds a stable civilization together. The *impurity* of the sexual revolution is primarily responsible for much of our contemporary social destabilization.

If you throw a frog into a shallow pan of boiling water, the frogs physical reactions are so rapid that he can and will leap out of the pan before he can be scalded. But if you place the same frog in a shallow pan of tepid water, then slowly raise the temperature to the boiling point, you can boil him alive without the frog's reacting to the gradually increasing temperature. *Gradualism* neutralizes the frogs natural defense mechanism of speedy physical reaction time. Are even we Christians in the West being gradually *morally* boiled alive?

Could anyone have foreseen even thirty years ago that the average movie film of the 1990's *produced for the general public* would have such lurid, completely gratuitous, sex scenes as to make the films unfit for children to watch? Just as an example: the recent movie "Schindler's List" has explicit fornicational and adulterous fully nude sex scenes. That *explicitness* is totally irrelevant to the plot, therefore it is by definition gratuitous.

Honestly, would the impact of "Schindler's List" have been reduced one iota by the absence of those scenes? So, why did a film of such stature include such scenes which were totally unnecessary -- gratuitous to the plot line? And why are many Catholic High schools in the U.S. recommending that teenagers see this film (and many other films which have the same problems)? Such a film plants *impure* images in the minds of our young. It does not take a moral theologian to know that such thoughts predictably produce later temptations to more impure thoughts and actions in our young. *And why are some otherwise totally orthodox Catholics seemingly oblivious to these inherent dangers in such a film?* These are serious questions our Christian generation should ponder over!

From its very beginning, the Church has taught the necessity of guarding the purity of our thoughts.

Scripture, Tradition, and the writings of the Fathers, are full of explicit warnings on this subject. Saint Paul specifically tells us not to unnecessarily even talk of such foul themes amongst ourselves. Why then, do some otherwise orthodox Christians become irritated and angry when the danger of impure thoughts is brought up? Why is the irritation most extreme *when various forms of entertainment are involved*?

In their heart of hearts do they still know impurity is impurity? *How much have we been gradually desensitized by our age*? Are we already proverbially "boiled frogs"? Sister Marianne quotes God the Father as saying explicitly of the 20th century, "I shall punish heresy, blasphemy, and *impurity*." How many of the "good Christians" of the 1990's (who still clearly understand what heresy and blasphemy are) still *fully* understand what impurity is? Have we forgotten the constant Christian teaching about guarding the purity of their thoughts?

Could the reader who is over fifty have foreseen forty years ago that in the 1990's homosexuals would be flagrantly demanding their "rights," such as the right to teach their "alternate life style" to children in our elementary schools? What would have happened thirty or forty years ago if anyone had even brought up such a subject? Even practicing Christians who strongly disagree with impure/disordered behavior can tend to become desensitized to the impurity around them - by the sheer all-pervasiveness of its presence.

In the course of a generation (1965 to 1995), the Judeo-Christian morals which were accepted and socially enforced by previous generations' working majorities of Catholics, Protestants, and Jews, have been systematically overturned in public practice. We can forget how rapidly things have fallen apart. The author cannot recall an historic precedent to (1) *the shear speed* of the current moral decline in the West, and (2) the rapidity or success of the desensitization of the vast majority of its Christian opponents.

The early Christians living in the pagan Roman Empire were inundated and surrounded by crass impurity just as we are. But the majority of their leadership was never *totally* desensitized to it. Sometimes they gradually fell over an extended period of time as St. Cyprian narrates in *The Lapsed*. But it never happened with our contemporary rapidity. At least the majority of their leadership never lost their sense of moral horror of pagan impurity, *and most of them never stopped publicly opposing it*! That is one of the main reasons they ultimately bested that immoral paganism. Led by their better Bishops, they ultimately converted the world.

Today, *does Pope John Paul II sound almost like a lone voice in the public wilderness protesting our public impurity and disorderedness?* Where are the thousands of leadership voices that should be PUBLICLY joining the Holy Father in his admonitions against disordered impurity which is epidemic here in the West? Sister Marianne also prophesied that many Church leaders who *should* be publicly protesting "heresy, blasphemy, and impurity" in the 20th century, instead they would "maintain silence."

10. Our Lady of Good Success

Sister Marianne was ordered by Our Lady to have a statue made of Our Lady holding the child Jesus. The story is too long to tell in full, but during the course of the sculpting by Senor Francisco del Castillo (a famous Ecuadoran sculptor) the face of Our Lady which till then was incomplete, was totally changed and finished in one night. The sculptor was stunned to find it complete the next morning. Sor Marianne testifies that she saw St. Francis, and the three archangels, Raphael, Michael, and Gabriel finish it in the twinkling of an eye at around 3:00 in the morning.

This statue is brought out of the convent and placed on the high altar twice a year for veneration by the faithful. The author has seen this statue on the high altar of the Church of the Immaculate Conception in Quito. Its beauty is extraordinary. Sr. Marianne, states that Our Lady informed her that through the presence of her statue, Mary would henceforward be the true prioress of the convent.

Statue of Our Lady of Good Success and the Child Jesus

The statue resides in the Convent of the Immaculate Conception in Quito, Equador. Twice a year it is brought out from the convent proper, and then placed on the high altar of the attached *Church of the Immaculate Conception*. In 1610, Our Lady instructed Sr. Marianne de Jesus Torres to have this statue made of her and of the child Jesus being held in her arms.

Under sworn testimony, Sr. Marianne testified that Our Lady gave the following command,

> "I ask and command you to have a statue of me made for the consolation and support of my monastery and the faithful of that time (the 20th century)... Gabriel, Michael and Raphael along with the whole angelic choir will secretly take charge of the making of my statue."

The Equadoran sculptor, Francisco del Castillo, was commissioned to begin work on the statue. When he had completed everything but the faces of Our Lady and the child Jesus, the following was reported by the nuns of the convent (In Equador called a monastery) on Jan. 16, 1611:

> "early in the morning (at 3:00 a.m.), the fervent nuns arose to pray... Upon reaching the choir they heard melodious harmonies ... they hastened to enter the choir (which was) shining with a celestial light ... and they saw that the angels had already finished the whole statue."

Later in the morning, the sculptor came to work and was stunned to see the statue had been totally completed the previous night. He later attested to the truth of this miraculous event in a sworn handwritten document.

A Painting of Sr. Marianne Measuring Our Lady

Our Lady commanded Sr. Marianne to have a statue made of her and the child Jesus. When Sr. Marianne asked Our Lady how big to make the statue, Our Lady told her to make it full size. Sr. Marianne then said she would need to give the scuptor the dimensions of the statue and asked what specific dimensions to give him. Our Lady told Marianne to take a seamstress' tape measure and measure her and give those dimensions to the sculptor.

The picture above hangs on the left wall of the Church of the Immaculate Conception a short distance from the sanctuary. The nuns commissioned this painting to commemorate this event.

Sister Marianne through humility asked our Lady that she (Marianne) and her part in the production of this statue should remain hidden. Our Lady told Sister Marianne:

> "As for your request that your name be hidden, this pleases me greatly, and I will do as you asked. Tell the bishop that it is the will of my most Holy Son and of mine that your name be hidden at all costs, both within as well as outside the cloister, for it is not fitting at this time that anyone know the details or origin of how this Statue came to be made. *But this knowledge will only become known to the general public in the 20th. Century.*
>
> "During this epoch the Church will find herself attacked by waves of a secret sect, and this Ecuadoran land will be agonizing because of the corruption of customs, unbridled luxury and extravagance, the impious press, and the laic education;
>
> "Know, beloved daughter, that when your name is made known in the 20th Century, there will be many who will not believe, claiming that this devotion is not pleasing to God.
>
> "A simple humble faith in the truth of my apparitions to you, my predilect child, will be reserved for humble and fervent souls docile to the inspirations of grace, for our Heavenly Father communicates his secrets to the simple of heart, and not to those whose hearts are inflated with pride, pretending to know what they do not, or self-satisfied with empty knowledge."

> *Comment*: It is only during the last ten years that Our Lady of Good Success and Sister Marianne's role in this devotion have begun to become generally known to many Ecuadorans. There was always a small cadre of friends of the Nuns of the Convent of the Immaculate Conception who knew of and practiced this devotion. It is only in the last 6 or 7 years that word of this devotion to Our Lady of Good Success and Sister Marianne have *begun* to spread to the rest of the world.

Sister Marianne continues about the Statue and devotion to Our Lady of Good Success:

> "The most Holy Trinity confirmed the desire of my Queen, assuring that God will bless all those who, by their support and help, contribute in the making of the Holy Statue, **as well as all those who help to spread this devotion throughout the centuries, making known its origin and these apparitions in the 20th century.** This will be a time of great corruption of customs, and this devotion will be the safeguard of this land during the times to come when it will no longer be a colony, but a free and libertine Republic. Let us weep, pray and do penance so that this time will not be of long duration."

Our Lady made further disclosures about this our 20th century to Sister Marianne in the following manner:

> "The sacred Sacrament of Holy Orders will be ridiculed, oppressed and despised, for in doing this, one scorns and defiles the Church of God, and even God himself, represented by his priests. *The Demon* will try to persecute the Ministers of the Lord in every possible way, and *he will labor with cruel and subtle astuteness to deviate them from the spirit of their vocation, corrupting many of them.* These [corrupted priests] who will thus scandalize the Christian people, will incite the hatred of the bad Christians and the enemies of the Roman Catholic and Apostolic Church to fall upon all the priests. *This apparent triumph of Satan will bring enormous sufferings to the good pastors of the Church, to the great majority of good priests, and to the Supreme Pastor and Vicar of Christ on earth*, who ... will shed secret and bitter tears in the presence of his God and Lord, beseeching light, sanctity and perfection for all the Clergy of the world, of which he is the King and Father.
>
> "Moreover, in these unhappy times there will be unbridled luxury which, acting thus to snare the rest into sin, will conquer innumerable frivolous souls who will lose themselves. **Innocence will almost no longer be found in children, nor modesty in women, and, *in this supreme moment of need of the Church, those whom it behooves to speak will fall silent.*"**

This prophecy is obviously not limited to the confines of Ecuador. Notice the mention of the suffering of the Holy Father and "the great majority of good priests." This is talking of a worldwide problem for the 20th century.

Sr. Marianne's biographer states that St. Michael in an apparition to Sister Marianne told her the following about devotion to Our Lady of Good Success at two different time periods.

> "Through this devotion Our Lord will grant great miracles, spiritual as well as temporal, first to your [Sr. Marianne's] community, so that in it he will always find a safeguard, [victim souls], and secondly, to the devout faithful, above all to those at the end of the 18th and 20th Centuries, for those times will see the chosen ones of his heart, times during which hell would be unleashed and many souls would be lost!"

Later the "child Jesus" appeared to Sr. Marianne and told her many things including:

> "Here [in the convent] I will have a secret few, and always unknown souls who will give me pleasure and will make amends to Me, disarming Me when **my Justice will be tried to the limit by the evils and sacrileges of the 20th Century."**[419]

As Sister Marianne predicted early in the 17th century, knowledge of the origin of the Statue and devotion to Our Lady of Good Success did not come to light in the world until late in the 20th century. The prophecies had been lost until rediscovered in the diocesan archives of Quito, Equador, in 1985. Knowledge of the identity of Sister Marianne and her part in this devotion was also for the most part hidden until the 20th century. Her prophecies concerning the state of the world and the Church almost four hundred years later have come true in minute detail.

We shall close this discussion of the prophecies of Sor Marianne de Jesus Torres by repeating two quotes, and then by making some observations.

---

[419] Again all of the biographical quotes herein in referenced to Sor Marianne de Jesus Torres are from an unpublished manuscript translational copy of the *Compendium* of the *Caudernon*.

(1) "My Justice will be tried to the limit by the evils and sacrileges of the 20th Century."

(2) *"THIS PUNISHMENT WILL BE FOR THE 20TH CENTURY."* ... 'I shall punish heresy, blasphemy, and impurity.'"

Could any intellectually honest observer of our century deny the possibility that mankind is being punished? Our general wars, civil wars, and persecutions have killed people on a scale unimaginable to previous centuries. Look at the massacres and "ethnic cleansings."

(1) World War I - an estimated casualty list of civilians and military of one and a half million.
(2) Stalin and Soviet Russia murdered three and a half million Ukrainian farmers in the early 1930's alone - dumping their bodies into mass graves.
(3) An estimated additional fifty-five to seventy-five million people were effectually murdered in the various Soviet concentration camps over a seventy year period.
(4) Word War II - an estimated civilian and military casualty list of six to seven million.
(5) Hitler and Nazi Germany probably murdered between four to six million Jews alone throughout Western Europe in the late 1930's and early 1940's – and three to fiver million gentiles.
(6) Early in WW II, the Soviet secret police (NKVD) mass murdered fifteen thousand Polish military officers and ten thousand civilians in the Katyn Forest Massacre.
(7) The various persecutions in Red China have accounted for the murder of over two hundred million people - a number admitted by Mao Tse Tung, and labeled "Hsao Mei." – [deprived of existence]
(8) The mass murders in communist coups in Africa in the middle part of this century cost an estimated six to seven million lives.
(9) As portrayed in the movie "The Killing Fields," the communists in Cambodia murdered over a million people in less than a decade.
(10) In the last three decades Moslem persecution of native Christians in Africa has cost a million people their lives - through outright murder or starvation.

(11) In this decade we have already witnessed the "ethnic cleansing" of several hundred thousand Bosnian Muslims by Bosnian Serbs - *Serbs who claim to be Christians.*

Not even Attila the Hun killed people on such a massive scale as this. Our killing is not localized. It is world-wide. This is massive inhumanity to man on an honestly unprecedented scale. As anyone who really knows the history of this century can affirm - the list above is just hitting the high spots of atrocities against God and man in this century!

Could any intellectually honest person deny the possibility that we are already being chastised through many different sufferings. **But there is hope.** Sr. Marianne predicts an end to this suffering, for her convent, the City of Quito, for Ecuador, and for the world, sometime in the future.

11. Fr. Balthassar Mas (17th Century)

> "I saw a land swallowed up by the sea and covered with water. But, afterwards, I saw that the sea receded little by little and the land could be seen again. The tops of the towers in the city rose again above the water and appeared more beautiful than before, and I was told that this land was England."[420]

This prophecy is remarkably similar to an earlier quote from St. Hildegard. We shall hear prophecies of disasters from every major European country. Here England is specifically mentioned, but included in visions of the future are Germany, France, Spain, Portugal, Italy, Poland, Belgium, Russia, Ukraine, Ireland, America, Columbia, Ecuador, Brazil, China, the Holy Land, Cyprus, Switzerland, and many other countries. The conditional chastisement if it should occur as predicted will quite literally be universal.

12. Ven. Bartholomew Holzhauser (17th Century)

> "*The fifth period of the Church, which began circa 1520,* will end with the arrival of the Holy Pope and of the powerful

[420] *Catholic Prophecy*, p. 32.

> Monarch who is called 'Help From God' because he will restore everything [in Christ].
>
> **"The fifth period is one of affliction, desolation, humiliation, and poverty for the Church**. Jesus Christ will purify His people through cruel wars, famines, plague, epidemics, and other horrible calamities. He will also **afflict and weaken the Latin Church with many heresies.** It is a period of defections, calamities and extermination. Those Christians who survive the sword, plague and famines, will be few on earth. Nations will fight against nations, and will be desolated by internecine dissensions."[421]

Holzhauser's statement about heresy afflicting the Latin Church is most apropos. This is one of the prophecies we were talking about in Chapter 2 — Sr. Marianne's prophecy of heresy for the 20th century is another. In previous centuries, the Eastern Rites were on occasion more heavily afflicted by heresy. There are numerous prophecies which single out the "Latin Rite" (versus the various Eastern Rites, e.g., Byzantine, Armenian, etc.) of the Roman Catholic Church, to be literally riddled with heresy during our specific time.

It is interesting to note that in the 20th Century it has been the Latin Rite which has had the heresy problems, not the Eastern Rite. A number of prophecies state that this will be a major cause of suffering for the Holy Father. An additional example of a heresy uniquely affecting the Latin Rite: The loss of faith in/questioning of the Doctrine of Transubstantion and the resultant Real Presence which afflicts many in the Latin Rite today *is virtually unheard of in the Eastern Rites.* Recent polls show that only 30% of American Catholics accept the Doctrine of the Transubstantion.

All of this may only be coincidental. However, the number of coincidences between these prophesies and facts about our own age does begin to rapidly accumulate as one reads more and more of these older prophecies. The other problem with the "coincidence" theory is that (as the reader can see) some of these centuries-old prophecies specifically name the 20th century.

---

[421] *Apocalypsis*, Bartholomew Holzhauser, 1850

A. PREDICTED HERESIES IN THE LATIN RITE OF THE CATHOLIC CHURCH

Here we will briefly interrupt our series of prophecies in order to examine the prophesied "Heresy Problem" within the *Latin* Rite of the Catholic Church. For those who are actually unaware of the problem, there is great theological confusion on many doctrinal issues even amongst many in the Latin Rite priesthood. For the reader who might be unaware of what the Eastern (sometimes called "Oriental") Rites of the Catholic Church are, please refer to the Glossary in the back of the book.

At this point, let it suffice to say that many of the Eastern Rites have their own Cardinals - who are part of the College of Cardinals of the Catholic Church. A current example is the Ukrainian Rite (a branch of the Byzantine Rite) whose Cardinal Lubachiewsky presides over the Ukrainian Rite from Lvov, Ukraine.

B. A RETURN TO HOLZHAUSER AND PROPHECIES

Now we will return to the flow of *Holzhauser's prophecies*.

> "Are we not to fear, during this period, that the Mohammedans will come again, working out their sinister schemes against the Latin Church?"[422]

This eventuality sounded relatively impossible when the speaker first read it twenty-four years ago, but today this possibility does not sound so improbable. The majority of Moslems, just like most Christians, simply wish to live their lives in peace and to be left alone. Unfortunately, most groups at some point in history have their extremists. The growing rise of Moslem Fundamentalism is well-known to all. If it continues its spread unabated, prophecies of a Mohammedan invasion of Western Europe might tragically come to pass.

> "During this period, many *men will abuse of the freedom of conscience conceded to them.* It is of such men that Jude, the Apostle, spoke when he said: 'These men blaspheme

[422] *Apocalypsis*, Bartholomew Holzhauser, 1850.

whatever they do not understand; and they corrupt whatever they know naturally as irrational animals do.

"During this unhappy period, there will be laxity in divine and human precepts. Discipline will suffer. *The Holy Canons will be completely disregarded*, and the Clergy will not respect the laws of the Church. Everyone will be carried away and led to believe and to do what he fancies, according to the manner of the flesh."

Anyone familiar with current conditions in the Western Church is aware how difficult a task it is for good bishops to enforce the disciplinary laws (Holy Canons) of the Church in general due to the prevailing spirit of rebellion.

"They will ridicule Christian simplicity; they will call it folly and nonsense, but they will have the highest regard for advanced knowledge, and for the skill by which the axioms of the law, the precepts of morality, the Holy Canons and religious dogmas are clouded by **senseless questions and elaborate arguments.** ***As a result, no principle at all, however holy, authentic, ancient, and certain it may be, will remain free of censure, criticism, false interpretations, modification, and delimitation by man.***"

Does the theological chaos described in this prophecy sound similar to the views of the "extreme higher critics" described in the "Higher Critics' Statements on Tradition" section in Chapter 1, and all of Chapter 2? Do the "senseless questions" sound like some pages out of Raymond Brown's books? Do the "elaborate arguments" sound like passages from the books of Kung, Schilebeex, Rahner or Tielhard de Chardin? Could their mutual questioning of Tradition, or the Divinely Inspired context of Scripture (and/or its historicity in any meaningful sense of the word) and of the dogmas of the Church be more clearly described by you or me today?

[Any reader who skipped over Chapter 2 may now be motivated to go back and read it carefully.]

1. Abortion and Contraception

Condemnation of abortion and unnatural illicit methods of birth control (contraception) is one of the earliest doctrines of the Church to be specifically spelled out in written form. This is fully evidenced in the DIDACHE. Holzhauser refers to the future questioning (by some members from within the Church) of virtually any *"principle at all, however holy, authentic, ancient, and certain it may be."* Current polls show that 80% of the Catholics of childbearing years in the U.S. "disagree with" the Church's rules against contraception and are currently practicing contraception. Similar polling results from Western Europe show roughly the same percentages.

2. The DIDACHE

Abortion and illicit methods of birth control (contraception) were condemned as excommunicable offenses in the *DIDACHE*. Outside of Scripture itself, the *DIDACHE* is possibly the oldest written disciplinary document we possess from the infant Church. The best scholarship dates the *DIDACHE*'s earliest publication as somewhere between 100 and 150 A.D.[423] During the infancy of the Church, the *DIDACHE* condemned both the practices of abortion and unnatural methods of birth control (contraception) under pain of excommunication. Why? Because the pagan world surrounding the Christian communities commonly practiced many methods of such birth control, ranging from contraceptive and abortifacient drugs to incantations. Some of the Christians were being infected with pagan thinking, so the Church had to impose the penalty of excommunication on such practices in order to stop them.

The Church's positions on abortion and contraception do not derive from Tradition alone. For instance, the Fathers[424] of the Church who addressed such issues universally applied Galatians 5:20, and Revelation 21:8 and 22:15 in their condemnation of such practices. In those original Greek language Scripture passages appear the following words; "mageia" (using magic) and "phar-

[423] Some Patrologists date this work from possibly as late as 160 "probably before the appearance of Montanism." [But this is not the majority opinion.] *Patrology*, Berthold Altaner, Herder and Herder, N.Y., 1960, p. 51.

[424] In this connection especially see the commentaries of Clement of Alexandria in his *Paidagogos*. See also Justin Martyr, Origen, Lactantius, Epiphanius, Ambrose, Jerome, Chrysostom, and especially commentaries on this subject by St. Augustine.

makeia" (using drugs) and "pharmakois"[425] (those who use such drugs). Our modern English words "pharmacy" and "pharmacist" come directly from the Greek "pharmakois." Its primary Scriptural usage relates to drugs.

It is an *extremely well-documented historical fact* that; in the time of the Apostolic Church it was a common pagan practice throughout the Roman Empire to use such drugs as contraceptives, and if that failed, secondly, to use drugs to induce abortion. These practices both the Apostolic Church and the commentaries of the Fathers[426] condemned as grievously sinful. These are not 20th century discoveries.[427]

It was these two practices of using drugs to stop conception, and to induce abortion, which the DIDACHE declared to be grounds for excommunication from the Church. Therefore, it is patently obvious that the teachings on abortion and contraception to be found in Pope Gregory IX's 13th Century *Decretals,* and in the 20th century decrees - Pius XI's *Castii Conubii* and Pope Paul VI's *Humanae Vitae,* are nothing new in the Church. As a matter of fact:

> "The list of such declarations would be interminable. In country after country and in every century, bishops and councils forbid "contraceptive potions," "herbs or other agents so you will not have children," "spilling the seed in coitus," "coitus interruptus, "Poisons of sterility," "avoiding children by evil acts," "putting material things in the vagina," and "causing temporary or permanent sterility."[428]

---

[425] The *New Vulgate* translates this term into the Latin, "Veneficis" is the ablative form of "Veneficus," of which the first and primary definition given is "poisoner or poisonous," i.e., "Poisoners" (Definition given in the largest scholars Latin-English Dictionary in print, *A New Latin Dictionary*, Short, Oxford, Clarendon Press). Unfortunately, almost all the English editions of the Bible poorly translate this word as "Sorcerer," which is an alternate, but is definitely not the primary meaning given in all Classical Latin Dictionaries. "Poisoner" is the closest to the original Greek meaning. e.g., The Greek word "pharmakois" does not signify "sorcerer."

[426] For a fuller treatment of some elements of this subject, see the section on the "SIXTH AND NINTH COMMANDMENTS" in *The Catholic Catechism*, John A. Hardon, S.J., Doubleday and Company, Garden City, N.Y. 1975. pp. 351-370.

[427] Ibid. p. 367.

[428] Ibid. p. 370.

There is absolutely no historical or scholarly doubt at all that disciplinary decrees against contraception and abortion are amongst the very oldest formal moral teachings of the infant Church.

If there had been any doubt that the DIDACHE'S teachings against abortion and contraception did not constitute teachings handed on from the Apostles, some of the disciples of the Apostles would have vociferously objected to the teachings in the DIDACHE. There is absolutely no record of any such protest. Therefore, there can be no reasonably justifiable doubt that these teachings ultimately came directly from the Apostles.

Today in the West, as 80% of the married laity of childbearing years are arguing with one of the oldest moral teachings of the Church, is this another example of a rampant heresy such as prophesied by Holzhauser, when *"no principle at all, however holy, authentic, ancient, and certain it may be, will remain free of censure, criticism, false interpretations, modification, and delimitation by man."?*

But one cannot lay all the blame for this state of affairs on the laity. It has been thirty years or more since the Church's doctrine on contraception has been clearly taught in the U.S. and Canada. For about fifteen years following the U.S. Roe vs. Wade Supreme Court decision legalizing abortion, the silence of the majority of the American clergy on abortion was almost deafening. During that fifteen years tremendous damage was done to the faithful's understanding of this issue. Today, many of our bishops and many of our priests are again courageously raising their voices against abortion. The laity should encourage and congratulate them for this. In today's climate it takes great courage for a priest or bishop to speak out on this issue. The faithful laity should also encourage them to repreach the Church's timeless teaching on contraception.

In the 1600's Holzhauser foresaw the eventual challenging of the very oldest and most venerable of the Church's teachings sometime prior to a great chastisement.

> "These are evil times, **a century full of dangers and calamities.** ***Heresy is everywhere, and the followers of heresy are in power almost everywhere.*** Bishops, prelates, and priests say that they are doing their duty, that they are vigilant, and that they live as befits their state in life. In like manner, therefore, they all seek excuses. *But God will permit*

> *a great evil against His Church: Heretics and tyrants will come suddenly and unexpectedly;* they will break into the Church while bishops, prelates, and priests are asleep. They will enter Italy and lay Rome waste; they will burn down the churches and destroy everything."[429]

Many, many, of the prophecies describe a sack of Rome for the future, and that this is foretold to be a resultant fruit of rampant heresy in the Latin Church which will cause much suffering for the Holy Father and faithful bishops. Holzhauser even specifically states that the worst of that period will occur during a 100 year period. After that century, he then foresees a period of consolation. There is absolutely nothing vague about Holzhauser's prophecies. They are very specific. Whether the century foretold is ours only time can tell.

> "The sixth period of the Church will begin with the powerful Monarch and the Holy Pontiff, as mentioned previously, and it will last until the revelation of Antichrist. In this period, God will console His Holy Church for the affliction and great tribulation which she has endured during the fifth period. All nations will become Catholic. Vocations will be abundant as never before, and all men will seek only the Kingdom of God and His justice. *Men will live in peace, and this will be granted because people will make their peace with God.* They will live under the protection of the Great Monarch and his successors."[430]

Here it would appear that the Great Monarch may have some successors. This possibility and its duration may depend upon cooperation with grace to extend the age of peace.

> "During the fifth period, we saw only calamities and devastation; oppression of Catholics by tyrants and heretics; executions of Kings, and conspiracies to set up republics. But, by the Hand of God Almighty, there occurs so wondrous a change during the sixth period that no one can humanly visualize it.[431]

[429] *Apocalypsis*, Bartholomew Holzhauser, 1850.
[430] *Apocalypsin*, Bartholomew Holzhauser, 1850, p. 68..
[431] Ibid. p. 68.

> "The Powerful Monarch, who will be sent by God, will uproot every Republic. He will submit everything to his authority, and he will show great zeal for the true Church of Christ. *The empire of the Mohammedans will be broken up, and this Monarch will reign in the East as well as in the West.* All nations will come to worship God in the true Catholic and Roman faith. There will be many Saints and Doctors (of the Church) on earth. Peace will reign over the whole earth because God will bind Satan for a number of years until the days of the Son of Perdition. No one will be able to pervert the word of God since, during the sixth period, there will be an ecumenic council which will be the greatest of all councils. By the grace of God, by the power of the Great Monarch, by the authority of the Holy Pontiff, and by the union of all the most devout princes, atheism and every heresy will be banished from the earth. ***The Council will define the true sense of Holy Scripture, and this will be believed and accepted by everyone.***"[432]

This is one of many prophecies to predict some great council of the Church in the future.

3. Potential Future Changes in Secular Governmental Forms

A number of the prophecies state that the Great Monarch will uproot all the Republics. This should not be construed as a condemnation of republican forms of government as such. The Church traditionally teaches that many different forms of government can legitimately fulfill the legitimate role of government. That includes republics. So what might be the ultimate causal source of this repeated prophecy that the Great King or Monarch will uproot republics?

Most modern political commentaries refer to the U.S. as a Democracy. That is probably the reason only a small minority of contemporary Americans are aware that the U.S. form of government is a Republic, not a Democracy. When Americans recite their "Pledge of Allegiance" they say in part, "... and to the *Republic* for which it stands, one nation, *under God*, ..." In 1973, the Supreme

[432] Ibid. p. 69.

Court of that American Republic in its legal decision of *Roe vs. Wade* legalized the murder of babies. In *Roe vs. Wade*, whether they knew it or not, the U.S. Supreme Court separated the U.S. Republic from God's law -- **"THOU SHALT NOT KILL."** Many other major Republics of Western Europe over the last few centuries have separated their nations laws from God's law.

Our modern Western Republics have not as a group been anchored in God's law. The fact is that most of the Western "Republics" established in the last two centuries have not formally recognized the absolute moral authority of God's law in His Decalogue. In their contemporary desire to separate "Church and State," they have effectually separated God and State. Which of the modern Republics constitutionally publicly recognize God's Ten Commandments as the moral basis of the law of their land?

Prior to the era of modern Western Republics, most Western Governments (no matter what their specific form) *publicly recognized God's Decalogue as the moral basis of their law*. Within those previous Western governments murder was murder, in that no one dared to attempt to repeal the Ten Commandments. Moral debate over law was rooted in the commonly accepted Judeo-Christian understanding of the "Ten Commandments." The moral base of their law was rooted in the authority of the Creator. Their moral base was *not* rooted in the vagaries of human opinion, i.e., they did not view codified law as a fruitful conclusion to popularity contests on morality.

In the same Old Testament wherein they learned that God had given them the Decalogue, they read of the sanctity of all human life. They knew they could not change law on subjects such as abortion because they recognized that they did not have the moral authority to do so. They publicly recognized that only God had such authority. They also knew God had publicly exercised that authority in the issuance of the Ten Commandments to Moses.

Our modern Western Republics never publicly *faced* that dilemma. Because they have never formally recognized God's unchanging moral law as the supreme basis of their civil laws, those Republics have not had to clearly face the issue that when they attempt to "legalize" abortion they are attempting to nullify God's law. Many modern Republics have vaguely given lip service to "the architect of the universe" in public utterance. At the same time they have gradually denied many of God's basic precepts in their law. Many of these Republics publicly recognized that the "architect of the universe" had "created man free." They never concomitantly recognized that almighty God had also created man with responsibility to obey His law. One cannot get much more basic than recognizing God's law that, "THOU SHALT NOT KILL."

God delivered the Decalogue to Moses, who in turn handed it on to the Chosen People. When he did so he also delivered to them a synoptic prophetic companion message:

> "Behold I set forth in your sight this day a blessing and a curse:
>
> A blessing, if you obey the commandments of the Lord your God, which I command you this day:
>
> *A curse, if you obey not the commandments.*"

The fifth of those commandments is *"Thou shalt not Kill!"*

Continuing the U.S. example, U.S. law (and the bulk of Western law) had previously recognized the rights of the unborn even in estate law. Even the unborn baby's right to inherit property was protected at law. How then could a court which had previously upheld the anticipated property rights of the unborn child overrule the same unborn child's right to life? The illogic of the situation is patently obvious even to a child.

The answer to this "illogic" lies not in the "form" of government, but in the fact that most modern Western Republics initially failed to *formally publicly* anchor the moral base of their civil law in God's Law. Also, our economies have not been based on the traditional Christian teachings on what is socially just. Popes Leo the XIII and Pius X issued encyclicals referring to the "modern" lack of God's order in our politics and our economic systems. As observed by Pope Pius XII back in mid-century (1952), what we have in this century is:

> "an economy without God, politics without God."[433]

[433] Pius XII's allocution to the Union of Men of Italian Catholic Action on Oct. 2, 1952.

John Paul II has continued these observations about the lack of God's law and justice in our modern political institutions.

The founders of most modern Republics said they merely wanted to separate Church and State. They ultimately separated God and State. There is a big difference between the two. It should surprise no Christian, Jew, or Moslem, that a government which leaves the morality of law up to human opinion -- that government might ultimately fall under the resultant chaos caused by the vagaries of *human* opinion versus the stability of God's law.

A recent appointee to the U.S. Supreme Court suggested that our basis in law could rest in the "Natural Law." The resultant hue and cry which went up from the established legal community was horrific. How dare anyone suggest that there was an objective moral standard against which codified law could be judged? For the majority of those in the legal profession, the moral base of law in the U.S. has devolved into nothing more substantive than the relativism of modern philosophy and popularity contests in personal opinion. The majority of the legal community will brook no objective restraint to their personal right to decide not only law, but also its moral base. Mortals have no such power or right. That power and right belongs to Almighty God alone.

4. A Return to Holzhauser's Prophecies

> "When everything has been ruined by war, *when Catholics are hard-pressed by* ***traitorous coreligionists*** *and heretics*, then the hand of Almighty God will work a marvelous change, something seemingly impossible according to human reason ..."[434]

Holzhauser here depicts a time just prior to the rise of a Great Monarch and Great Pope which we will hear more of in a moment. But his remark about traitorous co-religionists is one that we in our time should look at closely.

> "There will rise a valiant king anointed by God. He will rule supreme in temporal matters. The Pope will rule su-

[434] *Apocalypsis*, Bartholomew Holzhauser, 1850, p. 70.

> preme in spiritual matters at the same time. Persecution will cease and justice shall reign. He will root out false doctrines. All nations will adore God their Lord according to Catholic teaching. People will love justice, and peace will reign over the whole earth, *for Divine Power will bind Satan* ***for many years*** *until the coming of the Son of Perdition...*"
>
> "After desolation has reached its peak in England, peace will be restored and England will return to the Catholic faith with greater fervour than ever before..."[435]

One of the major values of Holzhauser is that he covers almost every major event foretold in detail. We see the growing secularization of the world and the subsequent injustice and suffering in consequence of that fact. There follow growing wars and tensions and finally afflictions of heresy and laxity which torment the Church itself. If all of this talk of universal peace and cessation of heresies and Mohammedans and Jews being converted sounds impossible, we must remember that Scripture itself talks of a time when there will be "one flock [or fold] and one shepherd,"[436] and general peace on earth. So to deny the possibility that such a thing could actually ever happen is tantamount to denying that the above passage of Scripture can come true at some time in the future.

---

435 *Ibid.*

436 John 10:16 Jesus in speaking to the Jews about Himself being the Good Shepherd. He tells them about the difference between the Good Shepherd and wolves. He is predicting that wolves and false shepherds will arise. Then he says, "And other sheep I have, that are not of this fold, them I must also bring, and they shall hear my voice, and there shall be one flock, 'one shepherd.'" Jesus is explaining to the Jews that people besides Jews enter into His plan of salvation, He is making reference to the Gentiles. Most scriptural commentators from the Fathers and Doctors have also interpreted this text to signify that at some point in time, the vast majority of the Jews and Gentiles will believe in Christ -- that then will be the ultimate fulfillment of the time of "one flock, one shepherd."

5. St. Louis-Marie Grignion De Montfort (18th Century)

De Montfort is so famous that we will dispense with any biographical details.

> "The power of Mary over all devils will be particularly outstanding in the last period of time. She will extend the Kingdom of Christ over the idolaters and Moslems, and there will come a glorious era when Mary is the Ruler and Queen of Hearts."

6. Capuchin Friar (18th Century)

> "All the ecclesiastics, both secular and regular, shall be stripped of their possessions and of every kind of property, and obliged to beg from lay persons their food and everything necessary for their support, and for the worship of God."[437]

> "*During these calamities the Pope shall die. ...* Through the death of the Supreme Pontiff the Church will be reduced to the most painful anarchy, because from three hostile powers (through their influence) three popes will be contemporaneously elected: one Italian, another German, the third Greek. This [the Greek], by force of arms, shall be placed on the throne."[438]

Many, many, of the prophecies refer to an Antipope for some time in the future during which great calamities occur to the Church.

> "During this time, much human blood will be shed in Italy, and many cities, country towns and castles [military fortresses] shall be brought to ruin, with the death of many thousands of persons. By the Catholic clergy and people *the true and lawful Pope* will be elected who shall be a man of great holiness and goodness of life."[439]

The statement "*the true and lawful Pope*" is taken by some to imply the possibility of an Untrue or Unlawful Pope having been

---

[437] *The Christian Trumpet*, p. 55.
[438] Ibid.
[439] Ibid.

forcibly placed on the throne of Peter. If that should come to pass, it wouldn't be the first time in history that a civil tyrant attempted such a maneuver.

> *"A scion of the Carolingian race, by all considered extinct,* will come to Rome and behold and admire the piety and clemency of this Pontiff, who will crown him, and declare him to be the legitimate Emperor of the Romans and from the chair of St. Peter the Pope will lift up the standard, the crucifix; and will give it to the new emperor.
>
> "This new emperor with the robust Italian and French people, and with those of other nations will form a most mighty host, called the Church Army, through which he shall destroy the Ottoman [Mohammedan?][440] Empire and all heresies."[441]

It must be born in mind that at the time these prophecies were written, the average person equated the Moslem religion (or power in the hands of Moslems) with the Ottoman Empire. Therefore, the term "Ottoman Empire" may merely refer to a future suppression of Moslem forces and influences.

> "The above mentioned new emperor, with the assistance of God and of the Pope, he will cooperate in the reformation of abuses; he will assume the direction of temporal governments; he will assign a decent pension to the Supreme Pontiff, and also to the bishops and clergy. And they all being detached from every earthly covetousness, will live in peace, which shall last till the End of Time."[442]

This prophecy is very clear in its chronology. Many of the other prophecies when tied in with this one give a quite broad picture of

[440] By the time of the writing of this prophecy, the Mogul Dynasty of the Ottoman Empire was already in serious decline, and at last disappeared in 1858 when the British dethroned its last Sultan. Therefore, it is most probable that the "Capuchin Friar" who made these prophecies would have viewed a future restoration of Moslem power as an "Ottoman" restoration.

[441] Ibid. p. 71

[442] Ibid.

the prophesied events to take place during the reign of some great future Christian King. The battles within which he will be engaged (if indeed all these prophecies are about the same man) will run from Northern to Southern Europe.

7. Bernhardt Rembordt (18th Century)

This is another prophet who describes struggles which shall take place during what appears to occur during this time of this "Roman Emperor."

> "*Cologne will be the site of a terrible battle.* Many foreigners will be slaughtered there; both men and women will fight for their Faith. It will be impossible to prevent this horrible devastation. People will wade up to their ankles in blood. At last, a foreign king will appear and win a victory for the cause of the righteous. The remaining enemy will retreat to *the Birch tree country*. There, the last battle will be fought for the just cause.
>
> "At that time France will be divided. The German Empire will choose a simple man as the Emperor, who will rule for a short time. His successor will be the man for whom the world has longed. *He will be called a 'Roman Emperor,'* and he will give peace to the world. A good and happy era will follow. God will be praised on earth, and war will be no more."[443]

The "Birch Tree Country" is a name which applies to the German territory known today as Westphalia. Many other prophecies refer to this future decisive battle as the Battle of Westphalia. Many other prophecies also refer to a previous battle which takes place in Cologne. Again, the message ends on a high note of hope that the Faith and the Church will rise above all of the growing problems which we have lived through during the last several centuries. And this hope is tied to talk of Catholic Emperors.

---

443 *The Prophets and Our times*, p. 178.

8. Old German Prophecy

We quote this prophecy out of historical context to show the similarity between many of the prophecies concerning a final battle wherein the forces of the Great King will defeat antichristian forces in Germany. As with many other prophecies it describes the forces of the North fighting the South. These prophecies consistently describe the forces of the North as those of Russia and Prussia. Some are so explicit as to describe the forces of the North as from the land of Moskva. A simple glance at a globe will show the listener that Moscow, the traditional capitol of Russia, is well North of the bulk of Western Europe.

> "When the world becomes godless: revolutions will break out against kings; fathers will be against sons and sons against fathers; dogma will be perverted; men will try to overthrow the Catholic Church; mankind will be lovers of pleasure. A terrible war will find the North fighting and South. *The South will be led by a Prince wearing a white coat with a cross on the front*; he will be lame afoot. *He will gather his forces at Bremen for Mass*. Then he will lead them into battle beyond Woerl near the Birch-tree country [Westphalia]. After a terrible battle at a brook running eastwards near Berdberg and Sondern, the South will be victorious."[444]

St. Hildegard also describes the Great Monarch as being lame. She also confirms that the final European battles conducted by the Great Monarch will be fought in Germany. Later, we will hear Catherine Emerick describe how he becomes lame.

9. Brother Anthony of Aachen (19 Century)

Many readers of brief presentations of these foretold battles fought in Europe by the Great King, later to be anointed Holy Roman Emperor, have wondered if there are not more details given

[444] *The Prophets and Our Times*, p. 143.

somewhere. There are at least dozens of prophecies which do so. For the interested reader, we present the following more detailed account. For the reader who merely wishes to push on, please proceed to the next prophecy of Fr. Nectou.

> "Some day war will break out again in Alsace. I saw the French in Alsace with Strassburg at their rear, and I saw Italians fighting with them [as allies of the French]. Suddenly, great transports of troops arrived from the French side. A two-day battle ended with the defeat of the Prussian army. The French pursued the Prussians over the Rhine in many directions. In a second battle, at Frankfurt, *the Prussians lost again and retreated as far as Siegburg,* ***where they joined with a Russian army.*** The Russians made common cause with the Prussians. It seemed to me as if Austrians also were aiding the French.
>
> "The battle of Siegburg was more horrible than any before, and its like will never occur again. After some days, the Prussians and Russians retreated and crossed below Bonn, to the left bank of the Rhine. Steadily pressed by their opponents, they retired to Cologne, which had been bombarded so much that only one-fourth of the city remained intact. Constantly in retreat, what was left of the Prussians moved to ***Westphalia*** where the last battle went against them. People greatly rejoiced because they were freed from the Prussians.
>
> "Then, a new Emperor, *about forty years old*, was elected in Germany, and he met the Pope. Meanwhile, an epidemic broke out in the regions devastated by war, and many people died. *After the battle of Westphalia, the French returned to their country, and from then on there was peace between the French and the Germans.* All exiles returned to their homes. When I begged God to take the terrible vision away, I heard a voice saying: 'Prussia must be humiliated in such a manner that it will never again bring sorrow to the Church.'"[445]

[445] Ibid. pp. 201-202.

GEOGRAPHIC CONFUSION FACTORS

Part of the problem with interpreting many prophecies is that over time, the meaning of geographic terms changes. What we call "Germany" in 1996 is not necessarily what we normally meant by Germany as short a time ago as 1989. Brother Aachen prophesies "a new Emperor, about forty years old, was elected in Germany" after his French troops win a final battle in Westphalia against "Prussians" and "Russians."

Does Brother Aachen mean by "Germany" the same thing we mean by "Germany"? Brother Aachen (a German) does not say the new emperor is German. He simply says he is elected in Germany. This man has been leading French troops (therefore he is probably French) against Prussian and Russian troops. Brother Aachen is most likely describing an election of a French leader as "a new Emperor," which election probably occurs somewhere in the area of the city of Cologne (French Spelling), or Köeln (German spelling of the same city). Many prophecies must be thought out over and over in order to understand them.

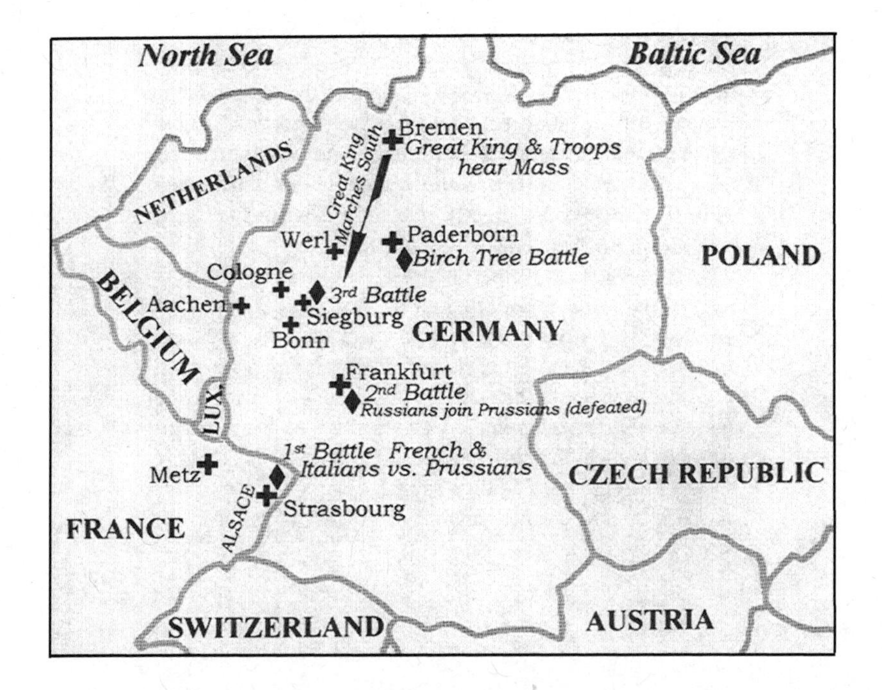

Locations of battles and related events foretold by Br. Anthony and other private profits.

People usually don't stop viewing natural events through the eyes of the land and culture of their birth just because they become prophets. The area around the city of Cologne (German spelling Köeln) has historically changed ownership many times between what we call Germany and France. According to the *Catholic Encyclopedia*, "in 794 he (Charlemagne) had made his residence at Aachen (Ai-la-Chapelle) *where the French and German languages of his people met*." Brother Aachen was German. He would therefore primarily view the area *(Köeln)* as German. A Frenchman from the same general era would probably claim that same city (*Fr. spelling Cologne*) as French. To make things even more complex, Brother Aachen distinguishes between Prussians and Germans, which many of the prophecies do. The Prussians are most likely primarily from the territory which we referred to as late as 1989 as East Germany.

10. Fr. Nectou

Again we return to Fr. Nectou:

> "When those things come to pass *from which the triumph of the Church will arise*, then will such confusion reign upon earth that people will think God has permitted them to have their own contrary will, and that the Providence of God is not concerned about the world. *The confusion will be so general that men will not be able to think aright*, as if God had withheld His Providence from mankind, and that, *during the worst crisis, the best that can be done would be to remain where God has placed us, and persevere in fervent prayers.* Two parties will be formed in France which will fight unto death. The party of evil will at first be stronger, and the good side will be weaker. At that time there will be such a terrible crisis that PEOPLE WILL BELIEVE THAT THE END OF THE WORLD HAS COME. Blood will flow in many large cities. The very elements will be confused. IT WILL BE LIKE A LITTLE GENERAL JUDGMENT."[446]
>
> COMMENT: Consider the following quote from the above prophecy: "When those things come to pass *from which the triumph of the Church will arise, the confusion will be so*

[446] *Catholic Prophecy*, pp. 47&48.

> *general that men will not be able to think aright*." If we were to attempt to discern whether that prophecy applied to our time, where would we begin? First of all, the prophecy states that the confusion will be general. It does not say that only the bad will be confused. Today, even many who are trying to be good Christians are confused as to what to believe and/or do on many moral issues.

If all of the conditionally foretold events should come to full fruition, we are told that many will believe it to be the end of the world. If such prophesied events should occur, those people familiar with them will not easily be mislead into believing that it is the end of the world. *Those who know their prophecy will know such events are prophesied to well precede the end of the world.* There is an additional point which should be covered. We are all human. Many people who hear these prophesies for the first time wonder where they might go if and when they see these foretold events coming to pass? Where is a place of refuge?

We should repeat a passage from that just quoted. "During the worst crisis, the best that can be done would be to remain where God has placed us, and persevere in fervent prayers." As St. Thomas Aquinas teaches; in the normal course of events, we usually are where God has placed us and wants us. We must have confidence and trust in God. If and when a chastisement comes either for us or some future generation, it would be more or less universal - no *safe* area.

In these prophecies, one reads that the condition of man does not change much from country to country. The evil that man is committing changes little from country to country. The warnings for the world given at Fatima were for the whole world. The promised punishments if men did not change were for the whole world. God's love of all and spiritual protection for those who love him is universal. We need to place our efforts in conversion of our own hearts first, and then pray and work for the conversion of others. That is our duty, that is our task, to faithfully fulfill our duties within our individual state in life.

Fr. Nectou continues:

> "A great multitude of people will lose their lives in those calamitous times, but the wicked will not prevail. They will

> indeed attempt to destroy the whole Church, but not enough time will be allowed them, because the frightful crisis will be of short duration. ***When all is considered lost, all will be found safe.*** *This disaster will come to pass shortly after the power of England begins to wane. This will be the sign.* As when the fig tree begins to sprout and produce leaves, it is a sure sign that summer is near. *England in her turn will experience a more frightful revolution than that of France. It will continue long enough for France to recover her strength; then she will help England to restore peace and order.*"[447]

Comment: England had continuously been a major power from before the time of this prophecy till shortly after the end of WW II, 50 years ago. Then her power began its wane and she began to lose her colonies one by one, losing virtually all of them by the 1970's. How by the means of unaided reason alone could Fr. Nectou have foreseen England's loss of her colonies almost two centuries before the event? One can see that these prophecies, far from merely being "national prophecy wars" are the writings of people from all over Europe serially describing basically the same events.

Fr. Nectou goes on:

> **"During this revolution, *which will very likely be general and not confined to France*,** Paris will be destroyed so completely that twenty years afterwards fathers walking over its ruins with their children will be asked by them what kind of a place that was; to whom they will answer: '*My child, this was a great city which God has destroyed on account of her crimes*.'
>
> "Yes, Paris will certainly be destroyed; but, before this happens, such signs and portents will be seen, that all good people will be induced to flee away from it. After these most frightful events, order will be restored everywhere. **Justice will reign throughout the whole world, and the counter-revolution will be accomplished.**
>
> "The triumph of the Church will then be so complete that nothing like it has ever been seen before, for this will be the last victory of the Church upon earth.

[447] Ibid. p. 48.

> *"Those Christians who are fortunate enough to survive will thank God for preserving them and giving them the privilege of beholding this glorious triumph of the Church."*[448]

This is the prophetic goal upon which we should keep our eyes fixed. This is the ultimate message of hope, a message of consolation. **"BE NOT AFRAID!"** The details of this prophecy are specific and in-depth. They are delivered by a former Jesuit provincial with a reputation for sanctity amongst his brother Jesuits. This is one of those classic cases in private prophecy where a Catholic has to either believe that the seer genuinely received a prophecy - or - he was crazy or a liar. But would such a man have a reputation for sanctity amongst his fellow Jesuits.[449] That is not likely. It is intellectually impossible to simply summarily dismiss such detailed prophecy. It is either real, or it is the product of either some form of insanity or a lie. Those are the two horns of the dilemma.

This is a prophecy proclaimed by a Frenchman who speaks of its applying to "the whole world." You will shortly hear other prophecies mention that immediately after three days of darkness which comes near the end of a chastisement the survivors will envy the dead. But this state of mind will last only a short while. Shortly after that the survivors will be infected with a contagious spirit of hope and optimism due to the most Christian state of affairs by then prevalent in the world. That would fit in very well with Fr. Nectou's prediction that, "Those Christians who are fortunate enough to survive will thank God for preserving them and giving them the privilege of beholding this glorious triumph of the Church."

> "A man disliked by France will be placed on the throne; a man of the House of Orleans will be made king. It is only after this event that the counterrevolution will begin."[450]

---

[448] Ibid.

[449] The author was Jesuit trained and is familiar with classic "Jesuit jokes." Therefore he is also aware of the potential for good-natured humorous responses this question might generate from priestly ranks outside the Society of Jesus. Fr. Nectou's prophecies are not signed "God, S.J."

[450] *The Christian Trumpet*, p. 46.

11. Jeanne le Royer (Sister of the Nativity) (18th Century)

Sr. Jeanne was born on February 24th, 1731, in Brittany, France, and became a nun in 1755. She entered the Monastery of St. Clare of Fougeres. This order of nuns was called the "Urbanists." Her religious name was "Sister of the Nativity." She was totally illiterate, and many years before the French Revolution she foretold it in great detail. In 1790, by command from God, she told all her visions and previsions to the Spiritual Director of her monastery, the Abbe Genet, in fifty conferences, who wrote them down. She said:

> *"The knowledge of these things shall contribute to the salvation of many souls, and form a treasure for the faithful of the last age of the world."*[451]

Comment: HERE AGAIN WE HAVE A PROPHET STATING THAT IT WILL BE OF GREAT ADVANTAGE TO BE CONVERSANT WITH THESE PROPHECIES -- EVEN TO THE POINT OF CONTRIBUTING TO THE SALVATION OF MANY SOULS. This is only one of the prophets who has said exactly the same thing. This is one of the author's strongest motivations in making these prophecies known. Sr. Jean continues:

> "I had a vision: Before the Father and the Son - both seated -- a virgin of incomparable beauty, representing the Church was kneeling. The Holy Ghost spread His wings over the virgin and two other persons. The wounds of Our Lord seemed alive. Leaning on the Cross with one hand, He offered to His Father with the other hand the chalice which the virgin had given to Him. She supported the Chalice which the Master held in the middle. The Father placed one hand on the cup and raised the other to bless the virgin.
>
> "I noticed that the chalice was only half-filled with blood, and I heard these words spoken by the Saviour at the moment of presentation: *'I shall not be fully satisfied until I am able to fill it right up to the brim.'* I understood then that the contents of the chalice represented the blood of the early martyrs, and that ***this vision had reference to the last***

[451] *Ibid*, p. 115.

> ***persecutions of the Christians, whose blood would fill the chalice, thereby completing the number of martyrs and predestined.*** For at the end of time, there will be as many martyrs as in the early Church, and even more, for the persecutions will be far more violent. Then the Last Judgment will no longer be delayed."[452]

That Sister Jeanne's vision covers a fairly broad sweep of history is betrayed by the following sequence from this vision.

> ***"I see in God that -- a long time before the rise of Antichrist -- the world will be afflicted with the many bloody wars.*** Peoples will rise against peoples, and nations will rise against nations, sometimes allied, sometimes enemies, in their fight against the same party. Armies will come into frightful collisions and will fill the earth with murder and carnage.[453]
>
> "As well as that, I see that the earth will be shaken in different places by frightful earthquakes. I see whole mountains cracking and splitting with a terrible din. *Only too happy will one be if one can escape with no more than a fright;* but no, I see come out of these gaping mountains whirlwinds of smoke, fire, sulphur, and tar, which reduce to cinders entire towns. ***All this and a thousand other disasters must come before the rise of the Man of Sin*** **(Antichrist)."**[454]

> COMMENT: Notice that in 1790 Sr. Jeanne says "*A long time before the rise of Antichrist -- the world will be afflicted with the many bloody wars*" and *"All this and a thousand other disasters must come before the rise of the Man of Sin"*

There have been many conflicts during the two centuries since Sr. Jeanne made that prophecy. But "*the World*" was not afflicted as such till World War I (1914-1918), which was dubbed at the time as "the war to end all wars." However, World War II began a mere twenty-one years later (1939-1945). Six years later the Korean War broke out (1950-1953) during which troops from all over the world fought under the banner of the United Nations against the combined armies of Communist China and North Korea. Only nineteen years

---

452 *Catholic Prophecy*, p, 54.
453 Ibid.
454 Ibid.

later the Vietnam War broke out (1964-1973) under the aegis of SEATO[455], which is a regional subjunct of the U.N. Not since the Crusades have troops from so many nations been embroiled in singular conflicts as they have been in the 20th century.

We again repeat Sr. Jeanne's prophecy, "*A long time before the rise of Antichrist -- the world will be afflicted with the many bloody wars." Would not a reasonable conclusion from this prophecy be that, it is still "a long time" till the "Rise of Antichrist."* That conclusion forms a consistent pattern in *approved* prophecies, the thesis that a significant period of time still remains before the coming of Antichrist.

> "I saw in the light of the Lord that the faith and our holy Religion would become weaker in almost every Christian kingdom. GOD HAS PERMITTED THAT THEY SHOULD BE CHASTISED BY THE WICKED IN ORDER TO AWAKEN THEM FROM THEIR APATHY. *And after the justice of God has been satisfied, He will pour out an abundance of graces on His Church, and He will spread the Faith and restore the discipline of the church in those countries where it had become tepid and lax.*
>
> "I saw in God that our Mother, Holy Church, will spread in many countries and will produce her fruits in abundance to compensate for the outrages she will have suffered from the impiety and the persecutions of her enemies."[456]

These are some of the many *messages of hope* upon which we should keep our souls, our minds, and our hearts riveted, particularly if a foretold chastisement should happen during our lifetime. And we must remember that according to Sr. Jeanne (and many other prophets), God permits a chastisement *to "awaken us from our apathy." That is a Divine Mercy.*

> *"I saw that the poor people, weary of the arduous labours and trials that God sent to them, shall then be thrilled with a joy that God will infuse in their good hearts.* The Church will become by her faith and by her love, more fervent and more flourishing than ever. *Our good Mother the Church will witness many amazing things, even on the part of her*

---

455 "SouthEast Asia Treaty Organization."

456 *Catholic Prophecy*, pp. 55&56.

> *former persecutors, for they will come forward and throw themselves at her feet, acknowledge her, and implore pardon from God and from her for all the crimes and outrages that they had perpetrated against her.* She will no longer regard them as her enemies, but she will instead welcome them as her own children."[457]

In ages past and present the poor we have had with us, and according to Christ, they will always be with us. He said, "The poor you will always have with you." But in simpler times before the advent of the industrial revolution, the poor at least had time for reflection. Their work entailed to some degree a sense of accomplishment. Their jobs for the most part were not dehumanizing.

Today a large percentage of the poor spend their lives in factories that even our modern psychologists and sociologists describe as enervating and dehumanizing. In centuries past only condemned felons were committed to such work conditions. According to *approved* prophecies, in the reign of peace to come even the poor will be accorded lives of dignity and will again experience a sense of accomplishment in their work.

One of the most interesting patterns in many prophecies is that they accurately predict specific social phenomena for later eras. These phenomena are later secularly recognized and corroborated by social scientists of a later age. In almost every case these social scientists are totally unaware of the fact that the phenomena were prophesied by Catholic prophets centuries in advance.

Sr. Jeanne continues:

> "I saw in God' s essence a numerous assembly of ministers of the Church, who like an army in battle array, and like a firm and unflinching column, shall sustain the rights of the church and of her Head, and shall restore its ancient discipline."[458]

Over and over we hear a description of a future chaos and disorder in the Church, lack of obedience to authority. Here again we hear the oft-repeated phrase about a restoration of former disciplines

---

[457] Ibid. p. 56.
[458] *The Christian Trumpet*, p. 116.

after the period of disorder and disobedience to God's law. The large assembly of pastors is probably the foretold Great Council.

There are many recognizable patterns in these prophecies. They come from many different centuries, countries, cultures, and from people of differing vocations. Some are priests, some are nuns, some are laity. Some are cloistered and some live in the world. Some are illiterate and some are highly educated. The patterns are not to be found in these prophets backgrounds. The consistent patterns which exist are in the prophesied events themselves, their disclosed causes, and the sincerity of the Christian lives of these prophets. Those patterns become more and more evident as one becomes familiar with a broader base of *approved* prophecy. Sr. Jeanne continues,

> "All the false religions will be abolished; all the abuses of the Revolution will be destroyed; the altars shall be reestablished, and *our religion will flourish more than ever.*"[459]

Sr. Jeanne goes on to describe the joy of the Church during a future period of peace.

> **"I see in God that the Church will enjoy a profound peace over a period which seems to me to be of a fairly long duration.** This respite will be the longest of all that will occur between the revolutions from now till the General Judgment.[460]
>
> "One day I found myself in a vast plain alone with God. Jesus appeared to me, and from the top of a small hill, showing to me a beautiful sun on the horizon, He said dolefully: 'The world is passing away and the time of My second coming draws near. When the sun is about to set, one knows that the day is nearly over and that the night will soon fall. *Centuries are like days for me.* Look at this sun, see how much it still has to travel, and estimate the time that is left to the world.'
>
> *"I looked intently and it seemed to me that the sun would set in two hours.* Jesus said: 'Do not forget that these

[459] *The Christian Trumpet*, p. 117.
[460] *Catholic Prophecy*, p. 57.

> are not millenaries, but only centuries, and they are few in number.' But I understood that Jesus reserved to Himself the knowledge of the exact number, and I did not wish to ask Him more. *It sufficed me to know that the peace of the Church and the restoration of discipline were to last a reasonably long time*."[461]

Once again we find reference to an extended period of peace and harmony for the Church and her members. Notice that there is no mention of Antichrist or the Parousia prior to this age of peace. This age of peace which Sr. Jeanne says seemed **"***to be of a fairly long duration***"** is prophesied to precede the coming of Antichrist and therefore precede the Parousia. Dozens of these *approved* prophecies state the same chronology of events:

(1) Mankind is warned of a "conditional" chastisement. It can be averted if mankind will heed God's prophetic warnings. If man does not so heed the warnings, a chastisement will occur which will seem so terrible that many people who are unfamiliar with prophecy will erroneously think it is the end of the world,
(2) which is followed by a calm grace-filled period of peace for the Church and the world,
(3) since people usually cannot withstand an extended period of peace and prosperity, a general falling away from the faith follows, and then,
(4) the beginning of events which leads to the coming of Antichrist.
(5) These events are prophesied to extend over "a fairly long duration" of time. Just exactly what "a fairly long duration" of time is, we do not know, but,
(6) **the series of events described in these *approved* private prophecies exclude the possibility that Antichrist and/or the Parousia are just around the corner.**

These prophecies are truly messages of consolation for a faithful Catholic. Every one of these prophets says that God is sending these prophetic warnings to console rather than to afflict the righteous. There is nothing for a good Christian to fear in them. On the contrary they are a source of hope. The reference to centuries

[461] *Catholic Prophecy*, pp. 58&59.

instead of millenaries is given from the Divine perspective and must be balanced with the statements about an era of peace *of a fairly long duration.* Could not five or fifteen centuries for that matter appear to be about two hours from the Divine perspective to which a "thousand years is as a day?"

This time-line could possibly also be a literal one implying only a few centuries left till the end of the world. But speculation accomplishes absolutely nothing since "no one knows the day nor the hour" of the Lord's Second Coming. Sr. Jean shows a healthy regard and appreciation for this principle when she says, "*It sufficed me to know that the peace of the Church and the restoration of discipline were to last a reasonably long time.*" That period of peace has not occurred yet. It is something to look forward to, if not for us, then perhaps for our children or grandchildren. As Mary said at Fatima, "In the end, my Immaculate Heart will triumph, and a certain period of peace will be given to the world."

Sr. Jeanne states further:

> "The storm began in France, *and France shall be the first theatre of its ravages after having been its forge.*
>
> "But the Church in Council assembled shall one day strike with anathemas, pull down and destroy the evil principles of that criminal constitution. What a consolation! What consolation, what joy for all the truly faithful!"[462]

Here we find another reference to a future Council of the Church, which prophesies the "Council" will increase the number of defined dogmas and positively affect the practice of the Faith.

12. The Ecstatic of Tours

> "Before the war breaks out again, food will be scarce and expensive. There will be little work for the workers, and fathers will hear their children crying for food. There will be earthquakes and signs in the sun. *Towards the end darkness will cover the earth.*"[463]

---

462 *The Christian Trumpet*, pp. 116&117.

463 *Catholic Prophecy*, p. 37.

This is another prophecy which predicts a general economic collapse. It will not be limited to France. Also, we are given the timing that the THREE DAYS OF DARKNESS WILL COME TOWARD THE END OF A CHASTISEMENT.

Many of the prophecies state that this Minor Chastisement (which is prophesied to precede Antichrist by a significant period of time) will be like a little general judgment. It appears to be a foretaste of the Major Chastisement or Tribulation of Antichrist and cataclysmic events foretold for the Parousia. It will contain many of the same *elements* foretold for the time of Antichrist and the Parousia, *but to a lesser degree*. For instance, this and other prophecies confirm there will be some "earthquakes and signs in the sun" during the Minor Chastisement, which is prior to the time of Antichrist.

> "*When everyone believes that peace is assured, when everyone least expects it, the great happenings will begin. Revolution will break out in Italy almost at the same time as in France.* For some time, the Church will be without a Pope. England, too, will have much to suffer."[464]

All the prophecies which discuss the issue state that the problems will begin in France and Italy at almost the same time. The reader has already seen an almost identical prophecy from Blessed Anna Maria Taigi. It is unclear from many of the prophecies whether the Church will actually be "without a Pope," or, there will be a Pope who will be in hiding. Other prophecies predict the murder of a Pope. There is the third possibility that these are two separate incidents. The prophecy continues,

> "The revolution will spread to every French town. Wholesale slaughter will take place. *This revolution will last only a few months* but it will be frightful; blood will flow everywhere because the malice of the wicked will reach its highest pitch. Victims will be innumerable. *Paris will look like a slaughter house.* Persecutions against the Church will be even greater, but it will not last long. All churches will be closed, but only for a very short time in those towns where disturbances are

---

464 Ibid.

> least. Priests will have to go into hiding. The wicked will try to obliterate everything religious, but they will not have enough time."[465]

Another repetitive part of the prophecies is that the height of the persecutions in France will last but a short time. It will not last long enough for the forces of evil to accomplish all of their goals. Also, this prophecy made in 1863 cannot be referring to the French Revolution; which was by then three quarters of a century old. This prophesied revolution in France is something which has not happened since the time of this prophecy.

> "Many bishops and priests will be put to death. *The Archbishop of Paris will be murdered.* Many other priests, in Paris, will have their throats cut because they will not have time to find a hiding place.[466]
>
> "In those days, France will receive no human assistance. She will be alone and helpless. At this juncture, the French people will turn back to God and implore the Sacred Heart of Jesus and Mary Immaculate.
>
> "*The French people will ask for the good King*, he who was chosen by God. He will come, this saviour whom God has spared for France, this king who is not wanted now because he is dear to God's Heart. He will ascend to the throne; he will free the Church and reassert the Pope's rights."[467]

Subsequent to this prophecy, Monsignor Darboy, the Archbishop of Paris was "executed" by leftist revolutionaries on May 24, 1871. This "execution"[468] was carried out by an order of the executive committee of the Commune of Paris during its infamous 70 days of rule. It occurred just as Our Lady had predicted to St. Catherine Laboure.

Since in the "legal" sense this was labeled an "execution" there is a question as to whether this was the murder predicted by the Ecstatic of Tours quoted above. But the Ecstatic immediately

[465] Ibid.

[466] Ibid.

[467] Ibid.

[468] Bishop Darboy was an innocent man. All he had done was try to be a good priest and bishop. He was murdered by these 18th Century communist revolutionaries.

continues with the contemporaneous prophecy that, "Many other priests, in Paris, will have their throats cut because they will not have time to find a hiding place." This definitely appears to be discussing another persecution of the Church in France, most specifically in Paris. There are other prophecies which make an almost identical statement about murder of priests in Rome at the height of an Italian crisis. That Italian crisis is prophesied to be almost contemporaneous with the violence in France.

13. Bl. Anna-Maria Taigi (19th Century)

Here we shall repeat Anna Maria's description of the three days of darkness to tie it in with the rest of her predictions.

> **"God will send two punishments; one will be in the form of wars, revolutions and dangers originating on earth, the other will be sent from Heaven.** There shall come over the whole earth an inner darkness that will last three days and three nights. Nothing will be visible, and the air will be pestilent and foul and will harm, though not exclusively, the enemies of religion.
>
> "During those three days of darkness artificial light will fail, only blessed candles will burn. *During those days of darkness, the faithful should remain in their houses, praying the Holy Rosary and asking God for mercy.*"[469]

Comment: Anna Maria is quoted in this book from several different sources. She is heavily quoted by numerous Catholic authors simply because she is so well-known. She is also so highly respected in the Church that she is one of a handful of private prophets to merit specific mention in various Catholic encyclopedias.

It is a major point of the prophecies that of the punishments to come during the chastisements that *most of them will have been created by man.* Man is responsible for the suffering to come -- NOT GOD. The chastisement which God per se will send, will be that which ends the formal chastisement, the three days of darkness

[469] *The Last Times*, Rev. Benjamín Martín Sánchez, SSD, Pub: Opus Reginae Sanctissimi Rosarii, Zamora, Espania, 1971, p. 47. [The author has quoted this prophecy several times throughout the book - utilizing several different versions. That does not mean that it has been interpolated. It is simply a function of style in the various translations from its original 19th Century Italian.]

in which all of the enemies of Him and of the people of God will perish. God sends His part of the chastisement as a mercy to end it all -- to save his people additional suffering. The rest He allows to happen to bring man to his senses.

Anna Maria continues:

> "All the enemies of the Church, whether known or unknown, will perish over the whole earth during that universal darkness, with the exception of a few who will be converted. St. Peter and St. Paul will intervene in the election of a new Pope."[470]

All of the above quotes from Anna Maria are included in her Beatification document in Rome.

Prophets repeatedly state that during the three days that almost every enemy of the Church still alive will die. The vast majority of those who survive will be God-fearing people. The prophecy that a Holy Father will have to flee Rome at some time during a chastisement repeats itself over and over again in these prophecies.

> "France shall fall into a frightful anarchy. *The French shall have a desperate civil war in the course of which even old men will take up arms.* The political parties, having exhausted their blood and their rage without being able to arrive at any satisfactory settlement, shall agree at the last extremity to have recourse to the Holy See. Then the Pope shall send to France a special legate ... In *consequence of the information received, his Holiness himself shall nominate a most Christian king for the government of France.*[471]
>
> "After the three days of darkness, St. Peter and St. Paul, having come down from Heaven will preach in the whole world and designate a new Pope. A great light will flash from their bodies and will settle upon the cardinal who is to become Pope. Christianity, then, will spread throughout the world. *He is the Holy Pontiff, chosen by God to withstand the storm.* At the end, he will have the gift of miracles, and his name shall be praised over the whole earth.[472]

---

[470] Ibid.
[471] *Catholic Prophecy*, p. 45.
[472] Ibid.

> "Whole nations will come back to the Church and the face of the earth will be renewed. ***Russia, England, and China will come into the Church.***"[473]

Notice that Blessed Anna Maria, an Italian, is emphasizing the importance of foretold events in France. For some reason, events in France appear to be central to all of this. Also, Anna Maria is only one of several prophets to predict that "Russia, England, and China" will at some point rejoin the Church more or less en masse. *The prophesied events engage the whole world, both in its foretold tribulation, and also in its joyful restoration.*

14. Nursing Nun of Bellay (19th Century)

> "All these things shall come to pass once the wicked have succeeded in circulating large numbers of bad books."

There are a number of prophecies which refer to the vast number of "bad books" which will be in print. They repeat over and over again that these "bad books" will be in large part responsible for the disordered thinking of some future time. Many of them add that "common people" (who will in a later age be able to read) will be lead astray by them. It is difficult for us to remember that as recently as one hundred and fifty years ago, the majority of the "common people" were illiterate.

This was not, however, universal. Many Catholic dioceses had "cathedral schools" where children from average families who wished to do so could receive an education free of charge. But only a small percentage availed themselves of the opportunity. Most of them instead sought to learn a trade. In those days a trade often provided a better and more reliable source of income than formal education did.

The predicted "leading astray" will not be unique to the common people. The prophets who discuss this issue simply make a somewhat startled announcement that "common people" will at some time in the future be able to read. The prophecies include the upper class and many of the clergy and episcopate in this being "lead astray by bad books." The good news is that according to the prophecies, many of the bishops who were previously wracked

---

[473] Ibid.

by indecision will, in the end, stand firm with the Pope. Many of these good bishops, according to a number of prophecies, will also distinguish themselves with extremely heroic martyrdom.

15. Venerable Anna-Katerina Emmerick (18th Century)

Sister Emmerick was an Augustinian nun. She was born in Germany in 1774, spent a life of sufferings, and died in 1824 in her native country. She bore the stigmata of Our Lord and went through continual suffering for Him. She lived on the Blessed Eucharist alone for many years.[474]

> *April 12, 1820*. "I had another vision of the great tribulation."

> *October 22, 1822*. "I saw the battle also. The enemies were far more numerous, but the small army of the faithful cut down whole rows [of enemy soldiers]. During the battle, the Blessed Virgin stood on a hill, wearing a suit of armor. It was a terrible war. *At the end, only a few fighters for the just cause survived, but the victory was theirs*."

This is one of many prophecies which state that "the just" will be heavily outnumbered in a chastisement. These prophecies say that Our Lady will miraculously help the predominantly Christian forces. Ven. Anna continues,

> *July 26, 1820*. "I have a vision of *the holy Emperor Henry*. I saw him at night kneeling alone at the foot of the main altar in a great and beautiful church ... and I saw the Blessed Virgin coming down all alone. She laid on the Altar a red cloth covered with white linen. She placed a book inlaid with precious stones. She lit the candles and the perpetual lamp ... Then came the Saviour Himself clad in priestly vestments.

---

[474] Anna Katerina's "works" were transcribed in part by a volunteer secretary, who was not deemed by some Churchmen to be particularly reliable. That having been said, it must be noted that as mentioned in the next two pages, the author has in his possession some printed copies of her prophecies describing in some startling details what is probably a post-1967 Mass. This copy was printed over 80 years prior to the post Vatican II changes in the Mass. This kind of apparent prophetic gift is difficult to explain away with the fact that she had a questionable secretary -- because the prophesied event appears to have already come true.

> He was carrying the chalice and the veil. Two Angels were serving Him and two more were following ... His chasuble was a full and heavy mantle in which red and white could be seen in transparency, and gleaming with jewels ... Although there was no altar bell, the cruets were there. The wine was as red as blood, and there was also some water. ***The Mass was short. The Gospel of St. John was not read at the end.*** When the Mass had ended, Mary came up to Henry (the Emperor), and she extended her right hand towards him, saying that it was in recognition of his purity. Then, she urged him not to falter. Thereupon I saw an angel, and he touched the sinew of his hip, like Jacob. *He (Henry) was in great pain; and from that day on he walked with a limp...*"[475]

16. Sometimes Things Are *Not Necessarily* What They First Appear to Be

[Here we interrupt the prophecies of Sr. Emmerick for the following comments, which may at first seem to be of interest only to students of liturgical history. *But that is not the case at all* -- as should become obvious by the end of the commentary.]

Some commentaries on this prophecy of Sr. Emmerick's which have been written since 1967, state that her prophecy that "The Gospel of St. John was not read at the end" is *proof-positive* that she was referring to the Mass we have had since 1967. The following example is taken from only one of many such commentaries,

> "It is interesting to note, too, that St. John's Gospel "was not read at the end." *This new development was foreseen 140 years ago by Sr. Emmerick.*"[476]

That commentary, which was written in 1970, assumes that Sr. Emerick is referring to the Latin Rite Mass which has been said in most parishes since 1967. But that was not necessarily so, because

[475] *Catholic Prophecy*, Yves Dupont, Tan Books and Publishers, 1970, p. 62.
[476] Ibid.

there were legitimate exceptions to the reading of the "Last Gospel" prior to 1967.[477]

That having been said, assuming this prophecy/vision is genuine, the author does personally consider it to be *highly probable* (but not certain) that the Mass which Sr. Emmerick saw in her vision was *some* post 1967 Latin Rite Mass. And *if so*, how could anyone without the gift of prophecy have foreseen 140 years ahead of time that:

(1) Some day the Last Gospel would not regularly be read (as it was at the vast majority of Latin Rite Masses of her time), and,

---

477 In 1570, Pope Pius V published his Papal Bull *Quo Primum*, which was intended to regulate the Latin Rite Masses. One of its requirements was that the "Last Gospel" (alternately known as the "Gospel of St. John") must be read at the end of Mass. Pope Paul VI's *New Order of the Mass*, which was promulgated in 1967, removed that previous requirement. *Quo Primum* made exceptions for any demonstrable local, monastic, or diocesan tradition, or a tradition within a religious order, which was different from the requirements proposed by *Quo Primum*, which tradition had to be of at least 200 years duration prior to the issuance of that document. This was particularly apropos with the "Last Gospel," since the "Last Gospel" itself was a very late addition to the Latin Rite. It does not stem from early Roman liturgies.

"The first evidence of the Gospel of St. John at the end of the Mass--it is a question here primarily of a private Mass--is found in the *Ordinarium* of the Dominicans, which was fixed in 1256" *The Mass of the Roman Rite: Its Origins and Development* (*Missarum Sollemnia*), Rev. Joseph A. Jungmann, S.J., Prof. of Theology, University of Innsbruck, Benziger Brothers, Inc. Vol. 2, p. 448.

Observe that even this provision is only for Dominican private (not public) Masses. Even as late as 1558, the issue of the "Last Gospel" was not firm even in Rome itself.

"When in the year 1558, the first general chapter of the Society of Jesus (the Jesuits), convened to choose a successor to St. Ignatius, expressed the desire to make the rite of the Mass uniform within the order, the last Gospel was one of the points that still hung in the balance even in Rome itself." Ibid. p. 449.

In the light of this background it should be easier to understand the relevancy of some of the following historical facts. Jungman states in 1955, "the Carthusians have not yet taken the last Gospel into their rite even today, just as they have not inserted the last blessing." (Ibid.) There were many other "exceptions," wherein entire orders or dioceses availed themselves of the "tradition" exceptions to *Quo Primum*. e.g., the Ambrosian Liturgy (which is said in the entire Diocese of Milan, Italy) since it was of great antiquity, never adopted the rubrics of *Quo Primum*. Another example, while the Dominicans did have the "Last Gospel" in their Mass (since they were the primary promoters of it to begin with), they never did accept the norms of *Quo Primum*, but under the terms of that Papal Bull, retained their traditional Eucharistic Liturgy.

(2) the Mass would have been shortened (but she could also have been describing a "Quo Primum" "low" Mass), and,

(3) there would be no altar bells for the altar servers to ring on several occasions during the Mass (bell ringing which since 1969 has become an uncommon practice)?

In case someone wonders if someone later tampered with or manipulated this prophecy; *the author has seen copies of it which were physically printed over 100 years ago -- over 80 years before the changes in the Mass. There was no after-the-fact tampering with this prophecy -- its physical validity prior to the beginning of the 20th century is indisputable!*

> "*August to October 1820.* 'I see more martyrs, not now but in the future ... I saw the secret sect relentlessly undermining the great Church. *All over the world, good and devout people, especially the clergy, were harassed, oppressed, and put into prison.* I had the feeling that they would become martyrs one day.
>
> "'Then, I saw an apparition of the Mother of God, and she said that the tribulation would be very great.'
>
> "*October 1, 1820.* 'The Church is in great danger. We must pray so that the Pope may not leave Rome; countless evils would result if he did.'
>
> "*In those days, Faith will fall very low, and it will be preserved in some places only.*"[478]

If this prophecy sounds like it could not be for our time, one has a right to his opinions. But with legitimate polls clearly showing that as of the mid-1980's, eighty percent of the Catholics of child bearing years were practicing illicit methods of birth control; how could anyone believe that the faith is being maintained whole and integral in anything but "a few places only." Wouldn't any realist also know that things are currently getting worse -- not better.

---

[478] Ibid. p. 69.

> *"I see many excommunicated ecclesiastics who do not seem to be concerned about it, nor even aware of it.* Yet, they are excommunicated whenever they cooperate to (sic) enterprises, enter into associations, and embrace opinions on which an anathema has been cast. It can be seen thereby that God ratifies the decrees, orders, and interdictions issued by the Head of the Church, and that he keeps them in force even though men show no concern for them, reject them, or laugh them to scorn."[479]

Here again we see facets of our age described in exactitude. In the so-called Catholic academic community, Church law is to a great degree laughed to scorn. Recent attempts by Rome to establish Catholic order in American Catholic universities is publicly met with derision and ridicule in the name of "academic freedom." The thought that the Church has a right and duty to regulate her own is met with open challenges.

Anna Katerina continues:

> "Then, I saw in the distance great legions approaching. In the foreground I saw a man on a white horse. Prisoners were set free and joined them. All the enemies were pursued. Then, I saw that the Church was being promptly rebuilt, and she was more magnificent than ever before."[480]

A commentary: Given the chronology of the other events Katerina has previously foretold, the man on the white horse is most probably the Great Monarch. *This prophecy could easily be mystical in its reference to him being on a horse, But many other prophecies also say that he will subsequently lead his troops into battle on a horse.* One prophecy states he will mount his horse from the right side. That is highly unusual.

Most horsemen in most cultures have mounted their horses from the left side. The only major historic counter-example has been the American Indian horsemen. There are two reasons most cultures mount a horse from the left-hand side, (1) most people are right-handed. It is easier for someone who is right-handed to

[479] Ibid.
[480] Ibid. p. 63.

mount his horse from the left. (2) A right handed cavalryman wears a hand-held weapon such as a sword on his left side. When wearing a sword or other weapon on ones left side, it is almost impossible to mount a horse from the right.

The natural ease of mounting from the left became custom in most of the world through military usage. If a man were to have continuous pain in his left hip, it would be much easier to mount from the right side. Several prophecies state that this great prince, monarch, or king, will walk with a limp caused by pain in his hip. One of them even discloses the source of that pain.

17. War on Horseback?

The prophecies state that during this period, Europe will have been ravaged by general and civil wars for several years before the rise of the Great King. A future general leading his troops on horseback may seem ludicrous to us in the late 20th century -- unless we review some 20th century precedents.

Hitler's highly mechanized German Army invaded Russia during WW II. Two years later when that same army retreated back to Germany in defeat, much of their transportation was provided by commandeered Russian horses pulling German cars and trucks for which the Wehrmacht no longer had spare parts or fuel.

In much the same way the Spanish Civil War began as a mechanized conflict and ended utilizing much horsepower. In the 1980's, the Afghan guerrillas who depended almost exclusively upon horsepower for transportation fought the modern Russian Army to a standstill. This has now happened again in mountainous Chechnia. The Russian army managed to push the Chechnians out of their capital but could not subsequently control the countryside. The Chechnian's guerrillas are now dependent on horsepower.

Modern warfare is highly dependent upon intact supply lines and/or well maintained roads especially in rugged terrain, without which, warfare quickly becomes primitive. Even when both those elements are in place, a non-mechanized force, if brilliantly led, can often fight a modern army to a standstill. After an extended period of general and civil war, having a military commander on horseback during a future "chastisement" might not be unrealistic at all. Many military historians might even call it humanly *predictable*.

18. Venerable Isabel Canori-Mora (1774-1825)

Isabel prophesied:

> "All men shall rise one against the other, and they shall kill one another without pity. During this sanguinary conflict the avenging arm of God will strike the wicked, and in His mighty power He will punish their pride and presumption. *God will employ the powers of hell for the extermination of these impious and heretical persons who desire to overthrow the Church and destroy it to its very foundation* ... Innumerable legions of demons will overrun the earth, and shall execute the orders of Divine justice by causing terrible calamities and disasters; they will attack everything; they shall injure individual persons and entire families ... Nothing on earth shall be spared. God will allow the demons to strike with death those impious men, because they gave themselves up to the infernal powers, and have formed with them a pact against the Catholic Church."[481]

> "*Happy will be all true and good Catholics*! They shall experience the powerful protection of the Holy Apostles, St. Peter and Paul, who will watch over them lest they be injured ... These spirits shall plunder every place where God has been outraged, despised, and blasphemed; the edifices they profaned will be pulled down and destroyed, and nothing but ruins shall remain of them."[482]

Comment: It is interesting to note the reference to "impious heretics" attempting to destroy the Church. The irony is that according to this and many other prophecies, at God's command it will ultimately be completely stopped by the demons themselves. Ironically, it will be the demons themselves who stop the blasphemies, sacrileges, and heresies which they have tempted poor sinners to perform. *In the denouement of this evil age even the demons from Hell will serve the will of God.*

This is not a novel prophetic concept. In much the same way the Apocalypse tells us that during the Reign of Antichrist, God

481 *The Prophets and Our Times*, p. 190.
482 *Christian Trumpet*, 1873.

will issue a direct command or encouragement to the "Kings and Antichrist" to destroy the "New Babylon." Scripture even tells us that those whom God shall cause to destroy "New Babylon" will lament the loss of the city. In spite of their rebellion against God, they will nevertheless on occasion be the instruments of His will in destroying evil.

If one takes the above prophecies literally, without the solace of Faith in God it becomes almost overwhelmingly terrifying. But now comes the aftermath - which is wonderful. Isabel describes what happens after the above described conflagration:

> "Then a great light appeared upon the earth which was the sign of the reconciliation of God with man. The angels conducted before the throne of the prince of the Apostles the small flock that had remained faithful to Jesus Christ. These good and zealous Christians testified to him the most profound respect, praising God and thanking the Apostles for having delivered them from the common destruction, and for having protected the Church of Jesus Christ by not permitting her to be infected with the false maxims of the world."[483]

Lastly: from the context of this and other prophecies it is clear that Isabel is referring to Sts. Peter and Paul protecting Christians as regards their faith. There is no absolute guarantee that Christians will not suffer physically. After further discussion of the chastisement, she continues:

> "St. Peter then chose the new Pope. The Church was again organized; religious orders were reestablished; the private families of ordinary Christians, through their great fervor and zeal for the glory of God, became like the most exemplary religious communities. Such is the glorious triumph reserved for the Catholic Church; she shall be praised, honored, and esteemed by all men."[484]

Many other prophecies say that almost the whole world will be Catholic during an age of peace which is to come. That pattern

---

483 *The Prophets and Our Times*, p. 191.
484 Ibid.

repeats itself over and over again in the prophecies. Other prophecies confirm that St. Peter in some manner will be instrumental in the selection of a new Pope.

When the author first read the above prophecy, he frankly was not favorably impressed. Not yet having read almost identical prophecies from numerous canonized Saints, and knowing virtually nothing of the miracles and holy life of Isabel Canori Mora, he thought this prophecy was some kind of pathetic Catholic Triumphalist delusion. The author has been there. Like his peers, he is the product of a skeptical age. But upon learning of many other very specific prophecies of Isabel that did come true as predicted, the author was finally intellectually forced to reserve intellectual judgment on the matter.

In the opinion of the author, the above prophecies of Isabel are related to the three days of darkness and its aftermath.

Military leader in addition to Great Monarch

19. Bug De Milhaus (d. 1848)

There are numerous prophecies which lead one to believe that the "Great King" will have many allies in his struggle. There are prophecies about a Polish military leader who will also fight side by side with the Great King. You are about to read a prophecy about a great Spanish military leader of the future. From correlations of literally hundreds of such prophecies which would take many volumes for a systematic presentation of their contents, it appears that early in the conflict, the man who is later to emerge as the "Great King" is *one of many* Catholic leaders fighting for the Faith. Only later does the "Great King" develop into their central commander.

Many prophecies suggest that Spain may become some kind of safe haven for Western European Catholics fleeing the fighting during the chastisement. Since these Spanish prophecies appear to be somewhat central to the outcome of European events, we will look briefly at them. The author has unfortunately never seen an original manuscript of the following prophecy, so it is simply described as it appears in Fr. Sanchez' book, *The Last Times*.

Bug de Milhas was born about the middle of the 18th century and died in 1848 when he was nearly one hundred years old. Because of his holy life he was venerated throughout the whole region of the Pyrenees, where he lived in the little village of Cominges. He made many predictions which have been fulfilled. He made the following prophecy about a future Battle of the Pyrenees.

Bug de Milhas predicts:

> "A war, in Europe, is announced by name and their prophecies will be fulfilled. That war will ravage all places. Pestilence and many other plagues will scatter terror every where. The fanaticism of false beliefs and of intolerant parties will fill many countries with victims. Iberia (Spain and Portugal) will be the asylum of all its refugees. Catholics fleeing from the fury of their enemies will seek refuge in Spain.
>
> "Then the region of the river Tajo (Spain and Portugal) will produce a valiant warrior similar to the Cid and he will be as religious as Ferdinand III who, planting the standard of the faith, will unite around himself innumerable armies. With his army he will go out to meet a formidable giant who, with his ferocious soldiers, will advance towards the conquest of the Peninsula.
>
> "The Pyrenees will witness the cruelest combat ever seen throughout the centuries. The battle will last three days. In vain, the fearsome giant will try to encourage his own to continue the fight, but the finger of God will already show him the end of his reign and his army will fall under the sword of the new Cid.
>
> "Then the victorious army, protected by their Supreme Creator, will cross provinces and seas and will carry the standard of the Cross even to the banks of the river Neva (the heart of Russia). The Catholic religion will triumph everywhere."[485]

There are a multitude of prophecies which say that faithful Christians will assemble their forces to meet invading Antichristian forces. Most of the prophecies clearly identify the Antichristian

[485] *The Last Times*, p. 62.

forces as those of Russia (notice the Russian reference immediately above) and Prussia. Many skeptics about prophecies claim that this and other prophecies are simply the product of overactive imaginations on the part of Catholic Triumphalists. The author submits rather, that the prophecies are too geographically broad in origin, come from too many different centuries and cultures, and too many of them come from canonized Saints and even Popes for that thesis to be credible to a conscientious secular scholar, let alone a serious believing Catholic.

20. Pope Pius IX (19th Century)

He was one of the Popes who was a confidant of Blessed Anna Maria Taigi mentioned elsewhere in this book. He was also the man cured of epilepsy by Isabel Canori Mora. Pius IX said:

> "There will be a great prodigy which will fill the world with awe. But this prodigy will be preceded by the triumph of ***a revolution during which the Church will go through ordeals that are beyond description.***"

Pius IX had already seen plenty of horrid revolutions. He had already been made a virtual prisoner in the Vatican. The Papal States had recently been taken from the Church leaving her almost destitute. In general, the position of the Church has gradually (at least since the time of Pius IX) gotten better and better versus revolutionaries with the single exception of behind the Iron Curtain. For him to say that a triumphant revolution would put the Church through ordeals "that are almost beyond description" had to be saying quite a lot for Pius IX. Therefore, it seems highly logical that this period of trial he spoke of is still ahead of us.

21. Melanie Calvat (The Seeress of LaSalette, 19th Century)

> "After a frightful war a Great king will arise and his reign will be marked by a wonderful peace and a great religious revival."

Again, if this prophecy comes to pass, it has to be for the future. Why? Because there has been no Great King accompanied by a great religious revival since the mid-1800's.

22. St. Don Bosco (19th Century)

Now we come to the prophecies of St. Don Bosco. He was a contemporary and confidant of Pope Pius IX whom we have just quoted. Founder of the Salesian Order, he was renowned for his miracles. He died in 1888. His order specialized in education of poor boys. He was famous amongst his students and members of his order for his prophetic dreams later coming true in minute detail. Through his humility he constantly referred to them as his "distractions," rather than attribute to himself this Divine favor.

As one interesting note the reader should be aware of the following. In one of his "dreams" or visions, he foresaw the work of his order which would in the future be accomplished in South America. He describes the course of a mystic journey in which he even got to "see" the physical locations of the Salesian order in many locations in South America. He describes the territory as if he is looking down on it from above. It sounds like the descriptions of a commercial airline captain describing the territory over which he is flying. In this journey (dream), St. Don Bosco describes geographical details which were actually unknown until the invention of modern aircraft and aerial mapping techniques were developed. One can read all of this in *Dreams, Visions & Prophecies of Don Bosco*, edited by Rev. Eugene M. Brown, Don Bosco Publications. This book is still in print. It makes fascinating reading.

In one of his prophetic dreams he saw the following which was attested to by the clerics John Boggero, Secundus Merlone, and Dominic Ruffino, and a layman, Caesar Chiala, who wrote down this dream. We still have their individual manuscripts which agree with each other in almost every detail.

> "The vast expanse of water is covered with a formidable array of ships in battle formation, prows fitted with sharp, spear like beaks capable of breaking through any defense. All are heavily armed with cannons, incendiary bombs, and firearms of all sorts -- even books -- and are heading toward one stately ship, mightier than them all. As they close in, they try to ram it, set it afire, and cripple it as much as possible.

"This stately vessel is shielded by a flotilla escort. Winds and waves are with the enemy. In the midst of this endless sea, two solid columns, a short distance apart, soar high into the sky: one is surmounted by a statue of the Immaculate Virgin at whose feet a large inscription reads: Help of Christians; the other, far loftier and sturdier, supports a Host of proportionate size and bears beneath it the inscription Salvation of believers.

"Standing at the helm, the Pope strains every muscle to steer his ship between the two columns from whose summits hang many anchors and strong hooks linked to chains."

"The entire enemy fleet closes in to intercept and sink the flagship at all costs. *They bombard it with everything they have: books and pamphlets, incendiary bombs, firearms, cannons.* At times a formidable ram splinters a gaping hole into its hull, but, immediately, a breeze from the two columns instantly seals the gash.

"Suddenly the Pope falls, seriously wounded. He is instantly helped up but, *struck down a second time, dies. A shout of victory rises from the enemy and wild rejoicing sweeps their ships. But no sooner is the Pope dead than another takes his place.* The captains of the auxiliary ships elected him so quickly that the news of the Pope's death coincides with that of his successor's election. The enemy's self-assurance wanes.

"Breaking through all resistance, the new Pope steers his ship safely between the two columns and moors it to the two columns; first, to the one surmounted by the Host, and then to the other, topped by the statue of the Virgin. At this point, something unexpected happens. The enemy ships panic and disperse, colliding with and scuttling each other."

The above was quoted from *Dreams, Visions & Prophecies of Don Bosco*, edited by Rev. Eugene M. Brown, Don Bosco Publications. This prophecy is highly mystical in approach and has puzzled some Catholics who assumed that the stricken pope spoken of is John Paul II. But the author does not think we can be sure from the context of this prophecy that John Paul is the stricken Pope prophesied by Don Bosco.

But *if* we assume for the purposes of argument that he is, then, here is a possible explanation. John Paul was shot before. Possibly he is the Pope who flees Rome in the company of several other cardinals and goes into hiding in a foreign country. Other prophecies say that Rome will be without a Pope for some time during the chastisement. *Some specifically state that the period will be 25 months.*

If this applies to the reign of John Paul, then he would subsequently be found and brutally murdered. Other prophecies say that when the Pope is murdered that the enemies of the Church will say to the good Catholics, "Your Pope is dead, what are you going to do now?" Possibly, it is at that juncture that the surviving cardinals almost immediately elect his successor. The prophecies are not specific. They are almost all part of "conditional" prophecies. Therefore, they will only become clear if the conditional prophecy comes to pass.

It is possible that Don Bosco's prophecy here speaks of another time in the future. But the prophecies speak of an age of peace beginning shortly after the murder of the exiled Pope. There may be more than one more major period of peace to come between now and the end of the world, but the prophecies seem to indicate otherwise.

23. Pope St. Pius X (20th Century)

Famous for his encyclicals against the modernists and their heresy, he once lamented that he thought he was the only man in the world of his time that understood how great were the dangers to the Church in the 20th century.

> *"I saw one of my successors taking to flight over the bodies of his brethren.* He will take refuge in disguise somewhere; and after a short retirement he will die a cruel death. **The present wickedness of the world *is only the beginning* of the sorrows which must take place before the end of the world."**[486]

[486] *Catholic Prophecy*, p. 22.

Pope St. Pius X died in 1914. In this case we are hearing a canonized Pope say that he saw in a vision one of his successors taking flight from Rome. No Pope has had to take flight from Rome since that time. This is another one of those cases where we either believe him and that his prophecy was genuine or we don't.

24. Fatima 1917 (20th Century)

The prophecy of a great chastisement was made at Fatima in 1917 in a series of locutions from Our Lady to the three children of Fatima. A fair number of details on this great event appear in this book's Introduction. As a brief reminder: In 1917, the Blessed Virgin appeared at Fatima, Portugal, to three young shepherds, *Lucia*, Francisco and Jacinta, ranging in age from ten to seven years. Seventy-thousand people witnessed the predicted miracle of the Sun.

Lucia is the only one of the three seers still alive. A few years after the miracles at Fatima, Lucy became first a Dorothean, and then a Descalced Carmelite nun. She presently lives in a Carmelite convent in Coimbra, north of Fatima, Portugal.

The Message, or secret of Fatima, has three parts. The first was the vision of hell. Immediately after that vision of Hell, Lucia tells us that the following occurred:

> "As if to ask for help, we raised our eyes to Our Lady, who told us, with kindness and sadness: '*You have seen hell where the souls of poor sinners go. To save them, God wishes to establish on earth the devotion to My Immaculate Heart. If people do what I tell you many souls will be saved and there will be peace.*'
>
> "But if it is not done and if the world does not cease offending God, Divine Justice will manifest itself with newer and even greater punishments. Russia will scatter her errors throughout the world, provoking wars and persecutions of the Church. The good will be martyred, the Holy Father will have much of suffer, and various nations will be destroyed..."

The Virgin then asked them to practice some acts of piety, to do much penance and make reparation, to pray so men would amend their lives and not offend Our Lord with their sins; she asked them to pray the rosary every day. The child, Jacinta, later said something she repeated on her death-bed:

> "If men will repent, God will pardon them, but if they do not amend their lives, there will come upon the earth the most terrible chastisement ever known."

C. THE PREDICTED GREAT SIGN

Another one of the prophecies made at Fatima in 1917 was that after having asked for inner conversions of the Catholics in the World and their saying the daily Rosary, Mary said:

> "If people do what I ask, many souls will be saved and there will be peace. The war (1st World War) is going to end. But *if people do not stop offending God*, another even worse, will begin in the reign of Pius XI.
>
> "When you see a night illuminated by an unknown light, know that it is the great sign that God will give you that *He is going to punish the world by means of war, hunger and persecution of the Church and of the Holy Father.*
>
> "To prevent it, I shall come to ask for the *Consecration of Russia* to my Immaculate Heart and the Communion of reparation on the first Saturdays. If people attend to my requests, Russia will be converted and the world will have peace."

On the evening of January 25, 1938, Sister Lucia (and the whole of Europe) saw the unknown light which Our Lady had predicted. Several months later, Hitler's invasion of Austria, which began his expansions/invasions, led to war in Europe. A short time later, Our Lord told Sister Lucia (the lone survivor of the three children of Fatima):

> "Ask, ask again insistently for the promulgation of reparation in honor of the Immaculate Heart of Mary on the First Saturdays. THE TIME IS COMING WHEN THE RIGOR OF MY JUSTICE WILL PUNISH THE CRIMES OF DIFFERENT NATIONS. SOME OF THEM WILL BE ANNIHILATED.

IN THE END THE SEVERITY OF MY JUSTICE WILL FALL MOST SEVERELY ON THOSE WHO SEEK TO DESTROY MY REIGN IN SOULS."

Comment: At that time, the few Catholics who knew the Fatima prophecies almost universally along with Sister Lucia accepted the "glow" in the sky as the foretold portent of war. And they were right. On the other hand, the scientific community attempted to explain away the "red glow" as the "northern lights," the Aurora Borealis. Any reader who has seen the northern lights knows that they are pale to pastel in hue and shade. They are never blood red, not ever.

Nine years before that in 1929, Our Lady had asked for the collegial consecration of Russia to Her Immaculate Heart, promising that it would be a sign of Russia's conversion. But when the consecration was not made at that time, Our Lord told Sr. Lucia that it would eventually be accomplished, but: "It will be too late; Russia will already have spread her errors throughout the world."[487]

After the collegial consecration made by the Pope in 1984, Lucia said: "The consecration will have an effect, but it is too late."

D. THE QUESTION OF HELL!

This section began with a discussion of Fatima. The entire expressed motive entailed in the revelations at Fatima turned around one central theme. Yes, there was the cause to avert war, epidemics, hunger , i.e., temporal suffering. **But the central core of the Fatima revelations and requests all centered around Our Lady's expressed desire to save souls, to keep them from going to Hell.** God does love us! The visions and prophecies related to the three children began with a "vision" of the reality of, "Hell, where poor sinners go."

Many in today's culture have a difficult time dealing with the concept and subject of Hell. But their difficulty is really a moot point from a Catholic perspective. That there is such a place as Hell, and that those who die unrepentant of grave (mortal) sin go

[487] Martin's edition of Lucia's Memoirs, Porto, 1973, Page 465. (Quoted from Akita, p. 63.)

there, is a defined teaching of the Church! The Church has always taught that from the time of the Apostles till now. In other words, a Catholic *must* believe that! The existence of Hell is no modern invention, nor is it an old-fashioned idea. It is a timeless truth. The Holy Father recently reiterated this point in his book, *Crossing the Threshold of Hope*, when he said,

> "The problem of hell has always disturbed great thinkers in the Church, beginning with Origen and continuing in our time with Mikhail Bulgakov and Hans Urs von Balthasar. In point of fact, the ancient councils rejected the theory of the *"final apocatastasis,"* according to which the world would be regenerated after destruction, and every creature would be saved, a theory which indirectly abolished hell. ... *And yet, the words of Christ are unequivocal.* In Mathew's Gospel He speaks clearly of those who will go to eternal punishment,"[488] (Emphasis the author's)

1. The Church Officially Teaches the Existence of Hell

The new *Catechism of The Catholic Church* clearly teaches "the existence of Hell and its eternity" and that souls "who die in a state of mortal sin" go there "Immediately after death."[489] This is nothing new in the Church for, "The Church has repeatedly defined this truth, e.g., in the profession of faith made in the following Ecumenical Councils; Second Council of Lyons (Denz., n.464) and in the Decree of Union in the Council of Florence (Denz., n 693) 'the souls of those who depart in mortal sin, ... go down immediately into hell,'."[490]

---

[488] *Crossing the Threshold of Hope*, Alfred A. Knopf, New York, 1994. Origin, an early Christian Writer of the 3rd century taught that there would be a *"final apocatastasis,"* a reconciling of all those who had "temporarily" gone to Hell. And that at this *"final apocatastasis,"* that all the souls would be reconciled with God and then live in happiness with Him for Eternity. This teaching of Origen was condemned by the 5th through 7th General Councils of the Church as a heresy.

[489] *Catechism of the Catholic Church*, St. Paul Books & Media, 1994, P. 270, #1035 & #1051.

[490] *Catholic Encyclopedia*, 1913 Edition, Vol. 7, p 208.

So, why is it that we so seldom hear of the subject of Hell -- especially from the pulpit? Has our materialism and fun-seeking become so all-pervasive and apparent that our priests are afraid to mention this unpleasant possibility to us? Do the majority of our priests themselves believe in the existence of Hell; that some people actually go there for eternity? Has one form or another of Origen's heretical thesis of the "final apocatastasis" subtly wormed its way back into the bosom of the Church? Or are we engaging a watered down variation of "Origenism," which thinks it is almost impossible for anyone to commit a mortal sin? That is *not* the message of Fatima!

At Fatima, Our Lady said,

> "You have seen hell where the souls of poor sinners go. To save them, God wishes to establish on earth the devotion to My Immaculate Heart. If people do what I tell you *many souls will be saved* and there will be peace."

2. The Church Officially Teaches That Some Souls Actually Go to Hell for Eternity

Our Lady here clearly states that *many souls* are in jeopardy. The Church has never formally defined a "percentage" of people who go either to Heaven or to Hell. This remains within the area of speculative theology. In other words, as long as someone admits:

(1) the existence of Hell, and
(2) that some souls (plural) do go there for eternity;

then they are free to "speculate" as to a "percentage" which go to either Heaven or Hell. But no one may challenge their Catholicity, their good standing in the Church, no matter what percentage they come up with in said speculation -- as long as it is a percentage expressing a plurality of form. The concept of a plural form is necessitated by the fact that *the official Church teaching relates this doctrine in the plural.*

As we know, some of the early Fathers of the Church took a patently pessimistic view on the percentage that go to Heaven. But if there is an extreme today, it would have to be that of an almost euphoric optimism which sometimes expresses itself in the belief that hardly anyone goes to Hell. Despite some current highly optimistic "percentage" speculations (even from amongst the ranks of unquestionably Catholic theologians) the Fatima message from Heaven (and the messages of many canonized Saints also quoted in this book) seem to confirm with the Fathers and Doctors of the Church their *teaching* that:

(1) there is a Hell,
(2) a plural number do go there, for eternity,
(3) their *opinions* that, it is not a mere handful of souls that do so.[491]

3. The Companion Question of Purgatory

This entire euphoric attitude regarding private eschatology (the situation of specific departed souls) goes beyond the current practical assumption that everyone (or almost everyone) goes immediately to Heaven. Let us for arguments sake, assume for a moment the position of Origen. He may falsely have assumed a "final apocatastasis," the belief that everyone is eventually saved. But at least he never assumed that everyone went immediately to heaven. At least he taught the traditional Christian belief that, for many departed souls, there is a temporary cleansing before one sees the Beatific Vision.

What happens at the average Catholic funeral today? Do people not talk as if it is assumed that the deceased is already living in perfect bliss with God? When is the last time the reader heard as part of a homily at a funeral, or at a Sunday Mass, a request to pray for the "suffering souls in Purgatory"? Has the Church changed Her belief in Purgatory, or is it just that pastors aren't teaching this doctrine any more?

The answer to that question is very straight forward. Belief in Purgatory is not just a traditional teaching. This may come as a shock to some readers, but, a Catholic must believe in Purgatory. It

---

[491] (As a matter fact, one would have to admit that the heavy majority of the opinions of the Fathers, [with Origen and a few other as exceptions] is that a very large number of souls choose the world to the point of rejecting God and therefore choose an eternal Hell.)

is a defined Dogma of the Church. At root the doctrine goes back in its seminal form to the infancy of the Church, and in that form is to be found in both Tradition and Scripture. The Council of Florence spoke of the doctrine of Purgatory. It was later declared a Dogma absolutely binding in Faith in 1563. The Council of Trent formally declared in part:

> "Since the Catholic Church, instructed by the Holy Ghost, has, following the sacred writings [Scripture] and the ancient tradition of the Fathers, taught in sacred councils, and very recently in this ecumenical synod **that there is a Purgatory,** and that the souls there detained are aided by the suffrages of the faithful, and chiefly by the acceptable sacrifice of the altar; the council commands the bishops that they strive diligently to the end that the sound doctrine of purgatory, transmitted by the Fathers and the sacred councils, be believed and maintained by the faithful of Christ, and everywhere taught and preached."[492]

This solemn "Decree Concerning Purgatory" was passed by the Fathers at Trent on Dec. 4, 1563. It was subsequently contemporaneously promulgated by Pope Pius IV (This was the last session held under Pius IV). It is not optional for a "Catholic" to believe in Purgatory. It is de fide.

Even in many parishes wherein the pastor does not orally specifically teach this doctrine, the practice of the Church does. e.g., The entire reason for the pre-funeral Rosary is to aid "the departed soul." If that soul were already in Heaven, why would we bother to pray for him or her? We pray for him or her because the traditional teaching of the Church is that the vast majority of us have some cleansing yet to perform after we die before we can actually enjoy the Beatific Vision, before we can come face to face with Our Lord and God.

Prayer for the departed (except the case of martyrs) is a practice which can be demonstrated to go back to the infant Church. Again, there is no point in praying for someone who is already in Heaven. In the only cases where we absolutely know that the soul is already

[492] *Canons and Decrees of the Council of Trent*, original Latin text with English translation, Rev. H.J. Schroeder, O.P., B. Herder Book Co., 1941. p. 214.

in heaven (a canonized saint) the shoe is on the other foot and we ask her or him to pray for us.

There are those who will tell you that the Church used to believe in Purgatory, but "changed" its doctrine on Purgatory at Vatican II.[493] On the contrary, the Council Fathers at Vatican II specifically reaffirmed the dogmatic teaching of Trent. They retaught as a dogma of faith a place of purgation or purification, which for some, must occur prior to the Glory of Heaven. In Vatican II's ***Dogmatic** Constitution On The Church,* the Council Fathers describe the current states of various souls until Christ comes in His glory at the Parousia,

> "When the Lord will come in glory, and all his angels with him (cf. Mt. 25:31), death will be no more and all things will be subject to him (Cf. 1 Cor. 15:26-27). But at the present time some of his disciples are pilgrims on earth. **Others have died and are being purified,** while still others are in glory, contemplating "in full light, God himself triune and one, exactly as he is."[494]

In this way the Fathers at Vatican II reconfirm the constant Catholic teaching on Purgatory ("Others have died and are being purified"), which the Council of Trent declared as a Dogma of the Church. The 1994, *Catechism of the Catholic Church,* teaches about Purgatory,

III. "THE FINAL PURIFICATION, OR PURGATORY"

> "All who die in God's Grace and friendship, but still imperfectly purified, are indeed assured of their eternal salvation; but after death they undergo purification, so as to achieve the holiness necessary to enter the joy of heaven.

---

493 That type of a statement is a contradiction in terms. By definition a Dogma can neither change nor be changed by anyone. It is a guarantee of its absolute truth. That is why a Catholic is absolutely bound in conscience to believe and fully accept a dogmatic teaching. Most people who make such a statement about Vatican II having changed the teaching on Purgatory simply do not know the history of their Faith well enough to know that the Council of Trent defined the doctrine of Purgatory as a Dogma.

494 *Vatican Council II, The Concilior and Post Concilior Documents, Vol 1.* Flannery, New Revised Edition, 1992. Dogmatic Constitution On The Church, Lumen Gentium, Chapter 7, The Pilgrim Church, p. 409.

"The Church gives the name *Purgatory* to this final purification of the elect, which is entirely different from the punishment of the damned."[495]

4. Message of Heede (20th Century)

The diocesan bulletin of Onasbruch, Germany, approved the supernatural character of the events of Heede. The following message can be found in "Charles de Actualidad," S. A. R. Edit. Ersa Madrid, 1195, with the Imprimatur of Dr. Garcia Lahiguera, Bishop.

In 1937, in the village of Heede, in the Diocese of Onasbruch, Germany, Our Lady began appearing to four little girls, whose names are: Anna Schulte, Greta and Maria Gauseforth and Susanna Bruns. According to the seers, the apparitions began the 1st of November, 1937 and terminated on November 3rd, 1940. The children reported that Our Lady said to them:

> "The world will have to drink the dregs of the chalice of divine wrath for their innumerable sins through which they have wounded the Sacred Heart of Jesus." [Then She admonished them]: "Pray ... pray much, especially for the conversion of sinners."[496]

In 1945, once again, the four little girls began to speak of new apparitions, but with a difference, this time it was Jesus Christ Himself Who spoke.

Therefore, the Bishop of Onasbruch sent two priests to Heede to investigate, priests who were ill-disposed towards them. But their report was favorable. *The parish pastor of Heede says as follows*:

> "We possess unequivocal and irrefutable evidence about the truth of these apparitions of Jesus Christ. The pastor and the chaplain who have made the investigation are fully convinced of the verity of these apparitions despite their notorious and systematic opposition to the revelations, despite their incredulity and distrust towards the events."[497]

---

495 *Catechism of the Catholic Church*, P. 268, #1030 & #1031

496 *The Last Times*, p. 37.

497 Ibid. p. 38.

The four children reported the following as the message Our Lord gave to them.

> "Humanity has not heeded My Blessed Mother, who appeared in Fatima, to exhort everyone to penitence. Now, I have come, in this last hour, to admonish the world. The times are grave. Men should do penance for their sins .... I am near. The earth will tremble and will suffer. It will be terrible. A minor judgment. ***For those who are not in a state of grace it will be frightful.*** The angels of My justice are now scattered all over the world. Men do not listen to My calls. They close their ears, resist My graces and refuse My mercy, My love and My merits. They will agonize in the blindness of their faults. Hatred and greed fills the hearts of men. All this is the work of Satan. The world sleeps in a dense darkness.
>
> This generation deserves to be annihilated, but I desire to show Myself as merciful. Great and terrible things are being prepared. *That which is about to happen will be terrible, like nothing ever since the beginning of the world.*"[498]

A CONSTANT PATTERN

The constant pattern of these prophecies repeats itself over and over. The basic message is that if men do not repent, the most terrible chastisement the world has ever known is going to come down on mankind's collective head. The second part of the pattern is that it is a message of hope and consolation for those who are conformed to God's will. As always, the words of Our Lord are, **"BE NOT AFRAID!"** The message of Heede continues.

> *"All those who have suffered, in these last times, are My martyrs and they prepare the newly converted of My Church.* That which will shortly happen, will greatly surpass everything that has ever happened until now. The Mother of God and the angels will intervene. **Hell will believe that victory is theirs, but I will seize it from them.** Many blaspheme Me and, because of this, I shall allow all kinds of misfortunes to rain upon the earth for, through this, many will be saved.

[498] Ibid. p. 38&39.

Blessed are those who suffer everything in reparation for those who offend Me.

"My beloved children the hour is near. Pray incessantly and you will not be confounded. I unite My elect. They will come together, at the same time, from all parts of the world and they will glorify Me. I come. Blessed are those who will be prepared. Blessed are those who hear Me."[499]

The prophecies all tell the same story. Only those who are hardened or desensitized to the obvious evil surrounding us find it ridiculous or hard to believe. And the good have nothing to fear.

5. Sister Elena Aiello (20th Century)

As stated earlier, Sr. Elena Aiello was founder of the Calabrians, an Italian order of nuns. Like most Stigmatics, she would suffer terribly and experience stark locutions on Good Friday. On that day in 1954 (April 16th), she received the following communication from Our Lord:

"The world is flooded by a deluge of corruption. The governments, of the people, have arisen as demons in human flesh and even though they speak of peace, they prepare for war with devastating weapons that can annihilate whole peoples and nations."[500]

"So ungrateful have they become towards My Sacred Heart and abusing My graces they have converted the world into a scene of crimes. Innumerable scandals carry souls to their ruin, especially the souls of the youth. They have given themselves, without restraint, to the pleasures of the world which have degenerated into perversions.

"The bad example of the parents produces, within the families, scandals and infidelities, instead of the practices of virtue and of prayer. The home, source of faith and holiness is stained and destroyed.

---

[499] Ibid. p. 39.
[500] *The Last Times*, p. 39.

> "The willfulness of men does not change and they stubbornly continue in their sins. The punishments and afflictions, God sends to make them become reasonable, are severe, but men are enraged as if they were wounded beasts, and harden their hearts against the grace of God.
>
> "The world no longer merits pardon, but deserves fire, destruction and death. *There must be much penance and prayers, by the faithful, to mitigate the deserved chastisement which is now detained by the intervention of My dear Mother,* who is Mother of all men. Near at hand is the scourge that will cleanse the earth of evil! Divine Justice clamours for satisfaction for the many offenses and evils which cover the earth. No more can be tolerated. Obstinate men, hardened in their faults, do not turn to God.
>
> "*The people do not subject themselves to the Church and despise the priests because there are so many among them who are the cause of scandals.*"[501]

As will be stated elsewhere in the book, the above is a vicious circle. Over and over again, Our Lord and Our Lady plead with us for prayers for Bishops, priests and religious. If not all of the clergy are what they might be, how much of that is the fault of laymen who have failed to pray for them as much as they might?

The following is a message from Our Lady to Sr. Aiello on the same date:

> "Listen well to what I tell you and announce it to everyone. My heart is saddened by the many afflictions which threaten the world. The justice of our Heavenly Father is gravely offended.
>
> "Men continue to live willfully in their sins. The wrath of God is near at hand. *The world will be visited by great misfortunes, by bloody revolutions, by terrible hurricanes and floods of rivers and seas.*
>
> "Raise your voice until the priests of God heed My messages and advise men that the time is near and if they do not convert and return to God through prayers and sacrifices, the world will be involved in a new war. The dictators,

---

[501] Ibid. p. 40.

> of the world, infernal creatures, will destroy the churches, profane the Holy Eucharist and destroy the most cherished and holy things. In that new pitiless war, much that men have constructed will be destroyed.
>
> "*Clouds with lightning rays of fire and a tempest of fire will pass over the whole world and the punishment will be the most terrible ever known in the history of mankind. It will last 70 hours.* The wicked will be crushed and eliminated. Many will be lost because they stubbornly remained in their sins. Then they will feel the force of light over darkness. *The hours of darkness are near... some nations will be purified while others will disappear entirely.*"

Immediately above are the previously quoted words of Our Lady to Sr. Aiello about the three days of darkness (70 hours). They are quoted here again in full so that the reader may see them in their full context. And again, I do not think that the clouds with lightning rays of fire refer to nuclear war. Many other prophecies about the three days of darkness refer to clouds so thick that it will be pitch black. Observe that here again we hear a prophecy repeating what we read from Fatima, prediction of the disappearance of some entire nations if there is no repentance.

> "I am bending over the world and detain the justice of God, otherwise, these things would have already happened. Prayer and sacrifices are needed. Men must return to God and to My Immaculate Heart, Mediatrix for men, then, at least, part of the world will be saved.
>
> "Speak out loudly. Propagate these words everywhere as a true echo of My voice. Make them known because it will help to save many souls and impede much destruction of the Church and the world."[502]

With the exception of her prophesy about the three days of darkness and the spiritual state of men and the Church, Sister Elena

[502] *The Last Times*, pp. 40&41. This entire message was reproduced in the magazine, "Heraldo de la Preciosa Sangre de Nuestro Senor," on Nov. 1957. It was, also, published in "Fatima ... 1960?" by Paul Ellis, with the Imprimatur of the Bishop of Cadiz-Cueta in 1959.

so far has not gone into specific details about secular affairs. But now, we will delve into them. Sister Elena describes events which will begin the chastisement.

> "*Russia will march upon all the nations of Europe*, particularly Italy, and will raise her flag over the dome of St. Peter's. Italy will be severely tried by a great revolution and Rome will be purified in blood for its many sins, especially those of impurity. The flock is about to be dispersed and the Pope will suffer greatly."

If this quote sounds familiar in tone, that is probably due to the fact that it is almost identical to one of those of Bl. Anna Maria Taigi and many other prophecies. Some commentators think some of Anna Maria's prophecies about turmoil in Italy have already been fulfilled. But Sr. Elena's 1959 prophecies definitely have not yet occurred. Russia has not marched upon "all the nations of Europe" nor raised her flag "over the dome of St. Peter's. Nor has Italy gone through a great revolution.

Likewise, her prophecy of *"Clouds with lightning rays of fire and a tempest of fire will pass over the whole world and the punishment will be the most terrible ever known in the history of mankind. It will last 70 hours."* This speaks of the three days of darkness which has not occurred. Sr. Elenas's prophecies give us somewhat of a schema or chronology for a conditional chastisement.

6. A Message of Lucia of Fatima

We read earlier of the vision of Hell which the three young children, Jacinta, Francisco, and Lucia received from Our Lady in 1917 at the Cova da Iria near Fatima, Portugal. What many have not heard is the following which was reported in 1961.

> **Note:** The following was given to Father Augustin Fuentes who was, at the time, the postulator of the Cause of Beatification of the two little seers of Fatima, Francisco and Jacinta.

"I bring you a message of extreme urgency: The Holy Father has permitted me to visit Lucia.

"She received me sadly, she was very thin and quite afflicted. Upon seeing me she said: 'Father, our Lady is very unhappy because they have not taken Her message of 1917 seriously. Neither the good nor the bad have paid any attention to it. *The good continue their way without preoccupying themselves with it, they do not heed Her celestial requests.* The bad walk through life swollen with perdition, not taking into account the punishment that threatens them. *Believe me, Father, God will chastise the world very soon.* Think, Father, about all the souls who will fall into *hell*. This will happen because no one prays, because they do not do penance.

'All this is the reason why the Blessed Virgin is sad. Father, tell everyone that our Lady has, frequently, announced to me that *many nations will disappear off the face of the earth.* ***Russia is the scourge chosen by God to punish mankind,*** if we, through prayer and the sacraments, do not obtain the grace of their conversion. Tell them, Father, tell them that the devil has begun a decisive battle against our Lady, because *what most afflicts the Immaculate Heart of Mary and the Sacred Heart of Jesus is the fall of the souls of religious and priests.*

'The devil knows that when religious and priests fail in their beautiful vocations they carry along with them many souls into *hell*.'"[503]

E. TWO OBSERVATIONS: (1) ON RUSSIA, (2) ON HELL

1. Communism, "A rose by any other name, is still a rose"

The message immediately above came from Lucy in 1961. In that message she speaks repeatedly of souls falling into hell. We

---

[502] Taken from the "Messagero del Cuore di Maria" No. 8-9 August-September, 1961, Rome, Italy. Referenced from p. 135 of *The Last Times*, Rev. Father, Benjamin Martin Sanches,, Opus Reginae Sacratissimi Rosarii, Universidad de Salamanca, Espania., 1972.

have also read the prophecy of a Russian invasion of Western Europe (if people do not repent) which comes from Sr. Elena Aiello two years previous in 1959. You have read the 19th century prophecy by Brother Aachen foretelling exactly the same thing, tying in (as many of the prophecies do) the Prussians (East Germans?) with the Russians in an invasion of Western Europe.

Does a "Russian invasion" seem no longer possible as of this writing in 1996? Does it seem that since the fall of the Berlin Wall and the "demise" of the Soviet Union, Communism is no longer a problem? It would probably behoove anyone under that impression to read some recent intelligence briefings on NATO's and the U.S. Military's concern over the remaining reality of a potential future threat to peace from that quarter. Additionally, despite what the reader may have heard, the Communist Party is far from dead in the former Soviet Union. The local Communist Party candidates (most often disguised as "Socialists") have been winning many local elections in areas of the former Soviet Union -- including Russia.

Men reported by the press to be "former" Communists have won a large percentage of elections not only in Russia, but in most of the former satellite nations of Russia in its Soviet Union. Many interviewees on network current events TV shows, as well as syndicated columnists sometimes explain this away as simply a result of the fact that the "former" Communists are the only ones who have contacts and know how to wield political power.

That may have been true when the Soviet Union first began to break up, but this statement is not accurate today. The fact is, today those "former" Communists usually call themselves "Socialists." The term "Soviet Union" is short for the "Union of Soviet Socialist Republics." Socialism is the claimed "short term" economic system of the Communists until they can mature into a pure Communist state, wherein theoretically, government would melt away as something no longer necessary. In the meantime, the Communists claim the necessity for "strong" centralized government in order to make this transition. This "strong" government they call the "*Dictatorship* of the Proletariat."

This is not the place to discuss whether top "Communists" ever intended to give up their power, i.e., how cynical they may have been. In any event, the men who rose to the top in the Communist

"Dictatorship of the Proletariat" had to be absolutely ruthless just to survive the intrigues within the Politburo and the power struggles within the secret police, the KGB. They had to demonstrate support for the utter brutality of that system just to survive within the Communist apparatus -- let alone to rise to top positions of power.

So when a "former" Communist states that he is now merely a "Socialist," *would it be logical or prudent to "assume" that very much has really changed in the mind and heart of such a man who was capable of doing the things necessary to rise to the top in such a brutal system?* Would a thoughtful observer doubt for a minute that such a man or woman would or could revert to type at the first real opportunity?

The author receives more or less regular reports on activities behind the former Iron Curtain from those who travel there regularly on various types of official business. The reader can be assured that very many "former" Communists are solidly in positions of power throughout the former Soviet Union. Given this situation, how difficult would it really be (if the current political, economic and social degeneration continues in Russia and other former Soviet States) to reinstall a "socialist dictatorship" and march with Russian or Soviet armies on Western Europe? That scenario is exactly what the prophecies predict is going to happen -- if people do not repent.

F. THE EXISTENCE OF HELL IS TAUGHT BY THE CHURCH AND WE ARE CALLED TO SAVE OTHERS FROM GOING THERE!

What is the purpose of all this talk of Hell in Lucia's message, to frighten us? No! It is assumed that a majority of this book's readers are adult Christians of sound faith who are in the state of grace. The purpose is to emphasize Mary's call for prayer, sacrifice and penance IN ORDER TO SAVE THE SOULS OF OTHERS. But there is a downside to personal refusal of this "call." In our charity we are supposed to answer this call for prayer, sacrifice, and penance for the salvation of souls. If we do not, is there a possibility that sometime in the future we might need such spiritual assistance from others -- perhaps to withstand some great temptation of our own, (despair, pride, loss of faith, etc.), and that when we need help, we shall receive as we gave? "Let him who stands, beware lest he fall." Let us charitably respond to Mary's call.

1. Sr. Agnes of Akita (20th Century)

Sister Agnes is a member of the Handmaids of the Eucharist. She is a humble nun living in a religious community in Akita, Japan. She received revelations from her guardian angel and the Blessed Virgin between 1975 and 1982. She received the stigmata of Our Lord in her right hand which was miraculously matched by a similar wound in the right hand of the statue of Our Lady in the convent chapel.

The veracity of these events and revelations has been attested to by her former Bishop, Bishop Ito of Niigata. They have been officially approved by proper Church authority. Later, in retirement, Bishop Ito said about the book *Akita* from which the following revelations to Sr. Agnes are quoted below, "I recommend this book and testify that its contents are true."[504]

> *FIRST MESSAGE* "Pray very much for the Pope, Bishops and Priests. ... Continue to pray very much very much."[505] "Do so not only because of your sins, but in reparation for the sins of all men. The world today by its ingratitude and outrages, wounds the most Sacred Heart of Our Lord. The wound on the hand of Mary is much deeper and more painful than yours."[506]
>
> *SECOND MESSAGE "In order that the world might know His anger, the Heavenly Father is preparing to inflict a great chastisement on all mankind.* With my Son I have intervened so many times to appease the wrath of the Father. I have prevented the coming of calamities by offering Him the sufferings of the Son on the Cross, His Precious Blood, and beloved souls who console Him forming a cohort of victim

---

504 *Akita, The Tears and Messages of Mary*, Rev. Teiji Yasuda, Pub: 101 Foundation, Asbury, N.J., 1989, (Quoted from the inside cover page.)

505 *Akita*, P. 36.

506 Ibid., p. 47.

> souls. *Prayer, penance and courageous sacrifices can soften the Father's anger.*"[507]
>
> *THE THIRD MESSAGE* "My dear daughter, listen well to what I have to say to you. You will inform your superior. As I told you, if men do not repent and better themselves, the Father will inflict a terrible punishment on all humanity. *It will be a punishment greater than the deluge, such as one will never have seen before. Fire will fall from the sky and will wipe out a great part of humanity*, the good as well as the bad, sparing neither priests nor faithful. The survivors will find themselves so desolate that they will envy the dead. The only arms which will remain for you will be the Rosary and the Sign left by My Son. Each day recite the prayers of the Rosary. With the Rosary, pray for the Pope, the bishops and the priests."[508]

There has been much conjecture about whether this refers to nuclear war. The author realizes that is a possibility. But if this prophecy is tied in with others such as those of Sr. Elena Aiello and Blessed Mary of Jesus Crucified quoted earlier, it seems most likely that what is being described is a God-sent chastisement. It sounds like another prophecy of the "darkness."

Sr. Agnes continues:

> **"The work of the devil will infiltrate even into the Church in such a way that one will see cardinals opposing cardinals, bishops against other bishops. *The priests who venerate Me will be scorned and opposed by their confreres,*** churches and altars sacked; the Church will be full of those who accept compromises and the demon will press many priests and consecrated souls to leave the service of the Lord.
>
> "The demon will be especially implacable against souls consecrated to God. The thought of the loss of so many souls is the cause of My sadness. If sins increase in number and gravity, there will be no longer pardon for them.

---

507 Ibid. p. 62

508 Ibid. pp. 77&78.

> "*Pray very much the prayers of the Rosary*. I alone am able still to save you from the calamities which approach. Those who place their confidence in me will be saved."[509]

We have just quoted *four revelations* from *four different decades* of the 20th century, one from Fatima (2nd decade), one from Heede (5th decade), Sr. Elena Aiello (6th decade), and Sr. Agnes of Akita (7th & 8th decades), all approved by competent Church authority. They all state that a chastisement of horrific proportions is about to befall mankind if people do not amend their ways. There are many, many, other prophecies almost identical in nature. We could, if we so chose, quadruple the number of independent prophecies which say exactly the same things!

Within a Catholic context, we are free to reject these seers and their messages if we choose to do so, and no one may challenge our orthodoxy for doing so. But would it be prudent to reject these good people out of hand? In any case, history shall tell us if these prophecies of good and pious Catholics, the Venerable, Blessed, and even canonized Saints, stigmatics, and Popes are the ravings of madmen or a true foretaste of the future -- in the sense that it *will* be the future if we do not as a people experience inner conversion.

You will notice in the prophecies of Sr. Agnes of Akita, that integral to them are unfaithful Churchmen who persecute good Churchmen. In order to understand the significance of unfaithful religious we will return in a moment to Sr. Marianne de Jesus Torres of the 17th century and a revelation given to her by the Child Jesus.

G. THE ROLE OF UNFAITHFUL CLERGY AND RELIGIOUS

1. Sr. Marianne de Jesus Tores

> "*Know, moreover, that Divine Justice releases terrible chastisements on entire nations, not only for sins of the people but for those of Priests and religious persons*. For

509 *Akita*, p. 78& 79.

> the latter are called, by the perfection of their state, to be the salt of the earth, the masters of truth, and the deflectors of the Divine Ire.
>
> "Straying from their divine mission, they degrade themselves in such a way that, before the eyes of God, *they are the ones who quicken the rigor of the punishments*. Because, detaching themselves from Me, they end up living only a superficial life of the soul, maintaining a distance from Me that is unworthy of my Ministers. With their frigidity and lack of confidence, they act as if I were a stranger to them."[510]

Later on the Child Jesus comments on the value of devout and faithful religious souls who sacrifice themselves for the sanctification and salvation of other priests and religious.

According to Sr. Marianne, the Child Jesus then said,

> "I am greatly pleased by religious souls that take upon themselves the sublime task of sanctifying the Clergy by means of their prayers, sacrifices, and penances. Throughout time I will choose for Myself such souls so that, uniting themselves to Me, they will labor, pray, *and suffer* for the attainment of this most noble end, with a special glory awaiting them in Heaven."

Any faithful religious or laity reading this book should take great encouragement from this message. The current suffering that faithful clergy, religious, and laity are going through is not for nothing. It can be especially efficacious if they offer up these sufferings for their brothers and sisters in Christ serving as clergy and religious who might be less faithful. *And we laymen should not take any consolation in the guilt herein applied to faithless religious.* If some of their lives are less than perfect, how much responsibility do we the laity bear for it, because of our tepidity and scarcity of prayer for the clergy and religious?

---

[510] *Unpublished Manuscript of Life of Sor Marianne de Jesus Torres*, This particular work is an English translation of an unpublished manuscript which is developed from the *Compendium* of the *Caudernon*. All of the quotes from Sor. Marianne de Jesus Torres in this book are taken from that unpublished manuscript. Therefore, there will not be footnotes giving page number citations, etc.

The mystical body is like a giant ring or circle. *We all help or hinder each other as we either cooperate or fail to cooperate with grace*. A positive charge (cooperation with grace) enlivens the whole ring. A negative drain (sin or rejection of grace) pulls some life from the self-same spiritual ring. Hear Mary's requests for prayers for bishops, priests and religious. *If some of them are less than perfect it follows that we as laymen have not prayed for them as much as we should have*. To use an expression of the day, *what goes around comes around.* In particular we must pray for the priests and religious to whom we owe so much. *Our Lady delivered the following prophecy to Sor Marianne specifically for the 20th century.*

> "That which is most sorrowful is that even in the secular clergy there will be much to be desired, for the Ministers of the Altar will have forgotten their sublime mission of identifying themselves with my Most Holy Son through means of knowing themselves and humble, daily and fervent prayer. They will live only a superficial life of the soul, without detaching themselves from material things, being too greatly attached to family and to riches. *They will think they can aspire to sanctity in the priestly state by means of practicing one or two virtues - without taking care to construct the solid foundation of a profound humility, without which no virtue can exist. How can anyone, without humility, give pleasure or delight to God?* For God resists the proud and exalts the humble and simple of heart, to whom He delights in manifesting and communicating His secrets."

2. God is in Control - Ultimately There Will Be Peace

We must cling to the fact that all of the prophecies say that God is in control, and that *should suffering come*, afterwards will arrive a period of triumph, consolation, and peace for the Church and all men of good will. This is what we should concentrate on, that in the end, Mary's Immaculate Heart will triumph. And it is our current efforts of prayer, sacrifice and suffering in union with God's providence which specifically will prepare the way for the upcoming period of triumph for the Church. If we increase our prayer, sacrifice and voluntary suffering, that peace can come *without a chastisement.*

Both the evils and the weaknesses Sor Marianne predicts for our century are there for us to see. If we of the late 20th or early 21st century should go through a chastisement, it will be because God knows it is necessary as a last resort to wake us from our lethargy. A chastisement would at least accomplish the cessation of the murder of millions of completely innocent babies per year. But how much more evil than the physical murder of our little ones is the spiritual homicide our age is performing on them? Our Lord told us, "For he who would scandalize one of these my little ones, it would be better for him if he had never been born." Our little ones are being scandalized -- their innocence being destroyed every day -- by our culture itself.

3. Our Culture Destroys Innocence

Our television programs are foul. As we drive our little children to Church they see suggestive and in some cases foul advertisements. Many children are having their innocence destroyed in their schools with sex education programs which in many cases are the antithesis of Christian standards. The prominently displayed magazines in the grocery stores where mothers take their children to shop for food are covered with lewd and suggestive pictures. The innocent babes and little ones whom Jesus loves the most are being scandalized and are having their innocence destroyed by our very culture itself. *If the culture won't change, will God destroy the culture to protect the little ones?*

Our Lady says at Fatima and Akita that she wants us to follow the path of conversion. QUESTION: *Have we truly followed "the path of conversion*?" Who among us is innocent of the blood of Christ? Everyone outside of our innocent babes and children is guilty to one degree or another of the blood of Christ on the cross. Can we turn to Christ and say, "Lord, look at my meritorious life, and stay your hand on account of it?"

Have we really practiced the inner conversion Our Lord and Our Lady have asked for? Vatican II tells us that we are all called to sanctity. It is not just Catholics who are called to sanctity - but every child of God, every one of us.

Are we in the process of achieving sanctity? It is not the ubiquitous "George" who is being called to sanctity, it is us - whether we are Catholic, Protestant, Jewish, Moslem, agnostic or atheist.[511] God is calling every one of us to conversion. Do we gladly suffer for the sins of others in order to save souls? Have we generously offered ourselves as a sacrifice to Our Lord? All saints do! Will we begin this path of conversion? ***It is never too late!*** The aversion or serious amelioration of a chastisement could depend upon any additional one of us now choosing to follow that path!

There are quite literally hundreds of other prophecies from many additional Catholics (including more canonized Saints) which we could quote here which conditionally prophesy the same things about events to come. But what good would that do? We have heard the message. Either we believe it or we don't! And we either accept Heaven's analysis and solutions or we don't!

If given a limited choice today of either maintaining the status quo with the attendant danger to the young -- or -- a chastisement, the author would vote for a chastisement. ***Why?*** Because souls are more important than either material prosperity or an extended life span. Several of the prophecies already quoted say that if we don't change, a chastisement is part of both God's justice AND HIS MERCY. *The mercy is to stop the current state of corruption.*

Fortunately, God has given us his plan for averting or ameliorating a chastisement -- all of the plan was spelled out at Fatima and restated at Akita, Japan. The plan is *our* prayer, sacrifice and penance. IT WILL EITHER BE INCREASED PRAYER, SACRIFICE AND PENANCE -- OR -- CHASTISEMENT. That is the message! God has given us the choice, it is ours. If we reject conversion, we opt for chastisement.

In the event that the world does not choose serious prayer, sacrifice, and penance, and we and/or our children should live to see this chastisement: *According to the prophecies - people who are not familiar with them and are unaware that God has a plan and is in total control - they will almost despair of hope.* Some of the prophecies even say that those who are unaware of the consolation

[511] These statements should not be considered as in any way sympathetic to the heresy of Agnostic "Indifferentism." The author is not meaning to imply that the Catholic Church and its Chief Vicar are not uniquely called to direct man to in his struggle to achieve final salvation for his soul. He is simply stating that God wishes all men to be saved, and therefore calls all to sanctity.

of these prophecies will be tempted to believe that it is the end of the world, or that the very Gates of Hell have prevailed against the Church.

But the prophecies say that those who are familiar with authentic prophecy and walk in faith -- they will pray and work in patient consolation in expectation of the Age of Mary. Our job is to give everyone hope. Our hope is in Our Lord's promise that He will be with us all days. The messages of Fatima and Akita emphasize this and ask for increased prayer, sacrifice, penance, *and trust in God's Divine Mercy.*

If we so accredit the "faith of human reason" to these prophecies we must remember that Christianity is a joy filled Faith. St. Luke tells us that when we see things such as these come to pass that we should lift up our heads for our salvation is at hand. Mary assures us that in the end her Immaculate Heart will triumph and that a certain period of peace shall be granted to the world. The prophecies themselves tell us of a miraculous and wonderful period of peace which is to follow. This is a message of hope and consolation for any man or woman of good will! **"BE NOT AFRAID!"**

4. These Prophecies are Devoid of Mention of Antichrist or the Parousia

One of the major purposes of this book is to demonstrate that the theme, "Antichrist and/or the Parousia are just around the corner" is not consistent with either Revelation, or the teaching of the Fathers, or a broad view of approved Catholic prophecy. *The reader has surely noticed that in none of these prophecies from Popes, or from those the Church has designated as canonized Saints, Blessed or Venerable, is there any inference whatsoever of an immediate approach of Antichrist.*

Quite the contrary, the message from *approved* sources is of a threatened "conditional" chastisement which substantially precedes Antichrist. According to these prophecies, if people meet God's condition of inner conversion a chastisement can and will be averted, and a great period of peace will be ushered in. According to these same *approved* prophecies, if people do not heed God's warning, a terrible chastisement will ensue, *which will be followed by "a great period of peace"* which precedes the Antichrist. This is a message of hope. **"BE NOT AFRAID!"**

Much more evidence in support of a period of peace between our time and that of Antichrist will be given later. Much of that information comes from Tradition and the commentaries of the Fathers of the Church. The author repeats the point that the thesis that the coming of "the" Antichrist is imminent is totally incompatible with the totality of Revelation. Does prophecy which implies Antichrist's immediate coming and the sequential Parousia meet St. Augustine's epithet, "He who indiscreetly announces the coming of Christ falls into a noxious error?"

For the reasons above, we have first established that Scripture and Catholic Scripture scholars clearly argue against an imminent coming of Antichrist at this time. Since the best way to fight fire is with fire; we have then presented *approved* Catholic private prophecies as an augmentation to arguments from Revelation. Such *approved* prophecies demonstrate that even a broad understanding and knowledge of "approved" private prophecy clearly argues against the imminent arrival of Antichrist or the Parousia.

The only possible source for a belief in an imminent arrival of Antichrist or the Parousia rests within an exclusive emphasis on *unnaproved* prophecy, which emphasis likewise ignores the totality of what is contained in Revelation, and the exegesis of the Revelation by the Fathers and Doctors of the Church. A faithful Catholic who is seeking truth within the context of what the Church approves will most likely find the combination of arguments from Revelation augmented by Catholic prophecy from *approved* sources highly persuasive.

5. The Age of Peace Foretold to Precede Antichrist

In the next chapter we will look at the various prophecies from *Church-approved* sources about the wondrous age of faith to precede the ultimate end times. That, and Heaven, is what we should keep our eyes of faith glued to! If it is true that we are to enter into a chastisement, *we need to be Christians of joyful calm, the type of people whom others will naturally turn to when the going gets truly rugged.* That is our job -- to sanctify the world by our example, prayer, sacrifice and penance -- just as we promise to do every day in our morning offering.

Whether the impending conditional chastisement is the one predicted for the time of a Great King, or *whether there is more than one chastisement in the ages to come, that we cannot know*. All that the prophecies are clear on is that through a series of struggles, a Great King and a great Pope usher in a *final* era of peace. **The only thing the *approved* prophecies *are* absolutely clear on is that one way or another, with or without a chastisement, we are headed for a wonderful era of peace. That era of peace *precedes* the very "end times." That is a message of hope! "BE NOT AFRAID!"**

A few things appear *absolutely* clear in prophecy from Church-approved sources.

(1) the current sinful state of mankind.
(2) the prediction that if mankind does not go through an inner conversion that there will be a chastisement to bring mankind to conversion.
(3) Whether man converts with or without a chastisement, *at least* one great period of peace stands between our generation and the coming of Antichrist.

With one possible exception, none of these things are part of Revelation.[512] But in basics the "approved" prophecies present a message of hope -- not a message of fear of the imminent coming of Antichrist. **"BE NOT AFRAID!"** The heart and soul of all these messages is the message of Fatima;

> **"In the end my Immaculate Heart will triumph, and a certain period of peace will be given to the world."**

Here another caution is in order. The foretold "period of peace" could be fifty or one hundred years down the road. There is no

[512] That possible exception is the "age" or "time" of peace at some time between now and the Antichrist. So many Catholic commentators from the Fathers till now have "seen" such a period of peace in the *Apocalypse*, that it would be brash to state that this particular item could not be of Faith or possibly contained within Revelation. See the next section for more detail.

guarantee that the "period of peace" is "just around the corner" any more than the reign of Antichrist is. Things could just gradually get worse over the course of the next century prior to resolution of the problem. We have no way of knowing.

Did that mere thought of more of the same, and then worse for the next century just send a chill or depression through the reader's heart? If it did, then we should be aware of several natural conclusions to be drawn from that. Emotionally, doesn't any normal human being desperately want to believe that the current suffering and trials and problems of our age will be over some time in the near future? Wouldn't such an individual even subconsciously prefer the reign of Antichrist to what our age is going through? After all, Antichrist will only rule for three and one half years -- and then the suffering is over. What a tremendous emotional appeal that idea must have for all of us at the subconscious level.

To expand on a point made earlier in the book, there is also a relaxation of personal responsibility in this idea. God in his providence has provided for the arrival of Antichrist at some time in the future. Therefore, it appears there is nothing we can do about that. There is no personal responsibility. But an extended period of suffering leading up to a chastisement, that heavily indicates personal responsibility.

Our Lady of Fatima said we are all responsible for ameliorating or averting a chastisement through our own personal prayers, work, sacrifices and suffering. Belief that Antichrist is just around the corner can emotionally (but illogically) relieve our consciences of personal responsibility to perform our normal religious duties, and especially to respond to the requests of Our Lady of Fatima.

Therein lies the greatest danger and the strongest emotional appeal of the contemporary "Antichrist" scenario to be found in many *non-approved* prophecies. It can strike any of us no matter how intelligent or well-educated we might be, because when it strikes, it does so at the subconscious level. It appeals to the subconsciously dormant desire in all of us to escape personal responsibility. If we are not alert to that potential danger, that type of blow can emotionally circumvent the intellects which God has given us.

6. Private Prophecy and the Age of Peace

Most Catholics who have bought into the idea that the Parousia or Antichrist are just around the corner were lead there by certain private prophecies from some *unapproved* sources. Everyone even remotely familiar with Scipture and Tradition can see that the persecution of Antichrist must precede the Parousia. Therefore, a prophecy which alleges the Parousia is close, by definition, must allege the Antichrist is even closer. But we have seen consistent indications of a period of peace to precede Antichrist from prophecies contained in both Tradition and Scripture. We have also seen that private prophecies from many Church-approved sources (which includes canonized Saints, Blessed, and Venerable) all clearly and consistently indicate a period of peace yet to precede the rise of Antichrist. Tradition and Scripture are part of the Deposit of Faith. Authentic private prophecy is not and can never be part of that deposit of Faith. So it is theologically difficult to go much further in comparisons than to state the obvious from reason. i.e., prophecies from (1) Tradition and Scripture, and (2) private prophecies from *approved sources, they appear to be in agreement on this issue of a period of peace preceding Antichrist. On the other hand, that type of apparent agreement cannot be posited about a comparison of (1) Tradition and Scripture and (2) certain recent prophecies from unapproved sources which imply that Antichrist and the Parousia are just around the corner. The only indication that Antichrist is just around the corner, rather than the Age of Peace, comes from sources which are not approved by the Church.*

CHAPTER 9

THE AGE OF PEACE WHICH PRECEDES THE ANTICHRIST

We have already read much about the foretold reign of Mary, the age of peace. The greatest council of the Church is prophesied to occur during this time. Vocations are foretold to flourish as never before. It will be the most glorious period of the Church since the age of the Apostles. There will be universal peace for a period of time. Heretics and pagans will enter the Church in vast numbers. A Pope/Popes of incredible sanctity shall rule the Church. Civil governments will be Catholic with a great Catholic Monarch or a series of them to maintain peace, order and tranquillity. It is almost too good to be true! But not necessarily. It may be the time of "one flock and one shepherd" which the Scriptures themselves testify to.

1. Scriptural Basis

Is there any intimation in Scripture in its prophetical works as to an Age of Peace? A number of Scriptural commentators state so. It must also be noted that all the great commentators on the Apocalypse (the Book of Revelation) pointedly remark the obvious, that the Book is highly mystical in nature. They also comment that the prophecies contained in that Book are not necessarily presented in perfect chronological order. Thus there is some chronological cross-referencing back and forth in this Book. Therefore it can be difficult to determine just exactly where a prophesied event fits chronologically.

Fr. Herman Kramer was possibly the best 20th century English speaking author on the Apocalypse. He completed his theological studies at St. Lawrence Seminary in Mt. Calvary, Wisconsin, and then processed to Innsbruck, Austria for his Theologate. Ill health forced his return to the U.S. where he completed his theological studies in St. Paul Seminary in St. Paul, MN. He then returned to his diocese in Sioux City, Iowa.

Besides his duties as a pastor, he also served for a number of years as chancellor of his diocese. Fr. Kramer continued his studies and ultimately could read and write fluently in seven languages. Over a thirty year period he extensively studied available source materials on the Apocalypse, its exegesis by the Fathers and Doctors, and major theologians of all ages vis-a-vis their eschatological commentaries. At the end of that study he produced his now-famous *The Book of Destiny*. Fr. Kramer in this work says the following in his commentary on Chapter 9 of the Apocalypse:

> *"The text gives no intimation about the interval of time between the first and second woe. It will be a time of wars developing into a world-revolution that will deluge the whole world with carnage and bloodshed. The three-and-a-half years of the reign of the Beast will be its climax.* The time of its beginning is wrapped in secrecy, and the duration of this time of slaughter is likewise a deep and dark secret. *Verses 20 and 21 presage a time of peace between the first reign of terror in the second woe and the reign of Antichrist."*[513]

Fr. Kramer's discussion of a "time of peace" is based upon the commentaries of all the great eschatological Scripture scholars in the history of the Church. This is especially applicable to those of the early Fathers, and then many commentaries of the 19th and 20th centuries. Many readers of the Apocalypse assume that its described events fit into a narrow time frame during the immediate period of Antichrist and the period to follow.

It was Fr. Kramer's contention that St. John in the Apocalypse is *in some ways* describing the entire sweep of history from the Resurrection of Our Lord up until the end of the world. This contention is anything but unique. It is also the opinion of a far-ranging number of Catholic Scripture scholars over the last 1000 years. In

---

[513] *The Book of Destiny*, Rev Herman Kramer, Buechler Pub. Co. 1955 p. 228 (Fr. Kramer is commenting upon Chpt. 9, V. 20 & 21.)

this context, it was Fr. Kramer's opinion that we (as of 1955) were probably on the eve of entering the beginning of the "Second Woe" foretold in the Book of Revelation.

Therefore the "Time of Peace" foretold in the Apocalypse that Fr. Kramer is talking about is (in Kramer's opinion) something which follows our time, but presages the Reign and time of Antichrist. [*The "first reign of terror in the second woe," which Fr. Kramer refers to, also fits in many ways the descriptions of the "chastisement" spoken of in approved private prophecies.*] In the opinion of many sound Catholic Scripture scholars, there is a Scriptural basis for a significant "Time of Peace" that is an interlude which comes before the Antichrist.

That *possible* interpretation is recognized by all the great eschatologists in the Church as a plausible interpretation. For a fuller understanding of this particular subject, the author recommends to the reader that he or she obtain a copy of Fr. Kramer's book (See Bibliography). This is another case where the Scriptures and/or the interpretations of Scriptural exegetes are consonant with many details contained in many private prophecies.

2. Tradition - St. Ephraem and the Age of Peace

There is also a large body of prophecy from Tradition which foretells an extensive period of peace just prior to the emergence of the end times and Antichrist. We will quote but one of the Fathers (who is also a Doctor) on this subject. The reason we have chosen this particular Father is that he poignantly ties in the period of peace with the reemergence of a "Roman Kingdom." The following passage is from a sermon of St. Ephraem's which appeared earlier in this book.

> "***Then the Lord from his glorious heaven shall set up his peace.*** And **the *kingdom* of the Romans shall rise in place of this latter people**, and establish its dominion upon the earth, even to its ends, and there shall be no one who will resist it. After iniquity shall have (subsequently) multiplied, and all creatures have become defiled, then Divine Justice shall appear, and shall wholly destroy the people, and coming forth from perdition, the man of iniquity shall be revealed

> upon the earth, the Seducer of men, and the disturber of the whole earth."[514]

The reader will notice that this period of peace which is foretold by St. Ephraem *to precede* "the man of iniquity" (Antichrist) has several key elements;

(1) This "peace" is directly "set up" by God Himself.
(2) It comes in very latter times.
(3) During this peace there is a reemergence of a "Roman Kingdom."
(4) Eventually the people cannot stand the prosperity of the peace, and subsequently "iniquity shall have multiplied, and all creatures have become defiled"
(5) From out of this general iniquity and defilement shall come the "man of iniquity," the seducer of men" (the Antichrist).

CONCLUSION: We have prophetic Scripture *and* Tradition telling us of some final period of peace which is established by God - during which what is variously described as some Roman "Power," "Kingdom," or "Empire" is established. Now we will turn to samples of private prophecies from various canonized Saints, Blessed and Venerable and see what they tell us of a period of peace which appears to be the same one.

3. St. Francis of Paula

St. Francis of Paula, some of whose prophecies appeared earlier, describes the founding of a last great religious order during an era of peace. According to St. Francis, the order will be called the Knights of the Cross ("Crusaders") who will be instrumental in a reevangelization process:

> "A new order will then be founded, that of the Cruciferi ("Cross-bearers") because their members will have the cross on their banners. This order will be comprised of three

[514] *The Sunday Sermons of the Great Fathers*, Vol. 4, Translated and edited by M.F. Toal, Henry Regnery Co. 1964, p. 355. [Again, see caveat in footnote on Ephraem in chpt. 4.]

> groups: the first group will be armed horsemen; the second group, priests, and the third, nurses. These Knights of the Cross ("Crusaders") will convert Mohammedans, heretics and fallen-away Christians to Christ."[515]

According to St. Francis de Paulo, this religious order will also be the last one to be founded in the Church.

4. Sr. Mechtilde of Helfta (13th Century)

Mechtilde never went through the formal canonization process.[516] However, she is traditionally referred to as a Saint in many Catholic reference works. Unquestionably, she is venerated as a Saint by the people of the area where she lived out her life. Sr. Mechtilde was born into a noble family in Saxony about 1210, and died at the Cistercian convent at Helfta, Saxony, probably in 1285. She was a highly celebrated medieval mystic whose revelations about the hereafter many scholars suspect were the "basis for Dante's *Divine Comedy*, and the poet's *Matelda* (Purgatory,)"[517]

When about twenty years old (1230 A.D.), while a "Beguine at Magdeburg" she began having visions, and;

> "Here, under the spiritual direction of the Dominicans, she led a life of prayer and extreme mortifications. Her heavenly inspirations and ecstatic visions became more frequent and were of such a nature that they dispelled from the mind of her confessor all doubt as to their Divine origin. By his order she reluctantly wrote her visions. Shortly after 1270, she joined the Cistercian nuns at Helfta, (Saxony), where she spent the remaining twelve years of her life, highly respected as one signally favoured by God, especially by her namesake St. Mechtilde of Hackeborn and by St. Gertrude the Great.

---

515 This quote of St. Francis' is taken from Cornelius a Lapide's commentary on "In Apoc. 17,7."

516 Sr. Mechtild is generally given the title of "Saint" even though she never formally went through the canonization process. However, this accolade is not as universally accorded as, say, with St. Hildegard, therefore the author has used "Sr." and not "Saint."

517 *Catholic Encyclopedia*, 1917 Edition, Vol. 5, pp. 106-107, "Mechtild of Magdeburg."

> Mechtilde left to the world a most wonderful book, in which she recorded her manifold inspirations and visions."[518]

All of the quotes hereinafter attributed to Sr. Mechtilde come from that book.

Sr. Mechtilde explained that *prior to the time of Antichrist an order of preachers* would come into existence. She described its members as follows:

> "They will be clad in a double garment, the undergarment white and the outer one red and fastened with a girdle. Their beards and hair will be unshorn. They will go barefooted, except in winter when they will wear red sandals with white thongs. They will have no possessions and will not be allowed to have gold or silver.
>
> "Each of them will bear at all times a staff which will be painted white and red and which will have a crook a span long. On one side of the staff will be portrayed the Passion of Christ and on the other side His Ascension into Heaven. No member of this order shall be younger than 24 years old. They will be priests, confessors, and good preachers."[519]

According to many prophecies, it will be the work of a "last" order which will in large part reevangelize the entire world toward the end of the Age of Peace. *According to Sr. Mechtilde, They will perform their mission in peace for 30 years;* then Antichrist will come. The author has, somewhere in his manuscripts, another prophecy which says that 25 years of good crops will be sufficient for them (the people in general) to forget. It possibly coincides with St. Mechtilde's prophecy of 30 years of peaceful evangelization.

5. St. Vincent Ferrer

St. Vincent gives a concise chronology of events beginning with the Great King, then the Age of Peace. Here St. Vincent describes the advent of the Great King,

---

518 Ibid. *Catholic Encyclopedia.*

519 *Revelations of Sister Mechtild of Magdeburg*, Morel, Regensburg Manz, 1869, page 208.

> "Armies from the West, East, and North will fight together in Italy, and the Eagle shall capture the false king, and all things shall be made obedient unto him, and there shall be a new reformation in the world."

Here St. Vincent first has spoken of the Eagle, the Great King, who will conquer the enemy, describes the subsequent peaceful era and tells of a "new reformation in the world." Next, he describes the Apostles of the end times, in a manner similar to that spoken of above by St. Francis and St. Mechtilde. Now he immediately tells us of what subsequently happens to destroy that reformation of the world to bring to an end that Age of Peace.

> "In the days of peace that are to come after the desolation of revolutions and wars -- before the end of the world -- *Christians will become so lax in their religion that they will refuse the sacrament of Confirmation, saying that "it is an unnecessary sacrament";* and **when the false prophet**, **the precursor of Anti-Christ comes, all who are not confirmed will apostasize, *while those who are confirmed will stand fast in their faith*,** and only a few will renounce Christ."[520]

Comment: That is a very specific and very well-known prophecy. It might be wise to pass this prophecy down in your family. Many of the prophecies state that a knowledge of these types of prophecies will save the soul of many a Christian in the latter times.

We are describing an age of incredible peace and prosperity. The earlier mentioned prophecy that, "Crops will be abundant as never before" is enough to gladden the cockles of our hearts. But *people usually cannot stand prosperity*.

CONCLUSION: Tradition, Scripture, and the private prophecies of many canonized Saints, Blessed, and Venerable are in agreement that there will be some wonderful period of peace before the specific end times -- before the advent of Antichrist. According to that scenario, Antichrist most probably will not be in our immediate future.

---

[520] *The Prophets & Our Times*, p. 155. This prophecy is also quoted by Fr. Pellegrino in the *Christian Trumpet*, and by Yves Dupont in *Catholic Prophecy*.

A. THE SCRIPTURALLY FORETOLD MASS CONVERSION OF THE JEWS: COULD IT HAPPEN DURING THE AGE OF PEACE, WHICH AGE WAS PREDICTED AT FATIMA?

> Romans 11: 25-27:
> "For I would not have you ignorant, brethren of this mystery, (lest you should be wise in your own conceits), that **blindness in part has happened in Israel, until the fullness of the Gentiles should come in,** And so all Israel should be saved, as it is written; 'There *shall come out of Sion, he that shall deliver, and shall turn away ungodliness from Jacob.*'"

As we have already read, any number of canonized Saints, such as St. Hildegarde, have predicted a conversion "for many Jews, Heathens, and heretics" (and other prophecies add Moslems to this group) during the "Age of Peace." According to many of the prophecies, this "Age of Peace" precedes the "Age of Antichrist" and the "Apostasy" which precedes it. The question about the timing of a mass conversion of the Jews is discussed at this point because many have conjectured if this foretold "Age of Peace" could be that time. The key to its understanding lies with the Scriptural phrase "*until the fullness of the Gentiles*."

1. The Fullness of the Gentiles

Scripture states that the "the fullness of the Gentiles" will have been achieved when on an observable basis the Gentiles will have stopped coming into the Church. That point is Scriptural and is not in any way based on opinion or conjecture. We also have the unanimous testimony of the Fathers of the Church that this is also of Apostolic Tradition.

It is important that we remember what was just said in Romans, "I would not have you ignorant, brethren *of this mystery,.*" Someone might object and say, "Fine, then why bring it up at all?" Because: The author of Romans says, "For *I would not have you ignorant*, brethren of this mystery, (lest you should be wise in your own conceits),." **In God's providence, He foresees that *it is important***

to us to know that this will come about. That is why God inspired the sacred writer to include it in Scripture, and reinforces its importance by informing us that He doesn't want us in ignorance on this subject.

Our Lord gave us the parable of the fig leaf, showing us that when we actually see before our very eyes *the predicted signs of the impending advent of Antichrist*, that then we can expect those signs to be fulfilled in the event. He told us that no one knows "the day nor the hour" (of his Second Coming), "except the Father in Heaven."[521] However, He did give us "proximate" signs to recognize the event when it occurs. While we cannot positively state when such a predicted event *will* happen, nevertheless, we can state that at this or that point (when those "proximate" signs are absent) that it will *not* happen then.

2. St. Jerome

Likewise, if we wish to see if the mystery of a mass conversion of the Jews will take place during the foretold "Age of Peace," let us compare the predicted signs of both events to see if they could be concomitant events. *St. Jerome*,[522] foreseeing the time of loss of faith of the Gentiles, said:

---

[521] According to the Magisterium,, this should not be taken literally. As far back as Pope St. Gregory the Great, we have direct Papal exegesis on this matter. "So too the Almighty Son says He does not know the day which He causes not to be known, not because He himself does not know it, but because He does not permit it to be known at all. ... Man (Jesus) for us, did indeed *in* His human nature know the day and the hour of the judgement, but nevertheless did not know this *from* His human nature ... because God-made-man knew the day and the hour of the judgement by the power of His Godhead .. Therefore He knows, as God and as Man, the day and the hour of the judgement; but for this reason, the Man (Jesus) is God. ... For how could anyone who confesses that the Wisdom of God is incarnate say that there is anything of which the Wisdom of God is ignorant?"

Quoted from the *Letter of Pope Gregory I to Eulogius, Patriarch of Alexandria,* August, 600 A.D. Referenced from *The Faith of the Early Fathers*, Vol. 3. Jurgens, pp. 311 & 312.

[522] Jerome's Commentary on Romans 11: 20-22 - Quoted by Fr. Sanchez in *Public And Private Prophecies About The Last Times*, Rev. Benjamin Martin Sanchez, Pub: Opus Reginae Sacratissimi Rosarii, University of Salamanca, 1972. p. 30.

> "*If for the crimes of the Jews* (crimes of unbelief), *the salvation passed to the Gentiles*; *by the incredulity of the Gentiles it will pass to the Jews*."

We learn that this will not be a universal "incredulity" on the part of the Gentiles from St. Mathew's Gospel. In Chapter 13:24-25 we learn of the continual mixture of the cockles (weeds) and the wheat "until the harvest" (until the end of time). So this time of the "fullness of the Gentiles" is probably a time when the vast majority of them will not believe. It is a relative thing, a loss of faith on the part of the Gentiles which will be unparalleled with anything up till that time. When this occurs, then will be the time for the conversion of Jews.

What St. Jerome is saying (and many other "Fathers" said) is that Israel is suffering at the present time, from a *temporary* blindness. But that blindness will last only as long as Gentiles in relatively significant numbers persevere in the Faith.

3. St. John Chrysostom

Earlier, we have quoted St. Jerome on this theme. Now we will quote another Father, St. John Chrysostom. In his commentary on Romans, he quotes Paul (in italics), and then comments,

> " *When the fulness of the Gentiles,* he [Paul] says, *shall have come in, then shall all Israel be saved,* at the time of His second coming, and the end of the world."

Obviously, St John Chrysostom states that the time of the conversion of the Jews will come very approximate to the "Second Coming," which he also interprets to be proximate to the end of the world. The exact timing of all of this is somehow vague in the writings of the Fathers. But that is to be expected -- there is mystery involved here.

4. *The Catechism of the Catholic Church*

Not everything contained in the *Catechism of the Catholic Church* has been declared De Fide, i.e., not everything in it has been declared as *binding* in faith. As repeatedly stated before, only in a small percentage of traditional teachings of the Church has She gone to the trouble to declare them as being de Fide. All that a ruling of De Fide accomplishes is to bind Catholics that they now *must* believe that which they already should believe. The Church teaches us in Her *Catechism*, that which we *can and should* safely believe in faith.

Another point of interest is: the Church teaches that one of the signs which must precede the Second Coming of Christ is the conversion of the bulk of the Jews to Christ, and that this event comes "in the wake" of the "full number (fullness) of the Gentiles. As the *Catechism of the Catholic Church* states,

> **"The glorious Messiah's coming is suspended at every moment of history until his recognition by 'all Israel,'** for 'a hardening has come upon part of Israel' in their unbelief' toward Jesus. ... The 'full inclusion' of the Jews in the Messiah's salvation, in the wake of 'the full number of the Gentiles' will enable the People of God to achieve 'the measure of the stature of the fullness of Christ,' in which 'God may be all in all.'"[523]

The *Catechism* clearly teaches here that the Second Coming, the Parousia, cannot happen until the conversion of "all Israel." Therefore, we can safely believe and should believe that Jesus' glorious Second Coming cannot happen until the world experiences the mass conversion of the Jews, which conversion is prophesied in Scripture and Tradition. If *anyone* attempts to tell you that the Second Coming can precede the conversion of the Jews, that person is out of step with the traditional teachings of the Church.

B. MORE ON THE AGE OF PEACE

Again, according to Fr. Kramer and many other Scripture scholars, Verses 20 and 21 of Chapter 9 of the Apocalypse presage a time of peace between the first reign of terror in the second woe

[523] *Catechism of the Catholic Church*, Libreria Editrice Vaticana, St. Paul Books and Media, 1994, #674, p. 176.

and the reign of Antichrist. It is a period of peace which precedes Antichrist. Numerous private prophecies which we have already reviewed clearly state that during an "Age of Peace" that, amongst other things, a large majority of people (at least in the West) will become serious practicing Catholics.

1. Sr. Bertina Bequillon

There is no way of knowing if that privately foretold "Age" is the same one as that apparently foretold in Scripture. In any event, the privately foretold "Age of Peace" is one within which the average Catholic will lead a holy life, the most poignant quote concerning this period may be Sr. Bertina Bequillon's:

> "A saint raises his arms to Heaven; he allays the wrath of God. He ascends the throne of Peter. At the same time, the Great Monarch ascends the throne of his ancestors. All is quiet now. Altars are set up again; religion comes to life again. What I see now is so wonderful that I am unable to express it."[524]

This hardly sounds like the time when the Gentiles will have ceased coming into the Church, on the contrary, it would be a time when Gentiles flock into the Church. Therefore, that particular "Age of Peace" most probably cannot be the time of the mass conversion of the Jews, which Scripture tells us will happen at the time of the "fullness of the Gentiles" (a period when the Gentiles stop entering the Church).

So, if the conversion of the Jews will not take place during the period of peace *preceding* Antichrist (and while it appears unlikely - there could be more than one), when *will* their mass conversion take place? We don't *know for sure*! Many commentators of the Scriptures have conjectured that (1) it happens (or at least begins) during the time of Enoch and Elias, or (2) others are of the opinion that it happens during the period between the death of Antichrist and the end of the world, or (3) a combination of 1&2. But again, no one knows. As *Hebrews* tells us, that is a mystery. Only God knows. All we know is that it appears highly improbable that it will

---

524 *Voix Prophetiques*, Curicquo, 1872, Vol. 1, p. 472.

happen during the great foretold "Age of Peace," and it definitely happens prior to the Parousia.

C. THE *GREAT COUNCIL* IN THE AGE OF PEACE

We have already heard a number of prophecies which predict a "Great Council" for sometime during the Age of Peace. Is there any possible Scriptural basis for this possibility? Fr. Kramer in his, *The Book of Destiny*, tells us the following vis-a-vis the Apocalypse:

1. Scriptural Basis? - Fr. Kramer

> "Chapters XI. 1-2 and XII. 7 argue for many and great evils in the Church. And those verses together with XII. 5 suggest a great conflict between the Church and the world-powers and the necessity of drastic measures of reform for the Church to free herself from the danger of contamination by the evils in the world and purify her from the prevalent internal evils. *The Seven Thunders may then be declarations of an ecumenical council* clearing up all that was left unfinished by the magisterial office of the Church, before God will permit Satan to exert his supreme efforts to destroy her from without. The Seven Thunders will strengthen the faithful and loyal clergy in their belief and practices, expel all who are addicted to corrupt lives and superstitions and manifest the unwavering stand of the Church on the then prevailing maxims of the world. ... Through the Seven Thunders, God gave him (St. John) a special revelation of great importance, indicating what would immediately precede the coming of Antichrist, but it was to remain a secret to the Church."[525]

Again, this interpretation by Fr. Kramer is *not* based upon interpretation of private prophecy. It is based upon his studies of the Scriptural commentaries of some of the greatest eschatological exegetes in the history of the Church. Fr. Kramer goes on to comment:

> "St. Paul likewise heard secret revelations which he was not allowed to communicate to the Church. *The Thunders do re-*

[525] *The Book of Destiny*, p. 242.

> *veal this: there will be special decisions made by the Church and these will complete the work of her magisterial office before the culmination of evil is due to arrive.* The decisions may be the "reed" by which the wicked are separated from the good and expelled from the Church."[526]

Now we will re-present some of the prophecies already seen in order to show the contiguity of them with Fr. Kramer's interpretation of the *Apocalypse:*

2. Holzhauser

> "By the grace of God, by the power of the Great Monarch, by the authority of the Holy Pontiff, and by the union of all the most devout princes, atheism and every heresy will be banished from the earth. *The Council will define the true sense of Holy Scripture, and this will be believed and accepted by everyone."*[527]

3. Jeanne de Royer – Sister Nativitas Clarissin of Fourgeres (1731-1798)

> "I see in God a great power, led by the Holy Ghost, which will restore order through a second upheaval. I see in God *a large assembly of pastors* who will uphold the rights of the church and of her Head. *They will restore the former disciplines.* I see, in particular, two servants of the Lord who will distinguish themselves in this glorious struggle and who, by the grace of Holy Ghost, will fill with ardent zeal the hearts of *this illustrious assembly.*"[528]

It certainly seems most likely that what Sr. Nativitas is describing is a Council of the Church. Sr. Nativitas gives a description of conditions following the Council.

> "I see in God that the Church will enjoy a profound peace over a period which seems to me to be of a fairly long dura-

---

[526] Ibid.

[527] *Catholic Prophecy*, p. 40.

[528] *The Christian Trumpet* p. 115.

> tion. This respite will be the longest of all that will occur between the revolutions from now till the General Judgment. The closer we draw to the General Judgment, the shorter will be the revolutions against the Church. The kind of peace that will follow each revolution will be shorter also. This is so because we are approaching the End of Time, and little time will be left for either the elect to do good or for the wicked to do evil."[529]

This prophesied council almost certainly takes place during the Age of Peace.

4. Ecstatic of Tours

> "*The Council will meet again after the victory*. But, this time, men will be obliged to obey; *There will be only one flock and one shepherd.* All men will acknowledge the Pope as the Universal Father, the King of all peoples. Thus mankind will be regenerated."

This prophecy comes from this French nun in the book of her revelations, *La Vielle de la Victoire du Christ*, which were recorded by her spiritual director in 1882. This particular prophecy comes immediately after prophesy of a "Great King" who has by then freed the Church. She refers to a Council meeting *again* after a final victory. She lived during the period of the First Vatican Council which had to break up due to violent revolutionary activity in Italy. That Council was never officially closed, since the Council Fathers thought they would be reconvening.

Some of the prophecies which we receive are word-for-word messages delivered by Our Lord or Mary. Others are general impressions which the prophet receives from visions, sometimes a combination of visions and locutions. It could be that the Council which the ecstatic saw for some time in the future she thought or assumed to be an extension of the "unclosed" First Vatican Council. It also could be that she was mistaken in this. But it is extremely interesting that she says that after the "Council" it will be a time during which "*There will be only one flock and one shepherd.*"

[529] *Catholic Prophecy*, p. 57.

That obviously could not be referring to the Ecumenical Councils of Vatican I or Vatican II.

5. Ven. Holzhauser

Now we will again show a prophecy of Holzhauser which casts all of these events into a concise compendium of occurrences during an Age of Peace. In the middle of these we see foretold a great Ecumenical Council.

> "The powerful Monarch, who will be sent by God, will uproot every republic. He will submit everything to his authority, and he will show great zeal for the true Church of Christ. The empire of the Mohammedans will be broken up, and this Monarch will reign in the East as well as in the West. All nations will come to worship God in the true Catholic and Roman faith. There will be many Saints and Doctors (of the Church) on earth. Peace will reign over the whole earth because God will bind Satan for a number of years until the days of the Son of Perdition. *No one will be able to pervert the word of God since, during the sixth period, there will be an ecumenic council which will be the greatest of all councils*. By the grace of God, by the power of the Great Monarch, by the authority of the Holy Pontiff, and by the union of all the most devout princes, atheism and every heresy will be banished from the earth. *The Council will define the true sense of Holy Scripture, and this will be believed and accepted by everyone*."[530]

Such Scriptural Exegetes as Cornelius Lapide, St. Robert Bellarmine (A Doctor of the Church) and Suarez, (and lately Fr. Kramer, whom we have quoted elsewhere in this book) all concluded in the light of Scripture that there would be some future "Great Council" of the Church. This was their interpretation of several passages of the Apocalypse. There have been two Ecumenical Councils since they wrote, Vatican I and Vatican II. Events surrounding Vatican Councils I and II, make it clear they do not fit the description of that "Great Council." The "Council" they speak of is in some way associated with events surrounding the end times preceding Antichrist.

---

530 *Catholic Prophecy*, p. 40.

The last sentence of Holzhauser is of particular interest. Scripture scholars have for centuries thought that at some future time the Church would eventually solemnly define the specific meanings of numerous of the certain difficult Scripture passages. According to this and other prophecies, it will happen to one degree or another sometime during a foretold Age of Peace.

D. THE END OF THE "AGE OF PEACE"

According to prophecies which we read above, one each from Sr. Vincent Ferrer and St. Mechtilde, when things go well, people will again fall into laxity. From prophecies it appears there will be two distinct periods of war: one during a chastisement, then comes a period of peace and prosperity, than another period of wars will follow the period of peace. According to the prophecies, *this second period of wars will lead to Antichrist.*

The Gospel, too, seems to confirm that there will be two different periods: the beginning of the end, and the end proper, with an intervening respite. The beginning of the end constitutes what theologians refer to as the "remote signs" of Antichrist. The end happenings constitute those referred to as the "proximate signs" of Antichrist.

Even with the sheer volume of Old Testament prophecy about the coming of the Messiah, the Old Testament Rabbis were also consistently wrong when they attempted to extend an educated guess as to the time of the Messiah's arrival. And they were dealing with prophecy of predestination -- not merely conditional prophecies. We do not know when either this chastisement or the privately foretold age of peace to follow it might occur. The author has numerous manuscripts in his possession from *approved prophets* themselves who *guessed* wrong about the time of a foretold chastisement. Almost everyone who gets into the "guessing game" as to when prophesied events will occur is ultimately proven to be wrong.

E. LIFE IN THE AGE OF PEACE

One of the greatest 20th century mystics is a saintly French parish priest, Père Lamy (1855-1931). His Christian spirituality was expressed by his bishop in the following manner, "I have in my diocese another Curé of Ars."

One of Lamy's great friends, the lay Catholic philosopher and theologian, Jacques Maritain, who wrote the Preface to Comte Paul Biver's famous biographical work, *Père Lamy.* Therein, Maritain described Lamy's gift of prophecy in this manner, (p.11)

> "As regards the prophetic gifts of Père Lamy, I only say here that to many, and especially to the Vicar General Dupin, he had formally foretold the War [World War I] some years before it broke out."

Père Lamy himself acknowledged his prophetic charism, (p.142)

> "She [the Bl. Virgin] has been good enough to lift for me a corner of the curtain which hides the future from us."

He said Our Lady told him about the coming of the Age of Peace;

> **"Peace will be given back to the world, but I shall not see it, ... War is big business.** The manufacturer of the aeroplane, the exploitation of the mines, the iron works, *all that will dwindle.* ***There will no longer be those great factories where morality withers and disappears.*** *The working class will be bound to turn back the land.*
>
> ***"When peace is given back to the world, big business will shrink to smaller proportions*** *and will stay there. Everything will grow less. ...When peace is given back to the world, plots of* [farm] *land will rise to more value than they have now.* ***Even if the old workmen insist on dying in towns, that will come to pass..."***

Our Lady told Père Lamy about the reflourishing of religion.

> **"The world will have to be reevangelized over again** ***and that will be work for a whole generation.*** ... The spiritual state of the first Christians will come back moreover, ***there will be so few men on earth."***

> "[from p.67] The monasteries will flourish again, the convents will fill up again. After these calamities, souls in great numbers will come and dwell in them again."

CHAPTER 10

THE AGE OF THE ANTICHRIST

The ultimate arrival of Antichrist is not a "conditional" prophecy. It comes from public prophecy of "predestination." *This is universally taught by the Fathers of the Church.* However, in the more recent past many good Christians have wondered if Communism/ Socialism was or is the Antichrist. Prior to that many Catholics and Protestants wondered if Napoleon, Hitler, or Stalin was he.

Today, as in the past, there are a number of sincere Catholics and Protestants who are confused as to whether Antichrist is an individual, a movement, or a series of calamities. Cardinal Ratzinger has publicly commented upon "a resurgence of Neo-Pelagianism" in the Church. With the appearance of its companion New Age movement, some Catholics have compared these recent developments with statements of Popes in this century about our living in an age which is Antichristian and anti-gospel. When they consider all of these happenings, *they have conjectured whether the "New Age Movement" might perhaps be THE Antichrist.* Several English language Catholic publications have *openly discussed* this "possibility" within the last five or six years.

Prior to an evaluation of that thesis or any other which could entertain the idea of the Antichrist's coming in our age, several observations are necessary.

(1) There have been both disasters and consolations for the Church in every age of the Church.

(2) In every age there have been Christians who contemplated contemporary disasters and wondered aloud if Antichrist might be coming in their time.

(3) Some of the Christians who so wondered were highly educated, highly intelligent, and emotionally stable Catholics. To so wonder is *not* the mark of a stupid person.
(4) Some who so wondered were even expert theologians.

One in particular was a Pope of the greatest personal sanctity, St. Gregory the Great. Additionally, he was brilliant and one of the greatest theologians in the history of the Church. So it is no badge of ignorance or credulity to prematurely wonder about or anticipate the arrival of the end times.

We will now discuss a *few* examples from amongst over a dozen which are available from throughout the history of the Church to firmly establish the points just made. Let us return again to St. Paul.

> "For the day of the Lord will not come unless the apostasy comes first, and the man of sin is revealed, the son of perdition who opposes and is exalted above all that is called God, or that is worshipped; so that he sits in the temple and gives himself out as if he were God. *Do you not remember that when I was still with you, I used to tell you these things?*"[531]

We know from Patristic writings that many early Christians thought Christ might return in a very short period of time. They knew from the Apostles that the Antichrist must precede the Second Coming of Christ. In 64 A.D., the Roman Emperor Nero had declared it a crime merely to be a Christian. For this and other acts performed by Nero, many 1st century Christians came to the conclusion that Nero was probably the Antichrist.

It has been the common opinion of the best Scriptural exegetes for well over fifteen hundred years that Paul wrote his "man of sin" warning to the Thessalonians in order to calm their fears that Antichrist had arrived in the person of the Roman Emperor Nero. So, we know even from Scripture that Christians (from the earliest days of the Church) have precipitously "wondered" if their age was ushering in the Antichrist. Christians have been engaged in this type of conjecture almost from the beginning of the Church, certainly even prior to all of the books of the Bible having been written. Every believing Christian longs for the heavenly Jerusalem.

---

[531] 2nd. Thessalonians, 2:3-6 *RSV. Catholic Edition*, 1965.

If looked at calmly, it is really quite natural for a Christian to want the present suffering to be over and for Our Lord to return in all His glory.

1. Scripture

At the time of Christ, believing Jews were able to determine from the predictions of the prophets where the Messiah would be born, many of His miracles, and His manner of death. But they did not know *when* He would come. Only when the specific events foretold of his arrival were in the process of fulfillment did they "know." Similarly, in particular we know from (1) the Book of Revelation (St. John), and (2) from Old Testament prophecies, and (3) from St. Paul, many details about the Antichrist, the events which precede his rise to power, his faked miracles, his final demise and many other things. As with the coming of the true Messiah, *what we do not know is when.* But we have signs to look for, just as the Chosen People had signs by which to recognize the Messiah when he arrived.

2. Tradition

The thesis that Christians of the Apostolic and Sub-Apostolic Ages received from the Apostles additional specific data about Antichrist is a thesis which no serious Patristic scholar can question. This thesis is also very clearly stated in Scripture. St. Paul's statement quoted above (which we have already quoted several times in this book) about the signs of the coming of Antichrist closes with:

> "And you know what is restraining him (the man of sin) *now* so that he may be revealed in his time."[532]

St. Paul does not elucidate further in that letter on what it is that restrains the coming of the Antichrist "now." He simply says to the Thessalonians, "you know." It is clear from this passage that the Thessalonians knew for certain, but from *Scripture alone* we know very little.

---

[532] 2nd Thessalonians, 2:6.

Many of those "things" which St. Paul says he orally taught to his flocks (as well as the oral teachings of the other Apostles) were passed on "Traditum" to the Apostles' disciples. They in turn passed them on to the Apostolic Fathers of the Church, who in turn passed then on to later Fathers. That is patently provable from the following point: It is obvious from the context of Paul's remark that it was common knowledge amongst the Christians of Thessalonica.

But we do not *know* today from Scripture what that specific thing is that retrains the coming of Antichrist. St. Jerome however, does refer to a "common tradition" amongst the Fathers as to what "restrains him." The reader will remember that this was discussed at some length earlier in the book.

The vast majority of the Fathers who wrote on the subject specifically tell us through Tradition that what restrains the Antichrist's coming is the final destruction of an Empire, which they interpreted to be a Roman Empire. St. Jerome even tells us, "it is the common teaching" among Christian writers. But, along with many other traditional teachings of the Church, this has *never* been defined as De Fide by the Church.

3. Is Eschatology Still Important in the 20th Century?

There are those Catholics who will tell you that to study doctrine concerning the Antichrist, or the latter, or end times, is either a waste of time or unimportant. *That opinion is even held by some orthodox Catholic scholars.*

If eschatology is a waste of time, then why is it treated with such importance in Scripture, in Tradition, and by the Magisterium?

(1) *Scripture* - Why did the Apostles emphasize this doctrine in sacred Scripture?

(2) *Tradition* - Why did the Fathers refer so often to the latter and end times and in particular to Antichrist in their writings? Some of the Fathers wrote entire books on the received doctrine on Antichrist.

(3) *Some modern writers state that the earliest Fathers wrote about eschatology because of* an early sense in the Church that Jesus Christ was going to return very soon.

They therefore somehow conclude that since we now know better, that eschatology is no longer *important.*

(4) But interest in eschatology is *not* limited to the very early Fathers. The "sense" of Christ's imminent return was long gone by the time of St. John Damascene in the mid-8th century, yet St. John wrote extensively on the Antichrist and the Parousia.

(5) *Magisterium* - Why have so many Popes written commentaries on general eschatology?

The sacred writers of Scripture and the Fathers heavily emphasized the importance of a Christian being conversant with the doctrines of the end times. Those who make light of eschatology, whether they know it or not, are violating one of the most central exhortations to be found in Revelation.

There are a number of "Prophetic Books" in the Old Testament. The "Book of Revelation" is the only "Prophetic Book" in the New Testament, in the sense that its *primary* purpose is to prophesy future events. It is a book begun and completed in mystery. *Here we are discussing mystery in the sense that there are pieces of information in the Book of the Apocalypse' prophesied events which are not supplied in that book.* The question remains: how much, if any, additional information is supplied by Tradition.

4. A Knowledge of Tradition Stops Many Eschatological Mistakes

Tradition fills in or clarifies a fair number of pieces *(though far from all)* of the prophetic jigsaw puzzle. God wills that, "No man knows the day nor the hour." If Tradition filled in *all* the missing pieces, everyone who read the Bible, *and*, knew "Tradition" would know the "day and the hour." There would be no "mystery" left about prophesied events which God in his providence wills there should remain about these foretold events. So, of what value is knowing the teachings of Tradition on eschatology? *The answer is that Tradition keeps us from making some very basic eschatological mistakes.*

Example:

(1) Many modern "Catholic" scholars think Antichrist is most probably (or well could be) some movement, or, a group of individuals. Consequently, it is not unusual to find otherwise orthodox lay Catholics who are terribly confused on this issue.
(2) (While we are not going to take the space to get into the merits of their following argument), such people will tell you that Scripture is not absolutely clear on this issue.
(3) Tradition, however, clarifies the point that Antichrist will be an individual, i.e., he *cannot* be a group or movement. The Fathers and Doctors teach that Antichrist will *appear* as an individual human being. No Father denies it. With only two exceptions, the Patristic writers also universally teach Antichrist will actually be a man (Origen and Hippolytus erroneously say he will be the Devil or a demon who merely *appears* to be a human being). But nonetheless, the Fathers universally teach Antichrist to *appear as an individual, he will not appear as a movement or group*. [It is also conjectural whether either of the two exceptions of Origin and Hippolytus would break the Pope Leo XIII's rule about specific denial by any Father.[533]]

The early Christians were familiar with the writings of Sts. Paul and John and the other sacred writers on the end times and particularly on the ultimate arrival of "the Man of Sin, the Son of Perdition" i.e., the Antichrist. They had many questions on this doctrine as is evidenced in the extensive writings of the early Fathers on the subject. They were intelligent human beings. The same questions came to their minds that come to ours when we read apocalyptic utterances throughout the N.T. The Fathers addressed

[533] Two of the qualifications for being a "full" Father of the Church are (1) general orthodoxy, and (2) holiness of life. As stated earlier, some of Origen's works were condemned as heretical by three Councils of the Church. That is why Origen is usually not included in lists of Fathers of the Church. Hippolytus became an anti-Pope, and was only reconciled with the Church on his death bed. For these well-known reasons, many Patrologists have conjectured concerning to what degree Hippolytus can be considered as fully meeting the qualifications for a Father of the Church. An alternative might be to view them simply as authoritative "Ecclesiastical Writers."

these apocalyptic issues from the totality of that which they had received either by word of mouth or by letter.

5. St. John's Apocalypse and Systematic Theology

It is in all of the senses mentioned above that Fr. Kramer makes the following observations,

> "In the knowledge of St. John, the Church surely possessed of divine truth all she possesses today though in a less developed form. **Hence for an interpretation, no one is restricted to the words of the text alone but may take *the Apocalypse as a poetic description of many truths written down later in the traditional writings of the great Fathers and Doctors*.**
>
> "If therefore an interpretation, which holds the doctrines of the Church of today to have been clearly outlined in the mind of the Sacred Writer and which understands these doctrines as portrayed in the historico-prophetical visions of the Apocalypse to be the same as those contained in the crystallized expressions of theology, will work out logically from beginning to end, such an interpretation should be justifiable. **And surely St. John had a clear knowledge of the doctrines which in later ages were crystallized by the church, and he might express them in symbolic language such as makes up the Apocalypse.**"[534]

Some of the above is somewhat complex in its logical development. It is a complex subject. However, the views stated *are* those held by most truly orthodox Catholic Scripture scholars and theologians of the 20th century.

Shorthand for Father Kramer's remarks above is the following: what St. John writes cryptically under the inspiration of the Holy Spirit, is more clearly explained (yet still veiled in degrees of mystery) by the Fathers of the Church in their expositions of that which comes from all aspects of Tradition and Scripture.

As St. John himself said in the final conclusion to his Gospel, in which he describes that which he has written therein:

---

[534] *The Book of Destiny*, Fr. Leonard Kramer, Buechler Pub. Co., Belleville, Il. 1955, p. 17.

> "This disciple [John] is the one who vouches for these things and has written them down, and we know that his testimony is true.
>
> "There was much else that Jesus did; and if it were written down in detail, I do not suppose the world itself would hold all the books that would be written."[535]

St. John is obviously describing much more detail than what was preserved in Scripture. The body of oral Tradition and exegesis - which the Fathers wrote down for us - at the very least most probably holds additional details which help us to understand more of the eschatological jigsaw puzzle. This is especially so after the beginning of the development of theology per se - let us arbitrarily say with St. Irenaeus. Fr. Kramer (and many other orthodox theologians) make the point that it is perfectly legitimate to interpret the Book of Revelation in the light of subsequent systematic theology which is based upon the totality of Apostolic Tradition.

6. The Church's Traditional Teaching on Eschatology

On many of the issues to follow, the Church has never provided a formal declaration on the proper interpretation of various Scripture passages. This is also the case with many of the materials which come to us from Tradition. There are only a few traditional teachings of the Church as to events (A) which must preceed the Parousia, and, (B) surrounding the Parousia itself;

(1) The Gospel must be preached throughout the whole world.
(2) There will be a great apostasy or religious defection
(3) The man of sin, the Antichrist must appear
(4) The Jews as a nation will be converted after the full number of the Gentiles enter the Church
(5) Elias is to come and restore all things
(6) there will be a final transformation of the universe, and the world will be purified by fire.
(7) the Parousia, the second coming of Christ,
(8) the bodily resurrection of the dead.
(9) the final judgment, death, heaven and hell.

[535] John 21:24-25, New Jerusalem Bible, Doubleday, 1985.

Given the paucity of dogmatic eschatological definitions it is very important to emphasize the teachings of the Fathers and Doctors of the Church in order to glean a sense for the traditional teaching of the Church in this area.

7. St. & Dr. Robert Bellarmine (1542-1621)

Many of the *Fathers and Doctors* will be quoted at various places in this section on the Antichrist. But for several reasons, the author will give special weight herein to the teachings of St. Robert Bellarmine. Of the thirty-two Doctors of the Church, Bellarmine is chronologically the last "Doctor" to specialize in extensive study of eschatology and subsequently write about the subject of the Antichrist.

Bellarmine died in 1621. Several of his contemporaries were also later declared to be "Doctors" of the Church. However, none of these "contemporaries" published an in-depth study of the subject material in this chapter. The only person to be declared a "Doctor" who lived after the time of Bellarmine and his contemporaries was St. Alphonsus Ligouri, who died in 1787. Ligouri, whose specialty was moral theology, made no great study of the end times or of Antichrist. So Bellarmine is the latest "Doctor of the Church" to make an in-depth study of the Church's teachings on Antichrist and to write extensively on this subject. For this reason, the author is emphasizing Bellarmine's teachings wherever they apply to the material that follows.

Bellarmine is known to scholars to be one of the most learned and both broadly and deeply read scholars in the history of the Church. He was aware of and familiar with the writings of the vast majority of the previous Fathers and Doctors of the Church. The most amazing aspect of Bellarmine is that he was not a theological gadfly. He learning was simply so vast that he was considered *the* living expert of his time on almost every subject he spent any serious effort studying. In addition to being publicly recognized as one of the most brilliant man of his age, he was also gifted with close to a photographic memory.

Successive Popes sought him out as a theological advisor. For this reason, he spent the majority of his most fruitful years posted in Rome.

> "In 1597 (Pope) Clement VIII recalled him to Rome and made him his own theologian and likewise Examiner of Bishops and Consultor of the Holy Office. Further, in 1599, he made him Cardinal-Priest of the title of Santa Maria *in via,* alleging as his reason for this promotion that *'the Church of God had not his equal in learning.*'"[536]

In the face of the Protestant movement, it was Robert Bellarmine who wrote the most incisive and telling Catholic commentary on their theology. For this reason his *De Controversiis* became famous throughout Europe in both Protestant and Catholic circles.

> "This monumental work was the earliest attempt to systematize the various controversies of the time and made an immense impression throughout Europe... Nor has it even yet been superseded as the classical book on its subject-matter."[537]

Because some Protestant theologians were proposing the idea that the Pope and/or the Papacy was the Antichrist, Bellarmine immersed himself in (1) the Scriptural passages dealing with Antichrist, and then (2) the writings of all the Fathers, Doctors, and great theologians on the subject. He synopsized his research and conclusions in his work *De Summo Pontifice* (On the Supreme Pontiff). All of the quotes from Bellarmine in this section are from that work.[538] Shortly we will begin our investigation into particular Scripture passages, Tradition, and the writings of particular Fathers, Doctors, and other eminent theologians of the Church on the subject of Antichrist.

---

[536] *Catholic Encyclopedia*, 1913 Edition, Vol. 2, p. 412.

[537] Ibid.

[538] All of the English quotes are translations of the author. While many of Bellarmine's works have been translated from their original Latin into French and German, very few have been translated into English. For each English quote presented, the Latin original will be shown here in the footnotes. All of the quotes are from *Bellarmini, Opera Omnia, Disputationum Roberti Bellarmini*. The Particular Quotes are from the section containing *De Controversiis - Christianae Fidei, Tomus Primus, Liber Tertius, De Summo Pontifice*, written in 1577. The quoted edition was printed under the aegis of Cardinal Archbishop Sforza at Naples in 1856. The only footnote reference for the following quotes of Bellarmine therefore will be the page number from this edition.

A. THE ESCHATOLOGY OF THE FATHERS AND DOCTORS

(1) **We will anchor the Fathers in St. John Damascene since he was the last of the Fathers.**

(2) **We will anchor the Doctors in St. Robert Bellarmine since he is the latest Doctor to deal with the subject of the end times in similar depth.**

Between them we have a reliable compendium of the traditional teachings of the Church on the Antichrist and the Parousia.

1. The Fathers and Doctors are Unanimous That "Antichrist Appears as an Individual"

The Church Fathers show unanimity through (1) their Oral Tradition (as ultimately contained in Patristic Writings), and (2) in their commentaries on Scripture on the following: *They all say that Antichrist will be an individual man***.** This is very important for a Christian to know, since during the foretold chastisement, the prophecies say many people will mistakenly think it is the end of the world (instead of a minor chastisement), and despair. If "the Chastisement" should occur in our times, in order to properly interpret the events of their times we minimally need to know the following; what we call the chastisement does not meet what Tradition, Scripture, the writings of the Fathers, as well as *approved* private prophecies tell us of the Antichrist or the Parousia.

2. The Book of Daniel, Other O.T. Prophetical Books and the Apocalypse

Many late 20th century Catholics may be surprised at the frequency of the following quotes from the Fathers on (1) the Book of Daniel, and (2) other Old Testament Prophetical Books, and (3) the Apocalypse. It is now uncommon to hear the Fathers quoted on *Eschatology*. That is unfortunate because *today these prophetical books are treated by most "higher critics" and their students as almost totally indecipherable code.*

Many higher critics claim these prophetic Scriptural books are only meant to impart a moral message. Those books are treated by most "higher critics" as mysteries wrapped in enigma which contain no prophetic messages about the end times. That was *not* the approach or teaching of the early Fathers and Doctors of the Church. And they stated that much of their exegesis on those books was what they had received from apostolic Tradition.

In the history of the Church, great Scriptural exegetes (e.g. Hippolytus, Ambrose, Augustine, Jerome, Thomas Aquinas, Bellarmine, Suarez, Cajetan, all but one of whom are saints) commonly wrote either full or partial commentaries at least on *Daniel*, and often on the other O.T. Prophetical works. They just as commonly and consistently quoted *Daniel* in companion with the book of the *Apocalypse*, which today we usually refer to as the Book of Revelation. *Of the Fathers who wrote Scriptural commentaries*, it is difficult therefore to think of one of them who did *not* write a commentary in one form or another on the *Book of Daniel in the eschatological sense*.

This commentarial tradition of comparing *Daniel* (and some other O.T. Books) with the *Apocalypse* carries through to the mid-twentieth century. Unfortunately, within the last few decades there has been a regrettable decrease in the study of eschatology, which decrease is prominently observable in many Catholic universities and seminaries.[539] However, one of the best and most recent in-depth scholarly studies of the subject is *The Book of Destiny.* In it Fr. Kramer states,

> "However, from the contents of the Apocalypse, it is perfectly plain, that St. John verbally copied many passages from the O.T. to give them fuller expression and to put them in a context where their true meaning can be easily understood. Such use of the prophets appears decisively intentional in many instances. Many prophecies of the Old Testament are just fragments, are mere glimpses of the future empire of the Messias. *St. John takes these fragments and pieces them together and shows the full import of each prophetic glimpse. His work is* ***not*** *a compilation of those prophecies*

[539] However there are some notable exceptions such as Fr. Vincent Micelli, S.J.'s, recently published, *The Antichrist*.

> *but is as concise as possible a statement of the revelations made to him.* Since those revelations were the completed visions, the glimpses of the Old Testament prophecies fit in here and there without an apparent conscious effort by the Apocalyptist."[540]

Herein Fr. Kramer has restated the continuous Catholic teaching on this matter since the earliest Fathers' commentaries on this subject. A little further on Fr. Kramer says,

> **"It is claimed that he refers to the book of Daniel in forty-five places. Isaias, Ezechiel and Zacharias are next most frequently in evidence.** And the book of Psalms has a large share in his attention. *With all that, the book is not a compilation but a logical unity from beginning to end.*"[541]

From the above it should be obvious to any reader that there is an implicit necessity for anyone studying the *Apocalypse* to at least be readily familiar with the *Book of Daniel*. Most advantageously such a student also should be familiar with at least *Isaiah*, *Ezekial* and *Zacharias*. For as St. Augustine observed, "The New Testament lies hid in the Old, and the Old is revealed in the New."

B. ST. JOHN DAMASCENE (DAMASCUS) (8TH CENTURY), HIS ESCHATOLOGY

In order to establish what Tradition and the Fathers tell us of the Antichrist, we will begin by quoting one of the Fathers at great length. Most Catholic scholars consider this Doctor of the Church to be the last of the Fathers.[542] He was truly one of the greatest saints and scholars of his age. He was immersed in the teachings, writings, and oral traditions of the Fathers who preceded him. He quoted from them as easily as today's Scripture scholars quote from the Bible. Also, *many manuscripts of early Christian writings*

---

540 *The Book of Destiny*, p. 5.

541 Ibid. p. 6.

542 There are however others who consider Sts. Anselm and Bonaventure to be additional "Fathers."

were available to him which in the course of time have been lost. Fortunately, he quoted from many of them in his writings.

Born around the year 674, he was ordained a priest sometime before the year 726 A.D. and lived to be an old man (certainly past the year 743). He had a consuming love for Our Lady, writing many treatises on her "Dormitian" ("Falling Asleep/Assumption"), body and soul, into Heaven. As his name indicates, he was from Damascus, Syria.

The following is quoted from St. John Damascene's, *Orthodox Faith*, Book Four, published by "Fathers of the Church, Inc." pp 398-400. *We can be sure that this is not his own private prophecy, or opinion, but rather it is from tradition for he says, "I shall add nothing of my own, but shall gather together into one, those things which have been worked out by the most eminent of teachers and make a compendium of them."*[543] St John says:

> "One should know that the *Antichrist* must come. Antichrist, to be sure, is everyone who does not confess that the Son of God came in the flesh, is perfect God, and became perfect man while at the same time He was God. In a peculiar and special sense, however, he who is to come at the consummation of the world is Antichrist. So, it is first necessary for the Gospel to have been preached to all the Gentiles, as the Lord said, *and then he shall come unto conviction of the impious Jews. For the Lord said to them: 'I am come in the name of the Father, and you receive me not: if another shall come in his own name, him you will receive.'* And the Apostle: 'Because they receive not the love of the truth, that they might be saved. Therefore God shall send them the operation of error, to believe lying: that all may be judged who have not believed the truth but have consented to iniquity. *Hence, the Jews did not receive the Lord Jesus Christ and God, although He was the Son of God, but the deceiver who says that he is God they will*

[543] This statement however does not and cannot certify that everything which he says is infallibly from oral Tradition with a capitol "T." St. John simply states that he is not deliberately inserting his own opinions but rather is quoting the teachings (which includes this section on Antichrist) which have been handed down to his time of the mid-8th century A.D.

receive. For, that he will call himself God, the angel who taught Daniel thus declares: 'He will make no account of the gods of his Fathers.' And the Apostle: 'Let no man deceive you by any means; for unless there come a revolt first, and the man of sin be revealed, the son of perdition, who opposeth and is lifted up above all that is called God or that is worshipped, so that he sitteth in the temple of God,' *he says -- not, however, in ours, but in the former one, that of the Jews, for he will not come to us, but to the Jews* (initially) -- not for the sake of Christ and Christ's, for which reason, also, he is called Antichrist.

"*The Gospel, then, must first be preached in all nations, 'and then that wicked one shall be revealed*: whose coming is according to the working of Satan, in all power and signs and lying wonders, in all seduction of iniquity to them that perish: whom the Lord shall kill with the words of his mouth and shall destroy with the coming of his brightness.' *Thus, the devil does not himself become man after the Incarnation of the Lord* -- God forbid --! *but a man is born of fornication* and receives into himself the whole operation of Satan, *for God permits the Devil to inhabit him, because He (God) foresees the future perversity of his will.*

"So, he is born of fornication,[544] as we said, and is brought up unnoticed; but of a sudden he rises up, revolts, and rules. During the first part of his reign -- of his tyranny, rather -- he plays more the part of sanctity; but when he gains complete control, he persecutes the Church of God and reveals all his wickedness. And he shall come 'in signs and lying wonders' -- sham ones and not real -- and he will seduce those whose intention rests on a rotten and unstable foundation and make them abandon the living God, 'inasmuch as to scandalize (if possible) even the elect.'

---

[544] Fr. Huchedé says, "St. John Damascus and some other Fathers are of the opinion that Antichrist will be an illegitimate offspring. *[Lib. iv, ch. 27. Orthodoxy of the Faith]*. Holy Scripture says nothing of this, at least in an explicit manner, and tradition bearing on it is *not* unanimous enough to merit for it anything more than a probable certainty." Referenced from *History of Antichrist*, Rev. P. Huchedé, Professor of Theology at the Grand Seminary of Laval, France, English Edition of 1884, Nicholas Bray, New York, Reprinted by Tan Books and Publishers.

> "And *Enock and Elias* the Thesbite will be sent and they shall 'turn the heart of the fathers to the children,' that is to say, turn the synagogue to our Lord Jesus Christ and the preaching of the Apostles. *And they will be destroyed by him.* Then the Lord will come from heaven in the same way that the holy Apostles saw Him going into Heaven, perfect God and perfect man, with glory and power; and he shall destroy the man of iniquity, the son of perdition, with the spirit of His mouth. So, let no one expect the Lord to come from the earth, but from Heaven, as He Himself has positively assured us."[545]

We have chosen St. John Damascene to begin this section for a number of reasons. He was a great Scripture expert, as were St. Chrysostom and St. Jerome, St. Augustine and many others. Like them, he was a true scholar as most of the Fathers were. He was a great Saint, which they also were. But most importantly, he is traditionally considered to be the last of the Fathers, with access to all of the prior study which had gone into the body of both /t/ radition, and /T/radition, relating to Antichrist. Additionally, he is centuries beyond the time that Churchmen were considering the imminent arrival of Antichrist. Therefore, his testimony clearly demonstrates that these eschatological doctrines are continuously vitally important in the Faith.

From St. John Damascene, one of the greatest Fathers of the Church, we know in one sense all of those who deny Christ are antichrists. But in a more specific sense a particular man called Antichrist is probably to be born of fornication, i.e., he would be an illegitimate child. Initially, he shall preach principally (but not exclusively) to the Jews who have not followed Christ. He will claim to be God and will sit in the temple in Jerusalem making such claims. He will himself be of Jewish blood "making no account of the Gods of his fathers." (The Jews would never accept a Gentile as their Messiah since their tradition demands that he be a Jew). Antichrist will be opposed by Enoch and Elias, whom he will kill. Shortly after he kills them, Jesus will slay him.

---

[545] *De Fide Orthodoxa,* St. John Damascene, quoted from The Fathersof the Chaurch, Vol. 37, (Pub: The Fathers of the Church, Inc., New York, Trans. by Frederick H. Chase, Jr., 1958), pp. 398-400.

As a final confirmation of just how strongly the last of the Fathers, St. John Damascene, held that it was of apostolic tradition that Antichrist will be an individual, we shall quote from the very last paragraph of his *De Fide Orthodoxa.* St. John closes *with a discussion of the very end of time,* thus driving this point inexorably home:

> "And so, with our souls again united to our bodies, which will have become incorrupt and put off incorruption, we shall rise again and stand before the terrible judgement seat of Christ. And *the Devil* and his demons, ***and his man***, which is to say, ***the Antichrist***, and the impious sinners will be given over to everlasting fire, which will not be a material fire such as we are accustomed to, but a fire such as God might know."[546]

1. St. Augustine and Other Fathers

There are many others of the Fathers who speak in as great or even greater detail than St. John Damascene of the coming of Antichrist. Earlier in the book, in chapter 4, pages 225-230, the reader saw specific texts from St. Jerome, St. John Chrysostom, St. Cyril of Jerusalem, and St. Ephraem of Edessa which make this abundantly clear. Now we shall see St. Augustine on this subject. In his commentaries on the Psalms, St. Augustine demonstrates in many cases that what the Psalms anticipated in a veiled form, is laid out more clearly in the New Testament. The following is quoted at length to assure the reader of its context.

> "19. [V. 20] *Arise, O Lord, let not man prevail.* The Psalmist sighs for the coming of the Judgement, but before it does come, *Let the Gentiles,* he asks, *be judged in thy sight.* In secret that is, under the eye of God, since the Judgement is pronounced in God's sight and only the handful of saints and just men are aware of it. [V. 21] ***Appoint, O Lord, a lawgiver over them.*** **This if I am not mistaken, will be *the* Antichrist to whom the Apostle (Paul) refers in the words: *When the man of sin shall be revealed*.** *Let the Gentiles know themselves to be but men;* and since they refuse to be set

[546] Ibid. p. 406.

> free by the Son of God, to belong to the Son of Man and become sons of men, in other words new men, **let them be slaves to *a human being***,... since they are themselves but men."[547] [emphasis - author's]

As we can see from the context, St. Augustine teaches that the "man of sin," the Antichrist is "*a* human being." There is no confusion in Augustine's mind about whether *the* Antichrist spoken of by Paul is an individual, rather than some consortium of causes and effects (as some modern scholars would have us to believe). It was the *universal* teaching of the Fathers that Antichrist will be an individual man.

When the Fathers are unanimous on a point of Doctrine, then it is of Tradition. In that case it is safely accepted as clearly of Catholic teaching. St. Robert Bellarmine, a Doctor of the Church, repeatedly made the observation that the Fathers are so unanimous on the point that the Antichrist will be an individual that this fact is unarguably a full teaching Tradition of the Church.

2. DIDACHE's Commentary on Antichrist

The other Fathers *amplify* many of these points, but the basics are here. *THE* Antichrist, first of all, is an individual man born as other men. Antichrist is not an organization, or a current of events or conditions. As one final confirmation of this unwavering testimony from Tradition let us turn to the "**DIDACHE**." It is understood to be,

> "the most important document of the SubApostolic period, the oldest source of ecclesiastical law which we possess. ... The chapter on the *parousia* of the Lord and the Christian duties arising therefrom constitutes the conclusion [of the DIDACHE]."[548]

---

547 *The Ancient Christian Writers, St. Augustine on the Psalms*, Dame Scholastica Hebgin & Dame Felicitas Corrigan, Vol. 1, Psalms 1-29. The Newman Press, Westminster, Maryland, 1960, p. 125.

548 *Patrology*, Quasten, Vol. 1, p. 30.

Most scholars date this document somewhere between 80 A.D. and 150 A.D. Quasten says, "the DIDACHE must have originated between 100 A.D. and 150 A.D."[549] Quoting and commenting on the words of Enoch, it expresses the Tradition extant at the writing of this document:

> *"In the last days there will multiply false prophets and corruptors and they shall be changed into wolves of their flocks. Charity will be converted into hatred. There will be an increase in iniquity; men will mutually hate each other, they will persecute and betray each other and* ***then there will appear the deceiver of the world saying he is the son of God.*** *He will make signs and do miracles. The earth will be given into* ***his*** *hands and* ***he*** *will do such iniquities as has never before been done throughout the centuries.*
>
> "Therefore, what men have created will be cleansed by fire and many will be scandalized and will perish, but those who persevere in their faith will be saved from the evil one. Then there will appear the signs of truth. First, the sign of the open heaven; second, the sign of the trumpets; third, the resurrection of the dead, but, not all according to what has been said. The Lord will come and all the saints with Him. Then the world will see the Lord coming upon the clouds of heaven."[550]

As we can see, this document from the infant Church also testifies that the belief of the earliest Christians (many of whom had been personally taught by the Apostles) clearly was; that the final Antichrist would be an individual human being.

> [COMMENT: It is also interesting to note that there is no reference at all to a specific N.T. Scripture canon of any kind whatsoever in the *DIDACHE*. This is *one* of the strongest arguments for the extreme early date of its composition.[551]

549 Ibid. p. 37.

550 *Enchiridion Patris*. #10

551 It was most probably not composed at one time by one author. There is extensive internal evidence to support this judgment that it's final form is a compilation of at least several documents. Its antiquity was so firmly established in the minds of Christians that both Eusebius Pamphilus and St. Athanasius had to later inform their flocks that it did not have equal authority with Scripture.

At this point the Church is still teaching very simply from what has been received from the totality of Tradition. At the point of the *DIDACHE*'s composition clear distinction is not yet being drawn between oral and written "tradition."]

3. The Fathers and Doctors Universally Teach That the Antichrist is an Individual

The reader has already read multiple quotes from Fathers and Doctors of the Church which clearly absolutely teach that *the* Antichrist spoken of in the New Testament will be an individual human being. But many modern Biblical commentaries state that this is not the case. St. Paul says in 2nd Thessalonians,

> "For the day of the Lord will not come unless the apostasy[552] comes first, and the man of sin is revealed, *the son of perdition* who opposes and is exalted above all that is called God, or that is worshipped; so that *he* sits in the temple and gives himself out as if *he* were God. *Do you not remember that when I was still with you, I used to tell you these things?*"[553]

In its commentary on this passage, the *New Jerome Biblical Commentary* states,

> "Description of the 'Man of Rebellion' is indebted to a prophetic depiction of the historical despot who caused apostacy (Dan 11:36-37). As vv 8-10 will make clear, **this rebel *(ho anomos)* is an imagined, symbolic figure representing a real evil**, the antithesis of faith."[554]

This Biblical commentary is largely a work of Raymond Brown, a higher critic Scripture scholar previously discussed at some length in the Chapter 2 (See Index). As we can see, this commentary ranges itself against the universal teaching of the Fathers and Doctors of

---

552 In some editions of the Bible, this word is translated as "revolt."

553 2nd Thessalonians, 2:3-5 *RSV, Catholic Edition*, 1965.

554 *The New Jerusalem Biblical Commentary*, edited by Raymond G. Brown, S.S., Joseph A. Fitzmyer S.J., Roland E. Murphy, O.Carm., Prentice Hall, Englewood Cliffs, N.J., 1988. pp. 873 & 874., Pr.

the Church on this subject. The Fathers and Doctors teach that *the* Antichrist spoken of by Paul in 2 Cor. will be a specific human being. Raymond Brown and his associates say he is an imaginary "symbolic figure." It cannot be both ways. Either the Fathers and Doctors of the Church are wrong, or Raymond Brown and his theological look-alikes are wrong! The Magisterium teaches us that when the Fathers are universal in their interpretation of a passage of Scripture, that that interpretation is of Faith.

> **"The Holy Fathers, are of supreme authority whenever they all interpret in one and the same manner any text of the Bible, ... for their unanimity clearly evinces that such interpretation has come down from the Apostles as a matter of Catholic faith."**[555]

We will now synopsize texts from the Fathers previously presented in this matter on the Antichrist's individuality:

(1) Sts. Irenaeus, Ambrose, Jerome, Augustine, Pope Gregory the Great, and Anselm (Antichrist's capital will be in Jerusalem) - Tertullian-F, Lactantius-F, St. Cyril of Jerusalem-F&D and St. Jerome-F&D (the individual Antichrist comes with a final destruction of the Roman Empire.)

(2) Jerome: it is "what all the ecclesiastical writers have handed down". Amongst others, that is the teaching of St. Ambrose -F&D, St. John Chrysostom-F&D, St. Augustine, St. Pros- per-F, St. Primatius-F, Theophilatus-F, Eucomenius-F, Aimon-F, St. Rupert-F and many other ancient Church writers. St. Ephrem - Final destruction of Roman Empire.

St. Cyril of Jerusalem - This *one* shall seize the power of the Roman Empire, and shall falsely style himself Christ. By the name of Christ he shall deceive the Jews, who are expecting the Anointed (71); and he shall seduce the gentiles by his magical illusions.

---

[555] *Providentissimus Deus*, Encyclical of Pope Leo XIII.

St. Ephream - *the man of iniquity* shall be revealed upon the earth, the Seducer of men, and the disturber of the whole earth.

St. Gregory the Great - *the mother of Antichrist*, etc.

St. Jerome - Nor do we think **him** to be the Devil or a demon (as some others do), but one of mankind in whom Satan shall dwell totally ... for he is *the man of sin the son of perdition, such that* ***he*** *will seat himself in the Temple as if he were God.*

St. John Damascene - **One should know that *the Antichrist* must come.** Antichrist, to be sure, is everyone who does not confess that the Son of God came in the flesh, is perfect God, and became perfect man while at the same time He was God. **In a peculiar and special sense, however, *he* who is to come at the consummation of the world is Antichrist.**

Now we will cover more of the foretold events which lead up to the particular appearance of *the* Antichrist. We will cover these events through an interspersion of Oral Tradition, Scripture, and excerpts from Scriptural commentaries of Fathers, Doctors, Saints, and other great theologians of the Church. *We will show the congruity* between all of the above and the private prophesies of many great Saints, Blessed and Venerable of the Church.

C. PRIVATE PROPHECIES ON AN INDIVIDUAL ANTICHRIST

1. St. Methodius

St. Methodius, Bishop and martyr, who lived in the fourth century, prophesied as follows:

"In the latter days of the world, Christians will become ungrateful for the great favors they will receive through the coming of the Great Monarch, by reason of the long period of peace and prosperity on earth which they will enjoy under his reign; Many men will then begin to doubt if the Christian Catholic Faith is really the only sanctifying faith and will

> think that perhaps the Jews are right because they are yet awaiting the Messias."[556]

2. St. Bridget of Sweden (14th Century)

St. Bridget is one of the greatest mystics in the history of the Church. From the age of seven she showed signs of receiving special graces which gave her understanding beyond her years. At the age of thirteen she was married and subsequently bore eight children. One of her daughters is St. Catherine of Sweden. After the death of her husband, St. Bridget founded an order of nuns, the Briggitines. In 1349 A.D. she traveled to Rome and (with the exception of a pilgrimage to the Holy Land) remained there until her death in 1373. In 1370 Pope Urban V confirmed the rule of her congregation. She was canonized a Saint on October 7, 1391, by Pope Bonafice IX.

Her revelations have been extremely well-known throughout the Church to this day. The reader will remember that they are specifically referenced in the *Catholic Encyclopedia* as those which are piously credible. They were also listed as such by Benedict XIV in his *De Servorum Dei Canonizatione et Beatificatione*.

St. Bridget says,

> "Before Antichrist comes, the portals of the Faith will be opened to great numbers of pagans."[557]

This is one of the remote signs of Antichrist. This probably happens during the Age of Peace.

3. St. Hildegard

According to her prophecy,

> "*At that period when Antichrist* ***shall be born****, there will be many wars and right order shall be destroyed on the earth.*

---

[556] Quoted from Dionysius of Luetzenburg's, *Life of Antichrist*, 1682. Chapter 7. As was discussed much earlier in the book under the section on chronological prophecies concerning the Antichrist, this quote cannot be actually proven to be from Methodius. But it is certainly from no later than the 6th century.

[557] *Life and Revelations of St. Bridget*, p. 168.

> Heresy will be rampant and the heretics will preach their errors openly without restraint. *Even among Christians doubt and skepticism will be entertained concerning the beliefs of Catholicism.*"[558]

The author interprets the above to mean one of two possible courses. Possibly Antichrist is born towards the end of the chastisement. This would correspond with the 30 years or more Age of Mary (Age of Peace) talked of earlier at the end of which things begin to fall apart -- which collapse could lead to Antichrist. The other possibility is that people will sufficiently correspond with grace that the Great King will have successors to extend the last of the Holy Roman Empires. It could be either scenario. Only God knows.

4. St. Bridget

St. Bridget gives a sign of the approach of Antichrist.

> "An apparent sign that the Antichrist is coming will be when Christians love error and when the unjust tred spirituality and justice under foot."[560]

D. MORE FROM THE FATHERS ON ANTICHRIST

1. St. Cyril of Jerusalem

St. Cyril, one of the great Eastern Fathers, was recognized by his peers as one of the preeminent Scripture scholars of his age. His knowledge of the writings of the "Fathers" who proceeded him was prodigious. His twenty three "Catecheses" were written circa

---

[558] *Details Concerning the Antichrist, According to Holy Scripture, Tradition and Private Revelation,* Professor Franz Spirago, Prague, Pub: R. Von Acken, Linden, Hanover, Germany, Imprimi Potest, Dr. Anton Podlasha, Vical General, Archdiocese of Prague, 1921, from the English translation of the Benedictine Fathers of Mr. Angel Monastery, St. Benedict, OR., dated June 19, 1949, p. 3.

[560] *Life and Revelations of St. Bridget*, p. 168.

348-350 A.D.[561] They are standard readings in Patristics courses. And the last five "catecheses" (#'s 19-23), commonly called the "Mystagogic Catecheses", are to this day "must reading" for all of those engaged in serious Liturgical studies. St. Cyril says in *Catechesis 15*,

> "and after these shall arise **Antichrist** ... and having by the signs and lying wonders of **his** magical deceit, beguiled the Jews, as though **he** were the expected Christ, **he** shall afterwards characterize **himself** by all kinds of excesses of cruelty and lawlessness .. And ***he* shall perpetrate such things for three years and six months**."[562]
>
> Notice that St. Cyril (both a Father and Doctor of the Church) in referring to the Antichrist specifically uses the words, "he," "his," and "himself," confirming that Antichrist is a specific man.

We find among many of the Fathers of the Church (St. Jerome, St. Augustine, St. Chrysostom, etc.) many specifics about the Antichrist. **William Bousset** (in his 19th century book *Antichrist*) was one of the first to claim that the stories of Antichrist were part of "the Antichrist legend." But he was ultimately forced to admit that in all the Fathers' doctrines pertaining to the Antichrist there exists "order, continuity and system" (Page 14); furthermore, that these revelations must be accepted as of tradition (Page 17); and that originally a secret doctrine concerning the Antichrist appears

---

[561] There has been a long scholarly debate for the last two centuries as to whether the last five "Mystagogic Catecheses" were actually written by Cyril circa 350, or whether they were composed by his successor, Bishop John of Jerusalem circa 390. There is no *absolutely* definitive evidence for either argument. There have been a handful of people (mostly Protestant - who did not like the highly sacramental character of the *Catecheses*) who questioned Cyril's authorship of all the *Catecheses*. But today all twenty three *Catecheses* are again commonly accepted by most scholars as Cyril's work. For an excellent synopsis of these arguments see, *The Byzantine-Slav Liturgy of St. John Chrysostom*, Rev. C. Kucharek, Alleluia Press, Allendale, N.J., 1971, also, *St. Cyril of Jerusalem's Lectures on the Christian Sacraments*, Edited by Lady Margaret - Professor of Divinity, University of Oxford, S.P.C.K., Longon, 1951.

[562] *The Catechetical Lectures of S. Cyril, Archbishop of Jerusalem*, A Library of the Fathers, Oxford, 1845, Cat. 15, p. 190. [This is an Anglican patrology series.]

to have been taught regarding the Antichrist as was recorded by Sulpicius Severus (*Historia* II, 14). **But St. Irenaeus denies there ever existed a "secret doctrine."**[563] But Bousset ultimately admits that since the earliest Christian records there has been no change in the teachings concerning the Antichrist (page 19). *THAT IS EXACTLY HOW ONE DESCRIBES TRADITION.*

2. St. Jerome

St. Jerome also says,

> "*Satan will exercise his influence over all the powers of* ***Antichrist****, both over those of* ***his body and of his soul*** - namely over his will, his intellect and his memory" [From his commentary on the Book of Daniel, Chpt. 7].

Notice that St. Jerome here clearly states that Antichrist will have a soul, ergo, he will be a specific individual. A movement, a time, or a set of circumstances cannot possess a soul. This can

---

[563] The author has quoted Bousset's thesis in its entirely for accuracy and continuity's sake. St. Irenaeus in his *Adversus Haereses* (Against Heresies) says that there was *no* secret doctrine. He states that; since he (Irenaeus) is a disciple of Polycarp, who was a disciple of St. John the Apostle, if there was any "secret doctrine" he would certainly know about it. Irenaeus said this in response to the Gnostic Heretics who claimed they knew "secret doctrines" which had been taught by the Apostles.

However, in the early Church there was such a thing as the "Disciplina Arcani," the "Discipline of the Secret." This had to do with keeping knowledge of the "*Sacred Mysteries*" from the non-Christian community. The first problem developed late in the first century and early in the second when the authorities heard about Christians "Eating the Body and drinking the Blood" (of Christ) in Communion. In order to turn the mob against the Christians, the enemies of the Church subsequently began spreading rumors that the Christians were cannibals. (e.g., See the apologetic writings of St. Justin Martyr and Tertullian.) The elements of the "Creed" and other items dealing with the Eucharistic Liturgy were only explained after someone was baptized into the Faith. (e.g., See St. Cyril's *Mystagogic Catecheses*. In addition, Sts. Augustine, Hilary, Leo, and the Gelasian Sacramentary also state that by ancient tradition the Creed in any form was to be learned by heart, and never consigned to writing.)

What *was* taught, was openly known by every baptized Christian. There was no "secret doctrine" *amongst the Christians themselves* about anything. Therefore, there is absolutely no historic evidence of any "secret doctrine" relating to the teachings about Antichrist, the latter or end times, or on anything else. Some of those teachings have simply been lost over time.

only apply to an individual. According to St. Jerome, the mother of Antichrist will be a Jewess from the vicinity of Babylon who will have led an immoral life and pretended before people to be a holy woman. Many of the Fathers say that Antichrist will be of Jewish extraction (St. Irenaeus, Ad. Her. Book 5; St. Jerome "In Daniele" II, 21; St. Ambrose, St. Augustine, Pope St. Gregory the Great; St. Anselm all declare this).

3. St. Hilary

St. Hilary clearly states about the Antichrist,

> "Antichrist **will teach** that Jesus Christ is not the Son of God, but is the wickedest of all criminals"[564]

Here we have another Doctor of the Church declaring that Antichrist is a specific individual.

4. St. Hippolytus

Hippolytus says that Antichrist will order all things that might remind men of Jesus Christ to be destroyed, for example, the shrine of the Holy Sepulcher on Mount Calvary and other holy places in Jerusalem and the Holy Land. He further says in the three and one-half years in which Antichrist will reign as World Emperor, **he** will prohibit under pain of death, the administering of the sacraments and the offering of the Holy Sacrifice of the Mass. Mass will be celebrated mostly in the forests and in secret places, as was the case in the first days of Christianity.[565]

E. THREE MORE PRIVATE PROPHECIES

1. St. Hildegard

> "*An unchaste woman will conceive* ***an unchaste son***. The wicked serpent, who deceived Adam, will influence this child in such a way that nothing good or virtuous will enter into

[564] De Trinitate, 6.
[565] "*De Consummatione Saeculi*" – Concerning the End of the Age(s).

him; nor, under the circumstances will it even be possible for any good to be in him."[566]

2. St. Bridget

"Just as children of God are born of a spiritual marriage, so **will *Antichrist spring from an accursed woman*** *who will pretend to lead a spiritual life, and from an accursed man, through whose agency, and with God's permission, the devil will accomplish his ends.*"[567]

3. Sister Nativitas

According to **Sister Nativitas** Antichrist will be a child prodigy:

"*Even before he is ten years old he will be more powerful and learned than other men* and, through his actions, it will be evident that he possesses greater genius, spirit and skill than other people. *The fullness of his powers will first manifest themselves when he reaches the age of 30 years* at which time his greatest heroic deeds will begin" (quoted from Hartmann's "Life and Revelations of Sister Nativitas," 1865.

F. RETURNING TO THE FATHERS

1. Sts. Hippolytus & Ephraem

St. Hippolytus and St. Ephraem (who is a Father and Doctor of the Church) both say that, after holding public deliberations, *the Jews will then offer Antichrist a royal crown. This view is also held by* Sts. Irenaeus, Hilary, Ambrose, Augustine, Jerome, John Damascene, and others.

---

[566] *Divinum Operorum.*

[567] *Life and Revelations of St. Bridget*, p. 168.

2. St. Irenaeus

St. Irenaeus was a disciple of St. Polycarp. Polycarp in turn was a disciple of St. John the Apostle, having studied under St. John. So Irenaeus was only one teaching generation away from the direct teaching of the Apostles. He was from the East himself (probably Smyrna) and it was either there or in Ephesus that Irenaeus became a disciple of and studied under St. Polycarp. He traveled from his native East and arrived in Gaul (France) and became the second Bishop of the city of Lyon in 177 A.D.

His reputation as a scholar and theologian became quickly known throughout the entire Church. He is regarded by all serious Catholic scholars as the best theologian of the 2nd century. His work *Adversus Haereses* (Against Heresies) is a classic, and the definitive work of the Church against the Gnostic Heresy. Until very recent manuscript discoveries of Gnostic writings, his book *Adversus Haereses* (which he wrote sometime between 180 to 199 A.D.,) was our most thorough exposition on the Gnostic doctrines.

St. Irenaeus further says:

> *"**The** Antichrist will deceive the Jews to such an extent that they will accept him as the Messias and worship him."*[568]

3. St. Ambrose

St. Ambrose was a 4th century Bishop of Milano, Italy. It was he who converted St. Augustine. According to St. Ambrose (also a Father and Doctor of the Church) Antichrist will attempt to prove from Holy Scripture that he is the Christ.[569]

4. St. Anselm

Here we are quoting another Doctor of the Church. Some scholars also consider him to be one of the last Fathers (this is not a common opinion).

---

568 *Adversus Haereses*, Book 5, Chapter 25.
569 St. Ambrose, In Lucam, 21.

> *"Towards the end of the world Antichrist will draw the hearts of the Jews to him* by his great generosity and sympathetic attitude so much so that they will praise him as a demi-god. The Jews will say to one another: "There is not a more virtuous, just and wise man than he to be found in our entire generation. Of all men, he certainly will be able to rescue us from all our miseries."[570]

*Where do all of these absolute statements from Fathers and Doctors of the Church about Antichrist emanate from***?** Most of these statements are not found as such in Scripture! So where *do* they come from? Can we believe these Fathers and Doctors of the Church just pulled them out of the air? THEY COME FROM ORAL TRADITION - PASSED DOWN FROM CHRISTIAN TO CHRISTIAN, BISHOP TO BISHOP, SAINT TO SAINT.

As Father Huchedé, the great eschatological scholar of the late 19th century says,

> "All the Fathers and theologians unanimously concur in this belief as to Antichrist's individuality. And consequently, his personal existence and future event must be considered as an object of divine faith, such as stated by Suarez and Bellarmine."[571]

5. St. Thomas Aquinas

In reference to Huchedé's statement, St. Thomas is known as the greatest systematic theologian in the history of the Church. He is also a Doctor of the Church. This is obviously no guarantee of infallibility, but his opinion is certainly a particularly weighty one *when it is one hundred percent consonant with the total teaching tradition of the Church.* St. Thomas said of the Antichrist while speaking of his evil influence,

> "***He*** will pervert some in his day by exterior persuasion."

---

570 *Details Concerning the Antichrist*, Dr. Franz Spirago, Pub: R. Von Acken, Lingen, (EMS), Hanover, Germany, 1922, p. 27.

571 History of Antichrist, Rev. P. Huchedé, Nicholas Bray, N.Y. 1884.

St. Thomas discusses the subject of who is the "head" of evil in the world, and makes the point that the Devil will not destroy Antichrist's free will. Rather, he will by the power of suggestion "infuse" his own wickedness into Antichrist more fully than in any other *human being*. St. Thomas begins his discussion with Paul's famous Scriptural quote from Thessalonians and then adds his own commentary.

> "*'As in Christ dwelt the fulness of the Godhead, so in Antichrist is the fulness of all wickedness.'* Not indeed as if **his *humanity*** were assumed by the devil into unity of person, as the humanity of Christ is by the Son of God; but that the devil by suggestion infuses his wickedness more copiously into **him** [Antichrist] than into all others."[572]

St. Thomas could not be clearer that the Antichrist is an individual human being. Thomas even utilizes the specific words "his *humanity*" - as an attribute of Antichrist.

6. St. and Dr. Robert Bellarmine

So, we have already heard St. John Damascene (the last Father of the Church), and St. & Dr. Thomas Aquinas (the greatest systematic theologian of the Church) state unequivocally that Antichrist will be an individual man. We close this section on whether it is the constant teaching of the Church that Antichrist is an individual man with a discussion of Bellarmine's commentaries on this issue.

As stated previously, Bellarmine is the last Doctor of the Church to make a detailed study of this subject. In his refutation of the charge that the Pope or the Papacy is the Antichrist, Bellarmine had written his *De Summo Pontifice*. The second heading in this work is entitled, "SECOND HEADING, **Antichrist is sure to be a certain individual man of the future**."[573]

---

[572] *Summa Theologica*, Thomas Aquinas, Part III, Q. 8, Art. 8, Benziger Bros. New York, 1947, Vol. II, p. 2081.

[573] Quoted from *Bellarmini, Opera Omnia, Disputationum Roberti Bellarmini*. The particular quotes are from the section containing *De Controversiis - Christianae Fidei, Tomus Primus, Liber Tertius, De Summo Pontifice*, written in 1577. The quoted edition was printed under the aegis of Cardinal Archbishop Sforza at Naples in 1856. "CAPUT II. *Antichristum certum quemdam hominem futurum." Liber Tertius*, p. 425.

In the body copy under that heading, Bellarmine says that it is the constant Catholic teaching that, "he (Antichrist) shall be one singular man."[574] Later he says about him being an individual,

> "For **all Catholics actually perceive Antichrist to be one certain man**, but all the previously referenced heretics in a manner peculiar to them [proprie] teach Antichrist not to be a single person, but rather [they teach] the Antichrist to be a single throne, or tyrannical kingdom, or the apostolic chair of those who preside over the [Catholic] Church."[575] [Emphasis the author's]

Bellarmine is countering the claim of certain "heretics" that the Antichrist will *not* be an individual, but in some manner is the Papacy or the Apostolic Chair of Peter, i.e., a series of Popes or the Papacy. Bellarmine goes on to discuss specific occurrences of this position in Bezae, Calvin and other Protestant divines. In his arguments for the "Catholic" position, Bellarmine freely quotes from Irenaeus, Hilary, Augustine, Jerome, Chrysostom and many other Fathers.

There are other similar quotes from Bellarmine which make the same point, that "all Catholics" actually perceive that the individual "man of sin" that St. Paul speaks of shall be a specific individual man.

The quotes presented here are but a few samples culled from the constant teaching tradition of the Church on this subject. If anyone calling himself or herself Catholic wishes today to take a different position, *he or she must understand they are flying in the face of the constant teachings of the Fathers, Doctors, and a consistent teaching tradition which the Fathers testify goes back to the apostles.*

---

574 Ibid. "ille sit unus homo singularis."

575 Ibid. "Catholici enim omnes, fore Antichristum unum quemdam hominem, et haeretici omnes citati docent, Antichristum *proprie* dictum non esse singularem personam, sed singularem thronam, sive regnum tyrranicum, ac sedem apostolicam eorum qui Ecclesiae praesident."

G. ANTICHRIST'S ORIGINS AND BACKGROUND

1. Pope St. Gregory the Great (6th Century F&D)

In St. Gregory, we have one of the greatest Saints, Popes, and Fathers and Doctors of the Church. He is also one of the greatest scholars in the Church's history, having studied in both the East and the West. Prior to becoming Pope, in 589 A.D., he began to serve as the Papal Legate for Pope Pelagius II in the court of the Byzantine Emperor in Constantinople. He held this position until 590, when upon the death of Pelagius II, he himself was elected Pope.

Regarding the Antichrist, St. Gregory said,

> "*Before the birth of her child,* ***the mother of Antichrist*** *will announce the advent of a Messias who will restore great prosperity to mankind.*"[576]

He declares that Antichrist is an individual man born to an individual woman. Pope St. Gregory wrote this towards the end of the 6th century. At the time that he wrote, the theology of the Church was already quite highly developed. This is no naive rustic speaking.

2. St. John Damascene

We have already heard St. John Damascene tell us Antichrist will be *a* man,

> "*born of fornication.*"

The constant Tradition of the Fathers is that Antichrist will be of Jewish extraction. Many of them state more specifically - from the Tribe of Dan (Sts. Hippolytus, Irenaeus, Augustine, Prosper, and Gregory the Great, as well as Theodoret). But this last opinion appears to be based upon their *personal interpretation* of the several books of the Old Testament, Genesis and Jeremiah.

---

576 *Morales* 23,15, Pope St. Gregory the Great.

The 1936 edition of the *Catholic Encyclopedia* observes in its article on the Antichrist that "many of the Fathers" accept the following thesis that,

> Antichrist will be of Jewish extraction, of the tribe of Dan, will be circumcized, will rebuild Jerusalem and the Jewish Temple, in which he will set himself up as God. Likewise, he is to begin his work of seduction among the Jews who will accept him as the Messias. Thus St. Irenaeus (Adversus Haereses, v. 30; MIGNE, P.G., VII, 1206) says of Antichrist: "Jeremias does not merely point out his sudden coming, but he even indicates the tribe from which he shall come, where he says: 'We shall hear the voice of his swift horses from Dan -- **he** shall come and devour the earth.'" (Jer. VIII, 16).
>
> St. Hippolytus, another bishop of the early Church, who suffered martyrdom in 235, wrote a treatise on Christ and Antichrist in which he says: "As Christ springs from the tribe of Juda, so Antichrist is to spring from the tribe of Dan. And that the case stands thus, we see also from the words of Jacob: 'Let Dan be a serpent, lying upon the ground, biting the horse's heel.' (Gen. XLIV, 17). What then is meant by the serpent but Antichrist," (De Antichristo, 6, 14: MIGNE, P.G. X, 736, 738).

H. APPARENT MIRACLES OF ANTICHRIST

1. St. Vincent Ferrer

> "Now he will be a veritable man, but so proud that, not only will he desire to have universal dominion in the whole world, but will even demand to be called a god, and will insist on receiving divine worship."[577]

[577] *The Angel of the Judgement*, S.M.C., Ave Maria Press, Notre Dame, Indiana, p. 105.

On the same subject, on another occasion, he said,

> "The first affliction to come on the world in a short space of time is the advent of the Antichrist, a diabolical man, who will bring distress on the whole world"[578]

> "Again Antichrist will direct his attacks *against simple folk* who, because their hearts are turned to Him in rectitude of intention, are so pleasing to God. *He will make use of magic, and produce lifelike apparitions, which are, after all, the merest trickery*. He will bring down fire from heaven, and make images speak, for the demon can cause their lips to move. **To all appearance, he will recall the dead spirit of your father, the phantom infants will seem to speak.**"[579]

If you have ever wondered how Antichrist will be able to put good Christians through such terrible experiences, can you imagine being a Catholic and hearing a one month old baby speak clearly? And,

> "You must know that Antichrist will perform other prodigies by the power of demons, and these will be true miracles according to the nature of things in themselves, *but false in regard to the definition of miracle* (i.e. by the power of God). For **he will cause images and babes of a month old to speak.** The followers of Antichrist will question these statues or babies, and they will make answer concerning this lord who has come in the latter times, affirming that he is the saviour. **The devil will move their lips and form the words they utter when they declare Antichrist to be the true saviour of the world; and in this way he will cause the destruction of many souls.**"[580]

The reader may be wondering how anyone could withstand such false signs and powers. But Scripture tells us that one third of mankind will. That one third will be primarily composed of believing

---

[578] Ibid. p. 103 (This comment was delivered by St. Vincent during a long sermon given on the 1st Sunday of Advent.

[579] Ibid. p. 10.

[580] Ibid. pp. 107&108

Christians who have a simple faith. According to St. Vincent, those of simple faith will actually stand up quite well. He observes that one of the major causes of their withstanding such trials is that the people of simple faith will also be conversant with the prophecies about Antichrist. Like St. Peter's brother Andrew, they will believe them. At the same time, the learned and the arrogant who are immersed in pride will swallow Antichrists's blandishments, hook, line and sinker. It is this last type which he discusses immediately below.

> "Those in the third category whom he will try to seduce are *learned folk*, such as masters and doctors of civil and canon law, who can argue and grasp proofs of things. *Against these Antichrist will weave spells of enchantment, bringing out the most subtle arguments, the most seductive reasoning, to render these learned men tongue-tied and incapable of answering*. It is not difficult to understand how this is done since the demon already holds their souls in the chains of sin; for ***the greater their knowledge the more heavily burdened will be their consciences if they do not live up to it***. If he can hold their souls in chains it is easy for him to bind a morsel of flesh like the tongue so that they cannot speak except what he chooses."[581]

Now St. Vincent gives us the simple antidote for "specious reasoning" which could *at any time* confuse us in our faith. There are those who would hold that, to a certain degree, what St. Vincent is describing for the time of Antichrist is happening to many Catholics right now.

> **"The remedy for this state of bondage is faith, which follows simple obedience and not argument or reasoning.** Argument may be good for the strengthening of the intelligence, but it is not the true foundation of faith. **Those whose faith rests on reason will lose it when they hear the specious reasoning of Antichrist.** Those on the contrary who rely on a firm belief founded on obedience will reply: 'Away with your arguments! Such reasonings are not the grounds of my faith."[582]

581 Ibid. p. 110
582 Ibid.

[Comment: The author remembers the first time he read a "scholar" (who claimed to be a Catholic in good standing, and whose faith appeared "to rest on reason") describing Pope John Paul II as a "Polish peasant." This of course happened shortly after the intelligencia of the "higher critics" discovered that John Paul II was sympathetic to the traditional teachings of the Church. *The fact is that the academic credentials of John Paul II are substantially superior to almost all of his critics*. A serious look at his academic background will convince any objective observer of that fact. No one attacked the Pope's standing as a full-blown member of Academe until the orthodoxy of his Papacy became a thorn in the side of extreme "higher critics."]

Returning to St. Vincent: Could it possibly be clearer that St. Vincent is telling us Antichrist will be an individual? Additionally, in the Apocalypse, we are in different places told that the "Beast," and the "False Prophet" and the "Antichrist" will be personally thrown into the same pool of Fire (Brimstone) where they will be tormented. You cannot torment a philosophy, or an idea, or an "organization" in Hell. Only individuals can be tormented in Hell. Ergo, we know from these and many other passages of Scripture that Antichrist will be an individual.

St. Vincent talks of the devastating effect Antichrist will have on weak ecclesiastics:

> **"The temporal lords and ecclesiastical prelates, for fear of losing power or position, will be on his side, since there will exist neither king nor prelate unless he wills it."**[583]

I. THE RETURN OF (H)ENOCH & ELIAS, AT THE TIME OF ANTICHRIST

There is a vast body of oral tradition, Scripture, and private prophecy, and commentary by Doctors of the Church concerning Enoch (sometimes spelled Henoch) and Elias (sometimes spelled Elijah), and the role they will play at the time of Antichrist.

[583] Ibid. p. 105.

1. Scriptural Basis

Genesis

We learn the following from Holy Scripture: *Enoch, the seventh Patriarch,* was taken up alive into heaven and was taken into Paradise when he was 365 years of age.

> "And all the years of Henoch were three hundred and sixty five years. And he walked with God, and was seen no more: because God took him."[584]

St. Paul

> "By faith, Henoch was translated ***that he should not see death***; and he was not found, because God had translated him"[585]

According to the Book of Ecclesiasticus, Enoch will come again to preach penance to the nations.

Ecclesiasticus

> *"Henoch* pleased God, and *was translated into paradise,* that he may give repentance to the nations."[586]

Now, *how would it be possible for Henoch to "give repentance to the nations" from Paradise?* This would appear to be a riddle. But this apparent riddle is solved in the New Testament and Oral Tradition, and is amplified through private prophecy -- as we shall shortly see.

Around the year 900 B.C., not far from Jericho, and in the presence of the prophet Eliseus, *Elias also was taken up into heaven in a blaze of light in a flaming chariot drawn by fiery horses.*[587] *Elias is now in Paradise according to Oral Tradition and the unanimous declarations of many of the Saints - Sts. Hildegard, Augustine and Thomas Aquinas just to name a few.*

---

584 Genesis 5:23-24
585 Paul's Epistle to the Hebrews c.11, v.5
586 Ecclesiasticus 44:16
587 4 book of Kings, 2:11, Ecclesiasticus; 48:.

Malachias

The prophet Malachias foretold that Elias would come again before the end of the world to convert the Jews.

> "Behold I will send you Elias the prophet, before the coming of the great and dreadful day of the lord.
>
> "And *he shall turn the heart of the fathers to the children*, and the heart of the children to their fathers; lest I come, and strike the earth with anathema." Mal. c.4, v.5

Now, let us look again at what it says in the Book of Ecclesiasticus:

> "Henoch pleased God, and was translated into paradise, that he might give repentance to the nations." (Ecclesiasticus c.48, v.10).

The Jews at the time of Christ knew and understood these prophecies. That is exactly why they asked Christ if he was Elias.

Above we have read Scriptural prophecies telling us that Enock and Elias did not die. So what happened to them? Scripture only tells us that Enoch was translated into "Paradise." So, (1) if they did not die, and (2) if (as both Tradition and Scripture tell us) every man who has suffered the affects of original sin must die in order to go to Heaven,[588] then, (3) this *Paradise* cannot be Heaven. It may be the "Paradise" of Adam and Eve, but Scripture does not say. It does logically follow that if they did not die, then in some manner they must experience death before the end of the world.

---

[588] Mary, the Mother of God, is the Immaculate Conception. "The Most Holy Virgin was in the first moment of her conception, by a unique gift of grace and privilege of Almighty God, in view of the merits of Jesus Christ, the redeemer of mankind, preserved free from all stain of original sin. According to this doctrine, she is the only human to have been granted the exception by God of not being born with original sin." (Quote originates from Pius IX's Papal Bull *Innefabilis*. The actual quote is received from *Fundamentals of Catholic Dogma*, Dr. Ludwig Ott, Fourth Edition, (First English Edition), Pub: The Mercier Press, Limited, 19 Maylor Street, Cork, Republic of Ireland, 1960, Reprinted by Tan Books and Publishrs, 1974, p. 199.

2. Tradition

St Irenaeus (F)

St. Irenaeus declares:

> ***"The disciples of the Apostles say*** [*Here Irenaeus is clearly citing Oral Tradition*] that they [Enoch and Elias] whose living bodies were taken up from this world, have been placed in an *earthly* paradise, where they will remain until the end of the world."[589]

Here, **St. Irenaeus clearly states** that ***it is of Apostolic oral tradition that Enoch and Elias are in an "earthly Paradise"*** awaiting the fulfillment of their mission at the end of time. This is only one of many unqualified statements about the end times by various Fathers and Doctors of the Church -- which they say come from apostolic Tradition.

There are Catholic theological works which say that Tradition adds nothing to Scripture as to the end times. It is difficult to see how anyone can maintain such a position in the light of all the clear doctrinal statements from the Fathers, which the Fathers unequivocally say are of apostolic Tradition. Again, *these Patristic testimonies do not teach a new or different doctrine*, they fill out some details of those found in Scripture.

3. More Scriptural Confirmation of the Return of "the Two Witnesses" - The Apocalypse

Scripture itself testifies to the existence and return of "two witnesses" who will "prophecy" for the enlightenment and encouragement of the faithful Christians at the time of Antichrist. According to St. John in the Apocalypse, the two witnesses (which Tradition identifies as Enoch and Elias) will carry on their mission against Antichrist for 1260 days (Apoc. c.11, v.3). Scripture gives us specific details about these "two witnesses" who are "given" at the time of Antichrist.

---

[589] *Adversus Haereses*, Liber 4, Cap. 30.

The Apocalypse:

> "And I will give unto my two witnesses, and they shall prophesy one thousand two hundred and sixty days, clothed in sackcloth." (Apoc. 11:3)
>
> "And when they shall have finished their testimony, the beast, that ascended out of the abyss, shall make war against them, and shall overcome them, and kill them. (11:7)
>
> "And their bodies shall lie in the streets of the great city, which is called spiritually, Sodom and Egypt, *where their Lord also was crucified*." (11:8)
>
> "And they of the tribes, and peoples, and tongues, and nations, shall see their bodies for three days and a half; and they shall not suffer their bodies to be laid in sepulchres." (11:9)
>
> "And they that dwell upon the earth shall rejoice over them, and make merry; and shall send gifts to one another, because **these two prophets** tormented them that dwelt upon the earth." (11:10)
>
> "And after three days and a half, the spirit of life from God entered into them. And they stood upon their feet, and great fear fell upon them that saw them." (11:11)
>
> "And they heard a great voice from heaven, saying to them: Come up hither. And they went up to heaven in a cloud: and their enemies saw them." (11:12)
>
> "And at that hour there was made a great earthquake, and the tenth part of the city fell: and there were slain in the earthquake names of seven thousand men; and the rest were cast into fear, and gave glory to the God of heaven." (11:13)

The Apocalypse does not directly identify the two "witnesses," but it does tell us many things about them such as they are "prophets" and will demonstrate miraculous powers from the first moment they are returned to earth. Scripture says the purpose of the "Two Witnesses" return is to convince men that Antichrist is a fraud and to convert them to Christ.

> "If anyone desires to harm them, fire will come out of their mouths, and will devour their enemies."
>
> "These (the two prophets) have power to shut heaven, so that it will not rain during the days of their prophesying; and they have power over the waters to turn them into blood, and to smite the earth with every plague as often as they desire."[590]

The punishments mentioned will bring many of Antichrist's followers to their senses.

J. TRADITION CLEARLY IDENTIFIES THE "TWO WITNESSES AS (H)ENOCK & ELIAS."

You have already read the testimony of St. Irenaeus that "The disciples of the Apostles say that they (Enoch and Elias) whose living bodies were taken up from this world, have been placed in an earthly paradise, where they will remain until the end of the world."

1. St. Hippolytus on Enock and Elias

St. Hippolytus, who died a Martyr, has briefly spoken of the effect of the miracles of the "two witnesses":

> "In those times, dew will not fall from the heavens nor rain from the clouds, nor will the earth bear any fruits. The sea will reek with a fearful stench because the rivers will have dried up and fresh water will no longer flow into it from the mountain torrents. Pestilence will spread over the world and, because there will be but few people left alive to bury the dead, the earth in many localities will be strewn with corpses. Unconsolable mourning, wailing and weeping will prevail everywhere. Men will consider those fortunate who died before them. Finally, *men will seek help from Antichrist and, because he will not be able to aid them, will come to the*

[590] Apoc. 11:5-6.

> *realization that he is not God.* When finally they understand how grossly he has deceived them, they will seek Jesus Christ. People will then cast away gold and silver and no one will even stop to pick it up."[591]

The quote "dew will not fall from the heavens nor rain from the clouds" is predicated of a miracle called down by the witnesses. Hippolytus was a man truly wedded to "Tradition." He defended his perception of Tradition on every possible occasion. His *Apostolic Tradition* is a classic patristic work. It is the oldest document we possess from the young Church which contains a large portion of the liturgy of the Eucharist. A man such as Hippolytus would **never** have made the statement above unless he felt he had absolute certainty that this was of apostolic teaching.

2. St Augustine (F&D)

In St. Augustine's *City of God*, he describes certain aspects that we know from Scripture and Tradition about the role of Antichrist and many events which will occur during his persecution of the Christians. He begins the following with a Scriptural quote from Mal. 4:5-6, and then fleshes out its meaning by quoting things which have been handed on through Oral Tradition -- and confirms that it is also the common belief of the Christians of his era.

Again, the following quote from *The City of God* begins with a passage from the Old Testament.

> "'And, behold, I will send to you Elias the Tishbite [alternate spelling Thesbite] before the great and signal day of the Lord come: and he shall turn the heart of the father to the son, and the heart of a man to his next of kin, lest I come and utterly smite the earth.' [Now Augustine continues his commentary on the end times which he has just begun with this O.T. passage.]
>
> "It is a familiar theme in the conversation and heart of the faithful, that in the last days before the judgement *the Jews shall believe in the true Christ,* that is, our Christ, *by*

[591] *Details Concerning the Antichrist,* Dr. Franz Spirago, Pub: R. Von Acken, Lingen, (EMS), Hanover, Germany, 1922.

means of this great and admirable prophet Elias who shall expound the law to them. **For not without reason do we hope that before the coming of our judge and Saviour, *Elias* shall come, *because we have good reason to believe that he is now alive.*** For, as Scripture most distinctly informs us, he was taken up from this life in a chariot of fire. When, therefore, he is come, *he will give a spiritual explanation of the law which the Jews at present understand carnally, and shall thus, 'turn the heart of the father to the son,"* that is, the heart of the fathers to their children; ... And the meaning is, that *the sons*, that is, *the Jews*, shall understand the law as the fathers, that is, the prophets, and among them Moses himself, understood it ... that the Jews also, who had previously hated, should then love the Son who is our Christ.'"[592] [Emphasis-the author's]

Augustine's meaning could not be clearer. He clearly states that it is the "common belief" amongst Christians (in 428 A.D.) that Elias will return during the "last days" for the conversion of the Jews.

3. St. Ephraem (F&D-4th/5th Cent) on Enock and Elias

St. Ephraem wrote heavily on the end times. Among other things he said about Enoch and Elias:

"And when the *son of perdition* has drawn to his purpose the whole world, Enoch and Elias shall be sent that they may confute the Evil one;"[593]

Again, how can any reasonable person (who is also familiar with the writings of the Fathers on this subject) maintain that Tradition

---

[592] *Basic Writings of Saint Augustine*, Edited by Whitney J. Oates, Chrm. Dept. of Classics, Princeton University, Random House, New York. Vol. II, p. 557 [Section on *The City of God*, Bk. 20, Chpt 29.]

[593] *The Sunday Sermons of the Great Fathers*, Vol. 4., p. 357. Ref. from *St. Ephraem, Syri, III,* Col. 188, Sermo II. St Ephraem also comments that in the end times there shall be a resurgence of a "Roman Power" during a period of peace which shall be granted to the world by God. At the end of this period of peace the Roman power shall be broken and Antichrist shall come. [See also footnote on this sermon, in Chapter 4, questioning Ephraem as a source of this sermon. But even if this were not authentic Ephraem, there are a multitude of other Fathers who say the same thing.]

adds nothing to Scripture about knowledge of the end times? The Apocalypse tells us of two witnesses. Tradition identifies them as Enoch and Elias.[594]

K. PRIVATE PROPHESY CONCERNING ENOCK AND ELIAS

1. St. Hildegard

> "*Enoch and Elias will be instructed by God in a most secret manner in Paradise*. God reveals to them the actions and condition of men that they may regard them with eyes of compassion. Because of this special preparation, these two holy men are more wise than all the wise men on the earth taken together. God will give them the task of opposing Antichrist and of bringing back those who have strayed from the way of salvation. *Both of these men, will say to people*: 'This accursed one (Antichrist) has been sent by the devil to lead

[594] A number of 20th century higher critical scholars analyze this case of Enoch and Elias strictly from Scripture - effectually ignoring Patristic Tradition and the commentaries of the Doctors on this point - which is extensive. As observed earlier in the book, even more orthodox scholars have because of these critical influences tended to ignore the Fathers in many key areas which are at variance with the "developing" theological theories of many 20th century theologians.

One scholar who normally quotes *both* from Traditon and Scripture is Ludwig Ott. But for some reason he does not present the Fathers or Doctors on this issue for the consideration of his readers. Ott states: "The conversion of the Jewish people is frequently brought into a causal connection with the coming-again of Elias, but *without sufficient foundation*." [Emphasis added] Quoted from *Fundamentals of Catholic Dogma,* Dr. Ludwig Ott, Fourth Edition, (First English Edition, Pub: The Mercier Press, Limited, 19 Maylor Street, Cork, Republic of Ireland, 1960)

[The "*sufficient foundation*" which Ott says is missing, is found first, in the writings of the Fathers on this subject, and second, in the various commentaries of the Doctors of the Church including St. Thomas and Bellarmine, who are in total agreement with the Fathers on this point.]

Ott now discusses the Book of Malachias, Ecclesiasticus, Luke, John, Matthew, etc.. But (unusual for Ott) for some reason he does not bring the writing Tradition of the Fathers to bear on this subject (nor the writings of the major Doctors of the Church). It is of course always a possibillity (even if a small one) that he was not particularly familiar with their eschatological writings vis-a-vis Enoch and Elias.

> men astray and into error; *we have been preserved by God in a hidden place*, where we did not experience the sorrows of men, *but God has now sent us to combat the heresy of this son of perdition.*' They will go into all cities and villages where previously Antichrist had broadcasted his heresies, and by the power of the Holy Spirit will perform wonderful miracles so that all nations will greatly marvel at them. Thus, as to a wedding feast, Christians will hasten to death by martyrdom which the son of perdition will have prepared for them in such numbers that those murderers will be unable even to count the slain; then the blood of these martyrs will flow like rivers." (St. Hildegard, *Scivias, Visio II*).

2. Blessed Dionysius of Leutzenburg (17th Century)

Dionysius was a celebrated German Carthusian preacher. A prodigious writer, he completed 150 written volumes including his *Life of Antichrist* and *The Last Things*. Accordingly, his "right thumb and forefinger are still preserved incorrupt."[596] He was known also for his scholarship and writings on the Fathers of the Church, and on the teaching traditions which had come down concerning Antichrist. In 1682 he published his famous "Life of Antichrist" ("Vita Antichristi"), which has the Imprimatur of both the Bishop of Mainz and the Superior General of the Capuchin Order. In Chapter 38 of his work on Antichrist he wrote:

> Enoch and Elias will be borne with the speed of lightning in a fiery chariot from Paradise to Jerusalem. There they will hasten into the Temple and announce that this godless being who is being honored in the Temple is he whom the prophets have foretold is the Antichrist. The two prophets will publicly denounce him. *They will reveal their own identity and will prove from Holy Scripture that their appearance on earth was promised by God. Elias will preach principally to the Jews and Enoch to the Mohammedans and other nations.*

[596] *Details Concerning the Antichrist*, Dr. Franz Spirago, Pub: R. Von Acken, Lingen, (EMS), Hanover, Germany, 1922.

3. Sr. (St.) Mechtild (d. 1301)

Even though Sr. Mechtild has never formally been taken through the canonization process of the Church, many times (due to the holiness of her life) she is referred to as *St.* Mechtild by the people of the region in which she lived and worked. Mechtild was Abbess of the Benedictine nun's cloister at Dieszenam-Ammersein in Bavaria. She possessed the gift of prophecy to an extraordinary degree. She says of Enoch and Elias;

> "***Both are in Paradise*, living in blessed happiness. *An angel will lead Enoch and Elias out of Paradise.*** The transparency and bliss which their bodies possessed there, will then disappear ... As soon as they behold the earth they will become afraid, just as people do who, when they first behold the sea, do not know how they will be able to traverse it. They will appear as preachers when the majority of the good have died as martyrs and for a long time will comfort the people... *Enoch and Elias will force Antichrist to a show-down***;** they will tell men who he is and through whose power [Satan's] he is working miracles. Then many men and women who had previously followed Antichrist, will be converted."[597]

4. St. John Damascene - on Enoch and Elias - *Tradition*

We shall now requote St. John Damascene on Enoch and Elias. A Doctor of the Church, as stated earlier, he is also generally considered to be the last of the Fathers.

> "And *Enoch and Elias* the Thesbite will be sent and they shall 'turn the heart of the fathers to the children,' that is to say, turn the synagogue to our Lord Jesus Christ and the preaching of the Apostles. *And they will be destroyed by him* (Antichrist)." [*De Fide Orthodoxa*]

---

[597] *Revelations of Sister Mechtild of Magdeburg*, Morel, Regensburg, Mainz, 1869, page 218.

L. ST. ROBERT BELLARMINE (F&D) ON ENOCH AND ELIAS

To close this section on the "two witnesses" we will again quote from St. Robert Bellarmine. Again the reader should remember that Bellarmine is the last Doctor of the Church to study the Antichrist in-depth. In his "FOURTH HEADING" of his *De Summo Pontifice* (subtitled, "First demonstration explains that the Antichrist has not yet come") Bellarmine explains: many "signs" given us in Scripture about Antichrist have not yet occurred in his time. Therefore Bellarmine logically concludes that despite the theological statements of various Protestant theologians, that Antichrist cannot yet have come. Here we are going to quote Bellarmine in an extensive passage, for he covers a number of issues being discussed in this chapter. Where appropriate, we will later requote him on certain passages. Bellarmine says,

> "For it must be known that in the divine letters [Scripture], the Holy Spirit to have given to us six sure signs concerning the coming of Antichrist: *two which preceed Antichrist himself,* namely the preaching of the Gospel in the whole world, and **the devastation of the Roman Empire:** the two contemporaneous men [the Two Witnesses], **which it is to be seen prophesied Enoch and Elias**, and the greatest and last persecution, and also that the public sacrifice [of the Mass] shall completely cease, the two following [signs] surely, the death of Antichrist after three and a half years [after his rise to power] and the end of the world; ***none of which signs we have seen at this time.***"[598] [Emphasis and parens, the authors]

Obviously Bellarmine holds with the traditional teaching of the Church on the point of Enoch and Elias being the "two witnesses."

---

[598] Tomus Primus, Liber Tertius, p. 431. "Sciendum est enim, Spiritum sanctum in divinis literis sex signa certa adventus Antichirsti nobis dedisse: duo praecedentia ipsum Antichristum, nempe praedicationem evangelii in toto mundo, et imperii romani desolationem: duo comitantia, videlicet praedicationem Henoch et Heliae, et persecutionem maximum et notissimum, ita ut publica sacra omnino ceseent: duo sequentia, nimirum, interitum Antichristi post tres annos cum medio, et finem mundi; quorum nullum adhuc videmus existere."

But Bellarmine goes even further and teaches,

> "The third demonstration arises from the coming of **Enoch and Elias,** ***who live even now and shall live until they shall come to oppose Antichrist himself,*** and to preserve the elect in the faith of Christ, and in the end shall convert the Jews, and it is certain that this has not yet been fulfilled."[599]

Bellarmine later expands on this theme and states that "they were taken up before death and even now "they live in "mortal flesh" ("ipsi duo sint rapti ante mortem, et adhuc vivant in carne mortale"). Bellarmine now backs up this position from multiple Scriptural sources from both the Old and New Testaments. He points out that the Tradition from various ecclesiastical writers as well as the writings of the Fathers is unanimous on this point. He then extensively quotes from Tertullian and Sts. Irenaeus, Jerome, Augustine, and Epiphanius.

He proceeds to systematically destroy the various arguments of those "heretics" who claim that Enoch and Elias are simply an allegorical expression of "all the faithful ministers whom God will excite to action at the time of Antichrist to preach the Gospel which -- is without doubt the position of Luther and Zwingli"[600]

Bellarmine (as were many of the Fathers he quotes) is quite conversant with the allegorical interpretation theories of this event. He points out that the opposite, the "proper" literal interpretation of Enoch and Elias returning at the time of Antichrist, is the teaching tradition of the Church. He further points out that the recent allegorical teaching of Protestant theologians on this point is an innovation (with which they hope to promote their thesis that the Pope and/or the Papacy is the Antichrist). Bellarmine points out that various Protestant theologians go so far as to state that the belief that Enock and Elais will return at the time of Antichrist is a childlike fantasy. Bellarmine responds:

---

599 "Tertio demonstratio sumitur ex adventu Henoch et Heliaae, qui adhuc vivunt, et ad hoc vivunt, ut venienti Antichristo se opponant, et conservent electos in fide Christi, et tandem Judaeos convertant: quod tamen certum est nondum esse impletum. *Liber Tertius*, p. 434.

600 "per Henoch et Heliam ... omnes ministros fideles, quos Deus excitat tempore Antichristi, qualis nimurum fuit Lutherus, et Zwinglius." Ibid. p. 434.

> "But it is easily seen that by us (Catholics) truly this is not a childish fantasy, but a most true concept, that Enoch and Elias shall personally return, and it is also seen that the contrary concept (that they will not personally return) is either absolutely heretical, or a serious error very close to heretical."[601]

Despite the constant teaching of the Church as encapsulated by Bellarmine, Catholic "extreme higher critics" took up this *allegorical interpretation* of the "Two Witnesses" two centuries later. Bellarmine fully understands the allegorical argument and rejects and destroys it from Scripture and Tradition in the writings of the Fathers. **There is absolutely nothing new about the extreme element of "allegory theories" of the "higher critics."**

M. ST. ROBERT BELLARMINE (D) STATES ANTICHRIST COMES AFTER DESTRUCTION OF A ROMAN EMPIRE

Here we feel compelled to return to an earlier theme in this book (begun in chapter 4) -- that the Fathers and Doctors commonly taught that the Antichrist comes at the end of a Roman Empire. Again, Bellarmine is the last Doctor of the Church to make an in-depth study of the Church's eschatological teachings. Bellarmine's statement that Antichrist comes after "**the entire destruction of a Roman Empire**" (quod erit Desolatio omnimoda romani empirii) is merely a nugget culled from Bellarmine's immense treatise on this subject. Bellarmine traces the histories of various branches of the Empire for just this purpose. He specifically discusses that at his time, the "Ten Kingdoms" as heirs of a previous unified Empire *do not yet exist* (Sciendum est enim, romanum imperium tandem dividendum in decem reges, quorum nullus erit vel dicetur rex romanorum).

Bellarmine states clearly that this is not just his opinion, but that *it is consistently set forth by both the Greek and Latin Fathers* (Ita exponunt graeci Patres et Latini). In support of this he immediately

---

[601] "Nobis vero non puerilis imaginatio, sed verissima sententia videtur, Henoch et Heliam in suis personis venturos, et contrarium, vel esse haeresim, vel errorem haeresi proximum" De Summo Pontifice, p. 434.

gives some examples from both Latin and Greek Fathers, e.g.; Sts. Cyril of Jerusalem, Chrysostom, Theophilactus, Oecomenius, Tertullian, Lactantius, Ambrose, and Jerome and later he cites Irenaeus. He therefore concludes that one of the "two signs having been given to us by the Holy Spirit," which signs precede the coming of Antichrist, has not arrived. That sign is the resurgence of a latter Roman Empire and its subsequent division into ten kingdoms. Therefore, he logically concluded that the Antichrist has not yet come.[602]

He then goes on to specifically discuss the issue that the Emperor(s) of the last Roman Empire (preceding Antichrist) will probably not even be Roman, nor is it likely that their actual capital will be Rome. In support of this he cites a series of precedents of previous emperors of the Roman Empire who have not ruled from Rome nor was Rome the capital of their empire - but it was still called the Roman Empire. He cites the examples of the Emperors Valens, Arcadius, Theodosius, Justinian, etc. He then comes to the Holy Roman Empire which began with Charlamagne. He traces the history of the Holy Roman Empire to the time of his writing and demonstrates that *it* also has not ended, *nor has it been divided up into ten kingdoms.*[603]

Bellarmine teaches that All Catholics understand Antichrist is an individual

He thus refutes that the Pope and/or the Papacy can be the Antichrist as many Protestant theologians of the time were claiming. **He pointed out that "*all* Catholics" surely understand that the Antichrist will be an individual**, it cannot be some collective form or set of circumstances such as the "heretics" believe.

Bellarmine develops the history of this theology from Scripture and Tradition through the writings of the Fathers. He does so simply to theologically defend the Papacy. Bellarmine develops this theme in extreme detail quoting from dozens and dozens of sources. Bellarmine also quotes freely from the Fathers in support of this destruction

[602] All of this is to be found in *Liber Tertius, De Summo Pontifice*, Caput V, pp. 432 & 433.
[603] Ibid.

of the Roman Empire as a sign preceding Antichrist. Some of the Fathers he quotes on this are Sts. Irenaeus, Cyril, Ambrose, Hilary, Chrysostom, and Jerome, and then Lactantius, and Tertullian. Bellarmine graphically demonstrates that this is the constant teaching of the Fathers. "***The strength of Bellarmine's teaching on this point may be adduced from the fact that he heads the "Second Proof" of why Antichrist cannot have yet arrived*** (second proof - a final destruction of the Roman Empire) ***as, "another sign to preceed the time of Antichrist.***" Bellarmine does not state that a Catholic absolutely has to believe this, but he argues that its teaching tradition is so strong that he considers it a "sign" preceeding the Antichrist."

The author recommends to the serious student of this subject who is also comfortable with Latin, the obtaining of Bellarmine's *De Summo Pontifice*. He recommends first, the reading of its *Headings IV & V* in particular, and second, the *De Summo Pontifice* in its entirety.

It must be fairly observed that extreme "higher critics" would not agree with Bellarmine's analysis. This is primarily because Bellarmine bases his theology in Tradition and Scripture as interpreted in the traditional teachings of the Fathers of the Church. Extreme "higher critics" pay absolutely no attention to the teachings of the Fathers and Doctors of the Church in this area, or in any other area. Most of them state that the Fathers were ignorant of the advantages of modern studies and that therefore their theological positions are archaic. All of this was discussed earlier in the section on the "debunkers."

It must also be added that some orthodox Catholic theologians are of the opinion that it is forms of government in general, or the social order of the world, that restrains the coming of Antichrist. That number includes St. Thomas Aquinas. Thomas also includes in this restraint a waiting for a future time when the Holy Spirit (who is the "restrainer") will no longer restrain him.[604] When the Spirit "is out of the way," and, "the thousand years are ended,"[605]

---

[604] *Sancti Thomae Aquinitatis, Opera Omnia*, Tomus XIII, Musurgia Publishers, New York, 1949, p. 579.

[605] It was this event which the people of Christendom feared at the approach of the beginning of the 2nd millennium. They thought that Satan was about to be loosed upon the world (which would ultimately lead to the coming of Antichrist). This is a testimony to the early Christian traditional belief that the "thousand years" or millennium is something which occurs prior to Antichrist. Some of them took this figure literally - rather than figuratively - as representing a period of time.

then "Satan shall be loosed from his confinement, and he shall go forth and he shall seduce the nations."[606]

However, the Fathers and the vast majority of Doctors of the Church are in agreement with Bellarmine on this point. i.e., They hold with the teaching that there will be a last Roman Empire which while it operates IT restrains the Antichrist. When it falls, the restraint is gone. An important point to learn from all of this is that there is a superior number of equally prestigious Catholic theologians (with Thomas Aquinas) who hold with the traditional teachings of the Fathers of the Church on this subject.

A faithful Catholic who follows the recommendations and course of the Fathers at Vatican II will assiduously search out and study the writings of the Fathers and Doctors of the Church in any area of theology. He or she will then weigh them heavily in considering any Catholic point of doctrine.

1. Fr. Kramer

Robert Bellarmine adjudicates that the tradition of the Fathers is so strong that it cannot be ignored, that it must be accepted as a traditional teaching of the Church. Is it possible for a modern Scripture scholar to support all or part of the Fathers teaching on this point from *non-patristic* evidence? In *The Book of Destiny* Fr. Kramer, a modern Scripture scholar, (perhaps without intending to) says that there is.

In his commentary on Rev. 13:1-8, Fr. Kramer compares it with the Book of Daniel in 7:7 and 8:8. Then Fr. Kramer states,

> "The fourth beast is evidently the Roman Empire. This fourth empire according to the angel ([Rev.] 7:23) is to become greater than all the foregoing. *That was not true of any of the kingdoms that succeeded Alexander [the Great]. It could only be true of the Roman Empire.* **The empire represented by the fourth beast will in the end be divided into ten**

[606] Ibid. Thomas here refers to his reading of Apoc. 20:7. Thomas now writes "Solvetur satanas de carcere suo, et exibit, et seducet gentes."

> **kingdoms.** This is a round number, the world's number of completion."[610]

Now he immediately begins to make a case for a literal interpretation of this which is identical to that of the Church Fathers.

> "In the description of that beast, the fourth empire blends into another empire of the future, with which the fourth beast does not fit the Kingdom of the Seleucidae at all. ***But it does not fit the [old] Roman Empire either in all details.***"[611]

Kramer now gives one paragraph of detailed analysis of the statement he has just made. Now, he immediately launches into his interpretation of the next passage.

> **"The ten horns will evidently be the principal kingdoms or empires that grew out of the ancient Roman Empire.** And lastly a godless one will subdue three of these ten empires; ***this has not occurred since Roman times, and it can point only to the future empire of the Antichrist.*** The further illustration of his activities *show the exposition of the Fathers to be obviously correct... and it is the only logical one.*"[612]

In Fr. Kramer's arguments and conclusions on this section of the *Book of Revelation*,

(1) his arguments and conclusions are not at all based on Tradition.

(2) His arguments and conclusions are totally based on,
  (a) overwhelming Scriptural internal evidence, plus
  (b) external evidence from history.

---

610 Ibid. p. 303.
611 Ibid.
612 Ibid.

(3) From these, Kramer reaches his final conclusion, that,

(4) the Fathers' teaching on Rev. 7:23, is "obviously correct ... and it is the only logical one."

2. St. Jerome

We have read much about how Antichrist comes at the end of a Roman Empire which has in the end been divided up into ten kingdoms. But how does the transfer of power from the ten kingdoms to Antichrist take place? We will now re-present a statement of St. Jerome quoted earlier in the book. Jerome is commenting on the *Book of Daniel*, particularly Chapters 7 and 8. Most specifically he comments upon the following.

> "The fourth beast shall be the fourth kingdom upon earth, which shall be greater than all kingdoms, and shall devour the whole earth, and shall tread it down and break it in pieces.
>
> "And the ten horns of the same kingdom, shall be ten kings: *and another shall rise up after them, and he shall be mightier than the former, and he* shall bring down three kings.
>
> "And he shall speak words against the High One, and shall crush the saints of the most High; and he shall think himself to be able to change times and laws, and they shall be delivered into his hand until a time, and times, and a half a time.

There is not room in a book of this scope to perform an in-depth analysis of this passage, which would include a comparison of it with other quotes from the *Book of Daniel* as well as quotes from the *Book of Revelation*. The *Book of Revelation* also describes the Antichrist as someone who will "think himself to be able to change times and laws, and they shall be delivered into his hand until a time, and times, and a half a time."

The Apocalypse says his reign will last 1,290 days, or three and one half years. The Fathers are unanimous in stating that "a time, and times, and a half a time" means one year, plus two years, plus a half a year, which equals three and a half years. 1,290 days is very close to three and a half years. 1,290 days equals 3.53 years, barely over three and a half years.

Both the *Book of Daniel* and the *Book of Revelation* speak of "ten horns." *The Fathers universally interpreted the ten horns to be ten kingdoms which will be in place just prior to the rise of Antichrist.* The fourth beast which is spoken of in Daniel, the Fathers all interpreted to be (1) that kingdom of Antichrist. (2) They taught that this fourth kingdom (the one of Antichrist) will rise out of the ten kingdoms which Antichrist will bring into subservience to himself. In his commentary on Daniel 7:7-8, St. Jerome quotes Daniel 7:7-8. Jerome then tells us how this passage is understood by "all ecclesiastical writers." In doing so, he also tells us how the transfer of power from the ten kingdoms of the fourth beast, to the kingdom, of Antichrist will come about.

Jerome's commentary below begins with a quote from the *Book of Daniel.* The text which precedes "and had ten horns," is added from the English edition of *The New Jerusalem Bible.* It has been added to assist the reader in understanding the Scriptural context within which Jerome is speaking. Jerome's commentary on that passage of Daniel comes from the *Corpus Christianorum, Series Latina.*

> "I saw another vision ... there before me was a fourth beast, fearful, terrifying, very strong; ... It was different from the previous beasts **and had ten horns.**
>
> "While I was looking at these horns, I saw another horn sprouting among them, a little one,[613] three of the original horns were pulled out by the roots to make way for it; and in this horn I saw eyes like human eyes, and a mouth full of boasting."

This ends Jerome's quote from Daniel, and now he begins his commentary.

---

[613] The *New Jerusalem Bible* in its footnotes says, the little horn is "Antiochus Epiphanes (175-164) who came to power only after getting rid of several of his claimants."

> "Therefore, let us state what all the ecclesiastical writers [omnes scriptores ecclesiastici] have passed down [tradiderunt] the following: At the consummation of the world [consummatione mundi], when the Kingdom of the Romans has been destroyed, when ten kings shall have divided the territory of the Romans between themselves, an eleventh [man] shall rise to [the kingship of] a small kingdom, who when he shall have overcome three of the ten kings, i.e., the king[s] of the Egyptians, of the Africans, and of the Ethiopians and consequently as we learn more manifestly - whom he shall have killed, the other seven kings shall submit their necks to the victor [the eleventh king]."[614]

The naming of the three kings is not universally taught by the Fathers.

N. MODERN CRITICS' ESCHATOLOGY RISES OR FALLS ON *DANIEL'S* "LITTLE HORN" HAVING EXCLUSIVELY BEEN ANTIOCHUS EPIPHANIES IV

The extreme high critics deny the eschatological teaching of the Fathers that; the *Book of Daniel's 4th kingdom is a future Roman Kingdom.* They deny the Fathers' teaching that; the "little horn" in the *Book of Daniel* is the foretold Antichrist to come at the end of time. Their denial of these Patristic teachings hinges upon the higher critic's claim that; *Daniel's* "little horn" was the 2nd Century B.C.'s Seleucid King Antiochus Epiphanies IV. The extreme higher critics have herein resurrected the seventeen century old argument of the pagan philosopher Porphyry - from Porphyry's work entitled *Against the Christians*.

---

[614] *Corpus Christianorum, Series Latina*, Vol. LXXV A, *S. Heironymi Presbyteri Opera, Pars I, Commentariorum in Danielem*, Pub: Turnholti, Typographi Brepols, Editores Pontifici, 1964, p. 844.

Author's translation from, "Ergo dicamus quod omnes scriptores ecclesiastici tradiderunt: in consummatione mundi, quando regnum destruendum est Romanorum, decem futuros reges qui orbem *romanum [some manuscript texts read romanorum] inter se diuidant, et undecim surrecturum esse paruulum regem qui tres reges de decem regibus superaturus sit, id est Aegyptiorum regem et Africae et Aethiopiae sicut in consequentibus manifestius discimus, quibus interfectis etiam septem alii reges victori colla submittent.

Virtually the entire case of modern critics for dismissing the Fathers on this point boils down to one statement. The *New Jerusalem Bible* (like almost all current Bible editions) says in its footnote that the "little horn" was "Antiochus Epiphanes (175-164 B.C.) who came to power only after getting rid of several of his claimants." That is classic of much of today's exegesis. It is the current higher critical wisdom on this point.

1. In 407 A.D. Jerome Destroyed The *Antiochus Argument*

Jeromes spends many pages of his commentary on the *Book of Daniel* demonstrating that he is thoroughly familiar with all our so-called modern arguments. He does so when he attacks the position of the pagan Porphyry, who was the first to promote these arguments. Porphyry first proposed these arguments in his 15 volume *Against the Christians,* written around 270 A.D. As quoted earlier in Chapter 2: The 1913 *Catholic Encyclopedia* comments on Porphyry's *Against the Christians,*

> "Only a few fragments, preserved in the works of the Christian Apologists, have come down to us. From these it appears that *he directed his attack along the lines of what we should now call historical criticism* of the Old Testament and comparative study of religions."[615]

This has been known for a long time. The author of this book is not breaking new ground by challenging the position of higher critics on this issue. *It was the basic arguments from Porphyry's "historical criticism" attack on the Book of Daniel which* (earlier in Chapter 2) *Fr. Steinmueller says that the modern critics adhere to.*

Conclusion: The idea that "the kingdom of Antiochus IV Epiphanies is the Fourth Empire in *Daniel*" is not new with 20th century critics. It has been successfully discredited by Catholics since St. Methodius first challenged it in the early 4th century A.D.

---

615 *Catholic Encyclopedia*, 1913 Editioon, Vol. 10, Article on "Neo-Platonism," p. 743.

In his *Commentary on the Book of Daniel,* St. Jerome specifically refutes Porpyry's historical arguments. Jerome rightly states that : Porphyry's *assumes* (without proof beyond his own conjecture) that sometime in the 160's B.C., some anonymous religious Jew made up the prophecies contained in the *Book of Daniel.* Jerome describes Porphyry's claim that this *anonymous* Jew (who Porphyry cannot identify) took the historical events of the previous three hundred years -- and placed that history in the mouth of Daniel as prophecy.

As Jerome points out in 407 A.D., *there is absolutely no real evidence for Porphyry's thesis other than Porphyry's conjecture.* In effect, Jerome points out the only person who has really "made something up" is Porphyry. Jerome accurately states that all of Porphyry's diatribes on this subject are simply based in denial of prophecy, Divine Intervention, and the miraculous. Jerome adds that this should not surprise us because it *is* coming from Porphyry, a pagan who is also a vicious enemy of Christianity. As the *Catholic Encyclopedia* observes in 1913 and Fr. Steinmueller observes in the 1950's, Porphyry's arguments have been taken up again in our time by "modern critics."

Counter History

Just as one counter argument, let us look at Daniel 8:23 at the following description of the power of the fourth kingdom,

> "**The Fourth beast shall be *the fourth kingdom* upon the earth**, *which shall be greater than all the kingdoms, and shall devour the whole earth, and shall tread it down and break it in pieces.*
>
> And the ten horns of the same kingdom shall be ten kings: and another shall rise up after them, and he shall be mightier than the former, and he shall bring down three kings."

Does history confirm that Antiochus IV Ipiphanies had that kind of power? That is what Porphyry and the modern higher critics wish us to believe, that at least in his time, the kingdom of Antiochus Epiphanies IV was the most powerful in the world. History tells us that is anything but so!

2. Giuseppi Ricciotti

Giuseppe Ricciotti is the preeminent 20th century Christian historian of Israel. In his two volume *History of Israel*, he tells us about Antiochus IV Epiphanes (Reigned, 175-163 B.C.).

> "He was the product of the fusion of his own eccentric temperament with the traditions of his Hellenic dynasty, *and also with the aristocracy of Rome, where he had lived fourteen years as a hostage*[616]
>
> "*Antiochus IV avoided coming to grips with Rome.* Instead he directed all his energies to the realization of the one project permitted him [by Rome], namely, to infuse his Hellenestic spirit ever more profoundly into *his diminished kingdom.*"[617]

The *Book of Daniel* describes the fourth kingdom as one which shall be "greater[618] than all the kingdoms," and shall devour "the whole earth and shall tread it down and break it in pieces." Does the man described above sound like someone in control of such a powerful kingdom? Ricciotti now gives even greater reason to doubt that Antiochus' Kingdom could be that described in Daniel.

> "in 168 [B.C.] ... he [Antiochus] again invaded the Delta and aimed at Alexandria... *Rome vetoed the project...* Laenas Pompilius ... presented himself to Antiochus, now within a few miles of Alexandria... The Roman communicated to him the demand of the Roman Senate that he retire from Egypt. Antiochus requested time to consider, but Pompilius traced a circle with his staff upon the ground around him and replied 'Deliberate right here.' ...Antiochus abandoned Egypt

---

616 *The History of Israel*, Giuseppi Ricciotti, Vols. 2, The Bruce Publishing Co., Milwaukee, 1955, p 43. [For full details of Antiochus' domination by the Romans, see *The House of Seleucus,* Edwin Robert Belvin, 2 Vols., Pub: Barns & Noble, Inc., New York, 1966, Vol. 2, *particularly his humiliation by Laenus Popilius and the Roman Senate,* see pp 138-145.]

617 Ibid.

618 Some "modern" translations translate this as "different from" rather than "greater than". That is a poor translation choice.

> and returned to Syria via Palestine. **The fact that just any patrician of Rome could treat an heir of Alexander the Great and of the kings of Persia in such a manner is an eloquent indication of the exact state of affairs.**"[619]

The *Book of Daniel* describes the fourth kingdom as one which will

> "devour the whole earth."

Antiochus did not do that, *and neither did any other Seleucid King. Daniel* says of the "little horn" that,

> "the ten horns of the same kingdom shall be ten kings: and another [the 'little horn'] shall rise up after them."

Antiochus was the eighth Seleucid King -- not the tenth. He did not rise up after ten previous kings. *Daniel* says of the "little horn,"

> "and he shall be mightier than the former [ten]."

On the contrary, Antiochus' Epiphanies power was not even a shade of his own grandfathers. *Daniel* says,

> "and he shall bring down three kings."

Antiochus didn't do that either.

As Ricciotti has already told us, Antiochus Epiphanes was publicly humiliated by Laenus Popilius and the Roman Senate before the entire world. Antiochus then went back home to Syrian Antioch the same way he had come -- through Palestine. The first to see him in the wake of that humiliation were the Palestinian Jews. **Antiochus was the ruler of the Seleucid Kingdom during a time that Rome ruled the "known world". He was dominated by and publicly humiliated by the Roman Empire all of his adult life.**

How could anyone familiar with this history expect us to believe that Antiochus' kingdom was the one foretold in *Daniel* to be "greater than all the kingdoms" which would "devour the whole earth." That thesis is ludicrous to anyone who knows the history of

---

[619] Ibid., p. 44-45.

the period. As we are about to read, Msgr. Knox is absolutely correct when he says that certain attempts to make Antiochus Epiphanes into the "little horn" in *Daniel* are ***"curiously forced."***

3. Msgr. Ronald Knox

In the 1950's, the famous 20th century British Scripture scholar Msgr. Ronald Knox[620] commented upon those who interpret this passage of *Daniel* to refer to Antiochus VI Epiphanies;

> "The little horn is usually identified with Antiochus Epiphanies (B.C.), the persecutor of the Machabees; but he was the eighth, not the tenth, of his line **and the explanations given of the 'three horns' displaced by him seem *curiously forced.'"*** [621] [emphasis added]

Frankly, Msgr. Knox's words, "curiously forced," are the most appropriate ones to describe all current tendencies to claim the "little horn" in the *Book of Daniel* refers exclusively to Antiochus Epiphanes IV -- and does not include the future Antichrist.

4. A Catholic Commentary

In 1953, the 1,300 page *A Catholic Commentary on Holy Scripture* made similar comments about higher critical claims that the "little horn" in *Daniel* is exclusively Antiochus Epiphanes IV.

> "Antiochus, however, and his impious achievements do not correspond exactly to the little horn. The death of Antiochus did not bring about either the end of the Syrian domination [of the Jews] or the rise of universal and abiding kingdom [which *Daniel* prophesies to occur after the death of the "little horn"]. Considering the close resemblance between

---

620 In 1949, Msgr. Knox made a new translation of the entire Bible at the request of the entire hierarchy of the Catholic Church in Great Britain. Knox's international reputation as a Scripture scholar is one of the finest in the 20th century.

621 *The Old Testament*, translation and commentary by Msgr. Ronald Knox, Vol. II - Job to Machabees, Pub. Sheed & Ward, Inc. New York, 1950, p. 1357

the 'Man of Lawlessness' or the Antichrist, as described by St. Paul in 2 Thess 2:3-12, and the little horn, **we hold that the little horn**[622] **... in a fuller and adequate sense is the Antichrist of whom Antichus was but a faint image."** ... It follows that the complete victory of the righteous people and the establishment of an ever-enduring kingdom will not be realized before the end of the world. **The fact must be stressed that Daniel's outlook extends much further than the Messianic age."**[623] [emphasis added]

The men responsible for this Catholic commentary are all highly credentialed Scripture scholars (see footnote). They take notice of the already (in the 1950's) current opinion of extreme higher critics that the "little horn" in *Daniel* is Antiochus Epiphanes IV. They (and Msgr. Knox) point out many glaring historic flaws in that higher critical theory. The historic flaws are so obvious that you don't need to be a Scripture scholar to recognize them as such.

The same arguments of the extreme higher critics on this point are basically the same today as they were in the 1950's. The extreme higher critics use those historically flawed arguments to deny the eschatology of the Fathers on *Daniel's* "little horn."

A correct understanding of the "little horn" is absolutely critical to an accurate understanding not only of the Book of Daniel, but also the Book of Revelation (and many other passages in the New Testament). Why? Because, if you accept the higher critical theory that Antiochus Epiphanes IV is **Daniel's** ***"little horn," then you will believe that,***

most of the Book of Daniel *deals with historic events which had already occurred over a century prior to the birth of*

---

[622] [In this interim they state that Antiochus is a literal and figurative type of the final Antichrist to come, but now continue that this passage ultimately refers to ***the Antichrist*** to come at the end of time.]

[623] *A Catholic Commentary on Holy Scripture,* Foreword by; Bernard Cardinal Griffin, Archbishop of Westminster, Editorial Committee -- Dom Bernard Orchard M.A. (Cantab), Rev. Edmund F Sutcliffe S.J., M.A. (Oxom.), L.S.S., Rev Reginald C Fuller D.D., L.S.S. Secretary of the Catholic Biblical Association, Dom Ralph Russell D.D., M.A., Pub: Thomas Nelson and Sons, New York, 1953, p. 634.

> *Jesus Christ -- and Daniel would hold no prophetic meaning for people of the 20th century and beyond.*

The Central Problem: ***Once you accept the higher critical theory that the "Little" Horn in Daniel is exclusively Antiochus Epiphanes IV, then the Book of Daniel essentially becomes a history text of the Old Testament period – and Daniel essentially ceases to be a prophetic book including prophecy for the end times..***

But, if you reject the historically inaccurate theories of the extreme higher critics, if you accept the teachings of the Fathers and almost all the Doctors on this point (that the "little horn" in **Daniel** ***is ultimately the foretold Antichrist). In that case,***

> *You will view the prophecies in the* Book of Daniel *about the forth kingdom and the little horn as eschatological prophecy for the future very end times. That in turn dramatically affects your understanding of the* Book of Revelation *and many other books in the* New Testament.

The higher critics' denial of the eschatological teachings of the Fathers is centrally dependent upon their historically flawed theory that; the "little horn" in **Daniel** ***is exclusively fulfilled by Antiochus Epiphanes IV.*** Extreme higher critical denial of Patristic eschatology is the major cause of our contemporary low state of the study of eschatology. *Conclusion:* it *is* highly academically respectable, and advisable, to expose the historic impossibility of the theory of the extreme higher critics that the "little horn" in *Daniel* is exclusively fulfilled by Antiochus.

5. Pagan Philosopher Porphyry - First to Propose This Argument in the 3rd Century

Porphyry and our "modern critics" would have us believe that a religious Jew from the time of Antiochus or shortly thereafter created prophecies out of Jewish history. These prophecies are claimed by Porphyry and modern critics to have culminated in the rule of Antiochus. Antiochus IV Epiphanies and his blasphemous treatment of the Temple in Jerusalem were as well-known and infamous to Jews as the 1941 attack on Pearl Harbour is to modern Americans. His humiliation at the hands of the Romans was well-known. There is no way any educated Jew at that time or at the time of Christ would have believed Antiochus' kingdom could have been the fourth kingdom of Daniel. It's historically ludicrous.

That theory of Porphyry and our modern extreme higher critics -- that Antiochus IV Epiphanies' kingdom is the fourth kingdom in *Daniel* -- that theory can convince only those who are not aware of both the history of Antiochus and the contents of the *Book of Daniel.*

St. Jerome and the other Fathers were fully aware of this conflict between the historical facts about Antiochus and the Book of Daniel's description of the fourth kingdom. That is one of many reasons they condemned and even ridiculed the historical arguments of Porphyry. They further understood that many things in *Daniel* and the *Book of Revelation* mutually applied to something which had to happen in the end times. That part of the prophecy could most certainly not have been fulfilled by the 2nd century B.C. kingdom of Antiochus IV Epiphanes.

As Jerome commented "Therefore ...all the ecclesiastical writers" have dismissed that interpretation and hold that the "little horn" spoken of in Daniel is the Antichrist. He immediately continues the quote above by referring to "in this horn I saw eyes like human eyes, and a mouth full of boasting."

> "Nor do we think him to be the Devil or a demon (as some others do), but one of mankind in whom Satan shall dwell totally ... his mouth uttering great boasts, for he is *the man of sin the son of perdition, such that he will seat himself in the Temple as if he were God."* [Here Jerome is directly quoting from St. Paul's description of the Antichrist of the end times in 2nd. Thessalonians, 2:15][624]

Jerome could not possibly be any clearer that this individual member of mankind, the "eleventh king" associated in *Daniel* with the fourth kingdom, is the Antichrist. Jerome does not say this just once, but repeatedly. He and the rest of the Fathers associate the "eleventh horn" with, "the man of sin the son of perdition" to whom St. Paul

---

624 *Corpus Christianorum* p. 844.
Ibid. "ne eum putemus, iuxta quorundam opinionem, uel diabolum esse uel daemonem, sed unum de hominibus in quo totus satanas habitaturus est corporaliter. *Et os loquens ingentia: Est* enim *homo peccati, filius perditionis, ita ut in templo Dei sedere audeat faciens se quasi Deum.*

refers in 2nd Thessalonians. Jerome even points out the error of some who think "the eleventh horn" (the Antichrist) will be the devil incarnate or a demon.

6. This Opinion That the Fourth Kingdom Will Be a Roman Kingdom Did Not End With the Fathers

This entire understanding "of all the ecclesiastical writers" is also held by the last Doctor of the Church to do an in-depth study of eschatology, St. Robert Bellarmine. As the reader has already seen, the modern Scripture scholar, Fr. Kramer, agrees with Bellarmine and the Fathers and says that interpretation of the Fathers "is the only logical one." Cardinal Newman agrees.

7. Cardinal Newman

Cardinal Newman is recognized by all as one of the greatest minds of the Church in the last several centuries. Pope Leo XII created Newman a Cardinal-Deacon in 1879. His thinking and analysis led to the discovery that the Church's t*heological understanding* of the doctrines taught in sacred Traditon and sacred Scripture developed over a period of time. These theses he set forth in his classic work, *Development of Christian Doctrine.* As Newman observed therein,

> **(1) No one doctrine can be named which starts complete at first** [vis-a-vis its theological development and full understanding], **and (2) gains nothing from the investigations of faith and (3) the attacks of heresy.**[625]

Newman gives examples: (a) the Arian heresy led to a theological development of the Church's doctrine of the Divinity of Christ. (b) the Monophysite heresy began the theological development of the Church's doctrine of the full Humanity of Christ.

---

[625] *Development of Christian Doctrine*, John Henry Cardinal Newman, Longmans, Green and Co. New York, 1927, p. 68.

No intellectually honest person who really knows Newman could or would accuse him of having his head buried in the past. He understood the history of the development of Church doctrine as part of *a coherent and cohesive theological continuum* till the end of time. That "continuum" organically develops in a linear manner from God's Revelation. It is always rooted in sacred Tradition and sacred Scripture and therefore within that growth in understanding it can never reverse or contradict its stated doctrines of the past.

Newman's testimony as to the eschatological beliefs of the Church is very similar, if not virtually identical to, that of St. & Dr. Robert Bellarmine's. In his 1838 discussion of the "Religion of Antichrist", Newman says,

> "[On the subject of the Antichrist] I shall confine myself to the interpretations of Scripture given by the early Fathers. ... My reason for doing so is simply this, - that on so difficult a subject as unfulfilled prophecy, I really can have no opinion of my own ... The opinion of any one person, even if he were the most fit to form one, could hardly be of any authority, or worth putting forward; whereas the judgement and views of the early Church claim and attract our especial regard, ... because they are put forward far more consistently and unanimously than those of any other set of teachers."[626]

On the subject of a final Roman Empire which precedes Antichrist, and which he subsequently dominates, Cardinal Newman accepts the teachings of the Fathers and says,

[626] *Tracts for the Times, Advent Sermons on Antichrist,* Pub: J.H. Parker, Londom, 1840, p. 16. [This was written eight years prior to his reception into the Catholic Church, while he was still an Anglican. But Notice: The similarity of Newman's position to that of Pope Leo XIII -- in his encyclical *Providentissimus Deus* -- vis-a-vis that where there is unanimity among the Fathers on doctrinal interpretation of Scripture "**clearly evinces that such interpretation has come down from the Apostles as a matter of Catholic faith.**"]

> "*Now this fourth beast in Daniel's vision is the Roman empire*; therefore 'the beast' on which the woman sat, is the Roman empire ... Further, the prophet Daniel explains the ten horns of the beast to be 'ten kings shall arise' out of this empire; in which John agrees, saying, 'The ten horns which thou sawest are ten kings, which have received no kingdom as yet, but receive power as kings one hour with the beast.[627] [emphasis added]

Scripture clearly indicates that three of the ten "kingdoms" will be suppressed by Antichrist. But nowhere in Scipture do we find a specific identification of which ones they will be. At the end of the interpretation which St. Jerome tells us "all ecclesiastical writers" hold to, he personally identifies the three kingdoms as those "of the Egyptians, of the Africans, and of the Ethiopians."

To the best of the author's knowledge, Jerome is the only Father to so identify the three kingdoms. Since this information does not appear in Scripture, where can it come from? The only logical conclusion is that Jerome receives it from tradition -- or a stickler for accuracy in detail such as Jerome would never repeat it. But with the attribution of the names of the three kingdoms surviving in the writing of only one Father, that particular point can hardly be seen as showing "unanimity" among the Fathers.

On the other hand, we have the writings of literally dozens of the Fathers and other ecclesiastical writers which have survived down to our time which do mutually teach several things,

(a) that the "little Horn" in Daniel is the future Antichrist, and
(b) that the fourth beast is the empire which spawns the Antichrist, and
(c) that there will be ten kingdoms as survivors of a Roman Empire in place just prior to the coming of Antichrist.

---

[627] Ibid. pp. 29-30. [Newman also thought these "kings" might be "democracies". Newman wrote this roughly fifty years after the violently Antichristian experience of the French Revolution. He was very cautious about modern forms of popular government.]

Not just Jerome, but "all the ecclesiastical writers" have passed down this teaching. Dozens of their Patristic manuscripts have survived down to our day which prove it.

CONCLUSIONS:

(1) Pope Leo's Encyclical *Providentissimus Deus* stated that, "The Holy Fathers ... are of supreme authority whenever they all interpret in one and the same manner any text of the Bible, *as pertaining to the doctrine of faith and morals*; for their unanimity clearly evinces that such interpretation has come down from the Apostles as a matter of Catholic faith."

Pope Leo gives the additional warning or monitum that no individual Father may specifically deny such an interpretation in order to meet the "supreme authority" criteria. No Father specifically denies the interpretation which Jerome describes as that "of all the ecclesiastical writers"

(2) Unlike many extreme higher critics, the Fathers did not treat the totality of the prophetic books of the Bible as indecipherable code. They handed on that which they had received from Apostolic Tradition.

(3) Unless one is total allegorist, even internal arguments from Scripture and other external arguments corroborate the teachings of the Fathers *on many of these points*.

(4) This is particularly true in the case of the eschatological teachings about the *Book of Daniel* and the *Book of Revelation* concerning the future kingdom or empire of Antichrist.

(5) Sooner or later, Western scholars must again begin to seriously search the Fathers for a fuller understanding of that which we receive from the Apostles about Antichrist.

(6) The Holy Father has recently called on all in *Ut Unum Sint* to "breath with both lungs." Perhaps a return to a searching of the Fathers, particularly of their Scriptural exegesis, will help those of us in the West to "breath with both lungs."

O. THE REBUILDING OF THE TEMPLE

1. St. Paul

St. Paul says in II Thess. 2:4, that Antichrist will also seat himself *in the temple* to be adored and will command men to adore him.

2. Many Fathers and Doctors Expand on This Theme

According to St. Hippolytus, St. John Damascene, 4:27, 15; St. Irenaeus, Ad. Her. 5, 25; St. Ephrem; St. Ambrose; St. Anselm, *the temple in which he will demand personal adoration is the temple at Jerusalem which Antichrist will by then have rebuilt.* It is doubtful that enough of the Fathers teach this for it to be seen as a unanimous teaching of the Fathers. But several prestigious ecclesiastical writers, Fathers and Doctors teach the following.

3. St. Hippolytus

The Savior raised up and showed his holy flesh like a temple, and he [Antichrist] will raise a temple of stone in Jerusalem.[628]

4. St. Irenaeus (F)

St. Irenaeus comments directly on the issue of the Temple as related to Antichrist:

[628] *De Antichristo*, 6, 14: MIGNE, P.G. X, 736, 738.

> "*At the time of his reign, Antichrist will command that Jerusalem be rebuilt in splendor*, and will make it a great and populous city, second to none in the world and will order his palace to be built there."[629]

Irenaeus does not posit this position as a possibility. Rather, he teaches it with clear authority, and in a manner which Irenaeus usually reserves for those things which he believes to be of Apostolic Tradition. He does not specifically say that the Temple will be rebuilt, but he does with assurety state that the City will be rebuilt. It is highly unlikely that if Jerusalem is totally rebuilt in splendor, the Temple would not be part of that rebuilding process.

5. St. Anselm (D)

St. Anselm who *is* a Doctor of the Church, says,

> "For, the Temple which Solomon built having been destroyed, in its place he (Antichrist) shall restore it, he shall circumcise himself, and he shall give forth the lie that he is the son of the omnipotent God."[630]

Let us finish with a passage from St. Paul which we have quoted earlier, in which the *Catholic Encyclopedia* (1936) edition assures us St. Paul is here prophesying concerning the Antichrist; "Without mentioning the name, St. Paul, in the Second Epistle to the Thessalonians (II, 1-10), gives a fuller description of the Antichrist."[631]

---

629 *The Catholic Encyclopedia, Revised and Enlarged Edition,* 1936, Littleton & Ives, Co., New York, Imprimatur, Cardinal Hayes, Archbishop of New York, 1936, Vol. No. 1, p 599.

630 *Corpus Christianorum, Continuo Medievalis, Vol. 45, Liber Anselmi de Antichristo*, p. 163. The Latin reads "Templum etiam destructum, quod Solomon edificavit, in statu suo reparabit et circumcidit se et filium Dei omnipotentis se mentietur."

631 *The Catholic Encyclopedia*, Ibid. p 599.

> "Let no one deceive you, for the day of the Lord will not come unless the apostasy comes first, and the man of sin is revealed, the son of perdition who opposes and is exalted above all that is called God, or that is worshipped; *so that he sits in the temple* and gives himself out as if he were God. Do you not remember that when I was still with you, I used to tell you these things?"

6. St. Ephraem (F&D)

St. Ephraem specifically states,

> "The man of evil will prepare, and coming he will enter Jerusalem; he will build up and establish Sion [Jerusalem? or the Jewish faith[632]], and will make himself God, and entering he will sit in *the temple*, as the Apostle has written (II Thess. ii. 4): *as if he were God.*"[633]

Ephraem says the Antichrist will "Build up and establish Sion" after entering Jerusalem. He says he will then enter and sit in "the temple." This has been interpreted by all the major commentators on Ephraem as a reference to the rebuilding of Jerusalem as Antichrist's capital, and, the rebuilding of the Temple of Jerusalem.

---

632 Sion. Originally Mt. Zion (alternate spelling - Sion). When King David established Jerusalem as his capitol, he brought the Ark of the Covenant to this mountain or tall hill which is situated in Jerusalem. Later, when David's son, King Solomon built the first Temple of Jerusalem, Solomon moved the Arc to the Temple.

Ultimately, Zion came to mean the Jewish faith. Therefore, it is not immediately clear whether Ephraem is referring to the City or to the Jewish religion. However, it is most likely that he means the City. The reason is that both Scripture and Tradition say that Antichrist will legalistically set aside the moral precepts of the Jewish law replacing it with licentiousness. Therefore, it is more probable that St. Ephraem is referring to the city itself.

633 *The Sunday Sermons of the Great Fathers*, Vol. 4, Translated and edited by M.F. Toal, Henry Regnery Co. 1964, p. 356.

P. THE FINDING OF THE ARK OF THE COVENANT?

According to many prophecies, the Jews will be stunned by Elias finding the Ark of the Covenant. Accordingly, this "finding" will create a great impression on the Jews at the time of Antichrist.

On July 30, 587 B.C., after a three month siege, Jerusalem was sacked and burned by King Nabuchodonosor and his Babylonian army. The remains of the burned-out Temple in Jerusalem were pulled down along with the walls of the City. The Judean King, Jehoiachin, his mother, high officials, almost the entire leadership of Judea (10,000 men with another 30,000 of their wives and children) were led in bondage to Babylon. There is no Scriptural mention of the Ark since that time. The Ark of the Covenant disappeared from the Temple, never to be seen again.

According to the Book of Machabees the following occurred. In obedience to a divine revelation, and before the destruction of Jerusalem by Nabuchodonosor, the prophet Jeremias had the Ark carried to Mount Nebo. Together with the Tabernacle and Altar of Incense, he concealed the Ark in a cave, and closed up its entrance.

1. Historical Importance of the Ark and Jeremiah

Much of what is to follow in reference to Enoch and Elias (particularly in reference to their rediscovery of the Ark of the Covenant) would not make much sense to the reader unless he or she is also conversant with the historical background of the Prophet Jeremiah. This is also true in regard to the major events which preceded Jeremiah, and his prophetic mission to the Kingdom of Juda.

God had called Jeremiah to preach repentance and to prophesy chastisement and punishment to Juda if they did not amend their ways. To the reader who is already conversant with this history, please bear with this review.

2. A Cryptic Chronology of O.T. Events Surrounding the Ark of the Covenant

1000 B.C.	King David has established the Jewish Kingdom in Jerusalem. There, on Mt. Sion, he places the Ark of the Covenant.
950-955	By the middle of King Solomon's reign (sometime between 950-955) the Temple of Solomon is completed after seven and one half years of construction, The Ark of the Covenant is carried in solemn procession from the City of David (Mt. Sion) to the newly completed Temple on Mt. Moria.
922	King Solomon dies. Shortly after this, internecine squabbles separate the Kingdom of Israel in the North from the Kingdom of Judah in the South. They remain separated for the next 750 years - till the reign of the Machabees.
869 B.C.	By now the Northern Kingdom of Israel has been corrupted by the Caananites to the point that they were worshipping the Caananite god, Baal.
869 B.C.	God sends Elijah the Prophet in hair-shirt and leather loin-cloth to preach to Israel repentance and return to Yahweh.
750 B.C.	Amos the Prophet is sent by God to preach repentance, to tell them (the Jews) that God will punish them if they remain unfaithful. They don't respond.
745 B.C.	King Tiglath-Pileser III of Assyria conquers and lays waste the kingdoms of both Israel and Juda. *THIS BEGINS THE PERIOD OF THE GREAT PROPHETS.*

724 B.C. Amos' terrible prophecy is fulfilled when the Assyrian King Shalamaneser captures Israel and leads 27,290 *Israelites* into captivity. They never return. These are the people referred to as the "Ten lost tribes of Israel."

721 B.C. Isaiah the Prophet - is sent to warn the Jews (in the Southern Kingdom of Judea) that God will punish them still further if they do not repent. He also foretells the Virgin Birth, that the Messiah will be a Galilean, that He will be both true God and true man. Isaiah predicts the ultimate downfall of Assyria and Babylon, the destruction of Jerusalem and the Temple, and that Israel will ultimately be helped by a Persian King who will be named Cyrus.

663 B.C. The Persian Empire begins.

649 B.C. The Persian King Ashurbanipal sacks Thebes. The Assyrian Empire goes as far as the land of Egypt. *DURING THIS PERIOD OF TIME, THE KINGDOM OF JUDA has been falling away from the faithful serving of Yahweh -- just as the Kingdom of Israel before it.*

621 B.C. Under Josiah, King of Judea, the feast of the Passover is celebrated in the Land of Judah for the first time in centuries. King Josiah tries to reestablish faithful ritual worship of Yahweh in Judea.

Comment: If one is not all that familiar with the Old Testament, one must be wondering - *what were all these terrible things the Jews were doing which caused God to send so many prophets to warn them and call them to repentance?* **How bad could it have really been?**

In 621, King Josiah called all of the people together in Jerusalem to tell them that they were returning to "ritual worship" of the Lord God Jehovah. As part of this process,

> "The Temple was purged of every object connected with the *false gods* ... the priests who had used them, the mediums and the soothsayers and the wizards and *the cult prostitutes*, were all driven away. The alien shrines around and beyond Jerusalem were ceremonially defiled, *particularly Tophet where the children had been sacrificed*, in the deep Valley of Ben-Hinnom which, was to give its hellenized name of Gahenna to be one of the names of Hell."[634] (emphasis mine)

What was just quoted are the historical facts as seen through the eyes of an historian. In order to assure ourselves his view is in accord with that of God's Word, let us turn to *Jeremiah* and read the words which he said God had commanded him to deliver to the people of Judea.

> "Because the children of Juda have done evil in my eyes, saith the Lord.
>
> "They have set their abominations in the house in which my name is called upon, to pollute it;
>
> "And they have built the high places [sacrificial altars] of Topheth, which is in the valley of the son of [H]ennom, ***to burn their sons, and their daughters in the fire*:** which I commanded them not, nor thought on in my heart.
>
> "Therefore behold the days shall come, saith the Lord, and it shall no more be called Topheth, nor the Valley of the son of (H)ennom: but the valley of slaughter: and they shall bury in Topheth, because there is no place.
>
> "And the carcasses of the people shall be meat for the fowls of the air, and there shall be none to drive them away.
>
> "And I shall cause to cease out of the cities of Juda, and out of the streets of Jerusalem, the voice of joy, and the voice

634 *The Founding of Christendom - A History of Christendom,* Warren H. Carroll, Christendom College Press, 1985, Vol. 1, p. 130.

of gladness, the voice of the bridegroom and the voice of the bride: for the land shall be desolate."[635]

In other words, **it had gotten so bad** that;

(1) Jewish priests were sacrificing to the false gods of the surrounding pagan nations.

(2) Prostitution associated with pagan religious cults was being practiced in the Temple of Solomon itself.

(3) **The Jews had actually been involved on a massive scale in burning their own children alive -- sacrificing them to pagan gods.**

(4) God sends Jeremiah to warn the people that unless they change their ways, quickly and wholeheartedly, He will destroy their peace and tranquillity to wake them up.

COMMENT: ***THAT* IS HOW BAD IT WAS!** But was it worse than it is in the United States, where we murder 1.5 million children per year through abortion? God sent Jeremiah to warn the people of Juda about many things, but of all of them, the murder of innocent children was something which He absolutely would not tolerate amongst his people. He would not tolerate *the mass murder of innocents*. This *was the Judeans' final outrage* for which God would chastise them if they did not repent and amend their ways. Would God view our murder of our "innocents" any less sternly?

It would appear that He has sent many 20th century Jeremiahs to warn us that if we do not stop murdering our babies through abortion -- He WILL do the same thing to us! Why would it surprise anyone that God in his mercy would send us warnings before he would allow a chastisement? Would such a person believe that God loves us less than He did the child-murdering generation of Judeans

[635] Jeremias, 7:30-34.

at the time of Jeremiah? He warned them! Their crimes against God and man caused their chastisement through the Babylonian Captivity.

609/608 B.C. In response to God's call, the Prophet Jeremiah warns the Kingdom of Judea to return to Yahweh, that Judea and surrounding kingdoms will serve the King of Babylon in slavery if Judea does not repent. Most of the Judeans do not believe Jeremiah, or if they do, they certainly do not respond.

597 B.C. **The Babylonian Exile predicted by both the Prophets Isaiah and Jeremiah comes to pass.** It begins in 597 and lasts until 537. Most of the Judeans are taken captive to Babylon.

It is during this period initiating the Babylonian Captivity that the following occurred.

3. Scriptural Account of Ark's Disappearance

> "It was contained in the same writing, how the prophet (Jeremiah), being warned by God, commanded that the Tabernacle and the Ark should accompany him till he came forth to the mountain where Moses went up, and saw the inheritance of God." (Jeremiah 2:4)

> "And when Jeremias came thither he found a hollow cave: and he carried in thither the ark, and the altar of incense, and so stopped the door.[636]

There are scholars who question whether the "fact" stated in the quote from 2nd Machabees above is, per se, an inspired text. Be that as it may, you are going to read a number of private prophecies which *exactly* corroborate the "historical facts" as described in 2nd Machabees.

---

[636] 2 Machabees, 2:4-5.

According to Machabees, immediately after Jeremiah "stopped (closed up) the door" of the cave:

> "Then some of them that followed him [Jeremias], came up to mark the place: but they could not find it.
>
> "And when Jeremias perceived it, he blamed them saying: *the place shall be unknown, till God gather together the congregation of the people [the Jews] and receive them to mercy.*"[637]

This time of gathering "together the congregation of the people *and receive them to mercy.*" is a reference to the prophesied time when the Jews will be converted more or less "en masse" to Christ and his Church.

It was a solid Rabinical opinion (found in many Rabinical writings of the two centuries preceding the advent of Christ) that when the Messiah came would be the time when the Ark of the Covenant would be rediscovered in Mt. Nebo. While that timing of rediscovery was incorrect, it helps to confirm the tradition of the Ark having been hidden in Mt. Nebo. Now we will quote the full passage from Machabees.

> "Then some of them that followed him [Jeremias], came up to mark the place: but they could not find it.
>
> "And when Jeremias perceived it, he blamed them saying: ***the place shall be unknown, till God gather together the congregation of the people (the Jews) and receive them to mercy.***
>
> **"And then the Lord will show these things, and the majesty of the Lord shall appear**,"[638] [i.e., the traditional interpretation of this passage is that it is related to the Ark which will physically reappear or be rediscovered at that time of the congregation of the Jews.]

Should this happen as described it would have a stunning effect on the Jews. The Ark is totally conjoined psychologically and

637 2 Machabees, 2:6-7
638 2 Machabees c.2, v.8

emotionally to the history of the Jewish people and their Covenant with God. It is so integral to their faith that a non-Jew has a difficult time comprehending how central the Ark is to the faith of a religious Jew.

First of all, the Ark contained the "Tablets of the Law" which were delivered into the hands of Moses by God Himself. It contains a vessel with some of the "Manna" with which the Jewish people were miraculously fed during their Exodus through the Desert of Sinai. It also contains the "Rod of Jesse." This Ark (should it be found by Enoch and Elias and shown by them to the Jewish people) would have an intellectual, psychological, and emotional impact on them almost beyond description. As a number of the prophecies say, the Jews will be so stunned that Enoch and Elias have found the Ark, they will literally accept it as God's confirmation of the authenticity of the "Two Witnesses" as His personal messengers.

4. Arguments Against the Ark Being at Mt. Nebo

There are some scholars who question whether or not the Ark ever returned to Israel from Egypt during the reign of Pharoah Shishak (alternate spellings, Sesac and Sheshonk).

> "Scholars believe that the Ark never returned to Jerusalem following Pharoah Shishak's plunder of the city: 'He carried off the treasures of the temple of the Lord and the treasures of the royal palace. He took everything...'" (1 Kings 14:25-26).[639]

The opinion of "scholars" referred to above is totally dependent upon their assumption that the Ark was ever in the possession of Pharoah Shishak in the first place. The article stops the quote at "He took everything..." That quote continues, "including all the gold shields which Solomon had made."

That last phrase generates an interesting question. That event occurred in 917 B.C., barely five years after the death of King Solomon. Since some individual items which Shishak "took" are

[639] *Biblical Archeology Review*, January/February, 1996, Vol. 22, Number 1.

mentioned, why did the most important Jewish artifact, the Ark of the Covenant, not get mentioned? This is no idle question. The Temple which King Solomon built was for two primary purposes (1) as a holy place for the ritual sacrifices of the Jewish priesthood representing the Jewish people, and (2) to house the Ark of the Covenant. Again, how reasonable is it that, if the Ark was truly lost, the chronicler of this event would mention Solomon's gold shields and ignore the loss of the Ark?

One could reply that this was an attempt to show just how thorough the pillage was, that it even got down to gold shields. But does that really answer the question? The key word in the quote from the Book of Kings is "treasure." Pharoah Shishak was after "treasure" or booty. The cover (or lid) of the Ark, called the "propitiatory" was made of solid gold. But the Ark itself was made of "setim wood," and only *covered* with a thin layer of beaten gold. Its gold content therefor was probably not that high. As booty, it would have constituted a lot of weight and bulk for not that much gold.

But Solomon's shields were made of solid gold, would be compact for transport, and they must have been worth a fortune. They surely represented "treasure." Therefore, Shishak's coming into their possession had to have represented an incredible financial loss. Pharoah Shishak was after golden treasure, not religious artifacts. There is no conclusive evidence of Shishak even having received the Ark. As a matter of fact, the eminent historian, Dr. Warren Carroll, comments on this event,

> "In the fifth year of King Rehoboam (917 B.C.) Sheshonk ravaged Palestine from end to end. He only spared Jerusalem upon receiving from [King] Rehoboam a tribute so large that the Israelite king had to strip the gold from his palace and even from parts of the temple to pay it."[640]

The logical conclusion is that Shishak carried off what King Rehoboam *offered* him in tribute. There is no evidence at all of Shishak per se having physically pillaged the Temple. There is no evidence that he had any hand in selecting the golden "treasure."

---

[640] *The Founding of Christendom, Vol. 1, A History of Christendom*, Warren Carroll, Christendom College Press, Front Royal, VA. 1985, p. 95.

There is another excellent argument against Rehoboam having offered the Ark of the Covenant as part of the payoff to Pharoah Shishak. After the death of king Solomon, his son, Rehoboam, succeeded to the throne. Due to his harsh treatment of the tribes of the North,

> "The ten tribes of the North promptly rose in revolt ... and established their independence under the name of the Kingdom of Israel."

Very shortly after that, Pharoah Shishak invaded Palestine.

Rehoboam was facing many challenges from the Kingdom of Israel to his authority as the successor of King Solomon. Being in possession of first, the Holy City, and second, the Temple of Solomon, and third, the Ark of the Covenant, were not just religiously important to Rehoboam. In the psychology of politics, all three were crucial to Rehoboam's political claim to inheritance of the throne *and authority* of his father, King Solomon.

By offering tribute to Shishak, Rehoboam had (1) saved Jerusalem itself from being sacked, and (2) the Temple was left standing. Is it reasonable to believe he would then have offered to Shishak the Ark of the Covenant, the third item which was crucial to his political claim? Again, there is no conclusive evidence at all of Pharoah Shishak ever coming into physical possession of the Ark. As a matter of fact, the logistical, political, and religious exigencies of the period argue heavily against it.

5. Coptic Argument Against Mt. Nebo

One of the "Sister Churches," the Copts, claim that they possess the Ark of the Covenant in a Monastery. The author has even seen investigative reports on television inquiring into this claim. It is not just Copts who put credence in this. Some of the Catholics and Orthodox in the area also believe it to be true.

The explanation of how the Copts reportedly came into the Ark's possession is this: Some time at or around the fall of Jerusalem in 70 A.D., that the Ark was smuggled out of Jerusalem by Jews who fled south to northeast Africa. The claim is that the Ark later fell into the hands of the Copts.

At this Coptic monastery, there is a guard who watches over what the Copts believe to be the Ark of the Covenant. The office of guarding this location is reportedly the job of one man. When a guard dies, a new one is appointed to take his place. No one but this guard is ever allowed in to see what is stated to be the Ark. Therefore, there is absolutely no academic research or reports on the existence and/or authenticity of such an object. There is also no Scriptural evidence to support this claim.

6. Bl. Dionysius of Luetzenburg

He prophesies that which is the traditional interpretation of the above quoted passage from the Book of Machabees:

> ***"After the discovery of the Ark of the Covenant*, Enoch and Elias will restore the Holy Sacrament of the Altar;** Because of the fact that the Ark of the Covenant will be in the possession of the two holy prophets and not in Antichrist's hands, the Jews will recognize that Jesus Christ is the true Messias. A great throng of Jews from all lands will then make their way to Mount Nebo."[641]

We have now heard both Scripture, Jewish Rabbinical Tradition (in the sense of confirming the Machabees account), a chronicler of Oral Tradition, and private prophecy state that the rediscovery of the Ark of the Covenant shall have a dramatic effect on the Jews. However, there is nothing the author has yet found in the writings of the Fathers which confirms this event. Therefore, it depends upon Rabbinical tradition, a highly probable interpretation of Scripture, and several private prophecies. But it is a highly interesting hypothesis.

Scripture itself speaks of the "abomination of desolations" during which the perpetual "Sacrifice" (the Sacrifice of the Eucharistic Liturgy) shall cease. Antichrist shall have outlawed the saying of Mass. Many prophecies state that during this period, the Mass will only be said in the "desert" (wilderness). The Christians will have fled the cities which are controlled by Antichrist. Certain priests will have gone into the wilderness to serve the Christians in hiding.

---

[641] Luetzenburg, *Antichristus* Chapter 39. According to both Tradition & Scripture, and private prophecy, the Antichrist shall have abolished the "the Holy Sacrament of the Altar;" (the Mass). That is part of the Scriptural "abomination of desolations."

7. Finding of the Ark Would Supersede the Impact of False Miracles of Antichrist

It must be remembered that it is not only the Jews who will be taken in by Antichrist. According to Scripture and Tradition there will be a large percentage of the Gentiles who will also at first believe in him -- *primarily because of his false miracles*. But if it happened, the discovery of the Ark by Elias would have a particularly telling effect upon the Jews living at that time. To them it would have to look like a confirmation from "Yahweh" that Elias speaks truly for God in support of the Divinity of His Christ. Discovery of the Ark would readily nullify the effect of all the false miracles of Antichrist.

Many Fathers of the Church wrote whole chapters on the various false miracles of Antichrist, based upon what had come down to them from tradition. Also, many approved private prophets have recorded specific examples of these false miracles. An example is one quoted by Dionysius of Leutsenburg from Bernardin de Busto,

> "Bernardin a Busto says: 'When a mother is carrying her infant in her arms or is laying it in its cradle, the babe will begin to speak and with clear and distinct voice will acknowledge the divinity of Antichrist, calling on its mother to completely abandon Christ and to turn to Antichrist! The child will reproach its parents for remaining godless and obstinate against Antichrist despite his many miracles. O, what anguish of soul will such parents suffer!'"[642]

Other private prophecies speak of false miracles involving crucifixes being made *to appear* to speak. These prophecies foretell the simulated (by Antichrist and Satan) speech emanating from these crucifixes to encourage people to worship the Antichrist.

Finally, according to both Scripture and Tradition, Antichrist will slay both Enoch and Elias in Jerusalem and will leave their bodies unburied; however, God will raise them again to life after three and a half days and will take them up into heaven before the eyes of their enemies.[643] *Antichrist will survive Enoch and Elias*

[642] Ibid. Chpt. 32.

[643] Apoc. c.11, v.3-12.

(apparently by only thirty days). According to Daniel, his reign will last 1290 days.[644] It is also stated in the Apocalypse (c.11, v.3) that he will live about 30 days after the preaching of Enoch and Elias which will last for 1260 days.

Q. THE DEATH OF ANTICHRIST

Tradition and Scripture taken together with numerous "approved" private prophecies, flesh out many details surrounding the death of Antichrist.

1. Scripture - St. John and the Apocalypse

In his Apocalypse St. John indicates that Antichrist will reign in Jerusalem, because that is where he will slay Enoch and Elias:

> "And when they [the two witnesses] have finished their testimony, the beast that ascends from the bottomless pit will make war upon them and conquer them and kill them, and their dead bodies will lie in the street of the great city which is allegorically called Sodom and Egypt, **where their Lord was crucified.**"[645]

From this and other Scriptural passages it is fairly apparent that the city being described is Jerusalem, where Our Lord was crucified. That is the most common Patristic exegesis.

Many of the prophecies from Tradition and private prophecy tell us that Antichrist will have killed "the two witnesses" (Enoch and Elias) because due to their miracles and preaching both the Jews and Gentiles will begin to turn away from him. He kills Enoch and Elias to show his power over them. But **according to Scripture's *Book of Revelation***, now an even greater event occurs to confound Antichrist (the beast):

> "For three days and a half men from the peoples and tribes and tongues and nations gaze at their dead bodies and refuse

---

[644] Daniel, c.12, v.11.

[645] Apolcalypse 11:7-8.

> to let them be placed in a tomb, and those who dwell on the earth will rejoice over them and make merry and exchange presents, because **these two prophets** had been a torment to those who dwell on the earth.
>
> "But after three and a half days *a breath of life* from God entered them, and they stood up on their feet, and great fear fell on those who saw them. **Then they heard a loud voice from heaven saying to them, "Come up hither." And in the sight of their foes, they went up to heaven in a cloud.** And at that hour there was a great earthquake, and a tenth of the city fell; seven thousand people were killed in the earthquake, *and the rest were terrified and gave glory to God of heaven.*"[646]

This last line is the key to understanding what happens next. According to Scripture, for three and a half days the fickle people have again returned to Antichrist. Due to this new display of power by the true God of the Christians, Antichrist's followers begin again to totally lose confidence in him.

2. Antichrist is Desperate, Attempts to Simulate the Ascension of Our Lord

Now, in a desperate bid to reclaim his authority with his followers, Antichrist will attempt (through the power of Satan) to simulate Christ's ascension into Heaven from a mountain. St. Jerome and St. Thomas Aquinas say it will be Mt. Olivet.

3. St. Thomas Aquinas

St. Thomas also specifically states that it will be St. Michael who will slay him during that attempted ascension from Mt. Olivet. In his commentary on 2 Thessalonians, Chapter 2, Verse 8, ("and the Lord Jesus will slay him with the breath of his mouth"), Thomas says,

[646] Ibid. 8-13.

"For Michael shall kill him on Mount Olivet from whence Christ ascended."[647]

4. St. Hildegard

St. Hildegard now tells us in her own private prophetic words (which she says were revealed to her by God) what transpires at this point.

> "After Enoch and Elias suffer physical death ... the spirit of life will reawaken them, raise them up into the clouds, and the rejoicing of that man's [Antichrist's] followers will change into fear, sorrow and dismay.
>
> "Then the son of corruption [Antichrist] will gather together a large group of people in order that his glory can be openly shown forth. He [Antichrist] will attempt to walk through the heavens so that any remnant of the Catholic Faith that might still remain throughout the world, [as a result of his ascension into heaven] might completely disappear.
>
> "In the sight of crowds standing around and listening [to Antichrist], he will order the higher strata of the sky to lift him up during his ascension into heaven, and the words of My loyal servant Paul will be fulfilled, and these are the words which Paul, who is full of the spirit of truth, says, 'and the Lord Jesus will slay him with the breath of his mouth and will destroy him with his glorious appearance at his coming. [Here the prophecy is quoting 2 Th. 2:8]
>
> "... **When the son of corruption ascends on high *through diabolical trickery*,** he will be thrust down again by the Divine Power. The fumes of sulphur and pitch will consume him such that the crowds standing nearby will flee into the mountains for protection. Such abject fear will seize all who see and hear these things that they will reject the Devil and his [spiritual] son [Antichrist] and be converted to the true faith through Baptism."[648]

647 The Latin reads "quia Michael interfecturus est eum in monte Oliveti unde Christus ascendit." This quote is from *Sancti Thomae Aquinitatis, Opera Omnia*, Tomus XIII, Musurgia Publishers, New York, 1949, p. 579.

648 *Hildegardis Divinum Operorum*, Visio 10, (Headings 35 and 36).

Many of the prophesies seem to indicate that Antichrist's ascension may be accomplished simply through what we today would call some advanced form of technology (trickery?). But it will appear magical/mystical to the onlookers. Other prophecies state that it will quite literally be by the power of Satan and the demons from hell that Antichrist will be able to rise into the air.

Some prophecies state that Michael the Archangel (as a messenger of Christ who will appear mystically riding through the heavens on a white horse) will actually strike Antichrist with a bolt of lightning and hurl him down to the earth upon the occurrence of Antichrist's false miracle of rising from Olivet. At that point, according to the prophecies (*and Scripture*) a chasm opens up in the ground and swallows up Antichrist (the beast), and the false prophet (the other beast).

It is from that chasm that the "fumes of sulphur and pitch" which St. Hildegarde discusses emanate. The Scriptures confirm the basics of all this. The "approved" private prophecies are in agreement with tradition and Scripture on the basics, and merely flesh out some additional details. Needless to say, these "details" are not "of faith."

R. THE "MILLENIUM"?

The traditional Catholic teaching is that the earth lasts only a reasonably short time after the death of Antichrist. But the attempts of many past theologians to "reason to" the exact length of that duration is an exercise in futility. To subsequently assign to it a length of forty-five days flies in the face of the Scriptural admonition that no one "knows the day nor the hour."

1. A Contemporary Problem Amongst Some Catholics

However, there is an even more deleterious tendency to be found in some *contemporary* Catholic speculation as to the "Coming of the Kingdom." This "worse" tendency is the now commonly heard theme that possibly Christ will physically rule for one thousand years with the Saints on earth -- sometime after the death of Antichrist but prior to the Final Judgement. This is actually nothing more than a resurrection of some of the main aspects of the previously condemned *Chiliast or Millenarianist heresy*. The entire Catholic Tradition on this subject from the time of the Fathers till now consistently teaches that the Parousia comes a reasonably short time after the death of Antichrist.

2. St. Robert Bellarmine (D)

We will now present the writing of Robert Bellarmine on the Catholic traditional teaching on this subject.

> "Heading Six. The sixth demonstration arises from the last sign, that follows Antichrist, which shall be the consummation of the world. For **Antichrist shall come a short time before the end of the world ... after Antichrist at once comes the last judgement**... the future reign of Antichrist shall be of one thousand two hundred and ninety days duration... Math. 24. 'This gospel of the kingdom shall be preached in the whole world, and then shall come the consummation (of the world)' that is, **a little after [Antichrist] shall come the end of the world.**"[649]

This is not just the teaching of St. Robert Bellarmine, a Doctor of the Church. It is the constant teaching of the Church. "Millennialists" associate the Millenium with the coming of Christ's kingdom. That is what they and Catholics refer to when they *escha-tologically* pray "Marana tha" which means "Our Lord, come." The difference lies in how they view that kingdom, *and when they see its coming*. The reader has earlier seen the following quote from Joseph Ratzinger,

> "...both Chiliasm [the teaching of a Millenium] and Montanism were declared heretical and were excluded from the universal church; for they both denied this vision [the "Christ is the end of the ages" vision] and awaited still

[649] "CAPUT VI. Sexta demonstratio sumitur ex ultimo signo consequente Antichristum, quod erit mundi consummatio. Nam Antichristi adventus erit paulo ante finem mundi. ... post Antichristum statim sequuturum ultimum judicium: ... 12. Antichristi regnum duraturum diebus mille ducentis et nonaginta. ... Matth. 24. Praedicabitur hoc evangelium regni in universo mundo in testimonium omnibus gentibus, et tunc erit consummatio, idest, paulo post erit finis mundi. p. 438.

> another period of more definitive salvation to follow after the age of Christ."[650]

The reader has also previously seen the following quote from the 1994 *Catechism of the Catholic Church* which states,

> "The Church has rejected *even modified forms* of this falsification of the kingdom to come under the name of millenarianism, especially the 'intrinsically perverse' political form of a secular messianism"[651]

As the reader can see, the Church rejects the teaching of a Millenarianism, "even modified forms" of it. We will now see the section of the *Catechism of the Catholic Church* which immediately precedes this last quote. This is a very succinct statement and deserves a very careful reading.

> "The Antichrist's deception already begins to take shape in the world every time the claim is made to realize within history that messianic hope which can only be realized beyond history through the eschatological judgement."[652]

Here, the Church is teaching that any "messianic hope" which occurs prior to the Final Judgement by Christ, is outside the teaching of the Church. If this is not absolutely clear in what the reader has just read, the Catechism immediately goes on to be absolutely specific on this point.

> ***"The Church will enter the glory of the kingdom only through this final Passover*, when she will follow the Lord in his death and Resurrection.** The kingdom will be fulfilled, then, not by a historic triumph of the Church through a progressive ascendency, *but only by God's victory over the final unleashing of evil* which will cause his bride

---

[650] *The Theology of History in St. Bonaventure*, Joseph Ratzinger, English Edition-translated by Zachary Hayes, O.F.M., Franciscan Herald Press, Chicago, 1971, p. 96.

[651] *Catechism of the Catholic Church*, Libreria Editrice Vaticana, St. Paul Books and Media, 1994., # 676, p. 177.

[652] Ibid.

> to come down from heaven. *God's triumph over the revolt of evil will take the form of the Last Judgement after the final cosmic upheaval of this passing world.*"[653]

The Church is specifically interpreting the *Book of the Apocalypse* here. There is absolutely no question as to what is being referred to. Therefore, when we as Catholics pray for the *escha-tological* kingdom -- we are praying to pass through "the final cosmic upheaval of this passing world" -- in order to arrive at the Glorious Eternal Kingdom of Christ.

The Traditional teaching of the Church is that - the Parousia comes relatively soon after the death of Antichrist

We should remember that St. Robert Bellarmine was the last Doctor of the Church to make an in-depth study of Her eschatology. His knowledge of the Scriptures, Tradition, and especially the writings of the Fathers is matched by few men in the history of the Church. He teaches,

> **"Antichrist shall come a short time before the end of the world ... after Antichrist at once comes the last judgement**... the future reign of Antichrist shall be of one thousand two hundred and ninety days duration... Matt. 24. 'This gospel of the kingdom shall be preached in the whole world, and then shall come the consummation (of the world)' that is, **a little after [Antichrist] shall come the end of the world.**"[654]

By the "end of the world" Bellarmine means, "the end of time." Bellarmine represents the traditional teaching of the Church on

[653] Ibid. #677.

[654] "CAPUT VI. Sexta demonstratio sumitur ex ultimo signo consequente Antichristum, quod erit mundi consummatio. Nam Antichristi adventus erit paulo ante finem mundi... post Antichristum statim sequuturum ultimum judicium:... 12. Antichristi regnum duraturum diebus mille ducentis et nonaginta... Matth. 24. Praedicabitur hoc evangelium regni in universo mundo in testimonium omnibus gentibus, et tunc erit consummatio, idest, paulo post erit finis mundi. p. 438.

this subject. In no way does the traditional teaching of the Church (either as expressed by the Catechism or Bellarmine) allow for an "earthly millennium" during the course of history, i.e., before the Last Judgement.

CAVEAT: Why is it then that today one hears a significant number of otherwise orthodox Catholics speaking as if they believe a literal "millennium," or the coming the fullness of "the Kingdom" before the end of time is possible. It is because of the sparsity of sound eschatology heard from the pulpit.

It is also a fact that most lay Catholics learn the greatest percentage of their doctrine from sermons and homilies. In the contemporary vacuum of sound eschatology heard from Catholic pulpits, they are highly subject to suggestion. *When they have never heard the Catholic doctrine*, they honestly have no reason not to believe what they hear from some of their confused Catholic brethren, or from our separated brethren who might believe in a literal millennium.

S. OUTSIDE INFLUENCES

Many Americans regularly hear non-Catholic fundamentalist preachers or Television evangelists preaching an earthly "millennium" of 1000 years. While such evangelists undoubtedly hold that theological belief in good faith (*along with a number of currently confused Catholics*) that "belief" stands condemned as part and parcel of the "Millenarist" heresy described earlier in this book. *The tragedy is that one now hears this coming from some Catholics, even from some otherwise orthodox Catholic priests.*

Through personal conversations with many laymen and even some priests who talk about a "millennium, the author knows they have received this idea primarily from non-Catholic influences. Most who accept such ideas have never heard sound Catholic eschatological teaching to counter it. Some have previously heard it preached, but it was so many years ago that they had genuinely forgotten. This class of person tends to vaguely remember such teaching when reminded of it. In most cases, they are having to "remember" back over thirty years.

1. Old Claims Revived About the Council of Nicea

One disquieting claim which is resurrecting itself is this: the claim that the Council of Nicea taught a millennial doctrine. There are numerous spurious or false copies of the documents of various Councils of the Church. The Council of Nicea is no exception.

It is extremely unlikely that the Council of Nicea promulgated any decree on a "Millennial" teaching. The reason for this is quite simple. **According to the historical sources, the Council of Nicea promulgated only three documents.** Of these, only one dealt with doctrinal content. That document is the famous Nicene Creed. The second is a series of twenty disciplinary canons, or rules. The third is the Synodal Decree (which is most likely an expanded form of its disciplinary Canon #12). There have been numerous claims over the years that there were other "acts" of the Council of Nicea. But scholarship has demonstrated all of these claims to be false. Charles Hefele's *History of the Councils* is publicly recognized by all scholars of the Councils as *the* definitive work on the subject.[655] Hefele says,

> "from the first no more acts of Nicea were known than the three documents already named -- the Creed, the twenty Canons, and the Synodal Decree. This is indicated by Eusebius, when he says, in his *Life of Constantine*[656] 'That which was unanimously adopted was taken down in writing, and signed by all.' So early as the year 350, Athanasius could give no other answer to a friend who wished to learn what passed at Nicea[657] If a complete copy of the acts had existed, Athanasius [who was in attendance at the Council] would certainly have known of it, and would have directed his friend to that.[658]
>
> In default of these acts of the Council of Nicea, which do not exist, and which have never existed, besides the three authentic documents already quoted, we may consider as

---

655 That is why it was reprinted over seventy years later in 1973 by AMF Pub. Co.

656 Liber iii, Ch. 14.

657 *Annales*, ad ann. 325, No. 62.

658 *History of the Christian Councils*, Vol. 1, Charles Joseph Hefele, D.D., 1894, pp. 263-264

> historical the accounts of the ancient Church historians, Eusebius, Socrates, Sozomen, Theodoret, and Rufinus, as well as some writings and saying of S. Athanasius, *de Decretis synodi Nicaenae*, and in his *Epistola ad Afros*."[659]

Again, the three authentic documents are; the Creed, Disciplinary Canons, and the Synodal Decree. Anyone who has read or recited the Nicene Creed knows it contains no such Millennial teaching. That leaves the disciplinary canons and the Decree. The canons (rules) are of a disciplinary rather than a doctrinal nature. There are only twenty of them.[660] None of those canons deals with dogmatic teachings or issues. The "Synodal Decree" appears to have been nothing more than an expanded version of Canon #12.[661] This canon dealt with the issue of when the Feast of Easter was to be celebrated (this had remained somewhat of an issue ever since the Quattordecim controversy of the 2nd Century). **None of these three documents makes any reference to any teaching of any kind about a Millenium.**

As Hefẹle points out, all the *ancient Church historians* state that the list of authentic documents emanating from the council are limited to these three - the creed, the canons, and the decree. Cases in point are *Eusebius, Socrates, Sozomen, and Theodoret*. In addition to that we have the testimony of St. Athanasius who was personally in attendance at the Council of Nicea. There were spurious copies of alleged documents or "acts" from the Council of Nicea being circulated by Arian and other heretics at various points in history. But the best scholarship of the last century also limits the authentic documents emanating from Nicea to those three identified by Hefele. None of those three makes any mention of a millennium.

If someone wishes to make a counter-claim against all the ancient Church histories and all the best contemporary scholarship - a counterclaim that the Council of Nicea declared for a belief in a

---

659 Ibid. 264.

660 Some copies broke one or two of the canons into two pieces. In those cases they may number them as twenty-one or twenty-two canons. But the total content of all the non-spurious copies are identical.

661 For details about the history of these documents, see Socrates' *Ecclesiastical History*, Book 1, Chapter 9.

Millennium - *then the burden of proof rests on those who make the claim! Let them come forth with serious scholarly proof of such a claim - with appropriate scholarly documentation of such a claim.*

2. A Specific Example of Outside Influences

One night in late January of 1996, the author watched several hours of a fundamentalist TV program.[662] The author was watching a general broadcast channel. No cable hookup was necessary, but only a TV antenna. In most large American cities you can see such regular programming on general broadcast channels funded by religious organizations.

This program is broadcast nightly. Every night they speak of the "Rapture," the "Antichrist," and the "Millenium." On this particular night, the program had two guests who are fundamentalist authors. One of the guests is so well-known from one of his recent books, that if the title of that book was stated here, is it doubtful that any American reader would fail to recognize the title.

The whole discussion centered around what is referred to by them as "The Rapture." For those unfamiliar with this terminology, this is the belief (in their words from that night),

> "The good news is, -- if you are a believer today, you are going to be *taken up* before this tragic scenario plays itself out, before the Antichrist comes."[663]

They preach and teach that all true believers in Jesus Christ will be physically taken up by Him just prior to the arrival of Antichrist. They teach that Jesus will physically remove such "believers" from the face of the earth in order to spare them from the persecutions of Antichrist. They get this idea from their interpretation of two lines from the Gospel of Mathew 24:40-41. ***It should be well-noted by the reader: The fundamentalist interpretation of this passage, as quoted above, is not to be found in the Fathers and other Scriptural commentaries which come to us from the infant and early Church.***

---

662 The author has watched such programming on many occasions in order to research the doctrine(s) portrayed on these programs.

663 Quote taken from the author's notes taken during that broadcast of late Jan. 1996.

3. The Catholic Teaching on Matt. 24:40-41

In fact, **the Catholic teaching is that this refers to the Second Coming of Christ**. Some Fundamentalists interpret Matt. 24:40-41 to refer to the "just" being taken up so as to escape the Tribulations of Antichrist. The Catholic teaching is quite different. The people who will be "*taken*" are those who are "saved" at the time of Christ's Second Coming. They are those who are taken up into the heavenly Jerusalem. Those who are "*left*" are those who die outside of salvation, therefore they are left behind.[664]

The moderator of the broadcast said that right after the Rapture, "The world is going to turn [for direction] to the preachers who are left the day after the Rapture -- boy are they going to be in a mess." The message is that anyone who is left was not a believer in Jesus Christ -- that includes all preachers who would be left. On this program they were previewing and promoting a book which "describes" what it will be like for those who are "left behind" after the "Rapture." Part of that book "Includes a letter to those on the other side" (of the Rapture). Immediately after that, they showed clips from a videotape promoting the theme of the book.

This videotape dramatically simulates TV interviews with ordinary citizens, politicians, and clergymen filmed on "the day after the Rapture." *The first simulated clergyman interviewed*, while not specifically identified as to denomination, *is wearing a black suit and a Catholic priest's white collar.* He explains that the Gospel tells us that "One day the tares [weeds] will be separated from the wheat." Then this actor whose manner of dress bears a striking resemblance to a Catholic priest explains that the people "who are gone" are the weeds or "tares." Now the world is freed to accept the new religion of man. This "priest" is presented as someone preparing the road for Antichrist.

Several interviews later, there is a night scene looking out on a crowd of people. Even in that dim light, the buildings and other objects in the backdrop of the crowd bear a striking resemblance to

[664] "At Christ's coming people will be engaged in their ordinary occupations. Here to *be taken* means to be saved, to *be left* is to be damned." *A Commentary on the New Testament*, Prepared by The Catholic Biblical Commissiojn - under the patronage of The Episcopal Committee of the Confraternity of Christian Doctrine, Pub: William H. Sadlier, Inc., 1942. p. 167.

St. Peter's Square in Rome - including basilisk. A male voice with a Slavic sounding accent (in fact remarkably similar to the Polish accent of Pope John Paul II) is addressing the crowd in a manner similar to the previously interviewed "priest." The voice (from an individual who is unseen) is saying things to the crowd which would obviously prepare them to accept the teachings of the Antichrist. If this was an attempt to impart a *subliminal* message, it failed. It wasn't nearly subtle enough for that.

One of the next striking aspects of the program is a bold uncompromising statement to which all the panelists nodded their assent. The statement is, "The Parousia [the Second Coming of Christ] takes place exactly seven years after the Rapture. So everyone who comes after the Rapture will know exactly when it [the Parousia] is going to happen."

But, *immediately after* the Scripture passage which they interpret to signify this physical "Rapture" (Mat. 24:40-41), Our Lord in verse 42 says, "Watch therefore, for you do not know on which day your Lord is coming." And whatever happened to Our Lord's admonition that no man knows the day and the hour of His Coming, "not even the angels of heaven" (Matt. 24:36.)? What about His other statements that His coming will be as unforeseen as "a thief in the night"? What about the fact that the Last Judgement is the end of time?

For men who claim their interpretation of Scripture is based simply on taking it literally as it stands, their understanding of Mathew (and a lot of other Scripture) on this point is anything but literal. Their interpretation is anything but taking Scripture simply as it presents itself. These men are apparently extremely selective about which passages of Scripture they will take literally and which ones they won't. So is everyone -- including the Catholic Church. **The key question is, *on whose authority do those "Rapturists" and "Millenarianists" make their selections of when to be and when not to be word-for-word literalists?***

If they claim their authority in the name of the Holy Spirit, then what does that say about their fellow "Millennialists" who do not agree with them -- as to the timing of either the Rapture or the Millennium? Why are there splits among them between the "pre-tribulation" and "post-tribulation" millennial types? Which ones of them receive their understanding from the Holy Spirit? They can't all be inspired by the Spirit, because they interpret differently.

That is a classic example of the theological confusion that "private interpretation" of Scripture leads to. Which takes us full circle to the original question, on whose authority do the Millenialists interpret Scripture? On whose authority do they decide when to be or not to be "proper" literalists? And when they agree to be literal on a millennium, on whose authority do they state their timing of a millennium, or its existence at all, or its duration of exactly 1000 years?

4. Other Programs

The Fathers of the Church are currently being rediscovered by some of our separated brethren in non-Catholic denominations. Amongst those called evangelicals, a number of them are recently heard quoting from some of the Fathers who accepted varying degrees of Millenarianism. These evangelicals are sincere people. However, the study of the Fathers is relatively new to most of them, and there is a great deal of material to cover in such a study.

Recently, some evangelicals have begun quoting from men such as Justin Martyr and St. Irenaeus, amongst others. (These are to be found on completely different channels and programs from those described in the section above.) From these statements of various Fathers, they believe that it can be demonstrated that Millennarianism was a universal belief of the infant Church. From a thorough reading of even the early Fathers it is easily demonstrated that this was anything but a universal teaching. They usually begin by quoting St. Justin Martyr because he is the earliest writer with unqualified credentials as an early Church Father to unquestionably state a belief in a Millenium.[665]

However, they cannot have thoroughly read Justin, because Justin himself tells us it was not a universal belief. St. Justin was martyred around 165 A.D. Around ten years previous to his martyrdom, he wrote his *The Dialogue with Trypho*, which is "the oldest

---

[665] Papias cannot be an Apostolic Father since he himself testified that he had been trained neither by the Apostles nor their immediate disciples. Only one of his works has survived.

extant Christian apology against Judaism."[666] Justin recounts a conversation with a Jewish friend whom he is attempting to convert to Christianity. In the *Dialogue*, Justin says that,

> "there will be a resurrection of the dead and a thousand years in Jerusalem."

However, Justin goes on to modify this statement with the caveat that this is *not* a universal belief among true Christians,

> "I signify to you that ***many*** who belong to the pure and pious faith and are true Christians believe otherwise"[667]

The earliest ecclesial writer with unchallenged Patristic credentials (who himself accepts Millenial doctrine) tells us clearly that belief in a millennium is denied by "many" Christians.

5. The Influence of Papias

Both Justin and Irenaeus misunderstood the first century Father, Papias, to have claimed he received this Millenium doctrine personally from the Apostle John. It was from the antiquity of Papias' testimony that they thought the Millennium was a received apostolic doctrine. Papias wrote but one work we know of, *The Explanation of the Sayings of the Lord.* What we possess of it is "only a few small fragments, mostly preserved as quotations within Eusebius."[668] But as the Father of Church History, Eusebius of Caesarea, makes clear in his *Historia Ecclesia*, Papias himself is candid that he did not directly hear any of the apostles speak about a millennium, nor their disciples either, but rather of their "acquaintances."[669]

Again, the final point of all of this is the traditional Catholic teaching which "rejects" a millennium. We also requote St. Robert

[666] *The Faith of the Early Fathers*, W. A. Jurgens, Vol. 1, The Liturgical Press, Collegeville, Mn. 1970, p. 58.

[667] *The Dialogue With Trypho*, Justin Martyr, Ch. 80.

[668] *The Faith of the Early Fathers*, Vol. 1, p. 38.

[669] *Historia Ecclesia*, 3,29,2. It is probable that neither Justin nor Irenaeus ever saw Papias' *Explanation*. If, for instance, Irenaeus had actually seen it, he would not have said that Papias was a hearer of the Apostle John, since Papias made it clear in this work that was not the case.

Bellarmine's succinct statement of the Church's traditional teaching about the relative brevity of time after Antichrist,

> "'This gospel of the kingdom shall be preached in the whole world, and then shall come the consummation (of the world)' that is, a little after [Antichrist] shall come the end of the world."

6. Christian Charity

These broadcasts are not unusual. Their theme of a physical millennium prior to the end of time is found in television broadcasts, books, videotapes, and pamphlets all over the U.S. and Canada. In a vacuum of solid eschatological teaching from Catholic pulpits, is it any wonder if some Catholics are starting to accept eschatological doctrines from outside sources?

Ideas such as the imminent coming of Antichrist and the Parousia are primarily found in two places today: private prophecy from sources unapproved by the Church, and some very sincere, yet non-Catholic fundamentalist preaching. If solid Catholic eschatology is not aggressively taught, it should surprise no one if Catholics succumb to condemned doctrines such as belief in a Millenium in "*even modified forms*."

But despite all of the interpretations of Scripture which are not consistent with the interpretations of the early Christians, these people in these TV broadcasts are our separated brethren in Christ. Their love for Jesus Christ is real, deep and unfeigned. Despite their not so subtle insinuations that Catholicism is somehow tied in the near future to promotion of Antichrist, that type of attitude should not be returned in kind. It should also be clearly understood that not all broadcasts of this kind speak of Catholicism in an unkindly spirit. Many of them, despite differences in doctrine, respect us as we respect them as our brothers and sisters in Christ.

When we die we will not be asked by Our Lord whether our brother was charitable to us. We will be asked if we were charitable to our brother. Despite our differences in some doctrines with the men discussed above, they believe in and accept Jesus Christ as their personal Savior just as we do. We must lovingly treat them as brethren no matter how a few of them might refer to us or treat us. Jesus expects no less.

7. Influences From Inside - Misinterpretation of Vatican II

There is a particular text in Vatican II's *Dogmatic Constitution on The Church* which certain Catholics interpret in conjunction with certain Scriptural texts to support the idea of a near millennium. Short of that, they interpret this text to be a very sure sign that the end of the world is near. The author has documents in his possession written by Catholics which support this thesis. He has also heard this text verbally presented as "proof" that we are near the end. The reader will see that text shortly.

One such Catholic hints that in this eschatological statement made by the Council Fathers, they were hinting that the "new heavens and a new earth" are to arrive in our century, or very shortly thereafter. They also, therefore, think that this is somehow to be associated with an earthly millennium, for example,

> "Everything makes us predict that the epoch about which the prophets speak will certainly be ... as a heaven anticipated upon the earth."

This is not quoting someone out of context. The author of the statement immediately above states just previously to that quote,

> "By 'Millennium' one understands properly the time which will exist between the second advent of Christ and the final judgement."

The Vatican text in question comes from the section entitled *Dogmatic Constitution on The Church*, "The Pilgrim Church." That Catholic writer quotes from that document in support of his thesis of a "millennium." Just prior to quoting the following passage from "The Pilgrim Church, that author asks,

> "Will the glorious epoch, the prophets announce [the Millennium] come soon? ... Vatican Council II tells us in the Dogmatic Constitution of the Church (chapter 7 of the eschatological disposition),"

Immediately after asking this rather pointed question, that author immediately continues his sentence with the quote below from "The Pilgrim Church"

> "Already *the final age of the world is with us* (cf. 1 Cor. 10:11) and *the renewal of the world is irrevocably under way*; it is even now anticipated in a certain real way, for the Church on earth is endowed already with a sanctity that is real though imperfect. However, until there be realized new heavens and a new earth in which justice dwells (cf. 2 Pet. 3:13) the pilgrim Church, in its sacraments and institutions, which belong to this present age, carries *the mark of this world which will pass*, and she takes her place among creatures which groan and travail yet and await the revelation of the sons of God (cf. Rom. 8:19-22)."[670]

The man's intent is to emphasize the words "Already *the final age of the world is with us*." But the Scriptural quote the Vatican II Fathers reference for this statement is 1 Cor. 10:11.

He then states that Polycarp, Irenaeus, and Justin held that view. [We have already discussed this and their dependence upon a common misunderstanding of Papias. It is obvious from the context that the author of the statement above is unaware of this misunderstanding on Papias.] Then the author says that Jerome states that "many ecclesiastics and martyrs followed this idea."

Jerome did say that, but Jerome was not thereby validating their belief in a millennium. His point was that since some "ecclesiastics and martyrs" who believed in a millennium were in theological error, that they did not do so with an evil intent, since many of them were ecclesiastics and martyrs. Jerome was simply pointing out that their belief was confused and in error on this point.

In fact, Jerome was one of the most vehement opponents of a millennium theory. In his commentary on Isaiah 60:1-3, he explains that the reason the Jews rejected Christ was because they had misinterpreted several O.T. *metaphors* about the "Messianic era", misinterpreted them in an earthly and carnal way. So when Jesus did not deliver to them an earthly pleasure kingdom, they rejected Him. In this sense, Jerome says,

> The Jews, and *our own semi Jews* (Christians who make the same mistake), who expect a golden and bejewelled Jerusalem from heaven, claim that these things will take place *in a thousand year reign*, ... that is to say those who long for earthly pleasures ... whose god is their belly"

Does Jerome sound as if has has any sympathy or respect for Millennial theory?

Clearly, this man has (probably inadvertently) grossly quoted St. Jerome out of context. He also made the above argument for a "Millennium" "to come soon," and misapplied the quote[671] from Vatican II's "The Pilgrim Church" in support of that argument. He is a post-Vatican II priest -- a professor of theology at a major seminary. He unquestionably wished to be a most faithful Catholic. But what he wrote was out of step with the teaching of the Church that, "The Church has rejected *even modified forms* of this falsification of the kingdom to come under the name of millennarianism."

T. CONCLUSION OF ARGUMENT

1. Private Prophecy Must Always Take a Poor Third Place to the Constant Teaching of the Magisterium

Many of the Catholics who are getting into this belief that the Antichrist and the Parousia or some kind of a Millennium are just around the corner are quoting the passage above from "The Pilgrim Church" in support of that argument. Their guess that the Council Fathers wished to warn the faithful about the immediate impending end of the world in this century, is without any foundation in fact. Then they must face the constant teaching of the Church about the chronology of the end times. That also does not jibe with their interpretation. Unfortunately, their final bastion seems to be to quote a number of prophecies (particularly from sources which are not approved by the Church) in support of their thesis. Here they have an additional problem.

As the reader has already seen in multiple examples, **prophecy from approved sources** coincides with the traditional teachings of the Church on the chronology of events in the end times. In this particular instance we will close with a prophecy of St. Hildegard, who is the most honored of all private prophets in the history of the Church. She is very clear on the point that Antichrist comes very near the end of the world when she says:

> "The son of perdition will come when the day declines and the sun sinks, that is when the end of time arrives and the world loses its stability."[672]

There are many other saints besides St. Hildegarde we could quote on this point. There are many other Doctors of the Church besides Robert Bellarmine we could have quoted on the Catholic teaching on both the "Millennium,' and the teaching that the end of the world comes a reasonably short time after Anticrist. The reader will recall that earlier in the book we did so with Sts. Augustine and Jerome in relation to a related matter.

The fact is that *prior to Augustine and Jerome* the Church had never taken a position on the issue of a millennium. That is because Millenarianism did not become an issue for a significant period of time after the beginning of the Church. Certainly, since the time of Augustine and Jerome, the Church's teaching on this matter has been universal and constant. This heresy was not raised again until the advent of the 16th century Anabaptists.

THE MAJOR POINTS ON MILLENARIANISM ARE:

I. PRIVATE PROPHECIES *FROM APPROVED SOURCES* (unlike some from unapproved sources) ARE CONSONANT WITH CATHOLIC TEACHING to the effect that; shortly after the death of Antichrist, or a little while after (or some other such similar phrasing) comes the Parousia, the Second Coming of Our Lord.

II. *But much more importantly this and similar phrases are found throughout the vast majority of the writings of the Fathers of the Church.* The only exceptions are some of the early Fathers who mistakenly received Papias' statements as if he had heard them from John. But Papias himself says he only heard it from some "acquaintances" of the Apostles.

III. The constant teaching of the Magisterium is that Millenarianism is rejected.

There is no chronological place in prophecy from approved sources for a Millennium prior to Antichrist, or between Antichrist and the Parousia. The teaching of the Fathers and Doctors is that the Second Coming of Christ is co-mediate with the Last Judgement. That is also the case with private prophecies from approved sources. Most importantly, the Church repudiates a Millennium "even in modified forms."

Prophecies of a Millenium from unnaproved sources run afoul of the Fathers, the Doctors, the Magisterium, and lastly, the prophecies of canonized Saints, Blessed, and Venerable. How can any thinking Catholic seriously hold private prophecies from unapproved sources up against such an array. Where such a thing happens, the answer probably lies in their being unaware that that is what they are doing; holding a belief in contradiction to the Magisterium, the vast majority of the Fathers and Doctors, and ancillarily, prophecy from approved sources of Saints, Blessed and Venerable.

At the Parousia comes the end of time and its history, the final judgment and eternity, -- no earthly Millenium. The new heavens and the new earth come after the Final Judgment. That is the teaching of the Fathers, Doctors and the Magisterium. It is also the consistent teaching of private prophecy from approved sources.

According to Catholic teaching, there cannot be (as some misguided Catholics currently think) a benign and strife-free entrance into "the Kingdom." "The Kingdom" comes only with "the Last Judgement after the final cosmic upheaval of this world." As the Catechism teaches,

> "The Church has rejected *even modified forms* of this falsification of the kingdom to come under the name of millenarianism."

2. The Cause of the Problem

Traditon, and particularly the Fathers and Doctors of the Church tell us that there is a specific series of events between now and the end of the world. According to those same sources there are a specific number of events yet to happen prior to the coming of Antichrist. More events must happen between the death of Antichrist and the Second Coming of Christ and its contemporaneous Last Judgement. The Magisterium rejects a Millennium even in "any modified form." Private prophecies from approved sources are totally consonant with all of the above.

So why are a growing number of Catholics falling into beliefs or thoughts which run afoul of the traditional eschatological teachings of the Church. Many of them are getting these ideas from private prophecy from unapproved sources. Many are getting some of their ideas from non-Catholic fundamentalist sources. *But the question remains, why are they believing those sources?* They are believing them because they have never heard the traditional eschatological teachings of the Church clearly taught.

3. The Solution

The majority of Catholics learn most of their doctrine from the pulpit. The fact is that if Catholics were being taught the traditional eschatological teachings from the pulpit, most of them would reject anything contradictory to that teaching. That was the case forty to fifty years ago. The solution to the problem is this -- and probably only this; for priests once again to preach the common teaching of the Church on the Antichrist and the end times.

For any priests who do not themselves know that doctrine, their Bishops can readily encapsulate a short treatise on the subject. They can quote the salient portions of the *Catechism* and the documents of Vatican II. The Bishops could readily expand those sources into a short treatise. This would make it easy to absorb for any priests who do not already know this teaching. But the only way the faithful will learn this is if the Bishops then instruct their parish priests to preach on this subject. THAT IS THE ONLY SOLUTION WITH A REASONABLE PROBABILITY OF SUCCESS.

Our Bishops are swamped with contemporary problems. It is always easy to criticize another man when one does not face the other man's problems. We *must* pray for our Bishops that they will discern the seriousness of this eschatological problem (vis-a-vis all the others they face) *before* it escalates much more than it already has. We *must* pray for our priests that they will listen to and respond to their Bishop's call to faithfully preach on eschatology when that call comes -- as it surely will. We *must* pray for the laity that they will respond in faith when they hear the traditional teaching of the Church on the end times preached by their priests.

We *must* pray for ourselves, that we will always faithfully follow the teachings of the Magisterium on eschatology, and on every other matter of Faith and Morals. We must pray for the understanding that much of the Faith is revealed in Mysteries -- which can never be exhaustively comprehended by our minds here on earth.

Come Holy Spirit, fill our hearts and minds and souls. Lead us to accept and understand the teaching of your Church which you constantly enlighten through your bishops as they are in union with Peter. May our Bishops diligently and faithfully teach and preach in season and out of season about the end, until some day it comes.

Romans 11: 25-27:

"For I would not have you ignorant brethren, of this mystery, (lest you should be wise in your own conceits), that blindness in part has happened in Israel, until the fullness of the Gentiles should come in, and so all Israel should be saved, as it is written; 'There shall come out of Sion, he that shall deliver, and shall turn away ungodliness from Jacob.'"

CHAPTER 11

FINAL CONCLUSIONS

1. It is *Very* Common for Prophets (and Those Who Hear Them), and Even Some Canonized Saints, to Seriously Misunderstand Some Aspect of the Prophecy They Have Received

One of the truly classic examples of this is St. Vincent Ferrer. The reader has earlier read of the astounding public miracles which St. Vincent performed almost daily for over twenty years. The reader will remember Vincent's saving of the stone mason falling off a building, and his raising of a dead woman before thousands of witnesses to confirm that Vincent was, "the Angel (messenger) of the Judgment." That confirmation occurred in 1403 A.D. So, why hasn't the end of the world come?

Due to the fame of St. Vincent, many Catholic scholars have been embarrassed by his prediction of his apparent designation as "Angel of the (Final) Judgement." They need not have been embarrassed. They, and possibly St. Vincent, have simply made several key assumptions. **First, they *assumed* he was the angel spoken of in Rev. 14:6-7.**

> "Then I saw *another* angel flying in mid-heaven, with an eternal gospel to proclaim to those who dwell on the earth, to every nation and tribe and tongue and people, and he said with a loud voice, 'Fear God and give him glory, for the hour of his judgment has come.'"

They assumed Vincent was the angel come to announce the imminent coming of the Final Judgement. There are a number of angels who announce various judgments in the *Book of Revelation*. Fr. Kramer now gives us a very lucid explanation of this assumptive process;

> "By designating him [St. Vincent] the angel of [Rev.] chapter XIV. 6, the commentators run into inexplicable difficulties. For St. Vincent emphatically and repeatedly asserted that the Day of wrath was to come 'soon, very soon, within a short time', *cito, bene cito et vaide breviter.* St. John [the apostle] also announced that the judgment was to come very quickly (Apoc. III. 11), *which meant it would **begin** to operate soon.*"
>
> "... Since St. Vincent uttered those prophecies, five centuries have elapsed, and the end of the world and the last judgment have not come."[673]

Fr. Kramer explains that it is most probable that St. Vincent was the "Eagle" (or angel) mentioned in Rev. 8:13. He points out that many early Scripture manuscripts refer to this same being alternately as an angel or an eagle. Fr. Kramer comments;

> "The near approach of the judgment expressed by St. Vincent in the words "*cito, bene cito, et valde breviter* [soon, very soon, within a short time]" is easily explained by seeing it as the next world-wide [at the time of Vincent] event without anything else of importance intervening and as identical with the three 'woes' announced by the 'eagle'."[674]

The second questionable assumption is that all the events foretold in the *Book of Revelation* happen within a short period of time. That is the current attitude by many 20th century Christians. But that was *not* always the case! *Many Scriptural exegetes have believed that the Book of Revelation describes all the major events to affect the Church, from the time of the death of Our Lord till the end of time.*

---

[673] *The Book of Destiny,* Leonard Kramer, Buechler Pub. Co., Bellevill, Il. 1955, p. 209.

[674] Ibid. p. 210.

Such exegetes think that we are right now at or near the beginning of the second "woe." The reign of *the* Antichrist is foretold to come at the end of the second "woe." Exegetes such as Fr. Kramer believe we may be just now coming out of the first stage of the second "woe" (the reader saw the quote from Fr. Kramer on this earlier in the book - See Index). Within that second "woe' there appears to be a period of peace indicated — a period of true peace which precedes the time of *the* Antichrist.

When that school of thought looks at the prophecies of St. Vincent, then St. Vincent's prophecies have *all* come true. ***The judgments entailed in the first "woe" have already occurred.*** Those of the beginning of the second "woe" might be near. But that would leave many events yet to occur prior to the coming of the Antichrist. According to this school of thought we have yet to enter a period of peace indicated in the second "woe", which would precede the Antichrist.

There is not room in a single volume work to now describe how our age fits into such an interpretation in the Books of *Revelation, Daniel, Psalms, Ezekial,* and many other Old Testament books of prophecy. That would have to await until another time.

2. Some Recent Prophecies

The author has read the contents of numerous recent prophecies which as yet are unapproved by the Church. Some of them *appear* to be consistent with the eschatological teachings of the Church. Some *definitely* do not. But ***only*** the Church can make a definitive ruling on any of these alleged apparitions and/or locutions.

A number of the alleged locutions speak of the approach of the Antichrist and the Parousia. There is no question that "approach" at all times draws ever nearer. But some of them appear to be strongly hinting at the Second Coming of Christ *before* the year 2000. If the reader should come across an alleged prophet, who claims the Second Coming of Christ has been foretold to them to come before the year 2000, then the reader must be aware of the absolute necessity of the outlined sequences foretold by the Church to precede His coming. It must be born in mind that even Church-approved prophets, some of them canonized Saints, sometimes can and do misunderstand in part that which they have been told.

3. Is it Reasonable or Probable that the Parousia Could Happen by the Year 2000?

This question was partially addressed in the introduction. But a thorough discussion could not be entered into at that point. As stated earlier, only a few of the Church's traditional eschatological teachings have formally been declared to be "De Fide." Outside of those De Fide teachings, a Catholic is going to seek eschatological answers in,

(1) Papal pronouncements (part of the ordinary Magisterium),

(2) Official teachings — such as are found in the 1994 *Catechism of the Catholic Church*

(3) Statements from the CDF and other arms of the Magisterium, and very importantly

(4) The teachings of the Fathers and Doctors — which the Fathers at Vatican Council II said were to be searched for a "more profound understanding" of Scripture.

"She [the Church] strives to reach day by day a more profound understanding of the sacred Scriptures, in order to provide her children with food from the divine words. **For this reason she [the Church] duly fosters the study of the Fathers, both Eastern and Western"**[675]

4. The Church's Teachings on the Chronology of the End Times

There are several teachings of the Church which clearly indicate a chronology of events which must precede the Second Coming of Christ. What do we know with certainty about the Parousia? It is the time when Christ shall come for the second time to "judge the living and the dead" — it is the "end of time." As the Fathers at Vatican Council II taught,

[675] *Vatican Council II, The Concilior and Post Concilior Documents, Vol 1.* Flannery, New Revised Edition, 1992, Dei Verbum, p. 763.

> "When the Lord will come in glory, and all his angels with him (cf. Mt. 25:31), *death will be no more* and all things will be subject to him (Cf. 1 Cor. 15:26-27). But at the present time some of his disciples are pilgrims on earth. **Others have died and are being purified**, while still others are in glory, contemplating 'in full light, God himself triune and one, exactly as he is.'"[676]

"Death will be no more." Our time as pilgrims on earth is over at the Second Coming. The time and place of purification (Purgatory) will be no more. It is the time of the "end of the world." After the Parousia with its Last Judgement comes our eternity — either in glory with Christ — or its only alternative.

So the Parousia is the last divinely scheduled event within time. All other "scheduled events" within time take place prior to the Parousia. So, what does the Church teach us must occur prior to the Parousia, the end of time? Firstly, the *Catechism of the Catholic Church* teaches,

> **"The glorious Messiah's coming is suspended at every moment of history until his recognition by 'all Israel**,' for 'a hardening has come upon part of Israel' in their unbelief toward Jesus.[568] ... The 'full inclusion' of the Jews in the Messiah's salvation, in the wake of 'the full number of the Gentiles'[571] will enable the People of God to achieve 'the measure of the stature of the fullness of Christ,' in which 'God may be all in all.'[572]"[677]

The Church clearly teaches the *en masse* conversion of the Jews must take place prior to the Parousia. As the reader has read, the Fathers and the Doctors clearly speak of a period of time of unknown duration during which the Jews shall be the primary leadership of the Church, after their mass conversion that is. That time could be very short. We simply do not know how long it will be. *But it should be allowed for in a chronology of events between now and the Parousia.*

---

[676] *Vatican Council II, The Concilior and Post Concilior Documents, Vol 1.* Flannery, New Revised Edition, 1992, Dei Verbum, p. 409.

[677] *Catechism of the Catholic Church,* #647, p. 176. The internal Footnote #568 cites Rom. 11:20-26 and Mat. 23:39. Footnote #571 cites Rom. 11:12, 25; cf Lk. 21:24.

Next, the Church teaches us that the Antichrist must come,

> "Before Christ's second coming the Church must pass through a final trial that will shake the faith of many believers.[573] The persecution that accompanies her pilgrimage on earth will unveil the 'mystery of iniquity' in the form of a religious deception ... The supreme religious deception is that of the Antichrist"[678]

This teaching could not be clearer. The coming of *the* Antichrist must precede the Parousia.

Along with these two events, others are traditionally included by the Church. These are synopsized in the *Catholic Biblical Encyclopedia, New Testament*, written by Steinmueller and Sullivan (the same Fr. Steinmueller quoted earlier in the book).

> "Before the Second Coming of Christ various preparatory signs must be fulfilled.
>
> (1) The gospel must be preached in the whole world (Matt. 24, 14; Mark 13, 10), even though many will not accept its message (Luke 18, 8).
>
> (2) The Jews as a nation will be converted after the full number of the Gentiles enter the Church (Rom. 11, 25f).
>
> (3) According to some scholars, Elias is to come and will restore all things (Matt. 17, 11).
>
> (4) Before Christ's Second Coming there will be a great apostasy or religious defection (Matt. 24, 10-12; Luke 18, 8; Thess. 2, 3j; 2 Tim. 3, 1-9), and the Antichrist will appear (2 Thess. 2, 3-12; 1 John 2, 18, 22; 2 John 7).
>
> (5) There will be a physical transformation of the universe (Matt. 24, 29; Mark 13, 24f; Luke 21, 25f), and the world will be purified by fire in the final general conflagration (2 Pet. 3, 5-7; cf. 1 Cor. 3, 13). Then only will

---

[678] Ibid.

> the Son of Man appear in heaven (Matt. 24, 30; Mark 13, 26; Luke 21, 27)."[679]

According to the traditional teaching of the Church all the items in 1-5 above must be accomplished prior to the 2nd Coming.

How much time is involved for the fulfillment of those events? We cannot know the maximum; but could we reasonably, with a fairly high probability consider a minimum?

(1) There are some who might tell us that #1 (preaching of the Gospel throughout the world) has been accomplished. Frankly, this author doubts it for a number of reasons. One should suffice to make the point. Missionaries in South America are still reporting running into new tribes of people who have never heard the message of the Gospel preached. Additionally, there are massive sections of Asia wherein the vast majority of the people have never heard the Gospel preached. How then could the Gospel have been preached through the whole world?

(2) It is undoubtedly intuitively obvious to all readers that the mass conversion of the Jews to Christianity has not taken place. As the reader has repeatedly seen in this book, the Fathers taught that this could not happen until the coming of Antichrist, which they said also entails the return of Enoch and Elias.

Elias in particular, is foretold in Scripture to convert the Jews. Numerous passages from both the Old and New Testament prophesy this. As only one example:

> "Behold, I will send you Elias the prophet, before the coming of the great and dreadful day of the Lord.
>
> And he *shall turn the heart of the fathers to the children,* and the heart of the children to their fathers; lest I come, and strike the earth with anathema." Mal. c.4, v.5

[679] *Catholic Biblical Encyclopedia, New Testament,* John E. Steinmueller, S.T.D., S.Scr.L., Consultor of the Pontifical Biblical Commission, Kathryn Sullivan, R.S.C.J., Ph.D., Research Professor of Sacred Scripture, Introduction by James M. Voste, O.P., S.T.M., S.Scr.D., Secretary of the Pontifical Biblical Commission, Pub: Joseph F. Wagner, Inc., New York City, 1949, p. 142.

The Fathers state that it is the Jews who are spoken of here. But it appears from both Tradition and Scripture that the *completion* of their mass conversion will most probably happen after the death of Antichrist. How much time will that take?

We have already described the Fathers' interpretation of the "fullness of the Gentiles." The reader is particularly referred to St. Jerome's discussion of this earlier in the book. Also, the mass apostasy which the Fathers theologically conjoined to the "fullness of the Gentiles" does not yet appear to have happened. According to the Fathers and the traditional teaching of the Church, that time of the "fullness of the Gentiles" must occur before the coming of Antichrist. How much time would be required for that to happen?

(3) We have already covered #3 (the coming of Elias).

(4) The *Book of Revelation* says Antichrist will reign for 1290 days. In the *Book of Danial* it is also described as "a time, times, and a half a time" (Dan. 7:25). The teaching of the Fathers and Doctors of the Church on this subject is very specific. They state that this 1,290 days in the *Book of Revelation*, and "a time, times, and a half a time" in the *Book of Daniel* refer to the same event — the duration of the reign of Antichrist. They say it is a "proper" (word-for-word) literal meaning — three and one half years. A number of the Fathers have been specifically quoted on this interpretation earlier in the book (See Index).

The Fathers clearly teach that Antichrist will appear as an individual man. They teach that he will be a temporal ruler with all regions of the earth subject to him (Scripture specifically says the same thing about the Antichrist's world-wide power). It was the common teaching of the Fathers that he would rule from Jerusalem ("the city where Our Lord was crucified"). In other words, the Antichrist will be highly identifiable and highly visible to the Christians who are alive at the time of his appearance and who do not despise prophecy.

5. Timeline Conclusion

The Church teaches that all the events mentioned above must happen prior to the Second Coming of Christ. By the time most of the first readers get this book, it will already be the Fall of 1996. According to the common teaching of the Fathers and Doctors, the Antichrist rules for three and one half years. If he has not made his appearance as a world-wide ruler by the summer of 1996, then how could the reign of Antichrist be complete before the year 2000?

It is only three and a half years from midsummer of 1996 to the year 2000. Therefore,

(a) If the Antichrist does not make his appearance by midsummer 1996, and,
(b) Since it is a formal teaching of the Church that the Parousia *cannot* occur prior to the death of Antichrist,
(c) If the Antichrist does not appear by midsummer 1996, then how would it be possible for the Parousia to occur *before the year* 2000? [Again, several recent prophecies appear to be hinting at this.]

This three and one half years for the reign of the Antichrist is only one of the items listed in #'s 1-5 above which must precede the Second Coming of Christ! In light of the time required for all of the items in #'s 1-5, this author honestly does not think there is even one chance in ten million that all the items in #'s 1-5 could be accomplished prior to the year 2000. As this sentence is being written, it is only five months till mid-summer 1996. What are the chances that the Antichrist is going to make his appearance in the next five months?

6. Another Event Foretold to Precede the Antichrist

In addition to the chronological difficulties described above, according to the Fathers and the majority of the Doctors of the Church there is an additional obstacle to an immediate coming of Antichrist. According to virtually all of the Fathers (who interpret the Scriptures quite literally on this point) some form of a "Roman Empire" or "Kingdom" must be in place shortly prior to the coming of Antichrist. This is subsequently broken up into Ten Kingdoms.

The Fathers and Doctors tell us that just prior to the coming of Antichrist, that as Scripture literally says, an existing empire will be divided up into Ten Kingdoms. St. Jerome tells us that it is some kind of "Roman Kingdom" and that "all the ecclesiastical writers [omnes scriptores ecclesiastici] have passed down [tradiderunt]" this teaching.[680] As the reader has already seen, St. & Dr. Robert Bellarmine tells us that the Tradition on this is so strong, that if it is not an outright heresy to deny it, it is certainly a grievous error.

There are some Medieval Doctors of the Church (including St. Thomas Aquinas) who say that this "Empire" could be interpreted in a mystical non-literal sense. But the majority of the later Doctors concur with the Fathers that this will be a "proper" literal event. *No literal Empire has developed. Nor has any event developed* which can clearly be interpreted in an allegorical way as fulfilling this Scripturally described event.

Therefore ***both*** *major signs foretold to specifically precede Antichrist* in Tradition and Scripture (the universal apostasy, and, the collapse of a final Roman Kingdom or Empire, as explained by the exegesis of the Fathers), *appear to be missing*. ***Therefore, for all of the reasons listed so far in this chapter, this most probably cannot be Antichrist's time.***

7. Another Probable Obstacle

There is another *pre-Antichrist event*, which appears to be foretold both in the *Book of Daniel* and the *Book of Revelation*, which likewise does not appear to have occurred. The writings of the Fathers also clearly confirm a period of peace in the last times, which is probably one which appears to be referred to in Daniel and in the Book of Revelation. This is not a dogmatically defined teaching of the Church. But it is the interpretation of many Fathers who wrote on the subject, and also of many of the Doctors of the Church as well as many sound Scriptural exegetes. It is something to be seriously considered.

8. Private Revelation

It appears to be a reasonable conjecture that this "peace" also may be the one reportedly foretold by Our Lady at Fatima. As the reader

[680] *Corpus Christianorum, Series Latina,* Vol. LXXV A, *S. Heironymi Presbyteri Opera, Pars I, Commentariorum in Danielem,* Pub: Turnholti, Typographi Brepols, Editores Pontifici, 1964, p. 844.

has seen, such a period of true peace is also foretold by a myriad of Saints, Blessed and Venerable to precede the time of Antichrist. Those private prophecies are obviously not matters of faith. But they ***are*** consistent with the writings of the Fathers and Doctors of the Church, as well as those of many Scriptural exegetes.

The combination of these four sources (1) Tradition (in particular -- the eschatological writings of the Fathers), (2) Scripture, and (3) The traditional teachings of the Magisterium on this subject, and *very ancillarily*, (4) APPROVED private prophecy, for any objective Christian observer should be strong enough to overcome any belief that the Antichrist and/or the Parousia are coming in the near future.

We must all be aware of and on our interior guard against the strong emotional escapist appeal of belief in an immediate appearance of Antichrist. We are promised by Revelation that Antichrist's coming, his three and a half year rule, then his death, will usher in the end to the horrible sufferings of the people of that age. Believing Christians, both Catholic and non-Catholics are likewise suffering greatly in our age. If we can believe the Antichrist is coming soon, then we can concomitantly believe that our suffering will end in a matter of a few years if he is to arrive now. We must all be on our guard against the "quick fix" appeal of a belief in the Antichrist coming soon.

In a sense, the "appeal" of Antichrist's advent ultimately lies within its promise of a determinate end to terrible suffering ***within a very short period of time.*** While it promises to be painful, the immediate advent of Antichrist can also subconsciously promise a relatively "quick fix" to the mind of a suffering Christian. Therein lies the escapist appeal of belief in his immediate coming — three *and a half years and then it's over* - the light at the end of the tunnel.

However, according to Tradition, Scripture, the writings of the Fathers and "approved" sources of private prophecy, our future does not contain Antichrist. It might contain a "chastisement." However, if that chastisement should occur sometime in our age, it would *not* be the "tribulation" of Antichrist.

UNLESS, one should see with one's own eyes and/or hear with one's own ears that which one has heard PROPHESIED OF Antichrist from Tradition and Scripture, in exact concord with the traditional teachings of the Church about Antichrist, one can rest

assured that it is most Probably not his time. Unless one should see and hear those conditions prevail, even if a chastisement should develop, *no matter how severe that chastisement might appear, it is not the tribulation of the Antichrist.*

On the other hand, if after reading this book the reader is still incredulous as to whether it is possible that there might come upon us or our successors a "Minor Chastisement" if mankind does not experience inner conversion, remember the dying words of Jacinta, one of the three children at Fatima:

> "If men will repent, God will pardon them, but if they do not amend their lives, there will come upon the earth the most terrible chastisement ever known."

It is Possible that certain contemporary alleged prophecies about a Possible Chastisement are being misunderstood as referring to the Tribulation of Antichrist.

9. "In the End, My Immaculate Heart Will Triumph"

But all of this is ultimately a message of hope, as Our Lady said at Fatima, "IN THE END MY IMMACULATE HEART WILL TRIUMPH, AND A CERTAIN PERIOD OF PEACE WILL BE GIVEN TO THE WORLD." Our Lady promises us a period of peace which might well be the one which appears to be described in the *Book of Daniel* and in the *Book of Revelation*. Such a period Scripturally falls within a period which would chronologically precede Antichrist. That period ushers in a rebirth of a Christian world for "a certain period of peace."

Depending on OUR cooperation With God's grace, we may have to go through "the most terrible chastisement ever known" to get to that period of true peace Our Lady promises. But the current period of suffering should end not in the increased suffering caused by Antichrist - but rather - in peace. NO ONE KNOWS WHEN. IT IS EVEN POSSIBLE THE PEACE COULD BEGIN SOMETIME EARLY IN THE THIRD MILLENNIUM. THAT IS OUR MESSAGE OF HOPE. It is the message of Our Lord, "BE NOT AFRAID! I GO BEFORE YOU ALWAYS. COME, FOLLOW ME, AND I WILL GIVE YOU REST."

10. Summary of Events Foretold to Precede the Parousia, the Second Coming of Christ

The items below which are in bold print come from the common teaching tradition of the Church. *Those things which are in all italics, are things taught by virtually all of the Fathers and Doctors, but which one cannot fairly describe as a formal teaching of the Church.* Those which are in plain type come from private prophecy from Saints, Blessed and Venerable. They also include the personal opinions of the author as to where we, in the late 20th century, might fit into this picture.

(1) There are dozens of prophecies from canonized Saints, Blessed and Venerable, predicting a great period of heresy within the "Latin Church." These prophecies state that the Eastern Church will not suffer the same problems to the same degree. That is what is referred to by many prophets as the "Minor Chastisement," to distinguish it from the "Tribulation" or "Major Chastisement" of Antichrist.

(2) That Minor Chastisement is conditional, in that, it may or may not happen, or it can be lessened through prayer, sacrifice or penance. This distinguishes it from the Major Chastisement or "Tribulation" of Antichrist — which is *not* conditional. *The Tribulation of Antichrist* will someday absolutely happen. It comes from prophecy of predestination.

THIS AUTHOR BELIEVES THAT WE MAY BE BETWEEN #'s 1 & 2 RIGHT NOW. That would put us somewhere near the end of the first "woe" foretold in the *Book of Revelation*!

(3) *An age of peace: "the Lord from his glorious heaven shall set up his* ***peace****... in the place of this latter people. ... and [after that] coming forth from perdition, the man of iniquity shall be revealed upon the earth, the Seducer of men, and the disturber of the whole earth."*

How long will it be before this "peace"[which clearly precedes the Antichrist, is established? [See St. Ephraem's quote on page 221]

(4) *The establishment of a Roman Kingdom or Empire* (which most likely occurs during this period of peace) *which is finally broken up into Ten Kingdoms — which the man of sin then dominates. Virtually all the Fathers clearly teach this. None explicityly denies it. Most of the Doctors teach it.*

(5) **Before Christ's Second Coming there must develop a great and universal apostasy. It cannot be regional or limited to certain regions of the earth. It comes toward the end of the Age of Peace.**

(6) **The preaching of the Gospel throughout all the world must be accomplished.**

(7) **The three and one half year (1,290 days) reign or tribulation of Antichrist must be completed. The Fathers and Doctors say this is a literal fact.**

(8) **The full conversion of the Jews.**

(9) **The time for conversion of the nations (and the balance of the Jews) which time follows the death of Antichrist.**

These things are foretold to happen prior to the Second Coming of Christ (the Parousia). ***What are the odds all of this can happen before the year 2000? What are the odds that even all that which precedes the coming of the Antichrist could happen by the year 2000?***

CHAPTER 12

A HYPOTHESIS ON A CHRONOLOGY OF PREDICTED EVENTS

Herein is presented the author's best guess at the chronology of the prophesied events to come. But here again we must make clear distinctions. Earlier in the book we gave St. Thomas Aquinas' descriptions of two different types of prophecy; that of "foreknowledge" and that of "predestination." We now repeat it.

> "According to St. Thomas Aquinas, future prophecy is divided into two subdivisions, namely that of *foreknowledge* and that of *predestination*. (See Summa II-II, Q clxxiv, a. 1). "According to Thomas ... *that of foreknowledge*, takes place when God reveals future events *which depend upon created free will* and which He (God) sees present from eternity. They have reference to life and death, to wars and dynasties, to the affairs of the Church and State, as well as the affairs of individual life. *That prophecy of predestination* takes place when God reveals what he alone will do, and what He sees present in eternity and in His absolute decree."[681]

Prophecy of "predestination" as contained in *Revelation* is of Faith. A Christian must hold its ultimate fulfillment to be certain.

Events including such items as the coming of Antichrist:

(1) the Two Witnesses who will oppose him,
(2) the two signs which precede his coming,
(3) "the" false prophet who serves him,

[681] *Catholic Encyclopedia,* 1913 Edition, Vol. XII.

These and many other prophecies of *predestination are* the traditional teachings of the Church. Knowledge of exactly how such prophetic events are to be interpreted is left to the Magisterium. *Short of a definitive/dogmatic statement from the Magisterium on a given predestination issue*, the Church teaches us to hearken to the teachings of the Fathers and Doctors on these subjects to determine the traditional teachings of the Church in such matters.

It must be remembered that all conditional prophecies (which are by definition those of foreknowledge) depend upon human co-operation with grace as to their outcome. This is what St. Thomas means by prophecies of,

> "future events *which depend upon created free will* and which He (God) sees present from eternity."

In other words, a conditionally prophesied event may or may not even occur. Such prophesied events depend upon whether or not people cooperate with God's requests and grace. Such is what happened at Nineveh.

If a chastisement comes, the majority of it will be manmade - will be made up of those things God allows men to do to themselves through their "created free will." According to the prophecies, only the elements of the three days of darkness might be God's contribution. And He would perform this act as part of His Divine Mercy to stop the killing, suffering, and carnage which man is inflicting upon himself. In other words, the chronology which follows includes prophecies of both "foreknowledge" and some of "predestination." There is a mixture of that which is definitely revealed to us by God, mixed with many additional details from the writings of the Fathers, to which is added many from private prophecy (which by definition are not matters of Divine faith).

THE CHRONOLOGY WHICH FOLLOWS IS SIMPLY A BEST GUESS OF THE AUTHOR'S. IT INCLUDES ITEMS WHICH *ARE* "OF FAITH," WITH SOME WHICH DEFINITELY ARE NOT -- CONCERNING WHICH POPE BENEDICT SAYS "ONE CANNOT GRANT THE ASSENT OF CATHOLIC FAITH," BUT,

> "In keeping with laws of prudence, one must give them the assent of human belief (assensus fidei humanae), in that such

revelations are probable and piously credible. Consequently it is possible to refuse to accept such revelations and to turn from them, as long as one does so with proper modesty, for good reasons, **and without the intention of setting himself up as superior.**

"Though an assent of Catholic faith be not due to such revelations, *they,* however, *deserve a human assent, according to the rules of prudence, by which they are probable, and piously credible,* as the revelations of Blessed Hildegarde, St. Bridget, and St. Catherine of Sienna."[682]

Any Catholic may reject any or all private prophecy without jeopardizing his or her good standing in the Church. Whether it would be prudent to reject *all* private prophecy is an entirely different matter. That could be tantamount to thinking one had more wisdom in these matters than a very large percentage of the canonized Saints, and the vast majority of the Popes.

A. The Lesson(s) of Prophecy in this Book

What lesson(s) could we learn from all of the public and approved private prophecies presented in this book. There is a particular story which seems to apply in this case:

According to the story, sometime in the Late Middle Ages six men went to visit a very famous monk. The six were men of wealth, position, and prestige. The monk was a man known first for his holiness and then for his wisdom. When they arrived at the monastery they inquired after the whereabouts of the monk. They thought they would find him either in chapel or in the scriptorium reading the Scriptures. Instead, they found him hoeing vegetables in the monastery garden. (The role of his religious order prescribed two hours of manual labor a day for each monk.)

They introduced themselves and talked with him for a while. Finally, one of them asked the holy monk, "If you discovered that the Lord Jesus was coming at this hour, what would you do?" The monk leaned on his hoe and said, "I'd keep hoeing a straight row.

---

682 *De Servorum Dei Canonizatione et Beatificatione*, Lib. II. Cap. 32, No.11.)

Our rule calls for me to work for one more hour today, and my superior has assigned me to hoe the garden."

The educated wealthy gentlemen were shocked. They had anticipated that he would have said he would rush to the chapel to await the Lord. Sensing their consternation the monk said to them,

> "In obeying the rule of my order I am obeying God. I fulfill my duty to God. I show my true love for God. If I would do something different if I discovered the Lord was coming at this time, then there is something wrong with the way I am living my life right now. If there is, I should change it right now. I should always live my life as if the Lord were coming for me right then. But right now I am supposed to be hoeing vegetables. So if the Lord comes right now, He is going to find me doing my job well, hoeing a straight row."

There is something wonderful all of us can learn from the wisdom of this learned but holy and simple man. There is time in our life for prayer, work at our jobs, work in our churches, play, relaxation, for those of us who are married - faithful love of our spouses, sacrifice and penance. Faithfully offering our lives to God is a wonderful sacrifice in itself. If we live our lives as if Jesus was right there with us all the time, we will live and ultimately die with few regrets.

St. Joseph was a man of great prayer. He was undoubtedly a conscientious, hard-working carpenter. And he was a wonderful father for Jesus when he was growing up. As long as we are engaged in honorable work, the vast majority of us don't need to change what we do for a living. We need to improve the way we live every moment of the life God has given us. In the normal course of events, we are where God wants us to be. Let us live our lives according to the rules of whatever state God has placed us in. But in all of this, like the Holy Family, let us lead lives of increased prayer, sacrifice and penance for the greater glory of God.

A Hypothetical Chronology Table

B. The Minor Chastisement

(1) At some time in the future, the corrupt faithless age we live in now will come to an end either through inner conversion of a sufficient number of people who turn to prayer, sacrifice, and penance, -- or there will be a chastisement (which can be ameliorated by a lesser number of people through inner conversion). This would be a Minor Chastisement preceding the Age of Peace. St. Louis De Montfort described this Age of Peace as the Age of Mary.

(2) If this chastisement is not averted through conversion, the Latin Church will be terribly afflicted by heresy and schism.

(3) The chastising elements will come in two forms, (a) manmade and (b) Heaven-sent.

(4) *Civil war will break out in France and Italy at almost the same time***.** This is the sign given by many prophets that the Chastisement has begun.

(5) This will spread to general wars, and, famine and pestilence (the usual by-products of war).

(6) At the same time there will be civil war on almost a worldwide scale. THIS IS TOTAL CHAOS.

(7) Earthquakes, tidal waves, floods and all other sorts of "natural" disasters will occur.

(8) Some Moslems will cause great trouble for the Church and Europe in general.

(9) Somewhere in all of this, an army composed of Russians will invade Western Europe *just when everyone thinks this impossible.*

(10) England will suffer a terrible civil war which starts after the French and Italians have gone into theirs.

(11) The Pope will flee Rome in the company of several other cardinals and go into hiding, be found, and cruelly murdered. What the exact extent of his travels will be we do not know, but some of the prophecies state that at one point he will be in Cologne.

(12) A man who will subsequently be known as a great saint will ultimately be elected Pope near the end of the chastisement.

(13) He will be heavily responsible for the French acceptance of a king to be their military and civil leader.

(14) **The Great King** will lead his forces (against terrible odds) until finally, after attending Mass at Bremen, he leads his troops to a victory in Cologne and then their *great final victory in Westphalia* (The Birch Tree country). It will be obvious to all that Christ -- through the agency of His Mother -- has taken a direct miraculous hand in the victory.

(15) The Russians and the Prussians will subsequently be totally defeated by the Great King. Their immediate end will begin when the Great King's forces (against terrible odds) deliver them a defeat near Cologne. The Russians and Prussians retreat to somewhere in Westphalia, Germany. They are crushed during a battle wherein a miraculous event will turn the tide in favor of the Christian forces.

(16) At some point, the Great King chases an invading Moslem army back to the Holy Land.

(17) Somewhere near the end of the chastisement, God sends **Three Days of Darkness**.

(18) The three days of darkness occur sometime after final and total victory over the Russians and Moslems.

[In the event that sufficient souls cooperate with requests for prayer, sacrifice and penance to avert a chastisement at this time; There is an alternate possible interpretive scenario, that the prophesied Great King and the Great Pope come *near the end of the Age of Peace* which is about to be described in the next outline section.

In the latter scenario, there is a great deal of civil war and general war which is ended by three day of darkness. Near the end of a lengthy ensuing period of peace, things again turn bad. It might be then that the great king comes to usher in a final period of peace which lasts only as long as he lives. That is an alternate possibility. The prophecies simply do not give sufficient details for us to tell.]

C. The Age of Peace

(1) Through a historically very unique series of events there will be a complete restoration of Christian culture in the West.

(2) The Great King will be crowned Holy Roman Emperor by the reigning Pope.

(3) The Great King will establish peace and justice in civil matters on a worldwide basis, and protect the primacy of the Church in spiritual matters. He will defend the poor. Organized and systematic exploitation of the poor will be brought to an end.

(4) The former disciplines of the Church are fully restored and order is re-established.

(5) *The Pope calls an Ecumenical Council* which will be viewed as the greatest in the history of the Church. It will Dogmatically define the theological meaning of many Scriptural texts not previously formally explicated.

(6) The world is spiritually and materially prosperous as never before and many Jews, Mohammedans, heathens and heretics will enter the Church.

(7) Extended prosperity causes people to begin to grow lax in the practice of their Faith.

(8) Wars and bad economic times break out again after some period of time during which the faithful fall into laxity. This prepares the way for the death of the last Holy Roman Emperor.

(9) After his death (or retirement) ten kings divide up the boundaries of the Holy Roman Empire which had been established.

(10) The Empire of the Great King is broken up into Ten Kingdoms. If the people cooperate sufficiently with grace during the Age of Peace -- that Age will be extended. Therefore, (dependent upon the degree of "cooperation") this division could happen centuries or a millennium later under one of the successors of the Great King. Several prophecies state this possibility.

(11) Many of the above events (except the Age of Peace) may never happen at all. First of all, they are conditional prophecies. Its possible that mankind will sufficiently cooperate with grace that many of these events are curtailed by such cooperation.

D. The Major Chastisement -- Antichrist

(1) *A great military leader*: the last (Roman) Empire, which has been divided up into "Ten Kingdoms" is dismantled by a great (but evil) military leader. Three of the Ten Kingdoms will not go along with this. They are crushed. See - *Book of Rev.* Ch. 13, Book of Dan. Ch. 7 & 8. Also see St. Jerome's commentary in this book that Antichirst will kill the three kings "of who will not bow to him"

(2) The "False Prophet" arrives -- the Precursor of Antichrist. He will "ape" the role that St. John the Baptist performed in preparing the people for the arrival of the Messiah.

(3) All of this prepares the way for the coming of Antichrist. He begins his rise to power at about the age of thirty. After he seizes total power he begins a three and one half year bestial persecution of the Church.

(4) During this period, Enoch and Elias, who have never died but have been maintained in "Paradise" return to the presence of men and preach to the people against Antichrist. Elias preaches primarily to the Jews and Enoch primarily to the Gentiles. It is the arrival of these "Two Witnesses" which foreshadows the foretold conversion of the Jews to Christianity.

(5) Antichrist finally kills them by his own hand in Jerusalem and their bodies lie in the street by his command for three and one-half days, at the end of which a voice from Heaven is heard by everyone present to command Enoch and Elias to arise. To the surprise and stark terror of the onlookers they do.

(6) Antichrist, stung again by this latest heavenly miracle, tries to restore his prestige with the Jews by simulating Christ's ascension from Mt. Olivet, and St. Michael casts him down screaming to his death.

E. The Four Last Things.

(1) After the death of Antichrist, a period of time of unknown duration is given to the remaining inhabitants of the earth to repent and accept Our Lord and the message of his Gospel. According to Our Lord's words in the Gospels, *"as in the days*

of Noe" the judgment will come upon mankind suddenly *"as a thief in the night"* when *"they married wives, and were given in marriage. They bought and sold, they planted and built."* In other words, **after the death of the Antichrist, there will be a time of sufficient duration for things to have gotten back to normal** (Matt 24:37-39 & Lk 17:26-30). Scripture gives no exact indication of how long, but according to Tradition, it will be a short period of time.

(2) Then Jesus comes in glory to judge the living and the dead. It is the end of the world and time. The *Four Last Things for all mankind, Death, Judgment, Heaven and Hell.*

(3) The exact time when these things happen is unknown to us for no one "knows the day or the hour." As to those things which come from outside Revelation, outside "Sacred Tradition and Sacred Scripture,"[683] i.e., private prophecy, no Catholic has to believe them, not even those from Fatima or Akita.

Epilogue

At least three quarters of the public and private prophecies the author should like to have shared have gone unrecited because of the single volume dimension of this book. The exact locations and conditions of the great battles during a chastisement, major events foretold for Italy, South and North America, Ukraine, Russia, Ireland and Spain, the roles played by man, various "Secret Sects" efforts to subvert the Church, these and many other areas have barely been touched upon. Prophecies of other great military leaders from Spain and Poland who will be lieutenants to the Great King - these we have not portrayed.

Also not included are in-depth prophetical descriptions of many key figures and events such as:

(1) The major false prophet who is the precursor for the Antichrist (who apes the role of John the Baptist with Our Lord).

(2) A particular military leader who will help set the stage for him.

[683] *Dei Verbum*, #'s 9 & 10.

(3) The voluminous Patristic writings on many specific "false" miracles of Antichrist.

(4) The writings of the Fathers and Doctors on the end times and Antichrist have of necessity been presented in a truncated overview format. *An entire book could and should be written on this subject alone.*

(5) Patristic writings on specific events which lead to the rise of Antichrist.

(6) Presentation of the vast wealth of exegesis from the Fathers and Doctors on the foretold time of "one flock and one shepherd," or the time of the "fullness of the Gentiles."

(7) Patristic integration of foretold events in the *Book of Daniel* and the *Apocalypse* concerning the end times.

There has not been room in a single volume edition for extensive presentations in any of these and many other areas.

Despite these deficiencies, the author hopes this book will accomplish some good and lead those who read it to be more hope-filled Christians. Most importantly, **let us remember that if the chastising elements of the "conditional" prophecies come to pass, according to Oral Tradition, Scripture, and private prophecy, they are a combination of (1) things that God allows men with free will to do to themselves, and (2) that which He allows to happen for their greater good.** ***Finally, He directly intervenes to end such chastisement as a Divine Mercy to stop the suffering.*** Let us all light a candle rather than curse the darkness. Let us all try our best to live lives of increased prayer, sacrifice and penance, for if we do, it will save many souls.

At Fatima Our Lady told the children, "Pray the Rosary every day to bring an end to the war" (World War I). At other times she told them that good Catholics should pray the Rosary every day to bring peace to the world. In the course of Christian history, conflict after conflict has been brought to a successful conclusion due to the "faithful" saying the Rosary and leading edifying lives. There are literally dozens of recorded examples of this throughout the history of Christendom.

F. This May be the Beginning of the Age of Mary!

As Our Lord has told a number of Saints in the last two centuries, the victory over the forces of evil in our time has been reserved by Him for His Mother, so that after the victory, the world will pay her the reverence He wishes her to be honored with.

If we wish to stop or ameliorate the threatened chastisement and hasten the Age of Peace, if we wish to interdict the current influence of Satan and his legions on which Bishop Sheen was quoted earlier, we must bond ourselves to devotion of Our Lord in the Blessed Eucharist and to Our Mother Mary and her Rosary. If we are not saying the daily Rosary, are we part of the problem, or part of the solution? If we do not adore Our Lord in the Holy Eucharist, are we part of the problem - and therefore not a part of the solution?

For those who wish to place themselves close to Our Lord's Sacred Heart and His protection, He has chosen in the latter times to make the Immaculate Heart of His mother a lightning rod of grace and a special place of refuge for us. Many believe that this idea of the special intercession of Our Lady in "latter times" is something which has sprung forth since the apparitions at Lourdes and Fatima. Nothing could be further from the truth. Listen to the 14th century words of St. Vincent Ferrer on this latter day association with Our Lady.

> "By revelation it is manifestly shown that the whole duration of the world rests on a certain conditional prolongation obtained by the Virgin Mary in the hope of the conversion and correction of the world..."[684]

St. Vincent said that roughly six centuries ago.

God so loved the world that He gave His only-begotten Son for us. His love for every one of us is intense beyond our comprehension. Every man and woman has joys and sufferings on this earth. How a Christian handles these joys and sufferings depends in large part on his relationship with God. How often do we gaze upon the Cross of Our Lord and how do we gaze?

---

[684] *Angel of the Judgement*, p. 98.

If as we look upon Our Lord on the Cross and we remember His words, "Who has suffered as I have suffered?," and if we remember His great love for us which kept Him from letting His chalice of suffering from passing Him by, -- it is much easier to offer up our own sufferings to our heavenly Father. He awaits these offerings of love. When we offer our puny but greatly appreciated love to Him, grace increases to save and improve ourselves and other members of the Mystical Body. This relationship is a mystery. We cannot plumb its depths. But we can with faith and love accept it, believe it, and cooperate with God's grace within its bounds.

This Wisdom of the Cross was beautifully described by St. Francis of Assisi many centuries ago. St. Francis is the first "Stigmatic" in the history of the Church, the first one to actually bear the wounds of Christ upon his person. As he lived the life of the Wisdom of the Cross, Francis said,

> "If we accept this (our cross) with patience, believing it is a cross the good Lord wishes us to bear, then we know perfect joy! The greatest gift God can give us is the grace to subject our selflove to bearing the cross of humiliation, or affliction, or danger, or torture, for the love of God."[685]

None of us has suffered as Our Lady suffered at the foot of the Cross. She loves us all with a burning charity which surpasses the love of any other creature. She awaits us to love her Son in her Rosary, to talk to her throughout each day, to call upon her when we skin our knee, or need help to button our blouse or shirt, or to tie our shoes. We need to approach her as we did our own moms when we were four or five years old. And she will hug and kiss away our tears more than our natural mothers could. "Mary, mother of Jesus, be a mother to me now." This is the constant prayer of Mother Teresa's nuns - which they tell us is one of the keys to their success in their apostolate.

Jesus awaits our love. He thirsts for souls. He desires 100% of our devotion. Mary will show us how to give 100% - especially if we ask her through her Rosary. Love - not fear - will get us to a total relationship with Our Lord and his mother.

---

685 *Wisdom's Fool*, Fr. Edward Doherty, Montfort Publications, Bay Shore, New York, 1975, p. 87.

That love has been described as "love in the dimension of the Cross."[686] Such love is the love that Jesus showed sinful man from the Cross. A short time from physical death, Our Lord said, "Forgive them Father, for they know not what they do." He allowed Himself to be physically destroyed by the mob, and the individual members of that mob. He loved, forgave, and prayed for that destructive mob and its individual members, not only from His Divine love, but also from the depths of his fully human soul.

***That* is the test of Christian love.** In Christ, do I love, truly forgive, and pray for my enemies? If I do, then I love in the "dimension of the Cross!" Out of such love our neo-pagan world can be reconverted to the love of Christ!

Do we have a role model? The moto of John Paul II's papacy is "Totus Tuus" - "All yours (Mary)." At his first meeting with a bishop, the Holy Father gives him a Rosary. He exhorts him to pray it every day. ***Ad Jesum per Mariam*** - to Jesus through Mary. When he was shot in St. Peter's square, Pope John Paul's first recorded words were a question, "Who would do this?" His next recorded words were, "*I forgive you.*" John Paul II has extraordinary Marian devotion. He is also able to extraordinarily "love in the dimension of the cross."

Our Lord wants us to fully join Him in the contemporary battle for souls. He wants us to join Him with and through our Mother Mary. We are invited to the wedding feast of Cana. If we go in a clean garment of good intention - the Mediatrix of Grace will intercede for us and the rest of the Mystical Body as she did for the embarrassed couple at Cana. Our Lady of Good Success, pray for us now and at the hour of our death. Amen.

That is the key to OUR happiness - union with Jesus and Mary. *Ad Jesum per Mariam* - to Jesus through Mary. Our Lord wants us to fully join Him in the contemporary battle for souls. He wants us to join Him with and through our Mother Mary. We are invited to the wedding feast of Cana. If we go in a clean garment of good intention - the Mediatrix of Grace will intercede for us and the rest of the Mystical Body as she did for the embarrassed couple at Cana. Our Lady of Good Success, pray for us now and at the hour of our death. Amen.

---

686 An expression of the NeoCatechumenal Way

FINAL CONCLUSORY REMARK:

The materials contained in this book from Tradition, Scripture, the exegesis of the Fathers and Doctors, and only ancillarily, *approved* Catholic private prophecy, lead to one inexorable conclusion:

AS THE HOLY FATHER KEEPS REPEATING THE WORDS OF OUR LORD,

> **"BE NOT AFRAID. I GO BEFORE YOU ALWAYS. COME, FOLLOW ME, AND I WILL GIVE YOU REST."**

THIS IS NOT A TIME TO EITHER FEAR THE ARRIVAL OF ANTICHRIST AND/OR THE END TIMES. THIS IS A TIME FOR HOPE, PRAYER, AND WORK TOWARD RENEWAL OF CONTEMPORARY AND FUTURE CHRISTIAN LIFE AND VIGOR. THIS IS THE TIME FOR THE NEW EVANGELIZATION THE HOLY FATHER IS CALLING FOR.

As Mary said at Fatima, "In the end my Immaculate Heart will triumph and a certain period of peace will be given to the world." IT IS ONLY A MATTER OF TIME TILL OUR LADY'S PROMISE IS FULFILLED! IT will happen - if not for us - then perhaps for our children or grandchildren.

If you feel that you have gotten anything useful out of this book, please remember the author in your prayers, that he may daily grow spiritually.

ACKNOWLEDGMENTS

Over the last ten years, I have had invaluable help from a number of people in the preparation of this book. There have been so many it would be impossible to name them all on one page. So I will first name those who expended large amounts of time for the longest periods.

First comes two people at the Archbishop Vehr Theological Library in Denver, Colorado.[1] My deepest thanks go to Mr. Hirum "Dig" Chinn and Joyce L. White, the chief librarian. For over ten years these two people assisted me in finding and obtaining copies of rare books and materials. Many of the long out of print materials which appear in this book were obtained through their direct and invaluable assistance.

My thanks to the publisher whose insistence finally brought this manuscript to completion.

Fifteen people performed critical reads on the second draft of the manuscript. I thank all of them. My special thanks to Mr. Anthony Lillis for his *many* invaluable suggestions for improvement of and additions to the manuscript.[2] I am also deeply indebted to Mr. Henry Stachyra for his critical reading and other invaluable assistance over the last year and a half. Thanks also to Mr. Joseph Stachyra for an early read when it was badly needed.

My gratitude goes to Mr. Wesley Stupar whose critical read led to a total rewrite of Chapter 11.

I also wish to express my gratitude to the numerous priests and especially the bishops who read this manuscript and gave me their extremely valuable advice and suggestions.

[1] Formerly the St. Thomas Seminary Theological Library.

[2] Any weak spots in this book are undoubtedly within areas where I did not follow Mr. Lillis' advice.

Those who independently translated materials or checked the author's translations, I give my heartfelt thanks to;

Mrs. Pat Frenette who translated some extremely difficult scholarly French materials, and,

To Mr. Pat O'brien who checked and offered many valuable suggestions to the author's Latin translations.

To the Irish theologian, Fr. Michael O'Carroll, I give my especial thanks for the theological critical reading he gave the manuscript - and for his many valuable suggestions.

To Dr. Warren Carroll I wish to offer my thanks for; several telephone conferences on some critical historic points in Old Testatment history, and some historic points surrounding the early synods and councils of the Church.

Thanks to Monica Blanchard, of Catholic University's *Institute of Christian Oriental Research,* for checking some contemporary analysis of works and sermons attributed to St. Ephraem.

To Sr. & Dr. Gertrude Joett at Catholic U., my thanks for rechecking sources of the documents emanating from the Council of Nicea - particularly in reference to the "Synodal Decree" of Nicea.

I wish to especially thank Mr. Fran Pierson of Pierson Graphics of Denver, Colorado. Under terrible time constraints (not of his own making) Mr. Pierson managed to produce the three maps for this book.

Most importantly I wish to thank my family for many years of patience, my son John for on-site research in Westphalian geography. I wish to offer not just thanks but grateful appreciation to my bride of twenty six years. It is primarily due to her long-suffering and support that this manuscript could have come to pass at all.

Finally, I thank our mother, Mary, for her constant intercession with her Son, Jesus Christ, on behalf of I and my family that we might remain faithful sons and daughters of His Church.

Desmond Birch

GLOSSARY OF TERMS

APPARITION: Is more or less a cognate of "Vision" (See Vision), with a slight addition. It has all the qualities of a vision, but in addition, part of an apparition usually entails that something is actually heard as well as seen. i.e. All apparitions are visions, but not all visions are apparitions (not all visions have an auditory element to them.) When an apparition is claimed, the Church requires proof of such, and then examines such "proofs" to determine that they are non-natural (they are not a product of imagination or hallucination), and further, that they in fact emanate from a supernatural, and not an evil non-natural source.

BLESSED: In terms of Sainthood, this is the second step. After being given the title "Venerable" a candidate for canonization may at some point be declared "Blessed." This confirms to the faithful that the commission has investigated and solemnly certifies that the reputation of sanctity with the faithful is justified, and that (always in the case of non-martyr candidates) at least two miracles are certified as genuine. The faithful are now allowed to "publicly" venerate the candidate as a Saint. (See "VENERABLE" & "SAINT")

CANON: Basically signifies a list of items. In the "Canon of sacred Scripture" are to be found the 46 books of the Old Testament, and the 27 books of the New Testament. First complete canon of Scripture as we know it today promulgated by Pope Damasus and the council of Rome with help from St. Jerome. (380/381)

CHRISTOLOGY: Comes from a combination of "Christ" plus the Greek "logia" meaning science or knowledge. A systematic scientific study of the person Jesus Christ, most importantly of the union in Him of His two natures, the union of his truly Divine and truly human natures. In theology this is called the "Hypostatic Union." The Fathers of the Church and the early General Councils they attended and led, studied this "person" of Jesus Christ very carefully. The orthodox definitions which they wrote at these Councils center around the revealed truths about Jesus' relationship with the Father and the "Hypostatic Union," the joining of the truly Divine and the truly human in Jesus Christ. (See "COUNCILS")

COGNATE: Allied by blood, kindred or having the same nature or quality; similar, related.

CONCUPISCENCE: Describes the state of man since the fall of Adam and Eve through Original Sin. Prior to that Original Sin, man's will was in full conformity with the will of God as He expressed it to them. The intellects of Adam and Eve were unclouded by earthly desires and passions. Yes, they enjoyed tasty food, looking at breathtakingly beautify flowers and vistas, loved to listen to beautiful sounds -- in those things they were just as we are. They also fully appreciated the beauty of their own bodies and intellects, but they knew that all of this was attributable to God, their Creator; unlike the state of man since the fall, they did not have a *false* pride in themselves. Their enjoyment of the delights of the Garden before the fall of man did not cloud their judgment or ability to think correctly -- which correct thought always leads us to fully conform our will to that of God. But since Original Sin, man is subject to his passions, enjoyments, desires, and false pride overriding his reason. Since the fall, man's intellect has been weakened, his judgment clouded by these inordinate desires, passions, enjoyments and pride. *That factor of being subject to the passions, which in turn clouds our judgment and affects our will -- that is concupiscence.*

COUNCILS: Authoritative gatherings of Bishops for discussing problems, for which they intend to find solutions, which they publish in the form of decrees. These problems/decrees can be on matters of either doctrine and/or morals, or they can be matters of discipline.

The Roman Catholic terms ecumenical or general apply to a council when all the Bishops of the world are called to attend and participate. In that case the assembly of those bishops is called ecumenical (which means universal). The first ecumenical council was the Council of Nicea held in 325 A.D., at Nicea (located in modern Western Turkey). The last ecumenical Council was that of Vatican II, held at Rome between 1962 and 1964. If the council is called for less than all of the world, then this is called a particular council. If in fact it is a council as such, it has legislative authority for the area it represents. In this sense, councils are different from episcopal conferences, in that such conferences have no legislative powers as such.

DE FIDE: A technical term in Latin which translates into its English equivalent, "OF FAITH." (***Once a "doctrine"*** [traditional teaching of the Church which every Catholic *should* believe] ***has been declared a "Dogma," (declared to be "De Fide) all Catholics from then on are bound in conscience and must believe in and accept it in Faith.*** In the course of time, as certain individuals or groups publicly/widely challenged a doctrine (traditional Church teaching), the Church has on occasion responded by declaring those traditional teachings to be "Dogmas" in order to make it clear for the Church members what they must believe. An alternate verbal expression utilized by Councils of the Church or Popes to express this has been for them to declare something to be "De Fide." The relationship between "Dogmas" and "doctrines" is similar to the following; just as all houses are buildings (but not all buildings are houses), all "Dogmas" are also doctrines (but not all doctrines have been declared Dogmas) Therefore, the two expressions "De Fide" and "Dogma" are essentially (vis-a-vis the belief of Catholics) equivalent expressions.

DOCETISM: A philosophy or system of thought with which the Apostles themselves had to contend. This philosophy taught that the earthly life of the truly Human nature in the Person of Christ was an illusion (e,g,, his Incarnation, birth, passion, death resurrection, etc.). They taught that he only "seemed" to be a man. They recognized the possibility of Jesus' Divinity. But they claimed that there was an irreconcilable chasm, even an antagonism between those things material and spiritual which made what we call the Hypostatic Union impossible.

There was an intellectual partnership between the Docetists and the Gnostics (who claimed a knowledge higher than, greater than the Gospel) which was united with dualistic elements of Platonic philosophy. This "dualism" sees any communication between the spiritual world and the material world as at best skewed, flawed (see the allegory of the Cave in Plato's Republic), or even illusory. All of these elements, Docetist philosophy, Gnostic claims to a knowledge higher than the Gospel, and Platonic dualism, were loosely combined in the teachings of the Docetists, which teachings ultimately denied the Christological Mysteries contained in Revelation. In contraposition to the Docetists, under the inspiration of the Holy Spirit, St. Paul and St. John wrote their highly Incarnational letters and Gospels which contained much doctrine most explicitly pronouncing the *Mystery of the Incarnation.*

DOCTOR OF THE CHURCH: This is a very special title accorded by the Church to certain Saints. This title indicates that the writings and/or preachings of such a person are useful to Christians *in any age of the Church*. Such men and women are also particularly known for the depth of understanding and the orthodoxy of their theological teachings. (There are a certain number of "ecclesiastical writers" whose writings and preaching have an application limited to and directed at problems and opportunities of their particular age. Such writings and preachings can be difficult to apply to other sets of conditions. Such are never named doctors.)

There is also a division of Doctors of the East and the West. Both the two women Doctors are of the West. They are St. Catherine of Sienna and St. Teresa of Avila. As an additional note, the term Doctor does not signify everything contained in their writings are De Fide.

DOCTRINE: Comes from the Latin word "Doctrina" which signifies "a teaching." A Doctrine of the Church is a traditional "teaching" which has been constantly substantially taught by the Fathers and/or the Doctors and Theologians of the Church. When in the opinion of the Magisterium, a "Doctrine" has been attacked broadly enough to create danger of the possibility of honest doubt in the minds of Church members as to what they are to believe on a given Doctrinal point, then, the Church can declare that Doctrine to be "Of Faith," or the Latin "De Fide." "Doctrine" as such should be received and believed by every member of the Church. For instance, the recently published *Catechism of the Catholic Church* (1994) contains 688 pages of tightly packed "Doctrine" which a Catholic can and should believe on the authority of the Church. Needless to say, the Church would hardly go through the process of declaring all those items in the Catechism to be "De Fide" since most Catholics faithfully accept such as the teachings of the Church without confusion. See "DE FIDE"

DOGMA: See "DE FIDE"

EASTERN RITE OR CHURCH: See "RITE"

ESCHATOLOGICAL: An adjectival form of "ESCHATOLOGY" see Eschatology.

ESCHATOLOGY: A field of "Systematic Theology" which deals with the "Last Things": death, Heaven, Hell, both the Particular and General Judgments of individuals, and finally Purgatory. Most of the Church's solemn teachings on this subject were defined at the Fourth Lateran Council in 1215 A.D., and in particular, the Catholic Doctrine on the existence of Purgatory being "De Fide" was reaffirmed and expanded at the Council of Trent in the 16th century. The Latin phrase "De Fide," meaning "Of Faith," signifies something a Catholic must believe in order to be a member of the Catholic Church in good standing. See De Fide.

As it applies to this book, eschatology usually refers to "General" eschatology. That particular subject deals with (a) those things dealing with the approach of the end of the world, (b) the resurrection of the body, (c) the general judgment, and (d) the final consummation of all things. Most of the material in this book obviously deals with item (a).

EXEGESIS: The investigation of the true sense of sacred Scripture. As both an art and a science it goes back to the Rabinical studies of the Old Testament prior to the birth of Our Lord. Its purpose is to determine exactly what a specific passage of Scripture says. The rules of the science are contained in Hermeneutics. (See Hermeneutics)

FATHERS OF THE CHURCH: Writers of the early centuries of the Church. The Church grants such men special recognition with the title "Father" in that She recognizes them as Her special witnesses of the Faith as held by the early Church.

"There are four marks also by which a writer is recognized as a Father of the Church. *a*) orthodox doctrine, *b) sanctity* of life, *c*) antiquity, and *d*) approval of the Church. Antiquity is easily decided. The patristic age, by today's common agreement, ends in the West with the death of St. Isidore of Seville in the year 626 A.D., and in the East with the death of St. John Damascene in 749 A.D. Unless one belong within the proper period to his locale, he cannot be called a Father. And it is perhaps worthwhile noting that those whose antiquity is so great that they were in fact the immediate associates of the Apostles are called the Apostolic Fathers.

The other three notes are less precise. To be regarded as a Father, one must have orthodox doctrine; *but this does not exclude all doctrinal error.* An occasional material heresy (See definitions of formal and material) can be found in the greater lights among the Fathers.[1] It does imply, however, a devotion to orthodoxy and a faithful adherence to the orthodox Church.

Even sanctity must be taken in a somewhat broad sense. St. Jerome had an abominable gift for invective. ... In general we may say that those to whom ecclesiastical tradition has accorded the title of saint fulfill the requirements of sanctity of life.

The last note of a Father, is the most nebulous of all. It is not necessary that there be express approbation, but there need be only such approbation as can be deduced from ecclesiastical usage."[2]

---

1 The Church draws a distinction between material heresy and formal heresy. A material heresy is one wherein the matter of something said or taught is heretical per se. A formal heresy is one wherein some individual promotes a material heresy with the full knowledge that the Church established by Jesus Christ formally condemns such as a heresy, however, the heretic continues to teach the heresy anyway. In the cases of a formal heretic, there is no ignorance of the fact that the Church established by Jesus Christ formally condemns such teaching as heretical, whereas, the material heretic is ignorant (for one reason or another) of that fact. A good example of this might be the teachings of Origin on a "final Apocatastasis."

2 *The Faith of the Early Fathers*, W.A. Jurgens, The Liturgical Press, Collegeville, MN. 1970. p. X from Introduction.

Dr. Roy DeFerrari makes the additional point on a qualification for being a "Father," "He must be an author whose works are still extant. Fathers are important, because they are quoted as authorities in theology. They are all people who wrote works that can be quoted. St. Anthony the Hermit, St. Lawrence, and St. Sebastion are not Fathers because they left no writings."[3]

In other words, through one avenue or another we must be in possession of some of a "Father's" writings.

FORMAL (vs. Material) HERESY: When an individual who has been baptized a Christian, and who claims to be a Christian, tenaciously rejects or questions an authorized teaching of the Catholic Church about a doctrine which the Church authorizes to be contained in sacred Tradition and/or sacred Scripture, that person is by definition a heretic.

The question which then remains is -- does that person know that what he or she is teaching is heresy? The term "FORMAL" is added to the word heretic to identify a particular heretic as one who knows that the doctrine he teaches is contrary to the teachings of the Church. When the heretic *knows* that something he or she is teaching runs contrary to the teachings of the Church, then his or her heresy is considered to be FORMAL. i.e., When the heretic has the *knowledge* that a doctrine he or she is teaching is condemned by the Church, and he or she continues to teach that condemned doctrine anyway, that is when a heresy and the heretic are described as formal. *The central issues are (1) knowledge, (2) intent, and therefore culpability.* The "Formal" heretic intends to teach a doctrine which he knows is contrary to Church teaching. (See "Material" Heresy.) This is a morally culpable act. Therefore, there is guilt involved.

[The knowledge factor can be very complex. For instance, does the alleged heretic also "know" that the Catholic Church is the one which has the fullness of the faith? This can be a very complex issue. Other concepts such as "vincible" and "invincible" ignorance can and do enter into whether or not someone is a formal, not just a material, heretic. If the reader wishes to investigate this further,

---

3 *Selections from the Works of the Fathers of the Church, St. Bazil,* General Foreword, Dr. Roy J. Deferrari, Daughters of St. Paul, St. Paul Editions, p. 4. Boston, 1950.

they should first consult a Catholic encyclopedia, and then proceed to a good theology text on the subject.]

In any case, no individual is qualified to judge whether someone is a formal or material heretic. Only the Church can decide such an issue. When there is a question of apparent heresy in someone's teaching, holy charity should cause us to presume that it is only material, *not* formal, until or if the Church should definitively tell us that it is formal.

HERMENEUTICS: A scientific set of rules by which "Exegetes" interpret sacred Scripture. The rules involve (*amongst many other things*) the criteria for determining whether the primary sense of a Scripture passage is literal, allegorical or some accommodated sense. The etymology of the word is Greek, coming from the Greek word "*hermeneus*" which signifies "interpreter." (See Exegete)

HYPOSTATIC UNION: A union of both the truly Divine and truly human natures in the one Divine "person" of Christ. The Church teaches (as defined at the Council of Chalcedon in 451 A.D.), that the two natures of Christ are mystically joined "in one person and one hypostasis." Hypostasis, a Greek work, is equivalent to our English word substance. This doctrine teaches that the Divine Christ takes to Himself, assumes, includes in His Divine Person a perfect human nature. That mystical union is real; it is not illusory.

INDIFFERENTISM: Agnostics, for instance, do not see the worship of God and the practice of religion as a serious duty of man to God. They are indifferent to such worship and practice. Within their beliefs, agnostics and many others who hold similar beliefs believe that one religion is as good as any other. God has revealed to us that this is not the case. God has revealed to us that other than Jesus Christ's, there is "no other name under heaven by which man can be saved." To deny this, therefore, constitutes heresy -- often referred to as the heresy of "Indifferentism."

KERYGMA: Comes from the Greek "*K*âr*ygma*" meaning "proclamation." Kerygma signifies an initial proclamation or preaching of the Gospel of Christ as distinguished from teaching or instruction. Thus, St. Paul tells us of his proclamation (Kerygma) of his gospel, which Jesus Christ personally revealed to him. Distinction example: St. Paul's Kerygma, or proclamation of the Gospel of Christ, was reaffirmed in the Vatican II Document, *Dei Verbum*. But that document was not itself *the* "Kerygma" in the strict sense of the word.

LOCUTION: A supernatural communication to someone's ear, imagination, or directly to someone's intellect. The locution is supernatural in the manner in which it is communicated. The manner is beyond the ordinary laws of nature.

MATERIAL (vs. Formal) HERESY: When an individual who has been baptized a Christian, and who claims to be a Christian, tenaciously rejects or questions an authorized teaching of the Catholic Church about a doctrine which the Church authorizes to be contained in sacred Tradition and/or sacred Scripture that person is by definition a heretic. The question which then remains is -- does that person know that what they are teaching is heresy? A material heretic is ignorant of the fact that what they are refusing to accept, or are questioning constitutes heresy. When such an individual is in such ignorance, they are called a material heretic because the individual has no intent to teach heresy. A case in point is Origin's doctrines of the "Pre-existence of Souls" and his idea of a "Final Apocatastasis." No one doubts that Origin taught these in good faith, that he was unaware that these ideas ran contrary to Church Doctrine. There is the charitable assumption that had he known he would have ceased teaching or describing these doctrines.

MORNING OFFERING: A prayer with which Catholics have traditionally begun their day for many centuries. Over those centuries there have been many forms or versions of this prayer. There are several versions extant today, but the most common is the following:

> "Oh my Jesus, through the sorrowful and Immaculate Heart of Mary I offer Thee all my prayers, works, joys, and sufferings of this day.
>
> For all the intentions of Thy Sacred Heart,in union with the holy sacrifice of the Mass throughout the world,
>
> for the intentions of all my associates,
> and in particular for the intentions of the Holy Father. Amen."

MYSTAGOGY: (Adj. Mystagogical): Mystagogues are "Mysteries." Mystagogic Catechesis or instructions are those given the candidates for Christian Initiation into the Church. There are instructions for those preparing to be baptized, and the more advanced catecheses for neophytes who have recently been baptized These instructions introduce and explain the Mysteries of Faith - particularly as they relate to the sacramental life of the Church.

OMNISCIENCE: God's knowledge of all things. Omniscience signifies infinite knowledge, knowledge without limit. By definition, only the One God can know all things. Neither man nor angel nor any creature has unlimited knowledge. That is why many writers will even use the word "Omniscience" as a synonym for God.

OMNISCIENT: An adjective describing "Omniscience" (See Omniscience)

ORTHODOX: Comes from the two Greek words "orthos" which means "correct," plus "doksa" which means "opinion." Early Christian writers coined the word "orthodox" to mean "faithful" (to the doctrines as received from Apostolic Tradition). In the Western Church, that is still the most common or frequent usage. Someone who is "Orthodox" is faithful to the teachings of the Magisterium. Over the course of time the word has acquired an additional meaning wherein it can also signify the "Orthodox" (as they call themselves) as members of those Churches which are not in full union with Rome, or the "Orthodox" Churches (again not in full union with Rome). Examples are the Greek or the Russian "Orthodox" Churchs. The Orthodox Churches have Episcopal Succession from the Apostles and the same seven sacraments. Their sacraments are recognized by Rome as valid. Example: In danger of death, a "Catholic" of either the Eastern or Western Church may go to an "Orthodox" priest to hear his or her confession if there is not a "Catholic" priest of the Latin or Eastern Rites available. The "Orthodox" are truly our brothers and sisters in the Faith. Essentially, the thing which separates the "Orthodox" from Rome is obedience to the Holy Father, the Bishop of Rome.

PAROUSIA: The Second Coming of Christ to the earth at the end of time. It is then that Christ shall establish His Kingdom.

PATRISTICS: Includes Patrology (the study of the writings of the Church Fathers and the science of their contents) but is broader in scope. It further includes the scientific study of their doctrine and theology. In this book when the term "PATRISTICS' or "PATRISTICAL" are used, for reasons of convenience it can be referring to either patristics or patristical theology.

PATRISTIC THEOLOGY: The Apostolic Fathers and most of the Subapostolic Fathers were for the most part content to simply repeat quotations which came to them from the Apostles. Eventually, defense of the Church against pagan calumnies and attacks required a *reasonable* or *reasoned* defense of the Church. With the arrival of the "Apologists" (in particular Justin Martyr in the middle of the 2nd century) philosophy was put at the disposal of the Church to defend her beliefs and practices through reason.

With the arrival of St. Irenaeus, the reasoned approach began to be applied internally - the Church in defense against heretical attack from within - particularly from the Gnostics. Simply parroting back quotes from either the Oral or Written Tradition was not sufficient to handle the Gnostics, many of whom were trained philosophers. Therefor, Irenaeus developed reasoned arguments from the totality of Apostolic Tradition - and specifically defended that totality.

Further doctrinal disputes lead to increased use of this tool to develop formulas of Christian Doctrine against other heretical movements. Ultimately, the use of the reason which God gave to man as part of his nature - applied through the reasoning tool of philosophy - was a major determining factor in the defense of orthodoxy at the various ecumenical councils. For instance, reasoned argument as a tool of defense of Traditional Christian belief was the best affective weapon against the attacks of the Arian heretics - who in 319 A.D. began attempting to deny the Divinity of Christ from Scripture.

This practice of applied reason eventually became systematic. The Fathers of the Church developed systematic approaches to an overall defense of the great Trinitarian, Christological, and Marian beliefs of the Church. They developed verbal formulas to express those beliefs. Out of these first attempts grew what today is called systematic theology - in which the interrelationships of all these beliefs are more fully understood and described.

PATROLOGY: Usually defined as the study of the lives, and doctrines in the writings of the Fathers of the Church.

PLATO: A Greek philosopher, lived 427-347 B.C. A student of Socrates, he preceded Aristotle. Known for his idealism (philosopher-king, etc.), Plato distrusted the accuracy of almost any sense knowledge (see Allegory of the Cave) or empirical investigation. He believed that true knowledge can only be gained through a release from the bonds of darkness of our material existence - into the light of universal ideas (which is primarily intellectual/spiritual). In this he is opposed to Aristotle who held that knowledge of some absolutes can be gained from sense knowledge, that the world contains many realities (truths) which the "agent intellect" can truly abstract from/through sensory perception and images.

PLATONIC DUALISM: Plato did see two realities, the earthly or material, and the intellectual/spiritual. But he held that absolute truth could only be found in the latter. Plato was realist enough to recognize and describe some earthly realities (e.g., lack of honesty in men, political vagaries leading to gross injustices, pain, suffering, etc.). These and other earthly evils (absence of truth) he equated with the material world - and ultimately sought truth only in the purely intellectual/spiritual. When extended to Neo-Platonism, these philosophical concepts influenced some Christian thinkers (such as Origen) to overemphasize the figurative or allegorical interpretations of Revelation over against the literal. It was also this Neo-Platonic philosophical approach to exegesis which led Origen to some extreme speculations (e.g., a final apocatastasis, and, pre-existence of human souls [including Jesus Christ's]), ideas which were later condemned by the Church.

POLYGENISM: A condemned theological theory which is first based upon the false premise that the original *theory* of evolution as expressed by Charles Darwin is now an established fact, second, that since it is an "established fact" that human beings do not descend from one original couple (Adam and Eve), but rather humankind descends from a multiplicity of different human ancestors. **In 1950, this theory of polygenism was specifically condemned by Pope Pius XII in his Encyclical** *Humani Generis*.

PRIMATIAL SEE: Primatial as in primary. The three original "Primatial Sees" of the Catholic Church up until after the Council of Nicea in 325 A.D. were in Rome, Alexandria (Egypt) and Antioch (Syria). While the Bishop of Rome always had ultimate juridical and doctrinal authority, in the ordinary course of events discipline and administration of the Church was administered by geographic territory. The "Primates" of Rome, Alexandria, and Antioch presided in matters of discipline and administration over their own respective territories. The Bishop of Rome (the Pope) over Europe and North Western Africa, the Bishop of Alexandria over North Eastern Africa, and the Bishop of Syrian Antioch over the Middle East and Asia. While not officially a Primary See but technically a subordinate of the Bishop of Antioch, the Diocese of Jerusalem (and therefore its Bishop) also had a primary place of honor and prestige which was also respected throughout the Church. One of the Fathers so often quoted in this book, St. Cyril of Jerusalem was Bishop of that Diocese beginning probably in 349 A.D. Also, see "SEE."

RITE: Comes from the Latin word "ritual." In its derived usage, the word "Rite" has several applied meanings depending upon its usage . It can refer to the liturgical formulae for various sacraments, such as "The Rite of Baptism" or "The Rite of Ordination." Rite also refers to various "Rites" or Branches of the Catholic Church. For instance, there is the "Latin" or "Roman" Rite which is directly overseen by the Bishop of Rome. That is the "Rite" that most Catholics of Western Europe and North and South America belong to. Additionally, there are other "Rites" such as the Byzantine (sometimes called Greek), Antiochene, Armenian, and others. They celebrate their liturgical functions according to their customs and traditions which go back at least to the 4th century A.D. However, in all sacramental essentials there are no differences between the Rites.

These various "Rites" developed primarily after the Council of Nicea in 325 A.D. The Eastern Rites are primarily those other than the Roman or Latin Rite. They developed East of Rome, primarily in the Middle East, Asia Minor and North Africa. As a further example, while some of the Catholics behind the former Iron Curtain are Roman Rite Catholics, the majority of them are Eastern Rite Catholics. There are also Easter Rite Catholics in the United States of America and Canada. That is why in many large cities in the U.S., besides the Latin Rite Bishop, you can find listed in the telephone book Bishops of the Ruthenian, Ukrainian, Maronite, Chaldean, and other Eastern Rites. They are fully in union with Rome. Many of them even have their own Cardinal who fully participates with the Cardinals of the Latin Rite in Papal elections.

SAINT: In the specific term, as in a "canonized" Saint, once a decree of "Canonization" has been issued by the Magisterium, Catholics are not only "free" to venerate someone as a Saint (as after someone has been declared "Blessed"), but *after* a decree of canonization, all Catholics are bound to accept that guarantee of Sainthood on the part of the official Church. (See first "VENERABLE," then, "BLESSED").

Others are accorded the title "Saint" by the Church. The official legally binding "canonization" process which is currently in force in the Church goes back only to the 17th century. Prior to that time, to one degree or another, the Bishop of the area within which the Saint lived their life usually made such a ruling. Historically, that Episcopal ruling stood unless overruled by Rome.

Initially, martyrs for the Faith appear to have been the only ones accorded the title of Saint. As is evidenced by inscriptions and paintings on the walls of the oldest Christian cemeteries and catacombs, Christians *from the infancy of the Church* venerated certain martyrs as Saints. But by the 3rd and 4th centuries, "Confessors" of the Faith, those who had given witness to the Faith under persecution were also being accorded that title by local Bishops. In affect, the Church recognized that they had gone through a living martyrdom. An obvious example of this is St. John the Evangelist. He was thrown into a pot of boiling oil but miraculously did not die. He had nevertheless gone through a "living martyrdom." Eventually, justified veneration as a Saint by the faithful, coupled with miracles performed during his or her life and others' associated with their intervention after their death -- those two things achieved the same credible guarantee of "Sanctity" in the mind of the Church.

Ultimately, veneration by the faithful is always the first sign of a potential for formal Sainthood. The non-formal part of the process actually begins from within the ranks of the Faithful.

SEE: "See" derives from the Latin word "Sedes" which means "seat" or "chair," or in some cases "throne." This is used to describe the seat or "Chair" of Peter, the center or seat of the Church's papal or Episcopal authority. Thus the "Papal See" is Rome, and an "Episcopal See" is the cathedral of the city within which the Bishop of any diocese resides. See "Primatial See."

THEOLOGY: St. Augustine gave this word its first *Christian* definition as "reasoning or discourse about the Deity." St. Thomas gave it its full modern Christian meaning, which is a science which investigates the contents of Christian belief by means of reason - enlightened by faith -- in order to acquire a deeper understanding of God and His Revelation.

THOMISM: The philosophy and theology taught by St. Thomas Aquinas. Virtually every Pope of the last seven hundred years (including the current Pope John Paul II) has endorsed the theology of St. Thomas as that which best explains Catholic thought and theology.

THOMISTIC: An adjective describing "Thomism" -- see "Thomism."

TRANSUBSTANTION: The complete change of the substance of bread and wine into the substance of Christ's Body and Blood by a validly ordained priest during the consecration at the Liturgy of the Eucharist. Only the "accidents" of the bread and wine remain after the consecration.

VENERABLE: Worthy of respect. Comes from the Latin "Venerabilis." In the canonization process, the title "Venerable" is a median step to being declared "Blessed." (See "BLESSED") i.e., in the case of non-martyrs, an initial preliminary investigation is begun by a commission in Rome into their reputation for sanctity of life, and the plausibility of causes for such reputation. The gathered evidence is examined, and once sufficient evidence of sanctity has been gathered (in the opinions of the Cardinals sitting on the

Commission) to justify the work (not to mention financial cost[4]) initiation of a formal investigation into someone being declared "Blessed," a decree to that affect is promulgated which the Pope signs. Once the Pope signs that decree establishing that formal investigation, "Thenceforward the servant of God is given the title of Venerable."[5] Basically, the title "Venerable" assures a Catholic that the Commission found sufficient evidence of sanctity of life to justify the rather prodigious amount of work necessary to complete the process to declare someone "Blessed." The title does not indicate a final Church decision on those issues.

VISION: A supernatural perception of some object that is not normally (naturally) visible. A vision is a revelation only when the object which is seen also discloses some hidden truth or mystery, of which a prophecy is one example.

WESTERN CHURCH or LATIN CHURCH: See "RITE."

[4] The estimated ordinary cost for the beatification process alone (in 1913 American dollars) was "not less than $20,000.00. " In 1995, that would be around a half-million American dollars.

[5] Catholic Encyclopedia, 1913 Edition, Vol. II, p. 367.

BIBLIOGRAPHY

The quotes in this book from St. Irenaeus' *Adversus Haereses* are quoted from the *The Library of the Fathers* series. Some quotes from John Damascene are from the *Fathers of the Church* series. Many quotes from the Fathers and Doctors come from a large number of individual volumes of these and other sets of books. In the interests of keeping the bibliography as brief as possible, (with a few exceptions) the only reference in the bibliography to individual volumes (as from *Ancient Christian Writers)* are the listings for the sets themselves. Individual volume listings which are quoted or synopsized from are in all cases found in the footnotes of the book.

1. *Akita, The Tears and Messages of Mary*, Rev. Teiji Yasuda, Pub: 101 Foundation, Asbury, N.J., 1989.
2. *Ancient Christian Writers*, Edited by Johannes Quasten & Walter Burghardt, S.J., The Newman Press, Westminster Maryland, 55 Vols. 1963. [Many of the Patristic quotes in *Trial, Tribulation and Triumph* come directly from this series. It is the best English language series of Patristic texts in print.]
3. *Angel of the Judgement, A Life of St. Vincent Ferrer*, S.M.C.,. Ave Maria Press, Notre Dame, Indiana, 1953. [Best English language biography of St. Vincent.]
4. *Sancti Thomae Aquinitatis*, *Opera Omnia*, Tomus XIII, Musurgia Publishers, New York, 1949.
5. *The Apostolic Tradition*, *Of St. Hippolytus of Rome*, Rev. Gregory Dix, Monk of Nashborn Abbey, Society for Promoting Christian Knowledge, London, 1937.
6. *Anselm of Canterbury*, *Why God became Man*, Translation, introduction and notes by Joseph M. Colleran, Magi Books, Inc., Albany, N.Y. 1969.

7. *Die Antichrist*, William Bousset, Gottingen, Ger. 1895.
8. *Apocalypsin*, Bartholomew Holzhauser, 1850.
9. *Apocalypsin*, Cornelius a Lapide
10. *Basic Writings of Saint Augustine*, Edited by Whitney J. Oates, Chrm. Dept. of Classics, Princeton University, Random House, New York. 1948, 2 Vols.
11. *Bellarmini, Opera Omnia, Disputationum Roberti Bellarmini, De Controversiis* [3 vol.] *Christianae Fidei, Tomus Primus, Liber Tertius, De Summo Pontifice*. [This edition was printed under the aegis of Cardinal Archbishop Sforza at Naples in 1856.]
12. *Bible, Revised Standard Version Catholic Edition*, National Council of Churches of Christ in the U.S., 1966.
13. *Bible, The Holy*, Douay Rhiems Version, Tan Books and Publishers, Inc. Rockford, Il. 1989.
14. *Bible, Greek Latin English New Testament Student's Workbook*, The Liturgical Press, Collegeville, MN., 1963. [This book is out of print, however, it is the very best English/Latin/Greek interlinear New Testament available, if you can find one.]
15. *Bible, The Nevarre*, Four Courts Press, Faculty of Theology @ the University of Navarre, 1988. [The particular value of this Bible (N.T. only) is that first, it is English/Latin interlinear, and second, it has a marvelous running series of excerpts from commentaries of the Fathers and Doctors of the Church.]
16. *Bible, The New Jerusalem*, Doubleday, 666 Fifth Ave, New York, New York 10103, 1985.
17. *Biblical Exegesis & Catholic Doctrine*, Raymond E. Brown, S.S., Paulist Press, New York/Mahwah, 1985.
18. *The New Jerusalem Biblical Commentary*, edited by Raymond G. Brown, S.S., Joseph A. Fitzmyer S.J., Roland E. Murphy, O.Carm., Prentice Hall, Englewood Cliffs, N.J., 1988. [While there is an admirable assemblage of Scriptural scholarship in this work, it is higher critical in its approach from start to finish. However, it is still an excellent resource book if one bears in mind that it is extremely allegorical in its approach.]
19. **The Old Testament,* 2 Vols., translated & edited by Msgr. Ronald Knox, Sheed & Ward, New York, 1950. [This edition has an excellent series of commentaries.]
20. *A Commentary on the New Testament*, Prepared by The Catholic Biblical Commission - under the patronage of The

Episcopal Committee of the Confraternity of Christian Doctrine, Pub: William H. Sadlier, Inc. 1942.

21. *The Book of Destiny*, Leonard Kramer, Buechler Pub. Co., Belleville, Il. 1955. [This book is available as a reprint from Tan Books and Publishers.There are some passages of this book which could be interpreted as having a millenarist leaning. To the degree that this is true - it is the only major weak spot in this book.]
22. *The Building of Christendom, A History of Christendom*, Warren H. Carroll, Christendom College Press, 1987. [Dr. Carroll is simply the best English language Church historian in print. This particular volume covers the period from the end of the Council of Nicea (325 A.D.) till 1150.]
23. *Butler's Lives of the Saints*, 4 Vol.
24. *The Byzantine-Slav Liturgy of St. John Chrysostom*, Rev. C. Kucharek, Alleluia Press, Allendale, N.J., 1971. ["This book is the most comprehensive work on the Byzantine Liturgy that has ever appeared in any modern language" - quoted from the jacket of the book. It is written by Fr. Casimir Kucharek, a Ukrainian Rite Catholic priest/scholar from Canada.]
25. *Canons and Decrees of the Council of Trent*, original Latin text with English translation, Rev. H.J. Schroeder, O.P., B. Herder Book Co., 1941.
26. *The Catechetical Lectures of S. Cyril, Archbishop of Jerusalem*, A Library of the Fathers, Oxford. (This is an Anglican Patrology series).
27. *Catechism of the Catholic Church*, Libreria Editrice Vaticana, St. Paul Books and Media, 1994.
28. *Catholic Biblical Encyclopedia, New Testament*, John E. Steinmueller, S.T.D., S.Scr.L., Consultor of the Pontifical Biblical Commission, Kathryn Sullivan, R.S.C. J., Ph.D. Research Professor of Sacred Scripture, Introduction by James-M. Voste, O.P., S.T.M., S.Scr.D., Secretary of the Pontifical Biblical Commission, Pub: Joseph F. Wagner, Inc. New York City, 1949. [This book is long out of print. If you can find one, it is an outstanding piece of orthodox Catholic exegesis.]
29. *The Catholic Catechism*, John A. Hardon, S.J., Doubleday & Co., 1974. [This book is still in print and is an excellent companion to the new *Catechism of the Catholic Church*.]

30. *A Catholic Commentary on Holy Scripture*, Editorial Committee: Dom Bernard Orchard - General Editor, Rev. Edmond F. Sutcliffe S.J., - Old Testament Editor, Rev. Reginald C. Fuller, - Secretary of the Catholic Biblical Association, Dom Ralph Russell - Hon. Secretary and Treasurer. Pub: Thomas Nelson and Sons, New York, 1953. Forward by Bernard Cardinal Griffin, 1953. [43 of the finest Catholic Scripture scholars of the 20th century contributed the articles produced this 1312 page work. They came from England, Ireland, Germany, Australia, Malta, Canada, many others in teaching residence at Rome's Pontifical Biblical Institute, and from the U.S.A. It if probably one of the finest single volume yet scholarly English language Scriptural commentaries of the 20th century. It is generally consistent with the traditional teachings of the Church, while at the same time, it acknowledges and utilizes the finest of textual criticism developed by faithful Scripture scholars in the 20th century.]
31. *Catholic Encyclopedia*, The Catholic Encyclopedia Press, Inc., 1913 Edition.
32. *The Catholic Encyclopedia, Revised and Enlarged Edition, Littleton & Ives, Co.*, New York, 1936.
33. *Catholic Prophecy*, Yves Dupont, Tan Books and Publishers, 1971. [This book while excellent in many aspects dedicates about forty percent of its space to some of the prophecies of Nostradamus - who is *not* approved by the Church.]
34. *Christian Initiation, A Comparative Study of the Interpretation of the Baptismal Liturgy in the Mystagogical Writings of Cyril of Jerusalem, John Chrysostom, Theodore of Mopsuestia, and Ambrose of Milan*, Hugh M. Riley, Edited by Johannes Quasten, Vol. 17 of *The Catholic University of America Studies in Christian Antiquity*, 1974.
35. *The Christian Trumpet*, Fr. Pellegrino, Thos B. Noonan & Co., Boston, 1873. [This book is long out of print. The reader might find a copy at a large seminary library.]
36. *The Communion of Saints, An Examination of the place of Christian dead in the belief, worship, and calendars of the Church*, Michael Pelham, Alcuin Club/SPCK, London, 1980. [This text is an Anglican work developed for a study of the Anglican Liturgy. Its view is specifically Anglican - not Catholic.]

37. *A Companion to Scripture Studies*, 3 Vols. II, Rev. John E. Steinmeuller, S.T.D., S.Scr.Lld., Joseph F. Wagner, Inc., 6th. Printing, 1948. [Out of print, this is still the series used by many orthodox Scripture scholars. It is viewed by them as the best faithful English language series for Scripture study.]
38. *Compendium of the Caudernon*, Padre Frei Bartolome Ochoa de Alacano y Gamboa. [Not in print -- from an unpublished English manuscript].
39. *The Consciousness of Christ*, William G. Most, Christendom College Press, 1980.
40. *Corpus Christianorum, Series Latina*, Pub: Turnholti, Typographi Brepols, Editores Pontifici.
41. *Corpus Christianorum, Continuo Medievalis*, 144 Vols. A Tertulliano ad Innocentium III, Pub: Turnholti, Typographi Brepols, Editores Pontifici. [Many of the Medieval quotes on the Antichrist, and on a latter Roman Empire are taken directly from this series. This is the most extensive source of Medieval Patristic and theological works. However, many of its introductory sections are written by extreme "higher critics."]
42. *Crossing the Threshold of Hope*, Alfred A. Knopf, New York, 1994.
43. *St. Cyril of Jerusalem's Lectures on the Christian Sacraments*, Edited by Lady Margaret - Professor of Divinity, University of Oxford, S.P.C.K., London, 1951. (Anglican commentary and introduction.)
44. *The Dawn of Empire: Rome's Rise to World Power,* R. M. Errington, Cornell University Press, Ithaca, N.Y., 1972. [This is one of the very best treatments of the early Rise and growthof the Roman Empire. This book specializes in the period from 264 B.C.-133 B.C. The mostly indirect but very real impact of the Roman Empire on the Jewish people during this period was immense. It is excellent reading for students of the Old Testament and the history of the Jewish people.]
45. *Denver Catholic Register*, 200 Josephine St., Denver, Co. U.S.A. [Roman Catholic Diocesan Newspaper].
46. *St. John of Damascus - Writings, De Fide Orthodoxa (or, An Exact Exposition of the Orthodox Faith), A New Translation,* translated and introduced by Frederic H. Chase, Jr,, Pub: The Catholic University of America Press, Washington, D.C., The

Fathers of the Church series, Vol. 37, First Printing 1958, Reprinted - 1970. [This volume is the very best English Language text available of the major writings of St. John Damascene. The particular value of Damascene is that; besides being the last Father of the Church ("the generally accepted date of his death is Sept. 4, 749"), he is an Eastern Father. The *De Fide Orthodoxa* is "the first great *Summa* of theology to appear in either the East or the West." Therein, he specifically intends to record the totality of great Eastern Theological tradition as it is received from apostolic Tradition.]

47. *De Servorum Dei Canonizatione et Beatificatione*, Pope Benedict XIV.
48. *Details Concerning the Antichrist*, Dr. Franz Spirago, Pub: R. Von Acken, Lingen, (EMS), Hanover, Germany, 1922. [Long out of print]
49. *Development of Christian Doctrine*, John Henry Cardinal Newman, Longmans, Green and Co. New York, 1927. [Contains the thought and theory of Doctrinal Development of Card. Newman. A landmark work which should be read by every serious student of the subject.]
50. *The Disputed Questions on Truth*, St. Thomas Aquinas, Henry Regnery Company, Chicago, 1953, 3 Vols.
51. *Divinum Operorum*, St. Hildegardis.
52. *Dogm Const. on the Catholic Faith*, First Vatican Council.
53. *Dreams, Visions & Prophecies of Don Bosco*, Edited by Rev. Eugene M. Brown, Don Bosco Publications, New Rochelle, N.Y. 1986. [Still in print and available from the publisher]
54. *Dynamics of World History*, Christopher Dawson, Edition of Sherwood Sugden & Company, 1978.
55. *Ecclesiastical History*, Eusebius Pamphilus, Bishop of Cæsarea, in Palestine, (completed in 325 A.D.) This edition edited and published by Baker Book House, Grand Rapids, Mi. 1984. [This is a Protestant text which betrays *many* non-Catholic interpretations and opinions in its commentary and footnotes].
56. *On The Epiclesis of the Eucharistic Liturgy and on the Consecration of the Font*, E.G. Cuthbert F. Atchley, Oxford University Press, London, 1935. [This book is written by an Anglican scholar and therefore holds with numerous interpretations which are Anglican rather than Catholic. But there is also much sound scholarship in this work.]

57. *Encyclopedia of Saints*, Clemens Jöckle, Alpine Fine Arts Collection (UK) Ltd., London, England, 1995. This is a book with many four color prints, and in many cases, has excellent biographical information. However, many of the opinions and pieces of data which are listed as legends are in fact not legends at all. Read only for basic data.
58. *The Eucharistic Prayer*, J. A. Jungman, S.J., English Edition - 3rd Printing, Pitman Press, Bath, England, 1960.
59. *Evangelium Vitae*, Origins, Encyclical of Pope John Paul II.
60. *The Faith of the Early Fathers*, W. A. Jurgens, 3 Vols. The Liturgical Press, Collegeville, Mn. 1970. [This is the only "affordable" compilation of selected writings from the Fathers. It is excellent, and still in print.]
61. *The Fathers of The Church*, 53 Vols., The Fathers of the Church, Inc., (Ed. Dr. Roy Deferrari), New York. Roman Catholic Patrology Series.
62. *Fire Within*, Thomas Dubay, F.M., Ignatius Press, 1989.
63. *The Founding of Christendom, Vol. 1, A History of Christendom*, Warren Carroll, Christendom College Press, Front Royal, VA. 1985. [This is the very best English language general history of the Old Testament and Christianity up till the Council of Nicea in 325 A.D. It is still in print.]
64. *St. Francis of Paulo, God's Miracle Worker Supreme*, Gino J Simi & Mario M. Segreti, Tan Books and Publishers, Inc., 1977.
65. *Fundamentals of Catholic Dogma*, Dr. Ludwig Ott, Fourth Edition, (First English Edition, Pub: The Mercier Press, Limited, 19 Maylor Street, Cork, Republic of Ireland, 1960), Reprinted by Tan Books and Publishrs, 1974, 541 pages. [This book is the best compendium of Catholic Dogma available in English. It is still available from Tan Books and Publishers, Rockford, Illinois.]
66. *From Newman to Congar, The Idea of Doctrinal Development from the Victorians to the Second Vatican Council*, Aidan Nichols, O.P., T&T Clark, Edinburgh, Scotland, 1990.
67. *The Gospel and Epistles of John, A Concise Commentary*, Raymond E. Brown, S.S., The Liturgical Press, Collegeville, MN., 1988, p. 15.
68. *Heraldo de la Preciosa Sangre de Nuestro Senor*, Salamanca, Espania, 1955.

69. *The History of Israel*, Giuseppi Ricciotti, two Vols., The Bruce Publishing Co., Milwaukee, 1955. [This is still the very best history of Israel. Long out of print, it can be obtained through good used book outlets].
70. *History of Antichrist*, Rev. P. Huchedé, Professor of Theology at the Grand Seminary of Laval, France, Nicholas Bray; New York, English Edition of 1884, [The original edition in French was published at Innsbruck, Austria in 1878. Several quotes attributed by Huchedé to certain Fathers are dated. For instance, this book was written prior to discovery of unarguable proof that the "Second Epistle of Clement to the Corinthians" was written by someone other than Pope St. Clement. But it is still an excellent, if brief, treatment of the subject].
71. *History of the Councils,* von Hefele, Karl Joseph, 5 Vols. T&T Clark, Edinburgh, 1883-1896. AMS English Edition reprint, AMS Press Inc. New York, 1972. [While this series is over a hundred years old, it is still the definitive work on the history of the various councils of the Church, particularly of the early councils. Its depth of information on its subjects is simply unmatched by any other source. That is undoubtedly the reason this book was reprinted after eighty years.]
72. *The Homilies of St. John Chrysostom, Archbishop of Constantinople, on the Gospel of St. Mathew*, Oxford, John Henry Parker, The Frederick Field Edition, 1843. [Anglican work].
73. *Gethsemane: Reflections on the Contemporary Theological Movement*, Joseph Cardinal Siri, Archbishop of Genoa, Franciscan Herald Press, Chicago (in cooperation with, Editions De La Fraternite De La Tres Sainte Vierge Marie, Rome, Italy), 1981. [This book is out of print but copies are still available from the publisher].
74. *The House of Seleucus,* Edwin Robert Bevan, MA, 2 Vols., Barnes & Noble, New York, 1966. [This book was first published in 1902. It was republished in 1966 for the simple reason that it is still the definitive work on the history of the Seleucid Empire.]
75. *Humani Generis,* Encyclical of Pope Pius XII, Aug. 12, 1950.
76. *The Interpretation of the Bible in the Church*, Pontifical Biblical Commission, Pub: Libreria Editrice Vaticana, Repub: Origins, CNS documentary Service, January 6, 1994, Vol. 23:

No. 29 -- [Since shortly after Vatican II, this commission has ceased to be an office or arm of the Magisterium. Therefore, its documents no longer hold Magisterial authority.] Also, see immediately below.

77. *Address of His Holiness Pope John Paul II and Document of the Pontifical Biblical Commission*, Libreria Editrice Vaticana, 1993. [Papal Address on issuance of *The Interpretation of the Bible in the Church*].
78. *Jesus God and Man*, Raymond E. Brown, S.S., The Bruce Publishing Co., Milwaukeee, Wi. 1967.
79. *Josephus, Complete Works*, (References quoted *Trial, Tribulation and Triumph* come from its sections; *The Antiquities of the Jews*, *The Wars of the Jews*), Kregel Publications, Grand Rapids, Mi. 1981. [This book contains many editorial comments from its editors. They are in the main very fundamentalist Protestant in character. The reader should be aware of this editorial bias at all times. This author quotes from this volume primarily because it is the most readily available English language edition in print.]
80. *L'Oservatore Romano* (official Vatican Newspaper published in Vatican City).
81. *A Latin-English Dictionary of St. Thomas Aquinas*, Roy J. Deferrari, Ph.D., LL.D., L.H.D., Dr.Ed., St. Paul Editions, Boston, 1960. [Deferrari was not only a classical linguist, he was also an eminent Patrologist and Church historian. His *St. Thomas Latin Dictionary* is one of a kind in English. This book is still available from the publisher].
82. *Liber Mirabilis*, 1524.
83. *Library of the Fathers*, James Parker & Co., Oxford, England [Mid to late 1800's].
84. *The Life and Prophecies of St. Hildegarde of Bingen*, Frank J. Bendish, Carlton Press, Inc., New York, 1971.
85. *The Life of St. Anthony the Great*, St. Athanasius, Pub.: Eastern Orthodox Books, Willitts, Ca. [This edition reprinted in 1976 from an 1850 edition. The *original* work was completed circa 357 A.D. by St. Athanasius, and was simply titled, *The Life of Anthony*.]
86. *Life and Works of St. Hildegard*, Schmelzeis, Herder, Froiburg, Ger. 1879. [Many of Hildegard's works and letters have

never been translated into English. As a matter of fact, some of her works are difficult to find even in their original Latin. For this reason, Schmelzeis and several other authors are the only available sources for some of Hildegard's writings in a modern language edition.]

87. *Martin's Edition of Lucia's Memoirs*, Porto, 1973.
88. *The Mass of the Roman Rite: Its Origins and Development* (*Missarum Sollemnia*), Rev. Joseph A. Jungmann, S.J., Prof. of Theology, University of Innsbruck, Benziger Brothers, Inc. Vol. 2. [While now somewhat dated, 1953-1955, this is still the most comprehensive general work on the history of the Roman Liturgy.]
89. *Messagero del Cuore di Maria* No. 8-9 August-September, 1961, Rome, Italy.
90. *A Monument to St. Jerome*, Edited by Francis X. Murphy, C.SS.R. - Forward by Cardinal Tisserant, Sheed and Ward, New York, 1952
91. *Motivatione della fede oggi in Teologia dall'esperienza dello spirito*, Nuovi Saggi VI, ed. Pauline, Roma 1978.
92. *The New Jerusalem Biblical Commentary*, edited by Raymond G. Brown, S.S., Joseph A. Fitzmyer S.J., Roland E. Murphy, O.Carm., Prentice Hall, Englewood Cliffs, N.J., 1988. [There is much valuable commentary in this volume. But regretably, in too many instances it favors theories of extreme higher criticism over the traditional teachings of the Church. It is therefore not consistently dependable for traditional Catholic exegesis.]
93. *Brother Nicholas, The Life of St. Nicholas of Flue*, G.R. Lamb, Sheed and Ward, N.Y., 1955.
94. *Patrologiæ Cursus Completus, Series Graeca*, 161 Vols., Migne, Paris au Petit-Montrouge, 1857-1866.
95. *Patrologiæ Cursus Completus, Series Latina*, 217 Vols., Migne, Paris au Petit-Montrouge, 1866-1889.
96. *Patrology*, Berthold Altaner, 1 Vol., Herder and Herder, N.Y., 1960.
97. *Patrology*, Johannes Quasten, (Prof. of Ancient Church History and Christian Archeology, Catholic University of America), 4 Vols., Spectrum Publishers Utrecht-Antwerp, 5th Printing, 1950- (1986. Vol. 4), Pub: Christian Classics, Inc. Westminster, Md. 1986.

98. *Père Lamy,* Comte Paul Biver, Translated from French by Msgr. John O'Connor, Preface by Jacques Maritain, [Original English Ed. Clonmore & Reynolds, Ltd., Dublin, Ireland. Impri. Pot. John Carol, Archbishop of Dublin, 1951, Tan Books and Pub. 1973.
99. *Peter Mohila, Metropolitan of Kiev (1633-47) Translation and evaluation of his "Orthodox Confession of Faith (1640*), (Doctoral Dissertation of) Ronald Peter Popivchak, Catholic University of America, Department of Theology, Washington, D.C., 1995. [If one can obtain a copy, this is an excellent treatment of contemporary theological approaches of the East with many valuable commentaries on differences between the Church of the East and West.]
100. *Priests for Life Magazine,* A publication produced by an association of Pro-Life Catholic priests from the U.S. and Canada.
101. *Proceedings of The Catholic Biblical Association of America, First General Meeting*, The Abbey Press, Meinrad, Ind. 1938.
102. *Prophecy and Hermeneutic in Early Christianity*, E. Earle Ellis, William B. Eerdmans Publishing Company, Grand Rapids, Mi., 1978. [First published in German as vol. 18 of *Wissenschaftliche Untersuchungen zum Neuen Testament*, J.C.B. Mohr (Paul Siebeck), Tübingen, Federal Republic of Germany, 1978.]
103. *The Prophets and Our Times*, Rev. Richard G. Culleton, 1943.
104. *Providentissimus Deus,* Encyclical issued by Pope Leo XIII.
105. *Public And Private Prophecies About The Last Times*, Rev. Benjamin Martin Sanchez, Pub: Opus Reginae Sacratissimi Rosarii, University of Salamanca, 1972.
106. *Renewal and Reconciliation, Retreat Conferences by Archbishop Fulton J. Sheen*. Minister-O-Media, Inc. 1976.
107. *Revelations of Sister Mechtild of Magdeburg*, Morel, Regensburg, Mainz, 1869.
108. *Sacra Scrittura e Teologia*, in Nuovi Saggi I, Karl Rahher, Ed. Paoline, Roma 1968.
109. *Sacramentum Mundi, An Encyclopedia of Theology*, General Editor - Karl Rahner, S.J., 6 Vols., English Edition, Herder & Herder, N.Y.

110. *The Scandal of the Incarnation, Irenaeus Against the Heresies*, Selected and Introduced by Hans Urs von Balthasar, Ignatius Press, San Francisco, 1990.
111. *St. Theresa of Avila, Collected Works*, ICS Publication, Institute of Carmelite Studies, Washington, D.D., 1976.
112. *A Still, Small Voice*, Fr. Benedict J. Groeschel, C.F.R., Ignatius Press, San Francisco, 1992.
113. *Summa Theologica*, St. Thomas Aquinas, First Complete American Edition, 3 Vols., Translated by Fathers of the English Dominican Province, Benzinger Bros. Inc. New York, 1947.
114. *That Hideous Strength*, Third Book of the Trilogy, C.S. Lewis, McMillan Publishing Co., Third Publishing, 1973.
115. *The Sunday Sermons of the Great Fathers*, four Vols., Translated and edited by M.F. Toal, Henry Regnery Co. 1964.
116. *The Terrors of the Year Two Thousand*, Etienne Gilson, St. Michael's College, Toronto, Canada, Garden City Press Cooperative, 1949.
117. *The Theology of History in St. Bonaventure*, Joseph Ratzinger, English Edition-translated by Zachary Hayes, O.F.M., Franciscan Herald Press, Chicago, 1971.
118. *Tracts for the Times*, Member of the University of Oxford, Vol. 5, Advent Sermons on Antichrist, John Henry Newman, Pub. J.H. Parker, Oxford, 1840.
119. *Trojan Horse in the City of God*, Dr. Deitrich von Hildegrand, Franciscan Herald Press, Chicago, 1967.
120. *Vita Antichristi*, Dionysius de Luetzenburg, 1682. [Imprimaturs: Bishop of Mainz, and, Superior-General of the Capuchin Order.]
121. *Vatican Council II, The Concilior and Post Concilior Documents, Vol 1*. Flannery, New Revised Edition, 1992.
122. *Voix Prophetiques*, Curicquo, 2 Vols., 1872.
123. *The Waves of the Mystical Bark*, Rudolph Gekner, 1623.
124. *Wife, Mother and Mystic*, (Blessed Anna-Maria Taigi), by Albert Besseirs, S.J., translated by Rev. Stephen Rigby, Sands & Co. Ltd., London, 1952, [Repub. by Tan Books & Publishers.]
125. *Wisdom's Fool*, Fr. Edward Doherty, Montfort Publications, Bay Shore, New York, 1975.
126. *The Works of Bonaventure, Mystical Opuscula*, Translated from the Latin by Jose de Vinck-Doctor Louvain University, St. Anthony Guild Press, Patterson, N.J., 1960.

INDEX

This index is arranged in both alphabetical *and* topical order, *and* in many cases, various topics are also cross-indexed.

Examples: A. Alpha listings: One of the major theses in the book is that an Age of Peace preceeds the coming (advent) of Antichrist. There is (A) an alphabetical listing for both "Antichrist" and "Age of Peace". Numerous page number listings appear immediately after both those heading.

B. Then, under major headings are many subheadings, some of which are merely alphabetical, some of which are (B) topical. One of those topical subheadings under "Antichrist" is listed as "Age of Peace precedes Antichrist." There you will find a quick reference to many (but not all) of the references to this topic throughout the book.

C. There is also a (C) cross-referenced listing of the same event under the major heading of "Age of Peace". That subheading is entitled, "Precedes Antichrist". Therefore, you can find this topic (the Age of Peace occuring prior to the reign of Antichrist) listed under both, "Antichrist" and under "Age of Peace".

A number of the entries in the index appear in *italicized print.* Almost all of them fall into two categories, (1) titles of books or manuscripts, (2) quotes or encapsulizations of quotes from Scripture, Tradition, or various Catholic private prophecies from Church-approved sources.

The dates listed after the names of the various Popes are the inclusive dates during which they held the Papacy.

A number of the index references are to be found in the footnotes. So if you do not find the referenced item in the regular body copy - then look in the footnote. If you do not find the indexed item on the referenced page (especially in the last several hundred pages), please check back one page and then forward one page.

A

C

D

E

F

G

H

I

J

M

N

O

P

T

Y

Z

Visit your local bookstore for other great titles from:

QUEENSHIP PUBLISHING

www.queenship.org

The Truth about Mary, Volume I
From Human Inventions to the Truths Taught by Scripture
ISBN # 1-882972-82-1

The Truth about Mary, Volume II
Mary in Scripture and the Historic Christian Faith
ISBN #1-882972-83-X

The Truth about Mary, Volume III
A Response to Fundamentalist Misconceptions and a Return to Historic Christianity
ISBN #1-882972-84-5

Jesus, Peter and the Keys
A Scriptural Handbook on the Papacy
ISBN #1-882972-80-5

The Gift of the Church
Current Questions and Objections about the Catholic Church and Down-to-Earth Answers
ISBN #1-882972-01-5

Facts on Acts (of Apostles)
ISBN #1-882972-65-1

Prepare for the Great Tribulation and the Era of Peace, Vol. III
ISBN #1-882972-72-4

The Coming Chastisement
ISBN #1-882972-41-X

The Light of Love
My Angel Shall Go Before Me
ISBN #1-882972-53-8

Marian Apparitions Today
Why So Many?
ISBN #1-882972-71-6

Lord Jesus Teach Me to Pray
A Seven-Week Course in Personal Prayer
ISBN #1-882972-55-4

A Guide to Healing the Family Tree
ISBN #1-882972-64-3